Bulgaria

THE ROUGH GUIDE

There are more than one hundred Rough Guide titles
covering destinations from Amsterdam to Zimbabwe

Forthcoming titles include
Dominican Republic • Melbourne • Laos • South India

Rough Guide Reference Series
Classical Music • European Football • The Internet • Jazz • Music USA
Opera • Reggae • Rock Music • World Music

Rough Guide Dictionary Phrasebooks
Czech • Dutch • French • German • Greek • Hindi & Urdu • Hungarian
Indonesian • Italian • Japanese • Mandarin Chinese • Mexican Spanish
Polish • Portuguese • Russian • Spanish • Thai • Turkish • Vietnamese
European Languages

Rough Guides on the Internet
www.roughguides.com

ROUGH GUIDE CREDITS

Text editor: Amanda Tomlin
Series editor: Mark Ellingham
Editorial: Martin Dunford, Jonathan Buckley, Jo Mead, Kate Berens, Ann-Marie Shaw, Paul Gray, Chris Schüler, Helena Smith, Judith Bamber, Kieran Falconer, Orla Duane, Olivia Eccleshall, Ruth Blackmore, Sophie Martin, Geoff Howard, Claire Saunders, Anna Sutton, Gavin Thomas, Alexander Mark Rogers (UK); Andrew Rosenberg, Andrew Taber (US)
Production: Susanne Hillen, Andy Hilliard, Link Hall, Helen Ostick, James Morris, Julia Bovis, Michelle Draycott, Cathy McElhinney

Cartography: Melissa Flack, Maxine Burke, Nichola Goodliffe, Ed Wright
Picture research: Eleanor Hill, Louise Boulton
Online editors: Alan Spicer, Kate Hands (UK); Geronimo Madrid (US)
Finance: John Fisher, Neeta Mistry, Katy Miesiaczek
Marketing & Publicity: Richard Trillo, Simon Carloss, Niki Smith, David Wearn (UK); Jean-Marie Kelly, SoRelle Braun (US)
Administration: Tania Hummel, Charlotte Marriott

PUBLISHING INFORMATION

This third edition published June 1999 by Rough Guides Ltd, 62–70 Shorts Gardens, London, WC2H 9AB.
Distributed by the Penguin Group:
Penguin Books Ltd, 27 Wrights Lane, London W8 5TZ
Penguin Books USA Inc., 375 Hudson Street, New York 10014, USA
Penguin Books Australia Ltd, 487 Maroondah Highway, PO Box 257, Ringwood, Victoria 3134, Australia
Penguin Books Canada Ltd, 10 Alcorn Avenue, Toronto, Ontario, Canada M4V 1E4
Penguin Books (NZ) Ltd, 182–190 Wairau Road, Auckland 10, New Zealand
Typeset in Linotron Univers and Century Old Style to an original design by Andrew Oliver.
Printed in England by Clays Ltd, St Ives PLC
Illustrations in Part One and Part Three by Edward Briant.

Bulgaria

THE ROUGH GUIDE

written and researched by

Jonathan Bousfield and Dan Richardson

with additional research by

Gabi Petkova and Vanya Ganozhava

THE ROUGH GUIDES

THE ROUGH GUIDES

TRAVEL GUIDES • PHRASEBOOKS • MUSIC AND REFERENCE GUIDES

 We set out to do something different when the first Rough Guide was published in 1982. Mark Ellingham, just out of university, was travelling in Greece. He brought along the popular guides of the day, but found they were all lacking in some way. They were either strong on ruins and museums but went on for pages without mentioning a beach or taverna. Or they were so conscious of the need to save money that they lost sight of Greece's cultural and historical significance. Also, none of the books told him anything about Greece's contemporary life – its politics, its culture, its people, and how they lived.

So with no job in prospect, Mark decided to write his own guidebook, one which aimed to provide practical information that was second to none, detailing the best beaches and the hottest clubs and restaurants, while also giving hard-hitting accounts of every sight, both famous and obscure, and providing up-to-the-minute information on contemporary culture. It was a guide that encouraged independent travellers to find the best of Greece, and was a great success, getting shortlisted for the Thomas Cook travel guide award,

and encouraging Mark, along with three friends, to expand the series.

The Rough Guide list grew rapidly and the letters flooded in, indicating a much broader readership than had been anticipated, but one which uniformly appreciated the Rough Guide mix of practical detail and humour, irreverence and enthusiasm. Things haven't changed. The same four friends who began the series are still the caretakers of the Rough Guide mission today: to provide the most reliable, up-to-date and entertaining information to independent-minded travellers of all ages, on all budgets.

We now publish more than 100 titles and have offices in London and New York. The travel guides are written and researched by a dedicated team of more than 100 authors, based in Britain, Europe, the USA and Australia. We have also created a unique series of dictionary phrasebooks to accompany the travel series, along with an acclaimed series of music guides, and a best-selling pocket guide to the Internet and World Wide Web. We also publish comprehensive travel information on our Web site:

www.roughguides.com

HELP US UPDATE

We've gone to a lot of effort to ensure that the third edition of *The Rough Guide to Bulgaria* is accurate and up-to-date. However, things change — places get "discovered", opening hours are notoriously fickle, restaurants and rooms raise prices or lower standards. If you feel we've got it wrong or left something out, we'd like to know, and if you can remember the address, the price, the time, the phone number, so much the better.

We'll credit all contributions, and send a copy of the next edition (or any other Rough Guide if you prefer) for the best letters. Please mark letters: "Rough Guide Bulgaria Update" and send to:
Rough Guides, 62–70 Shorts Gardens, London WC2H 9AB, or Rough Guides, 375 Hudson St, 9th floor, New York NY 10014.
Or send email to: mail@roughguides.co.uk
Online updates about this book can be found on Rough Guides' Web site at www.roughguides.com

ACKNOWLEDGEMENTS

Jonathan would like to thank Tim & Jane; Elka Beneva; Lyuba & Yuri Boyanin; Peter Carney; Niki Chavdarov; Velislava Chilingrova; David Conklin; Desi; Petâr Dimov; Nadya Drakova; Sonya Enilova; Diana Gergova; Ian Hall; Silvia Hinkova; Hristomir Hristov; Milkana Ivanova; Janne in Malko Târnovo; Yordan Kamenov; Brian Kenety; Antoaneta Kostova; Joshua Lanzara; Aglika Markova; Boryana Mateva; Bonnie McCassy; Christine Milner; Ivo Miltenov; Sue Morell; Ivan Nikolov; Stanimir Nyagolov; Maria Patronova; Juliette Peeva; Ilyan Petkov; Violeta Petkova; Alek Popov; Lyubomir Popyordanov; Carolina Ramos; Dominique Repellin; Lilyana Runevska; Ana Ruseva; Asen Salkin; Betsy Sergeant; Hristo Sharenkov; Bob Sinclair; Ivan Skabrin; Paul Snow; Teodosii Spasov; Svetla Stoyanova; Sevelina Todorova; Lyubomir Veselinov; Kosyu Zarev; Kristina Zecheva; the British Embassy in Sofia; the Bulgarian Embassy in London; the Bulgarian Ministry of Trade and Tourism; and the staff of Kirkby Stephen Library.

Dan would like to thank all those in Bulgaria who provided help, hospitality and kindness, including Ivan Scriabin and Peter Stefanov of the Pirin Tourism Forum; Punky and the AUB faculty in Blagoevgrad; Christina Jecheva at the Visitors Centre, and the whole Detective Squad in Sandanski; Raicho Budurov at the Smolyan Tourist Office; Lubomir, Kiril and the two Ivans at Odysseia-In; Georgi Mantarov, Deputy Mayor of Haskovo; Kotse Hadzhesky in Trigrad; Vasil Stefanov and the Angelev family in Manastir; Lucy Malcheva in Plovdiv; James Kidner at the British Embassy; Nick at Borovets; Lilla and the Uzunovs in Melnik. In Britain, thanks go to Judith Sleigh; Jo Rogers of the European Children's Trust; Jeremy North of the Know-How Fund; Svetla Konstantinova and others at the Bulgarian Embassy; and Dave Elliot.

Thanks also go to Amanda Tomlin; to Nick Thomson and Henry Barrkman for Basics research; Elaine Pollard for proofreading; Sam Kirby and Maxine Burke for the maps; Dr Annie Kay of the British Bulgarian Friendship Society for help with picture research; Cathy McElhinney for production; and Sam Cook for the index.

THE AUTHORS

Jonathan Bousfield has been writing for Rough Guides for more than ten years, since first contributing to the now defunct *Rough Guide to Yugoslavia*. As well as the *Rough Guide to Bulgaria*, he is co-author of the *Rough Guide to Austria* and is currently researching and writing a new *Rough Guide to Croatia*.

Dan Richardson was born in England in 1958. Before joining the Rough Guides in 1984, he worked as a sailor on the Red Sea, and as a commodities dealer in Peru. Since then he has travelled extensively in Russia and Eastern Europe and is the author of Rough Guides to *St Petersburg, Moscow* and *Hungary*. While in St Petersburg in 1992, he met his future wife Anna; they have a daughter, Sonia.

READERS' LETTERS

Christy Alvord; Keith Anderson; Gary Brooks; Adrian Cashman; Penny Clark; Per Clausen; Andrea Connell; Charlotte Cox; John Fitzmaurice; Susanne Flydtkjaer; Anthony Furness; Colin Groom; Harriet Hamilton; Sara Humphreys; Martin Hurme-Lundin; David John and Michelle Morris; Gary Joiner; Miriam Lewin; N. Lewis; Thomas Osterberg; Markku Paaskynen; A. Smith; Lena Roth; Joanne Rushby; Sinikka Torkkola; Rik Verdellen; Walter Wornick; Arhur Wiggers; and Tom Winnifrith.

CONTENTS

Introduction ix

| PART ONE | **BASICS** | 3 |

Getting there from Britain and Ireland 3
Getting there from North America 10
Getting there from Australia and New Zealand 12
Visas and red tape 14
Health and insurance 15
Costs, money and banks 18
Information and maps 20
Getting around 23

Accommodation 30
Eating and drinking 32
Mail, phones and the media 39
Holidays, festivals and entertainment 41
Outdoor activities and eco-tourism 48
Museums, churches and mosques 51
Police, trouble and sexual harassment 53
Directory 55

| PART TWO | **THE GUIDE** | 59 |

● CHAPTER 1: SOFIA 59–98

Arrival 62
Information 63
City transport 64
Accommodation 65
Around pl. Sveta Nedelya and bul. Knyaginya Mariya Luiza 70
Bul. Vitosha and the National History Museum 74
The Largo 76
Pl. Aleksandâr Batenberg 77
Bul. Tsar Osvooboditel 80

Pl. Aleksandâr Nevski 80
Ulitsa G S Rakovski 82
Inner ring road 84
Mount Vitosha 86
Kremikovtsi 90
Eating 91
Drinking 93
Entertainment 94
Listings 95

● CHAPTER 2: THE SOUTHWEST 99–143

Pernik 101
Zemen Monastery 102
Kyustendil 103
Dupnitsa 105
Rila Monastery 108
Samokov 113
Borovets 115
Malyovitsa 118

Blagoevgrad 118
Bansko 124
Gotse Delchev 130
Sandanski 132
Melnik 135
Rozhen Monastery 139
Rupite 140
Petrich 141

• CHAPTER 3: THE BALKAN RANGE AND THE DANUBIAN PLAIN 144–240

The Iskâr Gorge 147
Vratsa 149
Berkovitsa 153
Montana 155
Chiprovtsi 156
Lopushanski Monastery 158
Belogradchik 159
Magura Cave 160
Vidin 162
Ruse 170
The Rusenski Lom 178

Silistra 180
Dobrich 181
Pleven 189
Lovech 194
Troyan 196
Veliko Târnovo 201
Arbanasi 211
Tryavna 219
Gabrovo 223
Shumen 226
The Ludogorie 234

• CHAPTER 4: THE SREDNA GORA AND THE VALLEY OF THE ROSES 241–276

Koprivshtitsa 243
Panagyurishte 250
Hisar 251
Kazanlâk 257
The Shipka Pass 264

Stara Zagora 266
Sliven 269
Kotel 272
Zheravna 274

• CHAPTER 5: THE RHODOPES AND THE PLAIN OF THRACE 277–323

Pazardzhik 281
Plovdiv 282
Asenovgrad 301
Smolyan 308
Shiroka Lâka 310

Trigrad 311
Velingrad 315
Kârdzhali 318
Momchilgrad 321

• CHAPTER 6: THE BLACK SEA COAST 324–375

Varna 326
Golden Sands 343
Kranevo 344
Albena 344
Balchik 346
Rusalka 349

Sunny Beach 351
Nesebâr 352
Burgas 359
Sozopol 363
Sinemorets 371
The Strandzha 372

PART THREE CONTEXTS 377

The historical framework 379
The Macedonian question 397
Bulgaria's minorities 405
Books 411

Bulgarian music 415
Language 422
Glossary 425

Index 428

LIST OF MAPS

Bulgaria	x–xi
Bulgarian Railways	24
Chapter Divisions	57
Sofia	59
Sofia	66–67
Central Sofia	72–73
Dragalevtsi & Simeonovo	88
The Southwest	100
Rila Mountains	106–107
Blagoevgrad	119
Bansko	123
Melnik	136
The Balkan Range and the Danubian Plain	144–145
Vidin	163
Ruse	172–173
Dobrich	182
Pleven	190

Veliko Târnovo	202–203
Gabrovo	224
Shumen	228–229
The Sredna Gora and the Valley of the Roses	242–243
Koprivshtitsa	244
Kazanlâk	260
Stara Zagora	267
Sliven	269
The Rhodopes and the Plain of Thrace	278–279
Plovdiv	284–285
Old Plovdiv	290
The Black Sea Coast	325
Varna	328–329
Nesebâr	353
Burgas	360
Sozopol	364
Macedonia	398

MAP SYMBOLS

═══	Road	ⓘ	Tourist office
──	Minor road	⊠	Post office
⊪⊪⊪	Steps	⚏	Church (regional maps)
-----	Path/Trail	⌂	Monastery
──■──	Railway	⚏	Mosque
■─■─■	National border	✡	Synagogue
── ──	Chapter division boundary	──	Wall
──	River	■	Building
✗	Airport	⊞	Church (town maps)
◉	Hotel	⁺₊⁺	Cemetery
♦	Point of interest		Park
⋀⋀	Mountain range		National park
▲	Mountain peak		Woodland
⟋⟍	Cliff		Beach
ⓒ	Telephone		

INTRODUCTION

In many ways, **Bulgaria** is the forgotten country of the Balkans. Back in the days when it was one of the Soviet Union's most loyal East European allies, mention of the country brought few distinct images to mind. Despite being known as the site of extensive Black Sea package resorts and the source of several good wines, Bulgaria was too often dismissed as a dour, inward-looking place peopled by officious bureaucrats. If Westerners remained in the dark about the real Bulgaria, however, this was largely because the country's rulers didn't seem to want anybody to see it. Bizarre currency regulations, arbitrary border hassles, and restrictions on where you were allowed to stay made Bulgaria one of the most infuriating destinations in this part of the world. Happily all this has changed, but post-totalitarian Bulgaria still finds it difficult to emerge from the smokescreen imposed by more than four decades of Communist-inspired dullness. Even the process of democratic reform, although never lacking in drama, proved to be less newsworthy than the chaos and violence experienced by some of its Balkan neighbours. Worse, the war in the former Yugoslavia disrupted Bulgaria's land links with Western Europe, leaving the country cut off from a continent it was increasingly eager to join.

Bulgarians are frustrated by their country's lack of a clearly defined image abroad. Heirs to one of Europe's great civilizations, and guardians of Balkan Christian traditions, they have a keen sense of national identity distilled by centuries of turbulent history. In a constantly repeating cycle of grandeur, decline and national rebirth, successive Bulgarian states have striven to dominate the Balkan peninsula before succumbing to defeat and foreign tutelage, only to be regenerated by patriotic resistance to outside control.

The Bulgarian nation was formed in the seventh and eighth centuries when the **Bulgars**, warlike nomads from central Asia, assumed the leadership of Slav tribes in the lower Danube basin and took them on a spree of conquest in southeastern Europe. The resulting **First Bulgarian Kingdom**, after accepting Orthodox Christianity as the state religion, became the centre of Slavonic culture and spirituality before falling victim to a resurgent **Byzantine Empire** in the eleventh century. Recovery came a century later when the local aristocracy broke free from Constantinople and restored past glories in the shape of the **Second Bulgarian Kingdom**. However, the rise of Ottoman power in the fourteenth century ushered in the 500-year-long period of *Tursko robstvo* or "**Turkish bondage**" when the achievements of the medieval era were extinguished. Bulgarian art and culture recovered during the nineteenth-century **National Revival**, and the emergence of a potent revolutionary movement prepared the ground for Bulgaria's eventual **Liberation** in 1878, achieved with the help of Russian arms. However, Europe's other Great Powers conspired to limit the size of the infant state at the Berlin Congress of 1878, the first of a series of betrayals which denied Bulgarian claims to a territory which had long been considered an integral part of the historical Bulgarian state, **Macedonia**. In this century alone, Bulgaria has been to war three times (in the Balkan Wars of 1912–13, World War I, and World War II) to try and recover Macedonia, only to be defeated on each occasion. By 1945 it seemed like a country which had somehow missed out on its destiny, and rapidly turned in on itself during the subsequent deep sleep of Communism.

Bulgaria into the millennium

While undoubtedly more open to the outside world and more visitor-friendly than ever before, Bulgaria remains a country in transition. Back in the momentous winter of 1989, it looked as if it was dragging its feet on the road to democracy while others forged

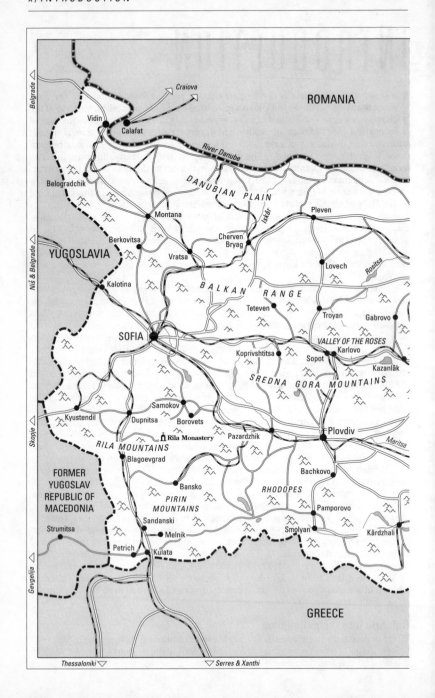

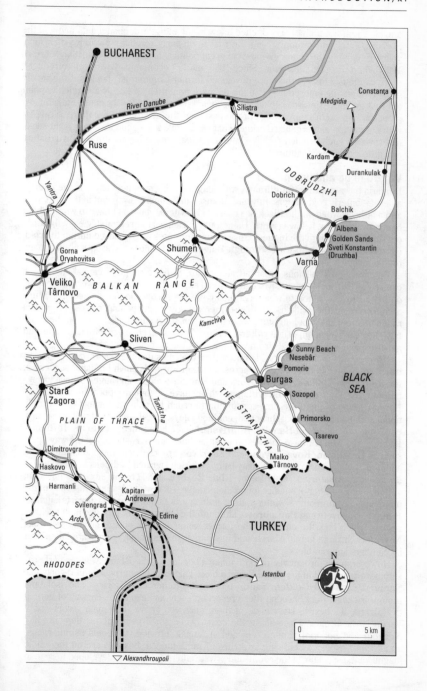

ahead. The Communist Party ditched a few of the old guard, changed its name to the Socialist Party and promptly won the first multi-party elections for more than forty years, remaining the country's most coherent political force, until the elections of April 1997, when the SDS took over. Since 1989, market economics have been introduced more cautiously than in the more developed former Communist states, but the steady growth of private enterprise is making its mark nonetheless. Locals are quick to point out that the move towards capitalism has meant poor conditions for many. Full employment and job security are things of the past, and the new business culture is riddled with corruption and organized crime. That said, while it's a good idea to remain sensitive towards such problems, they shouldn't affect your enjoyment of an invigorating and little-experienced culture.

Where to go and when

Bulgaria has a **continental climate**, with long, hot, dry summers and – in the interior at least – bitterly cold winters. July and August can be oppressively hot in the big cities, and a little crowded on the Black Sea coast – elsewhere, you won't have to worry about being swamped by fellow visitors. Using public transport is reasonably easy throughout the year, although the highest cross-mountain routes will be closed during the coldest months. Those who travel through Bulgaria too far out of season will find many tourist facilities shut.

Bulgaria's most obvious urban attractions are **Sofia**, a set-piece capital city whose centre was laid out by successive regimes as an expression of political power; and the second city **Plovdiv**, home to what is arguably the finest collection of nineteenth-century architecture in the Balkans. Both are increasingly cosmopolitan places, offering a range of street cafés and nightlife opportunities in short supply elsewhere in the country. They each form important cultural centres, being well endowed with museums and galleries, and are good bases from which to visit the rest of the interior.

However it's in the countryside rather than the cities that the real rewards of inland travel are to be found. You'll come across some of Europe's finest highland scenery in the **Rila**, **Pirin**, **Balkan**, **Sredna Gora** and **Rhodope** mountain ranges, whose valleys harbour the kind of **bucolic villages** which have all but disappeared in Western Europe. Many of them are time-consuming to reach by public transport, but if traditional architecture and goat-thronged, cobbled alleys appeal, any effort will be rewarded. While the villages of **Bansko**, **Koprivshtitsa** – a living memorial to the 1876 April Rising – and **Melnik** have the best tourist facilities, more rustic out-of-the-way spots such as **Brâshlyan**, **Kovachevitsa** and **Zheravna** are also well worth seeking out. In addition, the highland regions display Bulgaria's rich spiritual traditions in the shape of its many **monasteries**: **Bachkovo**, **Rila**, **Rozhen** and **Troyan** are the big four, although any number of smaller foundations make worthwhile destinations. Also in the mountains, a burgeoning winter tourist industry is taking shape in resorts such as **Bansko**, **Borovets** and **Pamporovo**, although the latter two are purpose-built package resorts which lack the charm of the former. Snow is thick on the ground from late November through to mid-March, and in summer the mountain resorts are taken over by climbers and ramblers.

However, most foreign visitors still make a beeline for the **Black Sea**, formerly the summer playground of the entire Eastern bloc. That said, big purpose-built resorts like **Sunny Beach** and **Golden Sands** tend to be rather characterless and isolating: though package tours based at these resorts present a cheap and easy way of getting to Bulgaria, it's best to steer clear of them once you arrive. The main resort-city of **Varna** is the liveliest place along the coast, while small peninsula settlements like **Nesebâr** and **Sozopol**, though crowded in August, provide traditional fishing-village architecture as well as enticing stretches of sand. Indeed, beaches are on the whole magnificent, especially in the south, and private enterprise is more developed here than anywhere else in the country, ensuring a plentiful supply of private rooms and good seafood restaurants. Although the climate remains mild all the year round, the Black Sea becomes deserted outside the main tourist season (July–Sept).

Elsewhere, few places are geared up to cater to Western-style, consumer-oriented tourism, although the rugged highlands that cut across the centre of the country are the best places to explore the heartlands of Bulgarian history and culture. The crafts towns and monasteries of the central Balkan Range were the places where Bulgarian culture recovered during the nineteenth-century National Revival, and are easily explored from the dramatically situated, citadel-encrusted town of **Veliko Târnovo**, medieval capital of the Second Bulgarian Kingdom. **Shumen**, main town of the north-west, is dour in comparison, but allows access to the remains of the Bulgarian state's first two capitals, **Pliska** and **Preslav**. Between the Balkan Range and the **Sredna Gora**, with its countless reminders of Bulgaria's nineteenth-century struggles against Turkish oppression, lies the **Valley of the Roses**, lined by a string of historic market towns and home to Bulgaria's renowned rose harvest in late May.

BULGARIA'S CLIMATE												
Average temperatures °F (°C)												
	Jan	Feb	Mar	Apr	May	Jun	Jul	Aug	Sep	Oct	Nov	Dec
Borovets												
°F	30	33	41	48	59	65	71	74	61	54	42	33
°C	(-1)	(1)	(5)	(9)	(15)	(19)	(22)	(23)	(16)	(12)	(6)	(1)
Plovdiv												
°F	33	34	44	54	62	73	74	76	65	55	45	36
°C	(1)	(3)	(7)	(12)	(17)	(23)	(23)	(24)	(19)	(13)	(8)	(3)
Varna												
°F	36	43	43	54	62	70	75	74	68	60	49	39
°C	(3)	(6)	(6)	(12)	(17)	(22)	(24)	(23)	(20)	(16)	(10)	(4)

THE

BASICS

GETTING THERE FROM BRITAIN AND IRELAND

Given Bulgaria's location on the southeast fringes of Europe, the overland journey from Britain and Ireland can be both time consuming and costly, however rewarding. By far the most convenient way to get there is to fly, although scheduled airline services to Sofia tend to be expensive. Alternative options include flying to another city in southeast Europe, such as Bucharest, Istanbul, Budapest or Thessaloniki, and continuing by land, or signing up for an inexpensive package holiday.

FLIGHTS

The sad fact is that, unlike Athens, Istanbul or Budapest, there's not enough volume in air traffic to Sofia to have created a **discount market**: finding the least expensive seat is a matter of scouring the newspapers, checking the independent travel specialists and utilizing any student/youth bargains you may be eligible for. **Peak times** for flights to Bulgaria are July and August and around the Easter, Christmas and New Year holidays. At these times be prepared to book well in advance.

Only BALKAN, the Bulgarian national airline, and British Airways offer **direct flights to Sofia**, from where you can pick up connecting flights to Plovdiv, Burgas and Varna. BALKAN has scheduled flights from London Heathrow five times a week (daily except Tues and Thurs), and the journey takes just over three hours; the food, however, is vile. An Apex return fare (which must be

booked at least two weeks ahead, must include at least one Saturday night away, and is valid for a maximum of three months) costs about £230 in low season and £250 during peak times. British Airways offers direct flights to Sofia three times a week (Tues, Thurs & Sun) for roughly the same price, although limited-period special offers may get you a small discount of about £10–20.

Discount flight agents sometimes sell seats on the BALKAN or BA London–Sofia service for a slightly cheaper price than the airline itself, but are more likely to offer special deals on **indirect flights** with other carriers, such as Lufthansa or Austrian Airlines, which can cost as little as £150 return. Eastern European specialists such as Scott's Tours (see overleaf) and Interchange (see p.6) can usually help with these, as can the Air Travel Advisory Bureau (☎0171/636 5000). Under 26s may get even better deals from **youth and student** travel firms such as USIT Campus or STA Travel.

Package tour operators may have a few discounted tickets on **charter flights** to Sofia, Plovdiv, or coastal destinations such as Varna, which work out far cheaper than scheduled flights but are rarely advertised in the press. You'll have to contact operators direct to find out what's on offer; Balkan Holidays are the obvious place to start. Similarly, you may find packages that fly from a regional airport that's more convenient than London.

You could also fly to another destination in **southeast Europe**, such as Budapest, Bucharest, Istanbul or Thessaloniki, and continue to Bulgaria overland. Flights to the Romanian capital Bucharest can be as expensive as those to Sofia, but cheap flights to Budapest, Istanbul and occasionally Thessaloniki are advertised in the press – as ever, check out local papers, or the travel pages of Sunday newspapers, or ring one of the agents in the "Discount Flight Agents" box overleaf.

PACKAGE DEALS

The main advantage of **package holidays** to Bulgaria is their low cost. Flight-plus-accommodation deals are often cheaper than the price of a scheduled airfare alone, and even the most independent of travellers should consider the package

DISCOUNT FLIGHT AGENTS AND AIRLINES

Council Travel, 28a Poland St, London W1V 3DB (☎0171/437 7767, *www.ciee.org*).
Flights and student discounts.

Joe Walsh Tours, 69 Upper O'Connell St, Dublin 2 (☎01/872 2555); 8–11 Baggot St, Dublin 2 (☎01/676 3053); 117 St Patrick St, Cork (☎021/277 959).
General budget fares agent.

North South Travel, Moulsham Mill Centre, Parkway, Chelmsford, Essex CM2 7PX (☎01245/492882).
Discount travel agency that contributes profits to support sustainable tourism and other projects in the developing world.

Scott's Tours, 159 Whitfield St, London W1P 5RY (☎0171/383 5353).
Specialists in discount flights to Eastern Europe and the CIS.

STA Travel, 86 Old Brompton Rd, London SW7 3LH; 117 Euston Rd, London NW1 2SX; 38 Store St, London WC1E 7BZ (all enquiries ☎0171/361 6161, *www.sta.travel.co.uk*); 25 Queen's Rd, Bristol BS8 1QE (☎0117/929 4399); 38 Sidney St, Cambridge CB2 3HX (☎01223/366966); 184 Byres Rd, Glasgow G1 1JH (☎0141/338 6000); 75 Deansgate, Manchester M3 2BW (☎0161/834 0668); 88 Vicar Lane, Leeds LS1 7JH (☎0113/244 9212); 9 St Mary's Place, Newcastle-upon-Tyne NE1 7PG (☎0191/233 2111); 36 George St, Oxford OX1 2OJ (☎01865/792800); and branches on uni-

versity campuses in Aberdeeen, Birmingham, Brighton, Bristol, Cambridge, Canterbury, Cardiff, Coventry, Durham, Glasgow, Leicestershire, Leeds, London, Loughborough, Manchester, Nottingham, Oxford, Sheffield and Warwick.
Worldwide specialists in low–cost flights and tours for students and under-26s.

Student & Group Travel, First Floor, 71 Dame St, Dublin 2 (☎01/677 7834).
Student specialists.

Trailfinders, 42–50 Earls Court Rd, London W8 6FT (☎0171/938 3366); 194 Kensington High St, London W8 7RG (☎0171/938 3939); 22–24 The Priory, Queensway, Birmingham B4 6BS (☎0121/236 1234); 48 Corn St, Bristol BS1 1HQ (☎0117/929 9000); 254–284 Sauchiehall St, Glasgow G2 3EH (☎0141/353 2224); 58 Deansgate, Manchester M3 2FF (☎0161/839 6969).
One of the best-informed and most efficient agents.

The Travel Bug, 125 Gloucester Rd, London SW7 4SF (☎0171/835 2000, *www.travel-bug.co.uk*); 597 Cheetham Hill Rd, Manchester M8 5EJ (☎0161/721 4000).
Large range of discounted tickets.

Travel Cuts, 295 Regent St, London W1 (☎0171/255 1944, *www.travelcuts.co.uk*).
Budget, student and youth travel specalists.

USIT Campus, 52 Grosvenor Gardens, London SW1 0AG (☎0171/730 3402, *www.campustravel.co.uk*); 541 Bristol Rd, Selly

option. Although they in theory tie you down to staying in one or two centres, there's nothing to prevent you from absenting yourself for a few days and indulging in a little exploration of your own. The most popular packages are **beach holidays** on the Black Sea coast, or winter **skiing** trips in highland resorts. The **season** for summer packages runs from mid-May to late September, peaking in the first two weeks of August. The winter season runs from December to March, peaking in mid-February.

There are also a number of other options: Balkan Holidays arranges numerous **two-centre trips**, combining coastal and mountain resorts, Bulgarian and Romanian, or Bulgarian and Turkish destinations, as well as fly-drive holidays with pre-booked accommodation. For a **city break** in Sofia, again try Balkan Holidays, or Interchange, a company specializing in travel to Eastern Europe,

who will tailor a flight-plus-accommodation deal to your needs.

HOLIDAYS ON THE COAST

The main **disadvantage** of package holidays on the Black Sea coast is the nature of the principal holiday resorts themselves. The purpose-built complexes are often over-large and some distance from the nearest town or village, ensuring that you experience little of Bulgarian life. **Beaches**, however, are generally spotless, and coastal waters warm, clean and safe. **Sunny Beach** (Slânchev Bryag) and **Golden Sands** (Zlatni Pyasâtsi) are the biggest (and most soulless) of the tourist complexes, chock full of restaurants, bars and discos, while **Albena** is almost as huge but rather more stylish, with excellent sports facilities. **Sveti Konstantin** is smaller, surrounded by woodlands and coves,

Oak, Birmingham B29 GAU (☎0121/414 1848); 61 Ditchling Rd, Brighton BN1 4SD (☎01273/570226); 37–39 Queen's Rd, Clifton, Bristol BS8 1QE (☎0117/929 2494); 5 Emmanuel St, Cambridge CB1 1NE (☎01223/324283); 53 Forest Rd, Edinburgh EH1 2QP (☎0131/225 6111, telesales 668 33303); 166 Deansgate, Manchester M3 3FE (☎0161/833 2046, telesales 273 1721); 105–106 St Aldates, Oxford OX1 1DD (☎01865/242067).
Student/youth specialists, with branches in YHA shops and on university campuses all over

the country. Also agents for InterRail and other train passes

USIT, Fountain Centre, College St, Belfast BT1 6ET (☎01232/324073); 10–11 Market Parade, Patrick St, Cork (☎021/270900); 33 Ferryquay St, Derry (☎01504/371888); 19 Aston Quay, Dublin 2 (☎01/602 1600 or 679 8833); Victoria Place, Eyre Square, Galway (☎091/565177); Central Buildings, O'Connell St, Limerick (☎061/415064); 36–37 Georges St, Waterford (☎051/72601).
Student and youth specialists for flights and trains.

AIRLINES

Austrian Airlines, 10 Wardour St, London W1V 4BJ (☎0171/434 7350, *www.aua.com*).

BALKAN, 322 Regent St, London W1 5AB (☎0171/637 7637).

British Airways, 156 Regent St, London W1R 5TA; 101–102 Cheapside, London EC2V 6DT; Victoria Place, Victoria Station, SW1W 9SJ; 146 New St, Birmingham B2 4HN; 41–43 Deansgate, Manchester M3 2AY; 6 New Broadmead, Union St, Bristol BS1 2DL; 66 Gordon St, Glasgow G1 3RS; 30–32 Frederick St, Edinburgh EH2 2JR (all enquiries ☎0345/222111, *www.british-airways.com*); 1 Fountain Centre, College St, Belfast BT1 6ET (☎01342/326566); Dublin reservations (☎1800/626747).

CSA (Czech Airways), 72–73 Margaret St, London W1N 8HA (☎0171/225 1898, *www.csa.cz*).

Lufthansa, 7–8 Conduit St, London W1R 9TG; Phoenix House, 78 Vincent St, Glasgow G2 5UB (☎0345/737747, *www.lufthansa.co.uk*).

Malév (Hungarian Airways), 1st floor, 22–25 Sackville St, London W1X 1DE (☎0171/439 0577).

Olympic Airways, 11 Conduit St, London W1R 0LP (☎0171/409 3400).

Tarom (Romanian Airways), 27 New Cavendish St, London W1M 7RL (☎0171/224 3693).

Turkish Airlines, 125 Pall Mall, London SW1 5EA (☎0171/766 9300, *www.turkishairlines.com*).

---

while villa complexes and holiday villages such as **Dyuni** or **Elenite** will appeal to holiday makers in search of something more tranquil. You could also stay in the attractive fishing port of **Nesebâr**, either in a hotel or an apartment in the old or new town.

Currently, Balkan Holidays is the only **tour operator** offering summer beach packages. Peak-season **prices** for holidays in Sunny Beach, Golden Sands, Albena and Dyuni hover around £300–350 for one week, and £350–400 for two, though prices are often £100 lower in May and September. Self-catering apartments in the old houses of Nesebâr cost about £285 per person for seven days in high season, dropping to £242 in May or September; apartments in the new town cost slightly less. It's worth noting, however, that **food and drink** prices in package resorts are usually three times as high as in the rest of

Bulgaria – Albena and Golden Sands are notoriously expensive, with prices around the same as you'd pay at home.

SKIING HOLIDAYS

Balkan Holidays, First Choice, Neilson and Crystal Holidays all offer one- and two-week winter holidays at the Rhodope resort of **Pamporovo**, where British tourists make up about 75 percent of the foreign guests, and **Borovets** in the Rila mountains, where they account for a stunning 90 percent. There are currently no UK operators offering packages to the other ski resorts such as **Bansko** and **Malyovitsa** in the Pirin and Rila mountains, or **Mount Vitosha**, just outside Sofia. At Borovets and Pamporovo, a week's stay can cost as little as £235 in December, early January or March, rising to £439–479 in the mid-February peak season. Remember, though, that equipment

PACKAGES, STUDY TOURS AND SPECIALIST OPERATORS

ACE Study Tours, Babraham, Cambridge CB2 4AP (☎01223/835055).
Fourteen-day study tours of monasteries (Zemen, Rila, Rozhen, Bachkovo) and National Revival architecture in historic towns (Melnik, Plovdiv, Veliko Târnovo and Koprivshtitsa) from £1005.

Balkan Holidays, 19 Conduit St, London W1R 9TD (☎0171/543 5555; flight-only ☎0171/543 5588).
Extensive range of beach, skiing and mountain and lake holidays; also flight-only deals and special interest tours for independent travellers.

Balkania Travel, 28 Hawgood St, London E3 3RU (☎538 8654, fax 537 9377).
Runs wine tours of Bulgaria, through its parent company, the UK wine importers Domaine Boyar.

British-Bulgarian Society, c/o Finsbury Library, 245 St John St, London EC1V 4NB (☎0171/837 2304).
Membership (£10 a year) gives access to cut-price natural history, wildlife, ornithology and textile (10 days from £800) tours, as well as lectures and social events.

Crystal Holidays, Crystal House, The Courtyard, Arlington Rd, Surbiton, Surrey KT6 6BW (☎0181/399 5144, email *travel@crystalholidays.co.uk* Web site *www.crystalholidays.co.uk*).
Ski packages to Borovets and Pamporovo, from £299 for seven nights.

DA Study Tours, Williamton House, Low Causeway, Culross, Fife KY12 8HL (☎01383/882200).
Offers an eight-day art-history tour with a spot of walking, featuring Sofia, Plovdiv, Koprivshtitsa, Kazanlâk, Dobârsko, Bansko, Melnik, Rila and Bachkovo, for £550.

Exodus, 9 Weir Rd, London SW12 0LT (☎0181/675 5550, email *sales@exodustravels.co.uk* Web site *www.exodustravels.co.uk*).
Seventeen-day hiking and camping tours in the Rila and Pirin mountains, in July, Aug and Sept only.

Explore Worldwide, 1 Frederick St, Aldershot, Hants GU11 1LQ (☎01252/760 000; email *info@explore.co.uk* Web site *www.explore.co.uk*).
A ten-day tour featuring Melnik, Rila, Sofia,

Plovdiv and four days' hiking in the Pirin and Rila ranges from £560–590, with a cheaper option of joining the tour in Bulgaria. Tours run May–Sept.

First Choice, First Choice House, London Rd, Crawley, West Sussex RH10 2GX (☎0870/754 2 574).
Ski packages to Borovets and Pamporovo, for £235–419 for seven nights.

Inghams, 10–18 Putney Hill, London SW15 6AX (☎0181/780 4444).
Ski packages to Borovets, from £289 for seven nights.

Interchange, Interchange House, 27 Stafford Rd, Croydon, Surrey CRO 4NG (☎0181/681 3612, *interchange@interchange.uk.com*).
Can arrange full-board homestays in Sofia (from £32 per person per night), as well as excursions with a car and a guide. Also offers flights to Sofia from London (from £239), and from Manchester via Frankfurt (from £309).

Limosa Holidays, Suffield House, Northrepps, Norfolk NR27 0LZ (☎01263/578143).
Runs birdwatching tours in May, June and Sept. The ten-day spring tour (£1125) features the Rhodopes, Black Sea coast and the Danube wetlands; the eight-day autumn tour (£895) is centred on the coast.

Neilson, 71 Houghside Rd, Pudsey, Leeds LS28 9BR (☎0990/994 444, email *sales@neilson.co.uk* Web site *www.neilson.co.uk.*
Ski packages to Pamporovo and Borovets, from £235 for seven nights.

Prospect Music and Art Tours, 454–458 Chiswick High Rd, London W4 5TT (☎0181/995 2151, fax 742 1969).
Runs a week-long art-history tour of Sofia, Kazanlâk, Plovdiv, Bistritsa Palace, Melnik and the monasteries of Rila, Bachkovo and Rozhen for £925; in May and Sept only.

Sherpa Expeditions, 131a Heston Rd, Hounslow, Mddx TW5 0RD (☎0181/577 2717, email *sherpa.sales@dial.pipex.com* Web site *www.sherpa-walking-holidays.co.uk*).
Runs trekking tours in the Rila and Pirin mountains staying in mountain chalets from July–Sept.

Silk Road Travel, 64 South William St, Dublin 2 (☎01/677 1029).
The Irish agents for Exodus.

and tuition (usually bookable in advance) will cost extra: about £30 a week for a lift pass, £20–30 for ski and boot rental, and £30–40 for six days' worth of skiing lessons – though many firms offer an all-inclusive ski pack for as little as £75.

MOUNTAIN AND LAKE HOLIDAYS

Aimed at those who enjoy highland scenery, these summer packages feature a mixture of guided walks, entertainments and optional excursions – and can be a good way to indulge in some independent travel as well. At present Balkan Holidays offers seven- or fourteen-night holidays in **Borovets** (from £317 or £377), **Pamporovo** (from £329 or £388) and **Bansko** (from £293 or £328), or a two-week **twin centre** holiday (from £379). While the opportunities for hiking are equally good at all three resorts, Bansko and Pamporovo have more to offer in terms of public transport than Borovets does, and Bansko itself has more charm and historic interest than the other two put together.

HIKING AND SPECIALIST HOLIDAYS

From June to mid-September several UK operators offer hiking holidays in the **Pirin and Rila mountains**. The amount of walking and type of accommodation varies, as do the included tours to sites such as Rila, Melnik, Plovdiv or Sofia. Exodus offers a seventeen-day package of which twelve nights are spent camping out (from £645), while Sherpa Expeditions uses mountain chalets for its eight-day hiking trips (from £790). The ten-day Explore Worldwide package (£560–590) stays in both hotels and chalets, but involves only four days' hiking. At the time of writing, no UK operator features the **Rhodopes**, but it is possible to join a tour in Bulgaria; see "Outdoor activities and eco-tourism" on p.48 for details and local contacts.

Specialist holidays and **study tours** cater for those with particular interests from monasteries to ornithology, wine or folk dancing. These tend to be pricier than the standard packages, but almost always include knowledgeable guides, and offer experiences that you don't get on regular tours. Membership of the British-Bulgarian Society gives access to natural history trips (15 days for £815), wildlife tours (14 days for £805) and ornithology holidays (seven or fourteen days from £590 or £825), the latter being a lot cheaper than the **birdwatching** tours offered by Limosa Holidays (eight or ten days for £895 or £1125). While Melnik, Rila, Plovdiv and Koprivshtitsa invariably feature on most **art history** tours' itineraries, other destinations vary, so it's worth comparing the packages carefully – DA Study Tours, Prospect Music and Art Tours, and ACE Study Tours all offer interesting packages. If it's **wine** you're keen on, you could consider Balkan Holidays' gastronomic tour including Plovdiv and Veliko Târnovo (seven or fourteen days from £479 or £516), or Balkania Travel's tailor-made wine tours for small groups and individuals.

BY TRAIN

The most direct **train routes** to Bulgaria (Dieppe–Paris–Milan–Venice–Zagreb–Belgrade–Sofia or Ostende–Brussels–Munich–Zagreb–Belgrade–Sofia) were disrupted by the war in Yugoslavia, which severed the connection between Zagreb and Belgrade. Although this is likely to be restored in the next few years, the only services currently running follow the slightly longer Budapest–Belgrade–Sofia route. Be warned that it is not safe to travel overnight unless you've booked a sleeper for the Yugoslav leg of the journey; women travellers should team up with a male companion or book the whole compartment for security. **Transit visas** for the Former Yugoslavia can be issued by the embassy or consulate in your home country (but not at the border). They cost £14/$24, providing that you already have a valid visa for Bulgaria.

A longer way of reaching Bulgaria by train is to travel **across Romania** to enter Bulgaria at the northern town of Ruse – a journey requiring two and a half days and a transit visa, available at border crossings or from the Romanian consulate in your home country for around £29/$47.

Perhaps the most roundabout train route to Bulgaria is London–Paris–Milan–Brindisi, followed by a ferry to Patras in **Greece**, from where you can continue by train to Sofia via Athens and Thessaloniki. An even more adventurous variation would be to take a ferry from Bari in Italy to Durrës in **Albania**, travelling by bus across Albania and the Former Yugoslav Republic of Macedonia before entering Bulgaria from the west. Albania is quite anarchic and certainly not for inexperienced travellers, but there's a fairly reliable bus service to Kyunstendil and Sofia in Bulgaria from Durrës and Tirana, operated by the Bulgarian company MATPU.

BUYING TICKETS

Buying a **through ticket** from London to Sofia is practically impossible, since Rail Europe can only sell tickets as far as **Budapest** in Hungary. Tickets are valid for no more than two months and do *not* allow stopovers en route. Both of the routes on offer entail travelling by Eurostar to Paris or Brussels and boarding an overnight train there, but discounts for under 26s only exist on the routing via Paris, where the standard one-way fare is £127 (£119 for under 26s), which is marginally cheaper than a single to Budapest via Brussels (£130). Anyone over 60 and holding a British Rail Senior Citizen Railcard qualifies for £10 off the standard fare via Paris, while by purchasing a Rail Europe Senior (RES) card for £5, you can reduce the fare to £90. On the Brussels route, RES-holders qualify for a discount fare of £92 which is not available otherwise. On top of all these prices, you must also add the cost of a couchette (£11). Return tickets cost twice the price of singles.

Once in Budapest, it is easy to buy an **onward ticket to Bulgaria** at the MÁV International Bookings office, VI, Andrassy út 36; expect to pay about £42 if you travel via Yugoslavia, and £66 via Romania.

If you want to stop off anywhere en route or travel across Europe as far as Turkey, you may do better to buy some kind of pass, though this is unlikely to work out any cheaper. **InterRail passes** cover 28 European countries (including Turkey and Morocco) grouped together in eight zones. As Bulgaria is in Zone H (together with Romania, Yugoslavia and Macedonia) you'll need to buy a one-month all-zones pass to cover the whole journey from the Channel Ports to Bulgaria and back again, which costs £259 for under 26s, and £349 for anyone older. A cheaper option is to buy a three-zone pass (£229/£309) as far as Greece, then catch a bus to Bulgaria for about $20 (less than you'd pay to travel the last leg by train). Note that InterRail passes do not cover travel between Britain and the continent, though holders are eligible for discounts on cross-Channel ferries and free travel on the Brindisi–Patras ferry between Italy and Greece.

As InterRail passes are supposedly only sold to those who can prove residence in Europe for six months prior to the date of application, people who aren't eligible (or can't find an agent who doesn't require proof) are obliged to consider other options, such as a Eurail or Eurodomino/ Freedom pass.

Eurail passes allow unlimited travel through seventeen countries in Europe, but as they don't cover Bulgaria nor any of the neighbouring states except Greece, they're only worth considering if you're travelling widely throughout Europe. Eurail passes come in numerous varieties, some with age restrictions and others allowing the option of first class travel. To give an idea, a fifteen-day Youth Pass valid for second-class travel costs £273, a one month pass £438, and a three month version £767.

The other option is a **Eurodomino/Freedom Pass**, which allows second-class travel for three, five or ten days within a one month period in any one country in Europe. Though you're unlikely to save any money by buying the pass covering

Bulgaria (three days costs £29; five days £39; and 10 days £68), it could be worth buying one if you're planning a few days travelling around a country where train fares are higher, before entering Bulgaria. Anyone is eligible for a Eurodomino/Freedom Pass, provided that they can prove that they do not reside in the country for which they have purchased the pass.

All the above passes can be bought at USIT Campus, or Wasteels (see box below) in the UK; InterRail passes are also available from Rail Europe/French Rail in Britain; and Eurail passes from selected agents in North America and Australia (see boxes on p.11 and p.13 for addresses).

If you're **moving on from Bulgaria** to another country, remember that international tickets purchased in Bulgaria can be very expensive, another reason for opting for an InterRail pass.

BY BUS

Although there are no direct **buses** from Britain to Bulgaria, it's worth contacting Britain's main international bus operators Eurolines or scanning local pages and listings magazines for news of what other companies are offering to Central Europe. Currently, the nearest you can get to Bulgaria by direct bus is **Budapest**: the Eurolines service departs on Monday, Friday and Saturday mornings from London's Victoria coach terminal, arriving in Budapest 27 hours later. A

TRAIN AND BUS ENQUIRIES

Rail Europe/French Rail, 179 Piccadilly, London W1V OBA (☎0990/084 8848). Tickets can be collected (but *not* purchased) from 10 Leak St, opposite the Eurostar arrivals terminal at Waterloo Station.

Eurolines All enquiries ☎01582/404 511.

Eurostar, EPS House, Waterloo Station, London SE1 8SE (nationwide reservations ☎0990/186186 or 03445/3030, *www.eurail.com/eurostar/eurostar/htm*).

USIT Campus, 52 Grosvenor Gardens, London SW1W OAG (☎0171/730 3402, *www.campustravel.co.uk*). See box on pp.4–5 for other branches around Britain and Ireland.

Wasteels, Victoria Station (by platform 2), London SW1V 1JY (☎0171/834 7066).

For train contacts in Australia, New Zealand and North America, see p.25.

---

return ticket costs £119 (£129 in July, Aug and Dec), or £109 (£119 peak rate) for under 26s, but off-season (mid-April–May & Nov) discount fares can be as low as £99 for both. From Budapest you can catch a train to Bulgaria via Serbia or Romania (see above).

However, there's an easier **connection via Prague**. The Eurolines bus from Victoria on Monday, Thursday, Friday and Sunday mornings arrives in Prague about 9am next day. In the vicinity of the bus terminal is the ticket office of the Bulgarian firm Diligence Express, which runs a daily bus to Sofia leaving at 6pm – so there's time for some sightseeing even if you decide not to stay in Prague. A return ticket to Prague costs £89 (£95 in July & Aug), or £79 (£85 peak rate) for under 26s, while Diligence charges about £60 return to Sofia – on top of which there's the cost of a double transit-visa through Serbia (£28). Each leg of the two-stage journey lasts 24 hours.

APPROACHING FROM TURKEY

Several Turkish bus operators run regular **services from Istanbul** to Plovdiv, Sofia, Varna, Burgas and elsewhere in Bulgaria. Prices on the Istanbul–Sofia route hover around $20–25 each way. Numerous travel agents in the central Sultanahmet district of town can reserve seats; otherwise head for west Istanbul's main bus station at Topkapi, where most of the bus operators have offices. Bear in mind, however, that Bulgarian–Turkish border crossings are usually clogged up with East European bus parties travelling to or from the Bosphorus, and long queues at the frontier (a wait of 5–8 hours is not uncommon) ensure that this option can be long, tedious, and difficult to timetable. Services from **other towns** in western Turkey such as Edirne, Bursa, Gebze and Yalova run to Plovdiv and Kârdzhali.

DRIVING TO BULGARIA

Driving to Bulgaria is plain sailing as far east as Hungary, following the E5 from the Belgian coast through Brussels, Cologne and Vienna, to Budapest. Thereafter the roads deteriorate, border crossings take longer and the risk of mishaps increases, whichever route you take. The most direct way is **through Yugoslavia**, still on the E5, from Belgrade down to the Dimitrovgrad/Kalotina crossing on the Bulgarian border. Though drivers avoided it during the Yugoslav wars and embassies strongly warn against it during crises, in "normal" times the road is less arduous than the alternative route **through Romania**, via Nadlac–Arad– Timisoara–Drobeta Turnu–Severin and then a ferry across the Danube to Vidin. Driving non-stop with no mishaps, the route via Yugoslavia should get you to Sofia in about 36 hours from Brussels or Calais, with the Romanian route taking four to five hours longer. Travellers will need a **transit visa** for Yugoslavia or Romania. Yugoslav visas can only be obtained though a Yugoslav consulate abroad; Romanian ones are available at border crossings as well as consulates (see box on p.8 for addresses).

A longer, but more agreeable approach through Europe is **via Italy and Greece**, catching a car-ferry to the Greek mainland and driving north-wards to Bulgaria. Besides the pleasure of driving through Italy and Greece, this route reveals the similarities and differences between Aegean and Pirin Macedonia and has the advantage of good roads and magnificent scenery for much of the way to Sofia past such prime attractions as Melnik, Bansko and Rila Monastery.

If you are planning to drive, the **AA** European Routes Department (☎0990/448866) can advise on all facets of driving to Bulgaria, including the best route to follow and the addresses of useful organizations. Remember that you'll need an **international driving licence**, available from the motoring organizations in your home country for a

small fee, together with an **international Green Card** from your insurance company. Both documents are obligatory in Hungary and recommended in the other countries you'll be driving through. For more on driving around Bulgaria, see p.26.

HITCHING TO BULGARIA

Quite apart from the obvious, and very real **dangers** involved, **hitching to Bulgaria** is not simple. Even when fully traversable the road down through Yugoslavia was notoriously bad for hitching, and the long route through Hungary and Romania is, if anything, worse. However, approaching **from Turkey or Greece** is feasible. Otherwise, the best idea seems to be to hitch as far as you can on the Western European highway network, heading through Germany and Austria as far as the Hungarian border and making for Budapest, from where you can complete the journey reasonably cheaply by public transport. It is worth looking into the possibility of **sharing a lift** at least part of the way. You can consult the noticeboard or post your own notice at Nomad Books, 781 Fulham Rd, London SW6 5HA (☎0171/736 4000), or check the "Connections" page in the travel magazine *Wanderlust*. Alternatively you could put your own free advert in *Wanderlust*, by writing to: Connections, *Wanderlust*, PO Box 1832, Windsor, Berks, SL4 6YP.

GETTING THERE FROM NORTH AMERICA

The only direct flights to Bulgaria from the USA are with BALKAN, the national airline. Alternative options include flying via another European country, or flying to another city in southeast Europe and continuing by land. See "Getting there from Britain and Ireland" and "Getting around" for information on routes and train passes.

FLIGHTS TO BULGARIA

Barring special offers, the cheapest of the airlines' published fares is usually an **Apex** ticket, although this will carry certain restrictions: you have to book – and pay – at least 21 days before departure, spend at least seven days abroad (maximum stay three months), and you tend to get penalized if you change your schedule. Many airlines offer youth or student fares to **under-26s**; a passport or driving licence are sufficient proof of

DISCOUNT TRAVEL COMPANIES, AIRLINES AND SPECIALIST OPERATORS

Council Travel, 205 E 42nd St, New York, NY 10017 (☎1-800/226 8624 or 212/661 1450, www.ciee.com), and branches in many other US cities.
Nationwide specialists in student travel.

Educational Travel Center, 438 N Frances St, Madison, WI 53703 (☎1-800/747 5551 or 608/256 5551, www.edtrav.com).
Student/youth and consolidator fares.

STA Travel, 10 Downing St, New York, NY 10014 (☎212/627 3111, www.sta-travel.com), and other branches in the Los Angeles, San Francisco and Boston areas.
Worldwide discount travel firm specializing in student/youth fares; also student IDs, travel insurance, car rental, train passes, etc.

TFI Tours International, 34 W 32nd St, New York, NY 10001 (☎800/745 8000 or 212/736 1140), and offices in Las Vegas and Miami.
Consolidator.

Travac, 989 Sixth Ave, New York NY 10018 (☎1-800/872 8800 or 212/563 3303).
Consolidator and charter broker, mostly to Europe.

Travel Avenue, 10 S Riverside, Suite 1404, Chicago, IL 60606 (☎1-800/333 3335 or 312/876 6866).
Discount travel agent.

Travel Cuts, 187 College St, Toronto, ON M5T 1P7 (☎800/667 2887 or 416/979 2406, www.travelcuts.com), and other branches all over Canada.
Specializing in student fares, IDs and other travel services.

NORTH AMERICAN AIRLINES

Austrian Airlines ☎1-800/843 0002, www.aua.com

BALKAN US ☎1-800/852 0944; Canada ☎1-800/668 1059

British Airways US ☎1-800/247 9297; Canada ☎1-800/668 1059

Czech Airlines (CSA) ☎1-800/223 2365, www.csa.cz

KLM US ☎1-800/374 7747; Canada ☎1-800/361 5073; www.klm.nl

Lufthansa US ☎1-800/645 3880; Canada ☎1-800/563 5954; www.lufthansa-usa.com

SPECIALIST TOUR OPERATORS

Adventure Center, 1311 63rd St, Suite 200, Emeryville, CA 94608; ☎1-800/227 8747 or 510/654 1879, www.adventure-center.com
Offers a "Byways of Bulgaria" tour including hiking and cultural sights from $690 (land-only).

Adventures Abroad, 2148-20800 Westminster Highway, Richmond, BC V6V 2W3; ☎1-800/665 3998 or 604/303 1099,
www.adventures-abroad.com
Offers two-week packages of Sofia and the countryside from $2722 including airfare (from New York), or $2895 (from LA).

Balkan Tourist USA 20 E46th St, New York, NY10017, New York, NY 10017; ☎1-800/822 1106 or 212/338 6838, wwwbalkanusa.com
Eastern European specialists, and a good source

of discount flights to Bulgaria. Also offers city breaks and organized tours including five nights in Sofia from $780, and a "Grand Tour of Bulgaria" from $1328; both include airfares from New York.

Carpati International, 72 Gypsy Trail Road, Carmel NY 10512; ☎1-800/447 8742, www.carpati.com
Offers a range of customized tours and packages,

Eastern Europe Tours, 600 Stewart St, 1222, Seattle, WA 98101; ☎1-800/641 3456 or 206/448 8400, www.imp-worldtours.com
Customized tours and packages including a seven-day "Classic Bulgaria" tour for $1679, and Bulgaria and the Black Sea" from $1925.

age, though these tickets are subject to availability and can have eccentric booking conditions.

You can normally – though by no means always – cut costs further by going through a **specialist** **flight agent**: either a **consolidator**, who buys up blocks of tickets from the airlines and sells them at a discount, or a **discount agent**, who in addition to dealing with cheap flights may also offer special student and youth fares and a range of other services such as travel insurance, rail passes, car rentals, tours and the like. Bear in mind, though, that penalties for changing your plans can be stiff. Remember too that these companies make their money by dealing in bulk – don't expect them to answer lots of questions. If you travel a lot, **discount travel clubs** are another option – the annual membership fee may be worth it for benefits such as cut-price air tickets and car rental.

Be advised, however, that the pool of travel companies is swimming with sharks – exercise caution and *never* deal with a company that demands cash up front or refuses to accept payment by credit card.

Air **fares** to Bulgaria are highest from around June to September and mid-December to mid-January; they drop during the "shoulder" season – April through May, and are lowest from November to mid-December and mid-January through March. Note that flying on weekends can add $60 to the round-trip fare; the following prices quoted below assume midweek travel, and exclude **taxes** (about US$70/CAN$60).

BALKAN offers the only non-stop **direct flights** from New York (JFK) to Sofia, operating on Mondays, with occasional Friday flights over Christmas, New Year and the peak season. Its cheapest fare (allowing up to thirty days stay) is currently $499 in the low season, $750 peak rate.

Alternatively you can fly to Sofia **via another European city**. Austrian Airlines via Vienna offers a good deal in low season, when a return (valid for one month) costs $425 from New York, $485 from Chicago or $575 from LA, though prices more than double during peak season. British Airways flies daily from New York via London for around $500 (low season), and Lufthansa flies daily from New York via Frankfurt or Munich for $525 (low season) and $1138 (high season), though occasionally offers special promotions from as low as $425. Czech Airlines also charges $525 (low season) from New York to Sofia via Prague, but only flies on certain days of the week, which vary depending on the time of year.

From **Canada**, your best bet is to fly KLM to Amsterdam, who can book the connecting Amsterdam to Sofia flight on BALKAN. The daily through service from Toronto to Sofia costs CAN$975 in low season and CAN$1840 at peak times, while the daily flight from Vancouver to Sofia starts at CAN$1550 in low season, up to CAN$2185 in high season.

A number of specialist operators run **package tours** to Bulgaria; although phone numbers are given in the box on the previous page, you're better off making **reservations** through your local travel agent, who will make all the phone calls, sort out the snafus and arrange flights, insurance and the like – all at no extra cost to you.

GETTING THERE FROM AUSTRALIA & NEW ZEALAND

There are no direct flights from Australia or New Zealand to Bulgaria. Travellers from

down under have to fly to Bangkok (with Air New Zealand, for example, or Qantas), stay overnight at their own expense, and connect with BALKAN's twice weekly Bangkok–Sofia flight. The return fare from Melbourne or Sydney to Sofia is about AUS$1500/NZ$1640 low season (Oct–March), rising to AUS$1900/NZ2200 in high season (April–Sept).

If you're visiting Bulgaria as part of more extensive travels within Europe, it may be worth-while looking into buying a **train pass**, which can be obtained through most travel agents; see "Getting There from Britain and Ireland" (p.3) and "Getting Around" (p.23) for more information.

AUSTRALIAN AND NEW ZEALAND TOUR OPERATORS, SPECIALIST AGENTS AND AIRLINES

Accent on Travel, 545 Queen St, Brisbane (☎07/3832 1777, *www.accentontravel.com.au*).

Anywhere Travel, 345 Anzac Parade, Kingsford, Sydney (☎02/9663 0411).

Budget Travel, 16 Fort St, Auckland (☎09/366 0061 or 0800/808040).

Destinations Unlimited, 3 Milford Rd, Milford, Auckland (☎09/373 4033).

Flight Centres,
Australia: Circular Quay, Sydney (☎02/9241 2422); Bourke St, Melbourne (☎03/9650 2899), plus other branches nationwide; Web site *www.flightcentre.com.au*

New Zealand: National Bank Towers, 205 Queen St, Auckland (☎09/209 6171); Shop 1M, National Mutual Arcade, 152 Hereford St, Christchurch (☎03/379 7145); 50–52 Willis St, Wellington (☎04/472 8101), and other branches throughout the country.

Harvey World Travel, Princess Highway, Kogarah, Sydney (☎02/567 6099, *www.harveyworld.com.au*), plus branches nationwide.

Northern Gateway, 22 Cavenagh St, Darwin (☎08/8941 1394).

Passport Travel, 11/401 St Kilda Rd, Melbourne (☎03/9867 3888).

STA Travel,
Australia: 855 St George St, Sydney (☎1300 360960 or 02/9212 1255); 256 Flinders St, Melbourne (☎03/9654 7266), plus other offices in Townsville, state capitals and major universities; Web site *www.statravel.com.au*

New Zealand: Travellers' Centre, 10 High St, Auckland (☎09/309 0458); 233 Cuba St, Wellington (☎04/385 0561); 90 Cashel St, Christchurch (☎03/379 9098), and other offices in Dunedin, Palmerston North, Hamilton and major universities.

Thomas Cook,
Australia: 330 Collins St, Melbourne (☎03/9602 3811), plus branches in Sydney and other state capitals; Web site *www.thomascook.com.au*

New Zealand: Shop 250a St Luke's Square, Auckland (☎09/849 2071), plus branches throughout the country.

Topdeck Travel, 65 Glenfell St, Adelaide (☎08/8232 7222).

Tymtro Travel, 428 George St, Sydney (☎02/9223 2211).

UTAG Travel, 122 Walker St, North Sydney (☎131398, *www.unimedia.co.au*), plus branches throughout Australia.

SPECIALIST AGENTS

Balkan Travel Service, Shop 6, Belvedere Arcade, 70 John St, Cabramatta, Sydney (☎02/9727 0305).
Eastern Europe specialists.

Eastern Europe Travel Bureau, Level 5 75 King Street, Sydney 2000 (☎02/9262 1144); Third floor, suite 313, 343 Little Collins St, Melbourne (☎03/9600 0299).
Offers Sofia stopovers and city tours, plus longer trips including Rila Monastery, Plovdiv and Varna. Can book accommodation in selected destinations and tailor-make short tours.

AIRLINES

Quantas 70 Hunter Street, Sydney, (☎131211); 154 Queen St, Auckland (☎357 8700 and 0800 808767).

Air New Zealand 5 Elizabeth St, Sydney (☎132476); 139 Queen St, Auckland (☎0800 737000 or 09/3573000).

RED TAPE: VISAS AND CARTES STATISTIQUES

All visitors to Bulgaria require a full (not visitors') passport, and EU and US citizens can remain in the country for up to thirty days without a visa, but will need a visa if intending to stay for longer. Australians, New Zealanders and Canadians will need a visa, unless they meet certain conditions (see below). However, as the rules change every year, it's wise to check with a Bulgarian embassy or consulate, whatever your nationality.

Currently Bulgarian visas are not available on arrival in the country, and can only be issued by Bulgarian embassies or consulates in other countries. Applying by post or in person, you should allow seven working days for the visa to be issued, unless you're willing to pay more for the so-called express service, in under seven days. Fees are payable in cash or by postal order only. No photos are required. Standard **tourist visas** are valid for three months and entitle you to thirty days' stay. In the case of **transit visas**, valid for three months and good for 24 hours' stay, you may be asked to show an onward flight ticket or a visa for your ultimate destination. If you're passing through Bulgaria and then returning by the same route, make sure you ask for a double-entry transit visa, otherwise you'll end up paying more. **Multiple visas**, valid for three or six months and allowing unlimited visits, are only issued to people working or studying in Bulgaria. Generally, it's best to get a tourist visa whatever your plans, since Bulgarian customs sometimes view transit ones as an implied slight on their country, and have been known to pester holders

to change large sums into leva as the price for gaining entry.

In **Britain** the costs of these visas are: tourist visa £36 (express issue £56); transit visa £36 (double-entry £42); and multiple visa £42 (six months £62), although the multiple visa is the only one that UK citizens are likely to need. In the **US**, tourist visas cost US$53 (express issue US$88); and multiple-entry visas US$63 (six months US$93; a year US$123). Note that while US citizens don't require a visa for less than thirty days' stay, they must pay a **border fee** of $20 on arrival.

Australians, Canadians and New Zealand citizens are obliged to have visas unless they can prove that they're on a package tour or can produce travel agency vouchers for at least three nights' pre-paid accommodation in Bulgaria, in which case they qualify for the so-called **visa-free option**. The cost of a tourist visa in Australia, New Zealand and Canada is AUS$75/NZ$100/CAN$78 (express issue AUS$124/NZ$145/CAN$113); for a transit visa AUS$61/NZ$71/CAN$63 (double-entry AUS$93/NZ$109/CAN$93); and a multiple visa AUS$89/NZ$101/CAN$123 (six months AUS$131/NZ$153/CAN$133).

It shouldn't be too difficult to obtain a **visa extension** if you want to stay in Bulgaria for more than thirty days, although the process may involve lots of queuing and paperwork. Head for the local police station (*politseiski uchastâk*), where you'll be advised on what forms to fill in and (possibly) questioned on your reasons for wanting to stay. Expect to pay a fee (currently the equivalent of around $20). If you're in Sofia, the place to go for visa extensions is the *MVR* (Interior Ministry) office at bul. Knyaginya Mariya Luiza 44. If you have any problems, contact your embassy (*posolstvo*) for further advice. For a list of embassies and consulates in Sofia, see p.96.

THE CARTE STATISTIQUE

A hangover from the Communist era, the **carte statistique** (known colloquially as the *zhâlta karta* or yellow card, though it can be white) is supposed to be issued to all independent travellers on arrival in Bulgaria, and date-stamped at reception whenever you check into and out of a hotel or campsite, or at the agency responsible

BULGARIAN EMBASSIES AND CONSULATES

Usual opening hours are Mon–Fri 9.30am–noon.

Australia 4 Carlotta Rd, Double Bay, Sydney, NSW (☎02/9327 7581).

Britain 186–188 Queen's Gate, London SW7 5HL (☎0171/584 9400 or 584 9433).

Canada 325 Stewart St, Ottawa, Ontario K1N 6K5 (☎613/789 3215).

Denmark Gamlehave Alle 7, 290 Charlottenlund, Copenhagen (☎39/642 484, fax 39/634 923).

Germany Abenstelle der Botschaft der Republik Bulgarien, Mauerstrasse 11, 10117 Berlin (☎30/201 0922, ☎ & fax 208 6838).

Greece 33 Stratigou Kallari St, Athens (☎1/674 8105–07); 2 Nicolau Manou St, Thessaloniki (☎31/829 210).

Ireland 22 Burlington Rd, Dublin 4 (☎1/660 3229, fax 1/660 3915).

The Netherlands 9 Duin roosweg, 2597 KJ, Den Haag (☎70/350 3051, fax 70/358 4688).

New Zealand No representation; visa applications should be made through the Bulgarian consulate in Australia (see above) or via local travel agents.

Sweden Karlavgen 29, 11431, Stockholm (☎ & fax 8/723 0938).

Turkey Kavakli dere, Ataturk bulvari 124, Ankara (☎312/426 7455); Amhet Adnan, Saygun cad. 44, Ulus–Levant, Istanbul (☎212/269 2216); Talat Pasha cad. 31, Edirne (☎284/212 5950).

USA 1621 22nd St N.W. 667–3870, Washington DC 20 008 (☎202/483 5885); 121 E 62nd St, New York, NY 10021 (☎212/935 4646).

---

for booking you a private room. In practice, however, supplies of the *carte* often run out, and officials simply write бк (for *bez karta*, without a card) in your passport, which could cause problems if another official later demands evidence that you've been registered with the authorities whilst in Bulgaria. If you *don't* get issued with a card, be sure that your passport is marked, and

insist on a stamped receipt (*faktura*) whenever you stay somewhere. In theory, you can be fined for unregistered nights, though officials are less zealous in applying the rule than they were under Communism.

If you are given a card, it's worth photocopying it against loss and acquiring at least a few stamps to your credit.

HEALTH AND INSURANCE

Though no inoculations are required for travel in Bulgaria, embassies advise visitors to check that they've been vaccinated against diptheria, tetanus, typhoid and hepatitis A, and recommend that anybody planning to spend a lot of time walking in the mountains be innoculated against tickborne encephylitis. However, most visitors suffer nothing worse than diarrhoea or sunburn, so stock up on preparations like Diocalm before you leave home, and protect yourself with a good sunscreen. While salads and fresh fruit are quite safe, it's risky to eat grilled snacks in provincial restaurants with a slow turnover. Tap water is safe to drink in all parts of the country.

Minor complaints can be solved at a pharmacy or **Apteka**, but if you require a doctor (*lekar*) or dentist (*zâbolekar*) head for the nearest **Poliklinika** or health centre, whose staff might

CYRILLIC CHECKLIST: HEALTH	
Pharmacy	аптека
Health centre	поликлиника
Herbal pharmacy	билкова аптека
Hospital	болница

speak English, German or French, and will almost certainly understand Russian. Urgent cases go to **hospitals** (*bolnitsa*) courtesy of the *bârza pomosht* or ambulance service (☎150 in most towns, service free), and emergency treatment is free of charge although you must pay for **medicines**. Although Bulgarian physicians are well-trained and competent, the equipment, facilities, auxiliary staff and aftercare in hospitals falls well below the standards to which Westerners are accustomed, so it's best to fly home in the case of anything serious.

Bear in mind that many pharmacies are not as widely stocked as at home, so you should **bring** with you a supply of razor blades, contraceptives and tampons, not to mention any specific medication that you require.

Bulgaria has a strong tradition of **herbal medicine** (though none, curiously, of homeopathy), and most towns will have a *Bilkova apteka* or herbal pharmacy offering a wide range of natural remedies. However, you'll need to speak Bulgarian, or enlist the help of a native speaker, if you want to understand what you're being offered.

INSURANCE

Before buying an insurance policy, check that you're not already covered. **Bank** and **credit cards** (particularly American Express) often provide certain levels of medical or other insurance, and travel insurance may also be included if you use a major credit or charge card to pay for your trip. You might, however, want to contact a specialist **travel insurance** company; your travel agent can usually recommend one, or see the boxes opposite.

Travel insurance **policies** vary: some are comprehensive, while others cover only certain risks (accidents, illnesses, delayed or lost luggage, cancelled flights, and so forth). Travellers coming from a country that has no reciprocal health agreement with Bulgaria should make sure to ask whether the policy pays medical costs up front or reimburses you later, and whether it provides for medical evacuation to your home country. For policies that include lost or stolen luggage, check exactly what is and isn't covered, and make sure the per-article limit will cover your most valuable possession. If you're planning to do any **"dangerous sports"** (skiing, mountaineering, and the like), be sure to ask whether these activities are covered: some policies add a surcharge.

To claim **compensation** back home you'll need receipts for any medicines purchased, or in the case of theft, an official police report. This is normally no problem, although be prepared to wait around; Bulgarian policemen are not the most efficient in the world when it comes to paperwork. If police are unwilling to issue a report, or try to charge you for it in dollars (not a common occurrence, but it has been known to happen), be persistent and invoke the name of your embassy (*posolstvo*).

BRITISH AND IRISH COVER

Britain, Ireland and other EU countries have a **reciprocal health agreement** with Bulgaria, entitling travellers to receive all medical treatment free of charge on production of a passport. If you have a good "all risks" **home insurance policy** it may well cover your possessions against loss or theft even when overseas, and many **private medical schemes** also cover you when abroad — make sure you know the procedure and the helpline number.

However, you may still want to buy a specialist travel insurance policy before you go. Most **travel agents** and **tour operators** will offer you insurance when you book your flight or holiday, and some will insist you take it. These policies are usually reasonable value, though as ever, you should check the small print. If you feel the cover is inadequate, or you want to compare prices, contact a specialist low-priced firm. Good value possibilities include USIT Campus or STA (see

TRAVEL INSURANCE COMPANIES IN BRITAIN AND IRELAND
Columbus Travel Insurance, 17 Devonshire Square, London EC2M 4SQ (☎0171/375 0011).
Endsleigh Insurance, 97–107 Southampton Row, London WC1B 4AG (☎0171/436 4451).
Liverpool Victoria Friendly Society, Frizzell House, County Gates, Bournemouth, Dorset BH1 2NF (☎01202/292333).
Sun Alliance, Sun Alliance House, 13–17 Dawson St, Dublin 2 (☎01/677 1851).

p.4), or any of the specialist companies listed in the box opposite. Expect to pay about £30 for a month's cover, though under 26s may pay as little as £20. Some companies refuse to cover travellers over 65, or charge a hefty premium. The best policies for **older travellers**, with no upper age limit, are offered by Age Concern (☎01883/346964)

NORTH AMERICAN COVER

Canadian provincial health plans typically provide some overseas medical coverage, although they are unlikely to pick up the full tab in

---

> **TRAVEL INSURANCE COMPANIES IN NORTH AMERICA**
>
> **Access America** ☎1-800/284 8300
>
> **Carefree Travel Insurance** ☎1-800/323 3149
>
> **Desjardins Travel Insurance** Canada ☎1-800/463 7830
>
> **International Student Insurance Service (ISIS)** sold by STA Travel ☎1-800/777 0112, www.sta-travel.com
>
> **Travel Guard** ☎1-800/826 1300, www.noel-group.com
>
> **Travel Insurance Services** ☎1-800/937 1387

---

the event of a mishap. Holders of official **student/teacher/youth cards** are entitled to accident coverage and hospital in-patient benefits – the annual membership is far less than the cost of comparable insurance. **Students** may also find that their student health coverage extends during the vacations and for one term beyond the date of last enrolment. **Homeowners' or renters'** insurance often covers theft or loss of documents, money and valuables while overseas.

If you're looking at buying a **specialist policy**, most travel agents will arrange travel insurance at no extra charge, or you can phone the companies listed above directly. The best **premiums** are usually available through student/youth travel agencies, such as those offered by STA, which come in two forms – with or without medical cover. The

current rates are $45/$35 (for up to 7 days); $60/$45 (8–15 days); $110/$85 (1 month); $140/$115 (45 days); $165/$135 (two months), and $50/$35 for each extra month thereafter. If you're planning to do any hazardous sports (skiing, mountaineering), be sure to check whether these are covered.

Remember that most North American travel policies apply only to items lost, stolen or damaged while in the custody of an identifiable, responsible third party – hotel porter, airline, luggage consignment, etc. Even in these cases you will have to contact the local police within a certain time limit to have a complete report made out so that your insurer can process the claim.

AUSTRALIAN AND NEW ZEALAND COVER

Travel insurance in Australia and New Zealand tends to be put together by the airlines and travel agent groups in conjunction with insurance companies. Most of the policies available are comparable in premium and coverage. A typical policy covering Bulgaria will **cost** Aus$190/NZ$220 for 31 days, Aus$270/NZ$320 for two months and A$330/NZ$400 for three months. Adventure sports are usually covered – except mountaineering with ropes, bungee jumping (some policies) and unassisted diving without an Open Water licence – but you should always check your policy first.

> **TRAVEL INSURANCE COMPANIES IN AUSTRALIAN AND NEW ZEALAND**
>
> **AFTA**, 181 Miller St, North Sydney (☎02/9928 4300); 485 La Trobe St, Melbourne (☎03/9601 8252); Level 7 Arthur Anderson Tower, 205 Queen St, Auckland (☎09/3730530).
>
> **Cover More**, Level 3/60 Miller St, North Sydney (☎02/9202 8000 or 1800/251881); 123 Camberwell Rd, Hawthorn, Melbourne (☎03/9811 9941); 6th floor 57–59 Symonds St, Auckland (☎09/3775958).
>
> **Ready Plan**, 141 Walker St, Dandenong, Melbourne (☎1300/555 017); tenth floor, 63 Albert St, Auckland (☎09/300 5333).

COSTS, MONEY AND BANKS

Bulgaria always was a relatively cheap country for tourists and, despite the shift to a market economy, it remains so due to the fall in value of its currency – the lev (plural: leva). The outlook is less bright for Bulgarians themselves, whose living standards have been eroded by inflation, and who count themselves lucky if they earn $20 a day.

While visitors on package holidays to the ski or beach resorts could probably subsist on **travellers' cheques**, anyone planning to travel around the country – especially in rural areas – will need to carry the bulk of their funds in **cash** (preferably US dollars and/or Deutschmarks, in a mixture of high and low denominations). To minimize the security risk, always carry your funds in a discreet moneybelt, worn under your clothing.

Visitors to Bulgaria must **declare** foreign currency in excess of $1000 on arrival and departure. Failure to do so will result in a fine, confiscation and possible prosecution.

COSTS

Despite price rises and comparatively high **costs** in Sofia, Plovdiv and along the coast, the **essentials** remain inexpensive. If you're camping and buying food in local markets, you can live on $20 a day. Staying in two-star hotels or private rooms and eating out regularly, $40–50 should be sufficient, while on a daily budget of $70 or above you can enjoy a very good life, staying in top-class hotels and taking taxis everywhere.

The most unpredictable factor is the cost of **accommodation**, which varies from region to region, as well as depending on the facilities, age and ownership of the place in question. Private rooms and B&Bs can cost anywhere from $6–20 per person and hotels are equally variable, with two-star places costing from $10–30 per person, three-star hotels from $40–80, and four- and five-star establishments from $90–150. There is less variation in the cost of hostels ($5–10), mountain chalets ($6–10) and campsites ($4–6), but their standards vary even more.

Once you've sorted out a bed for the night, your remaining daily costs can be very low. Public **transport** is cheap, with flat fares of about 40¢ on most urban transport and inexpensive rates on intercity buses and trains: travelling second-class by train, you can cross the entire country from east to west for $15, though international services to neighbouring countries are another matter (see p.8). Providing you avoid deluxe hotel restaurants, **eating** should likewise prove economical. An average evening meal with drinks will set you back $8–12, less if you stick to standard local food such as simple grills and salad. **Drinking** Bulgarian wine or spirits (about $3 and $5 a bottle respectively) will hit your liver harder than your wallet, and snatching a quick cup of coffee or a sandwich won't set you back more than about 60¢.

Most **museums** and tourist attractions charge foreigners about five times the amount paid by the natives, and with rates averaging $1–2, and a few places charging as much as $6, they can become a significant expense if you're on a very low budget.

CURRENCY

Since its catastrophic devaluation in 1996, Bulgaria's **currency**, the lev (literally, lion), has been managed by an IMF-appointed Currency Board, which has pegged it to the Deutschmark at a rate of DM1 = 1000 leva. Having stabilized the lev, the next stage in the programme (scheduled for the summer of 1999) is to slash three zeros off

---

Because of the uncertainty surrounding the future **value of the lev**, we've deliberately avoided quoting food, drink and museum prices in the Guide: you'll find the key to hotel prices explained in "Accommodation", p.30.

CYRILLIC CHECKLIST: MONEY AND BANKS

Bank	банка
Hard currency	валута
Exchange	обмяна

the currency and revalue it at a rate of 1:1. Assuming that plans don't go badly awry (as happened in Russia after a similar revaluation), this means that new, low-denomination banknotes will be issued and the long obsolete stotinka (100 stotinki = 1 lev) is due for a comeback. At the time of writing it is unclear whether the old notes will cease to be legal tender as soon as the new coins and banknotes are introduced, or remain in circulation at a thousandth of their face value. Travellers are advised to check with a Bulgarian bank as soon as they arrive, to ascertain which is the case and what the new notes look like.

Although almost all goods and services can be paid for in leva, **hard currency** (known as *valuta*) is often required when buying international bus and airline tickets. In the case of hotels, however, although they may quote prices in US dollars or DMs, many prefer payment in the leva equivalent.

BANKS AND EXCHANGE

Although the value of the lev is now determined by market forces, it remains a non-convertible currency, unavailable in banks outside Bulgaria. Inside Bulgaria, you can **change** money in banks, tourist offices, at reception desks of the bigger hotels, and at private exchange bureaux. There's usually a slight difference in the **rates** offered, with private bureaux offering the most generous terms – though beware of hefty commission charges, usually written in very small print so you don't notice initially. It's also worth noting that many private exchanges will only accept US$, DM and French francs, though in specific localities they may also take other currencies (eg, Greek drachmas in Plovdiv, or pounds sterling in Borovets).

The collapse of the Pârva Chastna Banka (First Private Bank) – whose billboards and empty premises are still highly visible – has left Bulbank the biggest of the high street **banks**, with branches in most Bulgarian towns. **Opening hours** are usually from Monday to Friday 9am–4pm. **Private exchange bureaux** are usually open until 5 or 6pm (longer in summer), and sometimes 24 hours. Wherever you change money, it makes sense to request a **receipt** (*smetka*) – which can, in theory, enable you to re-exchange surplus leva for hard

currency at the frontier before leaving, but don't depend on it. You can usually buy US$ (and, on occasion, DM and sterling) from bureaux with your excess leva, but the exchange rate may be disadvantageous.

THE BLACK MARKET

The realistic exchange rates now available in banks and private bureaux have all but demolished the appeal of the **black market** to visitors, but the demand for hard currency among Bulgarians remains strong. "Freelance" moneychangers may well offer you a slightly higher rate than the best of the exchange bureaux, but it's best to resist the temptation – the vast majority of them are either performing a sleight-of-hand or handing you a wad of duff notes.

TRAVELLERS' CHEQUES AND CREDIT CARDS

While it's a sensible precaution to carry a percentage of your funds in the form of **travellers' cheques**, they are certainly not convenient for everyday use, except in Sofia and the coastal and ski package-resorts. Elsewhere you'll be lucky to find a private exchange that will touch them, and even banks can be reluctant to accept any but the particular brand to which they're affiliated. Moreover, the only firms with affiliates in Bulgaria which can issue replacements for **lost or stolen** travellers cheques are **American Express** (c/o Megatours, ul. Levski 1, Sofia; ☎880 419 or 981 4201) and **Thomas Cook** (☎00-44-1733/318950; ask for reverse charges). If you can't find a branch of Bulbank (which accepts any brand bearing the Eurocard or Mastercard logo), a three- or four-star hotel is your best bet for changing cheques. In holiday resorts, be prepared for a **commission** charge of up to five percent.

Credit cards can be used to pay for car rental, and at top–notch restaurants and hotels in the major cities and resorts, but are virtually useless throughout most of Bulgaria. You can in theory get **cash advances** in leva with Eurocard, Access, Visa, Diners Club and Mastercard, but most banks are still either inequipped to deal with the procedure or simply can't be bothered. Again, Bulbank is likely to be able to handle transactions more efficiently than other banks. Certain cards can also be used to get cash from **ATMs**, which are still extremely rare in Bulgaria. If you do find one, it's likely to take Visa, Cirrus and Plus only.

INFORMATION AND MAPS

The job of promoting Bulgaria as a tourist destination is now handled by the trade sections (STIVs) of Bulgarian embassies abroad. Although often far from visitor-friendly or clued up about tourism, these are usually happy to supply booklets designed to whet your appetite – the motoring and camping maps and the *Tourist Calendar* of festivals are worth acquiring. However, you're likely to get more practical help from travel agencies specializing in Eastern Europe. Another

source of information is the Internet, where *www.travel-bulgaria.com* features up-to-date information on several regions of the country, while *www.interrrinet.bg* is full of useful facts and figures.

INFORMATION IN BULGARIA

Inside Bulgaria, **tourist information offices** in the Western European or North American sense are still in their infancy, and the few that exist are financed by the British Know-How Fund and other foreign organizations. These offices (in the Pirin, Stara Planina and western Rhodopes) are staffed by knowledgeable and enthusiastic young Bulgarians, keen to promote new initiatives, with faxes, email and the Internet at their fingertips. The Pirin Tourism Forum, in particular, has shown the way by publishing an excellent series of booklets detailing sights, excursions and other useful information on different areas within the Pirin.

However, that's not the case for the vast majority of **tourist agencies** in Bulgaria. Whilst towns and villages are now allowed to form their own voluntary associations, few of these have their own premises yet so are not accessible to tourists, and the vast majority of agencies that

TOURIST INFORMATION ABROAD

Australia Bulgarian Embassy, 4 Carlotta Rd, Double Bay, Sydney, NSW (☎02/9327 7581).

Eastern Europe Travel Bureau, Level 5 75 King St, Sydney 2000 (☎02/9262 1144); Third floor, Suite 313, 343 Little Collins St, Melbourne (☎03/9600 0299).

Britain Bulgarian Embassy, 186–188 Queen's Gate, London SW7 5HL (☎0171/589 8402, fax 589 4875).

Canada Bulgarian Embassy, 325 Stewart St, Ottawa, Ontario K1N 6K5 (☎416/789 5341, fax 789 3524).

Denmark Bulgarian Embassy, Gamlehave Alle 7, 290 Charlottenlund, Copenhagen (☎ & fax 39/633601).

Germany Botscaft Der Republik Bulgarien, Auf der Hostert 6, D-5300 Bonn, Bad Godesberg (☎228/351029). Mauerstrasse 11, 10117 Berlin (☎30/201 0922, fax 208 6838).

Ireland Bulgarian Embassy, 22 Burlington Rd, Dublin 4 (☎01/660 3229, fax 660 3915).

The Netherlands Bulgarian Embassy, 9 Duin roosweg, 2597 KJ, Den Haag (☎70/350 3051, fax 358 4688).

New Zealand Innovative Travel, 6th floor 160 Manchester St, Christchurch (☎03/3653910).

Sweden Bulgarian Embassy, Karlavgen 29, 11431, Stockholm (☎ & fax 8/411 3799).

USA Bulgarian Embassy, 1621 22nd St N.W. 667–3870, Washington DC 20 008 (☎202/387 7969, fax 234 7973); 121 E 62nd St, New York, NY 10021, New York (☎212/935 0485, fax 935 4646).

Balkan Tourist USA, 20 E 46th St #1003, New York, NY 10017 (☎800/822 1106, fax 212/6838, *www.balkanusa.com*).

you'll come across will be private operators who can arrange rooms, excursions or other services, but are unwilling or unable to provide unbiased information. Many of these agencies occupy the premises of the former state-owned travel company Balkantourist, whose name still appears on signs even though the organization was privatized years ago – as is also the case with another firm, Orbita, specializing in youth travel.

Most of the hotels previously owned by Balkantourist still advertize "tourist services" in the lobby, although the services in question are often limited to changing money and selling places on sightseeing tours. However, people are usually fairly helpful to stray tourists, providing

that you can find a common language: while staff in Sofia and the main coastal and ski resorts generally speak English, elsewhere they're more likely to understand Russian, German or French. Addresses of tourist offices and useful agencies appear in the relevant sections of the Guide.

MAPS

If you can read the Cyrillic alphabet, the best **general map** of Bulgaria is the 1:500,000 road map (*Pâtna Karta*) published by *Kartografiya* in Sofia, and sold on street stalls or at petrol stations throughout the country. If not, you should buy *Kümmerly and Frey* or *Freytag and Berndt's*

MAP OUTLETS

AUSTRALIA AND NEW ZEALAND

Map Land, 372 Little St, Melbourne (☎03/9670 4383, *www.mapland.com.au*).

The Map Shop, 16a Peel St, Adelaide (☎08/8231 2033, *www.mapshop.net.au*).

Perth Map Centre, 884 Hay St, Perth (☎08/9322 5733).

Specialty Maps, 58 Albert St, Auckland (☎09/307 2217).

Travel Bookshop, 3/175 Liverpool St, Sydney (☎02/9261 8200).

BRITAIN AND IRELAND

Blackwell's Map and Travel Shop, 53 Broad St, Oxford OX1 3BQ (☎01865/792792; *bookshop.blackwell.co.uk*).

Daunt Books, 83 Marylebone High St, London W1 (☎0171/224 2295); 193 Haverstock Hill, London NW3 4QL (☎0171/794 4006).

Easons Bookshop, 40 O'Connell St, Dublin 1 (☎01/873 3811).

Fred Hanna's Bookshop, 27–29 Nassau St, Dublin 2 (☎01/677 1255).

Hodges Figgis Bookshop, 56–58 Dawson St, Dublin 2 (☎01/677 4754).

James Thin Melven's Bookshop, 29 Union St, Inverness IV1 1QA (☎01463/233500, *www.jthn.co.uk*).

John Smith and Sons, 57–61 St Vincent St, Glasgow G2 5TB (☎0141/221 7472, *www.johnsmith.co.uk*).

National Map Centre, 22–24 Caxton St, London SW1 (☎0171/222 4945, *www.mapsworld.com*).

Stanfords, 12–14 Long Acre, London WC2 (☎0171/836 1321); 52 Grosvenor Gardens, London SW1W 0AG; 156 Regent St, London W1R 5TA (☎0171/43 4744); 29 Corn St, Bristol BS1 1HT (☎0117/929 9966); mail, phone or email order (☎0171/836 1321, *sales@stanfords.co.uk*).

The Travel Bookshop, 13–15 Blenheim Crescent, London W11 2EE (☎0171/229 5260, *www.thetravelbookshop.co.uk*).

Waterstone's, 91 Deansgate, Manchester M3 2BW (☎0161/832 1992, *www.waterstones.co.uk*) has the best map department of any branch in this UK-wide chain.

BULGARIA

Odysseia-ın, bul. Stamboliiski 20 (entrance on ul. Lavele), Sofia (☎02/890538).

continued overleaf

1:1,000,000 combined map of Romania and Bulgaria before leaving home, as either is preferable to the English-language maps sold in Bulgaria.

The availability of **town plans** (*plan-ukazatel*) in Communist times was always patchy, with none available in the localities they covered while stocks gathered dust hundreds of kilometres away. With no money for reprints – let alone updating – those still in circulation have been rendered out of date by the widespread renaming of streets in the 1990s. Post-Communist plans (printed on glossy paper and carrying adverts) now exist, but their coverage and distribution are limited. The main publisher, *Domino Press*, produces an excellent map of the Blagoevgrad region including plans of all the sites of interest, as well as street plans of Plovdiv, Haskovo and Varna (though the last is hard to find); while

Kartografiya publishes a map of Sofia that marks public transport routes and is available in Bulgarian or English versions.

If you're going walking in the mountains it pays to compare the various **hiking maps** available from Odysseia-In in Sofia (see box on previous page). The Bulgarian Tourist Union (BTS; БТС) publishes series on the Rhodopes, Stara Planina, Rila and Pirin ranges, whose accuracy depends on when they were last updated (between 1993 and 1997), and at worst can lead hikers into uncomfortable, if not hazardous, situations. *Kartografiya's* 1:55,000 maps of the Rila and Pirin mountains are a step in the right direction, if not wholly reliable, while the new 1:65,000 map of the Troyan Balkan range (available from tourist offices in Gabrovo, Tryavna and Troyan) is absolutely accurate, having been drawn up by the mountain rescue service, using military survey charts.

GETTING AROUND

The lack of investment in public transport over the past 10–15 years has left it in a sorry state, with semi-derelict stations, run-down vehicles and demoralized staff, and although private bus companies have taken up the slack on major routes, the state-owned network has drastically contracted. While transport remains cheap it is also slow, a failing compounded by Bulgaria's mountainous terrain and climatic extremes (which rapidly degrade tarmac), with train journeys between the north and south being particularly prone to roundabout routes and changes. Bear in mind, too, that schedules are designed to fit in with the working day. There may be several departures in the early morning, then nothing until mid-afternoon, with nothing at all on Sundays.

The fragmentation of the transport system is reflected in the **timetables** (*razpisanie*) in train and bus stations, which used to be on a clearly legible board but are nowadays often merely scribbled on a piece of paper stuck to the window of the ticket office. Usually, arrivals (*pristiga* or *pristigane*) are listed on one side, and departures (*trâgva* or *zaminavane*) on the other. To make things harder for travellers, the schedules of private buses are unlikely to be posted at all, and it's impossible to buy a national train timetable: in addition, any timetables that do exist are invariably in **Cyrillic**. To make things easier we've included a list of town names in Cyrillic at the beginning of each chapter, and a rundown of regional transport under the "Travel Details" at the end of each chapter.

BY TRAIN

Bulgarian State Railways (*BDZh*) can get you to most towns mentioned in this book, although trains are very slow by Western standards and delays are common on the longer routes. **Intercity** (*intersiti*) and **express** (*ekspresen vlak*) services only operate on the main trunk routes, but on everything except the humblest branch lines you'll find so-called **rapid** (*bârz vlak*) trains. Use these rather than the snail-like **pâtnicheski** (пътнически; literally "travellers", meaning "slow" in this context) services unless you're planning to alight at some particularly insignificant halt. Generally speaking, intercity services are the only ones which carry a **buffet car**, so if travelling on another type of train, make sure you

---

CYRILLIC CHECKLIST: GETTING AROUND

Bulgarian State Railways		**Slow service**	пътнически влак
(booking offices)	БДЖ	**Sleepers**	спален вагон
Timetables	разписание	**Left luggage office**	гардероб
Departures	тръгва (abbreviated	**Bus station**	автогара
	to Тр) or заминаване	**Filling station**	бензиностанция
Arrivals	пристига or прис	**Petrol**	бензин
	тигане (Пр)	**Motoring map**	пътна карта
Tickets	билети	**Street**	ул.
National train timetable	пътеводител	**Square**	пл.
Intercity service	интерсити	**Boulevard**	бул.
Express service	експресен влак	**Suburb**	кв.
Rapid service	бърз влак	**Block**	бл.

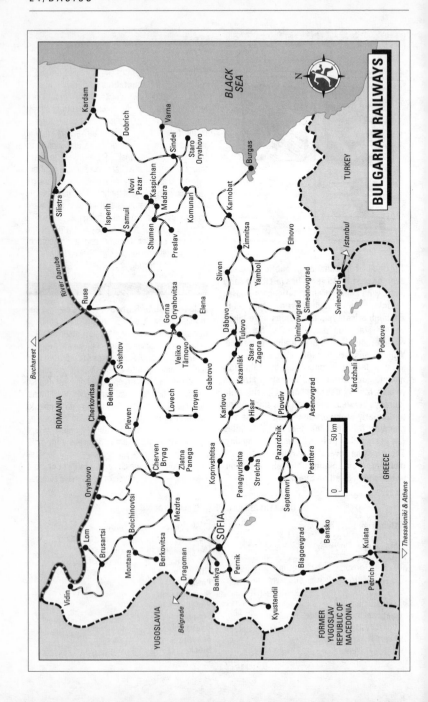

have enough food and drink to survive the journey. On timetables, the four types of services are indicated by the **abbreviations** ИЦ, Е, Б and П; express services are usually lettered in red. A **reservation** (*zapazeno myasto*; about 15¢ in addition to the basic ticket price) is compulsory on intercity and express services, and advisable for all other trains if you're travelling on summer weekends. You might find yourself paying a hefty surcharge if you board a train without one.

Though a **national timetable** (*pâtevoditel*) is extremely useful for frequent train travellers, the chances of obtaining one are slim, as they're snapped up immediately after publication each May. If you do get hold of a copy, note that trains running on a particular day only are indicated by a number in a circle (for example, 1 = Monday, 2 = Tuesday, and so forth). International services are printed in the Roman alphabet, rather than Cyrillic.

Long-distance/overnight trains have a wagon with reasonably priced **couchettes** (*kushet*; кушет) and/or **sleepers** (*spalen vagon*). At the time of writing you can travel from Sofia to Varna by sleeper for under $15, which probably works out cheaper than a night's accommodation. In order to secure a bed on the train, you need to reserve a day or two in advance, and, if possible, at least a week in advance in July or August.

Commonly, a single sign halfway down the platform is all that identifies a **station** (*gara*). If you're sitting at the back, you won't see this until the train starts up again, so try to sit up front. Most stations have a **left-luggage office** (*garderob*); in the large ones you may need to complete a form before stowing your gear.

PASSES

Unless you've already bought an **InterRail** or **Eurail** pass (see p.8) in order to get to Bulgaria, buying a train pass to travel around the country makes little sense. Indeed, the only one currently on offer is the **Eurodomino/Freedom Pass** (see p.8), which allows for three, five, or ten days second class travel within Bulgaria, but its cost (£29/£39/£68) will almost certainly exceed what you'd spend on fares without a pass – especially given that many destinations in Bulgaria can only be reached by bus.

You can also buy individual tickets for travel in Bulgaria in advance from your home country, though this doesn't work out any cheaper than doing so on the ground (in Australia, it will work

---

> **TRAIN CONTACTS**
>
> **USA AND CANADA** Rail Europe Canadian Reservations Centre, 2987 Dundas East, Suite 105, Mississauga, ON L4X 1M2 (☎1-800/361 7245); Rail Europe, 226 Westchester Ave, White Plains, NY 10604 (☎1-800/438 7245).
>
> **AUSTRALIA** Eastern Europe Travel Bureau, Level 5, 75 King Street, Sydney 2000 (☎02/9262 1144); Third floor, suite 313, 343 Little Collins St, Melbourne (☎03/9600 0299).
>
> *For train contacts in Britain, see p.9.*

out more expensive, as you pay double the booking fee); again, check with the train contacts listed in box above.

INTERCITY TICKETS

Bulgaria's main **intercity routes** are very busy in summer and on weekends throughout the year. It is wise – if not always essential – to **book** a day or two in advance; otherwise you'll probably have to spend the journey standing in the carriage corridor. In many large towns, it's possible to buy **tickets** (*bileti*) and make advance reservations from **railway bookings offices**, listed in the appropriate places in the Guide. Tickets can also be bought at the station just before travel (in out-of-the-way places, a ticket window will only open a few minutes before the train is due). If you arrive at a station too late to queue up and buy a ticket, you can **pay on the train** itself – with a surcharge of 30–40 percent.

INTERNATIONAL TICKETS

International tickets are handled by a separate organization, the Rila Agency. Although cities like Sofia and Ruse have international ticket counters in the stations – so you can buy a ticket immediately before travel if you're pressed for time – more often, Rila offices are located some distance away from stations, and you'll need to make sure you buy your ticket well in advance. We've given addresses where appropriate in the Guide.

Generally speaking, **prices** of tickets to Romania, Hungary and other former Eastern bloc countries are quite reasonable (at the time of writing, a one-way ticket from Sofia to Bucharest costs about $15), but increase significantly if travelling to hard currency countries like Greece or Turkey, where fares are comparable with those in the West.

BY BUS

In many parts of Bulgaria it's necessary – or easier – to travel by **bus** (*avtobus* or, colloquially, *reis*), especially in the Rhodopes and the Pirin, where few of the attractions are accessible by train. Each town of any size has a bus **station** (*avtogara*, автогара), or sometimes two, as buses operated by private companies may use another depot (often just a parking lot); in cities, this duplication can result in three or four terminals (as detailed in the Guide). Since the buses run by **private companies** are usually newer than the vehicles owned by municipalities, they tend to be more comfortable and faster, particularly if the route follows a highway through the lowlands rather than mountain roads. The drawback is that infomation on schedules is harder to obtain as few companies post timetables, so that you may have to ask at several kiosks to get the full picture. In some cases the vehicles are **minibuses**, and leave as soon as they're full; such services are called *marshrutni taxi*.

TICKETS

As a general rule, tickets are sold until five minutes before departure, although it's advisable to buy them an hour or two in advance if travelling on a route serving major towns – especially during summer or at weekends. Note that if you're catching a **bus that originates elsewhere**, tickets are only sold when the bus arrives, in which case you need to queue outside the shuttered ticket hatch. *Tova li e gisheto za bileti za...?* means "Is this where I get tickets to...?" (remember that a shake of the head means "yes" and a nod "no"). On **rural routes**, tickets are often sold by the driver rather than at the terminal. If you're aiming for a campsite or monastery along a bus route, ask the driver for the *spirkata za kampinga (or monastira)*, or call *Spri!* (Stop!) as it hoves into sight.

CITY BUSES

On **urban transport** – trams and buses in Sofia, buses and trolleybuses everywhere else – there's usually a **flat fare** (seldom more than 40¢) on all routes. In Sofia, **tickets** are bought beforehand and then punched in a machine on board, so it's sensible to buy a bunch of ten tickets (from street kiosks next to tram and bus stops) as soon as you arrive. Fare dodgers pay a spot fine. Elsewhere in Bulgaria, tickets are sold by an on-board conductor. Routes are sometimes displayed on each bus

stop (*spirka*) together with the times of the first and last services, but many of these signs are so old that it's best to check with the locals before jumping aboard. In some regions, private companies operate, so on a few routes you'll encounter a plethora of different coloured buses and minibuses, identifiable only by a scribbled route number posted in the windscreen.

INTERNATIONAL BUSES

Since the end of Communism, a plethora of **international bus services** has sprung up, connecting Bulgaria's main towns and cities with neighbouring countries and further afield. As you'd expect, the main point of departure is Sofia – whence you can reach any country in Southern and Central Europe – but there are also several regional towns where you can pick up a bus to Turkey, Greece, Albania or the former Yugoslavia. Many of the companies running buses to Turkey are Turkish; the chief Bulgarian operators are MATPU and Diligence Express. Tickets are priced in leva, dollars or Deutschmarks, but you can pay in most currencies at the prevailing rate of exchange. Details appear in the relevant section of the Guide.

BY TAXI

Providing you don't get ripped off, **taxis** are a reasonably priced and useful way of getting around in towns and cities, or reaching places that aren't accessible by public transport. All licensed taxis are metered, and generally charge about 20¢ initially, plus 20¢ per kilometre thereafter during the day (twice as much at night), except for taxis on the Black Sea coast, whose rates are 3-4 times higher (though city taxis in Varna and Burgas charge normal rates). The minority of taxi drivers out to take advantage of foreigners tend to hang around airports, major train stations and city centre hotels, so it's best to go looking for a taxi elsewhere if you have the option. We've given phone numbers of some reputable taxi firms in the relevant sections of the Guide, though it is unlikely that anyone on the other end of the line will speak English.

BY CAR

Foreigners may drive in Bulgaria using their national **driving licence** (though, should you stay longer than six months, it must be translated and legalized), but most of the neighbouring countries require an international licence. It is obligatory to have third-party **insurance** plus a "Green" or "Blue" card – the latter can be bought at the frontier. Entering Bulgaria, your vehicle will be registered with a special **"visa tag"** or *carnet de passage* which must be presented on leaving – a rule intended to prevent foreigners from selling their cars. As **car theft** is endemic and Bulgaria is a major transit route for stolen vehicles, drivers bringing their own car should be sure to carry their log book (and make photocopies of it), their driving licence and *carnet de passage*, and take every precaution against the documents and the vehicle being stolen. Use guarded parking lots wherever possible, and never leave vehicles on sidestreets unless fitted with wheel locks and immobilizers.

Upon arrival in Bulgaria, an **entrance fee** is payable on all motor vehicles (car/van $10; minibus seating eight or more $60), plus a **disinfection fee** (car $2; van/minibus $4) – though EU citzens are exempt from the former charge.

FUEL, MAPS AND SIGNS

Petrol (*benzin*, бензин) in Bulgaria – slightly cheaper than in Britain and Western Europe, and slightly more expensive than in the USA – can sometimes be hard to find. Although you'll find **filling stations** (*benzinostantsiya*, бензиностанция) on the main road exits from most large towns, and spaced 30–40km apart along the highways, they're few and far between once you get off the beaten track, so fill up wherever you can. Octane values aren't always what is stated on the pump, so higher capacity engines may make plinking noises, while fuel injection vehicles sometimes have problems with dirty petrol purchased

at out-of-the-way stations. The most reliable sources are the 24-hour stations run by Shell and BP, which occupy prime sites on **principal trunk routes** such as the E83 near Yablanitsa, the E79 near Blagoevgrad, the E80 near Pazardzhik, national route 86 between Plovdiv and Asenovgrad, and the E772 between Aitos and Burgas, where you can also buy Super and **lead-free** (*bez oloven*) petrol. Filling stations are often marked on the Cyrillic-script **motoring maps** (*pâtna karta*, пътна карта) available from bookshops and street stalls.

Names signposted along the highways appear in both alphabets, and although the system of transliteration is slightly different from the one used in this book, they're recognizably similar. Other road **signs** are basically identical to those employed in the West.

ROADS, TRAFFIC AND SPEED LIMITS

Roads in Bulgaria tend to be inconsistently numbered (some highways carry two or three designations), and even trunk routes (marked in red on maps) have the same bumpy, pot-holed surfaces as the minor roads (indicated in yellow.) There are stretches of **dual carriageway** (*magistala*) between Sofia and Plovdiv (on which the first **tolls** in the country were introduced in 1996), and betwen Sofia and Pravets, but travel is pretty slow going elsewhere. If following the main Sofia–Burgas, Sofia–Varna, Sofia–Vidin, Sofia–Kulata or Plovdiv–Kapitan Andreevo routes, expect to be stuck behind long files of slow-moving freight **traffic** for large stretches of the journey. Traffic on other routes can be very light, but a combination of poor road manners and abysmal surface quality should prevent you from

---

STREET NAMES

Any visitor to Bulgaria is bound to experience some confusion over **street names**. During the Communist period, towns vied with each other to name their principal thoroughfares or main squares after revolutionary personalities or events, and there was barely a settlement that didn't have something named after **V I Lenin**, **Georgi Dimitrov** (first leader of the postwar socialist state), and **Vasil Kolarov** (his loyal disciple); not to mention the key date in Bulgarian Communist history, **9 septemvri** (the day on which the monarchy was toppled in 1944).

After November 1989, when the Communists were forced to proceed with democratic reforms, the removal of ideologically loaded street names became an issue. While Lenin, Dimitrov and Kolarov have disappeared, the fates of other names from the Communist era are in the hands of the local councils. Those dominated by the BSP (the ex-Communists) are obviously keener to preserve names pertaining to left-wing heroes, but inconsistency prevails even where names have been changed. In most cases, both the street name and the appropriate street sign have been changed; in others, the name has been changed but the old signs remain; and even where new names have been signposted, the locals may continue to use the old one.

getting anywhere quickly. Potholes, farm carts and wandering animals make it unsafe to drive **after dark**.

In urban areas buses have the right of way and parking is restricted to specified spots. **Speed limits** in built-up areas (60 kph), on the open road (80 kph), and highways (120 kph) are reduced to 50 kph, 70 kph or 100 kph for minibuses or cars with caravans or trailers.

ACCIDENTS, FINES AND THEFT

Mountainous Bulgaria has lots of hairpin bends, and in rural areas it's important to watch out for farm animals and carts. Motorists are legally obliged to report **accidents** and, in case of injury, render assistance where appropriate while waiting for the police (*Politsiya*). **Spot-fines** for trivial offences are common practice; the police have been known to abuse this by demanding payment in dollars and pocketing the cash. Requests for a receipt might put a stop to this – or make things worse. In the event of arrest, insist on being allowed to contact your embassy (see Sofia "Listings" for addresses). **Drinking and driving** is absolutely prohibited, punishable with a heavy fine or imprisonment. Note that **flashing the lights** of your car does not mean "I am prepared to give way to you" but "get the hell out of my way".

In the event of being in an acccident or having your car stolen, the **bureaucratic procedures** are nightmarish. You will need a police report (which can take 2–3 days) that must be taken to the local prosecutor's office for stamping (involving another delay), and then be stamped by the local customs office, which may insist that the document is authorized by the regional office in another town. All this is done in Bulgarian, so unless you're lucky enough to find an official who speaks English, there is also the cost of hiring an interpeter to consider, not to mention accommodation costs and other related expenses for the duration. If the vehicle was brought into Bulgaria you won't be allowed to leave the country without it, even if the car is a total write-off.

CAR RENTAL

Car rental can be arranged through Avis, Budget Europcar and Hertz offices in Sofia and other major cities. Most Bulgarian travel agents act as repesentatives for one of these firms or one of their domestic equivalents, the most widespread of which is Intercar. You'll also find car rental desks in the lobby of each town's principal hotel. In general, the cars offered by the big Western firms are better maintained than those leased by the smaller Bulgarian outfits, with **prices** averaging around $50 a day for a cranky Lada and upwards of $70 for a Western Golf-style equivalent.

You may find it cheaper to **book direct in advance** from your home country with one of the major car rental companies (see box opposite for contacts), or take advantage of some of the prebooked car rental deals offered by the package holiday companies. Booked through a package company, a week with unlimited mileage in a Fiat Cinquecento can cost as low as $250 on the coast and $300 in the ski resorts. For insurance and driving licence regulations see p.27.

Another option is to rent a car **with a driver**, relieving you of the worries associated with road use in a strange country. Any of the rental firms can oblige, or, if you have Bulgarian friends, it's relatively easy to find someone to drive you around for a negotiable sum. Making arrangements unofficially, you can probably get a car with a driver for $30–40 a day, plus petrol costs and any expenses incurred if an overnight stay is required.

HITCHING

Hitching (*autostop*) is fairly widespread in rural Bulgaria, where local drivers are used to giving lifts to villagers in the absence of buses, but motorists are less accommodating on busier routes, where bus and train services are better. In addition, now that robberies and rapes are far more common, both drivers and hitch-hikers are a lot more cautious than they used to be. **Women** are strongly advised *not* to hitch, and even male travellers should exercise caution about which lifts to accept.

It's best to carry a **sign** in Cyrillic if you're heading for somewhere distant; see the boxes at the beginning of each chapter in the Guide for a rundown of the chief place names in each region. It used to be possible to get a clue to drivers' movements from their number plates, whose initial letter(s) indicated the town where the vehicle was registered (П = Plovdiv; C = Sofia; Бл = Blagoevgrad, etc), but the introduction of new licence plates using a different coding system has made this method less reliable nowadays.

CAR RENTAL COMPANIES

AUSTRALIA

Avis ☎1800/225 533
Budget ☎1300/362 848
Citroën Peugeot Euro Lease ☎02/9949 1711

Hertz ☎133039
Renault Eurodrive ☎02/9299 3344

BRITAIN AND IRELAND

Avis ☎0990/900500
Budget Britain 0800/18181; Ireland ☎0990/327711

Europcar ☎0345/222 525
Hertz ☎0990/996699

BULGARIA

Avis Sofia ☎02/273 8023 or 988167; Varna ☎052/500832 or 361491
Budget Sofia ☎02/871682; Varna ☎052/361955

Europcar Sofia ☎02/720157; Burgas ☎056/83896; Plovdiv ☎032/557197; Varna ☎052/435054
Hertz Sofia ☎02/791477 or 722590; Varna ☎052/650210

NEW ZEALAND

Avis ☎0800/655 111 or 09/579 5231
Budget ☎0800/652 227

Hertz ☎0800/655 955

US AND CANADA

Avis ☎1-800/331 1084, *www.avis.com*
Budget ☎1-800/527 0700; *www.budgetrentacar.com*

Dollar ☎1-800/800 6000; *www.dollarcar.com*
Hertz US ☎1-800/654 3001; Canada ☎1-800/263 0600; *www.hertz.com*

BY AIR

Daily **BALKAN flights** are the quickest way to travel between Sofia and the Danubian and Black Sea ports, and given the length of the train journey (6–8hr) a flight to Varna or Burgas is worth considering. The difference in cost is considerable, however: **fares** from Sofia work out at about $65 one way for non-Bulgarians, as opposed to about $10 by bus or train. You'll need to book the day before (most flights leave around 7–8am), if not two or three days in advance for services to the coast.

ACCOMMODATION

Accommodation in Bulgaria is currently in a state of flux, what with the privatization of former state-owned hotels and a burgeoning number of new private places. While the choice of accommodation is undeniably wider than it was in the early 1990s, standards and prices vary far more than previously, and you can no longer get an idea of what a hotel is like purely from its star-rating. In addition, things are changing all the time – generally for the better, but not always so.

HOTELS

In Communist times, Westerners were restricted to staying in **hotels** run by the state-owned chains Balkantourist and Interhoteli. Cheaper establishments frequented by Bulgarians were off limits, although they would often claim to be full up rather than admit this. These days, although you may be turned away by less expensive establishments – often because the facilities are so bad that they can't believe you'd want to stay there – you can, in theory, stay where you wish.

This is just as well, as the stock of hotels from Communist times is generally in poor shape, either simply due to lack of money for refurbishment – which tends to be the case in small towns with not much tourist trade – or because the hotel is being deliberately run down prior to **privatization**, so that the buyers can acquire it at a knock-down rate, which is particularly common in the ski and coastal resorts.

Meanwhile, hundreds of **new hotels** have opened in the main cities and resorts, along highways and even in remote villages where you wouldn't expect to find anything. While some belong to hotel chains, the majority are small, often family-run establishments – sometimes termed *Mini Hotels* – which tend to be cleaner, friendlier and more attractive than the older, ex-state hotels.

As a consequence of all this, there is little or no consistency in how **rates** are calculated. Some hotels charge on a per-person basis (which may or may not include breakfast), while others oblige solo travellers to pay for a double room (at reduced rates, or full cost) if there isn't a single available. For similar reasons, you can't be sure whether or not they'll accept **credit cards**; four- and five-star hotels are fairly certain to, the odds are 50:50 in three-star places, and anywhere with fewer stars or off the beaten track is very unlikely to. Although we've cited prices in dollars, most places prefer that you **pay in leva**.

It's seldom necessary to make **reservations**, other than during festivals or at popular rustic retreats such as Kovachevitsa in July or August. Although we've given phone numbers throughout the Guide, the odds of getting a hotel receptionist who speaks English aren't good except in four- or five-star hotels or places with an email address; however, faxes sent in English will probably be translated and acted upon. Alternatively, most tourist offices can call on your behalf, but may charge a small fee.

As a new private two-star hotel is often much nicer than an old three-star block, the system of **star ratings** (from one-star up to five) is fairly irrelevant, and it's safer to base your assumptions on the age of places. Hotels built in Communist times tend to conform to a few models. Postwar one-star places are gloomy warrens with shared facilities in the corridor and a sink in the room if you're lucky, while two-star hotels of the 1950s

CYRILLIC CHECKLIST: ACCOMMODATION	
Accommodation bureau	квартирно бюро
Hotel	хотел
Private rooms	частни квартири
Hostel	туристическа спалня
Mountain chalet	хижа
Rest home	почивна станция ог почивен дом
Campsite	къмпинг

ACCOMMODATION PRICE CODES

All **accommodation** in this book has been categorized according to the following price codes. The prices quoted are for the cheapest double room in high season.

① $9 and under   ③ $18–36   ⑤ $60–90   ⑦ $120–150
② $9–18   ④ $36–60   ⑥ $90–120   ⑧ $150 and over

and early 1960s are mid-rise prefab blocks of matchbox rooms with ensuite bathrooms and erractic plumbing, where the only amenity that can be taken for granted is a bar. Three-star hotels built in the 1970s and 1980s tend to be high-rise or cuboid blocks with overblown lobbies and restaurants and cheesy basement nightclubs, while four- and five-star hotels usually feature similar facilities, but in a more luxurious style and managed with efficiency.

Private hotels opened during the 1990s tend to be a lot smaller and occupy houses in towns, or alpine-style villas in the mountains. Most run to ensuite bathrooms, and the ritzier ones to cable TV and mini-bars. Though shoddier efforts are already showing their age, the majority are comfortable, clean and well looked after by owner-managers who have sunk their savings into the venture and have every reason to make it succeed. Most places have a small taverna and summer garden, and some have saunas, solariums, fitness centres or even swimming pools.

Another factor worth considering is the time of year. In the old one- and two-star hotels, hot water may only be available in the morning and evening, which is rarely a problem at the height of summer but can be a real pain in winter, when rooms in even three-star establishments may be poorly heated. If travelling at this time of year, it's a good idea to opt for a family hotel or a private room (see below), where the provision of basic comforts can be taken for granted

PRIVATE ROOMS

Private rooms (*chastni kvartiri*) are available in Sofia, Plovdiv, Ruse, Varna and a number of other tourist destinations. They're bookable through local tourist offices, **accommodation bureaux** (*kvartirno byuro*), and private or cooperative firms that specialize in renting out rooms – addresses are given in the Guide. Even when the bureaux are closed (from early September onwards in smaller coastal towns), you can often find a room **unofficially**, by asking around, although this will mean foregoing a date stamp on your *carte statistique* (see p.14). If you stay in someone's home you're meant to **register with the police** within 24 hours. While agencies should register you automatically, few hosts take these formalities seriously.

The size and quality of private rooms varies enormously (it's rarely possible to inspect the place first), but they are always clean. Spacious rooms in nice old houses seem to be the rule in smaller resorts such as Sozopol and Nesebâr on the coast, and Koprivshtitsa inland, while in the cities private rooms are almost invariably situated in apartment buildings. They are often let by pensioners, who find it hard to afford repairs but keep things tidy. In mountain areas the houses can be warm and cosy or ramshackle and primitive, depending on the wealth of the owner. While some are **B&Bs**, the majority are not, though few landladies will refuse to provide breakfast for a few dollars extra.

Prices vary according to where you are. Expect to pay $20 for a double room and $16 for a single in Sofia; $15 for a double and $10 for a single in Varna; and on a per-person basis almost everywhere else, from $5–12 in Sozopol, $6–20 in the Rhodopes and Pirin, and $3–5 off the beaten track in northern Bulgaria.

YOUTH HOTELS AND REST HOMES

Bulgaria has a range of other types of accommodation that are more or less available to foreign tourists. Orbita, the former state agency for youth tourism, has led the way by turning its chain of **youth hotels** that once hosted a large number of young travellers from fellow socialist countries into "normal" hotels where anyone can stay. More uncertain is the future of the **rest homes** (*pochivni stantsii* or *pochiven dom*), owned by trade unions and factories, for the use of their workers. Many are no more than frugal holiday camps, but those built for the Communist *nomenklatura* can be quite sumptuous – the former Politburo ones at Arkutino and Sandanski, especially. Some have already opened their doors to foreigners, and others may be open to persuasion, though you have to be pretty desperate to stay in a *Voennen Klub* (used by soldiers in transit between their homes and garrisons).

CAMPSITES, HOSTELS, CHALETS AND MONASTERIES

While most towns of interest once had a **campsite** (*kamping*) on their outskirts, many have now closed down or face an uncertain future, and it is only on the coast and at Pamporovo and Rila that they are they still going strong. Most of these charge around $3–5 to pitch a tent, and also have two-person **chalets** available for rent at around $4.50–6 a night. Note that many campsites close down in early September, as soon as the summer rush has slackened. **Camping rough** is illegal and punishable with a fine.

Cheap, very basic **hostels** (*turisticheska spalnya*) lurk in the backstreets of many provincial towns. In some, you'll be offered a bunk in a large, 20-bed dorm; in others you may be in a 2- or 4-bed room. Prices range from $3–6 per person; contact the Bulgarian Youth Hostel Association, bul. Vassil Levski 75, Sofia 1000 (☎02/883821) for details. In highland areas favoured by hikers there are scores of **mountain chalets** (*hizhi*), some primitive, others more like comfortable hotels. Costs at all but the most expensive will rarely come to more than $5–6 per night. Upon arrival you may have to wait for the custodian to turn up before being allocated a bed. You can **reserve** beds in some parts of the country through local tourist offices or Odysseia-In in Sofia (see p21).

The larger of Bulgaria's **monasteries** traditionally accommodated guests in their cells, but closed their doors to Westerners in the early 1980s. Nowadays it's up to the individual monastery to decide, with popular ones such as Rila, Troyan and Bachkovo allowing foreigners to stay there for $5–15 per person. The rooms are usually quite comfortable, with a wash-basin and some form of heating, but you're unlikley to find hot water laid on.

EATING AND DRINKING

Bulgaria is stuffed full of vegetable plots and orchards ("Bulgar" used to be a synonym for "market gardener" in several Balkan countries), and fresh fruit and vegetables are half the secret of Bulgarian food. In the villages, almost all the food comes straight from the land and is organic or free range, as few people can afford pesticides or chemical fertilizers. In the towns, however, 45 years of collectivized agriculture and catering have conspired to impose a certain conformity on restaurants, and the high quality and range of cooking you'll experience as a guest in a Bulgarian home is still rarely reflected in the country's eating establishments.

Grilled meat dishes predominate everywhere, and, despite the wide range and quality of the vegetables available, **vegetarians** may well be frustrated by the lack of animal-free options. Though the newer restaurants tend to offer more variety, menus remain pretty unimaginative, with a limited choice of dishes on offer. There is, however, an increasing variety of **street food** available, although traditional Bulgarian pastries and snacks are often a bit too stodgy and greasy for Western tastes.

In big towns and coastal resorts, **food shops** (*hranitelni stoki*) are reasonably well stocked with

CYRILLIC CHECKLIST: EATING AND DRINKING			
Breakfast/snack	закуски	Skara-bira	скара-бира
Bread	хляб	Restaurant	ресторант
Supermarket	магазин на самообслужване	Vegetarian restaurant	вегетариански ресторант
Food shop	хранителни стоки	Self-service restaurant	експресресторант
Outdoor market	пазар		
Indoor market	хали	Folk restaurant, inn	ханб ханче
Café	кафе	Mehana, tavern	механа
Patisserie	сладкарница	Café-bar	кафе-аперитиф

useful domestic picnic ingredients such as fresh bread, cheese (kashkaval Vitosha is made from cow's milk; kashkaval Balkan from ewe's milk), sausages (pastârma is a spicy beef salami; sudzhuk a flat home-cured sausage), smoked leg of ham (pushen but) and dairy products, as well as tinned goods, packet soups, conserves and chocolates imported from Greece or Turkey. In rural areas, food shops are much more sparsely provisioned, with shelves lined with jars of Bulgarian jam, packets of dry biscuits, and little else. Instant **coffee** is usually vile, and **tea** is either Chinese or herbal, so it's wise to bring both if you're planning on self-catering.

Fresh fruit and veg is best bought in the outdoor **markets** (pazar) which you'll find in most towns and villages. Here smallholding peasants from the outlying districts sell whatever produce is currently in season, as well as herbs, nuts, sunflower seeds, dried fruit and pulses. Many towns also have old-style, municipally run **indoor markets** (hali), though these tend to be sad, half-abandoned affairs with little to offer. Ad hoc street stalls often sell foreign produce such as bananas, coffee and chocolate. City-centre **bakeries** tend to produce fresh bread (hlyab, хляб) throughout the day. In smaller towns and villages, shops selling bread stand empty for much of the day, until an arbitrarily timed delivery attracts queues of shoppers.

BREAKFASTS, SNACKS AND STREET FOOD

Traditionally, food was eaten in the fields or pastures, or consumed on returning home – which meant subsisting on bread, cheese, vegetables and fruit throughout the day until an evening meal of stew or grilled meat. Nowadays, people eat rather less frugally, but the habit of picking up a bite to eat in the morning and continuing to nibble at **snacks** throughout the day still remains. In general, the best advice is to keep an eye out for signs advertising zakuski (закуски), a generic term meaning either breakfast or any daytime snack.

In towns and cities, a typical **breakfast** tends to consist of an espresso coffee and a cigarette, followed by another round of the same if one still feels any hunger. Few restaurants, except for fast-food or self-service places, open for breakfast, and the most convenient places to pick up snack food are the stalls and kiosks that tend to congregate around main thoroughfares, train and bus stations. You can also pick up a pastry from a **patisserie** (see overleaf), to be washed down with one of two traditional breakfast drinks: yoghurt (kiselo mlyako), or boza, a browny-coloured millet drink.

The most common **Bulgarian snack food** is banitsa (often referred to by its diminutive form, banichka, or known in some areas as byurek), a flaky pastry filled with cheese or, on occasion, meat. At its best, the banitsa is a delicious light bite, although it's invariably quite stodgy by the time it reaches the streets. Mlechna banitsa (literally "milk banitsa") is a richer, sweeter version made using eggs and dusted with icing sugar, while the Rhodopska banitsa, found only in the Rhodopes, is more like a soufflé filled with cheese.

Equally popular is the kifla, a small bread roll usually made from slightly sweetened dough and with a vein of marmalade running through the middle, although you will probably encounter more savoury variants, filled either with cheese (sâs sirene), or a small hot-dog-type sausage (s krenvirsh). Similar is the sirenka, a small bread bun with a cheese filling. Other favourites among street vendors are ponichki, deep-fried lumps of dough, not unlike doughnuts, and *palachinki* or pancakes, usually stuffed with cheese.

Street stands also sell grilled snacks, which are the likeliest cause of an upset stomach for travellers. *Kebapcheta* are wads of mincemeat (traditionally a combination of lamb, pork and veal, although the precise mix depends on what's available) served with a hunk of bread; *kyufte* is the same in meatball form; while *nadenitsa* is a spicy sausage. In autumn and winter, vendors emerge peddling corn on the cob (*tsarevitsa*), and throughout the year incorrigible snack-munchers can find solace in the *fâstâtsi*, or roast nuts, and *semki*, sunflower seeds, sold everywhere in paper cones.

All these traditional snacks are rivalled in popularity by **hot dogs**, **hamburgers** and **pizzas**, which, with a few honourable exceptions, tend to be revolting. The hot dogs are of doubtful composition and gristly consistency; hamburgers often amount to a slice of luncheon meat on a tepid bun, smothered in ketchup; while pizzas are typically rubbery slices with inferior Bulgarian cheese, ham and fish substituted for mozzarella, salami and anchovies. The same goes for open (usually toasted) **sandwiches** (*sandvichi*), sold at many kiosks, cafés and bars. Typical toppings are *kashkaval*, a hard, cheddar-like cheese; *salam*, an unappetizing slice of pinkish, pork-based meat; *kayma*, a mincemeat paste; *shunka*, ham; or *kombiniran*, a mixture of two or more of the above. Never order any of them without first inspecting what's on offer.

Cakes and **pastries** are sold throughout the day in a **patisserie** or *sladkarnitsa*. Many of Bulgaria's sweet dishes were originally imported from the Middle East by the Turks – the syrupy *baklava* (referred to in some establishments as *triguna*), the nut-filled *revane*, and the gooey rich *kadaif* being the most common. Turkish Delight (*lokum*) and *halva* are also firm favourites. Betraying a more Central European ancestry are the variety of cakes (*torta*) on offer, with buttercream (*maselna*), fruit (*frukti*) or chocolate (*shokoladova*) filling. *Garash*, a layered chocolate cake, is the most widely available. **Ice cream** – *sladoled* – is sold everywhere on the streets in summer.

RESTAURANTS AND MEALS

Although **restaurants** (*restorant*) vary widely in terms of decor and service, it's rare to find any cuisine but Bulgarian, outside of Sofia, and the range of dishes can be pretty limited – in some cases the waiter will merely rattle through a list of what's on that evening. Higher prices in top-notch restaurants don't necessarily imply a wider choice – merely a better quality of meat. Restaurants are usually **open** between about 11am and 11pm, although many close for a few hours in the afternoon. It's very difficult to get food after 11pm outside big city hotels or package resorts, and in provincial towns you'll be lucky to find anywhere open after 10pm.

The growth in new private places has largely put paid to the former dominance of hotel restaurants, which used to be a focus for the social life of the local elite in provincial towns, but are now mostly sad and soulless affairs. New restaurants catering to the nouveaux riches usually offer slightly more exotic menus than you'll find at the Communist-era restaurants in National Revival-period mansions in Plovdiv or Sozopol, where the food and service often fail to match the setting. As a rule though, you'd do better in a **mehana** or taverna, which concentrates on grills, salads and other traditional staples, and usually has tables outdoors and music in the evening. A **han** (хан) or **hanche** (ханче) – literally an "inn" – is likewise usually decorated in the folk-style and features traditional cooking, while **skara-bira** are a lower form of culinary life serving little more than beer and kebabs and, in rural areas at least, traditionally a male-only preserve. In towns, you'll also find **self-service** restaurants (*ekspres-restorant*), which are invariably cheap, but often with reason.

With the exception of deluxe hotel restaurants in the capital, none of these places will **cost** the earth, and providing you avoid imported drinks, the bill should be very modest indeed: in most cases, a three-course meal for two, with a bottle of wine, will rarely exceed $15, except in Sofia, Plovdiv and the coastal resorts, where you can expect to pay $20–30 for the same.

WHAT TO EAT

If you're looking for nothing more than a quick and inexpensive stomach-filler, most restaurants serve filling **soups** accompanied by copious amounts of bread. *Bob*, a spicy bean soup, *shkembe chorba* or tripe soup, and *tarator*, a cold soup made from yoghurt and cucumber, are the three most common varieties.

Salads in Bulgaria are usually eaten as a starter, or as the accompaniment to a stiff aperitif,

VEGETARIANS IN BULGARIA

Traditional Bulgarian cuisine excels in **vegetable dishes**; the snag is trying to find places that serve them. Vegetarian restaurants (*vegetarianski restorant*, вегетариански ресторант) used to exist in most major towns, but began to lose their appeal in the mid-1980s as supplies of agricultural produce from the countryside deteriorated. Most of them were privatized and turned into something else.

Standard menus usually include an omelette (*omlet*), either with cheese or mushroom filling, along with *kashkaval pane*, hard cheese fried in breadcrumbs or batter; *kartofi s sirene*, french fries with grated white cheese; *sirene po shopski*, cheese baked in an earthenware pot with a spicy tomato sauce; and *pâlneni chushki*, peppers stuffed with cheese. One popular meatless dish is *mishmash*, scrambled eggs with chopped peppers

and tomatoes; and there's also a vegetarian version of the oven-baked stew *gyuvech* (ask for *posten gyuvech*), although in many cases this turns out to be the same thing as *mishmash*. Any of these would suffice as a main meal; otherwise you're limited to choosing from vegetable side dishes, which are less widely available. If you're lucky, you may encounter fried courgettes (*pârzheni tikvichki*); aubergines (*patlidzhan*) covered in yogurt (*s kiselo mlyako*); peppers stuffed with egg and cheese and fried in breadcrumbs (*chushka byurek*); eggs fried on spinach (*pârzheni yaitsa s pyure ot spanak*); or potato purée (*pyure ot kartofi*). The spiciest dish is *kyopoolu* – mashed aubergine with garlic and chilli.

When in doubt, use the phrase *postno yadene* (literally "fasting food") to ensure that you receive something that's genuinely meat free.

rather like *meze* in Turkey. Most common are those formed from the following vegetables, whether singly or in combination: cabbage (*zele*), tomatoes (*domati*), cucumber (*krastavitsi*) and peppers (*piperki* or *chushki*). A *meshana salata* (mixed salad) consists of cucumbers and tomatoes; a *Shopska salata* is the same topped with grated white cheese, while a *selska salata* features peppers and spices. Two yogurt-based salads are *mlechna salata* (like *tarator* but thicker, with nuts) and *snezhanka* (pickled cucumbers covered in yoghurt). Other oft-encountered **starters** are *pârzheni chushki*, baked peppers; *lukanka*, a spicy salami-like sausage; and *sudzhuk* – all of which make an excellent accompaniment to a round of drinks.

Mainstay of any Bulgarian restaurant menu are the **grilled meats**, of which *kebapcheta* and *kyufte* (see "Breakfast, Snacks and Street Food", p.33) are the most common. More substantial are chops (*pârzhola* or *kotlet*), or fillets (*file* or *kare*), which are invariably *teleshko* (veal) or *svinsko* (pork). Main courses may be served with a set *garnitura* (usually fries and the occasional vegetable), although sometimes you'll find these items listed individually on the menu and will have to order them separately. In the grander restaurants the main course will be accompanied by potatoes (*kartofi*) and a couple of vegetables, as well as bread: sometimes a *pitka* or small bread bun, or more rarely a *simitla*, a glazed bun made from chickpea flour. Lower down the scale, you may just

get fried potatoes (*pârzheni kartofi*) and a couple of slices of bread. You're usually expected to specify how many slices (*filiya*) you want.

Mehanas and touristy folk-style restaurants are the likeliest places to get **traditional Bulgarian dishes** baked and served in earthenware pots. The best known is *gyuvech* (which literally means "earthenware dish"), a rich stew comprising peppers, aubergines, and beans, to which are added either meat or meat stock. *Kavarma*, a spicy meat stew (often pork), is prepared in a similar fashion, and tastes something like Hungarian goulash. Two other traditional recipes which you may come across are *sarmi*, cabbage leaves stuffed with rice and mincemeat; and *imam bayaldi*, aubergine stuffed with all manner of vegetables, meat and herbs – a Turkish dish, whose name translates as "the priest burst", found in the south of the country.

Finally, along the coast and around the highland lakes and reservoirs there's **fish** (*riba*) – most often fried or grilled, but sometimes in a soup or stew – and nearly always of a higher standard than the meat dishes. Most coastal snack bars and restaurants offer *tsatsa* or *popche*, small white fish which are deep fried in batter and served with fries; and *skumriya* (mackerel), delicious when grilled. *Skumriya na keramidi* (literally "mackerel on a tile"), is baked in an earthenware container, usually with a rich tomato sauce. In parts of the Rhodopes and Pirin you'll also find mountain trout, as well as calamari, shark and other *riba ot Byalo*

More (fish from the White Sea, as Bulgarians call the Aegean).

DRINKING

Private enterprise has vastly increased the number of **places to drink**, and all town centres now have a healthy sprinkling of **kiosks** serving coffee, soft drinks and basic snack food, usually with plastic chairs and tables on the adjoining pavement. Some of them serve beer, vodka, and other strong drinks, and stay open well after nightfall, but for the most part they're a daytime, fairweather phenomenon. A more traditional venue is the **sladkarnitsa** (сладкарница), a Bulgarian version of the Central European café, many of which serve cakes as well as alcohol.

Evening drinking tends to take place in restaurants (where it's quite common for tables to be monopolized by drinkers rather than diners), or in the vast number of **bars** operating under the generic title of *kafe-aperitiv* (кафе-аперитиф). Some are no more than a converted garage or basement room, though many of them – in Sofia, Plovdiv and along the coast in particular – compare favourably with anything found in the average Western European town. Here you can get the full range of domestic alcoholic and non-alcoholic drinks, as well as imported spirits and canned beers, and all kinds of cocktails in the flashier places.

Coffee can be excellent or vile, so it pays to look before ordering. If they've got a machine behind the counter, you can order a *kafe espresso* or a *kapuchino* with reasonable confidence and maybe feel emboldened to ask if they also do *turska* (Turkish coffee) or *Viensko kafe* (Viennese coffee), which comes with a dollop of ice cream on top. If not, you risk getting a revolting brew from some kind of instant coffee under the generic title of *neskafe*, or *nes*. Coffee is often drunk in tandem with a glass of **juice** (*sok*), usually a pretty artificial concoction such as *tropik*, a cocktail of citrus fruits, or the sickly green *kivi* (kiwi). *Naturalen sok* (natural fruit juice) is usually imported and costs more. Delicious domestically produced fruit juices (*nektar*, or *fruktovi sok*) are sometimes sold bottled in supermarkets and food shops, but rarely appear in cafés or bars. **Tea** (*chay*) is available in most cafés; specify *cheren chay* or black tea unless you want some herbal concoction.

Other *bezalkoholni* (non-alcoholic) choices include *gazirana voda* (gaseous mineral water), or international beverages such as Coca Cola, Pepsi, Fanta and Sprite.

BULGARIAN WINE

From having an insular **wine** industry before World War II, Bulgaria has muscled its way into the forefront of the world's export market, specializing in robust red wines of basic but solid quality. Tried and tested grapes like Cabernet Sauvignon and Merlot have been planted in different regions (such as Pomorie, Haskovo, Asenovgrad or Suhindol), under whose name they're sold with phenomenal success abroad. Inside Bulgaria there's a greater variety and more differentiation between the various blended wines, all of which cost less than $3 a bottle in supermarkets and *mehanas*.

Among the **reds** are full-bodied Cabernet; heavier, mellower Melnik and Gâmza; rich, dark Mavrud; and the smooth, strawberry-flavoured Haskovski Merlot. Sweet Pamid, first grown by the Thracians and verging on rosé, is blended with Mavrud to produce Trakiya, or with Melnik wine to make Pirin, while Madara is obtained from concentrated Gâmza and Dimyat grapes (a similar mix is used for the more acidic Târnovo). Asenovgradski Mavrud and the red Muscatel Slavyanska are both dessert wines.

The sweeter **whites** are preferable to Dimyat unless you like your wine very dry. Of these, Karlovski and Rilski Misket (Muscatels) and Tamyanka are widely available, but the golden-coloured Evksinograd is much harder to find. Of the dry whites, Traminer Han Krum is the one to look for, while Preslav is a decent **rosé**.

In wine-growing areas, many tavernas and restaurants offer **home-made wine** (*domashno vino*), often straight from the cask (*nalivno*). There is never a problem ordering by the glass (*chasha*).

SPIRITS

Native **spirits** are highly potent and cost little more than $3 a bottle. They are drunk diluted with water in the case of *mastika* (like ouzo in Greece or raki in Turkey), or downed in one, Balkan-style, in the form of *rakiya*, or brandy. *Slivova rakiya* is made from plums, *Kaisieva rakiya* from apricots, and *grozdova* from grapes – *Pomorska rakiya* is the best example of the latter. *Rakiya* is always accompanied by a soft drink

BULGARIAN FOOD AND DRINK TERMS

Basics

Imate li...?	Do you have...?	*Nazdrave!*	Cheers!	
Az sâm vegetarianets/ vegetarianka	I am a vegetarian	*Hlyab*	bread	хляб
		Kifli	rolls	кифли
Ima li postno yadene?	Do you have any vegetarian dishes?	*Kiselo Mlyako*	yoghurt	кисело мляко
		Maslo	butter	масло
Ima li neshto bez meso?	Do you have anything without meat?	*Med*	honey	мед
		Mlyako	milk	мляко
Molya, donesete mi/ni...	Please bring me/us....	*Piper*	pepper	пипер
Listata	the menu	*Sol*	salt	сол
Smetkata, molya	The bill, please	*Yaitse*	egg	яйце
Dve biri	two beers	*Zahar*	sugar	захар

Appetizers, Soups (*supi*) and Salads (*salati*)

Bob	spicy bean soup	Боб	*Postna supa*	vegetable soup	постна супа
Bulyon	consommé	бульон	*Salata shopska*	mixed salad, topped with grated cheese	шопска салата
Chorba	broth, thick soup	чорба			
Kyopolu	aubergine, pepper and tomato salad	кьопоолу	*Shkembe chorba*	tripe soup	шкембе чорба
Lyutenitsa	piquant sauce of red peppers and herbs	лютеница	*Tarator*	yoghurt and cucumber soup	таратор

Meat (*meso*)

Drebolii	giblets	дреболии	*Kyufteta*	meatballs	кюфте
Ezik	tongue	език	*Mozâk*	brains	мозък
File	fillet	филе	*Musaka*	moussaka	мусака
Gyuvech	meat and veg stew baked in a pot	гювеч	*Pârzhola*	grilled cutlet	пържола
			Pile	chicken	пилешко
			Ptitsi	poultry	птици
Imam Bayaldi	stuffed aubergines (lit. "the Imam burst")	Имам Баялди	*Salam*	salami	салам
			Shishcheta	lamb or pork shish kebabs	шишета
			Slanina	bacon	сланина
Kare	fillet or loin chop	каре	*Svinsko* (*s kiselo zele*)	pork (and sauerkraut)	свинско (с кисело зеле)
Kebapche	shish kebab	кебапче			
Kebapcheta	grilled, spicy sausage-shaped meatballs	кебапчета			

Terms

cheverme	barbecue	чеверме	*pârzheni*	fried	пържни
divech	game	дивеч	*pecheno*	roast	печно
na skara	grilled	на скара	*zadusheno*	braised	задушено

continued overleaf

BULGARIAN FOOD AND DRINK TERMS (cont)

Fish (*riba*)

Byala riba	pike perch	бяла рива	Lefer	bluefish	лефер
Chiga	sterlet	чига	Midi	mussels	миди
Esetra	sturgeon	есетра	Palamud	tuna	паламчи
Haiver	roe	хайвер	Pâstârva	trout	пъстърва
Kalkan	turbot	калан	Sharan	carp	шаран
Karagyoz	Black Sea herring	карагъоз	Skumriya	mackerel	скумрия
Kefal	grey mullet	кефал	Som	sheatfish	сом

Vegetables (*zelenchutsi*)

Chesân	garlic	чесън	Morkovi	carrots	моркови
Chushki	peppers	чушки	Pârzheni kartofi	chips/french fries	пържени картофи
Domati	tomatoes	домати			
Gâbi	mushrooms	гъби	Praz	leeks	праз
Grah	peas	грах	(Presen) luk	(spring) onions	(пресен) лук
Karfiol	cauliflower	карфиол	Sini domati	aubergines	сини домати
Kartofi	potatoes	картофи	Spanak	spinach	спанак
Krastavitsa	cucumber	краставица	Tikvichki	courgettes	тиквички
Luk	onions	лук	Zelen fasul	runner beans	зелен фасол
Maslini	olives	маслини			

Fruit (*plodove*) and cheese (*sirene*)

Chereshi	cherries	череши	Vishni	morello cherries	вишни
Dinya	watermelon	диня	Yabâlki	apples	ябълки
Grozde	grapes	грозде	Yagodi	strawberries	ягоди
Kaisii	apricots	каисий	Kashkaval	hard, Edam-type cheese	кашкавал
Krushi	pears	круши			
Limon	lemon	лимон	Pusheno sirene	smoked cheese	пушено сирене
Malini	raspberries	малини			
Praskovi	peaches	прaskови	Sirene	salty, feta-type cheese	сирене
Slivi	plums	сливи			

Drinks (*napitki*)

Goreshti napitki	hot drinks	голеши напитки	Sok portokal	orange juice	сок портокал
Kafee expreso	espresso	кафе еспресо	Aperitivi	aperitifs	аперитиви
Neskafee	instant coffee	нескафе	Rakiya	brandy	ракия
Chai	tea	чай	Vino	wine	вино
Bezalkoholni napitki	soft drinks	безалкохолни напитки	Shardone	Chardonnay	Шардоне
			Bira	beer	бира
Voda	water	вода	Nalivna	draught	наливна

and a salad or appetizer. Vodka is also widely drunk: domestic brands like *Tsarevets* are the cheapest, although Russian and Scandinavian brands are widely available. Imported whisky is cheaper than in the West, but much of it is counterfeit (*mente*). Buy it from the bigger outlets, and avoid stuff sold by the smaller kiosks and street traders.

In bars and restaurants spirits are sold by the gramme. *Pedeset grama* (50g or 5cl) is roughly equivalent to a British double measure, *sto grama* (10cl) a quadruple. You'll see plenty of men downing *sto grama* at 11am, or even earlier, although Bulgarians maintain that they're not such heavy drinkers as the Russians.

BEER

Bulgarian **beer** (*bira*) is pretty unexciting but perfectly drinkable. The most popular brands are *Zagorka* from Stara Zagora, *Astika* from Haskovo and *Kamenitza* from Plovdiv, all of which are lager-type beers whose regular versions have 10 percent alcohol, and their "specials" 11 or 12 percent. While *Pirin*, brewed in Blagoevgrad and

available in the southwest, and *Plevensko Pivo* from the northern town of Pleven, also have a following, true drinkers sniff at *Ariana* from Sofia, which is only 4.5 percent alcohol. A 50cl bottle of regular *Kamenitza* or *Zagorka* rarely costs more than 75¢ in a bar or restaurant, while a 33cl bottle of *Astika* or a "special" will set you back about $1. Imported German, Austrian, Czech or Danish beers are also widely available, at about twice the price. An increasingly number of bars offer **draft beer** (*nalivna bira*) as well as bottled – either Bulgarian or an imported brand.

COMMUNICATIONS: MAIL, PHONES AND MEDIA

In recent years Bulgaria's telephone system has improved and expanded rapidly, while the postal service, although slower to modernize, also functions reasonably efficiently. Email is gaining ground, particularly amongst those Bulgarians involved in tourism or other international concerns, although cybercafés have yet to arrive in the country.

POST OFFICES AND MAIL

Most **post offices** (*poshta*) are open from 8.30am to 5.30pm from Monday to Saturday, although those in the larger towns tend to open an extra thirty minutes or so either side. It's not always easy to identify the right counter (*gishe*) to queue up at; look for signs advertising the sale of *marki* (stamps) or the despatch of *pisma* (letters) and

koleti (parcels). **Stamps** are best bought at the post office, although **envelopes** (*plikove*) are sold at street kiosks. **Mail** can take 7–10 days to reach Britain and 2–3 weeks to the US; less than half that time if you send it *bârza* (express) or *vâzdushna* (airmail). It's reasonably cheap to send **parcels** home from Bulgaria, although items have to be brought into the post office and a customs declaration filled out before being wrapped up on the premises (only books and magazines are exempt from this procedure).

Poste restante services are available at the major post office in every sizable town. Mail can be claimed by showing your passport (ask *Ima li pisma za mene* – is there any mail for me?), and letters should be addressed писма до поискване, централна поща, followed by the name of the town. Letters from Western Europe generally take around a week to arrive in Bulgaria, those from North America two weeks, and Bulgarian postal officers are apt to misfile or return mail to the sender if it's not claimed

CYRILLIC CHECKLIST:	COMMUNICATIONS
Post office	поща
Poste restante	писма до поискване
Express mail	бърза
Air mail	въздушна
Stamps	марки
Letters	писма
Envelopes	пликове
Parcels	колети
Telephone	телефон
Phone card	фонкарта

immediately, so don't hold high hopes for poste restante communications.

When writing **letters to Bulgaria**, remember that the postcode and name of the town comes first, the street and number second, and the name of the addressee last: eg. 9000, Varna, ul. Nevazhno 40, Mr Todor Aleksandrov.

PHONES

Although Bulgaria's **telephone system** has greatly improved in recent years, it remains patchy. Because investment has been concentrated on business communications, international and trunk calls are often easier than local ones, especially using the new public telephones taking **phonecards** (*fonkarta*). These can usually be found in post offices, hotel lobbies and major public buildings such as cultural centres and concert halls. There are two systems, using separate phones and non-interchangeable cards, *Bulfon* (whose phones are orange) and *Betkom* (with blue phones). It's best to carry both cards as you never know which system will be available (in some towns one has a monopoly). You can use them to make any kind of direct-dial call for the same cost as you'd pay in a telephone office or private house. Phonecards are sold at post offices and many shops and kiosks.

In the absence of a cardphone you'll have to fall back on the **telephone offices** (*telefon*, телефон) attached to post offices, where you are assigned a cabin and pay for your call afterwards. The telephone section is usually open longer than other parts of the post office, often as late as 11pm in major cities and 24 hours in Sofia. As most hotels levy extortionate surcharges on **international calls**, you'll almost always save money by going through a phone office instead. Note that Bulgaria is one of the few countries in Europe with **no peak or off-peak rates**, so you can call at any time without worrying about extra costs.

Domestic calls can be fraught with difficulties in rural areas, where getting a connection between the main town and a village may necessitate going through the telephone office, as direct-dialling isn't possible. Another peculiarity is that within such regions, the **phone codes** for settlements differ from those used when calling long distance or from abroad. For example, the national code for Melnik is ☎07437, but within the Pirin region its prefix is ☎997437. If you can't

get though using the prefix starting with ☎0, try using ☎99 instead. In this book, all codes are given in the zero-form, unless they *only* work as ☎99 calls.

Holders of **calling cards** should phone their company's customer service line to find out if they provide service in Bulgaria, and if so, what the toll-free access code is. In theory, it is possible to use AT&T or Sprint cards to call home collect and pay at local rates, by dialling ☎008 /001010, but often in practice the Bulgarian operator tends to cut you off after thirty seconds. At the time of writing, holders of MCI, Telstra, Optus and NZ Telecom cards cannot use them to call out of Bulgaria. GSM **mobile phones** can be used in the big cities and coastal resorts but coverage is extremely patchy elsewhere.

THE MEDIA

English-language newspapers and magazines are not widely available in Bulgaria, although you may find recent copies of *Time*, *Newsweek*, the *Financial Times* and the *Herald Tribune* on the bigger newsstands in Sofia, Plovdiv and Varna. English tabloids appear regularly at the package resorts along the coast, and in Sofia there's an English-language weekly paper called *The Sofia Echo*, which is an excellent source of local news.

THE BULGARIAN PRESS

The collapse of censorship after November 1989 and the disappearance of turgid propaganda organs such as the former party newspaper *Rabotnichesko Delo* ("Workers' Deeds") have resulted in a lively domestic media scene. The

---

INTERNATIONAL TELEPHONE CODES

To **dial abroad direct from Bulgaria**, first use the international code listed below and then the STD (area) code, remembering to omit the initial 0.
UK ☎0044
USA & Canada ☎001
Australia ☎0061
New Zealand ☎0064

To **call Bulgaria from abroad**, use the following international access codes, followed by the area code (omitting the initial 0) and the local number.

From the UK ☎00359
From USA & Canada ☎0113 59
From Australia & New Zealand ☎0011359

two principal **daily newspapers** are 24 Часа (*24 Chasa*, "24 Hours") and Труд (*Trud* or "Work"), tabloids that mix news reporting with racy articles about Hollywood starlets or the antics of the Bulgarian mafia. The tone of both titles is overwhelmingly conservative, reflecting the nostalgia of people who find market economics, high inflation and growing Western influence slightly disorientating. Of the four "serious" dailies, Дума (*Duma*, "The Word") is the organ of the Bulgarian Socialist Party, while Демокрация (*Demokratsiya*, "Democracy") acts as a mouthpiece for the right-of-centre Union of Democratic Forces; and serious journalistic content is often undermined by frequent political slanging matches between the two. The other two heavies, Континент (*Kontinent*) and Стандарт (*Standart*), aim for impartiality, although the fact that they're run by figures previously active in Communist-era journalism ensures that they're distrusted by most democrats.

A gaggle of lesser, predominantly weekly titles have also emerged offering a hitherto forbidden diet of celebrity gossip, lurid crime stories, and improbable tales of the paranormal. The glossiest publication is Бляськ (*Blyasâk*, "Glitter"), which basically rehashes stories from the Western tabloids.

TV AND RADIO

Bulgaria's two domestic **TV channels**, Kanal 1 and Efir 2, which peddle old imported soaps, b-movies from the west and cheesy game shows, are augmented by two foreign stations: TV5 Europe, an international French-language channel, and Russian TV. The latter, originally imported to foster Bulgarian–Soviet friendship, was becoming an embarrassment by the mid-Eighties, when it provided Bulgarians with a window on *glasnost* denied to them by their own government. In addition, **cable** and **satellite TV** have caught on in a big way, to the extent that many hotels and bars feature Sky or MTV, while in the ethnic Turkish regions, household dishes point towards Turkey.

The best way to catch up on news is the **BBC World Service** on short wave (available on the following frequencies, depending on the time of day: Mhz 15.07, 12.09, 9.41, 6.18) or in Sofia on VHF (91Mhz).

HOLIDAYS, FESTIVALS AND ENTERTAINMENT

With the collapse of Communism, several ideological holidays have disappeared from the Bulgarian calendar to be replaced by traditional Orthodox festivals such as Easter and Christmas. In addition, there's an increasing observance of local festivals and saint's days, marked by the holding of special services, feasting, or simply by lighting candles next to an icon of the appropriate saint. Though traditional folk customs are still observed by many people, when it comes to entertainment tastes are much the same as in the West.

FESTIVALS

In Communist times virtually all **festivals** were organized and funded by the state under the auspices of the Party, and "unofficial" events such as Rockers' festivals or Muslim pilgrimages were firmly discouraged. Today, there are almost no ideological constraints but little money either, so that while the diversity of festivals is far greater, there's less certainty of them actually taking place, particularly in the case of events that require major funding.

For lovers of **classical music and ballet**, the major events remain the **Sofia Music Weeks** (late-May to late-June), the **March Music Days** in Ruse, the international **chamber music** festival in Plovdiv (mid-June), and the **symphonic music** festival in Haskovo (end of Oct). In addition, there's whatever is featured during the **Varna Summer** (mid-June to mid-August), Sozopol's **Apollonia Festival** (beginning of Sept) or the **Trakiisko Lyato** in Plovdiv (early Aug) – though none of these three are exclusively devoted to classical music.

While you can also hear some **jazz** during the Varna Summer and Apollonia Festival, a better bet is one of the **international festivals** in Haskovo (Sept or early Oct), Ruse (late Oct), Blagoevgrad or Sofia (both in Nov). Though big names from the West are thin on the ground, top performers from Bulgaria, the Former Yugoslavia and the Soviet Union often play there, and the general standard of musicianship is high.

There's less to look forward to in the way of **pop** music during the Apollonia and Trakiisko Lyato festivals, unless you go for Balkan clones of Boyzone or the Russian diva of pop, Alla Pugachova – though the annual **Rockers' Festival** is a gas if you can find out exactly where and when it's on (see p.282).

Comedy is even less rewarding, with no stand-up circuit to tap into even if you understood the language, now that the once-vaunted **Festival of Humour and Satire** at Gabrovo is practically in the terminal ward. However, drama and poetry are both alive and kicking, and can be seen at the **Theatre Days** in Blagoevgrad (Bulgaria's equivalent of the Edinburgh festival) and the **Young Poets** festival in Haskovo (both late April/early May) – though you obviously need to understand Bulgarian to enjoy them.

FOLKLORE FESTIVALS

Bulgaria's **folklore festivals** vary enormously in size and character, from parades of floats through the streets, to gatherings on highland meadows, or a few musicians playing on the village square while everyone dances the *horo*. While the **Rose Carnival** at Kazanlâk in the Valley of the Roses

If you want to visit some of the more hard-to-reach folklore festivals, the Sofia-based tourist agency Lyub Travel (ul. Milin Kamâk 11; ☎02/702 287, fax 02/963 4427; email *boyanin@mail.techno-link.com*), often runs **organized excursions** to such events, or can arrange them to order if the money's right.

(early June) is fairly cheesy, you're bound to enjoy some of the acts at the **international festivals** in Burgas and Plovdiv in August, featuring dance troupes from all over Europe and the Near East.

A more distinctly Bulgarian event is the **Koprivshtitsa Folklore Festival**, the largest gathering of traditional singers and musicians, from every region of the country; formerly held every five years, it now occurs annually (in August). Other highland music festivals include the annual **Rozhenski Sâbor** at Rozhen in the Rhodopes, and the biennial **Pirin Pee** at the Predel Pass (both in August) – the largest gatherings of musicians from the Rhodopes and Pirin regions. These regions also host the annual **Pirin Folklore Festival** in Sandanski (Sept), and the bi- or triennial **Balkan Folklore Festival** in Blagoevgrad (anytime between June and September), both of which have acquired an international flavour due to the area's historic ties with neighbouring Macedonia, Greece and Turkey. In the summer, throughout the Pirin and Rhodope regions (and sometimes in Sofia, Plovdov and other major cities), a plethora of civic and festive events commemorating the **Ilinden** uprising of 1903, takes place on two separate dates a week apart, depending on whether it is pegged to the Old or New Style calendar (see below).

While descendants of refugees from Aegean Thrace celebrate their roots at the **Gathering of the Beautiful Trakiya** in Haskovo (May) and the **Thracian Festival** at Madzharovo (Sept), **Macedonian**, **Pomak** and **Vlach traditions** are celebrated in the Rhodope villages of Dorkovo (first Sunday in August) and Zabârdo (Aug 15), and there's a festival of **Gypsy music** in Stara Zagora (late June or early July). Another event not to be missed is the annual **Bagpipe Festival** at Mugla, which unfortunately coincides with the festival at Dorkovo (first Sunday in August).

Another, spectacular manifestation of Bulgarian folk culture is the **Kukeri processions** of mummers in nightmarish costumes, carrying flaming torches throughout the streets of Razlog, Sandanski, Pernik and Petrich on New Year's Eve and January 1. In Blagoevgrad the processions take place as early as December 25, while in Shiroka Lâka they don't appear until March.

Nor does the list of festivals end there, for many of the events above incorporate aspects of religious or agricultural rites which are interwoven with customs and traditions that still feature prominently in Bulgarian life. We've listed the festivals specific to

NATIONAL HOLIDAYS AND SPECIFIC EVENTS

You'll find shops, banks and restaurants closed on major **national holidays**, although the occasional café, exchange bureau or provision shop may open up in big cities or resorts.

Jan 1 New Year's Day
March 3 Liberation of Bulgaria
Easter Sunday (see below)
Easter Monday (see below)
May 1 Labour Day
May 24 Day of Slavonic Education and Culture
Dec 25 Christmas Day

SPECIFIC EVENTS

Events occuring on the cusp of two months are listed under the earlier date.

JANUARY

Kukeri processions in Razlog, Sandanski, Pernik and Petrich (New Year's Eve/Jan 1).

Jordanovden celebrations at Koprivshtitsa (Jan 6).

Christmas (Old Style) celebrated by female carol singers at Dobârsko (Jan 6/7).

Festival of orchestral music in Plovdiv (early Jan).

FEBRUARY

Trifon Zarazen celebrated in Melnik, Sandanski, and Vishovgrad near Veliko Târnovo (Feb 14).

MARCH–APRIL

Kukeri at Shiroka Lâka (First weekend in March).

March Music Days Classical music festival in Ruse (Last two weeks in March).

Todorovden Horse races at Koprivshtitsa, Dobrinishte and Katarino near Razlog (First Sat of Lent).

Day of My Town festival in Sandanski (End of April).

Easter Nationwide church services on Thusday and Saturay night, a Great Easter Concert in Bansko, and Kukeri rites at Eleshnitsa (Easter Monday).

Lazarovden Lazaruvane displays in the City Garden, Stara Zagora, and Dragalevtsi (Sat before Palm Sunday).

Theatre Days in Blagoevgrad (Late April/early May).

Young Poets Festival in Haskovo (Late April/early May).

MAY

Procession of icons from Bachkovo Monastery to Ayazmoto (25 days after Easter Sunday).

Gergyovden Sacrifices and feasting at Chiprovtsi, Slatolin (near Montana) and the Monastery of St George near Hadzhidimovo (outside Gotse Delchev). Also Muslim/Christian gatherings at Ak Yazula Baba Tekke near Obrochiste, and Demir Baba Tekke near Sveshtari (May 6).

Measuring of the Milk festivals in Rhodope highland villages (May 21).

Celebration of Bansko Traditions in Bansko (May 17–24).

Classial Guitar Festival in Gotse Delchev (Late May).

Gathering of the Beautiful Trakiya Thracian folklore festival in Haskovo (Last weekend in May).

Sofia Music Weeks Festival of classical music and ballet (Late May to late June).

Festival of Humour and Satire in Gabrovo (Every 2 or 3 years).

Trakia Pee Thracian folk music festival in Stara Zagora (Last week of May or first week of June).

JUNE

Macedonian Folk Songs festival in Blagoevgrad (Every two or three years)

Rockers' Festival (classic cars and bikes) off the highway between Pazardzhik and Plovdiv.

Fire-dancing at Bâlgari in the Strandzha (June 4 or nearest weekend).

Kazanlâk Rose Festival, with folk music and parades in Kazanlâk (First weekend in June).

Chamber music festival in Plovdiv (mid-June).

Folklore and crafts displays at Etâra, near Gabrovo (June 24).

Gypsy music festival in Ayzama Park, Stara Zagora (Late June or early July).

Varna Summer Festival of classical music, folk-lore and jazz (Mid-June to mid-Aug)

JULY

Ilinden (New Style) Services at churches and monasteries named after St Elijah, and civic events throughout the Pirin region. Also a Christian/Muslim gathering at Demir Baba Tekke, near Sveshtari (July 20 or the last Sun in July).

Macendonian Sâbor at Rozhen, near Melnik (Last weekend in July).

AUGUST

Ilinden (Old Style) Ilindenski sâbor at Popovi Livadi near Gotse Delchev (Aug 2 or nearest weekend).

Pirin Pee folklore festival at the Predel Pass in the Pirin Mountains (Every 2 years).

continued overleaf

NATIONAL HOLIDAYS AND SPECIFIC EVENTS (cont)

Bagpipe festival at Mugla in the Rhodopes (First Sun in Aug).

Folklore festival (Macedonian, Pomak and Vlach) at Dorkovo (First Sun in Aug).

Trakiisko Lyato classical, pop and folk music, and an international folklore festival in Plovdiv (Early Aug)

Folk music festival in Koprivshtitsa (Aug 15 or nearest weekend).

Golyama Bogoroditsa Parade of icons at Troyan and Bachkovo monasteries (Aug 15).

Folk music festival at Zabârdo (Aug 15).

Karakachani festival (folk music and feasting) at the Blue Rocks outside Sliven (Third weekend in Aug).

Birthday of St John of Rila celebrated at Rila Monastery (Aug 18).

Dânovisti gathering at the Seven lakes in the Rila Mountains (Aug 19–28).

Golyama Bogroditsa (Aug 29).

Gypsy festival at Osikovitsa near Botevgrad Nearest weekend to (Aug 29).

International festival of folk music in Burgas (Late Aug).

Rozhenski Sâbor folklore festival at Rozhen in the Rhodopes (Last weekend in Aug).

SEPTEMBER
Thracian Festival of music, dancing and wrestling in Madzharovo (First week in Sept).

Apollonia Festival classical, jazz, rock and theatre festival (First 7–10 days of Sept).

Balklan Folklore festival in Blagoevgrad (Every 2 or 3 years).

Pirin Folklore Festival in Sandanski (second weekend in Sept).

Malka Bogoroditsa parade of icons at Rozhen Monastery (Sept 8).

Krâstovden pilgrimage to Krâstova gora (Sept 14).

Jazz Festival in Haskovo (Late Sept or early Oct).

OCTOBER
Autumn Festival in Blagoevgrad

Bansko Day Massed male choirs in Bansko (Oct 8).

Gotse Delchev Day in Gotse Delchev Oct 18

Wine harvest festival in Melnik (Oct 18).

Feast day of St John of Rila celebrated at Rila Monastery (Oct 19).

International Jazz Forum in Ruse (Last week of Oct).

Symphonic Music Festival in Haskovo (End of Oct).

NOVEMBER
International Jazz Festival in Blagoevgrad

International Jazz Festival in Sofia (Second week in Nov).

DECEMBER
Kukeri rites in Blagoevgrad (Dec 25)

---

particular places separately from the Saints' days that are widely observed at churches, but not worth going out of your way to attend. Those festivals scheduled to take place every two or three years are entirely subject to getting enough funding.

SEASONAL RITES AND RELIGIOUS FESTIVALS

Most traditional Bulgarian festivals relate to different stages of the agricultural year and are rooted in paganism, but the pantheon of Orthodox saints and holy days imparts a Christian framework to the seasonal calendar. Although the nearest most tourists get to this cycle of **rural celebrations** is a glimpse of festive costumes in museums, a surprising number of customs are still upheld and can

be witnessed if you're in rural areas at the right time. Given that many are scheduled around **Orthodox festivals**, it's unfortunate for visitors that Bulgarians themselves are often confused over whether these should be dated by the Old or New Style calendar, and the rule varies from place to place for no apparent reason. To confuse things further, the major **Islamic festivals** observed by Bulgarian Muslims follow a separate calendar, but several popular feasts fall on Orthodox holy days and are attended by Christians as well.

SEASONAL RITES

In Christian areas, the festive calendar begins with **New Year's Day** or St Basil's Day – also known as *survaki* – when young children go from house to house offering New Year wishes to the householders by slapping them on the back with a *survaknitsa* – a bunch of twigs adorned with brightly coloured threads and dried fruit. In some villages in southwestern Bulgaria, New Year's Day is also marked by processions of villagers wearing animal masks, a ritual similar to those performed on *Kukerov den* (see below).

In wine-producing areas, vines are pruned and sprinkled with wine for good luck and casks of young wine from last year's harvest are broached on St Tryphon's Day, **Trifon Zarazen** (Feb 14). A more widespread festival associated with the start of the agricultural year in arable or pastoral regions is **Kukerov den**, the Day of the *Kukeri*, on the first Sunday before Lent. Processions are led through the village by dancing, leaping men dressed up in animal costumes and grotesque masks, augmented by a girdle of goat or sheep bells and extravagantly tasselled trousers. In urban centres such as Razog, Petrich and Pernik, the festival is conflated with *survaki* and held on New Year's Eve or New Year's Day.

The advent of spring, **Baba Marta** (literally, "Granny March"), is celebrated on March 1, when peasant households embark on a round of spring-cleaning – symbolically sweeping the winter months away. On the same day people present each other with **martenitsa**, good-luck charms made of red and white woollen threads with tassels or furry bobbles on the end, that are worn until the sighting of the first migrating stork or budding bush (when the charms are hung on its branches). **Todorovden**, or St Theodor's Day, on the first Saturday of Lent, is still marked by horse-races in Koprivshtitsa, Dobrinishte and Katarino, while another widespread springtime fertility rite is *lazaruvane* which takes place on St Lazar's Day, or **Lazarovden** (the Saturday before Palm Sunday), when village maidens considered fit for marriage perform ritual dances, songs and games. **Gergyovden**, St George's Day (May 6), is an occasion for sacrificing and roasting sheep, to celebrate the end of spring.

The coming of summer is traditionally marked by the feast day of **SS Konstantin and Elena** (May 21 by the New Style calendar, May 4 by the Old). Many pastoral Rhodope villages hold a festival known as the **Measuring of the Milk** or *Predoi*, intended to ensure good milk yields for the rest of the year, which includes the practice of milking a ewe so that the milk dribbles through the wedding ring of a young bride before falling into the pail; while in a few remote villages in the Strandzha hills, they go in for the ancient pagan custom of **fire-dancing** barefoot on hot coals.

Other church holidays tend to coincide with the changing of the seasons. **St Marina's Day** (July 17) has always been a popular midsummer feast day, and **Enyovden**, the birthday of St John the Baptist (June 24), is still regarded as the best time to pick medicinal herbs. The beginning of autumn is marked by the major religious festival of *Golyama Bogoroditsa* (see overleaf). While Melnik and other wine-growing areas rejoice in their harvest on October 18, elsewhere, the end of the farming year is traditionally celebrated on St Demitrius' Day, **Dimitrovden** (Oct 26).

ORTHODOX FESTIVALS

While the majority of Bulgarians who profess to be Christians may not fast or pay much attention to saint's days, they're sure to attend at least one of the high festivals such as Easter, the Feast of the Assumption or Christmas, while those with a strong commitment abstain from meat and even dairy products over **Lent**.

On Palm Sunday (*Tsvetnitsa* or *Varbnitsa*), people everywhere buy willow branches and hang them up at home in preparation for the **Easter** services in churches on Thursday night (the eve of Good Friday) and Saturday night (the eve of Easter Sunday). At the latter the priest emerges from behind the iconostasis at midnight bearing a candle symbolizing the Resurrection; the congregation light their own candles from this and file

---

EASTER

The **Orthodox Easter** occurs roughly a week later than in Western Europe, and its exact timing varies from year to year. Certain other festivals (chiefly Lent) and saint's days are also timed in relation to

Easter, rather than occuring on a fixed date. Barring divine intervention at the Millennia, Easter Sunday is scheduled to fall thus:

2000 April 30
2001 April 15

2002 May 5
2003 April 27

outside to walk around the church three times. Painted eggs (prepared by families beforehand) are then knocked together and eaten; the first egg to be made is always painted red to symbolize the blood of Christ and put aside – either to be buried in the fields to ensure fertility or kept in the home to bring good luck. On Easter Sunday married couples traditionally visit the best man at their wedding and have roast lamb for lunch.

Lamb is also on the menu for the **Golyama Bogoroditsa**, or Feast of the Assumption of the Virgin, which occasions big gatherings at any church or monastery dedicated to her, picnics in the grounds of the Dragalevski and Lopoushanski monasteries, and a parade of icons at Troyan and Bachkovo. The feast is generally observed on its New Style date (Aug 15), but Christian Gypsies celebrate it according to the Old Style calendar (Aug 29). **Malka Bogoroditsa**, the Feast of the Birth of the Virgin, is also marked in both calandars, by a parade of icons at Rozhen Monastery (Sept 8) and services at Sandanski's Church of SS Kozma and Demyan (Sept 16).

Of the many other saint's days in the Orthodox calendar, three engender particularly impressive crowds and spectacles: the birthday (Aug 18) and feast day (Oct 19) of **St John of Rila** at the Rila Monastery; and the **pilgrimage to Krâstova gora** on the eve of **Krâstovden** (Sept 14). The mountain-top shrine of Krâstova gora is Bulgaria's chief pilgrimage site (see p.304) and attracts New Age cultists as well as mainstream Christians.

Christmas (*koleda*) is a family and neighbourly affair which most people celebrate on December 25 according to the Gregorian calendar, though traditionalists do so on January 6/7 by the Old calendar, and those who can afford it might even celebrate both. A traditional practice in villages is the *koleduvane*, whereby young men go from house to house singing carols under the leadership of a *stanenik*, charged with the baking of a specially decorated loaf of bread which the singers take with them on their rounds.

In olden times, the pagan New Year rites of *suvraki* were followed by an affirmation of Christianity called **Yordanovden**, celebrating Christ's baptism in the River Jordan. Once widespread throughout the Balkans, this involved casting a wooden cross into a river, which local lads dived in to retrieve, while their elders collected bottles of water blessed by the priest. Given the state of Bulgaria's rivers, it's probably for the best that this ritual is nowadays only performed at Koprivshtitsa in the Sredna Gora (Jan 6).

MUSLIM FESTIVALS

Bulgaria's Muslim minority is no less observant of **Islamic festivals**, converging on mosques and holy sites in order to celebrate the more important holidays. If you're in Bulgaria at the right time, these gatherings can be observed in Sofia and Plovdiv, or towns in areas of Muslim settlement, such as Shumen, Razgrad and Dobrich in the north; Pazardzhik, Kârdzhali, Haskovo and Momchilgrad in the south.

During **Ramadan** (*Ramazan*), the month of daylight abstention from food, water, tobacco or sexual relations, cafés and restaurants still open for business, and the degree to which the fast is observed varies from individual to individual, but

---

ORTHODOX SAINT'S DAYS

Where there are two dates below, it is because the saint's day is celebrated either on the date in the Old Calendar or on the date in the New Calendar, or sometimes both.

Yordanovden (Jordan Day) Jan 6
Trifon Zarazen (St Tryphon's Day) Feb 14
Todorovden (St Theodor's Day) First Sat of Lent
Lazarovden (St Lazar's Day) Sat before Palm Sunday
Gergyovden (St George's Day) May 6
SS Cyril and Methodius May 11
SS Konstantin and Elena May 4 and May 24
Ilinden (St Elijah's Day) July 20 and Aug 2
Golyama Bogodroditsa (Feast of the Assumption) Aug 15 and Aug 29

St John of Rila (birthday) Aug 18
Malka Bogoroditsa (Birth of the Virgin) Sept 6 and Sept 16
Krâstovden (Day of the Holy Cross) Sept 14
St John of Rila (feast day) Oct 19
Dimitrovden (St Demetrius' Day) Oct 26
Arhangelovden (Archangels Michael and Gabriel) Nov 8
Nikulen (St Nicholas' Day) Dec 6
Koleda (Christmas) Dec 25 and Jan 6/7

MUSLIM FESTIVALS

Since the **Islamic calendar** is lunar, dates of festivals tend to drift backwards eleven days each year relative to the Gregorian calendar, but as the start of Ramadan depends on the visibility of the new moon at Mecca and elsewhere, it is impossible to predict the dates of the Sheker Bayram holiday, at the end of Ramadan, or the Kurban Bayram, with total accuracy – so these dates are only approximate.

Sheker Bayram	*Kurban Bayram*
January 6–8 2000	March 17–19 2000
December 27–29 2001	March 6–8 2001
December 16–18 2002	February 23–25 2002
December 5–7 2003	February 12–14 2003

everyone enjoys the three-day **Sheker Bayram** (Sugar Holiday) at the end of Ramadan, celebrated with family get-togethers and the giving of presents and sweets to children. Another major event is the **Kurban Bayram** (Festival of the Sacrifice), which is marked by the ritual slaughter of sheep and goats, feasting and dancing.

Outdoor feasts are an important aspect of Muslim culture in Bulgaria, and one that is shared by their Christian compatriots. Many people from both faiths come to picnic and enjoy themselves at localities revered by Muslims (usually a dervish mausoleum, or *Tekke*). Happily for everyone, the Aliani festival of **Hidrelez** at the beginning of summer coincides with the Orthodox feast of Gergyovden (May 6). Foreigners are welcome to attend, but anyone squeamish about animal slaughter should stay away. Bulgarian Muslims are not averse to drinking alcohol on these occasions.

ENTERTAINMENT

Most Bulgarians have little spare money, and the range of **entertainment** on offer reflects this. Thanks to past state subsidies most provincial towns have a **theatre** and most big cities an **opera house**, but their programmes have been curtailed in recent years – though financial cut-backs have had less effect on **puppet theatre** (*kuklen teatâr*, куклен театър), a popular art form with children.

Although Bulgaria is renowned for its **folk music**, visitors are only likely to see it performed in three situations: at folklore festivals (see p.42); by regional ensembles such as the Pirin Song and Dance troupe; or as part of the entertainments laid on for package tourists. If young Bulgarians listen to folk music at all, it tends to be the pop-folk crossover music from neighbouring Serbia rather than the home-grown stuff.

There's little in the way of a domestic **rock** tradition, and regular gig venues are few and far between, although Sofia has a few live music bars, and the capital sometimes plays host to foreign bands. Most radio stations play predominantly Western pop (including a lot of European techno, popular among Bulgarians of all ages, who regard it as an example of Western cultural sophistication). Stalls selling cheap cassettes of Western bands are a feature of most street markets, although new copyright laws are slowly forcing the sellers of pirated tapes underground.

FOOTBALL

No list of entertainments in Bulgaria would be complete without a mention of the country's favourite sport, **football**. Teams in the premier division (*"A" Grupa*) usually play on Sunday afternoons, although some of the big matches take place on Saturdays. Tickets are generally dirt cheap and sold at booths outside the grounds on the day of the match. Due to Bulgaria's harsh winters, the football **season** (mid-August to mid-May) is interrupted by a two-month break in January and February. Most Bulgarian stadia are dilapidated, uncovered affairs with rickety bench seating, though some clubs – notably CSKA in Sofia and Neftohimik in Burgas – have installed plastic bucket-seating to meet UEFA safety guidelines.

While CSKA Sofia and Levski Sofia remain the most successful and popular **teams**, in recent seasons powerful private sponsors have done much to ensure high league positions for Neftohimik Burgas and Liteks Lovech (the champions in 1998). Matches between these clubs are always big occasions, as are any derbies involving teams from the capital (CSKA, Levski, Lokomotiv and Slavia).

Matches involving the Bulgarian national team (fourth in the World Cup in 1994, but largely ineffectual ever since) are the only ones for which advance purchase of tickets, from the stadium box office, is advisable. **International matches** are usually held at the Vasil Levski Stadium in Sofia, or in Burgas.

If you can decipher Cyrillic script, the daily sports papers *7 Dni Sport* and *Meridian Match* are the best sources of football **information**, and carry full details of British and other European league matches in their Monday editions. Internet users can check out several Web sites (see box below).

FOOTBALL WEB SITES
www.bfu.online.bg/
Official homepage of the Bulgarian Football Association.

www.belloweb.se/cska/
CSKA's unofficial Web site.

www.members.aol.com/Serdica/levski.html
Levski's unofficial Web site.

OUTDOOR ACTIVITIES AND ECO-TOURISM

While Bulgaria is well known for its skiing (see p.5 for details), few foreigners realize its potential for activities such as hiking, climbing and caving, nor the country's wonderful natural history. Bulgaria's mountains and lowlands are incredibly rich in wildlife – especially flora and birds – as the country has features of both the Balkan and Mediterranean eco-systems, and is visited by hundreds of migratory species. Whilst many people may prefer to book a tour through a specialist operator abroad (see box on p.6), it's perfectly possible to arrange adventure and eco-tourism trips through various agencies in Bulgaria.

HIKING

Hiking was first popularized in Bulgaria in the late nineteenth century, when it had patriotic connotations. During Communist times it was regarded as an ideal activity for citizens, and a network of trails and chalets (*hizhi*) was created throughout the mountains. Though not as well signposted as they could be, the hundreds of trails can be combined in an almost infinite variety of routes. The main hiking areas are the Pirin and Rila national parks, the central and western Rhodopes, and the Stara Planina.

The **Pirin Mountains** (p.118–135) are the wildest, most picturesque range in Bulgaria, with 45 peaks over 2590m, deep valleys, kastic massifs and more than 200 glacial lakes, mainly in the northern part of the range, which has the finest panoramic views. Further north, the **Rila Mountains** (p.105–118) include the highest peak

in the Balkan peninsula and Bulgaria's greatest monastery, and are characterized by magnificent coniferous forests and alpine scenery, abloom with wildflowers all year. Here too there are many lakes, including a cluster that attracts sun-worshippers. Both ranges abut the **Rhodopes** (p.300–321), which are lower, but arguably the loveliest range in Bulgaria, with a mixture of pine forests, crags, highland meadows and villages of stone houses, not to mention the fantastic caves and birdlife around the Trigrad Gorge.

In the **Stara planina** or Balkan Range (p.145–160), the fir-clad heights of the northwest are relatively uncharted, but their ill-marked trails reward the efforts of those with time to spare. Villages such as Berkovitsa and Chiprovtsi provide the best access to higher altitudes. The central Stara Planina between the Valley of the Roses and the Danubian plain has better maintained trails, and is best approached from Karlovo in the south or Cherni Osam and Apriltsi in the north.

If you're planning to go hiking **independently** you should visit Odysseia-In in Sofia (see box on p.50) first, to stock up on hiking **maps** (see p.21) and advice; they can also book accommodation in some areas. If you don't fancy heading off on your own, you could join Odysseia-In's weekly scheduled hiking groups for $35 per day, including bed and board. These run throughout the hiking season (mid-June to late October). Alternatively, you could **hire a guide** and tailor-make your own itinerary for $20 per person per day, plus all expenses for yourself and the guide. Guides can be hired from SunShine Tours (see p.50) or through tourist offices in the Pirin and Rhodopes.

CLIMBING AND CAVING

Bulgaria's mountainous terrain means that the opportunities for **climbing** are practically limitless. The most popular areas with mountaineers and rock-climbers are Mt Malyovitsa (p.118) in the Rila Mountains; the karst region to the north of Mt Vihren (p.129) in the Pirin range; the Iskâr Gorge (p.147), Vratsa (p.149) and Belogradchik (p.159) in the Stara Planina; and the Blue Rocks outside Sliven (p.270). Though no foreign operator runs package tours, individuals can go climbing **with a guide** from Odysseia-In for $25–30 per person per day. On top of this, you'll need to pay for his – and your own – accommodation, meals, transport and equipment rental (if required).

Of the hundreds of **caves** in Bulgaria (mostly in the Stara Planina and western Rhodopes), a dozen have been fitted with walkways and lighting and opened to the public. The most famous are the Magura Cave (p.160), with its prehistoric paintings; the Yagodina Cave, with its stalactites and cave pearls, and the awesome Devil's Throat near Trigrad (p.312). Scores of others that are equally spectacular are only known to Bulgarian cavers, who welcome contacts with their foreign counterparts. By getting in touch with the Bulgarian Federation of Speleologists you can be sure of finding someone who speaks English; local cavers such as "Kotse" Hadzhesky at Trigrad (see p.312) can also arrange **caving expeditions**, but you may need an interpreter to set the ball rolling. Alternatively, individuals can hire a guide from Odysseia-In for $25–30 per day plus expenses.

MOUNTAIN-BIKING

Mountain-biking is slowly catching on in Bulgaria, especially in the Pirin, Rhodopes and Stara Planina, where you can rent bikes from hotels in Bansko and Pamporovo and tourist offices in Apriltsi, Gabrovo, Teteven, Troyan and Tryavna. From a climatic standpoint, mid-June to late September is the ideal time for biking in the Pirin, while in the Rhodopes it's feasible until mid-October. Though there are plenty of dirt roads and tracks, the challenge is to find a locality with a mixture of mountainous, undulating and flat terrain, where you can get above the tree-line for a panoramic view – such as the area between Pamporovo and Trigrad. Trails are less developed in the Stara Planina, but there are several places in the region where you can rent bikes for only $5 a day (see p.185 for details).

You can also rent bikes ($10 per day, plus $200 deposit) from Odysseia-In in Sofia, where there are five bike shops stocking a range of imported models and spares, mainly for the Scott and Bianchi brands. High quality models such as the Scott Tempico actually cost less to **buy** in Sofia than they do in Britain.

WHITEWATER RAFTING

Whitewater rafting is still in its infancy as a sport, and there are no operators at present that regularly schedule rafting trips. In any case, the opportunity for doing so is limited to May and June, when the Struma and Arda rivers are swollen by snow-melt. Because of its proximity to Sofia, the Kresna Gorge on the River Struma is the easiest place to go rafting. Odysseia-In may be able to organize a trip, for around $30 per person per day, plus expenses.

BIRDWATCHING

Bulgaria is great for **birdwatching**, being a nesting ground for most European species in spring (May–June) and on the migratory path of many Asian ones in autumn (Sept to mid-Oct), totalling around 400 species in all. There's plenty to see at any time, owing to the diversity of ecological niches and the fact that farmers use less pesticides and insecticides than in Western Europe. Though birdlife can be seen anywhere, the richest concentrations are in the Rhodope Mountains, along the Black Coast and the floodplain of the River Danube.

In the **Rhodopes**, the Trigrad gorge (see p.312) is notable for Pallid swifts, Crag martins, Pot-bellied dippers and, above all, the rare, elusive Wallcreeper, while the local caves harbour six types of bat. Although eagles, hawks and falcons can be seen all over the highlands, the best sites for observing raptors are in the Arda gorge near Madzharovo (see p.320), which boasts rare Eastern and Imperial eagles, Egyptian, Black and Griffon vultures, Black storks, Blue Rock thrushes, Chukars, Nuthatches and Barred, Orphean and Olivaceous warblers.

The **Black Sea coast** has an even greater variety of birdlife, especially during the great autumn migration, when flocks of raptors fly over the lakes and marshes around Burgas (see p.361), which teem with Black and White storks, Marsh Harriers and Mediterranean gulls, while Black-winged stilts and avocets feed in the lagoons and terns fish offshore. In spring, the salt-pans and reed-marshes sustain White and Dalmatian pelicans, Great White and Little egrets, Bearded and Penduline tits, Red-necked Phalarope and Broad-billed sandpipers. Cape Kaliakra (see p.348) is likewise good for observing birds of passage (larks, pipits, wagtails, wheatears and warblers besides larger migants like storks and buzzards), while in spring you'll see Alpine swifts, Pied wheatears and the rare Finch's wheatear (found nowhere else in Europe). On Lake Durankulak (see p.350), Spanish sparrows breed in the nests of storks and there's a small nesting colony of Paddyfield warblers. Pygmy cormorants are also around in

September, along with Ruddy and Ferruginous shelducks (the latter an endangered species).

In spring, especially, another major site is **Lake Srebărna** (p.181) on the Danube floodplain, which is frequented by around eighty migratory species and has a nesting colony of Dalmatian pelicans. Its rich variety of wildfowl includes "Wheezing" Penduline tits, egrets, several kinds of warblers, and seventy types of heron. Black- and Red-necked grebes attend their floating nests, and Whiskered and White-winged Black terns drift on the open water. Further west the lowlands are home to Pygmy cormorants, Glossy ibises and Marsh harriers.

For **information** on all these sites, contact the Bulgarian Society for the Protection of Birds,

---

USEFUL CONTACTS IN BULGARIA

WILDLIFE ORGANIZATIONS

Bulgarian Society for the Protection of Birds (BDZP), 1172 Sofia P.O. Box 114, zh.k. "Dianabad", bl. 42, et. V, apt. 34 (☎ & fax 02/689 413).
The national ornithological society, with affiliates around the country.

Bulgarian–Swiss Biodiversity Conservation Programme, 1000 Sofia, ul. Graf Ignatiev 38-B (☎ & fax 02/980 4131).
Coordinates the regional projects listed below.

Dobrudzha Project, 4000 Plovdiv, ul. Rodopi 114 (☎032/267625, fax 02/980 4131).
Responsible for wildlife in the Dobrudzha and Cape Kaliakra region.

Northern Coastal Wetlands Zone Project, 9000 Varna, P.O. Box 492 (☎ & fax 052/302 536, email bspbvnbr@mbox.digsys.bg).
Responsible for wildlife around Kamchiya, Shabla and Lake Durankulak.

Poda Project, 8011 Burgas, bl. 403, apt. 8, P.O. Box 9 (☎056/550 718).
Runs the Poda bird reserve outside Burgas.

Ropotamo Project, 8011 Burgas, komplex "Meden rudnik" no. 444, B, VI (☎056/559 797).
Oversees the Ropotamo estuary, with an outstation at Primorsko (☎05561/2959, fax 3000).

Rozhen–Srednogorie Project, 1113 Sofia, ul. Akademik Bonchev bl. 23 (☎02/713 3777, email dpeev@jph.bio.acad.bg).
Bulgarian Academy of Sciences group monitoring rare flora and ecological niches in the western Rhodopes.

Strandzha Project, 1000 Sofia, ul. Graf Ignatiev 38-B (☎ & fax 02/980 4131).
Monitors the flora and fauna of the Strandzha Hills.

Eastern Rhodopes Project, 6480 Madzharovo, ul D. Madzharov, bl. 42 apt. 2 (☎0370/304, email bspbicer@main.infotel.bg).
Runs the vulture reserve in the Arda gorges near Madzharovo.

ADVENTURE TOURISM

Bulgarian Federation of Speleologists (BFS), 1140 Sofia, bul. Levski 75 (☎ & fax 02/878 812).
Umbrella organization for local caving groups throughout Bulgaria.

Odysseia-in, 1000 Sofia, bul. Stamboliiski 20 (☎02/989 0538, fax 980 3200, email odysseia@omega.bg; Web site www.intererinet.bg/clients/odysseia).
Bulgaria's leading adventure tourism agency, offering all kinds of individual and group tours.

Their shop, Stenata (ul. Tsar Boris I 117) sells camping and climbing equipment, and rents out mountain bikes.

SunShineTours, 1111 Sofia, ul. Shipchenski prohod 47 (☎02/971 3628, fax 973 3048, email sunshine@techno-link.com).
Wildlife, hiking, cultural heritage and archeological study tours, tailor-made for groups and individuals.

which can recommend local guides and advise on all matters ornithological. Odysseia-In runs a 15-day birdwatching tour which visits all the main sites mentioned above, and costs from $450–500 per person, including all expenses except the cost of getting to Bulgaria (based on a group of at least seven people).

ZOOLOGY, BOTANY AND GEOLOGY

Aside from birds, Bulgaria's fauna includes most of the Balkan and Mediterranean **reptiles** (over fifty species) and **mammals**. Mountainous areas are the habitat of bears, boars, wolves, wild cats, deer, foxes and badgers, while jackals can be found in the Strandzha, and otters and coypu in the coastal wetlands. However they are all pretty reclusive, so you shouldn't expect to see too much in the course of walking in these areas – aside from **butterflies** and moths, of which Bulgaria boasts some 1100 species. Of more recherché interest are the 75 species of **cave fauna**, including eight kinds of bats.

Bulgaria's flora is extremely diverse due to the three types of climate (continental, Mediterranean and steppe) within its borders. Almost a third of the country is covered in **trees**, with conifers (Corsican, Scots, Macedonian and white pine, fir, spruce and juniper) predominating in the high mountains of the Pirin, Rila and west-ern Rhodopes, and deciduous trees (oak, beech, hornbeam, elm, ash, hazel and lime) in the Stara Planina, Sredna Gora and Strandzha. The Rila, Pirin and Rhodopes are especially rich in **wild-flowers**, **herbs and fungi**, including some species that became extinct elsewhere in Europe centuries ago and others that are unique to Bulgaria, such as *Astragalus physocalyx*, *Glycyrrhiza glabra*, *Haberlea rhodopensis*, *Prunus laurocerasus*, *Ramondia sorbica*, *Rheum rhaponticum* and *Rhododendron ponticum*.

If geology is your passion, Bulgaria is great for **rock formations and minerals**. The Pirin range has some spectacular glacial and karstic features, while the Rhodopes abound in odd rock formations such as the Miraculous Bridges (see p.306), the Stone Wedding and others in the Kârdzhali region (see p.318); fantastic caves like the Devil's Throat near Trigrad (see p.312); and all kinds of gemstones and crystals. In northern Bulgaria the finest rockscapes are at Belogradchik (see p.159), Vratsa (see p.149), the Iskâr Gorge (see p.147) and outside Sliven (see p.269).

Odysseia-In can arrange a fifteen-day **botany tour** for groups of at least a dozen people, while SunShine Tours runs two- to three-week nature and hiking tours for smaller groups or individuals.

MUSEUMS, CHURCHES AND MOSQUES

Bulgaria's museums and art galleries were quite well provided for by a postwar state eager to instil in its inhabitants a strong sense of history and a pride in national culture. Civic pride comes into it too: every town in the country was determined to display at least some evidence of its contribution to Bulgarian history, whether in the shape of a small archeological museum, a restored nineteenth-century house, or the former home of a famous revolutionary. Religious monuments fared less well: while the most prestigious of them were paraded as examples of Bulgarian achievement, the vast majority were allowed to fall into neglect and disuse. Since 1989, however, Orthodox and Muslim communities have spent a lot of money on returning churches and mosques to their former glory.**

MUSEUMS

Most towns and cities have a central **history museum** or *istoricheski muzei*, (bigger centres will also have an **archeological museum**, *arheoloshki muzei*), designed to showcase the achievements of the ancient Thracians, the medieval Bulgarian empires, and the struggles of the Bulgarian peoples to overcome Turkish oppression. The style is often didactic, relying on sequences of texts and photographs past which schoolchildren slowly file, and English-language translations are extremely rare. However, presentation is usually good, and the wealth of

Neolithic and Thracian artefacts make the effort worthwhile.

The same may be said of Bulgaria's outstanding **ethnographic museums** (*etnografski muzei*), where rural traditions are faithfully documented with an array of folk costumes and craft implements – although Bulgarian texts explaining their use are rare, and English-language translations virtually non-existent. Localities of particular ethnographic importance have been preserved, either whole or in part, as **heritage villages** or **museum towns** (old Plovdiv, Tryavna, Nesebâr and Sozopol are just four examples). Buildings falling within such an *arhitekturen rezervat* are carefully reconstructed according to traditional building methods, and the best examples of vernacular architecture are often opened to the public as a *kâshta-muzei*, or **House-Museum**.

OPENING HOURS AND ENTRANCE FEES

The most frustrating aspect of Bulgarian museums is their failure to observe their own **opening hours**. Although the officially advertised working hours of all Bulgaria's tourist attractions are quoted in the Guide, they should always be taken with a pinch of salt. In much of Bulgaria, financial hardships, staff shortages and a general lack of customers ensure that most museums close earlier than posted, take longer lunchbreaks, or simply don't bother opening at all. Many museums devoted to historical personalities or important cultural figures may open during the academic year to cater for parties of schoolchildren, before closing their doors over the summer. That said, most of the museums in well-visited places such as Sofia, Plovdiv and Koprivshtitsa can be relied upon to open as advertised. The same applies to museums on the Black Sea coast during the summer season, although things become much more unpredictable from September through to June. Generally speaking, **opening hours** are Tuesday to Sunday, between 8am and noon and from 2pm to 5.30pm, although many work from Monday to Friday and close for the weekend. Big museums in Sofia, Plovdiv and Varna tend to do without the break for lunch, and may stay open until 6 or 7pm during the summer.

Entrance fees for foreigners are usually in the region of $1–2, and can be as much as $5–6, as museums struggle to raise revenue. A **student card** may secure reductions, but there's no guarantee that it will. Many museums offer a *beseda* or **guided tour** with commentary for an extra charge, though there's a fairly slim chance of finding an English-speaking member of staff (French or Russian speakers may have better luck).

CHURCHES AND MONASTERIES

During the Communist period, **religious buildings** considered to be of particular architectural or cultural importance were removed from church control and taken under the state's wing. Although their transformation into "museums" was at odds with their spiritual purpose, this policy did ensure that large amounts of cash were channelled into their restoration and upkeep. Now that ecclesiastical properties have been returned to the ownership of the Bulgarian Orthodox Church, many historical churches and chapels, previously used as exhibition halls or tourist attractions, have become places of worship again, but lack funds for repairs and can only afford to do the work slowly, which may entail long periods of closure.

Another reason why you'll find the doors of many churches firmly shut is general unease about crime, with many priests fearing for their precious icons and only opening up just before services. The morning liturgy – which commemorates the Last Supper – begins at 8 or 9am, and there may also be an evening service at 5 or 6pm; both usually take about one and a half hours. As Bulgarians often wander in halfway through to savour a few moments of prayer before crossing themselves and departing, you shouldn't feel embarrassed about doing the same. The period between about 4pm or 5pm, just before the evening service, tends to be the best time for looking around. There are no hard and fast rules regarding what to wear in a Bulgarian church, although bare arms for females, and bare legs for males, are often regarded as a sign of disrespect.

The gates of **monasteries** tend to be open to all-comers from dawn until dusk. The more famous monasteries, among them Rila, Troyan, Bachkovo and Dryanovo, are used to receiving visitors all year round, and you can wander through

CYRILLIC CHECKLIST: MUSEUMS	
History museum	исторически музей
Ethnographic museum	етнографски музей
Archeological museum	археолошюси музей
House-Museum	къща-музей
Guided tour	беседа

the galleried monastery courtyards more or less at will. Some of the smaller foundations, however, will only have a handful of monks or nuns in residence, so you may again discover that churches and chapels within the monastic precinct are locked. Somebody will probably open up, though, if you show persistent interest.

MOSQUES

Five hundred years of Turkish occupation left Bulgaria with some of the finest **Islamic architecture** in the Balkans. Prestige mosques (such as the *Tombul Dzhamiya* in Shumen) were restored and opened to the public by the Communist authorities, but the vast majority suffered as a result of the government's anti-Turkish policies. Many were left to slide into disrepair while others were demolished – especially during the mid-1980s, when the so-called "Regeneration Process" (see p.407) was at its height. Surviving mosques in Muslim areas have now been returned to the Islamic community and many Pomak villages that were formerly forbidden from building their own mosques are now doing so. Outside of purely Muslim areas, mosques are rarely open other than at prayer times due to acts of racist vandalism or the theft of kilims and other valuables, which are spirited across the border to be sold to dealers in Istanbul.

ARCHITECTURE AND ETIQUETTE

The basic **layout** of a mosque is a carpet-covered square with a *mihrab* cut into the eastern end facing Mecca; from this niche the *imam* or priest leads the congregation in prayer, the women grouped behind the men on a balcony or behind a low balustrade. Because the Islamic faith prohibits reproduction of the human form, the richest mosques tend to be covered in passages from the Koran and non-figurative decoration of tiles and ornamented plaster. Visitors are allowed in mosques but should observe certain **proprieties**: shoes must be removed before entering, women have to cover their heads, arms and legs, and you may be asked to leave a small donation. Using the Islamic greeting *salaam aleikum* (Peace be upon you) will be appreciated as a courteous gesture, and you should avoid walking in front of someone who is kneeling in prayer, as it is considered very rude.

POLICE, TROUBLE AND SEXUAL HARASSMENT

Despite an increase in theft, corruption and mafia-style organized crime over the last decade, Bulgaria still feels an unthreatening country in which to travel, and most tourists will have little or no contact with the Bulgarian police (*Politsiya*, Полиция). **However, everyone is required to carry ID at all times, so it's a good idea to keep your passport on you, together with your *carte statistique* (see p.14) – or a photocopy of both – to satisfy any policeman making a casual check.**

There are a few basic commonsense rules to follow if you want to avoid the attention of the Bulgarian police. **Camping rough** is not recommended, and driving with any quantity of **alcohol** in the blood whatsoever is strictly forbidden and carries stiff penalties. Given Bulgaria's position on the overland route to Turkey and beyond, an equal lack of mercy is shown to anyone caught in possession of **drugs**, for whom years in jail are likely.

Most of the negative stories concerning the Bulgarian police relate to **crossing the border** to or from Turkey or Former Yugoslavia, where cops and customs officials are notorious for extorting cash. Over the past couple of years society has become much more aware of the abuses committed by those in uniform, but it will take some time before all the bad habits of the past are abandoned.

CRIME AND THE POLICE

Bulgaria's **crime rate** has mushroomed since the collapse of the totalitarian system, engendering a great deal of fear and insecurity among the law-abiding majority. While mafia killings make headlines, however, small-time thieves are much more likely to pose a hazard to visitors. Again, a few commonsense precautions will help you avoid trouble: display cameras as little as possible, never leave your valuables in your room, and keep large sums of cash in a moneybelt, out of sight. Don't travel without insurance (see p.16), and be sure to make a photocopy of your passport (including your entry stamp, visa and *carte statistique*, if you have one). If you do have anything stolen, go to the police immediately, and get a report detailing the things you've lost.

Petty theft is most widespread on the coast, where the police are so blasé about it that they take an age to fill out a report, and may even demand payment for doing so. The average Black Sea thief isn't only interested in grabbing your money or your camera, but also items of clothing such as trendy T-shirts and replica football kits. In Sofia and Plovdiv, **pickpockets** are more of a problem, especially in the capital at night, around the *Sheraton Hotel*, Central Station and city centre underpasses. When travelling around Bulgaria, don't fall asleep on train journeys and try to book a couchette or sleeper if you're travelling overnight – it's always more secure than the (often unlit) regular carriages. Foreign embassies also advise visitors not to accept any food or drink from strangers in case it is drugged.

Car theft is endemic, with foreign cars and 4WD vehicles particularly sought after. It's always worth paying to park in a guarded lot (*ohranen parking*), and avoid leaving your vehicle on the street unless it's equipped with immobilizers and wheel locks. Never leave anything of value on display, wherever you park. If your car *is* stolen, the ensuing hassles can take up to a week to sort out. Because details of your car are written into your passport, you can't leave the country without it unless you obtain letters from (in turn) the police, customs and the public prosecutor.

If you're unfortunate enough to be **arrested** yourself, wait until you can explain matters to someone in English if at all possible (misunderstandings in a foreign language can only make things worse), and then request that your **consulate** be notified (see p.96 for Sofia "Listings" for addresses). Note that while consulates can be helpful in some respects, they will never lend cash to nationals who've run out or been robbed.

One aspect of Bulgarian crime you're bound to become aware of, but unlikely to be directly affected by, is the growth of mafia-style organizations operating drug-smuggling networks and **protection rackets**. Amost as dangerous are the (outwardly legitimate) insurance and security firms who use hired muscle to enforce their rule. Whether working legally as bodyguards or illegally as mafia heavies, these bodybuilders and ex-sportsmen (known as **bortsi**, or "wrestlers" to the locals) are instantly recognizable from their short-cropped hair, big biceps, mobile phones and fast foreign cars. Their excess of brawn over brain makes them the butt of many jokes, but they are widely resented and feared. Never argue with a *borets*: most people, including the police, are so scared of them that they'll rarely intervene on your behalf.

SEXUAL HARASSMENT

Modern feminism has made few inroads into what is a predominantly patriarchal society, and **women** travelling alone in Bulgaria can expect to encounter stares, comments and sometimes worse from macho types. Reports of women on overnight international trains experiencing harrassment from sleeping-car attendents and other passengers are on the rise, so it's wise to have a travelling companion if at all possible. Generally, however, older Bulgarian men tend to be quite gallant, and it's the young, arrogant *nouveaux riches* that are prone to sexist excesses. Local women deal with unwanted attentions with a firm display of indifference, and this should be enough to cope with most situations – if not, holler *Pomosht!* (Help!) or *Politsiya!*

Remember that local attitudes tend to be conservative, particularly in rural areas, where "immodest" attire can sometimes arouse strong feelings. However, most young, especially urban, Bulgarians have spent the 1990s casting off the country's erstwhile sartorial straitjacket, and Western fashions and hairstyles no longer attract disapproval.

DIRECTORY

ADDRESSES Like everything else in Bulgaria, addresses are normally written in the Cyrillic alphabet. In the text of the Guide, they're transcribed into Roman script according to the system explained in "Language", on p.422. The most common abbreviations are ул. (*ul.*) for "street" (*ulitsa*), пл. (*pl.*) for "square" (*ploshtad*) and бул. (*bul.*) for *bulevard*, although these designations are omitted altogether when the meaning is clear from the context. In large towns, you also see the abbreviation ж.к. for "housing estate". The street number of a building is given after the name of the street. Addresses in the high-rise suburbs (*kvartal*, abbreviated to *kv*, кв) include the building number (*blok*, shortened to *bl*, бл), a letter denoting the entrance (*vhod*), Roman numerals signifying the floor (*etazh*), and finally the number of the apartment itself.

BODY LANGUAGE Although a shake of the head means yes and a nod means no according to local custom, natives sometimes shake or nod their head in the "usual" way when talking with foreigners. Bulgarians are tolerant of misunderstandings over gestures, but it must be disconcerting for them to have a chat with someone who constantly nods "no, no". Anyone waving at you is probably signalling "come here" or "step inside", not "goodbye".

CHILDREN Many package deals offer child reductions, with the most suitable of the Black Sea destinations for kids being Albena, Golden Sands and Rusalka; elsewhere in Bulgaria don't expect much in the way of child-oriented facilities. While baby food and disposable nappies are available in shops, it's best to bring a supply of your preferred brand. More positively, Bulgarians dote on children, and they are seldom made to feel unwelcome in restaurants or hotels – though few adults see anything amiss in smoking right next to babies.

CIGARETTES Tobacco is a major crop in Bulgaria, so smoking is almost a patriotic duty. The range of *tsigari* on offer in street kiosks varies from place to place, so while you can find imported (or counterfeit) Marlboro, Rothmans and Camel on sale in Sofia or Varna for around $1.50 a packet, you may have problems getting even Bulgarian brands, such as Victory or Byal Sredets, in the villages. Smoking is prohibited in public buildings (notably train and bus terminals) and in many self-service restaurants and patisseries, but elsewhere, smokers rule. Matches are called *kibrit*.

CONTRACEPTIVES Although condoms are available from pharmacies and some street kiosks, you'd be wise to bring some from home. This advice most definitely applies to all other forms of contraception.

ELECTRICITY 220 volts AC. Round two-pin plugs are used, so bring an adaptor.

DRUGS Bulgaria is a major route for narcotics – mostly Turkish heroin, sent overland to Albania and thence by sea to Italy, but also cocaine, transported through Varna. The affects of this trade on Bulgarian society have been fairly slight so far, but in cities like Plovdiv, Sofia and Varna, drugs are now used to an extent that would have been inconceivable in Communist times. Penalties for possession are extremely severe and Bulgarian prisons are just as bad as in *Midnight Express*, so you would be mad to have anything to do with drugs here.

GAY LIFE The mere idea of homosexuality raises hackles in what is essentially a conservative and patriarchal society, and whilst gay issues are beginning to be discussed in the media and the paper *Kurier* includes gay adverts in its lonely hearts column, homosexuals still tend to keep a low profile. While homosexual acts between men over the age of 21 are not officially illegal, there are heavy restrictions on vague things like "scandalous homosexuality" or "homosexual acts leading to perversions" – which basically means that the authorities have the right to arrest you for any homosexual act. Liberalization of the laws governing homosexuality was on the cards in the immediate aftermath of democratization, but has latterly faded from the political agenda. This is partly due to irrational anxieties about AIDS, but is also symptomatic of a more general feeling that the introduction of Western-style personal freedoms since 1989 has done much to disrupt the traditionally homogenous nature of Bulgarian society.

Consequently, a gay scene as such is non-existent, except in Sofia, where a gay club called *Spartakus* exists in the pedestrian underpass outside Sofia University, though it's a private members club, and they may not let casual visitors in.

LAUNDRY Laundrettes (*peralnya*, пералня), let alone dry cleaners (*himichesko chistene*, [имическо чистене], are exceedingly rare in Bulgaria, and are usually found in distant suburban housing estates where travellers are unlikely to go. At the larger hotels, it's possible to have cleaning done on the premises, but this can be quite costly. Most Bulgarian holiday-makers just do it in the sink and hang it up on the balcony to dry.

LEFT LUGGAGE Most train stations have a left-luggage office or *garderob* (гардероб); in the larger towns these will be open 24hr. Bus stations will usually have a *garderob* as well, but opening times are more restricted and staff take more frequent breaks (*pauza*). To store each item of baggage should cost no more than a few cents.

NATURISM was once forbidden on the Black Sea's beaches, and the sight of naked foreigners being bundled into police cars provided frequent amusement for the locals. Topless bathing is now pretty much *de rigueur* among young Bulgarian holiday-makers, and nude sunbathing quite common on the quieter beaches. "Official" nudist beaches are yet to be established, although each Black Sea resort has a stretch of sand where naturism is tolerated. Generally speaking, it's acceptable to strip off anywhere on the coast providing you find a quiet cove, or a relatively isolated stretch of beach situated a discreet distance away from the main family sunbathing areas.

PHOTOGRAPHIC SUPPLIES Internationally known brands of colour print film are widely available in most big towns and along the coast, and a growing number of photo shops will develop films in one or two hours. More specialized items, such as decent black-and-white film, film for transparencies and camera batteries, can be difficult to find outside Sofia, so it's best to stock up before leaving home.

PROSTITUTION Most hotels of three-stars or above have prostitutes hanging around the lobby and bar, who proposition solo male travellers. In Sofia they often work in tandem with thieves and it's not unusual for clients to be mugged or have their room turned over. For drivers, it's worth noting that some motels along the truck routes to Greece and Turkey are little more than bordellos (called *publichen dom*, or "public house" in Bulgarian, should anybody try to warn you off).

SHOPPING HOURS Big city shops are generally open Monday to Friday from 8.30am (or earlier) until 6pm (or later, in the case of neighbourhood stores); on Saturdays they close at 2pm. In rural areas and small towns, a kind of unofficial siesta may prevail between noon and 3pm.

SNAKES Of the two kinds of poisionous snakes in Bulgaria, the most venomous is the nose-horned viper (*Vipera ammodytes*, locally known as *pepelanka*). Although vipers instinctively shun contact with humans, you should avoid going barefoot, turning over rocks or sticking your hands into dark crevices anywhere off the beaten track.

SUPERSTITIONS Bulgarians regard putting your handbag on the floor as a sure sign that you'll lose all your money, while seeing a spider in the house or laying out extra cutlery by mistake means that you'll have a guest. When buying flowers for somebody, make certain there's an odd-number of blooms; even-numbered bouquets are for funerals.

TIME Two hours ahead of GMT; seven hours ahead of EST. Bulgarian Summer Time lasts from the beginning of April to the end of September.

TOILETS Public toilets (тоалетни, *toaletni*) are found at all train stations, most bus stations, and in central parks in towns. They're usually quite appalling, despite the presence of a caretaker or cleaner, to whom you pay a small fee (*taksa*) on entering. Many toilets will clog if you put paper down them, so take the hint if a wastebasket is provided. *Mâzhe* (Мъжеъ or M) are men; *zheni* (Женъ or Ж) or *dami* (Дами, Д) are women.

WATER (*voda*) is safe to drink from all taps and drinking fountains, though bottled mineral water is also widely available.

PART TWO

THE
GUIDE

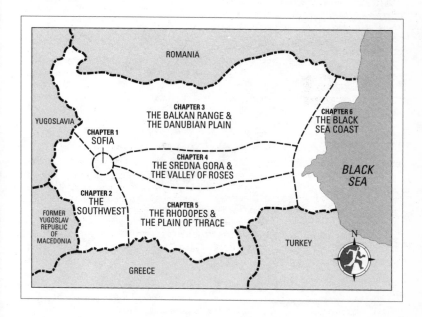

CHAPTER ONE

SOFIA

According to its motto, **SOFIA** "grows but does not age": a tribute to the mushrooming suburbs occupied by one-tenth of Bulgaria's population, and a cryptic reference to its ancient origins. Although various Byzantine ruins and a couple of mosques attest to a long and colourful history, little else in the city is of any real vintage. Sofia's finest architecture

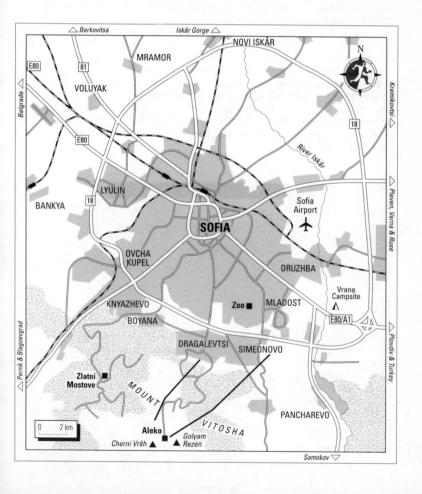

post-dates Bulgaria's liberation, when the capital of the infant state was laid out on a grid pattern in imitation of Western capitals – although the peeling stucco of its turn-of-the-century buildings lends an air of Balkan dilapidation to the capital's wide, tree-shaded boulevards. The close historical relationship between Bulgaria and Russia reveals itself in the capital's public buildings, foremost of which is the **Aleksandâr Nevski church**, a magnificent Byzantine–Muscovite confection. The socialist era, too, produced its shrines – most notably the ghoulish **mausoleum of Georgi Dimitrov** on the renamed Aleksandâr Batenberg square.

The mixture of chaos and decay which characterizes most of Sofia's points of arrival makes it an unwelcoming city for first-time visitors. However once you've settled in and begun to explore, you'll find Sofia surprisingly laid back for a capital city. Hardly a great European metropolis brimming with fine sights, the place comes into its own on fine spring and summer days, when the downtown streets and their pavement cafés begin to buzz with life. Urban pursuits can be easily combined with the outdoor recreational possibilities offered by verdant **Mount Vitosha**, just 12km south of the centre. Also on the fringes of the city, the medieval frescos at the **Boyana Church** (although you can only see copies now that the originals are out of bounds), and those at the **Kremikovtsi monastery**, make essential viewing for anyone interested in Orthodox art. Sightseeing apart, things can seem low-key here for those with sophisticated cosmopolitan tastes: entertainment in Sofia still revolves around an evening promenade in one of the city's parks, followed by a coffee in a nearby café, and haute cuisine has never been one of Bulgaria's fortés. Nightlife boils down to the odd disco and a few bars, plus lots of drama and serious music, especially during the **Sofia Music Weeks**, which take place each June.

CYRILLIC PLACE NAMES	
SOFIA	CJABZ
ALEKO	FKTRJ
BANKYA	<FYRZ
BOYANA	<JZYF
DRAGALEVTSI	LHFUFKTDWB
KNYAZHEVO	RYZ:TDJ
KREMIKOVTSI	RHTVBRJDWB
SIMEONOVO	CBVTJYJDJ
VITOSHA	DBNJIF
ZLATNI MOSTOVE	PKFNYB VJCNJDT
BUL. KNYAGINYA MARIYA LUIZA	<EK. RYZUBYZ VFHBZ KEBPF
BUL. STAMBOLIISKI	<EK. CNFV<JKBBCRB
BUL. TSAR OSVOBODITEL	<EK. WFH JCDJ<JLBNTK
BUL. VITOSHA	<EK. DBNJIF
PLOSHTAD SVETA NEDELYA	GKJOFL CDTNF YTLTKZ
PLOSHTAD ALEKSANDÂR	GKJOFL FKTRCFYL´´)H
BATENBERG	<FNTY<THU
THE LARGO	KFHUJNJ
TSENTRALNA GARA	WTYNHFKYF UFHF
UL. G S RAKOVSKI	EK. U. C. HFRJDCRB

Some history

Sofia's first inhabitants were the **Serdi**, a Thracian tribe who settled here some 3000 years ago. Their Roman conquerors named it Serdica, a walled city that reached its zenith under Emperor Constantine in the early fourth century. Serdica owed its importance to the position it occupied on the *diagonis*, the Roman road which linked Constantinople with modern Belgrade on the Danube, providing the Balkans with its main commercial and strategic artery. However, the empire's foes also used the road as a quick route to the riches of Constantinople, and Serdica was frequently under attack – most notably from the Huns, who sacked the city in the fifth century. Once rebuilt by the emperor Justinian, Serdica became one of the Byzantine Empire's most important strongpoints in the Balkans.

Migrating Slavs began to filter into the city in the seventh century, becoming the dominant force in the region after Serdica's capture by the Bulgar Khan Krum in 809. The city continued to flourish under the Bulgarians, although few medieval cultural monuments remain, save for the thirteenth-century **Boyana church**. Re-named Sredets by the Slavs (and subsequently Triaditsa by the Byzantines), the city became known as Sofia sometime in the fourteenth century, most probably taking its name from the ancient **Church of Sveta Sofia** (Holy Wisdom) which still stands in the city centre. Five centuries of Ottoman rule began with the city's capture in 1382, during which time Sofia thrived as a market centre, though little material evidence of the Ottoman period remains save for a couple of **mosques**.

Economic decline set in during the nineteenth century, hastened by earthquakes in 1852. Sofia was a minor provincial centre at the time of the Liberation in 1878, when defeat of the Ottoman Empire by Russian forces paved the way for the foundation of an independent Bulgarian state. Sofia was chosen to become the new capital of the country in preference to more prestigious centres (such as Târnovo in central Bulgaria) because of its geographical location: situated on a wide plain fringed by mountains, Sofia combined defensibility with the potential for future growth. It was also thought that it would occupy a central position in any Bulgarian state which included (as was then hoped) Macedonia. The Bulgarians were keen to stamp their identity on the city right at the outset. Mosques were demolished or turned to other uses, and 6000 of the city's Turks chose to emigrate. Sofia underwent rapid development after 1878, although progress sometimes sat uneasily beside backwardness and poverty. The Czech historian and educationalist Konstantin Jireček – one of many foreign experts brought in to help run the new state – dubbed Sofia *boklukopolis* ("trashville") in recognition of its chaotic post-Liberation appearance. However foreign observers were on the whole impressed by the way in which the Bulgarians speedily improvised a capital city out of nothing. "I had expected a semi-barbaric Eastern town," remarked Frank Cox, the *Morning Post*'s Balkan correspondent in 1913, "but I found a modern capital, small but orderly, clean and well-managed....but oh, so deadly dull". Despite its increasing prosperity, Sofia didn't experience much of a belle époque, save for the lavish palace balls presided over by the mercurial Tsar Ferdinand, and the weekly dances at the military club.

The city experienced more frenetic growth during the postwar era of "socialist construction", and a veneer of Stalinist monumentalism was added to the city centre in the shape of buildings like the **Party House**, a stern-looking expression of political authority. Sofia's rising population was housed in the endless high-rise suburbs (places with declamatory names like Mladost – "youth", Druzhba – "Friendship", and Nadezhda – "hope") that girdle the city today.

Sadly, the factories that used to employ the inhabitants of these suburbs went into a steep decline during the 1980s, collapsing totally in the 1990s. Like most of Bulgaria, Sofia has had problems finding its feet in the years following the demise of Communism. An upsurge in private enterprise, however invigorating, has gone hand in hand with rising unemployment and declining living standards for the majority. One of the most visible symptoms of social change has been the emergence of a large stray dog population in Sofia's downtown streets. Officially there are 35,000 of the beasts roaming the city, but the real figure may be up to three times higher. Although pretty docile during the day, the dog packs become territorial at night, when lone pedestrians can become the victims of massed barking, or worse.

Arrival

Bus #84, which runs every ten to fifteen minutes, connects **Sofia airport**, 10km east of town, with the Orlov Most (see p.85), from where you can walk into the

---

THE SHOPS

The vast majority of Sofia's inhabitants are of **Shop descent** – the Shops being the original peasant population from the surrounding countryside who have migrated to the city in vast numbers over the past hundred years. Although you can still tell a Shop by his or her accent, which is flatter than standard Bulgarian – they say *desno* instead of *dyasno* for "right"; *levo* instead of *lyavo* for "left" – the other ethnographic features that made them a distinct group a century ago have now all but disappeared.

At the time of the Liberation many Shops – especially those living around the foothills of Mount Vitosha – still lived in an extended family community known as a **zadruga**, an arrangement once common to the entire South Slav area. In a *zadruga*, several married brothers and cousins pooled their lands and lived together under the rule of a *domovladika* (literally "head of the household"), who would apportion tasks and look after the accounts. *Zadruga* members tended to specialize in different jobs (one may be a miller, one an innkeeper, another a priest, and so on) in order to keep the community self-sufficient. The growth of Sofia disrupted the traditional rural economy, signalling the end of the *zadruga* system. It was perhaps the sudden impact of urbanization that earned the Shops a reputation for being the nation's heaviest **drinkers**. Writing in the 1880s, the Czech observer Konstantin Jireček remarked that "Sofia is the one area of the country where you can actually see drunken Bulgarians on a regular basis". Indeed the expression "to drink like in Sofia" was in common use in late nineteenth-century Bulgaria.

Some of the villages around Sofia still preserve age-old **Shop Lenten customs**. Voluyak, 10km northwest of Sofia on the Berkovitsa road, still celebrates the Dzhamala festival (forty days before Easter on odd-numbered years), when a camel (actually a wooden sled dressed in skins) is hauled through the streets before being symbolically killed and returned to life again, in what is essentially a Dionysaic death-and-rebirth ritual of ancient origins. The neighbouring village of Mramor is the Sofia district's main centre for celebrations linked with Todorovden (St Theodore's day, the first Saturday of Lent), when people from all over the Shop area congregate – usually bringing their horses and carts – for a day of feasting and carousing.

> The **telephone area code** for Sofia is ☎02.

city centre. On leaving the international arrivals terminal, head to the left for about 200 metres to find the **bus stop**, where there's also a small kiosk selling tickets (see p.64). If you arrive after the kiosk has closed, pay the driver. Buses run between about 7am and 11pm.

Taxi drivers tend to charge foreigners fresh off the plane a hefty $20–30 for the ride into town. If you utter the odd word of Bulgarian or appear to know where you're going, you might get away with paying about half that.

By train

Trains arrive at the Central Station (*Tsentralna gara*), a concrete barn twenty minutes' walk north of the city centre. Trams #1 and #7 will take you from the station forecourt to pl. Sveta Nedelya, within easy reach of accommodation bureaux, central hotels and the important sights. If you're merely pausing in Sofia between trains, the Central Station is not the kind of place where you would want to sleep rough. By day it's pretty civilized, but at night the dimly lit underground walkways begin to fill up with teenage runaways, the homeless, and other displaced characters, making it a target for regular police raids. For details on **leaving Sofia by train**, see "Moving on from Sofia" on p.97.

By bus

Most inter-city services – especially those run by private bus companies – arrive at a sprawling bus park opposite the central station, just behind the *Hotel Princess* (formerly the *Novotel Evropa*, the name by which many locals still refer to it). Services not using this bus park stop at one of three other **bus stations**, all of them some way out of the centre. Services from points north and northeast of Sofia use the **Avtogara Poduyane** (sometimes referred to as *Avtogara Iztok*) terminal on ul. Todorini Kukli (bus #75 runs from here to Orlov Most, otherwise head one block north from the station and cross to the opposite side of bul. Vladimir Vazov to catch trolleybus #1 to bul. Vasil Levski); buses from the southwest use **Ovcha Kupel**, halfway down bul. Tsar Boris III (take tram #5 to the National History Museum, bang in the heart of the city); buses from the southeast use the **Yug** terminal, on bul. Dragan Tsankov, beneath the overpass known as Nadlez Dârvenitsa just beyond the *Hotel Moskva* (trams #2 and #19 take you from Nadlez Dârvenitsa to the central bul. Graf Ignatiev).

International services either use the bus park behind the *Hotel Princess* (see above), or pull into one of two **international bus offices**: one at Dame Gruev 38, ten minutes' walk west from the city centre; the other at bul. Knyaginya Mariya Luiza 84, ten minutes' north of the centre. For details on **leaving Sofia by bus**, see "Moving on from Sofia" on p.97.

Information

Getting official information about Sofia can be difficult. The new **national information centre**, at pl. Sveta Nedelya 1 (Mon–Fri 9am–5pm), doesn't always have the answers to specific queries about the capital, though the staff are English-speaking and friendly. They also have plenty of information and brochures on

USEFUL TRAVEL AGENTS IN SOFIA

Bâlgarski Turisticheski Sâyuz (Bulgarian Tourist Union or BTS), pedestrian underpass, bul. Levski 75 (☎980 1285, fax 802414). Information on and reservations for mountain huts throughout the country. Also sells hiking maps.

Lyub Travel, 4th floor, Milin Kamak 11 (☎702287, fax 963 4427, email *boyanin@techno-link.com*). Specialists in one- and two-day excursions in small groups, focusing on folk celebrations and rural areas that are difficult to get to independently. Only accepts enquiries by phone, fax or email.

Odysseia-In, Stamboliiski 20 (entrance round the corner on ul. Lavele; ☎989

0538, fax 980 3200) *odysseia@omega.bg* Information on and reservations in private hotels in Sofia, mountain huts, rural hotels, monasteries and village homestays. Specialists in hiking tours and activity holidays. Also sells hiking maps.

Orbita, bul. Hristo Botev 48 (☎800102, fax 988 5814). Reservations in hotels belonging to the *Orbita* chain in Sofia, Batak, Lovech, Pleven, Primorsko, Shumen, Silistra, Sunny Beach and Varna. Also sells international airline tickets.

TIR, Lavele 22 (☎880139 or 981 3140, fax 803101 or 981 4948). Reservations in hotels – usually three-star and above – throughout Bulgaria. Car rental services.

other parts of Bulgaria. For general advice on Bulgaria, it's also worth contacting an independent **travel agent** (see box above), who can act as a fixer during your stay in the country, arranging tours or booking accommodation in advance.

You'll find several reasonable **city maps**, featuring public transport routes and post-Communist street names, on sale at newsstands and street stalls. For **listings**, the monthly English-language brochure *Sofia City Info Guide* (free from big hotels – try the lobby of the *Sheraton* if you can't find one elsewhere) has comprehensive details of what's on in town as well as advice for new arrivals in the city. There's also a weekly English-language **newspaper**, the *Sofia Echo*, available from central newsstands.

City transport

Sofia is a surprisingly well-organized city when it comes to **getting about**. An extensive bus, trolleybus and tram network extends to just about everywhere you're likely to want to go, and inexpensive taxis fill the gaps. **Public transport** is cheap and reasonably efficient, with intertwining networks of buses (*avtobus*), trolleybuses (*troleibus*) and trams (*tramvai*). Most services run from about 4am until 11.30pm. Triple-digit route numbers indicate express buses, which stop less frequently and are useful for travelling across town in a hurry. The main problem is lack of information: while some bus and tram stops are well-marked, others are merely corroded metal poles displaying no information about which services call there or how often. Always be prepared to ask the locals, and buy a good city map if possible.

There's a flat fare on all urban routes (currently around 15¢), and **tickets** (*bileti*) for buses, trolleys and trams can be bought from street kiosks or, sometimes, from the driver. All tickets must be punched on board the vehicle: inspections are frequent and there are spot-fines for fare-dodgers – officially around $3, although unscrupulous inspectors sometimes make foreigners pay much more. If you're staying in Sofia any length of time, a one-day ticket (*karta za edin den*; around 70¢) or a five-day ticket (*karta za pet dena*; around $2) is a sound investment, but can only be bought from kiosks.

Taxis aren't particularly expensive either, charging the equivalent of 20¢ per km until 10pm, 25–30¢ per km after that. There's a taxi rank at the northern end of bul. Vitosha; otherwise vehicles hang around at most big intersections. You can order them by phone (try OK Supertaxi ☎2121, or Inex Taxi ☎91919), but don't expect to get through to an English-speaker. Sofia taxi drivers don't always have a detailed knowledge of their own city, and clients are usually expected to supply directions themselves. The overcharging of foreigners is fairly endemic, and there's little you can do to prevent this except check that meters are working and be firm with obvious transgressors. It's a good idea to stick to reputable firms like OK and Inex, though if you're staying in Sofia for any length of time you're unlikely to escape without being ripped off at least once.

Accommodation

In general, you'll find yourself paying more in Sofia than elsewhere in the country for a decent place to stay, with the majority of the high-rise socialist-era **hotels** charging rates out of proportion to the level of service they provide. However, small **family-run pensions**, offering comfortable rooms at reasonable prices, are beginning to appear in the city centre, and they're very well established in outlying village suburbs like Simeonovo and Dragalevtsi.

A **private room** is still the best-value way of getting a place close to the action, although the quality of accommodation varies considerably. Rooms are usually clean, but often feature decor that hasn't changed since the 1950s. Centrally located private rooms can be booked through Balkantourist, Stamboliiski 27 (daily 8am–9pm) and in the airport arrivals hall (daily 9am–last flight) for $20 a double ($16 for single occupancy), with reductions for stays of longer than three nights. Best of the smaller agencies is the Markela bureau, in a kiosk opposite the Banya Bashi Mosque at bul. Knyaginya Mariya Luiza 23A (Mon–Sat 9am–6pm; ☎981 6421), which has doubles for $16, singles for $12.

The only reliable **campsite** is at **Vrana**, 10km southeast of the centre beside the main E80 highway to Plovdiv and Istanbul (open all year; ☎781213). The quiet, wooded site has gone slightly to seed, although there's ample space for tents and trailers, ensuite bungalows (③) and a restaurant. It's on the north side of the highway, so if you're approaching from central Sofia you'll have to do a U-turn some 500m after the site entrance and retrace your steps. Arriving by public transport,

ACCOMMODATION PRICE CODES			
All **accommodation** in this book has been categorized according to the following price codes. The prices quoted are for the cheapest double room in high season. For more details, see p.30.			
① $9 and under	③ $18–36	⑤ $60–90	⑦ $120–150
② $9–18	④ $36–60	⑥ $90–120	⑧ $150 and over

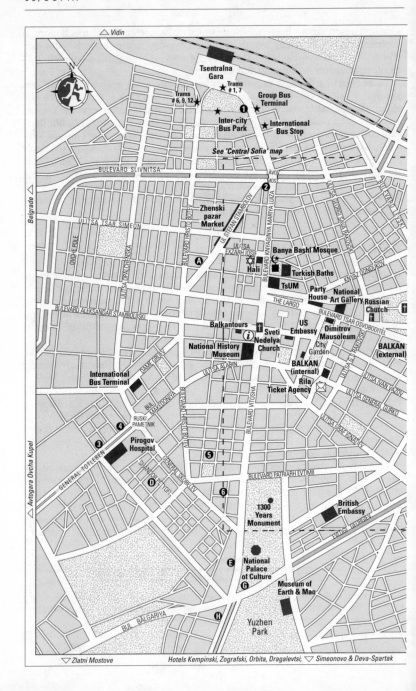

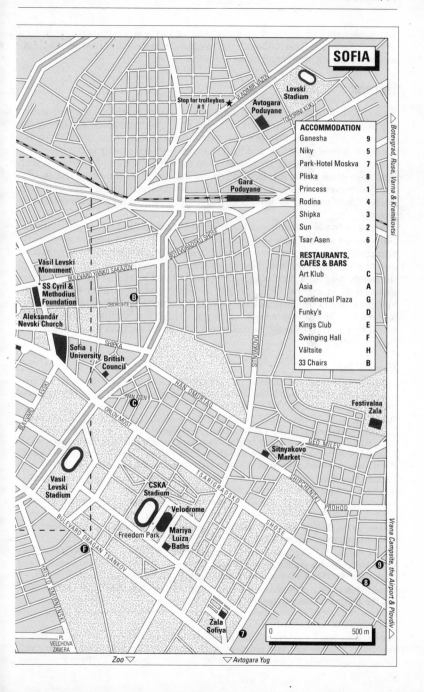

SOFIA

ACCOMMODATION

Ganesha	9
Niky	5
Park-Hotel Moskva	7
Pliska	8
Princess	1
Rodina	4
Shipka	3
Sun	2
Tsar Asen	6

RESTAURANTS, CAFES & BARS

Art Klub	C
Asia	A
Continental Plaza	G
Funky's	D
Kings Club	E
Swinging Hall	F
Vâltsite	H
33 Chairs	B

take trolleybus #4 from Orlov Most to the last stop: the site is immediately in front of you through the trees, although you might have to walk towards the main highway to work your way round to the entrance.

Hotels

Your choice of **hotel** will depend a great deal on how much you are prepared to pay in order to be near the heart of things. Places within walking distance of the centre tend to charge Western European prices without offering anything like the same degree of service, and budget alternatives are usually best avoided: the cheap hotels between the train station and the city centre are, for the most part, little more than seedy flop houses renting out rooms by the hour. The smaller family-run hotels tend to be comfortable and moderately priced, but they have limited space and can fill up quickly, so it's advisable to make **reservations** in advance.

Many of the best family-run establishments are in out-of-town locations like **Simeonovo** and **Dragalevtsi**, 8km to the south. Neither village is particularly attractive, and the journey into central Sofia by public transport involves at least one change. However both places provide easy access to Mount Vitosha, and the hotels here offer good standards of comfort and service at the kind of prices unheard of in central Sofia. To get to Simeonovo, take tram #2 or #19 to Velchova Zavera (the first stop after emerging from the park), then take bus #67 to the end of the line; otherwise catch tram #12 to the Hladilnika terminus, followed by bus #98. Dragalevtsi can be reached by taking tram #12 to Hladilnika, then bus #93 or #98.

Central Sofia

Baldzhieva, ul. Tsar Asen 23 (☎981 1257 or 872914). Relatively small, privately owned hotel in a nicely refurbished town house just one block west of bul. Vitosha. Rooms are clean and cosy, all with phone, fridge, TV and WC. ④.

Bâlgariya, bul. Tsar Osvoboditel 4 (☎870191). In the midst of the city's main tourist sights, Sofia's premier hotel at the turn of the century, the *Bâlgariya* preserves something of its old Central European charm with big, bright, atmospheric rooms. The service is not always what it should be for a hotel of this price, though, and the staff won't reveal which room Mustafa Kemal Atatatürk lived in when he was here as the Ottoman defence attaché in 1913. ⑥.

Balkan Sheraton, pl. Sveta Nedelya 5 (☎981 6541, fax 980 6464). Sofia's most expensive hotel; occupying a prime site on the city's central square. Housing a casino, and excellent (if expensive) restaurants and cafés, it's ideal for business, but not really a tourist choice unless you're loaded with cash. ⑧.

Enny, Pop Bogomil 46 (☎834395). Small and simple downtown hotel just off bul. Knyaginya Mariya Luiza, with cramped but clean rooms, and shared facilities. ③.

Gloria Palace, bul. Knyaginya Mariya Luiza 20 (☎980 7895, fax 980 7894). Neat new place with comfortable but slightly cramped rooms: all have ensuite shower, minibar, cable TV and air-conditioning. There's a nice, glass-roofed top-floor bar. Breakfast included. ⑦.

Grand Hotel Sofia, pl. Narodno Sâbranie 4 (☎987 8821, fax 988 1308). Modern hotel opposite the Bulgarian National Assembly. Comfortable but a bit bland, although many rooms have excellent views of the square. Contains a couple of posh restaurants and a nightclub with cabaret. ⑥.

Maria Luisa, bul. Knyaginya Mariya Luiza 29 (☎91044, fax 980 3355). New hotel in turn-of-the-century building with flash neo-classical interior decor. Rooms are small but come with the usual business-standard comforts – shower, minibar and satellite TV. Even if you're not staying here, it's worth dropping in to try the sumptuous cakes at the ground-floor café. Breakfast included. ⑦.

Maya, Trapezitsa 4 (☎894611). Small family-run pension on the second floor of an apartment block opposite the Largo. There's only a handful of rooms, but they're spacious affairs with settees, fridge and cable TV. ④.

Niky, ul. Neofit Rilski 16 (☎511915). Modest place in a converted apartment block just off the main bul. Vitosha. The rooms are tiny, but most have TV and shower. ③.

Princess, bul. Knyaginya Mariya Luiza 131 (☎320011, 31261). Formerly the *Novotel Evropa* – many locals still know it by that name – now owned by a Turkish chain. Standard business high-rise located between the train station and the town centre – hardly an upmarket area of town. ⑦.

Rila, ul. Kaloyan 6 (☎980 8865, 981 3386). High-rise hotel that used to be the exclusive preserve of Communist party officials, and now houses provincial deputies attending sessions of the Bulgarian parliament. Well-appointed business hotel, slap in the heart of things but somewhat lacking in atmosphere. Contains a good fitness club and restaurant, but the bar and café tend to shut down after 10pm. ⑥.

Rodina, bul. Totleben 8 (☎919803, fax 951584). Another business travellers' preserve just southwest of the city centre. Perfectly acceptable, but a bit overpriced for what it is. ⑥.

Shipka, bul. Totleben 34A (☎91960). Plain, friendly place on the southwestern fringes of the centre, within easy walking range of the sights. Most rooms have been recently refurbished with spic-and-span ensuite bathrooms. Formerly an army-only hotel, and visiting officers still stay here. Breakfast included. ⑤.

Slavyanska Beseda, ul. Slavyanska 3 (☎880441). Affordable mid-range choice, well placed for central Sofia's major sights, but lacking in both character and attentive staff. Worth considering if the smaller (and better value) family-run hotels are full. ④.

Sun, bul. Knyaginya Mariya Luiza 89 (☎833670 or 831833). New business hotel in a refurbished apartment block. Rooms are comfortable and tastefully furnished, although the position – at the grubby end of the main road to the train station – is hardly the best. Breakfast included. ⑥.

Tsar Asen, ul. Tsar Asen 68 (☎547801). Pleasant, family-run pension nestling in residential streets just west of the NDK. ③.

Outside the centre

Deva Spartak, bul. Arsenalski 4 (☎661261 or 658389, fax 662537). Small and intimate hotel with tidy modern rooms, all with ensuite shower, minibar and satellite TV. There's a covered swimming pool next door, and the city centre is a dull but unstrenuous 20-minute walk away. Tram #6 from the Central Station or the NDK to the end of the line. ⑤.

Ganesha, Al. Humboldt 26 (☎ & fax 707936, 718798 or 732992). A converted apartment block on a suburban street, mid-way between the city centre and the airport. The neat rooms have ensuite shower, satellite TV and a small balcony. Take bus #213 or #313 from the train station, or bus #84 from the airport, and get off at the *Hotel Pliska* stop. ③.

Kempinski Zografski, bul. Dzheims Bauchâr 100 (☎62518 or 683251). The best of Sofia's business hotels by far, featuring a multitude of restaurants and sports facilities. The only drawback is that it's 2.5km south of the centre. In 1980, the pope's would-be assassin, Mehmet Ali Agca, stayed in room 911 under the name of "Yogander Singh". Take tram #12 from the Central Station or ul. Graf Ignatiev. ⑦.

Orbita, bul. Dzheims Bauchâr 76 (☎657447 or 881019). Characterless but comfortable, modern hotel between Yuzhen Park and the suburban foothills of Mount Vitosha. Tram #12 from the Central Station or ul. Graf Ignatiev. ④.

Park Hotel Moskva, ul. Nezabravka 25 (☎656737 or 71261). Modern, high-rise affair much patronized by tour groups. Nice wooded location on the fringes of Borisova Gradina. Tram #2 from pl. Sveta Nedelya, or #2 or #19 from ul. Graf Ignatiev. ⑤.

Simeonovo

Accommodation in Simeonovo and Dragalevtsi is marked on the map on p.88.

Atlantik, ul. devedesetta (19-ta) 2 (☎963 3365 or 635 1369, fax 635 2132). Large modern hotel adorned with mock castle towers. All rooms come with comfortable furnishings, small but clean bathrooms and TV. Breakfast included. There's a panoramic restaurant on the top floor with good views of the city below. ④.

Bozhur, Bozhur 23 (☎635 1950, fax 635 2040). Small family house converted into two 2- to 4-person holiday apartments ($50 per apartment), each featuring sitting room, bedroom, bathroom and satellite TV. Ideal for families. Breakfast included. ④.

Traders, Bozhur 18 (☎635 2013, fax 635 1309). Large, new and very plush hotel with bright modern rooms, each with bath, TV and fridge. Breakfast included. ⑤.

Yaneva, Kraibrezhna 15 (☎635 2354). Small family-run place just uphill from the final stop on the #67 bus route. Simple but clean rooms, all with ensuite facilities and TV. Breakfast included; half-board available on request. ③.

Zdravets, Zdravets 10 (☎635 1617). Smallish but very comfortable establishment on a quiet street uphill from the main road, with two single and two double rooms, all with ensuite facilities and TV. ③.

Zhasmin, Simeonovsko shose 126 (☎635 1121 or 635 1069). Another family-run place with a small open-air swimming pool and ensuite rooms, all with satellite TV. Breakfast is included in the price, and there's a good restaurant attached. ③.

Dragalevtsi

Orhideya, Angel Bukureshtliev 9 (☎672739 or 671886). Cosy rooms with newish furnishings, cool tiled floors and cable TV, but communal bathrooms. ③.

Snezhanka, Elena Snezhina 8 (☎ & fax 672944). Seven simple but homely doubles, all ensuite with satellite TV, some with small balconies. Breakfast included. ④.

Vitosha, Elena Snezhina 16 (☎672154 or 671969). Big alpine chalet-style house with rooms featuring ensuite bathroom, cable TV and phone. There's a nice garden café, too. ④.

The City

The heart of Sofia fits compactly within the irregular octagon formed by the city's inner ring road. Most of the sights are found inside this **central area** within easy walking distance of each other, and the grid-like pattern of streets radiating outwards from the main square, **pl. Sveta Nedelya**, makes orientation relatively easy. Sveta Nedelya is a good place from which to begin explorations of the capital, although there's no single obvious sightseeing route to follow. It's a good idea to sample the area around Sveta Nedelya first, before embarking on a trip to the set-piece **public buildings** and **squares** to the east. Within striking distance are the refreshing open spaces of the city's main **parks**, a brisk walk or tram ride away from the centre. Expeditions to **Mt Vitosha** and the **suburbs** nestling in its foothills require more time and reliance on public transport.

Around Ploshtad Sveta Nedelya and bul. Knyaginya Mariya Luiza

Ploshtad Sveta Nedelya – Sveta Nedelya square – is Sofia's hub, straddling the capital's principal north–south and east–west thoroughfares and providing easy access to the main business and shopping districts – such as they are. Until recently the square carried the name of Lenin, whose huge statue – now demolished – dominated the southern end. With his removal, the central focus of the square has returned northward to the **church** after which it was originally named. The square elongates to join **bul. Knyaginya Mariya Luiza** to the north – the *Balkan Sheraton* hotel and the TsUM department store guard the entrance to the broad street-cum-square known as **the Largo**, main route to the tourist attractions of east central Sofia – while to the south lies bul. Vitosha, the city's principal thoroughfare.

The Church of Sveta Nedelya

Trams rattle round a paved island that bears the **Church of Sveta Nedelya**. Standing upon the former site of Serdica's chief crossroads, the current building was constructed after the Liberation as the successor to a line of churches that has stood here since medieval times. In those days aristocratic families built private chapels and endowed the monastic schools that formed the nucleus of the *Varosh* – the old Bulgarian quarter. During the Ottoman period it was known as the Church of Sveti Kral – the "Blessed King" – on account of the remains of the medieval Serbian monarch, Stefan Urosh, kept here. In 1925 it almost claimed another king, when bombs exploded among high dignitaries attending a funeral mass, killing 123 people but failing to harm their intended victims, Tsar Boris and his cabinet. The Communists – whose attempted revolution had been crushed in 1923 – were naturally blamed, but denied all responsibility. Leading revolutionary Georgi Dimitrov later laid claim to the attack, but the postwar Communist regime tended to ascribe it to "ultra leftists".

The Church Historical Museum and the Chapel of Sveta Petka Paraskeva

On the southern side of the square, an ochre building with attractive red and green tiling houses both the Theology Faculty and, on the first floor, the **Church Historical Museum** (Mon–Fri 9am–noon & 2–5pm; $1), a collection of icons, ceremonial priestly robes, bejewelled crosses and incense holders. The best of Bulgaria's religious art is found elsewhere – notably in the National History Museum (see p.75), or the crypt of the Aleksandâr Nevski memorial church, see p.81) – and the display here does little more than fill in the gaps. Highlights include two sixteenth-century icons (*Virgin and Child* and *Crucifixion*) from the Black Sea town of Sozopol (see p.363), which remained an important icon-painting centre throughout the Ottoman occupation; and some *pafti* (women's belt buckles) engraved with the forms of saints Dimitâr and George.

Round the corner heading east along ul. Sâborna, a low door leads down into the subterranean **Chapel of Sveta Petka Paraskeva**, a medieval foundation now dwarfed beneath turn-of-the-century buildings. Built in the thirteenth century by Tsar Kaloyan as a palace chapel, it's central Sofia's most atmospheric church, crammed with daytime shoppers muttering prayers or planting candles next to the icons — which far from being mere museum exhibits, are here the objects of genuine devotion. Alongside icons of Sveta Petka herself are powerful depictions of saints George, Dimitâr and Mina (a fourth-century Egyptian known in the West as Menas), the warrior saints so important to Balkan Christians.

The Banya Bashi mosque and the Turkish baths

North of the square, **bul. Knyaginya Mariya Luiza** was the "most horrible street in Europe" for Arthur Symons when he was here in 1903, a "kind of mongrel East"

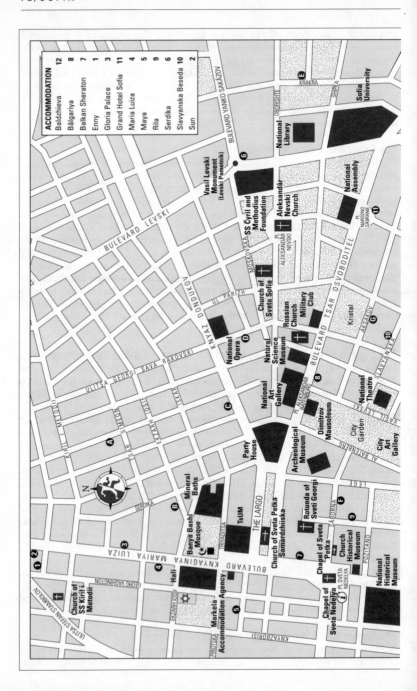

ACCOMMODATION

Baldzhieva	12
Bălgariya	8
Balkan Sheraton	7
Enny	1
Gloria Palace	3
Grand Hotel Sofia	11
Maria Luiza	4
Maya	5
Rila	9
Serdika	6
Slavyanska Beseda	10
Sun	2

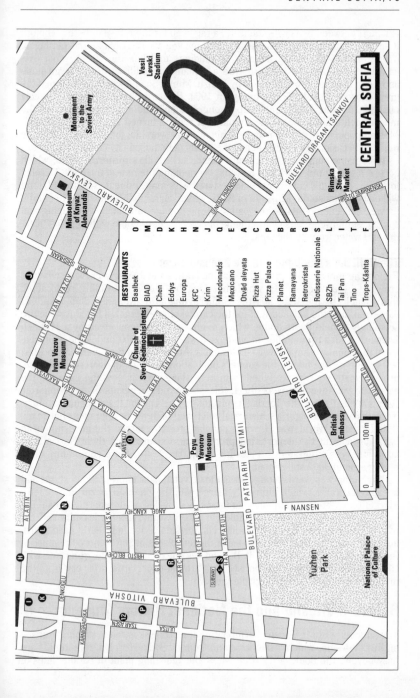

CENTRAL SOFIA

Vasil Levski Stadium

Monument to the Soviet Army

Mausoleum of Knyaz Aleksandŭr

Ivan Vazov Museum

Church of Sveti Sedmochislentsi

Peyu Yavorov Museum

British Embassy

Rimska Stena Market

Yuzhen Park

National Palace of Culture

RESTAURANTS

Baalbek	O
BIAD	M
Chen	D
Eddys	K
Europa	H
KFC	N
Krim	J
Macdonalds	Q
Mexicano	E
Otvŭd aleyata	A
Pizza Hut	C
Pizza Palace	P
Planet	B
Ramayana	R
Retrokristal	G
Rotisserie Nationale	S
SBZh	L
Tai Pan	I
Tino	T
Trops-Kăshta	F

0   100 m

SUBWAY

existing "between two civilizations . . . a rag-heap for the refuse of both". Though it has been considerably cleaned up since then you can see what he was getting at, if only in the dilapidated mixture of buildings that line the street. Most eye-catching is the **Banya Bashi mosque**: a "Sultan-style" edifice with one large dome and a single minaret, built in 1576 by Hadzhi Mimar Sonah, who also designed the great mosque at Edirne in Turkey. In 1960, Bernard Newman noted "scarcely enough Turks in Sofia to make up a congregation", and in subsequent years the mosque fell into disuse as the Communist regime turned against the country's Muslim population. Now it is once again open for worship, the discreet call of the muezzin occasionally wafting above the heads of bemused city-centre shoppers.

As its name suggests, the mosque stands near Sofia's **mineral baths**, which occupy a stately mock-oriental building overlooking the rear of the park. Derelict for many years, it's currently being restored with money donated by the EU, and will one day house the Museum of Sofia, which currently has nowhere to exhibit its vast collection. Outside the baths, people lounge on benches gossiping and spitting sunflower seeds or fragments of *kebapcheta*, or come with jugs to collect mineral water from public taps.

The Hali, the synagogue and the Zhenski pazar

Facing the mosque is the market hall or **Hali**, an elaborately carved structure crowned by a clock tower, which has long been closed awaiting restoration. Immediately to the west lies the **Sofia synagogue** (Mon–Fri 9am–5pm, Sat 9am–1pm; ring the bell and wait for the caretaker to emerge), a fanciful structure seemingly upheld by its dome, which might have been conceived by a Moorish Leonardo with a premonition of airships. It was built in 1910, and is the main centre of the country's small Jewish community. At the time of the Liberation in 1877, Jews made up one fifth of the capital's population, living in an overcrowded maze of narrow streets that stretched from here along what is now the Largo to the east. The vast majority were the Ladin-speaking descendants of the Sephardic Jews expelled from the Iberian peninsula at the end of the fifteenth century. Notwithstanding Bulgaria's historical tolerance of Jews (a tolerance that manifested itself in World War II, when popular pressure forced the government to back down from the deportation programme demanded by their Nazi allies), large numbers emigrated to Palestine in the late 1940s, but a community numbering around 3000 still remains.

Continuing westwards along Ekzarh Iosif, you'll pass unpretentious shops and cheap restaurants, which ultimately merge with the **Zhenski pazar** or Women's Market on ul. Stefan Stambolov, an intensely crowded affair where you can find everything from fruit and vegetables to fake designer-label tracksuits and car parts. Peasants from the surrounding countryside arrive here early each morning to sell their produce, and it's one of the few places in Sofia where the pulse of the Balkans of old can still be felt. Beyond lies one of Sofia's **older quarters**, with rutted cobblestones and low houses built around courtyards: a far cry from the modern housing estates that girdle the town.

Bulevard Vitosha and the National History Museum

The silhouette of Mt Vitosha surmounting the rooftops is the first thing you see on **bul. Vitosha**, which stretches south from pl. Sveta Nedelya. Its foothills are hazy beyond the boulevard's tram wires, the vanishing point of parallel lines of

> ## MOVING THE NATIONAL HISTORY MUSEUM
>
> In 1998 it was agreed in principle to move the National History Museum to a new site in the suburb of Boyana, allowing it's current city-centre home to revert to its former function as Palace of Justice. No date has been fixed for the move as yet – indeed whether it will take place at all remains the subject of much conjecture. In the meantime, look out for changes.

greyish buildings, most of which date from the inter-war years. Lined with pavement cafés and the capital's more stylish shops, Vitosha is an invigorating street to stroll along, though, other than the unmissable **National History Museum**, there's little in the way of specific sights.

The National History Museum

Sofia's **National History Museum** (Tues–Thurs, Sat & Sun 10.30am–5.30pm, Fri 2–5.30pm; $4) occupies the former Palace of Justice at the northern end of the boulevard. The museum is a superbly arranged affair marred only by dim lighting and inconsistent labelling. The archeological relics on the ground floor cover the history of the Bulgarian lands up until the medieval period, while the first floor concentrates on the politics and culture of Bulgaria's nineteenth-century renaissance. Some of the museum's best-known treasures occasionally go on tour abroad, so be prepared for some unexplained gaps in the collection.

ANCIENT ARTEFACTS

Halls 1–4 contain artefacts left by various Neolithic cultures between the seventh and third millennia BC – including stone **goddess figures** found near Varna and inscribed with rams, birds, chevrons, labyrinths and other motifs associated with the Great Earth Mother. Pride of place, however, goes to the great gold and silver hoards associated with the **Thracians**, who inhabited the eastern Balkans during the pre-Christian era. Earliest of these is the hoard of golden vessels found near the village of **Vâlchitrân** in northern Bulgaria, and thought to date from about 1300 BC. The various cups and goblets appear quite simple and functional, save for one item consisting of three small containers linked by a trident-like handle. Possibly intended for the ceremonial mixing of liquids, this triple-vessel no doubt had ritual significance for the tribal chieftain who owned it.

THE ROGOZEN TREASURE

Next comes the **Rogozen treasure**, a hoard of 165 silver vessels unearthed in the village of Rogozen near Vratsa. This was in all probability a family treasure, accumulated by wealthy nobles of the Triballi tribe somewhere between 500 and 350 BC. The scenes that decorate many of the vessels portray typically Thracian concerns: hunting trips involving a variety of wild beasts, and archetypal goddess figures – one in a chariot drawn by winged horses, another riding a golden-headed lioness.

THE PANAGYURISHTE TREASURE AND THE LETNITSA PLAQUES

More sumptuous still is the golden **treasure of Panagyurishte**, a collection of eight *rhyta* (drinking vessels) and one *phiale* (a kind of plate) made by Greek artisans of the Dardanelles area and imported into Thrace by a wealthy chieftain.

Each *rhyton* is designed in the shape of an animal's head, with mythological scenes shown in relief around the side. One amphora-shaped *rhyton* features handles in the form of centaurs and a procession of naked warriors round the main body of the vessel.

Further artefacts and jewellery from the Thracian period include a series of fourth-century BC horse trappings found at **Letnitsa** near Lovech: small silver plaques with gilded images of mythical beasts and a hunter on horseback. Rather like a modern cartoon strip, the plaques appear to tell a story common to many European cultures: that of a horse-riding hero who slays a serpent in order to win the heart of a maiden and deliver the kingdom from famine. The Thracians were particularly keen on heroic horsemen (see p.333), a fondness that is reflected in the modern Orthodox Church's reverence for saints such as George and Dimitâr.

BULGARIAN TREASURES
Bas reliefs, ceramics, silverware and frescos (halls 10–11) give some idea of the artistic heights attained during the medieval era, when Pliska, Preslav and Veliko Târnovo enjoyed their heyday as capitals, although these pale before the superb collection of **ecclesiastical art** displayed upstairs. Designed to show how the Bulgarian Church kept national culture alive during five centuries of Ottoman rule, the display whisks you through the various schools of **icon painting** which flourished in rural Bulgaria throughout the Ottoman period, and contains several examples of the **frescos** that decorated Bulgarian monasteries. An early example is the sixteenth-century *Last Judgement* from the Church of the Nativity in Arbanasi, in which true believers are transported to a paradise stocked with exotic beasts while the ungodly are suspended over fires or have spikes inserted in their backside. Equally outstanding is the *Wheel of Life* by Zahari Zograf, the nineteenth-century artist who did more than most to weld the Byzantine trad-itions of icon painting with the folk art of the Bulgarian peasantry. Several rooms are devoted to the leading lights of the nineteenth-century **National Revival**, when progressive Bulgarians struggled for education, civic reforms and, ultimately, independence, giving rise to revolutionaries like Vasil Levski and Hristo Botev, whose banners and proclamations are prominently featured.

The corridor connecting both wings of the upper floor exhibits a wonderful collection of nineteenth-century **folk costumes** and **carpets**, plus a beautiful and very cosy-looking **room from Teteven**, furnished in the National Revival style.

The Largo

The broad road stretching eastward from pl. Sveta Nedelya, **the Largo**, was one of the major showpieces of postwar Sofia, not least because of the political symbolism embodied in its most imposing edifice: the Communist Party headquarters. Flanked on three sides by severely monumental buildings, this elongated plaza was built on the ruins of central Sofia, which had been pulverized by British and American bombers in the autumn of 1944. Its yellow-painted stones are the start of a kilometre-long stretch of bright yellow cobblestones which, leading through pl. Aleksandâr Batenberg and along bul. Tsar Osvoboditel, forms a kind of processional way linking many of the capital's key sights.

The Church of Sveta Petka Samardzhiiska and the Rotunda of Sveti Georgi

The northern side of the Largo is dominated by a large postwar structure that houses the Council of Ministers (Bulgaria's cabinet) and Sofia's main department store, the **TsUM** (ЦУМ, pronounced "Tsoom"), alongside which runs an arcade lined with the stalls of street traders.

An underpass gives access to a sunken plaza laid out with café tables, whose bright awnings contrast with the weathered brick-and-stone **Church of Sveta Petka Samardzhiiska**, girded with concrete platforms, its tiled rooftop poking above street level. Originally built in the fourteenth century, the church gained the epithet *samardzhiiska* in the nineteenth century, when it was adopted by the Saddlers' Guild as their private chapel. Despite conscientious restoration, the surviving sixteenth-century frescos are now patchy and difficult to see, but you can make out portraits of several bearded and be-haloed figures, one of which is St John of Rila, medieval Bulgaria's leading holy man.

On the south side of the Largo, the *Hotel Balkan Sheraton* casts its sombre wings around a courtyard containing Sofia's oldest church, the fourth-century **Rotunda of Sveti Georgi** (summer 8am–7pm, winter hours are variable due to lack of heating; donation requested). Outwardly dour, with a red brick exterior, the church contains some incandescent frescos under the dome. Most of them, including the central image of Christ the Pantokrator and the surrounding frieze of 22 prophets, are fourteenth century, but many of the frescos below are much older. Another ring of prophets dates from the twelfth century, when Bulgaria was under Byzantine control, and some ninth-century floral designs, in the northern niche, date from the First Bulgarian Empire, when the newly Christianized state subjected unwilling aristocrats to mass baptisms in this very church.

The Party House

Of the buildings surrounding the Largo, the white, colonnaded supertanker of the **Party House**, or *partiinyat dom*, is by far the most arresting structure. Besides housing sporadic Communist Party congresses, the building accommodated the office of the Central Committee (*Tsentralen Komitet*), and featured in a popular joke: A man cycles up to the building and leans his bike against it, whereupon a policeman shouts: "Hey! You can't leave that there, a high Soviet delegation is due to arrive any minute." "That's okay," replies the cyclist, "I'll chain it up".

After November 1989, public pressure mounted to have the Communists evicted from the building: initially without much result. Anti-Communist demonstrations in August 1990 did, however, succeed in getting rid of the enormous **red star** traditionally perched above the roof. Though the National Assembly decided on August 24 to have all Communist iconography removed from public buildings, the red star atop the Party House failed to shift. Within two days the building had been torched by an angry mob – smoke-blackened walls at the rear of the building still bear testimony to their discontent. The party was finally ejected in early 1992, after which the Party House served briefly as a cinema. Its ultimate fate is yet to be decided.

Ploshtad Aleksandâr Batenberg

If the Bulgarian Communist Party had a soul it would doubtless still hover over the cobbled expanse of **pl. Aleksandâr Batenberg**, formerly pl. Deveti

Septemvri or 9 September square – where major anniversaries were celebrated with **parades**. These took place on May 1 and September 9 (the date of the Communist coup in 1944), and featured a familiar repertoire of Communist spectacle: red-scarved Young Pioneers, brigades of workers bearing portraits of their leaders, mass callisthenics, and floats carrying tableaux symbolizing the achievements of socialist construction. The anniversary of the Bolshevik Revolution (November 7) was marked by soldiers goose-stepping and armoured vehicles grinding across the plaza in emulation of mightier parades in Moscow. Militia cordons kept the uninvited at a distance (events were televised nationwide), and the regimented proceedings – known as "spontaneous demonstrations of the people" during the Stalinist era – were a tiresome obligation for many participants. "We have seen so many of these demonstrations which humiliate human dignity, where normal people are expected to applaud some paltry mediocrity who has proclaimed himself a demi-god and condescendingly waves to them from the heights of his police inviolability", wrote dissident writer Georgi Markov (criticisms like these eventually cost Markov his life, killed by a Bulgarian agent wielding a poisoned umbrella in 1978).

Hastily renamed "Democracy Square" after November 1989, the square has now reverted to its original prewar title, honouring the young German aristocrat who was chosen to be the newly independent country's first monarch in 1878. As an idealistic 22-year-old Aleksandâr had volunteered to fight alongside Bulgaria's Russian liberators during the War of Independence, yet it was his loss of Russian backing in 1886 – when Bulgaria declared union with Eastern Roumelia without first securing the approval of her big Slav brother – that brought his six-year reign to a premature close.

The National Archeological Museum

At the square's western end, on the corner of ul. Lege, stands an ivy-clad nine-domed building, formerly the *Buyuk Djami* or "Big Mosque", dating from 1494, and now housing the **National Archeological Museum** (Tues–Sun 10am–5pm; $1.50). Bulgaria's most valuable treasures are concentrated in the National History Museum (see p.75), and the Thracian pottery and silverware on display here has a more workaday feel. However, some individual items stand out, such as an eighth-century BC bronze figurine of a stag found at Sevlievo near Pleven, and there are plentiful Greek and Roman finds from around the country. Most famous of these is the **Stela of Anaxander**, a sixth-century BC gravestone from the ancient Greek colony of Apollonia (now Sozopol) on the Black Sea coast.

Upstairs there's an extensive collection of frescos plucked from crumbling church walls throughout Bulgaria. A cycle of paintings from the (now ruined) Church of St George the Great in Nesebâr shows the martyrdom of the saint, who had nails hammered into his feet before being strangled.

Dimitrov's Mausoleum

Party leaders used to take the salute from atop the austere white mausoleum on the southern side of the square. Now standing empty, the mausoleum was built to house the embalmed body of **Georgi Dimitrov**, the first leader of the People's Republic of Bulgaria (see opposite). Following his death in July 1949 while on a visit to Moscow, **Dimitrov's Mausoleum** was erected in six days and nights, in time for the body's return. Watched over by goose-stepping sentries wearing red-braided tunics and plumed hats, the mausoleum used to be open to visitors three afternoons a week. Suitably reverential citizens would file through antiseptic corridors into the dim, guarded vault where Dimitrov's corpse was displayed (though it was said that only the arms and head were original; the rest was wax). In July 1990, Dimitrov's body was quietly removed from the mausoleum and cremated; his ashes were buried in plot 212 of the Sofia city graveyard, next to his mother. The future of his erstwhile tomb remains uncertain, although it may be turned into a Pantheon honouring those who fought and died for Bulgaria's freedom in the nineteenth century. In recent years it has served as the backdrop for grandiose outdoor opera productions which, funds permitting, are mounted here annually in July.

The National Art Gallery

Opposite the mausoleum stands the former royal palace, which was once so dilapidated that Tsar "Foxy" Ferdinand had to sleep under scaffolding to prevent the roof falling in on him. The palace began life as the Ottoman *Konak* where Vasil Levski (see p.256) was tortured prior to his execution, before having the current neo-classical facade tacked onto it by Ferdinand's predecessor, Knyaz Aleksandâr. Inside is the **National Art Gallery** (Tues–Sun 10.30am–6pm; $1), a

---

GEORGI DIMITROV (1882–1949)

Both a distinguished anti-fascist campaigner and one of the twentieth century's great villains, **Georgi Dimitrov** still casts an ambiguous shadow over modern Bulgaria. Born into a humble background, he was a teenage apprentice printer when he converted to Communism, and, with characteristic nerve, doctored the speeches of reactionary MPs before they went to press – the prelude to a lifelong militant career. He organized Party cells, unions, strikes and propaganda inside Bulgaria, emigrating to Moscow after the failure of the September Uprising of 1923. Once in the Soviet Union he rose quickly through the ranks of the Comintern or Communist International, and it was while on Comintern business in Berlin that he was arrested by the Nazis on March 9, 1933 and charged with instigating the Reichstag fire. The subsequent show trial in Leipzig became an international cause célèbre, with Dimitrov (despite months of maltreatment by the Gestapo) conducting his own defence and succeeding in making Herman Goering, his prosecutor, appear to be both a liar and a fool. This, and the international attention the trial had received, ensured his acquittal in February 1934. He again took refuge in Moscow, and managed to survive Stalin's purges by betraying fellow Bulgarians also exiled in the USSR. Loyalty to Stalin managed to win him the post of secretary-general of the Comintern in 1935, where he became implicated even further in the liquidation of East European communists who didn't quite fit into the Soviet leader's plans.

During World War II Dimitrov masterminded the Bulgarian Communist Party's strategy of infiltrating and subverting the anti-fascist opposition, returning to the country himself in November 1945. He was prime minister from 1946 until his death in 1949, presiding over a period of intense social change: sweeping nationalization and industrialization proceeding hand-in-hand with the ruthless crushing of all political opposition. Under Dimitrov's leadership thousands of Bulgarians were brutally killed, and countless others packed off to concentration camps, in a near-genocidal attempt to rub out the Bulgarian bourgeoisie.

Until recently every town in Bulgaria had at least one street named after Dimitrov; nowadays, memories of the man are fast disappearing from national life.

fairly uninspiring collection that reveals how dependent on Western models Bulgarian painting has been. The works that stand out are those which heavily exploit the nostalgia for folk styles and motifs: notably Tsanko Lavrenov's pictures of old Plovdiv, and the near-naive canvases of fellow Plovdivite Zlatyu Boyadzhiev. The fusion of modern art and folk art which characterizes the work of Bulgaria's greatest twentieth-century painter, Vladimir Dimitrov-Maistor (see p.103), is represented by several stylized pictures of peasant girls. The artist had a strong interest in oriental religions, and his admirers have always detected a mystical quality in his depictions of Bulgarian rural life.

Housed in the same building is the **Ethnographic Museum** (Tues–Sun 11am–4pm; $1), which mounts a different, themed exhibition every year. Whatever's on show, it usually includes a wealth of folk costumes and textiles.

Bulevard Tsar Osvoboditel and around

Bulevard Tsar Osvoboditel heads out of pl. Aleksandâr Batenberg's eastern end, an attractive thoroughfare partially lined with chestnut trees. The **Natural Science Museum** at no. 1 (daily 10am–6pm; $1), presents a thorough cataloguing of Bulgarian and worldwide wildlife, both stuffed and pickled. Tanks containing live snakes and lizards line the stairs, domestic grass snakes vying for attention with central American geckos, pythons and anacondas. At teatime, live rodents are lowered into the tanks of the larger reptiles. There's also a small gift shop selling minerals and fossils. Immediately beyond the museum, the **Russian church** is an unmistakable, zany firecracker of a building with an exuberant exterior of bright yellow tiles, five gilded domes and an emerald spire, concealing a dark, candlewax-scented interior. Officially dedicated to St Nicholas the Blessed, the church was built in 1913 at the behest of a Tsarist diplomat, Semontovski-Kurilo, who feared for his soul to worship in Bulgarian churches, which he believed to be schismatic.

Towards National Assembly Square

Continuing eastward along Tsar Osvoboditel is a small square of greenery known popularly as **Kristal**, after the café that shelters on its southern flank. Opposite the park on the northern side of the boulevard is the recently spruced-up neoclassical facade of the **military club**, once the centre of post-Liberation Bulgaria's high society, and the place where the Zveno (a radical political group that attracted young right-wing officers) hatched several conspiracies in the inter-war years.

Bulevard Tsar Osvoboditel opens out into pl. Narodno sâbranie – **National Assembly Square**. On the northern side stands a cream building housing the *Narodno sâbranie* itself – Bulgaria's **National Assembly**, the facade of which bears the motto *sâedinenieto pravi silata* (unity is strength). Directly opposite, a semicircular plaza encloses the Monument to the Liberators, which gives pride of place to a statue of the *Tsar Osvoboditel*, or "Tsar Liberator" himself, Alexander II of Russia.

Ploshtad Aleksandâr Nevski

The area immediately north of bul. Ruski is dominated by **pl. Aleksandâr Nevski**, another of Sofia's set-piece squares, an expanse of greenery and paving stones (overlaying what was, in Roman times, the necropolis of Serdica) overlooked by the twinkling domes of the Aleksandâr Nevski memorial church. Entering the square from the western end, however, you first encounter the brown brick **Church of Sveta Sofia**. Dating from late Roman times, but much rebuilt after numerous invasions and earthquakes (the last one in 1858), the church still follows the classic Byzantine plan of a regular cross with a dome at the intersection. It was turned into a mosque by the Ottomans, and locals believed that it was haunted nightly by the ghost of Constantine the Great's daughter Sofia, founder of the first church to stand on this site. Around the back an engraved boulder marks the **grave of Ivan Vazov** (p.82), who requested that he be buried amid the daily life of his people; you'll notice his statue, seated with book in hand, in a park nearby. Set beside the southern wall of the church is the Tomb of the Unknown Soldier, flanked by two recumbent lions.

The Aleksandâr Nevski memorial church

One of the finest pieces of architecture in the Balkans and certainly Sofia's crowning glory, the **Aleksandâr Nevski memorial church** honours the 200,000 Russian casualties of the 1877–78 War of Liberation, particularly the defenders of the Shipka pass. Financed by public subscription and built between 1882 and 1924 to the designs of St Petersburg architect Pomerantsev, it's a magnificent structure, bulging with domes and half-domes and glittering with 18lb of gold leaf donated by the Soviet Union in 1960. Within the cavernous interior, a white-bearded God glowers down from the main cupola, an angelic sunburst covers the central vault, and as a parting shot a *Day of Judgement* looms above the exit. Expressive frescos lacking the stiffness of Byzantine portraiture depict episodes from the life of Christ in rich tones, and the grandeur of the iconostasis is enhanced by twin thrones with columns of onyx and alabaster.

Orthodox congregations stand or kneel during services, although the weak and the elderly traditionally lean or sit on benches round the side. The church's capacity of 5000 is ample for daily **services** (usually in the morning at around 9.30am, and in the evening at about 5pm), which can be spectacular affairs, rich with incense, candlelight and sonorous chanting.

The **crypt**, entered from the outside, contains a superb **collection of icons** (daily except Tues 10.30am–12.30pm & 2–6.30pm; $2) from all over the country. They're mostly eighteenth- and nineteenth-century pieces, but look out for some medieval gems from the coastal town of Nesebâr, home to a prolific icon-painting school, and source of the oldest icon on display here, a serene, white-bearded St Nicholas. Other highlights include a fourteenth-century wood-carved bas-relief from Sozopol showing saints George and Dimitâr riding together against some common foe. The horsemen are regarded as brother-saints in the Balkans, not least because their feast days (May 6 for George, October 26 for Dimitâr) play an important ritual role in marking the beginnings of the summer and winter cycles in the agricultural year. They're often pictured together in Bulgarian art, with St George invariably riding a white steed, Dimitâr a red one.

The SS Cyril and Methodius Foundation

An imposing gallery on the northeastern edge of the cathedral square houses the **SS Cyril and Methodius Foundation** (daily 11am–6pm), an international art collection largely based on the donations of rich Bulgarians living abroad (and the occasional philanthropic foreigner – Robert Maxwell was one early benefactor). The ground floor contains a sizeable collection of Indian miniatures, manuscripts and sculpture. Next door, a series of nineeenth-century Burmese wall hangings overlook a crowd of wooden Buddhas, including one gilt example sitting cross-legged on the backs of three elephants. Upstairs, second-division French artists take up a lot of space, although there are a couple of Delacroix sketches, a small Picasso etching (*The Visions of Count d'Orgas* from 1966), and a mesmerizing *Lucifer* by turn-of-the-century German symbolist Franz von Stück. In the basement (not always open, unfortunately), Thracian grave stones from an ancient necropolis excavated nearby surround a reconstructed mortuary chapel dating from late Roman times.

Ulitsa G S Rakovski and around

Central Sofia's southeastern quarter is one of the inner city's liveliest areas, its City Garden and pavement cafés providing the focus for social life during the day, its theatres and restaurants in the evening. The area's main thoroughfares are **ul. G S Rakovski**, a workaday street lined with office blocks, and **ul. Graf Ignatiev**, which is the capital's most important shopping district after bul. Vitosha. Government buildings and residental houses mingle in the quiet streets inbetween, along with a couple of worthwhile literary museums.

Around the City Garden

Directly behind the Dimitrov Mausoleum, the well-tended flowerbeds of the **City Garden** (*Gradskata gradina*) invariably attract chess-playing senior citizens and office workers taking their lunch break. Several fountains splash opposite the **Ivan Vazov National Theatre**, a handsome Neoclassical edifice, which provides a welcome contrast to the other sombre ministerial buildings along ul. Vasil Levski. Decked out in red, white and gold, it features Gobelin tapestries and Panagyurishte hangings inside. At the southern end of the park, ul. General Gurko is home to the **City Art Gallery** (daily 8am–5.30pm), a showcase for contemporary Bulgarian paintings, drawings and sculpture.

Two blocks east of the City Garden at the corner of ul. Rakovski and ul. Vazov is the **Ivan Vazov House-Museum** (Tues & Sun 1–7pm, Thurs 1–5pm, Fri & Sat 9am–5pm), where Bulgaria's greatest novelist lived from 1895 until his death in 1921. Most of the rooms are decked out in turn-of-the-century wallpaper and traditional Bulgarian floor coverings, making this one of the few places in town where the atmosphere of the old, post-Liberation Sofia still reigns. Downstairs a words-and-pictures display details the main events of Vazov's life, from childhood in Sopot (see p.254) through exile in Odessa (where he wrote *Under the Yoke*, the epic novel of nineteenth-century Bulgarian life) to old age in Sofia: the dining room where he suffered a fatal heart attack is preserved in its original state. Period rooms upstairs include the writer's study, where visitors are greeted by the stuffed remains of Vazov's beloved dog, Bobi. The unfortunate hound was run over by a tram just outside the house before being whisked off to the taxidermist by Vazov's youngest brother Boris.

The Museum of Peyu Yavorov

Continuing south along ul. Rakovski you soon come to the **Museum of Peyu Yavorov** in a secession-style house at no. 136 (Tues & Sun 1–7pm, Thurs 1–5pm, Fri & Sat 9am–5pm). One of the most compelling figures in Bulgarian literature (see box opposite), Yavorov lived in a modest first-floor flat here for eleven

PEYU YAVOROV (1878–1914)

Man of action, poet and charismatic loner, **Peyu Kracholov** was born in the dusty provincial backwater of Chirpan. At the age of sixteen, he was forced by an unsympathetic father, to abandon his studies and take up work as a telegraph operator. It was in the post offices of provincial towns like Sliven and Pomorie that the introverted Yavorov started to write the sombre, romantic symbolist poetry for which he became famous. Changing his name to Yavorov because it sounded more earthy (*Yavor* means "sycamore tree"), he was instantly received into Sofia's literary world, hung out with all the major writers of the day (including Vazov, who championed his work), and became editor of the top literary magazine *Misâl*. A star while still in his twenties, Yavorov nevertheless yearned for more than the salon-bound cultural life of the capital. Tiring of his youthful passion for socialism, he threw himself into the struggle to free Macedonia from the Ottoman Empire, fighting as a guerrilla in the mountains and writing a biography of the movement's leader, Gotse Delchev (see p.131). The death of Delchev and the failure of the Ilinden Uprising (see p.141) in 1903 left Yavorov disillusioned, but he continued to serve as an unofficial ambassador for the Macedonian cause, and returned to the fray as a *voyvoda* (guerilla leader) in the Balkan Wars, liberating the Aegean town of Kavala from Ottoman rule in 1912.

Yavorov's other great passion was writing love poetry to the two women with whom he had obsessive affairs. The first was Mina Todorova, teenage daughter of Petko Todorov, a fellow-member of the *Misâl* circle. Despite being an ardent admirer of Yavorov's writings, Todorov was horrified by the idea of having a penniless revolutionary poet as a son-in-law. Banned from seeing her, Yavorov wrote Mina love letters in verse, offering them to *Misâl* for publication at the same time. Mina died of tuberculosis in 1910, and it was at her graveside in Paris that Yavorov struck up a friendship with the next object of his affections, Lora Karavelova. The daughter of former Prime Minister Petko Karavelov (and niece of the Bulgarian revolutionary Lyuben Karavelov), Lora was one of Sofia's most modern, emancipated women, and she and Yavorov soon became the city's favourite intellectual couple. They married almost immediately, but Lora found Yavorov – already wed to Macedonia and his own writing – a distant, difficult person to live with. By early 1913 Lora was convinced (probably without reason) that Yavorov was having an affair with Dora Konova, the fiancée of a friend. They argued, and Lora threatened to shoot herself. Whether intentionally or not, the gun went off. Yavorov was tried for her murder – and speedily acquitted, despite the popular feeling that he was the guilty party. Abandoned by his friends and living in extreme poverty, Yavorov then turned a gun on himself, but at the first attempt lost only his eyesight. A few months later, at his second attempt, he succeeded in taking his life.

months in 1913. Among the period furniture and traditional rugs are some evocative personal effects, such as the knife and binoculars given to him by Macedonian freedom fighters Gotse Delchev and Yane Sandanski respectively. Quite by chance, the photographs of Yavorov and wife Lora which hang in the sitting-room have been separated by a large crack which has recently appeared in the wall – a poignant reminder of their tragic end.

Ulitsa Graf Ignatiev

Cutting across ul. Rakovski is **ul. Graf Ignatiev**, a meandering thoroughfare lined with shops, and named after the Russian count (and grandfather of

Canadian novelist, Michael Ignatiev) who persuaded Tsar Aleksandâr to support Bulgarian liberation. In the small garden beside the intersection with ul. Tsar Shishman stands the **Church of Sveti Sedmochislentsi**, literally the "Holy Seven", referring to Cyril, Methodius and their followers, the seven saints who brought Christianity to the Slavs. It was built on the site of the so-called "Black Mosque", an edifice which served as Sofia's main prison immediately after the Liberation. Prisoners used to sell hand-made trinkets to passing city folk in order to pay for their food. British barrister James A Samuelson bought a belt made of beads from a prisoner on death row in 1887, "for which" he wrote, "I, of course, gave him a trifle".

The inner ring road and beyond

Girdling the city centre is the broad sweep of Sofia's **inner ring road**, built in imitation of the wide boulevards of other European capitals such as Paris, Vienna and Budapest. There's little of architectural interest along its length, save for a scattering of monuments and buildings around the eastern end of pl. Aleksandâr Nevski and bul. Tsar Osvoboditel. A hundred metres north of the Nevski church, at the intersection with Yanko Sakâzov, stands the weathered stone **Vasil Levski Monument** (*Levski pametnik*), marking the spot where the "Apostle of Freedom" (see p.256) was hanged by the Ottoman authorities in 1873.

From there it's a brief stroll south to **Sofia University**, the country's most prestigious educational establishment. Founded a decade after the Liberation, it was named after Kliment Ohridski, a pupil of Cyril and Methodius, who as ninth-century bishop of Ohrid in western Macedonia had an important impact on the flowering of Slav culture. Not previously known for their radicalism, Sofia's students were at the heart of demonstrations in June 1990 protesting at the alleged unfairness of Bulgaria's first post-Communist elections. Barricades went up in front of the university, provoking fears that Bulgaria's nascent democracy would descend into confrontation, but government concessions to the opposition prevented any real violence.

Continuing along bul. Levski from the university, the **mausoleum of Knyaz Aleksandâr Batenberg** (Mon–Fri 9am–noon & 2–5pm) occupies a small park at the corner of ul. Slavyanska. Despite being deposed in 1886 and living in exile in Graz until his death in 1893, Bulgaria's first post-Liberation ruler always wanted to be buried in Sofia, and his successor Ferdinand obliged by having the mausoleum erected in his honour. It took so long to build, however, that Aleksandâr's corpse spent five years in the Rotunda of St George before finally taking up residence here. A neo-Baroque cupola-topped structure holds his plain marble sarcophagus, draped with a Bulgarian flag, but other than a couple of military tunics, worn by the prince when visiting front-line troops in the Serb-Bulgarian war of 1885, there's little to see.

Immediately opposite the mausoleum stands the towering **Monument to the Soviet Army**, erected in honour of the "liberation" of Bulgaria in 1944. Although allied to Nazi Germany during World War II, the Bulgarians always shrank from declaring war on the Soviet Union, mindful of the long tradition of Russo-Bulgarian friendship. The Soviets, however, regarded Bulgaria as ripe for conquest, and despite the Bulgarian government's readiness to change sides as the war neared its end, the Red Army invaded anyway. Centrepiece of the monument is a Red Army soldier flanked by a worker and a peasant woman with a child, an archetypal symbol of Bulgaro-Soviet friendship: you'll see it in monuments and fading propaganda billboards throughout the land.

Orlov Most and Borisova Gradina (Freedom Park)

To the east, the modest dribble of the River Perlovska is spanned by **Orlov Most** or Eagle Bridge, crowned with four ferocious-looking birds of prey. Set amid weeping willows, the bridge marks the spot where liberated prisoners of war were greeted by their victorious Russian allies and compatriots in the war of 1878. From here the main highway to Plovdiv (formerly bul. Lenin, it has now reverted to its original name of Tsarigradsko shose) heads southeast, flanked on one side by Sofia's largest park, **Borisova Gradina** (literally "Boris' Garden", although many locals still use its Communist-era name, *Park na svobodata* or "Freedom Park"). Partially influenced by St James' Park in London, it was laid out during the reign of Tsar Boris III, and harbours a rich variety of flowers and trees, becoming more densely wooded the further southeast you go. With its lily ponds, bandstands and crisscrossing paths, it's an ideal place for an aimless stroll, although many of Sofia's principal sports facilities are situated here too.

Guarding the northern entrance to the park, the elegant bowl of the Vasil Levski stadium is home to the national soccer side, and also harbours the **National Museum of Physical Culture and Sport** (officially Tues–Fri 10am–6pm). In the years following the Liberation, sporting activity was considered an effective way of raising general standards of health, education and readiness for war, as various sepia photographs of turn-of-the-century rifle clubs and cycling associations (each with their own ceremonial tunics and hats) attest. Other relics range from the absorbing – skiing equipment used by Bulgaria's inter-war alpinists – to the downright bizarre – the hairnet of "legendary" 800m runner Grigorii Pedan – but there's not yet any material relating to more recent national heroes such as world high jump champion Stefka Kostadinova or 1994's European Footballer of the Year, Hristo Stoichkov. Unsurprisingly, there's no mention of the alleged steroid-gobbling exploits of Bulgaria's scandal-shrouded weightlifting team either.

Yuzhen Park and the NDK

On summer evenings city-centre office workers, shoppers and youngsters pour down bul. Vitosha to **Yuzhen Park** (literally, "Southern Park") to drink coffee or stroll between increasingly weed-choked flowerbeds. Outshining Borisova Gradina as an evening parade ground for the city's youth, the park also holds two structures symbolizing Bulgaria's achievements.

The **Thirteen Hundred Years Monument** is boldly (some say hideously) modernist: huge wrench-shaped blocks emerging from a pit that represents centuries of servitude, garnished with anguished-looking figures (one of whom, it's rumoured, bears the features of former Party leader Todor Zhivkov) and inscribed with nineteenth-century freedom fighter Vasil Levski's maxim: "We are in time and time is in us" ("We transform it and it transforms us" he continued, to clarify the message).

At the top end of the park, the gleaming **NDK** or **National Palace of Culture** (*Natsionalen Dvorets na Kulturata*) rears up like a spaceship come to earth. Covering an area of 17,000 square metres, the complex contains concert halls, congress facilities, press centres, a disco and a subterranean arcade packed with clothes stalls selling cheap T-shirts and jeans. The building originally bore the name of Lyudmila Zhivkova, daughter of Todor Zhivkov, who died of a brain tumour while still in her thirties. Lyudmila was a powerful figure, running the ministry of culture like a personal fiefdom, but her interest in eastern religions and her efforts to promote Bulgarian culture abroad made her quite popular among Bulgarian intellectuals. But the most telling aspect of the NDK was its colossal cost, and with this in mind, Sofians invented a sarcastic pun on its initials, which can also stand for "another hole in the belt".

South of the NDK, the park degenerates into overgrown patches of grass traversed by badly maintained pathways, and there's not much point in venturing further unless you're keen to investigate the geological exhibits in the **Museum of Earth and Man** (*Muzei na Zemyata i Horata*; Tues–Sat 10am–6pm; 70¢) at bul. Cherni Vrâh 4. Housed in a former armoury, it's a worthy but dull display of the world's minerals and the techniques used to mine them; most striking are the enormous quartz crystals of varying hues crowding the main hall.

The Zoopark

Of all Sofia's city-bound attractions, the **Zoopark** (daily 9am–5pm; 30¢), 3km southeast of Yuzhen Park, is the only one you can't really walk to from the centre. While the large complex of concrete compounds has seen better days, and many of its cages stand empty, there are enough beasts on display to make a visit worthwhile if zoos are your thing. The tigers, leopards and bears (the latter occupying a large pit at the zoo's western gate) are currently the biggest draws. There are several alfresco cafés inside the zoo, but not much in the way of substantial food, and there is very little shade, particularly at the height of summer.

To get to the zoo, catch tram #2, #12 or #19 from Graf Ignatiev to pl. Velchova Zavera (the first stop after emerging from the park), and change to bus #67 (get off at the second stop) or #102, which terminates at the zoo's eastern gate.

Mount Vitosha

A wooded mass of granite 19km long by 17km wide, **MOUNT VITOSHA,** whose foothills begin some 7km from the city centre, is very much a part of the capital and is the source of its pure water and fresh breezes. *Sofiantsi* come here to picnic, gather wild herbs and berries, savour magnificent views or to ski, and the ascent of its highest peak, **Cherni Vrâh**, has become a traditional test of stamina for hikers. Vitosha's two main recreation centres, connected to the city by asphalt road, are **Aleko**, just above the treeline and within easy reach of the summit, and **Zlatni Mostove**, on the wooded western flanks of the mountain. Both give access to Cherni Vrâh; Aleko is the closer, but the longer ascent from Zlatni Mostove takes you through more varied terrain.

Routes from central Sofia to Vitosha pass through the villages (suburbs, really) nestling beneath its foothills: **Boyana** is the site of a famed medieval church, while **Dragalevtsi**, with an attractive wood-shrouded **monastery** just above it, and **Simeonovo** are the starting points for the ski lifts to Aleko. None of the above villages however, are worthy stopoffs in their own right: despite their status as exclusive suburbs for Sofia's post-Communist nouveaux-riches, they remain drab, uninspiring little places overshadowed by the glory of the mountain above.

Skiing is possible on Vitosha from late December through to mid-March, with Aleko providing access to the principal pistes. There's a small winter resort here with three hotels, where you can enquire about equipment rental and sign up for ski schools. However, Aleko currently doesn't feature in any of the package holiday brochures, and independent travellers interested in skiing on Vitosha would probably be better off staying in the small hotels in the village suburbs of Simeonovo and Dragalevtsi below, from where they can ascend the mountain by ski lift.

Getting to Vitosha

Public transport to Mt Vitosha is fairly straightforward, with **buses** for Dragalevtsi, Simeonovo and Aleko starting from the **Hladilnika** terminus on Sofia's southern outskirts, at the end of tram routes #9 and #12. After disembarking from the tram, head through a small bazaar area and turn left: buses for Vitosha destinations depart from stands 300m away at the end of the street. You can take bus #66 straight to Aleko or head instead for the Aleko-bound lifts at Dragalevtsi and Simeonovo. Which one you choose will largely depend on what day it is: both the Dragalevtsi chair lift and Simeonovo gondola only definitely work at weekends and during school holidays, and can't be relied upon the rest of the time. In addition, they're usually closed for maintenance in May and October. From the Hladilnika terminus, bus #64 goes to Dragalevtsi village then Boyana Church every 20–30 minutes; bus #66 goes to Aleko approximately every 30 minutes; bus #93 goes to the Dragalevtsi chair lift every 30 minutes, but only when the chair lift is running; bus #98 goes to Dragalevtsi village and Simeonovo village every 20–30 minutes; and bus #122 goes to the Simeonovo gondola every 30–40 minutes, but only when the gondola is running.

Buses for Zlatni Mostove leave from the **Ovcha Kupel** bus station southwest of the city centre, on the main road to Pernik, Blagoevgrad and Greece. To get there, take tram #5 from behind the National History Museum (also known as Palace of Justice or *Sâdebna Palata*) and travel eleven stops until you see the grubby concrete bus station buildings on your right. From here, bus #61 goes to Zlatni Mostove (Mon–Sat 7 daily; Sun every 30min), and bus #62 goes to Kopitoto (Mon–Sat 3 daily; Sun roughly hourly).

In addition, you can get to Simeonovo village on bus #67 (every 20–30 minutes) from **pl. Velchova Zavera** (on tram routes #2, #12 and #19).

As a rule, there are more buses to Vitosha on Sundays than on other days of the week, especially if you're aiming for Zlatni Mostove. **Journey times** from Sofia to any of the Mount Vitosha destinations take between 30 minutes and an hour, depending on the traffic and weather conditions. Sofia public transport tickets and travelcards are valid for all the above services except for buses #61, #62 and #66, for which seperate tickets must be bought from kiosks at the relevant terminals.

Dragalevtsi and Simeonovo

Arriving in **DRAGALEVTSI**, 3km south of the Hladilnika terminus, you'll either be dropped in the centre of the village or at the **Dragalevtsi chair lift** ($1 each way to Aleko), some 30 minutes' walk above the village square. Ascending to Aleko via the **Bai Krâstyo** middle station in about 20 minutes, the lift offers excellent views of Sofia stretched out on the plain to the north. An asphalt path winds up from the Dragalevtsi lift station to **Dragalevski monastery**, a peaceful spot enshrouded by beech woods which serves as the summer residence of the Bulgarian patriarch. There's a fourteenth-century church – the only part of the original monastery that remains – and cells around its leafy courtyard; which

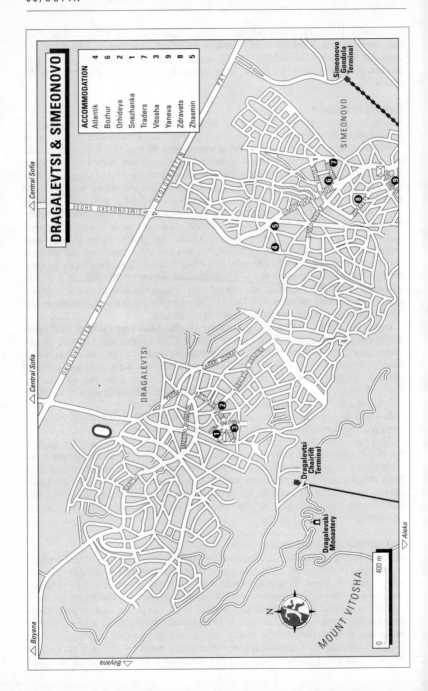

DRAGALEVTSI & SIMEONOVO

ACCOMMODATION

Atlantik	4
Bozhur	6
Orhideya	2
Snezhanka	1
Traders	7
Vitosha	3
Yaneva	9
Zdravets	8
Zhasmin	5

Central Sofia

Central Sofia

Boyana

Boyana

Aleko

DRAGALEVTSI

SIMEONOVO

Simeonovo Gondola Terminal

Dragalevtsi Chairlift Terminal

Dragalevski Monastery

MOUNT VITOSHA

OKOLOVRASTEN PAT

SIMEONOVSKO SHOSE

SIMEONOVSKO SHOSE

N

400 m

0

during the nineteenth century sheltered the revolutionary Vasil Levski. The monastery comes alive on August 15, the **Feast of the Assumption** (*Uspenie Bogorodichno* or more colloquially *Golyama Bogoroditsa*), when families from far and wide spend the day picnicking in the grounds or praying to the Virgin, the monastery's patron.

From Dragalevtsi, you can catch bus #98 to **SIMEONOVO**, the next village-suburb to the east, and terminus of the **Simeonovo gondola** ($1.50 each way to Aleko), which gives great views of the Sofia plain. For details of accommodation in Simeonovo and Dragalevtsi, see p.70.

Aleko

Some twenty minutes beyond Dragalevtsi, bus #66 arrives at **ALEKO**, an expanding **winter sports centre** with three hotels (the *Prostor*, *Moreni* and *Shtastlivetsa*), and a range of pistes to suit all grades of skiers. During the summer, the area is packed with weekending *Sofiantsi* enjoying picnics or taking advantage of the numerous hiking possibilities that radiate outwards from the *Shtastlivetsa Hotel*, the area's central point of reference. The resort takes its name from nineteenth-century writer Aleko Konstantinov (see p.170): in 1895, back in the days when hill-walking was an expression of patriotic love for the country rather than mere recreation, Konstantinov led a party of three hundred idealistic Bulgarians (Ivan Vazov was an enthusiastic participant) in an assault on Vitosha's highest point, Cherni Vrâh – a climb that marked the beginning of alpine pursuits in Bulgaria.

The chair lift from Aleko to Stenata, the crag which overlooks Aleko, usually works on summer weekends. If not, it's quite easy to scramble up there in 15–20 minutes. From here, you can see the 2290m **Cherni Vrâh** ("black peak") straight ahead, a clump of rocks surround by a grassy plateau – an easy 15-minute hike.

Boyana

Two kilometres northwest of Dragalevtsi – and connected by bus #64 – lies **BOYANA**, another affluent village suburb in the shadow of Vitosha. Just above Boyana's village square is a small garden surrounding the ivy-covered **Boyana church**, home to a justly famed set of **medieval frescos**, largely executed in 1259. With their realism and rejection of the Byzantine style, these anticipate the work of Giotto, which heralded the beginning of the Italian Renaissance. As well as biblical themes, the unknown artist drew on contemporary life for inspiration: clothing the saints in medieval Bulgarian dress and setting garlic, radishes and bread – the peasants' staples – on the table in the *Last Supper*. Perhaps the finest portraits are those of Boyana's patrons, Desislava and Sebastocrator Kaloyan (depicted holding the church in the customary fashion), and the haloed figures of the king and queen, Asen and Irina. Unfortunately, you need official permission from the Bulgarian Ministry of Culture to see the frescos, so most visitors make do with the replicas housed in the nearby **museum** (Tues–Sun 9am–5pm; $1), where you can also watch an English-language video (for an additional $1) about the history of the church.

Zlatni Mostove

From Sofia's Ovcha Kupel bus station, buses #61 and #62 ascend through the forests that cloak the western shoulder of Vitosha. Bus #62 forks left to wind its way up to the **Kopitoto** area on a spur of the mountain, where there's a TV mast, a hotel-restaurant (currently undergoing restoration) and numerous woodland walks, while bus #61 carries on to **ZLATNI MOSTOVE** ("golden bridges"). This area of mixed deciduous and evergreen forest is centred around the so-called **Stone River**, a ribbon of huge boulders running down the mountainside that was once the moraine of an ancient glacier. Beneath the boulders burbles a rivulet that used to attract gold-panners, hence the locality's name. Tracks lead from the bus stop in all directions, past trade union-owned rest homes and small shacks selling drinks and snacks. The most popular walking route is a well-signed, medium-difficulty ascent of Cherni Vrâh, taking 2–3 hours. The path leads up the side of the Stone River, passing the Kumata and Konyarnika huts before emerging above the treeline onto the grassy mountain top.

Kremikovtsi

Twenty kilometres northeast of Sofia, nestling in a crook of the Balkan mountains, the village of **KREMIKOVTSI** is home to one of western Bulgaria's most charming ecclesiastical attractions, the fourteenth-century **monastery of St George**. Occupying a spur of a fir-shrouded hill overlooking the village, the original monastery church lurks in a small courtyard, dwarfed by a more modern church built at the beginning of this century. The original church's interior is covered with vibrant frescos dating from the 1500s, evidence that wealthy Bulgarian nobles were spending considerable sums of money on religious art even at the height of the Ottoman occupation. A picture of St George, seated on a throne and using a dragon as a footrest, straddles the archway leading through to the naos, the inner sanctum of the church. The naos itself is dominated by a rendition of the Virgin Mary behind the altar, arms outstretched in a protective gesture. Look out, too, for a niche on the right bearing another portrayal of St George, this time riding his horse and planting a spear in the dragon's throat.

The best time **to visit** the monastery is at the weekend or on one of the big feast days, as the caretaker who unlocks the church for visitors can be difficult to track down at other times. The monastery attracts most visitors on St George's Day (*Gyergyovden*, May 6), although it also gets pretty busy on other big holidays, notably Assumption (*Golyama Bogoroditsa*, August 15) and the Birth of the Virgin (*Malka Bogoroditsa*, September 8). Note that there's nowhere to eat or drink in the village, save for a couple of rudimentary cafés, so bring your own supplies.

Getting to Kremikovtsi

Tram #22 runs from Knyaz Dondukov to the **Avtogara Iztok** in the northeastern suburbs (on some signs Avtogara Iztok is called "Avtostantsia Iztok", to differentiate it from Avtogara Poduyane, which is sometimes also misleadingly referred to as Avtogara Iztok by locals), where you change to **bus** #117. The bus passes the sprawling Kremikovtsi steel works before entering Kremikovtsi village: get off at the village library (*chitalishte*), a two-storey concrete building where the bus veers off to the right. Instead of following the route of the bus, bear left uphill through the village, and the monastery is about thirty minutes' walk; you should be able to pick out the church's cupola and bell tower on the hillside ahead.

If you're **driving**, head out of Sofia along Botevgradsko shose for about 10km, then turn left to Kremikovtsi at the KAT (traffic police) checkpoint.

Eating

While none of Sofia's restaurants could be classed as truly outstanding, you'll at least find a greater choice than anywhere else in the country. Mainstream restaurants aiming at modern European cuisine tend to be disappointing, and you would be better off sticking to the increasing number of establishments rediscovering the virtues of **traditional Bulgarian cooking**. Many of these restaurants feature **live music** – usually an inoffensive mixture of folk and international easy-listening. There's also a number of **foreign-cuisine** restaurants which, although few would pass muster in their homelands, add to the variety. Decent, inexpensive Chinese restaurants are thick on the ground, especially in the streets just west of the centre around the Zhenski pazar. Summer brings out the best in the city, when places with **outdoor seating** remain packed well into the evening.

For daytime snacks, the many **fast-food** joints around the Banya Bashi Mosque and along bul. Vitosha serve *kyofteta*, *kebapcheta* and other indigenous dishes. The salads and sandwiches at *Kenar*, bul. Vitosha 19 and Stamboliiski 55, feature traditional Bulgarian ingredients and rarely disappoint, while *Mimas*, on the corner of Graf Ignatiev and bul. Levski, offers the city's best kebabs and burgers and stays open well into the early hours. For even later dining, try *Kravai*, on the northeastern corner of Yuzhen Park at Frityof Nansen 1, a 24hr Chinese takeaway. Elsewhere, fast food in Sofia is pretty uninspiring, so you may want to stick to one of the international chains such as *KFC* at Graf Ignatiev 6 and Stamboliiski 28; *Macdonald's* at pl. Slaveykov; *Pizza Hut* at Knyaz Dondukov 7; and the Greek-owned burger palace *Goodys* on pl. Sveta Nedelya. For details of the city's **cafés**, many of which serve light snacks, cakes and lunches, see "Drinking" on p.93.

Restaurants

For most visitors, eating in a **restaurant** is relatively cheap, especially if you stay out of deluxe hotels and avoid imported drinks; even in the topnotch establishments, a three-course meal with drink rarely exceeds $8–10 per person. Most restaurants open from about 11am until 11pm, with some closing one day a week, often Sunday. We've included telephone numbers below, of those restaurants where **reservations** are a good idea at weekends.

Bulgarian and international cuisine

33 Chairs, Asen Zlatarov 14 (☎442981). Expensive, top-quality restaurant fifteen minutes southeast of the centre. It has an extensive French-Bulgarian menu and is popular with the business community.

BIAD, General Gurko 16. Busy central restaurant which doubles as one of Sofia's main venues for live folk-pop performers.

Continental Plaza, corner of bul. Vitosha and bul. Bâlgariya, behind the NDK (☎951 5430). Elite hangout with expensive international food and a high-society clientele.

Europa, ul. Alabin 34. Good chicken dishes at moderate prices, in a basement next to the cinema of the same name.

Krim, Slavyanska 17 (☎870131). Upmarket food, including the occasional Russian speciality, served in a nineteenth-century mansion. There's a nice garden, and live music on summer evenings. The atmosphere is quite snooty, and it's best to reserve in advance.

Otvâd aleyata, zad shkafa ("Beyond the alley, behind the cupboard"), Budapeshta 31 (☎835581). Upmarket place hidden away in residential streets northeast of the centre, with pleasant garden seating and Art-Nouveauish touches inside. The food is a mixture of modern European and traditional Bulgarian. The main courses don't always live up to their billing but the sweets are excellent.

Planet, Ekzarh Iosif 37 (☎981 1713). International food served in glitzy surroundings, attracting an upmarket, but youthful and arty crowd. It's also a cool place to drink: bar stools are arranged around a large central stage where musicians (jazz, rock and cabaret) perform.

Retrokristal, pl. Kristal. Upmarket venue above the Kristal café, with antique-shop decor and attentive service. The menu offers an imaginative spin on traditional Bulgarian favourites with some excellent salads and a good range of vegetarian courses.

Rotisserie Nationale, Neofit Riski 40 (☎9801717). This atmospheric cellar-like restuarant has a good reputation and offers a classy international menu. Dress is smart and reservations are essential.

SBZh (Union of Bulgarian Journalists), Graf Ignatiev 4. Good-quality Bulgarian food served in a spacious dining room with an inter-war ambience of faded gentility.

Tino, bul. Levski 22. Fairly standard choice of Bulgarian dishes, with big portions, reliable quality, and reasonably cheap prices. There's some outdoor seating, but it's on quite a noisy street.

Trops-kâshta, Sâborna. Excellent-value self-service restaurant offering tasty Bulgarian standards. Closes at 9pm. There's another branch just east of pl. Sveta Nedelya on ul. Sâborna.

Vâltsite, Vitosha 140 (525032). Upmarket place offering an imaginative crossover of Bulgarian and international cuisine. Noted for good service, big salads, and a large choice of vegetarian dishes, although the portions are small, so you'll have to order two or three veggie dishes to make a meal.

Asian, Latin American and Italian cuisine

Asia, Chiprovtsi 4. One of the better Chinese restaurants in the streets around the Zhenski pazar. It's always crowded, and serves enormous portions, but doggy bags are provided on request.

Baalbek, Vasil Levski 4. Highly regarded Lebanese establishment, with a sit-down restaurant upstairs and fast food counter, serving kebabs, shawarma and falafel, on the ground floor.

Chen, ul. Rakovski 86. Relatively expensive Chinese restaurant opposite the opera, though you're paying for the attentive service and chic ambience rather than the food.

Eddy's, bul. Vitosha 4. Tex-Mex place in a basement near the National History Museum. The food doesn't always live up to the atmosphere: the regular live music (usually local bands playing rock and blues covers) makes it a lively, if noisy place to spend an evening. Stays open til 3am.

King's Club, bul. Vitosha 108. Indonesian restaurant serving lots of saté and fried rice dishes.

Mexicano, Krakra 11 (☎446598). Quite classy restaurant situated in the headquarters of the Union of Bulgarian Architects. The food is authentic, and an elegant garden makes this a good place to spend a summer evening.

Pizza Palace, bul. Vitosha 34. Probably the best of the city-centre pizzerias, with acceptable if not-quite-Italian food and attentive staff; it's busy, and with a fast turnover.

Ramayana, Hristo Belchev 32. Indian restaurant with a pleasant garden, one block east of bul. Vitosha. There's a wide range of vegetarian dishes, though the food might disappoint real fans of eastern cuisine.

Sekura, in the *Kempinski Zografski* hotel, bul. Dzheims Bauchâr 100 (☎62518). Top-class Japanese restaurant: a meal with saké will set you back a small fortune by any standards.

Tai Pan, Alabin 46. Chinese restaurant near the National History Museum offering mid-price, reasonably authentic, Eastern food.

Drinking

Drinking in Sofia is a predominantly daytime or early evening activity, centring on the city's numerous cafés or the ubiquitous kiosks that dole out coffee, juice and sometimes alcohol. **Cafés** tend to close at around 8 or 9pm, after which the choice is pretty much limited to restaurants and hotel bars – although Western-European-style **bars** are on the increase, especially in the streets bordering bul. Vitosha. Most drinking venues lie on or near central Sofia's main thoroughfare, bul. Vitosha, or in the grid of streets that lies to either side of it; there's little point in straying beyond this area unless seeking out a specific place listed below. Most bars in Sofia close between 11pm and midnight, unless otherwise stated below.

Cafés and bars

Art Klub, Ivan Asen II 4. Café-bar near Orlov Most, specializing in live and taped jazz.

At the Mayors', ul. Parizh. Vast basement beer hall with massive tables (expect to share), featuring live music or a DJ. Good service, lively locals and chicken-and-chips-style snacks.

Bohemi, bul. Levski 55. Beer-hall-style venue on two levels with plenty of outdoor seating. Imported and local beers, and a substantial choice of nibbles, but rather indifferent service.

Café-bar 703, Tsar Shishman 24. Popular city-centre bar near the church of Sveti Sedmochislentsi, with dark red decor and a couple of cosy snug bars.

Dvete Furkli, Kârnigradska 14. Small daytime café and cake shop just off bul. Vitosha. It's the best of the central cafés, with great quality cakes and good service.

Funky's Pub, Shandor Petyofi 26A. Lively bar in a suburban basement, serving Belgian beer and pricey food. Nightly live music is provided by local bands playing Western rock covers. Expect to pay a cover charge of about $1.50. Open until 2am.

Jimmy's Sladoledena kâshta, General Parensov 25. Mecca for ice cream (both eat-in and take-out), as well as the usual coffee-and-cake café fare.

JJ Murphy's, Karnigradska 6. Themed Irish pub one block west of bul. Vitosha, with a mixed Bulgarian and expat clientele. Open til 1am, food served til 11pm.

Maimunarnika, Borisova Gradina. Dull kiosk serving drinks in the city's biggest park (it's just behind the Velodrome). Acts as a meeting place for the city's grunge and metal-fixated youth on summer evenings, and sometimes hosts gigs on Friday and Saturday nights if the weather is fine.

Makrit, Patriarh Eftimii 61. Wicker furniture and pot plants make this one of the best places in central Sofia for a relaxed, intimate drink.

Mr Punch, ul. Rakovski 114 (entrance round the corner on ul. Stefan Karadzha). Roomy pub-style basement venue with large eating area and loud live music (mostly rock cover bands). Cover charge is approx $1.

Planet, Ekzarh Iosif 37. Stylish cross between bar, restaurant and nightclub (see "restaurants" opposite).

Rock Café Luciano, corner of Vasil Levski and General Gurko. Large, lively basement bar with a substantial snack food menu, and video screens playing loud rock.

Schweik, Vitosha 1A. International beers (including excellent Czech ones) and sausagey snacks in a basement just off bul. Vitosha.

Swinging Hall, Dragan Tsankov 8. Modern suburban bar serving imported drinks at Western prices. Live music (usually pop/rock or jazz) on two stages. Open well after midnight. Cover charge is approx $1.

Tequila, Levski Pametnik. Classy but often heaving late-night drinking joint above the *Hotel Serdika*. Cover charge is approx $1.

Vienska Sladkarnitsa, Parchevich 36. Popular city-centre place serving good-value cocktails, along with cakes and ice cream.

Entertainment

Sofia's real forte is **drama, ballet and classical music**, all of which are of a high standard and very inexpensive. **Youth culture** is less prevalent, although it is beginning to make its presence felt. Cultural listings are usually to be found in the back pages of the daily press; otherwise **information and tickets** for most venues are available from the Concert Bureau at bul. Tsar Osvoboditel 2 (Mon–Fri 8am–noon & 3–7pm), or in the NDK centre. You can also get information on theatres and concerts by telephoning ☎171, but don't bank on getting a foreign-language speaker.

The most popular form of entertainment for many locals is the **cinema** – and the flood of (subtitled) American movies sweeping the country means that you won't have any problems understanding the dialogue. The biggest of the cinemas in the city centre are the Serdika, bul. Yanko Sakâzov 1; Vitosha, on the corner of Vitosha and Patriarh Eftimii; Evropa Palace, Alabin 34; and Novo Kino Slaveykov, pl. Slaveykov. Dom na Kinoto, Ekzarh Iosif 37, shows **cult films** and Hollywood classics.

Theatre

Plays are, naturally, performed in Bulgarian, so not knowing the language is a distinct drawback, but the general standard of performances can make a visit to the theatre rewarding. Performances at the *Kuklen teatâr*, or puppet theatre, General Gurko 14, are popular with children.

Dramatichen Teatâr Sofia, bul. Yanko Sakâzov 23A. Big productions and musicals.

Malâk gradski teatâr "zad kanala", bul. Yanko Sakâzov 25. The best place to see modern works in a small, intimate auditorium, next door to the *Dramatichen Teatâr Sofia*.

Mladezhki teatâr, pl. Narodno sâbranie. Youth theatre, with consistently good avant-garde productions.

Naroden Teatâr Ivan Vazov, Vasil Levski 1A. Works by eminent Bulgarians and classical writers performed by the national theatre company.

Sâlza i Smyah, Slavyanska 5. The oldest professional theatre company in Sofia, dating from 1892, and maintaining a reputation for challenging drama.

Satirichen teatâr Aleko Konstantinov, Stefan Karadzha 26. The place to go for comedy and cabaret.

Music

The National Palace of Culture, or **NDK**, is the venue for many of the bigger symphonic concerts or operatic productions; otherwise **symphonic music** can be heard at the Zala Bâlgariya, Benkovski 1, or the Zala Slaveykov, pl. Slaveykov. The traditional home of **opera and ballet** is the Narodna Opera, bul. Dondukov 58 (☎877011). The Stefan Makedonski State Musical Theatre, Panayot Volov 3 (☎442321), tends to concentrate on lighter operetta and musicals.

Festivals to look out for are the **Sofia Music Weeks** (late May to late June), featuring international soloists and ensembles; the **Music Evenings** (early Dec), concentrating on the best native classical musicians; and the November **Jazz Festival**. Festival events take place in the NDK and in the Zala Univerziada, Shipchenski prohod 2 (tram #20 from the Levski monument).

Popular music

Apart from the glut of cabaret bands playing cover versions to diners at the city's hotels and restaurants, Sofia has little in the way of a local contemporary **music scene**. There's no shortage of local grunge, rap and metal bands, but venues to see them are few and far between. Groups playing cover versions of anything from Pink Floyd to country and western to punk appear at *Funky's Pub*, *Mr Punch*, *Swingin' Hall* (see "Cafés and bars", p.93), *Biblioteka* (see discos, below), or at *Eddy's* (see "Restaurants", p.92). Other gigs occasionally take place in cultural centres and student halls, but it's difficult to get to know of them, unless you keep your eyes peeled for hastily photocopied, Cyrillic-script fly posters. Bulgarian pop stars, and the occasional Western act who can be bothered to make the trip, play in the NDK or in the large multipurpose halls such as Zala Universiada, Shipchenski prohod 2.

Discos

There's not much in the way of an established club scene in Sofia, and hip late-night venues change from one year to the next. Places worth checking out (expect to pay a cover charge of about $1 in each of them) include *Aliby*, an invigorating outdoor summer venue in the velodrome in Borisova Gradina, playing everything from techno to folk-pop; *Biblioteka*, in the basement of the National Library building on Oborishte, a busy youthful rock and pop oriented disco featuring regular live bands; *Chervilo*, a fashionable place in the military club on Tsar Osvoboditel which has different styles of music on different nights of the week; and *Yalta*, ul. Aksakov 31, a pulsating weekend pick-up venue of many years' standing, opposite the university.

Football

Sofia has two **football teams** with a mass following. Levski, originally the Interior Ministry (that is, the police and the secret services) team, have been the most successful in recent years, winning a string of first division championships. They play either at the national Vasil Levski stadium at the western end of Borisova Gradina or at their own Stadion Georgi Asparuhov, northeast of the city centre on Todorini kukli (tram #1 from bul. Levski). Levski's bitter rivals are the Bulgarian Army club CSKA, who play at Stadion CSKA in the middle of the Borisova Gradina park. The capital's two other clubs are Slaviya, who play at Sporten Kompleks Slaviya just behind the Ovcha Kupel bus station (tram #5 from behind the National History Museum), and Lokomotiv, whose ground is on bul. Rozhen in the northwestern suburb of Nadezhda (tram #12 from the train station). Derby matches between Sofia sides, as well as matches involving the national side, take place at the Vasil Levski stadium at the western end of Borisova Gradina. **Tickets** for regular league games (rarely costing more than $1 or so) are usually sold at turnstiles on the day of the match. For international fixtures, buy tickets from the stadium box office as far in advance as possible.

Listings

Airlines Aeroflot, bul. Tsar Osvoboditel 2 (☎980 0067); Air France, bul. Sâborna 2 (☎981 7830); Air Ukraine, bul. Stamboliiski 24 (☎873181); Alitalia, Graf Ignatiev 40 (☎981 6702); Austrian Airlines, bul. Knyaginya Mariya Luiza 68 (☎931 1472); Balkan, pl. Narodno sâbranie 12 (☎880663); British Airways, ul. Alabin 58 (☎981 7000); Czech Airlines, bul. Sâborna 9

(☎815289); JAT (Yugoslavia), bul. Vasil Levski 1 (☎988 0419); KLM, bul. Vasil Levski 82a (☎894919); LOT, Stamboliiski 27 (☎980 3293); Lufthansa, bul. Sâborna 9 (☎980 4101); Malev, Patriarh Eftimii 19 (☎884061); Olympic, bul. Stamboliiski 46 (☎981 4545); Swissair, bul. Knyaginya Mariya Luiza 66 (☎931 0871); and Turkish Airlines, Sâborna 11A (☎883596).

American Express Megatours, ul. Levski 1 (☎880419 or 981 4201).

Bookstalls The outdoor bookstalls at pl. Slaveykov and in the pedestrian subway outside Sofia University often have foreign-language books, as well as out-of-print art books and Bulgarian–English dictionaries.

Car rental Avis, Tsar Kaloyan 8 (☎981 4960), at the airport (☎738023), and at the *Balkan Sheraton* and *Kempinski Zografski* hotels; Budget, at the *Rodina* hotel (☎544782); Europcar, Pozitano 8 (☎860864, fax 883593), at the airport (☎720157), and at the *Kempinski Zografski*, *Orbita*, and *Rodina* hotels; Eurodollar, bul. Vitosha 25 (☎875779, fax 981 0884), at the airport (☎657102), and at the *Kempinski Zografski* hotel; Hertz, General Gurko 10 (☎980 0461, fax 885729) and at the airport (☎791447).

Car repairs BMW and Rover at Daru Car, Iliya Beshkov 2, Druzhba (☎798247, fax 799053); Peugeot at Sofia France Auto, 10km out along Tsarigradsko Shose (☎971 2444); Renault at Pro Mobile, Georgi Bonchev 2 (☎720225); Volkswagen at Unitrade X, Momina Cheshma 12, Druzhba 2 (☎793753, fax 793772). Otherwise seek advice at the Union of Bulgarian Motorists, ul. Sveta Sofia 6 (☎883856; ☎146 for the breakdown service). There's also a cluster of shops selling spare parts (*avtochasti*) along ul. Kozlodui near the central station.

Currency exchange There's no shortage of exchange bureaux on bul. Vitosha and neighbouring roads, which will exchange cash only, but beware of high commission rates charged by those on the central boulevards (even though many of them display "no commission" signs). For travellers' cheques and credit card advances, Bulbank on pl. Sveta Nedelya, is the most reliable bank.

Dry cleaning Hemiisko Chishchenie, Knyaginya Maria Luiza 17.

Embassies and consulates Albania, Krakra 10 (☎946 1222); Austria, Shipka 4 (☎981 1721); Belgium, pl. Velchova Zavera 1 (☎963 3622); Denmark, bul. Tsar Osvoboditel 10 (☎980 0830); France, Oborishte 29 (☎946 1579); Germany, Frederik Zholiyo Kyuri 25 (☎963 4518); Greece, Evlogi Georgiev 103 (☎946 1027); Hungary, ul. 6 Septemvri 57 (☎963 0460); Italy, Shipka 2 (☎980 7747); Macedonia, Frederik Zholiyo Kyuri 17 (☎701003); Netherlands, Galichitsa 38 (☎962 5785); Romania, Shipchenski prohod 1 (Tues 2–5pm, Wed & Thur 10am–noon; ☎971 2858); Russia, Dragan Tsankov 28 (☎963 0914); South Africa, Vasil Aprilov 3 (☎442916); Spain, Sheinovo 27 (☎9433034); Sweden, Alfred Nobel 4 (☎971 2431); Switzerland, Shipka 33 (☎943 3068); Turkey, bul. Levski 80 (☎980 2270); UK, bul. Levski 38 (Mon–Thurs 9am–noon & 2–3.30pm, Fri 9am–noon; ☎980 1220); USA, Sâborna 1 (☎980 5241: consular section at Kapitan Andreev 1; Mon–Fri 9am–5pm); Yugoslavia, Shipka 7 (Mon–Fri 9am–noon; ☎943 4590). Australians, Canadians and New Zealanders have no representation in Sofia, but the British Embassy will help. Irish citizens should contact their nearest embassy (in Budapest, Hungary ☎00361/302 9600, fax 302 9599) to find out which English-speaking embassy in Sofia is currently looking after their interests.

Hiking and camping equipment Stenata, Knyaz Boris I 117.

Hospitals The city's main casualty department is at Pirogov Emergency Hospital, opposite the *Rodina* hotel, at bul. General Totleben 21 (☎51531). For an ambulance call ☎150.

Libraries British Council, Tulovo 7 (Mon–Fri 9am–noon & 2–5pm); American Centre, Kârnigradska 18 (daily 1–5pm).

Markets The main fruit, vegetable and bric-a-brac market is Zhenski Pazar (literally "the women's market") on Stefan Stambolov. There are also good fruit and veg markets at Rimska stena, just south of the city centre at ul. Hristo Smirnenski; and, best of all, Sitnyakovo, 2km southeast of the centre on ul Shipchenski prohod (tram #20 from Knyaz Dondukov).

Newspapers Foreign newspapers can be bought from the newsstand in the basement of the *Balkan Sheraton* hotel.

Opticians bul. Knyaginya Mariya Luiza 54.

Pharmacies 24hr service at the following: pl. Sveta Nedelya 5; Pârva Chastna Apoteka, Tsar Asen 42.

Photographic supplies Pozitano 24A.

Post office General Gurko 6 (Mon–Sat 7am–8.30pm, Sun 7am–1pm).

Radio BBC World Service (91.0 VHF). The usual English-language services, punctuated by news in Bulgarian every couple of hours.

Shopping The main stores are around the bul. Vitosha, bul. Stamboliiski, Graf Ignatiev area. TsUM at the western end of the Largo stocks everything from shoelaces to satellite dishes,

---

MOVING ON FROM SOFIA

If you're **flying** out of Sofia, call ☎722414 for information on domestic flights, or ☎720672 for international services; bus #84 runs every ten to fifteen minutes from the Orlov Most to the airport, 10km east of town. A full list of airline addresses and telephone numbers appears on pp.95–96.

When leaving Sofia **by train**, remember that tickets for lines covering the northern half of Bulgaria (including the routes to Lom, Vidin, Ruse and Varna) are sold on the ground floor of the station; all others in the basement. The system of platform numbering is incredibly confusing (each platform is also divided into *iztok* – eastern – and *zapad* – western – sections, referred to as *i* and *z* respectively on the departures board), so allow plenty of time to catch your train. Beware, also, of pickpockets, beggars and con merchants who offer to help you onto your train, then make aggressive demands for money. To beat the queues, you can make **advance bookings** at the **Transport Service Centre**, or TsKTON, in the basement shopping arcade below the NDK (Mon–Fri 7am–7.30pm, Sat 7am–2.30pm; ☎590136). The same office handles bookings for sleeper services, as well as selling tickets for **international trains**. International tickets can also be bought from a counter in the Central Station or from the Rila Bureau, General Gurko 5 (Mon–Fri 8am–7pm, Sat 9am–2pm; ☎870777).

The Transport Service Centre sells advance tickets for some **inter-city bus services**, but in many cases you'll have to trek out to the relevant bus station in order to buy a ticket. The most important of these is the **bus park opposite the central station**, where a confusing array of private companies operates services to the provinces. Unfortunately there's no timetable information, and the only thing to do is to arrive early and look for destinations and departure times posted in individual bus windscreens. The biggest of the private bus companies, **Group**, uses a bus park on the opposite side of bul. Knyaginya Mariya Luiza: at least there's a small ticket kiosk here where you can check departure details and make reservations in advance. A few services still use the old state-run bus stations in suburban Sofia – Avtogara Poduyane, Avtogara Ovcha Kupel and Avtogara Yug – which serve different out-of-town regions: see "travel details" overleaf for an idea of which one to head for. To get to **Avtogara Poduyane** (destinations to the north and northeast) on ul. Todorini Kukli, take bus #75 from Orlov Most, or trolleybus #1 from bul. Levski. For **Avtogara Ovcha Kupel** (destinations to the south) take tram #5 from behind the National History Museum, and get off at the eleventh stop; for **Avtogara Yug** (destinations to the southeast), on bul. Dragan Tsankov, catch tram #2 from pl. Sveta Nedelya, or #2 or #19 from Graf Ignatiev. Alight at the stop called Nadlez Dârvenitsa, just beyond the *Park-Hotel Moskva*, and the bus station is immediately beneath you. There are two **international terminals** offering services to Greece, the Former Yugolsavian Republic of Macedonia, Turkey and even further afield; one is at Damian Gruev 38 (☎525004), ten minutes' walk west from the city centre, and the other at Knyaginya Mariya Luiza 84 (☎832665), ten minutes north of the centre.

but it's not the great department store it used to be. For luxury goods head to the shops around the southern end of bul. Vitosha and in the NDK centre. The Bulgarian Association of Craftsmen has a shop selling folksy gifts at bul. Vitosha 14. The souvenir shop in the Ethnographic Museum (round the corner from the ticket office; see p.80) sells woodcarving, embroidery, woollen kilims and folk CDs. Stalls selling paintings, reproduction icons, antiques, lace and embroidery are concentrated around pl. Aleksandâr Nevski and the pedestrian underpass between TsUM and the *Balkan Sheraton*.

Swimming Banya Mariya Luiza outdoor pool in the middle of Borisova Gradina is the place to head for in summer, and is the nearest thing to a beach you'll find this far inland. Otherwise, try the Deva Spartak indoor and outdoor pools, next to the hotel of the same name, bul. Arsenalski (tram #6 from pl. Vâzrazhdane to the end).

Taxis Inex Taxi ☎91919; OK Supertaxi ☎2121.

Telephones ul. Stefan Karadzha, behind the post office (open 24hrs).

Visa extensions Available at the Interior Ministry (*MVR*) building at bul. Knyaginya Mariya Luiza 44.

travel details

Trains

Sofia to: Burgas (6 daily; 6hr 30min); Kazanlâk (6 daily; 3–4hr); Koprivshtitsa (5 daily; 1hr 40min); Pleven (hourly; 3hr); Plovdiv (8 daily; 2hr 30min); Ruse (5 daily; 7hr); Varna (5 daily; 8hr 30min); Vidin (5 daily; 5hr).

Buses

In addition to the scheduled services listed below, a large number of inter-city buses leave from the **bus park opposite the Central Station**. Though there are no regular timetables – destinations and departure times are displayed in the windscreens of the buses – there are usually hourly buses to Plovdiv, and a couple of buses a day to other provincial centres.

Group bus park to: Ahtopol (summer only 1 daily; 8hr 30min); Burgas (2 daily; 7hr); Dobrich (1 daily; 7hr); Gabrovo (2 daily; 3hr 30min); Kârdzhali (3 daily; 5hr); Kiten (summer only 1 daily; 8hr); Lovech (1 daily; 3hr); Nesebâr (summer only 1 daily; 7hr 30min); Razgrad (1 daily; 6hr); Ruse (1 daily; 5hr); Silistra (1 daily; 7hr); Sozopol (summer only 1 daily; 7hr 30min); Svilengrad (1 daily; 5hr); Varna (2 daily; 7hr); Veliko Târnovo (2 daily; 4hr); Vidin (1 daily; 5hr).

Avtogara Ovcha Kupel to: Bansko (3 daily; 3hr); Blagoevgrad (3 daily; 2hr); Dupnitsa (10 daily; 1hr 30min); Gotse Delchev (2 daily; 4hr); Kyustendil (hourly; 2hr); Melnik (1 daily; 4hr); Rila Monastery (summer only 1 daily; 2hr 30min); Rila village (2 daily; 2hr 10min); Sandanski (2 daily; 3hr 30min).

Avtogara Poduyane to: Botevgrad (hourly; 1hr); Gabrovo (1 daily; 3hr 30min); Pravets (4 daily; 1hr); Teteven (2 daily; 2hr 20min); Troyan (3 daily; 3hr).

Avtogara Yug to: Borovets (2 daily; 1hr 30min); Panagyurishte (3 daily; 2hr); Samokov (hourly; 1hr); Velingrad (3 daily; 3hr).

Flights

Sofia to: Burgas (1 daily; 1hr); Gorna Oryahovitsa (1 daily; 45min); Kârdzhali (3 weekly; 1hr); Ruse (1 daily; 45min); Varna (2 daily; 1hr).

International trains

Sofia to: Belgrade (1 daily; 8hr); Budapest (1 daily; 16hr); Bucharest (4 daily; 11hr); Istanbul (1 daily; 15hr); Kiev (1 daily; 38hr); Lviv (1 daily; 31hr); Moscow (2 daily; 45hr); St Petersburg (1 daily; 65hr); Thessaloniki (2 daily; 10hr); Vilnius (1 daily; 51hr).

International buses

Sofia to: Athens (1 daily; 30hr); Bursa (2 weekly, on Tues & Sun; 14hr); Istanbul (2 weekly, on Tues & Sun; 10hr); Ohrid (1 daily; 9hr); Skopje (3 daily; 5hr); Thessaloniki (2 daily; 18hr); Tirana (2 weekly, on Fri & Sun; 20hr).

CHAPTER TWO

THE SOUTHWEST

The landscape of Bulgaria south of the capital is dominated by the River Struma, which rises on the southern slopes of Mt Vitosha before sweeping west then south through a series of arid gorges and fertile flood plains. Both the main southbound train route and the E79 highway to Greece follow the Struma Valley for much of its length, skirting some of the country's most grandiose scenery on the way. Although the major towns along the route are pleasant enough, most of the area's real attractions lie in the mountains to the east.

Formerly noted for their bandits and hermits, the **Rila and Pirin ranges** contain Bulgaria's highest, stormiest peaks: swathed in forests and dotted with alpine lakes they reward exploration by anyone prepared to hike or risk their car's suspension on the backroads. In the Rila range **Borovets** and **Malyovitsa** are major **winter sports** centres, both within easy striking distance from Sofia. On the way you pass through the historic crafts town of **Samokov**, whose artists adorned **Rila Monastery**, the most revered of Bulgarian holy places. The Pirin range is wilder and less developed, although its highest peak, **Mt Vihren**, is accessible from **Bansko**, whose nest of old stone houses makes it easily the most attractive of the mountain towns. On the southern fringes of the Pirin range near the Greek border, the monastery of **Rozhen** lies at the end of a great hike from the village of **Melnik**, known both for its wine and its vernacular architecture.

Slightly nearer to Sofia, the route leading west towards the Former Yugoslav Republic of Macedonia takes you past the ancient **monastery of Zemen** and the spa town of **Kyustendil**, which retains a smattering of Ottoman-period remains.

CYRILLIC PLACE NAMES

BANSKO	БАНСКО	KYUSTENDIL	КЮСТЕНДИЛ
BISTRITSA	БИСТРИЦА	LESHTEN	ЛЕЩЕН
BLAGOEVGRAD	БЛАГОЕВГРАД	MALYOVITSA	МАЛЬОВИЦА
BOROVETS	БОРОВЕЦ	MELNIK	МЕЛНИК
DELCHEVO	ДЕЛЧЕВО	PERNIK	ПЕРНИК
DOBÂRSKO	ДОБЪРСКО	PETRICH	ПЕТРИЧ
DOBRINISHTE	ДОБРИНИЩЕ	RADOMIR	РАДОМИР
DOLEN	ДОЛЕН	RILA	РИЛА
DRAGOMAN	ДРАГОМАН	ROZHEN	РОЖЕН
DUPNITSA	ДУПНИЦА	RUPITE	РУПИТЕ
GOTSE	ГОЦЕ ДЕЛЧЕВ	SAMOKOV	САМОКОВ
DELCHEV		SANDANSKI	САНДАНСКИ
KALOTINA	КАЛОТИНА	SAPAREVA	САПАРЕВА БАНЯ
KARLANOVO	КАРЛАНОВО	BANYA	
KOCHERINOVO	КОЧЕРИНОВО	SIMITLI	СИМИТЛИ
KOVACHEVITSA	КОВАЧЕВИЦА	ZEMEN	ЗЕМЕН

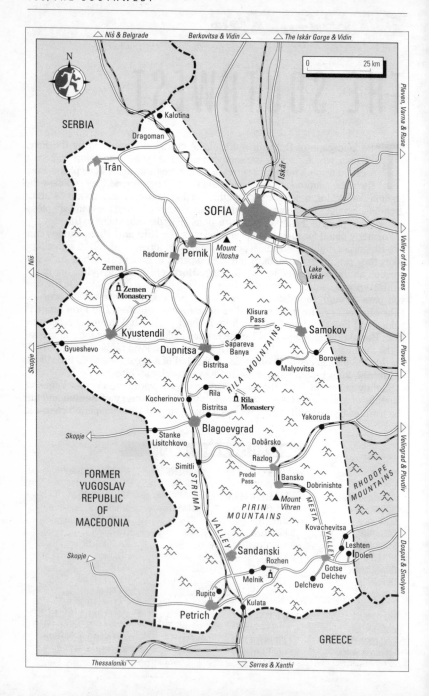

If you're planning any **hiking** in the Rila or Pirin mountains, the Sofia-based adventure tourism specialists Odysseia-In (see p.21 for details) stocks a complete range of maps, and can latch individual travellers onto its weekly hiking tours (mid-June to late October) for $35 a day, including bed and board. For information on other activities in the Rila or Pirin mountains, such as **climbing** or **whitewater rafting**, see "Outdoor activities and eco-tourism" in Basics, p.48.

Destinations like these – along with many others in the southwest – are possible day trips from the capital.

SOUTHWEST OF THE CAPITAL

Aside from its rugged yet fertile landscape and lack of tourists, the chief attractions of the region to the southwest of the capital are the small, reclusive **Zemen Monastery** and the mellow spa town of **Kyustendil**. Three or four slow trains a day between Sofia and Kyustendil stop at Zemen, making it possible to visit the monastery before catching a later train on to Kyustendil; unfortunately, buses between Kyustendil and Sofia take a more direct route, bypassing Zemen. Both buses and trains, though, initially pass through some of Bulgaria's most dismal urban-industrial sprawl, centred around the mining and smelting settlements of **Pernik** and **Radomir**.

Pernik and Radomir

Although both have played a significant role in Bulgarian history, by no stretch of the imagination could **Pernik** or **Radomir** be called attractive, and if you can avoid them, so much the better. Motorists heading south on the E79 can escape with a mere brush of Pernik's eastern outskirts, but train travellers en route to Kyustendil or Dupnitsa will – at least briefly – find themselves in both towns, since the line from Sofia passes through Pernik then divides at Radomir.

Pernik

The remains of a fortress on Krakra Pernishki hill and the derivation of its name – from the Slav god of thunder, Perun – are the sole traces of antiquity in **PERNIK**. After 1891 this hitherto agricultural village became Bulgaria's largest centre of coal mining – an industry that, until recently, employed most of the population. Hence the city's only real attraction is the rarely open **Mining Museum** (officially Mon–Fri 8am–noon & 1–6pm), which is reached from the train and bus stations by heading down ul. Târgovska as far as the high-rise *Hotel Struma* (③), then following the pedestrianized expanse of bul. Krakra Pernishki to its end. During the Communist era miners received wages almost 70 percent higher than other industrial workers and enjoyed early retirement, subsidized holidays and other benefits. Today, however, the mining industry has all but collapsed, and working-class communities like Pernik have fallen on hard times. Nearby at ul. Fizkultura 2, there's a small **History Museum** (again opening times are unpredictable, but officially Tues–Sun 9am–noon & 2–5pm), which holds a collection of ancient Thracian grave tablets found at a nearby sanctuary, as well as a few ethnographical oddments relating to the *kukeri* rites.

Pernik's New Year's **Festival of the Kukeri** represents the city's only real source of excitement, re-enacting the old *survakari* and *kukeri* rites, originally intended to ward off evil spirits and promote fertility respectively. About 3500 costumed dancers dressed as Yetis or nightmare apparitions and armed with wooden swords or axes participate, yelling and chanting. Alas for Pernik the festival's future is uncertain, but happily for tourists, such rites can also be witnessed in Razlog, Bansko, Blagoevgrad and Petrich.

Radomir

On the slopes of "Bare Mountain" in a valley to the southwest, **RADOMIR** developed in conjunction with Pernik, on whose coal and power its industries depended, and now shares Pernik's plight. Historically, the town is renowned as the site of the short-lived **Radomir Republic**, proclaimed by soldiers returning from the front in 1918, who began marching on Sofia to punish those responsible for Bulgaria's entry into World War I. Prevented from doing so by German troops, they so alarmed the government that it released the Agrarian leader Stamboliiski to avert a revolution. Radomir's socialist credentials were enhanced by the town's proximity to the **birthplace of Georgi Dimitrov**, in the village of Kovachevtsi 10km to the west.

Zemen Monastery

Lacking the high walls, tiers of cells and decorative facades that make Rila outstanding, **ZEMEN MONASTERY** (*Zemenski manastir*) seems humble by comparison, and its small twelfth-century cruciform **Church of St Ivan the Theologian** appears similarly modest from the outside. Inside, however, are some of Bulgaria's finest surviving **medieval frescos**, sensitively restored between 1970 and 1974. The frescos – produced by anonymous artists during the 1350s for local noble Konstantin Deyan – are examples of the Macedonian School of painting, which was somewhat cruder and less formalized than the predominant style of Târnovo. Against a background of cool blues and greys, the saints with their golden halos and finery are depicted in hierarchies (including Deyan and his wife Doya); while the narrative scenes are mainly rendered in hues of ochre, with dark blues and reds employed to highlight the gravity of episodes like the *Treason of Judas* and the *Judgement of Pilate*. The monastery is 3km southwest of Zemen itself, overlooking the town from a secluded hillside site. It's easy to find, however: on leaving the train station, turn right along the main road through the village and keep going.

To the southwest of Zemen, the River Struma has carved a rugged nineteen-kilometre-long defile between two massifs, known as the **Zemenski Prolom**. Various **rock formations** – dubbed the Cart Rails, the Dovecote, and so on by locals – are visible from the carriage window when the trains aren't plunging through a series of tunnels to escape the precipitous gorge; drivers will miss this view, however, as the road skirts round the gorge to the south. On inaccessible bone-dry crags you can also see the ruins of ancient forts, believed to have once defended the long-vanished town of Zemlen against incursions by the Byzantine Empire. The gorge ends near the village of Râzhdavitsa, beyond which lies the broad **Kyustendil plain** – which locals proudly describe as the "largest orchard in Bulgaria". Fragrant in spring, the plain is richly coloured during autumn by the red apples, yellow pears and lustrous grapes that hang profusely in the **orchards** and vineyards.

Kyustendil

Bisected by the River Bansko, the town of **KYUSTENDIL**, with its fertile plain and thermal springs, has attracted conquerors since Thracian times. The Romans developed this into the "town of baths", and the Turks who settled here in large numbers after the fourteenth century constructed the *hamams* and mosques that gave Kyustendil its oriental character. Some of this atmosphere lingers on in the old backstreets, although the centre of town has undergone considerable modernization, most of it tasteful. The town's wide, tree-shaded avenues lined with cafés are as agreeable as any in Bulgaria but specific sights are limited, so you could easily see all it has to offer in an afternoon. **Buses** to Kyustendil leave Sofia approximately every hour (about 2hr), and Blagoevgrad five times a day (1hr 30min). **Trains** run three or four times daily from Sofia (about 2hr).

The Town

Both the bus and train stations are near the northern end of **bul. Bâlgariya**, just beyond the high-rise landmark *Hotel Velbâzhd*. From here it's a ten-minute walk along bul. Bâlgariya to the centre, provided you don't stop at any of the cafés en route, nor detour left onto a square featuring a modern **art gallery** (Tues–Sun 9.30–11.45am & 2–6pm; free). The gallery is devoted to the work of local painter **Vladimir Dimitrov-Maistor**, who earned the honorific title of "Master" by treating uplifting themes in a vigorous, if uniform, style. Smitten by Eastern philosophy, Dimitrov saw parallels in it with the values of Bulgaria's peasantry, and a recurring image in his paintings is of innocent maidens surrounded by fruit and flowers. The bearded mystic considered himself beyond contemporary morality and had an exceptionally close relationship with his sister Yordana (whose portrait hangs upstairs beside his). A daughter, still living in Sofia, is said to have resulted from this union. Other rooms in the gallery display peasant scenes by Stoyan Venev, Asen Vasiliev's Parisian "Flappers", and photos and artefacts of the IMRO and the Ilinden uprising (see p.141).

Further off to the left you'll see a low red-tiled building that was once a **Dervish Bath**, with a pipe that still gushes scalding water. A couple of blocks south is the **Chifte Bathhouse** (Mon, Tues & Thurs–Sat 5.30am–8.30pm, Wed & Sun 5.30am–12.50pm), a shabby postwar conversion of another, larger Ottoman bath, whose hot (74°C), sulphate-rich waters are used in several sanatoria for the treatment of gynecological and nervous disorders. Behind the baths stands the sixteenth-century **Ahmed Bey Dzhamiya**, an impressive mosque with a tie-beamed porch, overlooking the excavated foundations of a Roman bath.

From here, you can turn right to reach **pl. Velbâzhd**, a modernized square featuring a **memorial to Todor Aleksandrov**, the Macedonian revolutionary assassinated by a group of his own colleagues within the IMRO in 1924. Though not in Macedonia itself, Kyustendil occupied a special role in the struggles for Macedonian liberation at the turn of the century, with groups of heavily armed guerrillas regularly descending on the town before crossing the border into Ottoman territory. Beneath the chestnut trees at the southwest corner of the square, the **Church of Sveta Bogoroditsa** contains a collection of nineteenth-century icons, some featuring Greek-language inscriptions that have been partially scratched away by zealous Bulgarians eager to erase memories of Hellenic influence. Behind the church is the **Maiorska kâshta**, a National Revival-style house that now harbours a café.

Backtracking along bul. Demokratsiya, you'll pass the tumbledown, overgrown **Fetih Mehmed Dzhamiya**, its minaret etched with hexagonal patterns, an effect achieved by inserting red tiles into the darker brown brickwork. Just to the east, traders and shoppers from the Former Yugoslav Republic of Macedonia crowd the daily **market**, south of which pathways begin the ascent of **Hisarlâk hill**, shrouded in wooded parkland. Near the summit you can see the **ruins** of what was originally an extensive Roman settlement around the *Asclepion*, the sacred baths where Emperor Trajan cured his skin complaint and renamed the town Ulpia Pautalia to mark the occasion. Intermingled are the remains of a medieval fortress once occupied by the boyar Deyan. The Ottomans, who supplanted his rule over the region during the mid-fourteenth century, designated their new acquisition "Konstantin's land" – *Kostandinili* in Turkish – which eventually gave rise to the name of the town.

Practicalities

With no tourist office, the best source of **information** is the receptionist in your **hotel**. The three-star *Hotel Velbâzhd* (☎078/20246; ③) is close to the bus station, but gloomy and lifeless, while the *Pautalia* (☎078/24561; ③), on the corner of bul. Bâlgariya and pl. Velbâzhd, is right in the heart of things but noisy until past midnight due to the neighbouring cafés. If you don't mind paying for a taxi, though, the best option is the *Hisarlâka* (☎078/25479; ③), below the ruins on Hisarlâk hill, which has a sauna and fitness centre and a fine view over town. In addition to the hotel **restaurants**, the best places to head for food are the branch of the pizza chain *Planet Italia*, at Bâlgariya 20, or the *Zlatno Pile* chicken joint on the side-street leading to the Fetih Mehmed mosque. For **drinks**, the outdoor cafés on bul. Bâlgariya stay open until at least midnight.

Moving on from Kyustendil

The MATPU office in Kyustendil bus station can make bookings on the twice daily buses to Skopje (3hr) and the lakeside resort of Ohrid (10hr) in the **Former Yugoslav Republic of Macedonia**, as well as on the four buses a week to Durrës (15hr) and Tirana (16hr) in **Albania**. All these cross the border at **GYUESHEVO**, where you can expect delays of more than an hour. Twenty kilometres northwest of Kyustendil there's also a crossing point into **Serbia**, but with no buses travelling this route, you'll have to rely on taxis. Make sure you have a valid Yugoslav visa before setting out (see p.14 in Basics).

If you're heading southwards towards Greece, it's a toss-up between catching a bus to Blagoevgrad (5 daily; 1hr 30min), a good base for trips to Rila or the Pirin, or the nearer town of Dupnitsa (8 daily; 1hr), which has fewer connections and is no place to get stranded. The only thing in Dupnitsa's favour is that the road there crosses the **Kadin Most**, a famous old **bridge over the Struma**, whose five-arched 17-metre span was constructed after 1463 to guarantee the Ottoman lines of communication between the Danube and Salonika, although local legends advance different explanations. According to one, Vizier Isak Pasha took pity on a maiden separated from her betrothed by the river, and had it built as a wedding present – hence its original name, the Bride's Bridge. Another tale has it that the builder, Manuil, suggested to his brothers that they appease the river god by offering one of their wives as a sacrifice, the victim being whichever one arrived first with her husband's lunch. Manuil's wife turned up and was promptly immured, weeping and begging that they leave holes so that she might see daylight and continue to suckle her child.

THE RILA MOUNTAINS

South of Sofia, Mt Vitosha gives way with barely a pause to the **Rila Mountains**, an area of wild highlands enclosing fertile valleys. If you're heading down the main southbound route towards Greece you'll only see the lowland town of **Dupnitsa** and the western fringes of the range, although this is the best direction from which to approach **Rila Monastery**, the finest in Bulgaria. The region's **ski resorts** and **hiking centres** are easier to reach via the town of **Samokov**, which has good transport links with Sofia.

Dupnitsa and around

Heading south from Sofia, the first town in the Struma Valley of any significance is **DUPNITSA**, which is still known to many locals by its Communist-era name **Stanke Dimitrov** (Stanketo for short). Its only real claim to fame is its **tobacco** industry: every year some eight million kilos of the stuff passes through Dupnitsa's warehouses and processing plants, the river is tinted a nicotine yellow, and you can see huge quantities of tobacco growing, or spread out to dry, throughout the surrounding countryside. However, the only reason for travellers to come here is to catch a bus to more appealing destinations.

If you have to kill an hour, there are a couple of monuments worth a look. Just off the modernized main square is a sixteenth-century **mosque**, whose simple domed structure has an elegance that displays Ottoman architecture's debt to Byzantine church building; it's now used by local artists as a gallery. Behind it is the **Okoliiskata kâshta**, a house of the same period that once served as the *konak* of the Ottoman governor.

A more exciting prospect is to follow some of the **hiking trails** into the Rila Mountains, that begin a few kilometres southeast of town at the village of **BISTRITSA**. From here, you can follow a path to the *Otovitsa* hut, with the shortest most southerly route leading to the *Byal Kladenets* chalet. About seven hours'

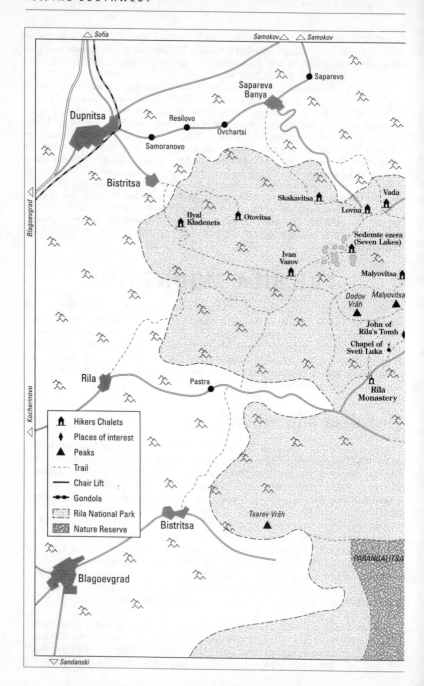

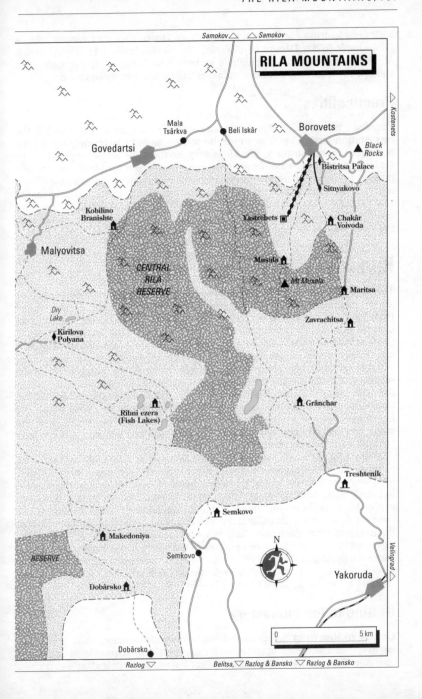

RILA MOUNTAINS

walk from Bistritsa another lodge, *Ivan Vazov*, is well placed for various hikes – for example to Mt Damga (1hr 30min), the Seven Lakes (2hr 30min) or Mt Malyovitsa (6hr 30min). The altitude up here is well over 1524m, so make sure you ask about current weather conditions and travel properly equipped.

Practicalities

Dupnitsa's **train station** is about fifteen minutes' walk from the centre, while the **bus station** lurks a block or so off the main square. Unfortunately for anyone hoping to reach Bistritsa or Rila Monastery, no timetable is displayed in the bus station and the ticket-windows are often closed, making it hard to obtain any information. In theory, there are three buses a day directly to the monastery and another one or two to Rila village, where you can change buses. Avoid having to stay the night in Dupnitsa, as the *Rila* **hotel** (☎0701/25015; ②) by the main square is decrepit and depressing, with no hot water, though there's a nice **restaurant**, the *Panorama*, in the hilltop park overlooking the square.

Rila Monastery

The single road leading to **Rila Monastery** passes first through **Rila village**, a sleepy community with a few cafés, a food store and the *Orbita* hotel (☎093754/2167; ③), but being 27km from the monastery, it doesn't make a good base for sightseeing. Beyond the village, the road enters the narrowing valley of the foaming River Rilska, fed by innumerable springs from the surrounding pine- and beech-covered mountains. Even today there's a palpable sense of isolation, and it's easy to see why **John of Rila** (*Ivan Rilski*) chose this valley to escape the savagery of feudal life and the laxity of the established monasteries at the end of the ninth century. To disciples drawn to his hermit's cell, John preached that "he who would be chief among you must be as he that doth serve". What began as a hermitage became an important spiritual centre after his death, and the monastery forged links with others in the Balkans and played a major role in Orthodox Christianity throughout the Middle Ages.

As the best known of Bulgaria's monasteries – justly famed for both its architecture and its mountainous setting – Rila Monastery receives a stream of visitors, who now arrive by bus or car rather than on foot or by mule, as did pilgrims in the old days. Although most visitors come on packaged day-trips, it is perfectly possible to get here independently, and the abundance of trails leading off into the densely forested hills make an extended stay more than worthwhile. Though the monastery gates are open daily to visitors from dawn till dusk, some of the sights within the complex keep more restricted hours. If you want to see (or take part in) a **service**, morning prayers start at 8am, evening prayers at 5pm. Apart from Easter, the two main religious **festivals** celebrated here are the birthday (August 18) and feast day (October 19) of St John of Rila.

Getting to the monastery

Getting to Rila from Sofia comes down to how much money or time you're willing to spend. The easiest option is to take one of the **day-trips** offered by the tour operators (see p.64) and the capital's bigger hotels, which cost about $40 per person including lunch. In summer only, a daily **bus** leaves Sofia's Ovcha Kupel terminal at 10.20am, with an extra one at 6.30am on Fridays, Saturdays and Sundays. These run directly to the monastery but head back only forty minutes later, so you would need to stay overnight. Otherwise, you can catch one of the hourly buses from Sofia's Ovcha Kupel terminal, or a **train** from the Central Station, to Blagoevgrad, where you can pick up local buses to Rila village, then change to another bus to the monastery itself (2–3 daily). Be sure to set off early, and check timetables carefully at each stage of the journey in order to plan your return trip. If you're approaching Rila **from the south**, Blagoevgrad is again the best transport hub to aim for.

Accommodation

Staying in the monastery's cosy guest "cells" has some appeal if you don't mind the lack of hot water, or that the gates close at 10pm (the porter can be roused until midnight), but those on a tight budget may baulk at paying $15 per person at the lodgings office in the southeast corner of the yard, when there's a **hostel** just beyond the monastery's east gate, above the *Rila* restaurant, that charges $5 for a dorm bed (no showers). Just downhill from here lies the *Tsarev Vrâh* (☎07054/2280, email *tzarev@infonet.techno-link.com*; ④), the newer and nearer of the two **hotels**. The older but still agreeable *Rilets* (☎07054/2106; ③) lies fifteen minutes' walk up the main road; cross over the bridge and turn right into the woods. A left turn here brings you to *Bor* **camping**, a primitive but beautiful site on the riverbank, while for hot showers, comfortable chalets and all amenities carry on 500m up the main road to *Camping Zodiak* (☎07054/2291; chalets ②).

ST JOHN OF RILA (880–946)

John of Rila, known to his compatriots as **Ivan Rilski**, was one of many ninth-century hermits and mystics who took to the wilds of Bulgaria and Macedonia in search of solitude and enlightenment. Having acquired a reputation as a wise man and healer, he finally yielded to his followers and established a monastery high in the Rila Valley, where he could combine the virtues of a religious community with ascetic solitude. It's said that he took steps to embalm himself by consuming herbs and potions, and his corpse was believed to possess curative powers. As a result, Rila became famous throughout the Balkans as a pilgrimage site.

In the Middle Ages, the bones of saints were important symbols that added legitimacy to the rule of whoever could establish control over them, so Tsar Petâr had **John of Rila's remains** moved to Sofia in the mid-900s. In 1183 they were stolen from here by the Hungarian King Béla III, who carted them off to the Catholic city of Esztergom, whose bishop reputedly went blind after denying that the bones were those of a saint and only regained his sight after publically recanting. Their return to Sofia in 1187 was secured by the Byzantine Emperor Isaac Angelus, to win support against the rebellion of the Bulgarian nobles Petâr and Asen, though this didn't prevent Asen from capturing the city and bearing the bones off to his new capital, Veliko Târnovo, in 1194. They finally returned to Rila in 1469 – though St John's right hand toured Russia in the sixteenth century to raise funds for the restoration of Bulgarian monasteries. The left hand, encased in a silver casket, is occasionally put on display by the monastery authorities.

There's no reason to stay at either of the other two campsites, 5–10km back down the valley towards Rila village.

The monastery

Founded in 1335, 4km from St John's original hermitage, Rila Monastery was plundered during the eighteenth century, and repairs had hardly begun when the whole structure burned down in 1833. Its rebuilding was presented as a religious and patriotic duty: urged on by Neofit Rilski, public donations were plentiful and master craftsmen such as Aleksii Rilets and Pavel Milenkov gave their services for free. Work continued in stages throughout the nineteenth century, and the east wing was built as recently as 1961 to display the monastery's treasures, recognized by UNESCO as part of the World Cultural Heritage. Like the old monastery, it's ringed by mighty walls, giving it the outward appearance of a fortress.

Once you get through the west gate, however, this impression is dispelled by the harmonious beauty of the interior, which even the milling crowds don't seriously mar. Graceful arches surrounding the flagstoned courtyard support tiers of monastic cells, and stairways ascend to top-floor balconies which – viewed from below – resemble the outstretched petals of flowers. Bold red stripes and black-and-white check patterns enliven the facade, contrasting with the sombre mountains behind, and creating a visual harmony between the cloisters and the church within.

The monastery church

The **monastery church** has undulating lines, combining red and black designs with arches and a diversity of cupolas. Richly coloured **frescos** shelter beneath the porch and within the interior – a mixture of scenes from rural life and Orthodox iconography, executed by muralists from Razlog, Bansko and Samokov, including nineteenth-century Bulgaria's greatest artist Zahari Zograf. The murals on the church's exterior include archetypal images of cataclysm: the fall of Constantinople, apocalypses and visions of hell, plagued by the bat-winged demons that seemingly loomed large in the Bulgarian imagination. The wrongdoings of sinners are portrayed with a love of grotesque detail; one picture shows rich men quaffing wine around a table, ignoring the pleas of a begging leper whose legs are being gnawed by dogs.

Inside the church, the **iconostasis** is particularly splendid: almost 10m wide and covered by a mass of intricate carvings and gold leaf, it's one of the finest achievements of the Samokov woodcarvers (see p.114). A chapel on the right of the nave contains the **heart of Tsar Boris III**, buried beneath a simple wooden cross. Boris died of a mystery illness after a visit to Berlin in 1944, prompting many to speculate that he'd been poisoned by his Nazi hosts. After 1945, the Bulgarian Communists scattered his remains in the Iskâr gorge in order to prevent his grave from becoming the focus of anti-Communist sentiment, but the former monarch's principal organ survived, to be ceremonially interred here in 1993.

Beside the church rises **Hrelyo's Tower**, the sole remaining building from the fourteenth century, which you can sometimes ascend in order to visit the top-floor chapel. Its founder – a local noble – apocryphally took refuge as a monk here and was supposedly strangled in the tower; hence the inscription upon it: "Thy wife sobs and grieves, weeping bitterly, consumed by sorrow".

Other parts of the monastery

Huge cauldrons that were once used to feed pilgrims occupy the old **kitchen** on the ground floor of the north wing, where the soot-encrusted ceiling has the shape and texture of a gigantic termites' nest. Various rooms await inspection on the floors above, where the spartan refectory contrasts with the more salubrious, panelled guest rooms, named after the towns which endowed them.

The **ethnographic collection** on the second floor of the north wing (daily 8am–5pm) is most notable for its carpets and silverware, while beneath the modern east wing there's a wealth of objects in the **treasury** (same times). These include icons and medieval gospels; Rila's charter from Tsar Ivan Shishman, written on leather and sealed with gold in 1378; the door of the original monastery church; and a miniature **cross** made by the monk Raphael during the 1790s. Composed of 140 biblical tableaux containing more than 1500 human figures (each the size of a grain of rice), this took twelve years for Raphael to carve with a needle, and cost him his eyesight.

Around the monastery

From the monastery's eastern gate, a path descends towards the river and the **Church of the Presentation of the Virgin**, a decrepit late eighteenth-century structure surrounded by the graves of several generations of monks. The chapel on the church's upper storey is richly decorated with scenes from the life of the Virgin. A painting in the porch shows the Archangel Michael stomping on the body of a bearded wrongdoer. Look out for the *kostnitsa* or **ossary** on the ground floor, housing the skulls of former monks.

Rila Monastery is the starting point for numerous **hikes** (see box overleaf, as well as an agreeable short stroll to the **St John of Rila's cave** (2hr return trip). The trail begins by the road about 2km beyond the east gate: a fairly obvious path bears left about 100m past the *Bachkova cheshma* restaurant, leading up through the woods to the **Chapel of Sveti Luka** after twenty minutes. The chapel, named after a nephew of St John of Rila who acted as the ageing hermit's servant, contains frescos depicting him with three other hermit-stars of the Bulgarian–Macedonian borderlands: Gavril of Leshnovo, Prohor of Pchinya, and Ioakim of Osogovo. Twenty minutes further on, the **Chapel of St John of Rila** is built into the rock beside the cave or **"Miracle Hole"** where he spent his last twenty years. Traditionally, pilgrims were required to enter the hole before proceeding to the monastery, and the conscience-smitten were regularly unable to do so. These people were judged to be sinners and forced to go home to repent for a year before coming back to Rila.

Eating, drinking and entertainment

For **snacks**, pick up some delicious bread from the bakery run by monks, just outside the east gate. Alongside is a *skara-bira* that's fine for *kebapcheta* or soup, while downhill behind the bakery, the *Rila* restaurant features a wider menu with a cocktail bar, but has rude staff and overcharges, making the **restaurants** in the *Tsarev Vrâh*, *Rilets* or *Camping Zodiak* better bets. **Nightlife** revolves around the subterranean bar at the *Rilets*, which hosts a **disco** if enough people turn up.

HIKING IN THE RILA MOUNTAINS

The **Rila National Park**, established in 1992, covers almost half the Rila mountain range (including its fourteen highest peaks), with a network of **hiking** trails and chalets built in Communist times. These are slowly being refurbished with an eye to eco-tourism, though most are still rudimentary, and information on vacancies or the weather remains scarce. For any of the hikes below, **food** supplies and a **map** of the mountains are essential, and it's prudent to pack a **tent** in case the chalets are full or you need to take shelter. It's strictly forbidden to pick flowers or light fires (except at designated spots).

A noticeboard in the car park maps out the options for hikers **starting from Rila Monastery**. From here, two trails (which later converge at Dodov Vrâh) lead to the **Ivan Vazov** chalet – about six hours' hard slog. From the right-hand trail another path branches off towards **Mt Malyovitsa**, which can also be approached from *Suhoto ezero*, or "Dry Lake" (you'll need to camp overnight there), or by bus from the direction of Samokov. Paths to the Dry Lake itself begin at the Kirilova Polyana (aka "Partisans Meadow"), 5km east of Rila monastery; the whole walk takes about five hours.

Southeast of Rila, the *Ribnite ezera* (**Fish Lakes**) are another feasible destination, with a chalet nearby. You can reach them by following the road to its end, and then following the Rilska up to its source in the mountains, or by a trail bearing southeast about halfway along the road, which crosses the ridge and passes some smaller lakes en route. Both walks take six to seven hours.

Due south of Rila is another chalet, **Makedoniya**, accessible by several paths originating from the minor road forking off a few kilometres west of the monastery. From the chalet it's a day's hike west down to **Bistritsa** (from where buses run to Blagoevgrad), or a few hours' walk east to the **Semkovo** hut, which can also be reached from the Fish Lakes and may serve as a way-station for walkers making longer hikes (2–3 days) towards the Pirin or Rhodope mountains. Semkovo lies on the way to Belitsa and Yakoruda, two villages linked by bus or train to Razlog, Bansko and Velingrad. Hikers can also descend from here to the village of **Dobârsko** (see p.128) via the chalet of the same name. Alternatively, the **Grânchar** hut (named "Boris Hadzhisotirov" on older maps), due east of the Fish Lakes, serves hikers bound for Mt Musala and Borovets, or those pursuing a more easterly path down to Yakoruda.

Samokov, Borovets and Malyovitsa

With a car, it's easy to get to the historic town of **Samokov** and the mountain resorts **Borovets** and **Malyovitsa** on a day-trip from Sofia, but to appreciate them – and for anyone reliant on public transport – it's more realistic to allow two or three days. If you're planning to head on to Rila Monastery, bear in mind that it's almost easier to *walk* across the mountains than get there by bus from Samokov, which will add at least another day to your itinerary.

Happily, the one-hour journey **from Sofia to Samokov** isn't difficult, with half-hourly buses and minibuses from the capital's Yug terminal following the River Iskâr past **Lake Pancharevo**, a centre for water sports. Entering the defile between the Lozhen and Plana massifs, you should be able to glimpse the ruined fortress of **Urvich**, where Tsar Shishman allegedly withstood the Turks for seven years; on the opposite bank, **Zheleznitsa monastery** lurks deep in the forest.

Beyond the defile lies the massive **Iskâr Dam** and **Lake Iskâr** – a man-made body of water 16km long, sometimes known as the "Sea of Sofia".

Samokov

Though it lacks the cachet of antiquity, **SAMOKOV** has a tradition of skilled work, art and popular socialism second to none in Bulgaria. Founded as a mining community in the fourteenth century, it soon became one of the busiest manu-facturing centres in the Turkish empire (its name derives from the Bulgarian verb "to forge"), where all kinds of crafts guilds flourished, particularly weavers and tailors, who turned flax (still a major product) into uniforms for the Ottoman army. From the seventeenth century until the end of Turkish rule, Samokov's stature eclipsed that of Sofia and Kyustendil – and was raised even higher by the artistry of its woodworkers and painters, who decorated Bulgaria's finest monas-teries. The town's working-class and artisan traditions also gave rise to one of Bulgaria's most interesting experiments in socialism, the Samokov Commune (see box below). Though foreign tourists from nearby Borovets are sometimes bussed in to wander around during the day, the place isn't really geared up for tourism, so it's best to digest what there is and move on.

The town centre

There's plenty of evidence of Samokov's past in and around the **centre**, although modern urban planning has left its monuments marooned in a sea of crumbling paving stones. The ornate **fountain** or *cheshma* on the main square is a legacy of the Turks, who considered running water an essential part of civilized living. Close by stands the only one of Samokov's once-numerous mosques to survive, the **Bairakli dzhamiya** (Mon & Thurs–Sun 9am–noon & 1–5pm), preserved as a monument to the skills of local builders rather than as a place of worship.

THE SAMOKOV COMMUNE

Like many other Bulgarian towns, the election of a non-Communist town council in October 1991 led to a revision of Samokov's political history. However, this is one place where the role of the Left in the town's development is too great to be ignored. Social progress was slow in the region until 1910, when a slump in the local iron-working industry provoked the declaration of the **Samokov Commune**. Within months of coming to power, the socialist-dominated council inspected factory con-ditions, supplied workers' quarters with sewers and electricity, granted books and clothing, and levied a progressive income tax. It also flew a red flag from the town hall until ordered to desist by the interior minister, and claimed rent for a palace built on municipal land, which so infuriated Tsar Ferdinand that he had a new road built to bypass Samokov en route to Borovets.

Even though it increased its vote during the 1912 election, the Commune was overthrown by the police and conservatives, but the ideals behind it remained in the popular consciousness, helping to inspire another left-wing victory in the local elections of 1919. The history of the Commune was naturally tailored to suit the needs of postwar Communist propaganda, but Dimitrov was right in calling it the "first practical attempt of the working people to govern themselves in the name of their own interests, against the blood-suckers, *chorbadzhii* and capitalists".

Commissioned by the pasha in 1840, its design betrays Bulgarian influences: the roof-line mimics the shape of a *kobilitsa*, or yoke, while the interior decoration relies upon plant motifs rather than arabesques, with a magnificent sunset beneath the dome – a piece of orthodox iconography. On Monday mornings, the environs of the mosque and main square are taken over by a big **market** selling everything from counterfeit sportswear to homemade rugs and woodcarvings, with the odd antique as well as lots of complete junk.

Just off the square to the east, the **History Museum** (Mon–Sat 8am–noon & 1–5pm) traces Samokov's evolution up to the present day. The town's industrial past is remembered in a sequence of models illustrating the mining and smelting of iron ore: one shows a gargantuan, waterwheel-powered set of bellows used to force air into the furnaces. Elsewhere the accent is on the various trades that made Samokov famous as a craft centre, with displays of ceramics, ironmongery, engraving and printing – the latter started by one Nikola Karastoyanov, who opened Bulgaria's first printing house here in the early nineteenth century.

However, it's the **Samokov school of icon painters,** on the first floor of the museum, that receives the most attention, with pictures and personal effects of the Vienna-trained Hristo Dimitrov and his sons Dimitâr and Zahari. The latter, subsequently known as **Zahari Zograf**, is remembered as the greatest and most prolific of Bulgarian nineteenth-century painters. A few of his personal belongings are here, and his gravestone, now so worn as to be virtually illegible, lies in the museum corridor. A gallery of icon painting upstairs contains works by lesser-known colleagues, as well as examples of the increasingly secular subjects tackled by this generation: note especially the animated, Brueghelesque figures of Nikola Obrazopisov's 1892 painting *Peasants dancing the Horo.*

South of the main square: woodcarving, icons and frescos

Ulitsa Boris Hadzhisotirov leads south from the main square towards the old Bulgarian residential quarter of town, and the *metoh*, or **Convent of Sveta Bogoroditsa** at no. 77. In the porch of the convent church there's a fine nineteenth-century painting of a winged Virgin Mary who extends her cloak to shelter the believers – the local priests and their flock – who herd beneath it. The church interior features colourful modern murals by local artists, imitating the folksy style of Zograf and his generation, while outside, a cobbled alley leads past a ramshackle collection of nunnery buildings and a beautifully maintained garden. A little way further on, the walled **Church of Sveti Nikolai** features cast-iron weathercocks on each of its three cupolas.

Although such skilful wrought-ironwork embodied the fusion of art and industry during the town's commercial heyday, greater fame accrued to the **Samokov school of woodcarvers**. Collectively, this refers to local artisans (some of whom studied on Mt Athos in Greece in the late eighteenth century), in particular to a group formed in the early nineteenth century, primarily to make the iconostasis for Rila Monastery. Although executed in 1793, the iconostasis of Samokov's **Metropolitan Church** on ul. Zahari Zograf, a couple of blocks south of Sveti Nikolai, is characteristic of their work. It's covered with intricate figures linked by plant-like traceries, interspersed with rosettes – which sometimes took the form of a six-petalled narcissus. The church's collection of icons presents the Samokov painting school at its best, with Hristo Dimitrov's *Enthroned Jesus* a particular highlight.

KALASHNIKOVS AND SS-23s

One aspect of Samokov's industrial heritage that's less well known is its association with the military, especially during Communist times, when its skilled socialist workers were regarded as ideal labour for the arms industry. To Samokov's artisans fell the task of designing new firearms and training cadres for use at the **shooting range** near the stadium, where, today, tourists can fire Russian handguns and AK47s (closed Mondays and Tuesdays). The $13 fee includes five rounds of ammunition, with further supplies costing 60¢ a round. Booking is through the tourist office in Borovets (see p.116).

Fortunately for all, the right to fire was never extended to the long-range **SS-23 missiles** stationed in the hills outside town during the 1980s. After diplomats had agreed to return the missiles to Russia, disarmament inspectors were perturbed to find that "five or six" nuclear warheads were apparently missing, but finally put it down to an accountancy error rather than loss or theft.

Barring the occasional angel, Samokov woodcarvers generally avoided depicting human figures, preferring to represent eagles, sparrowhawks, dragons, falcons and, above all, plants. A large iconostasis required several years' work, and most woodcarvers undertook less ambitious commissions, such as fitting *minderi* and panelled ceilings in the homes of wealthy citizens. These still exist in a few **old houses** among the backstreets south of ul. Hadzhisotirov, which are known after the names of their onetime owners: Saraf, Marikin, Ksenofontov, Obrazopisov and Kokoshov.

Frescos by Samokov artists decorate the **Belyova church**, 4km south of town on the Borovets road, most notably the serried ranks of saints provided by Nikola Obrazopisov, the most sought-after of Samokov painters after Zograf himself.

Practicalities

Other than a few householders who let rooms out in the height of summer, there's no tourist **accommodation** in Samokov as such; the best bet is to head for nearby **Borovets**, 10km south of town, where there's plenty of choice (see below). Alternatives further out include a motel (②) and campsite at **Govedartsi**, 11km along the road to Malyovitsa, or the *Belchanitsa* hostel (②), in the small spa resort of **Belchinski Bani**, 15km west of town on the road to Dupnitsa. Aside from a smattering of **cafés** on the main square, eating and drinking opportunities in Samokov are scarce.

Moving on from Samokov, there are buses roughly every hour to Borovets (the last one leaves at 7pm) and seven daily to Govedartsi, but none to Malyovitsa. For Rila Monastery you need to take the 10am bus to Dupnitsa and change there (see p.105). Dupnitsa-bound buses go by way of **Sapareva Banya**, Bulgaria's most ferocious mineral baths, whose hottest spring is fed by a super-heated geyser (102°C) gushing 550 gallons of sulphurous water a minute.

Borovets

Near the turn of the century, Prince Ferdinand of Bulgaria built three villas and a hunting lodge among the aromatic pine woods covering the northern slopes of Mt Musala, a mile above sea level. The Mamrikoff family – after whom a verb meaning "to steal from an exalted position" was coined – and other wealthy folk did likewise, founding an exclusive colony, Tchamkoria, from which **BOROVETS** has developed. Effectively nationalized for the benefit of union and Party members in 1949, Borovets became a major **winter sports** resort in the 1960s, and is now largely geared towards package tourism. It is also a popular place for Bulgarians to escape the heat during July and August, but pretty quiet during the intermediate months before and after the skiing season.

Competitively priced **package holidays** ensure that you get lodgings, skiing equipment and tuition – none of which is assured if you just turn up on spec. Also, most package operators offer lift-passes and "ski packs" (including equipment rental) for a lower cost than you pay on the spot, making package holidays even more worthwhile.

Skiing

The official **skiing** season lasts from mid-December to mid-April, though the snow-cover is most reliable in late February and early March. Off to the west of the *Hotel Rila*, the **nursery slopes** are served by ten **drag lifts** (9.30am–4.50pm), and overlooked by a steep slope topped by the *Sitnyakovo* chalet, once one of Ferdinand's villas, that's accessible by **chair lift** (same hours; winter only) from behind the *Hotel Rila*. Experienced skiers favour the pistes on the western ridge of the mountain, which can be reached by a five-kilometre-long **gondola** (9am–4.30pm; closed Tues morning) running from near the *Hotel Samokov* up to *Yastrebets*, a former royal hunting lodge (now a hotel). Another chair lift serves the two ski jumps (55m & 75m long), while there are also shuttle-buses to the start of three cross-country runs at Shiroka Polyana, 2km away.

Hiking

The **tourist office** in the *Hotel Rila* (Mon–Fri 9am–5pm) can organize various excursions, including **hikes from Borovets** during the summer months, with beds guaranteed in mountain chalets if required. The *Yastrebets* hotel (4hr 30min walk or 35min by gondola) is the starting point for the ascent of **Mt Musala**, the highest peak in Bulgaria (2925m). The first leg (1hr) brings you to the *Musala* chalet at the foot of the mountain, whence it's an hour and forty minutes' walk to the summit. From Mt Musala it's six hours' trek southwards to the *Grânchar* chalet, where one path leads down to Yakoruda on the narrow-gauge railway line **to Bansko**; the other **to the Fish Lakes** (5hr) where, after sleeping at the *Ribni Ezera* chalet, hikers can push on to **Rila Monastery** (5–6hr).

If these sound too much effort, you could try an easy, ninety-minute walk to the **Black Rocks** (*Cherveni skali*), east of Borovets. A row of crags with sheer drops on both sides, they were used by the secret police in the late 1940s as a killing ground for "enemies of the people", who were simply pushed off to their deaths. The trail begins after the *Hotel St Ivan Rilski*, entering the woods beside a cross-braced fence. Bear right at the fork 100m later, then left downhill and left at the next fork; when you reach the farm buildings take the middle, gravelled route and turn left at the fork onto a sandy track that gets narrower and stonier en route to a picnic area near the Black Rocks.

Another easy walk is to head up the *Yastrebets* road, past the *Breza* and *Flora* hotels, for about 15 minutes, till you see a nondescript gate on the right shortly after the gondola-lift crosses over the road. This is the entrance to the little-known

THE DÂNOVISTI

The Rila Mountains' Seven Lakes are a place of pilgrimage for the **Dânovisti** or "White Brotherhood", members of a sect founded in the 1930s by a Bulgarian, Dânov. Combining Orthodox Christianity with meditation, sun-worship, vegetarianism and yoga, the sect was widely popular in Bulgaria before the war and tolerated by both church and state until the Communist era, when it was obliged to go underground. Having re-emerged in the 1990s, Dânovism is now regarded as another example of the richness of Bulgarian spiritual culture (besides Orthodoxy, paganism, faith-healing and clairvoyancy), whose most famous living adherent is the fashion designer, Paco Raban. On August 19–28 each year, the Dânovisti gather to camp by the shores of the lakes and worship the sun with pan-rhythmic dances. You may also encounter them at Christian/New Age pilgrimage sites like Krâstova gora (see p.304) and Rupite (p.140).

Bistritsa Palace (Tues–Sun 9.30am–noon & 1–3.30pm). A rambling whitewashed mansion with carved wooden balconies, it was built as a hunting lodge for Tsar Ferdinand (who entertained Kaiser Wilhelm of Germany here in 1913) and used by his son, Boris, before passing into the hands of Bulgaria's Communist elite, and being opened to the public a few years ago. The interior is decorated in a mixture of High Victoriana and Samokov woodcarvings, and bristles with animal heads and pelts, while heraldic lions crown the lamposts that illuminate its landscaped grounds.

You might also wander down into the **village of Borovets** (take the turning near *Bonkers*, running past the *Maharani* restaurant), whose simple wooden church, opposite a shop near the post office, doubles as a workshop for a woodcarver who sells statues and picture frames.

Practicalities

Borovets has seven three-star hotels, all of which are grouped around the central bus terminal, but finding **accommodation** from December through to April can still be a problem if you're not on a package or haven't booked in advance. At any other time of year, there should be plenty of beds, although places may close for a while off-season. Remember, however, that rooms cost significantly more if you arrive on spec – about $25 per person for a double room – than if you come on a package. Alternatively, you could try one of the two "vacation villages" at the northeastern end of the resort: *Yagoda* (☎00359/7128343; ⑤), a huddle of wooden villas with pointed roofs, or *Malina* (☎00359/7128435), where you can rent your own log cabin, many of which have saunas, for $40 per person, per night (based on four people sharing).

There are a number of places to **eat and drink** in the vicinity of the *Hotel Rila*, including *Franco's Pizzeria* and, unusually, a curry restaurant. *BJ's* disco bar is the liveliest **nightspot** (all drinks except beer half-price before 10pm), followed by the *Black Tiger* karaoke bar, and the *White Magic*, which plays ski videos. *Bonkers* is a raucous venue for (usually awful) local dance bands. Other diversions include ten-pin bowling, billiards, swimming and a (mixed, naked bathing) sauna at the *Hotel Samokov*, all of which non-residents can use for a small fee. Last but not least, ski buffs can commission a commemorative **video** of their performance on the slopes – ask at the *White Magic* bar.

Malyovitsa and beyond

Beyond Govedartsi to the southwest of Samokov, a branch road snakes up to **MALYOVITSA**, 1750m above sea level. This is another ski resort with all mod cons, pistes, a slalom track and nursery slopes on the neighbouring peak from which its name derives. Though Malyovitsa doesn't really compare with Borovets as a **skiing** centre, it's a good starting point for **walks in the mountains**, particularly the trek to Rila Monastery. Climbers' huts and the trails themselves are marked on *BTS* maps of the Rila Mountains, which should be available from the *Hotel Malyovitsa*. The one-hour ascent to the *Malyovitsa* chalet above the resort constitutes the first leg of several hikes: from here it's seven hours' walk to the beautiful **Seven Lakes** (*Sedemte ezera*) cabin, or six hours to the *Ivan Vazov* lodge, depending on which trail you follow after the Urdin Lakes. Blasted crags surround another lake, *Strashnoto ezero*, which lies to the east of the *Malyovitsa* cabin. Refuges there, and to the north of the Dry Lake (*Suhoto ezero*), serve as way-stations along the route to the chalet beside the **Fish Lakes**: nine hours' hike in all. The most popular trail leads south to **Mt Malyovitsa** and **Rila Monastery**. Climbing the 2729-metre mountain takes about three hours, an easier ascent than by the steeper southern face. Afterwards, follow the path west along the ridge before taking the trail branching left, which leads to the monastery in the thickly wooded valley below (a further 3–4hr). For more information on hiking in the Rila range, see the map on pp.106–107 and the box on p.112.

THE PIRIN RANGE AND THE FAR SOUTH

Like the Rila Mountains, the **Pirin range** can be approached from two directions. Heading down the Struma Valley towards the Greek border, the only places worth stopping at are the lively university town of **Blagoevgrad**, and **Sandanski**, jumping-off point for such destinations as the weird and wonderful **Melnik**, **Rozhen** and **Rupite**. Though communications with Pirin's eastern flank tend to centre round Velingrad and Plovdiv, some buses make their way across the Predel pass to **Bansko**, the region's best base for hiking and skiing, and down the Mesta Valley to **Gotse Delchev**, another attractive town surounded by some interesting villages. Above all, the **Pirin Mountains**, a glorious glacial landscape of peaks and lakes, offer some of the finest walking in Europe.

Blagoevgrad

Administrative capital of the Pirin region, **BLAGOEVGRAD**'s concrete suburbs and factories suggest a workaday town with little to tempt you away from the highway, but in reality it's the coolest place in southwest Bulgaria. While the lovingly restored old quarter and modern civic centre are the legacy of Zhivkov's decision to host an international summit here in 1988, the buzz is generated by 20,000 **university students**, the vast majority of them female (males brag of a ratio of 14:1, but six or seven to one seems likelier), making Blagoevgrad's cafés and clubs the most stylish – and flirtatious – in Bulgaria.

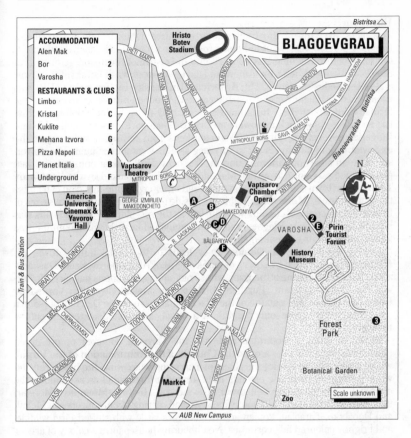

BLAGOEVGRAD

ACCOMMODATION
Alen Mak   1
Bor   2
Varosha   3

RESTAURANTS & CLUBS
Limbo   D
Kristal   C
Kuklite   E
Mehana Izvora   G
Pizza Napoli   A
Planet Italia   B
Underground   F

If that's not sufficient reason to visit, Blagoevgrad is a good place for **contacts** of all kinds, from the foreign students and staff of the American University to the Pirin Tourist Forum, or even the party headquarters of VMRO if you're so inclined. And with its lively **cultural life** and useful **transport** links to the rest of the Pirin, Blagoevgrad makes an ideal base. Hang around for a few days and you'll start to recognize (and be recognized by) the people you met last night in a bar.

Historically Blagoevgrad was an important crafts town, predominantly inhabited by Turks from the sixteenth century until their flight in 1912, after which it was settled by Bulgarian peasants and displaced Macedonians. In 1950 it was renamed Blagoevgrad in honour of **Dimitâr Blagoev**, the founder of Bulgarian (and Russian) Marxism, and has chosen to stick with it in the post-Communist era because citizens either absolved Blagoev of any blame for Communism, or rejected restoring the former Turkish name, *Gorna Dzhumaya* – bestowed instead on a vile brand of cigarettes from one of the local **tobacco** factories. Oddly, although Blagoevgrad produces most of Bulgaria's cigarettes, the popular, local brand *Victory* is notoriously difficult to get hold of.

The Town

Travellers **arriving** at the train station or adjacent bus terminals, on ul. Sv. Dimitâr Solunski, may want to book a room through MATPU (see below) across the road, before catching bus #2 or #3 into the centre of town, and getting off at the *Hotel Alen Mak*, near the American University, or pl. Vasil Levski at the lower end of the pedestrian zone. The **American University in Bulgaria** (AUB) was established in Blagoevgrad in 1991 because the council offered it free use of the former Communist Party headquarters – a canny move by local politicians that the Socialists (now back in power) are happy to support. Funded by the US and Bulgarian governments, it has 660-odd students from across the Balkans and the ex-Soviet Union, but this is set to increase as a new campus is built. The university, with an adjacent **Cinemax** and the **Yavorov Hall**, sits at one end of a vast plaza named pl. Georgi Izmirilev Makedoncheto, itself flanked by the **Vaptsarov Theatre**, the town council, the post office and other civic buildings. You can't miss the controversial "**Moneybags**" tableaux beside the theatre: displaying a series of bronze figures, one absconding with the loot as the rest slumber, the tableaux was banished from Sofia to Blagoevgrad, then languished near the station until it was finally moved to its present position.

East of the square, ul. Dimitâr Talev leads to the social hub of town, **pl. Bâlgariya**, surrounded by scores of **cafés** on Todor Aleksandrov, Raiko Daskalov and other sidestreets near the river, whose old houses and shops had facelifts during the Communist era. Further north on pl. Makedoniya, the **Vaptsarov Chamber Opera** and a statue of the Macedonian hero Gotse Delchev presage a residential area whose only "sight" is a small, abandoned sixteenth-century **mosque**.

Better to cross a footbridge and visit the **Varosha**, an area of preserved nineteenth-century houses around the **Church of the Annunciation of the Virgin**, whose fluid roof-line mimics the shape of a carrying yoke, while the black, red and white pattern on its facade extends right around a three-sided arcade linking the church to a freestanding bell tower. The nearby **History Museum** (Mon–Fri 9am–noon & 1–6pm) exhibits some fine icons and carvings from churches in Melnik and Dobârsko: Thracian, Roman and Greek relics jostle with stuffed Pirin wildlife, and brightly coloured folk costumes. Neighbouring houses form a colony of artists' **studios and workshops**, with crafts demonstrations (ask at the Pirin Tourism Forum for details), art for sale in the *Stanislav Gallery*, and a **puppet theatre** to round things off. Farther south is a large daily outdoor **market**, at its most lively on Saturdays, with sections for fresh produce, clothes and electrical goods.

Alternatively, it's only ten minutes' walk to the attractive **Forest Park**, where you'll find a small **zoo** and a **botanical garden**, with a rosarium and species from both the Rila and the Pirin mountains, dotted with interesting rock forms.

Practicalities

The best source of **information** – not only on Blagoevgrad but the whole region – is the Pirin Tourist Forum (Mon–Fri 8.30am–6.30pm and sometimes Sat 10am–4pm; ☎ and fax 073/65458, email *scabrin@pop3.aubg.bg*) near the *Hotel Varosha*, which can arrange anything from a "Kidnapping Picnic" to a room in a highland village. Students and staff at the American University (where English is the *lingua franca*) can also be helpful if approached with due consideration.

The cheapest **accommodation** available is a private room, booked through the 24hr MATPU agency (☎073/32793), opposite the station, which charges $5 per

BLAGOEVGRAD CULTURE AND FESTIVALS

Blagoevgrad is home to some prestigious cultural institutions and festivals: its **theatre** and **chamber opera** (both named after the poet Nikola Vaptsarov) are among the best in the provinces, and the **Pirin Folk Ensemble** (based at the Yavorov Hall) is the most popular troupe in Bulgaria. A **children's piano competition** takes place at the chamber opera in late February or early March, while the **Theatre Days** (late April–early May) are Bulgaria's equivalent of the Edinburgh Festival, with drama companies from all over Bulgaria and the Former Yugoslav Republic of Macedonia competing for prizes at the Vaptsarov Theatre. In addition, there's the **Autumn Festival** and **Magic of Bulgarian Voices Tryptich** every October, and the international **Jazz Festival** in November, while the mega **Macedonian Folk Songs** and **Balkan Folklore** festivals take place every two or three years, in June and late September. Due to the presence of the university, the New Year celebrations in Blagoevgrad have become Westernized, with fairy lights and Santa Clauses round the square, while the traditional **Kukeri** festival takes place on December 25, rather than January 1.

person per night. Blagoevgrad's two three-star hotels cost the same, but are completely different: the *Alen Mak* (☎073/23031, fax 20713; ④) is a large, soulless conference venue near the main square, while the cosy *Varosha* (☎073/80444; ④) occupies a converted inn just uphill from the Church of the Annunciation. Both have ensuite facilities, phones and TV. A very last resort is the *Bor* (☎073/22491; ②), a less salubrious hotel at the top of a steep flight of steps in the park – it's hell to reach after dark or with luggage.

Good places **to eat** and watch the streetlife are *Pizza Napoli* – which does tastier pizzas than *Planet Italia* – or almost any of the cafés on Todor Aleksandrov, if you just fancy salad, soup and grills. Though most places stop serving food an hour or so earlier, you can usually keep drinking till midnight. To enjoy Bulgarian cuisine in comfort, track down *Mehana Izvora* near the river, which also has live folk music, or *Kuklite* in the Varosha, a former favourite with the university crowd, but now fallen out of fashion. The coolest place to **drink** is the air-conditioned *Kristal* on the corner of pl. Bålgariya, which, like the *Tip Top* sandwich bar next door on ul. Miziya, is open 24-hours.

After midnight, **clubbers** gravitate to two basements off pl. Bålgariya. *Underground*, recognizable by its London tube sign, is a split-level cellar with three bars (one for beer only), where you can indulge in unrestrained but trouble-free drinking and dancing to hard rock, soul or salsa; while *Limbo*, just uphill on ul. Miziya, is a similar set-up playing rap and techno. Both charge a small admission charge at weekends, and stay open till dawn if enough people remain standing.

Moving on from Blagoevgrad

Next to the train station on ul. Sv. Dimitâr Solunski are Blagoevgrad's two intercity **bus stations**: a private one that's just a parking lot, with hourly services to Sofia, Dupnitsa and Sandanski, plus a few to Petrich; and the *avtogara*, with older, more run-down buses to the same destinations, plus Kyustendil, Bansko, Samokov, Gotse Delchev and Petrich. There's also one daily bus from here to Melnik (at 4.20pm), but it isn't very reliable, so you're better off catching a

THE MACEDONIAN QUESTION

Before the First Balkan War of 1912, the Pirin region was part of **Macedonia**, that swathe of Ottoman territory from Skopje to the Aegean, whose jigsaw of peoples – Slavs, Greeks, Albanians and Turks, chiefly – drove diplomats grappling with the Macedonian Question to despair. The Slavs of Macedonia share so many cultural, linguistic and religious affinities with the Bulgarians that the latter have always considered them to be the western branch of the Bulgarian nation. Given their common struggle against Ottoman oppression, and the fact that much of Macedonia was incorporated into the medieval Bulgarian empire, it's clear why aspirations for a future "reunion" of Bulgaria and Macedonia have constantly lurked beneath the surface of Bulgarian politics.

Today this entity is split between Greece, Bulgaria and the **Former Yugoslav Republic of Macedonia (FYROM)**, whose cumbersome title was forced upon it by Greece to emphasize that the new state had no claim on the territory or cultural legacy of Greek Macedonia. In Tito's time great efforts were made to foster a Macedonian identity distinct from Bulgaria's, which has underpinned the claims to be an independent state. Bulgarians regard it with mixed feelings, admiring and envying its relative prosperity but mildly exasperated by its political pretensions. Despite the revival of Macedonian **nationalist parties** in the Pirin – whose bickering pales beside the feuds within the IMRO earlier this century (see p.141 and p.399) – the vast majority of the region's inhabitants have little interest in their aims nor any wish to fight over them.

That might change if the Former Yugoslav Republic of Macedonia is destabilized by the conflict in neighbouring Kosovo, where the Albanians' struggle for independence from Serbia is opposed by the West and Russia for fear of kindred separatism among the Albanians of Macedonia igniting a war over the same territory that Greece, Bulgaria and Serbia have already fought over three times this century (four, if you count the First Balkan War against Turkey). Though its stance has been moderate, the Bulgarian government's disavowal of any claim on Macedonia as its territory stands *at present* implies the right to reconsider in the event of it being violated by others. For more on the Macedonian Question, see Contexts p.397.

morning bus to Sandanski and another bus on from there (see p.132). The MATPU agency runs coaches from the private bus station to **Greece** (daily to Thessaloniki, Seres and Athens, four times weekly to Edessa) crossing the border at Kulata, and to the **Former Yugoslav Republic of Macedonia** (daily except Sun to Bitola), via the border crossing at Stanke Lisichkovo, 26km west of Blagoevgrad.

Heading south towards Greece you're struck by the contrast between the arid highlands and the fertile bed of the **Struma Valley**, for while the region has one of the lowest rainfalls in Bulgaria, the Struma flows even in autumn. In May and June when it's swollen by snowmelt you can experience the thrill of **whitewater rafting**, organized by Odeyssia-in (see p.64). Otherwise, sit back and enjoy the scenery beyond **SIMITLI** (where a branch road heads off east towards Bansko), as the E-79 enters the **Kresna Gorge**, while trains forge their way through thirteen tunnels before reaching Sandanski (see p.132). If you're driving along here, beware of the stream of trucks thundering along a two-lane country road designated as a European highway.

Bansko and the mountains

Bansko, the nicest of the small Pirin mountain towns, makes a good jumping-off point for some amazing hikes in the **Pirin National Park**, and is a transport nexus with buses to the Struma and Mesta valleys flanking the Pirin range, and trains to Velingrad in the western Rhodopes. It also gives easy access to a couple of attractive, traditional villages **Dobrinishte** and **Dobârsko**, both of which are surrounded by stunning countryside.

The road from the Struma Valley follows the River Gradevska that separates the Rila and Pirin ranges, and crosses the **PREDEL PASS**, the site of the **Pirin Pee folklore festival** where 2000 amateur musicians and dancers from towns and villages throughout the region perform on a series of small stages. The festival is held every two years (next scheduled for 1999) over a weekend in August. For the exact date, enquire at the tourist office in Blagoevgrad, Bansko or Sandanski.

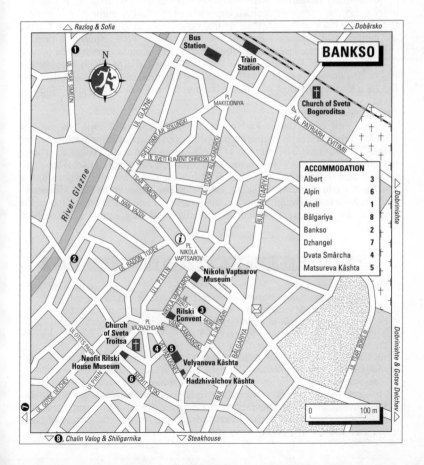

The route also passes through **RAZLOG**, 6km north of Bansko, which is a less attractive town, notable only for its **Kukeri rites** on January 1, when large processions of costumed revellers take over the centre.

Bansko

Winter lasts for almost half the year in **BANSKO**, a town of just under 10,000 people nestled among greenery in the shadow of ice-capped Mt Vihren, the highest peak in the Pirin range. Founded by exiled clans in the fifteenth century, Bansko has lived by trade and hard graft – growing tobacco at an altitude of 1000m above sea level – and remains an agricultural town, despite a big move into tourism. Though popular with Sofians as a winter ski and summer alpine resort, most tourists arrive on Friday and leave on Sunday, so local tavernas often close during the week while their owners work in the fields, and Bansko goes to bed early.

Unlike many Bulgarian towns, its modernized centre co-exists easily with the older quarters, a maze of cobbled lanes where the timber-framed stone houses hide behind thick walls with stout double doors, built to withstand siege. During the centuries of Ottoman rule, Christian households were required to provide "hospitality" to travellers bearing the sultan's seal of authorization, and preyed upon by rapacious Bashibazouks – irregular troops charged with keeping the Bulgarians cowed. Instead, Bansko's houses nurtured men bent on redeeming Bulgaria from oppression, who figure large in the nation's history and culture.

Arrival and information

The **bus and train stations** are on the northern fringes of town, ten minutes' walk from the central pl. Vaptsarov, where Bansko's **tourist information centre** (Mon–Fri 9am–1pm & 3–7pm; ☎07443/5048) lurks in an arcade below the Palace of Culture. Though not always open as advertised, it can supply a useful brochure on the Bansko region and help with accommodation in town or elsewhere, and is also the place to get advice on skiing (see below) or hiking in the Pirin Mountains (p.129). Note that although many of Bansko's sights and hotels are signposted in English, the **signs** are intended for motorists and may signify a roundabout approach.

SKIING AND MOUNTAIN BIKING AROUND BANSKO

Skiing is practised around Bansko from December until March, though its facilities are less extensive than at Borovets (see p.115), and scattered among various localities. The main areas are **Chalin Valog**, 4km southwest of town, which has a 1500-metre ski run with chair lifts and two 300-metre practice slopes with ski-tows, and **Shiligarnika**, higher up the tortuous mountain road (30–40 min by bus from town). Though all grades are catered for, Bansko is the best resort in Bulgaria for advanced skiers. Instructors speak various foreign languages and there's a range of equipment for hire – for details, ask at the tourist office in Bansko.

Another activity that's recently caught on is **mountain-biking**, with several of the hotels renting out bikes. One popular route is to the Belizmata Reservoir, 3km southwest of town; cross the bridge near the *Bansko Hotel* and go straight until the first field track, or follow the road from the *Aneli Hotel* to the barracks and then take the track through the field.

Accommodation

With around forty **hotels** and **B&Bs** in Bansko, tourists are not only spoilt for choice but get a better deal than anywhere else in Bulgaria. Ensuite bathrooms are universal, and other facilities on par with the best private hotels in Sofia. Moreover, everywhere charges on a per-person basis, so solo travellers aren't obliged to pay for an unwanted bed. The rates below are for a double room, including breakfast.

Albert, ul. Byalo More 12 (☎07443/4264). Pleasant, cosy family hotel off pl. Vâzrazhdane. All rooms with TV and phone, though the thinness of the walls can make it a bit too intimate for comfort. ③.

Alpin, Neofit Rilski 6 (☎ & fax 07443/5100). Centrally located, traditional-style building that can accommodate large groups. Sauna, garden, ski rental and transport to the ski slopes. ③.

Aneli, Tsar Simeon 1 (☎ & fax 07443/4298). Two modern blocks in the suburbs across the river, 15min walk from the centre. Well run and comfortable, with a pool, sauna and Russian *banya*, it also rents out skis, mountain bikes and motorbikes. ②.

Bâlgariya, Hristo Matev 2 (☎ & fax 07443/3006). A bit far from the centre but excellent value for money, with a sauna, solarium and fitness centre. There's also cable TV and a minibar in every room. ②.

Bansko, ul. Glazne 17 (☎07443/4275, email *bansko@bis.bg*). Five minutes from pl. Vâzrazhdane, this hotel is perhaps the best in town, with high standards and excellent management. All rooms have satellite TV, direct-dial phone and minibar, and there's also a gym, sauna and bike rental. ⑥.

Dzhangal, ul. Gotse Delchev 24 (☎07443/2661). Located in a quiet area 10min walk from the centre, with a garden, barbecue and sauna. The owner is an expert woodcarver and offers lessons in the art. ③.

Dvata Smârcha, Velyan Ognev 2 (☎07443/2632). Named after the two spruces that shade its garden, this pleasant family hotel serves delicious food, but is very noisy due to three tavernas in the vicinity. Its B&B rates are among the lowest in Bansko. ②.

Izvorite, Chalin Valog (☎07443/2202, fax 07443/2637). Comfy alpine-style hotel near the Chalin Valog and Pioneer ski runs, 4km from town. All rooms have TV, phone and minibar, and there's also a sauna, and ski instruction and rental. ③.

Matsureva kâshta, Velyan Ognev 7 (☎07443/2714). Small family-run hotel furnished in the traditional Bansko style, just off pl. Vâzrazhdane. ③.

Pl. Nikola Vaptsarov

Bansko's modern, pedestrianized zone is centred around **pl. Nikola Vaptsarov**, named after the revolutionary poet. On the corner of the square, near a postwar statue of Vaptsarov in a declamatory pose, is the house where he was born, now the **Nikola Vaptsarov Museum** (Mon–Fri 8am–6pm, Sat–Sun 8am–noon & 2–6pm), which recreates his childhood home and expounds on his life and poetry (in Bulgarian only). An engineer by training, he shared the Futurists' enthusiasm for the machine age and joined the wartime resistance with the courage of his Communist convictions. Vaptsarov's final poem was composed in a Sofia prison as he awaited execution in 1942:

The fight is hard and pitiless
The fight is epic, as they say:
I fell. Another takes my place –
Why single out a name!
After the firing squad – the worms.
Thus does the simple logic go.
But in the storm we'll be with you
My people, for we loved you so.

Ironically, Vaptsarov's father, Yonko, had connections at court from the days when he was an influential figure in Macedonian politics, but his demise in 1939 meant that no one was able to prevent Nikola from being shot by Boris III's lackeys. Attached to the museum is a **crafts exhibition** of textiles, woodcarvings and paintings by local artists, some of which are for sale. The carpets are simply patterned (with green and black stripes predominating) and nothing for serious collectors to get excited about, but as authentic handmade local crafts they make nice souvenirs, and cost less here than in Sofia.

Pl. Vâzrazhdane and around

Bansko's old town begins a short way uphill on **pl. Vâzrazhdane**, dominated by a large monument to an even more renowned son of Bansko, Otets (Father) Paisii, also known as Paisii of Hilendar (1722–73), author of the *Slav-Bulgarian History*. Begun in 1745, when Paisii became a monk at the Bulgarian monastery on Mount Athos, but not finished until 1762, this seminal work exalted the nation's past glories and inspired generations of Bulgarian nationalists.

On the south side of pl. Vâzrazhdane, the **Church of Sveta Troitsa** owes its existence to the efforts of another patriot associated with Bansko, Neofit Rilski. Born in 1793, Neofit was a key figure in the nineteenth-century resurgence of Bulgarian education and church life, in the face of Turkish restrictions and Greek influence, and led the campaign to restore Rila Monastery and build the local church. To accomplish this required a bribe to the governor and to the official witness of the "discovery" of an icon on the site (which qualified it as "holy ground" suitable for a Christian place of worship). A wall was then raised to conceal the townsfolks' enlargement of the church beyond the size set by Turkish clerks – for which the mayor of Bansko was jailed for five years. A monument in the churchyard remembers Peyu Yavorov (see p.83), poet and *Voyvoda*, or "war leader", who celebrated Bansko's liberation from the Turks in October 1912 by proclaiming "Throw away your fezzes, brothers! From today you are free Bulgarians".

Behind the church, the **Neofit Rilski House-Museum** (daily 9am–noon & 2–5pm) contains reconstructions of an eighteenth-century schoolroom and a collection of Rilski's works – textbooks, anthologies and the first Bulgarian grammar – though he never actually lived or taught here.

At the northeast corner of pl. Vâzrazhdane, the **Rilski Convent** (*Rilski Metoh*) has now been restored to the Orthodox Church and is once again a nunnery affiliated to Rila Monastery. The building still contains, however, an **Icon Museum** (Mon–Fri 9am–noon & 2–5pm) from Communist times, showing the achievements of Bansko's nineteenth-century icon painters – a school largely centred around the Vienna-educated Toma Vishanov, who, with pupils Dimitâr and Simeon Molerov, travelled from village to village decorating local churches. One highlight is an anonymous *Wheel of Time*, in which everyday village scenes are encircled by portrayals of the different ages of man.

A couple of minutes' walk south of pl. Vâzrazhdane, the **Velyanova kâshta**, at Velyan Ognev 5 (Mon–Fri 9am–noon & 2–5pm), is a typical stone house, with nineteenth-century furnishings and rugs, giving an idea of how citizens once lived. Alas, you can no longer visit the **Hadzhivâlchova kâshta** at no. 11, recalling the eighteenth-century merchant Hadzhi Vâlcho, who exploited Bansko's position midway between the Danube and the Aegean to create a minor trading empire. Reputedly the uncle of Neofit Rilski, Vâlcho was a major patron of the arts

Like other Pirin towns, Bansko takes its **festivals** seriously. Though its New Year **Kukeri rites** are outclassed by a larger event in Razlog, Bansko makes amends with the **Great Easter Concert** on the second day of the Orthodox Easter; the **Celebration of Bansko Traditions** (May 17–24), featuring comedy, culinary and crafts competions; and **Bansko Day** (October 5), when you can hear the **male choirs** for which the region is known. The town also makes a good base for visiting nearby festivals at the Predel Pass (see p.123), Dobrinishte or Dobârsko (see overleaf).

who was instrumental in encouraging the early flowering of the Bansko icon school, and donated large sums to both Rila and Zografski monasteries.

Church of Sveta Bogoroditsa and the market

Across town, east of the train station, the early nineteenth-century **Church of Sveta Bogoroditsa** is an atmospheric, semi-submerged structure beside the town cemetery, though most of its treasures – including the central doors of the iconostasis, painted by Toma Vishanov – have been moved to the Icon Museum.

Last but not least, the **market** that enlivens ul. Tsar Simeon on Sunday mornings, is worth a visit for its handwoven blankets, rugs and clothing which are on sale alongside workaday objects such as cowbells, saddles and harnesses.

Eating, drinking and nightlife

Eating and **drinking** are practically synonymous in Bansko, with nearly forty tavernas offering much the same menu and drinks served in pottery beakers. As chefs and owners change frequently, places that were good turn bad or vice versa, so you might as well choose somewhere on the basis of its music or its seating. Local specialities include *chomlek* (meat and potato stew), *katino meze* (fried meat with garlic and mushrooms) and *kapama* (meat, rice and pickled cabbage stew). For a change of cuisine, try the cheap-and-cheerful *Steakhouse* on ul. Sterfan Stambolov. If you just want a drink or an ice cream or beer, a dozen café-bars along Tsar Simeon vie for custom. **Nightlife** boils down to more of the same plus whatever's cooking at the *Vihren* disco on ul. Nikola Vaptsarov.

Around Bansko

Lying between two major ranges of mountains, Bansko and its surrounding countryside has some great walks. The village of **Dobârsko**, north of town, gives access to the huge network of hikes in the Rila Mountains (see p.112), while **Dobrinishte**, 6km east, serves as an excellent starting point for walks in the **Pirin Mountains**, Bulgaria's wildest range.

The heart of the Pirin massif consists of 45 peaks, all of which are more than 2590m tall, snow-capped for much of the year and subject to such powerful winds and violent storms that the early Slavs were convinced that this was the abode of the Thunder God, Perun. Pure water tarns and short-lived wildflowers abound in the highland valleys, and the slopes are a botanist's delight, with clumps of Scots, Corsican, Macedonian and white pine. The **Pirin National Park** covers 40,447 hectares of this terrain including the Bayuvi Dupki–Dzhindzhritsa and Yulen biosphere reserves. Its mountains are predominantly granite, with scores of glacial cirques, at the bottom of which are 186 lakes, but there is also a karst region of limestone crags and caves. The highest peaks and most of the lakes are in the northern Pirin, which is crisscrossed with hiking **trails** between *hizhi* – simple chalets connected to the outside world by radio telephone. Although, by law, they are forbidden to turn anyone away, you could end up on a bed in the corridor if all the rooms are occupied, so it's wise to book ahead.

Dobârsko

Twenty-three kilometres north of Bansko is the delightful village of **DOBÂRSKO**, whose seventeenth-century **Church of SS Teodor Tiron and Teodor Stratilat** contains a much-hyped picture of Christ's ascension described in one tourist brochure as "Jesus in a space rocket". Dobârsko is also known for its vibrant tradition of **carol singing** (*koleduvane*) on January 6–7, which is prac-tised – uniquely for Bulgaria – by women. There are nice walks in the vicinity, such as to the **Shtrokaloto Waterfall** (10min), while the *Dobârsko* chalet in the hills is the starting point for **hikes in the Rila Mountains** to the *Makedoniya* chalet, the Fish Lakes and beyond (see p.112).

To **get there** from Bansko, you need to change buses in Razlog, though a taxi all the way is an affordable alternative. Should you wish to stay in the village, the *Hotel Dobârsko* (☎997406/273; ①) offers cheap **accommodation** and meals, and has a sauna.

Dobrinishte

Even if you're not going hiking, **DOBRINISHTE** is an attractive village to visit, where sheep- and cattle-breeding, lumbering and woodcarving are the main indus-tries, augumented by a bit of tourism. Its attractions include three water-powered **fulling mills** (*valyavitsi*) for beating wool into felt; the nineteenth-century **Church of Petâr i Pavel**, with lovely iconostasis by Debârsko woodcarvers; a garden of mountain edelweiss flowers; and three outdoor pools fed by hot mineral springs, where you can bathe. Dobrinishte is also known for its **festivals**, with horse races on **Todorovden**, St Theodor's day (the first Sunday of Lent), and folk rituals and music on **Ilinden**, the second Sunday in August. There are also good walks to be enjoyed in the vicinity – for example to the **Valyavitsa Falls** (30min), in the area known as Sveta Nikola.

Despite being so near Bansko, there is no bus service and only five trains a day (two of which leave ridiculously early), so you may have to resort to a taxi to get there and back. If you want to **stay**, the best of the family hotels is the *Viola* (☎07447/2303; ③), on the outskirts of the village, which has TV and fireplaces in most of rooms.

Moving on from Bansko and Dobrinishte

From Bansko there are fairly frequent **buses** to Blagoevgrad (see p.118) via the Predel Pass, and to the southern Pirin town of Gotse Delchev (see p.130). In addi-tion, there are five daily services to Sofia (via Dupnitsa), as well as early morning services to Plovdiv (via Pazardzhik) and Petrich. Besides the Sofia-bound buses that pass through Razlog, there are also three local ones a day that terminate there.

Alternatively, you could take advantage of the **narrow-gauge railway** from Dobrinishte to Septemvri, via Bansko, Razlog and the spa resort of Velingrad (see p.315). There are four trains a day plus an extra one terminating at Velingrad on

HIKING IN THE PIRIN

If you're considering **hiking in the Pirin**, it's essential to get a good map. The *Domino CityGuide* to the Blagoevgrad region includes one detailing all the trails below, and is more user friendly than BTS maps or Kartografiya's 1:55,000 map of the Pirin, despite their greater detail. At a pinch, you could make do with the brochure from the tourist office in Bansko, which is also the place to ask about staying in *hizhi* and reserving beds. Besides this, stout boots, warm waterproof clothing, a sleeping bag and food are essential. You can camp at designated spots (not within nature reserves), but only during the summer; inexperienced hikers should avoid high peaks and snowy ground and, ideally, join a group familiar with the mountains, or hire a guide through the tourist office.

The **trails** below cover only part of the northern Pirin; determined hikers could continue farther south towards Gotse Delchev or Melnik. Staying within the region of Bansko and Dobrinishte, you can still enjoy the Pirin at its best on a two- or three-day hike around Mt Vihren and the lakes, on a circuit beginning or ending at a chalet that's accessible by road from Bansko or Dobrinishte. By taking a taxi instead of walking to the chalet you'll be fit to start hiking immediately. As the road from Bansko to the *Vihren* chalet is more direct than the journey from Dobrinishte to the *Bezbog* hut, it's easier to start from Bansko and end at Dobrinishte, although it's feasible to complete the circuit in either direction.

From Bansko, take the minor road heading south, which forks after 6km. The right-hand, better surfaced fork leads to the *Bunderitsa* hut 8km away, and on past the **Baikushev Fir** – a mighty tree 1300 years old – to the larger *Vihren* chalet, 2km beyond. From here on the scenery is magnificent, whether you make the two-and-a-half hour ascent of **Mt Vihren** (2914m), Bulgaria's second highest peak – with the option of carrying on into the karst region (see below) – or trek westwards past lakes and **Mt Todorin** (2746m) to the *Demyanitsa* chalet (4hr). For those with more time, there's a trail (3hr) south to the **Tevno Ezero** (Dark Lake) in the heart of the Pirin, and another to the *Yane Sandanski* hut, a base for weekend hikers from Sandanski. Otherwise, head eastwards to the *Bezbog* hut, on a trail (4hr 30min) that skirts the **Yulen Nature Reserve**, passing unforgetable vistas.

Starting **from Dobrinishte** entails reaching the *Gotse Delchev* hut by a 12km mountain road that peters out into a track. In the vicinity of the hut is the 45m-high **Visokata Ela** (Tall Fir), the tallest in the Pirin Mountains, and a **chair lift** to the *Bezbog* (Godforsaken) chalet, 700m higher up, which is also accessible by footpath (2hr 30min). Beside the lakes near the chalet there are signposted trails to the **Bezbog Peak** (1hr 30min) or a larger cluster of lakes at **Popovski Tsirkus** (1hr 30min), not to mention the *Demyanitsa* hut, if you're doing the circuit in the other direction.

Another possibility is to explore the **karst region** north of Mt Vihren, where the trail from Mt Vihren to the *Yavorov* chalet (7hr) is the longest, hardest and most exciting in the Pirin, crossing spectacular cols, serpentines and other rock formations. The most memorable part is the **Koncheto** (Horse), a 1500-metre-long ridge less than a metre wide, above an abyss; a steel rope provides a handhold. From the *Yavorov* chalet the trail continues past the **Bayuvi Dupki–Dzhindzhirtsa Reserve**, a massif ringed by karstic cirques and peaks over 2800m tall, down to the Predel Pass (see p.123).

Mondays, Saturdays and Sundays. The scenic route goes through Avramovi Kolibi, the highest station on the Balkan Peninsula – but be warned that it takes almost five hours to reach Velingrad, less than 60km away.

Gotse Delchev and around

Despite being named after Macedonia's greatest revolutionary (see box), **GOTSE DELCHEV** is one of the Pirin's mellowest towns, set in a wide valley watered by the Mesta and suffused with a bucolic air, cows stalking the bus station and tobacco leaves drying in back gardens. Though short on sights, Gotse boasts a vivacious café society and several **festivals**, with folklore events around the time of the Orthodox Easter, Gotse Delchev Day on October 18, and an international classical guitar festival in late May, not to mention one of Bulgaria's best **Folk Song and Dance Ensembles.** In addition, Gotse is the jumping-off point for several attractive highland villages in the region, such as **Leshten**, **Kovachevitsa** and **Delchovo**.

Gotse Delchev

From the bus station, ul. Vancharska leads past a red-brick synagogue (long since converted into apartments), to some nineteenth-century **crafts workshops** at the lower end of the main shopping street, ul. Târgovska, a cobbled boulevard lined with cherry trees and crumbling houses. On ul. Botev, which crosses it, the old Prokopov House contains a **History Museum** (Tues–Sat 10am–noon & 2–6pm) with a collection of folk costumes, and artefacts from Nicopolis ad Nestrum (see opposite), but a better set-piece is the **Rifat Bei kâshta** (same hours), embodying the lifestyle and crafts of the National Revival era. It's located beside the Delchecska River on the far side of the canal, near a 500-year-old, 24m-high plane tree called *Chinarbei*.

Practicalities

While the **tourist information centre** (☎0751/22086) in the town hall is still new enough to be unsure of its opening hours, its brochure's maps, details of festivals, walks and local beauty spots are very useful. Staff there can also make reservations in rooms in the highland villages, as well as at **hotels** in town. The *Malamovata Kâshta* (☎0751/29135; ③) occupies a restored nineteenth-century mansion at ul. Hristo Botev 25, and contains one of the best **restaurants** in town, while the equally comfortable *Hristoff*, at Byalo More 10 (☎0751/29113; ③), boasts a rooftop swimming pool. Of the **cafés**, *Gradina* on ul. Tsaritsa Ioanna is a popular outdoor place with cheesy live music, but there's no shortage of other similar places to choose from.

The **Greek frontier** is just 20km south of Gotse, and a new border post near Ilinden is scheduled to open in 1999, when bus links with Dhrama, the first big town on the Greek side, will follow. For the time being, however, Gotse is a bit cut off from the main southbound routes and **moving on** can be problematic. Barring the 7.20am bus to Petrich (daily except Tues & Thurs) and a 1pm bus to Dospat (Mon, Wed & Fri) that's the sole link to the western Rhodopes, most head north towards Blagoevgrad, Bansko or Sofia, while the villages around Gotse are only served on alternate days, if at all.

Highland villages around Gotse

Village tourism is the new cottage industry and buzzword in the region, as wealthy Sofians pay to live in authentic highland hamlets, consume local food and

The Whore of Babylon fresco at Rila

Bread delivery, Sofia

Bulevard Vitosha, Sofia

Alexandâr Nevski Church, Sofia

The Tsaravets citadel, Veliko Târnovo

Rila Monastery

Field with wildflowers, southwest Bulgaria

The Varosh quarter, Veliko Târnovo

Traditional house, Bozhentsi

Thracian tomb, Kazanlâk

The Madara Horseman

GOTSE DELCHEV (1872–1903)

Born in Kukush (now Kilkis in northern Greece) and inspired by Balkan revolutionaries Vasil Levski and Hristo Botev, **Gotse Delchev** dedicated himself to the cause of a free Macedonia, organizing a network of underground cells for the IMRO (p.141 and p.399) while publicly leading the life of a teacher. An enlightened and unusually liberal revolutionary, he was similar to his idol Levski in refusing to target local Turks, declaring that they too were victims of Ottoman oppression. Whilst undoubtedly in the Bulgarian revolutionary tradition, he stood for an **autonomous Macedonia** as part of some future Balkan federation, as opposed to the right-wing, Sofia-based *Vârhovisti* or Supremists, who sought its union with Bulgaria.

Killed in a skirmish with Turkish troops three months before the long awaited and abortive Ilinden uprising, Delchev neither witnessed nor was tarnished by the IMRO's decline into sectarian butchery, and is still honoured as a hero in both Bulgaria and the Former Yugoslav Republic of Macedonia, where his moustached portrait hangs in many a café. Initially buried in Rila Monastery, his bones were taken after World War II to the Macedonian capital Skopje, where his tomb lies in the courtyard of the Church of Sveti Spas.

The only biography of Delchev in the English language is Mercia Macdermott's *Freedom or Death* (see p.413 in *Contexts*). Researched in Bulgaria during the Communist period, it tends to exaggerate his role as an ardent socialist and Bulgarian nationalist, but is an inspiring account nonetheless.

wine and bliss out on the scenery – yet still enjoy decent bathrooms and cable TV. In fact, amenities vary from village to village – or house to house in places – from tastefully modernized stone houses to spartan lodgings with a local *Baba* (Granny). Gotse's tourist office can suggest options and phone on your behalf.

Unfortunately, this rural idyll is poorly served by **buses**. Currently, there is one on alternate days to Kovachevitsa, via Leshten, and none at all to Dolen, while Delchevo is served by two buses on a Monday and Friday (leaving Gotse Delchev at 8am and 4pm), though this service may be discontinued. Local **taxis** are the only other option, with prices depending on the state of the road – the one to Kovachevitsa is awful, whereas Delchevo is an easy drive.

Leshten and Kovachevitsa

East of Gotse the highlands belong to the Rhodopes, not the Pirin. The land is dry and stony, with Muslim and Christian villages dotted amongst stunted oaks, acacias and wild thyme, and subsisting on goats and tobacco. Once you've turned off the Dospat road onto the (unsigned) mountain road to Kovachevitsa, you'll pass the **ruins of Nicopolis ad Nestrum**, once a staging point on the Roman road from Constantinople to the Adriactic, and climb up into the mountains, leaving civilization behind.

After 10km of potholes it's a relief to reach **LESHTEN**, a pretty, picture-postcard village whose thirty-five inhabitants can be outnumbered by guests in the fifteen traditional homes (☎ & fax 07527/448), refurbished by the owner of the restaurant beside the church. All rooms have a double bed, TV, ensuite bathroom and underfloor heating; rates are $50 per person per night, and for an extra charge you'll get a kitchen stocked with food (otherwise, you can eat at his restaurant).

KOVACHEVITSA lies another 8km or so uphill, past a Pomak (Muslim) village that prefers strangers not to stop. Twice the size of Leshten and less sanitized, Kovachevitsa's National Revival houses and scenic vistas have made it a popular film location (more than fifteen movies have been shot here). The most comfortable places to stay are the *Zhechevata* (☎07527/461 or 02/810305), *Kapsazovite* (☎07527/443 or 02/9811671) and *Milchevata* (☎07527/445 or 02/43394) houses – which charge $21 per head B&B – and the *Spasovta kâshta* (☎075227/414 or 02/243083), charging from $15–19; though you can pay as little as $8–10 at the *Daskalovata* (☎07527/412) or *Bayatevata* (☎07527/413) houses.

In both villages, hosts can advise on **walks** in the hills, and arrange **horse-riding** or private transport to Melnik and other hard-to-reach places.

Dolen

Farther from Gotse but only 3km off the Dospat road, the large village of **DOLEN** seems more authentic due to its mixed Christian-Pomak population, amazingly ramshackle houses and barnyard smells. The oldest part of the village lies off downhill to the right as you approach the newer bit. In either you can expect shrugs when asking directions to the *Tashkov* villa or *Sofproekt* holiday home (☎02/880838), two ventures run by a Sofian which the locals seem to know nothing about yet. Both cost $6 per person per night B&B.

Delchevo and beyond

Nine kilometres in the opposite direction from Gotse, the village of **DELCHEVO** in the foothills of the southern Pirin is blessed by meadows, forests and streams, but its houses are built in the frugal Rhodope style rather than mortared and multi-storeyed in the Pirin fashion – the circle of houses around the church is especially fine. You'll need to book a week ahead at the *Tanchev* (☎0751/23722; ②), *Penkov* (☎0751/28842; ②), or *Dokuzov* (☎0751/2662; ②) **guest houses**, if you're planning to attend the celebration of **Konstantin and Elena's day** (May 21) on Sveti Konstantin peak, forty minutes' walk from the village, or the **Ilindenski Sâbor** folklore festival at nearby Popovi Livadi on August 2.

From Delchevo there are pleasant **walks** to the **Sveta Bogoroditsa Monastery** (30–40min), the ruined medieval fortress of **Momina Kula** (1hr 20min) or the highland resort of **Popovi Livadi** (2hr), whose hikers' chalet marks the beginning of some longer trails to the *Pirin* hut (10hr) and other sites in the Pirin National Park. There's also a spectacular **road** though the mountains **to Rozhen and Melnik**, but with no buses and little traffic of any kind along its beaten-up 80km, anyone travelling this way will have to hire a taxi.

Sandanski

On the other side of the mountains from Gotse, **SANDANSKI** enjoys the warmest, sunniest climate in Bulgaria, with alpine breezes mellowing its Mediterranean aridity, and hot mineral springs whose curative effects have been appreciated since Roman times – making it a **health resort** *par excellence*. You don't have to be ill to enjoy the baths and pampering at the "Hydro" – great if you've just been hiking in the mountains – nor the town's festivals, restaurants and *korso*, centred around Ul. Makedoniya. Moreover, Sandanski offers the best public transport access to Melnik, Rozhen and Rupite – the chief attractions in the far south – plus another way into the Pirin range, via the mountain resort of Popina Lâka and the *Yane Sandanski* chalet.

Sandanski's modern appearance belies its origins as Desudava, a settlement of the Thracian Medi tribe and the likely birthplace of **Spartacus**, who led the great slave revolt against the Roman Empire in the first century BC. The revolt originated in Sicily, where Spartacus – like other Medi – had been deported to labour on the island's estates following the Roman conquest of Thrace. While a Spartacus monument is visible from the highway, vestiges of the past in the centre of town relate to the Orthodox **saints Kozma and Damyan**, local brothers whose healing skills earned them the accolade *Sveti Vrach* (Blessed Doctor) – also the town's name prior to the Turkish conquest. A provincial *chiflik* under Ottoman rule, it rivalled Melnik as a market town in the nineteenth century and surpassed it after disaster befell Melnik in 1913. The town's present name, bestowed in 1949, pays tribute to the nineteenth-century Macedonian freedom fighter Yane Sandanski.

The Town

Sandanski's **train station** is 4km west of town, but services are met by a bus into the centre, where the **bus station** is a few blocks downhill from the main square, **pl. Bålgariya**. Head straight for the **Visitors Centre** in the civic complex (daily 10am–7pm; ☎0746/2403, email *bicc@omega.bg*), whose friendly staff can book rooms, supply maps and information, arrange mountain guides and may rent out mountain bikes in the future. They also run excursions to Melnik and Rozhen Monastery (see overleaf), and maintain an up-to-date timetable of both state and private buses – the latter leave from behind the civic complex.

Halfway down ul. Makedoniya, which runs through the centre of town to the park, on the left-hand side is the **Archeological Museum** (Mon–Sat 9am–noon & 2–6pm). Built over a late Roman/early Byzantine villa with a walk-round display of a mosaic floor found *in situ*, beside the remains of an Episcopal Basilica, its upper floor is filled with funerary stoneware from the necropolis of Muletarovo, including a child's sarcophagus with bull- and ram-head reliefs. Votive tablets feature Zeus and Hera or a hunter figure presumed to be Artemis – carved in a vigorous, almost naive style suggesting that Desudava was a predominantly Thracian, rather than a Roman or Hellenic, town.

A hundred metres or so beyond the museum, on the other side of the road, lies the ziggurat-shaped *Hotel Sandanski* (see overleaf), and beyond that a 192-acre **park** planted with more than 200 exotic species including Japanese ginkos and

---

FESTIVALS

As the cultural centre of the southern Pirin, Sandanski hosts several **festivals** besides the two mentioned overleaf (all on pl. Bålgariya unless stated otherwise). The most boisterous are the competition for local **Kukeri** groups on January 1 – with grotesquely costumed, chanting celebrants – and **Trifon Zarazen** (February 14), when prizes are given for the best young wines and everyone gets drunk. The **Sandanski Spring** beauty pageant in March is followed by the **Day of My Town** at the end of April, which combines folk dancing on the square with a religious festival outside the Church of Kozma and Damyan. Over Easter there's an **art exhibition**, and finally, the **Pirin Folklore Festival** takes place on the second weekend of September, a play-off between pop-folk groups in the summer theatre in the park, with prizes awarded on the Sunday.

Californian sequoias. Its large outdoor warm **pool** (May–Sept daily 9am–8pm), water-slides, boating lake and paths into the hills are all open to the public.

The nineteenth-century **Church of Sv. Sv. Bezsrebrenitsi Kozma i Demyan**, on the northern edge of the town, by the town cemetery, is the focus of the festivals of *Golyama Bogoroditsa* (August 15) and *Malka Bogoroditsa* (September 16), invoking the Virgin's protection of mothers and children. Even if you're not around then, the church is worth seeing for its fine murals and iconostasis.

Practicalities

With nine **hotels** in town you can afford to be choosy. Your best bet is to go for a comfortable hotel like the *Aneli*, just uphill from pl. Bålgariya (☎0746/8952; ②), the equally central but smaller *Sv. Sv. Konstantin i Elena*, 50m along ul. Makedoniya, from the square (☎0746/2423; ①), or the *Andoni* on ul. Voden (☎0746/3149; ②). If money's no object, go for the Balkans' largest spa-hotel, the *Hotel Sandanski*, also known as the Hydro, at the end of ul. Makedoniya (☎0746/0746/5165; ⑤), with all mod cons and sports facilities. Booking through the Visitors Centre gets you a big discount on rooms, and two kinds of medical treatment for $7. If you don't mind being 4km from town, the former Politburo resort *Sveti Vrach* (☎0746/8626; ②–⑧) has equally good facilities and a wonderful setting with a Henry Moore sculpture and a duck lake in the grounds; for real opulence take the Presidential suite ($220) once enjoyed by Todor Zhivkov. Both the *Sandanski* and the *Sveti Vrach* have large, heated indoor pools.

The *Melnik* and *Sveti Vrach* tavernas, on Makedoniya, and the *Riviera*, in a side-street to the left off the main road west of pl. Bålgariya, serve good, cheap Bulgarian **meals**. A few Russian or Spanish dishes feature on the menus at the *Davidoff* and *El Camino*, near the corner of ul. Makedoniya and Hristo Smirnenski, while, if you want to eat Greek, you should track down *Karat* on the same sidestreet as the *Hotel Andoni*, which turns off ul. Makedoniya beside a stand-up barbecue joint serving spicy ribs. For fish, try the *Evropa*, beside the ruins of the Episcopal Basilica, which has a nice terrace, a violinist and a singer.

Though there are **bureaux de change** on ul. Makedoniya, nowhere in Sandanski gives cash advances on credit cards – the nearest place this can be done is Blagoevgrad. You can change travellers' cheques at the *Sandanski*.

Melnik and Rozhen Monastery

Deservedly the most popular destination in the southern Pirin, the tiny town of **Melnik**, 20km southeast of Sandanski, is known for its robust red wine, impressive houses and natural surroundings. An ideal place to relax, favoured by Sofians and foreign diplomats at weekends, it's readily accessible by car via the E79, or on one of the five public buses daily (plus a private one), from Sandanski. In addition, the Sandanski Visitors Centre organizes a minibus excursion on Saturdays (10am) that includes the **Rozhen Monastery** and **Rupite** – ideal for those who wish to see them all but haven't much time. Tickets ($7) are on sale throughout the week, and the trip can be arranged on other days for groups of at least six passengers, with a day's notice.

The route from Sandanski passes tobacco fields hugging the roadside above the fertile bed of the Struma, before snaking into hills that become arid and rocky, swelling into desolate mountains stretching towards Greece and the Aegean. Roads deteriorate and faded notices attest to the border zone that previously existed here. If you're not in a hurry, stay at least one night in Melnik and walk over the hills to the Rozhen Monastery – one of Bulgaria's oldest, most picturesque foundations.

Melnik

Approaching **MELNIK** you'll catch glimpses of the wall of mountains that allowed the townsfolk to thumb their noses at the Byzantine Empire in the eleventh century. Melnik hides until the last moment, encircled by hard-edged crags, scree slopes and sandstone cones. Its straggling main street is lined with tavernas, whitewashed stone houses on timber props festooned with flowers, and vines overhanging cobbled alleys and narrow courtyards. Rooms for rent and wine for sale make it plain that the locals are used to tourists, while the new hotels being built attest to the sums that outsiders are now investing, yet it remains to be seen if this will reverse Melnik's extraordinary decline, from a town of 20,000 in 1880 to a village of 267 people today. A century ago the population was largely Greek, making it a unique outpost of Hellenic civilization in a Slav sea, whence mules departed laden with wine for foreign lands. But the economy waned towards the end of the century and the Second Balkan War of 1913 destroyed the town, sundered its trade routes and provoked a bout of ethnic cleansing. Today, memories of this Greek past have faded and it's hard to imagine so many extra houses, despite the scores of ruins on the hillsides.

Melnik's **layout** is simple, with a single main street running alongside a (usually dry) riverbed spanned by rickety footbridges, then diverging into two gullies. Due to the terrain, houses expand outwards, with the living quarters on the upper floors being larger than the lower barred and shuttered levels that function as cellars or barns. Tiny backstreets invite aimless wandering, while the hillsides abound in tortoises and lizards.

The Town

Of the seventy-two churches active in Melnik's heyday, barely a dozen now exist, and a mere handful still function or are worth noting as ruins. Uphill to the right between the first and second bridges, the **Petâr and Pavel Church** dates from the nineteenth century and has an iconostasis painted in a bold, almost naive style, the lowest row of panels depicting the Fall, while scaly fishes flank the crucifix above the altar screen. There are turbaned Turkish gravestones in the crypt and medieval frescos in the nave.

On the left bank of the river, shaded by 500-year-old plane trees, a cobbled square is overlooked by the derelict former **Konak** of the Turkish governor, a tall white edifice with Moorish scalloped arches. At the outset of the Balkan War, police chief Karim Bey had 27 eminent citizens arrested and murdered to instil fear into the population. Ironically, the erstwhile **jail** beside the Konak is now a cosy hotel.

On the other side of the riverbed, the **Church of Sveti Nikolai Chudotvorets** (St Nicholas the Wonder-worker) was a metropolitan church in the eighteenth century and is still the one favoured for weddings and funerals. Perched on the hillside, it is notable for its minaret-like bell tower and a long veranda overlooking the village. Inside, a wooden bishop's throne decorated with light blue floral patterns

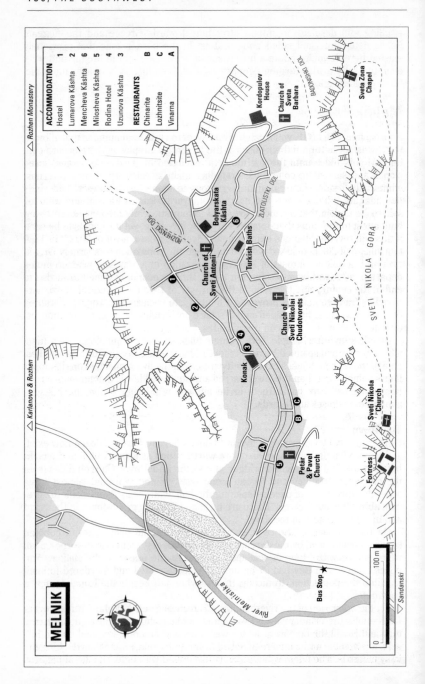

MELNIK

△ Rozhen Monastery

△ Karlanovo & Rozhen

▽ Sandanski

ACCOMMODATION
Hostel   1
Lumarova Kåshta   2
Mencheva Kåshta   6
Milosheva Kåshta   5
Rodina Hotel   4
Uzunova Kåshta   3

RESTAURANTS
Chinarite   B
Lozhnitsite   C
Vinarna   A

Kordopulov House
Church of Sveta Barbara
Sveta Zona Chapel

BADINSKI DOL

Bolyarskata Kåshta
Church of Sveti Antonii
Turkish Baths
ZLATOUSTKI DOL
Church of Sveti Nikolai Chudotvorets
Konak
SVETI NIKOLA GORA
SVETI NIKOLA GORA
Sveti Nikola Church
Fortress
Petår & Pavel Church

River Melnishka
Bus Stop

N

0   100 m

offsets a fine iconostasis where St Nicholas is portrayed seated on a throne, and St John the Baptist holds his own severed head above a narrative sequence of events in the Garden of Eden.

On a hillock near the fork in the gully, the ruined **Bolyarskata kâshta** was the residence of Melnik's thirteenth-century overlord, Alexei Slav, who invited rich Greeks – then persecuted in Plovdiv – to settle here; the house was inhabited until early this century. Nearby are the ruins of the nineteenth-century basilica of **Sveti Antonii**, a healer of the mentally ill.

The right-hand gulley runs on past the overgrown remains of a **Turkish bath** towards some of Melnik's most picturesque National Revival houses. Pride of place goes to the **Kordopulov House** (Tues–Sun 8am–noon & 1.30–6pm), protruding from a rocky shoulder above the gully, its 24 windows surveying every approach. Above the ground floor, now a taverna, the spacious rooms are intimate, the reception room a superb fusion of Turkish and Bulgarian crafts, with painted panelling, rows of cushioned *minder* lining three walls, an intricate latticework ceiling and a multitude of stained-glass windows. The Kordopulov (or Kordopoulos) who built the house in 1754 was a rich merchant of Greek extraction known for his anti-Ottoman sympathies, who prudently installed a secret room as a refuge for the family in emergencies. Below ground are the wine cellars, huge wooden barrels occupying vast caverns cut from the hillside, connected to the vineyards at the rear of the house by a network of tunnels. Further up the valley yet more ruins include the shell of the medieval **Church of Sveta Barbara**.

Around Sveti Nikola Gora

To stretch your legs before hiking to Rozhen Monastery, explore the scattered ruins atop **Sveti Nikola Gora**, south of Melnik, where the start of the trail is signposted near the Church of Sv. Nikolai Chudotvorets. The path soon turns into a dry stream-bed then forks after ten minutes. By walking east along the ridge you can reach the **Sveta Zona Chapel**, by an isolated house overlooking Melnik, where Zona's name-day (April 1) sees an overnight vigil and the blessing of children by day. From here a path turns west, passing the remains of a monastery en route to the eighteenth-century **Sveti Nikola Church**, its apses baring traces of frescos of Adam and Eve, and the dramatic tumbled ramparts of Alexei Slav's **fortress**. To return to Melnik, follow the path down past a derelict modern building. The entire hike takes about an hour, with fine **views** all the way.

Practicalities

Buses stop on the outskirts of Melnik, with at least two a day carrying on to Rozhen and returning half an hour later. There's no tourist office, but the Pirin Tourist Forum brochure, or your landlord, should yield any **information** required. The nearest **bank** is in Sandanski, so make sure you change enough money in advance. The Visitors Centre in Sandanski can reserve accommodation if the phone lines are working, which is advisable if you're coming for the weekend or a festival, or set on a particular establishment.

Most of the family-run **B&Bs** charge $10 per head; a bit more for a room with ensuite facilities. The agreeable *Uzunova Kâshta* (☎07437/270; ③) and *Rodina Hotel* (☎07437/249; ③) are both quiet and central, while the *Milusheva Kâshta* (☎07437/326; ③) and cut-price *Mencheva Kâshta* (☎07437/339; ②) are both near noisy tavernas. The *Lumarova Kâshta* (☎07437/2483) is a bit of a hike uphill, but

---

MELNIK WINE AND FESTIVALS

Justly famed throughout Bulgaria, full-bodied red **Melnik wine** once enjoyed an international reputation through the wine trade organized by the merchants of Dubrovnik, which enriched Alexei Slav and continued under Ottoman rule. Locals even boast that Winston Churchill ordered the wine for his son's wedding. Nowadays it provides a modest livelihood – tavernas slosh it around and locals are keen to flog tourists their homebrew – but the wine sold here isn't any cheaper than in a Sofia supermarket, and can even be dearer. The vineyards are planted with small, dark grapes of the variety known as Melnik Broad Vine, introduced from Syria in the fourteenth century. After harvesting, the grapes are allowed to cool in basements before being pressed and left to ferment in the chilly cellars that riddle the hills around Melnik.

Wine is central to two of Melnik's **festivals**. On **Trifon Zarezan** (February 14) the vineyards are ritually pruned and sprinkled with wine to ensure a bumper crop, and families sample the young wine from last year's harvest. The **harvest** can fall any time from late September to mid-October, but is always celebrated on October 18. Another festival with *horo* dancing occurs on the last Sunday in August.

---

has great views. You can also rent **rooms** or apartments by asking around near the first footbridge, and there's a cheap, 60-bed **hostel** (☎07437/2181) in the backstreets off the Rozhenski dol.

Half-a-dozen **places to eat** offer similar dishes at similar prices, and all stop serving food by 10pm. The *Chinarite* and *Loznitsite* are the liveliest, but the *Vinarna* is better food-wise. Venues for **drinking** include all the above, plus a dozen signposted cellars (*izba*) or tavernas, higher uphill or in the ravines. While the locals aren't a problem, enough outsiders visit Melnik and get drunk to make **safety** an issue; don't visit outlying tavernas after dark unless there's enough of you to deter trouble-makers.

Rozhen and the monastery

Rozhen Monastery makes a great excursion from Melnik, and although it's accessible by bus, anyone who's able would do better to walk and enjoy the scenery. The classic **trail over the hills** (6.5km; 1hr 30min) is signposted in Melnik and later marked by paint. About twenty minutes beyond the point where the watercourse widens, take the right-hand gully and follow it for ten minutes, before tackling a steep, stony path to the crest of the ridge, where your efforts will be rewarded by a stunning view of knife-edged crags and mushroom-like slabs of hard rock poised upon eroded columns. In Robert Littell's thriller *The October Circle*, it's here that the blind Witch of Melnik resides, foretelling the townsfolks' destiny for lumps of sugar in lieu of silver coins – a character based on the real-life oracle Baba Vanga (see p.140). The only scary part of the hike is the final, downhill stretch to the monastery, which is perilously steep and narrow – though it may be widened soon.

A **longer route** (2hr 30min) with nice scenery and few gradients involves heading southeast to the village of Zlatolist and then north to Rozhen. The trail begins in Melnik in the first gully on the right, beyond the Kordopulov house; ignore subsequent paths to the right until the watercourse divides after about 15 minutes, at which point take the right-hand gully and then a fairly obvious track over a pass and down into a broad vale. From there it's a level (but unshaded) hike to **ZLATOLIST**, which has nowhere to eat or drink but will soon be able to boast a **nunnery** built in honour of local wise woman Prepodobna Stoyna (1883–1933), a precursor of Baba Vanga. Pass through the village and take the left fork, whence a 4WD track leads to Rozhen monastery.

If you'd rather catch a **bus** (two daily; 15min) or walk the 7km (1hr 30min) along the **road from Melnik to Rozhen**, look out for the 100m-tall sandstone pyramids and the ramshackle village of **KARLANOVO**, where an old mill has been turned into a **hotel** (☎07437/231; ②) and taverna. Unlike both the trails described above, the road brings you to Rozhen village first instead of the monastery.

Rozhen monastery

Sited on a plateau above the village, **Rozhen Monastery** (*Rozhenski manastir;* dawn to dusk) is small and outwardly austere, having survived looting and burning many times since its foundation in the twelfth century, on the site of an earlier monastery. Dedicated to the "Mother of God's Nativity", its name derives from the ancient form of the word *roden*, meaning "born". The irregular courtyard is intimate and unadorned, save for trestles supporting a canopy of vines whose root is as thick as a thigh. In the **bakery** the oven and walls consist of the same mud-and-straw bricks, giving the entire room the texture of a very coarse wholemeal loaf. Only at the far end, where cell is stacked upon cell, does the woodwork display the finesse found at Rila. The **cells** themselves are arranged to give some idea of monastic life through the ages. The accent is on asceticism, although the vivid colours of rugs and cushions counterpoint the simplicity of the furnishings, and it's clear that leading clerics led a somewhat softer life than their charges, enjoying the use of silver coffee sets and book-holders inlaid with mother of pearl. To see monastic ritual at its best, attend the **Rozhenski Sâbor** on the day of the Holy Virgin (September 8), when icons are paraded around the grounds and symbolic offerings are made.

Within the monastery, the **Church of the Birth of the Holy Virgin**'s cloister shelters a battered *Judgement Day*, which shows the righteous assisted up one side of the ladder to heaven by angels, while sinners attempting to climb the other side are tossed by demons into the mouth of a large red serpent. The torments of hell are vividly depicted on the right, where the damned meet a gory end (prodded by toasting forks and suchlike). Inside the narthex, delicately restored murals include the varied sea-beasts of a *Miraculous Draught of Fishes*, and a splendid *Dormition of the Virgin*. Inside the church itself, the endless ranks of saints covering the walls are eclipsed by a magnificent iconostasis, the work of Debâr artisans. Flowers, birds, fishes and flounces swirl about the richly coloured icons, and the whole screen – unusually wide in proportion to its height – is a triumph of the woodcarver's art.

Sandanski's grave

Downhill from the monastery is the nineteenth-century **Church of Sv. Sv. Kiril i Metodii**, behind which lies the grave of the great Macedonian freedom fighter, **Yane Sandanski** (1872–1915), inscribed with one of his favourite rallying cries: "To live is to struggle: the slave struggles for freedom; the free man, for perfection!" For three days in July culminating on the last Sunday the surrounding hillside hosts a **Macedonian Sâbor** (Gathering) with music, speeches and drinking, where the police are kept busy by scuffles between supporters of the rival factions, VMRO and OMO-Ilinden, both of which mark the anniversary of the Ilinden uprising on July 20 *and* the first Sunday in August (in deference to Old Style date of the event).

Rozhen village
In the valley below, **ROZHEN** is a village of whitewashed, vine-shrouded houses with a workaday feel, where you can enjoy traditional **food** and local wine on the terrace of the *Hanche Rozhen*. If you feel like staying, there are plush **apartments** at the *Complex Rozhena* (☎07437/211; ③), uphill from the road out of the village, which also has a restaurant. A little further on towards Melnik, a signpost points into the woods to the **Church of Sv. Iliya**, where the **grave of Todor Aleksandrov** is an important a shrine for VMRO. One of the main leaders of the Macedonian revolutionary movement after Sandanski's death, Aleksandrov was assassinated by more right-wing colleagues in 1924 for agreeing to co-operate with the Communists in formenting revolution.

The borderlands

The lower reaches of the Struma Valley are borderlands in all but name, with streams of trucks converging on the crossing **into Greece** at **KULATA**, which has a motel and all-year campsite but little else to detain you from heading straight for the 24-hour checkpoint. The other, more tenuous flow of traffic is southwest towards Petrich – the only town in the region – and the **ZLATAREVO** crossing **into the Former Yugoslav Republic of Macedonia**. However, unless you have a car, it's far easier to enter either country on a coach from Sofia or Blagoevgrad than it is to cross over from Kulata or Petrich – so there's little necessity to visit either. That said, it's hard to resist the supernatural hype of **Rupite** – a New Age pilgrimage spot as well as a Christian one – and **Petrich** might appeal to some.

Rupite

Twelve kilometres northeast of Petrich, **RUPITE** is famed in Bulgaria as the home village and burial place of the oracle **Baba Vanga**. Legend has it that at the age of six, she witnessed an angel who offered her the choice between sight and clairvoyance, and she chose the latter. Vanga's subsequent prophecies and healing skills gained her a wide following (including Politburo members), and her vision of Varna engulfed by water was vindicated when it was discovered that the city stood upon an underground lake – from which day on high-rise building was prohibited. In old age she had fewer VIP visitors but her predictions were still heeded – not least by people choosing their Lottery numbers. During the 1994 World Cup Vanga let it be known that the final would be contested by two names beginning with the letter "B". Though Bulgaria lost to Italy in the semi-finals, her supporters still asserted that the prophecy was correct. "She meant Brazil and Baggio," they sagely proclaimed.

After her death in 1996, Vanga was buried in the **Sveta Petka Church**, a postmodern fusion of Slav and Byzantine design, decorated with expressionist murals and icons by the contemporary artist Svetlin Rusev. Its location in the crater of an extinct volcano makes the site even more special for Bulgarian New Agers, who believe it's a powerful energy node – sceptics can simply enjoy the **rock forma-tions** and **birdlife** in the vicinity of the village. There are no hotels as yet, but ask-ing around will probably turn up a bed in someone's house.

Getting to Rupite (and back) by **bus** from Petrich or Blagoevgrad is fraught with uncertainty, with only one or two services a day. If you're able to come on a Saturday, then a far better option is the excursion to Rupite, Melnik and Rozhen, offered by the Sandanski Visitors Centre (see p.133).

Petrich and around

PETRICH is strictly for connoisseurs of Balkan towns that have got rich quick by shady means – sanctions-busting during the UN embargo on Yugoslavia in its case – with more dollar **millionaires** and top-of-the-range cars than anywhere in Bulgaria. Before the war transformed its fortunes, this was a sleepy town of migrants from surrounding villages overlooking the fertile Strumeshnitsa Valley, whose excellent climate produces Bulgaria's earliest crops of cherries, melons and grapes, and superb **peaches**. Other than its pavement cafés, there are few

---

THE IMRO

Nowadays there's little reminder of the years between 1923 and 1934, when Petrich was the "murder capital" of Bulgaria, rife with so many hired killers that the price of an assassination dropped to $6. The warring factions then controlling the region descended from the most legendary of Balkan revolutionary movements, the **IMRO** (VMRO in Bulgarian). The **Internal Macedonian Revolutionary Organization** was founded in Salonika in 1893 by schoolmasters Damian Gruev and Hristo Tatarchev, to liberate Macedonia from Ottoman rule by mass insurrec-tion; to which end, activists like Gotse Delchev built up a "shadow" administration complete with schools, taxation and a postal service, besides sending *cheti*, or armed bands, to wage guerrilla war in the hills.

From the beginning, the IMRO was crippled by internal dissent and soon became divided between those who regarded Macedonia as a natural part of Bulgaria and those who saw it as an autonomous unit, either within Bulgaria or some future Balkan federation. Following Delchev's death, the Sofia-based *Vârhovisti* (Supremists) who regarded IMRO as a tool of the Bulgarian state persuaded its leaders to launch an uprising on *Ilinden* (St Elijah's Day), 2 August 1903. Like the April Rising of 1876, the **Ilinden uprising** was distinguished by heroic resistance (the insurgents held out for three months) and savage Turkish reprisals.

Although the Turks were finally driven out in 1912, Bulgaria, Greece and Serbia quarrelled over the spoils and partitioned Macedonia – Greece and Serbia taking the lion's share. After World War I, a battered IMRO regrouped in the Pirin region, using towns like Petrich as bases for cross-border raids, while the internal struggle between the *Vârhovisti* and autonomists turned fratricidal. Its new leadership oblig-ed Bulgaria's oligarchs by sending IMRO fighters to overthrow the Agrarian government and crush the 1923 uprising, but as the need for their services declined and relations with Greece and Serbia improved the government would no longer tolerate the opium-growing and rackets that financed IMRO's activites, and in 1934 "bloody" Tsankov sent in troops to end its sway over southwestern Bulgaria.

attractions aside from the **Old Town Songs** festival on the first weekend in September and boisterous **Kukeri rites** at New Year, unless you count the **museum** beneath the town hall (Mon–Fri 9am–4pm), harbouring some relics of Romano-Thracian Petra and more recent history involving the IMRO (see box on previous page).

Samuel's fortress

In a park 20km southwest of Petrich stand the ruins of **Samuilova krepost**, or "Samuel's fortress", site of a monument to perhaps the most infamous event in Bulgarian history. After being defeated in battle at Strumitsa in 1014, fourteen thousand Bulgarian prisoners were blinded on the orders of the Byzantine emperor **Basil the Bulgar-slayer**, except one man in every hundred to guide the victims back to Tsar Samuel in Ohrid (now in the Former Yugoslav Republic of Macedonia), who died of apoplexy at the ghastly sight. Two buses a day link Petrich with the fortress.

Practicalities

Petrich's only tourist **accommodation** is the three-star *Hotel Bâlgariya*, Dimo Hadzhidimov 5 (☎0745/2234; ③), directly opposite the bus station. If you're heading for the Former Yugoslav Republic of Macedonia, ask about buses to the town of Strumitsa across the border, which run once or twice a week. Otherwise there's a dearth of public transport to the frontier, and the lack of traffic on the Strumitsa-bound road makes hitching a bit risky – be prepared to pay for a taxi.

travel details

Trains

Bansko to: Dobrinishte (5 daily; 10min); Razlog (3–4 daily; 15min); Septemvri (3 daily; 5hr); Velingrad (3–4 daily; 4hr 30min).

Blagoevgrad to: Dupnitsa (7 daily; 45min); Kocherinovo (4 daily; 15–30min); Sandanski (4–6 daily; 1hr–2hr 15min); Sofia (4–6 daily; 2hr 30min–3hr 30min).

Dupnitsa to: Kocherinovo (4 daily; 15–30min); Kulata (5 daily; 2hr–3hr 45min); Sofia (5–7 daily; 2hr–2hr 45min).

Kocherinovo to: Blagoevgrad (4 daily; 15–30min); Dupnitsa (4 daily; 15–30min); Sofia (4 daily; 2hr 15min–3hr 15min).

Kulata to: Dupnitsa (5 daily; 2hr–3hr 45min); Sandanski (5 daily; 1hr 30min); Sofia (4 daily; 4hr 30min).

Kyustendil to: Gyueshevo (2 daily; 1hr 15min); Pernik (6 daily; 1hr 30min–2hr); Radomir (6 daily; 1hr 15min–1hr 30min); Sofia (3 daily; 2–3hr); Zemen (7 daily; 30min–1hr).

Pernik to: Kyustendil (6 daily; 1hr 30min–2hr); Sofia (every 30min; 45min).

Petrich to: Sandanski (6–7 daily; 45min).

Radomir to: Kyustendil (6 daily; 1hr 15min–1hr 30min).

Razlog to: Bansko (3–4 daily; 15min); Dobrinishte (3 daily; 25min); Septemvri (4 daily; 4hr 45min); Velingrad (4 daily; 4hr 15min).

Sandanski to: Blagoevgrad (4–6 daily; 1hr–2hr 15min); Dupnitsa (4–6 daily; 2–3hr); Kulata (5 daily; 1hr 30min); Petrich (6–7 daily; 45min); Sofia (4–7 daily; 3–5hr).

Sofia to: Blagoevgrad (4–6 daily; 2hr 30min–3hr 30min); Dupnitsa (5–7 daily; 2hr–2hr 45min); Kocherinovo (4 daily; 2hr 15min–3hr 15min); Kyustendil (3 daily; 2–3hr); Pernik (every 30min; 45min); Sandanski (4–7 daily; 3–5hr); Zemen (5 daily; 1hr 30min–1hr 45min).

Zemen to: Kyustendil (7 daily; 30min–1hr); Sofia (5 daily; 1hr 30min–1hr 45min).

Buses

Bansko to: Blagoevgrad (6–8 daily; 1hr); Dupnitsa (5 daily; 1hr 45min); Gotse Delchev (12 daily; 1hr); Petrich (1 daily; 2hr 30min); Plovdiv (1 daily; 4hr); Razlog (6–8 daily; 30min); Sofia (5 daily; 2hr 30min).

Blagoevgrad to: Bansko (6–8 daily; 1hr); Dobrinishte (1 daily; 1hr 15min); Dupnitsa (hourly; 45min); Gabrovo (2 daily on Wed, Sat & Sun; 6–8hr); Gotse Delchev (10 daily; 2hr); Kyustendil (5 daily; 1hr 30min); Melnik (1 daily; 1hr 30min); Petrich (3 daily; 1hr 30min); Plovdiv (1 daily; 4hr 30min); Razlog (2 daily; 1hr 30min); Rila village (hourly; 35min); Sandanski (4 daily; 1hr); Samokov (1 daily; 2hr); Simitli (every 30min; 20min); Sofia (hourly; 1hr 30min); Velingrad (1 daily; 2hr 15min).

Dupnitsa to: Bansko (5 daily; 1hr 45min); Bistritsa (every 30min; 25min); Blagoevgrad (hourly; 45min); Kyustendil (8 daily; 50min); Rila Monastery (3 daily; 1hr); Rila village (5 daily; 30min); Samokov (2 daily; 1hr); Sofia (hourly; 50min).

Gotse Delchev to: Bansko (12 daily; 1hr); Blagoevgrad (6 daily; 2hr); Dospat (1 daily Mon, Wed & Fri; 2hr); Kovachevitsa (3–4 weekly; 45min); Petrich (1 daily except Tues & Thurs; 4hr); Razlog (2 daily; 1hr 15min); Sofia (2 daily; 4hr).

Kyustendil to: Blagoevgrad (5 daily; 1hr 30min); Dupnitsa (8 daily; 50min); Sofia (hourly; 1hr 45min).

Melnik to: Blagoevgrad (1 daily; 1hr 30min); Sandanski (6 daily; 30min).

Petrich to: Bansko (1 daily; 2hr 30min); Blagoevgrad (3 daily; 1hr 30min); Gotse Delchev (1 daily except Tues & Thurs; 4hr); Kulata (5 daily; 25min); Sandanski (4 daily; 30min).

Rila village to: Blagoevgrad (hourly; 35min); Dupnitsa (5 daily; 30min); Rila Monastery (2–3 daily; 30min).

Samokov to: Blagoevgrad (1 daily; 2hr); Borovets (hourly; 30min); Dupnitsa (2 daily; 1hr); Govedartsi (6 daily; 40min); Plovdiv (1 daily; 1hr 45min); Sandanski (1 daily; 3hr); Sofia (every 30min–1hr; 1hr).

Sandanski to: Blagoevgrad (7 daily; 1hr); Gotse Delchev (1 daily except Tues & Thurs; 1hr); Melnik (6 daily; 30min); Petrich (4 daily; 30min); Samokov (1 daily; 3hr); Sofia (8–9 daily; 3hr 30min).

Sofia *Avtogara Yug* to: Samokov (every 30min; 1hr).

Avtogara Ovcha Kupel to: Bansko (1 daily; 2hr 30min); Blagoevgrad (hourly; 1hr 30min); Dupnitsa (hourly; 50min); Gotse Delchev (2 daily; 4hr); Kyustendil (hourly; 1hr 45min); Rila Monastery (June–Aug 1–2 daily; 2hr 30min); Samokov (every 30min; 1hr); Sandanski (8–9 daily; 3hr 30min).

International trains

Blagoevgrad to: Thessaloniki (1 daily; 7hr 45min).

Dupnitsa to: Thessaloniki (1 daily; 8hr).

Sandanski to: Thessaloniki (1 daily; 6hr 30min).

International buses

Blagoevgrad to: Athens (1 daily; 14–16hr); Bitola (1 daily except Sun; 8–9hr); Thessaloniki (2–3 daily; 11–12hr).

Kyustendil to: Bitola (1 daily; 7hr 30min); Durrës (4 weekly on Sun, Tues, Wed & Fri; 15hr); Ohrid (July & Aug 1 daily; 9hr 40min); Skopje (1 daily; 3hr); Tirana (4 weekly on Sun, Tues, Wed & Fri; 16hr).

CHAPTER THREE

THE BALKAN RANGE AND THE DANUBIAN PLAIN

T he Balkan Range cuts right across the country, a forbidding swathe of rock known to the Bulgarians as the **Stara planina** – the "Old Mountains". To the ancients they were the Haemus, lair of brigands and supposed home of the North Wind. In the seventh and eighth centuries, the Balkan Mountains were the birthplace of the Bulgarian nation-state. It was here, first at Pliska, and later at Preslav, that the Bulgar khans established and ruled over a feu-

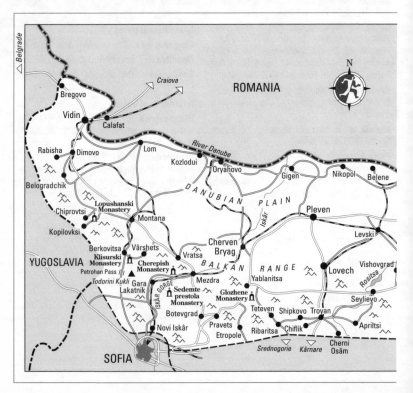

dal realm – known to historians as the "First Bulgarian Kingdom". Here too, after a period of Byzantine control, the Bulgarian nobility (the bolyari) proclaimed the "Second Kingdom" and established a new and magnificent capital at Veliko Târnovo. During the Ottoman occupation, the villages and monasteries of the Stara planina helped to preserve Bulgarian traditions, preparing the ground for the re-emergence of native culture during the nineteenth-century National Revival.

Given the mountainous topography and the vagaries of the road and train network, **routes** through the Balkan Range are many and complex. The main north-bound route from Sofia to the Danubian citadel town of **Vidin** provides access to a range of off-the-beaten-track destinations in the rural northwest, with settlements like **Vratsa**, **Berkovitsa**, **Chiprovtsi** and **Belogradchik** giving access to the stupendous – and very varied – mountainscapes of the western Balkan Range. For those heading for the central and eastern Balkan Range, east–west routes between Sofia and the sea skirt the highest peaks, and tend to be much quicker than north–south routes across the backbone of the Range. Hence many people approach the area by train from either the Sofia–Burgas line through the Valley of the Roses (see Chapter Four), or the Sofia–Varna line which arcs round the mountains to the north. The latter gives access to three potential urban bases from which to explore the area: **Pleven**, whose numerous museums commemorate a celebrated episode from the War of Liberation, when Bulgarian independence was

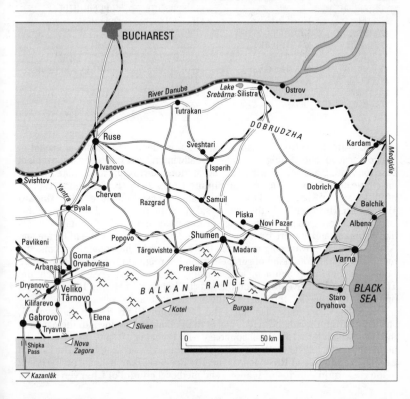

CYRILLIC PLACE NAMES

APRILTSI	АПРИЛЦИ	LOVECH	ЛОВЕЧ
ARBANASI	АРБАНАСИ	MADARA	МАДАРА
BELOGRADCHIK	БЕЛОГРАДЧИК	MEZDRA	МЕЗДРА
BERKOVITSA	БЕРКОВИЦА	MONTANA	МОНТАНА
BOTEVGRAD	БОТЕВГРАД	NIKOPOL	НИКОПОЛ
BOZHENTSI	БОЖЕНЦИ	NOVI PAZAR	НОВИ ПАЗАР
BYALA	БЯЛА	ORYAHOVO	ОРЯХОВО
CHERNI OSÂM	ЧЕРНИ ОСЬМ	PLAKOVO	ПЛАКОВО
CHERVEN	ЧЕРВЕН	PLEVEN	ПЛЕВЕН
CHERVEN BRYAG	ЧЕРВЕН БРЯГ	PLISKA	ПЛИСКА
CHIPROVTSI	ЧИПРОВЦИ	PRAVETS	ПРАВЕЦ
DOBRICH	ДОБРИЧ	PRESLAV	ПРЕСЛАВ
DRYANOVO	ДРЯНОВО	RAZGRAD	РАЗГРАД
ELENA	ЕЛЕНА	RUSE	РУСЕ
ETÂR	ЕТЬР	SEVLIEVO	СЕВЛИЕВО
ETROPOLE	ЕТРОПОЛЕ	SHUMEN	ШУМЕН
GABROVO	ГАБРОВО	SILISTRA	СИЛИСТРА
GIGEN	ГИГЕН	SVESHTARI	СВЕЩАРИ
GORNA ORYAHOVITSA	ГОРНА ОРЯХОВИЦА	SVISHTOV	СВИЩОВ
		TÂRGOVISHTE	ТЬРГОВИЩЕ
ISPERIH	ИСПЕРИХ	TETEVEN	ТЕТЕВЕН
IVANOVO	ИВАНОВО	TROYAN	ТРОЯН
KAPINOVO	КАПИНОВО	TRYAVNA	ТРЯВНА
KARDAM	КАРДАМ	TSAREVA LIVADA	ЦАРЕВА ЛИВАДА
KILIFAREVO	КИЛИФАРЕВО	VELIKO TÂRNOVO	ВЕЛИКО ТЬРНОВО
KOZLODUI	КОЗЛОДУЙ	VIDIN	ВИДИН
LAKATNIK	ЛАКАТНИК	VRATSA	ВРАЦА
LOM	ЛОМ	YABLANITSA	ЯБЛАНИЦА

wrested with the aid of Russian arms; the aforementioned medieval capital of Veliko Târnovo, one of Bulgaria's most visually impressive cities and a convenient base for visiting a string of nearby medieval **monasteries** and a yet more brilliant ensemble of craftworking towns; and **Shumen**, close to the First Kingdom capitals of Pliska and Preslav, as well as the enigmatic cliff-face sculpture of the **Madara Horseman**. However it's in the countryside that the real rewards of travel in this region lie. There's an increasing range of accommodation both in heritage villages like **Arbanasi** and in more traditional rural settlements such as **Cherni Osâm** and **Apriltsi**, the latter two being important trail heads for hiking routes south into the mountains. A different kind of rural environment reigns in the rolling hills of the Ludogorie north of Shumen, an enticingly undeveloped area in which the **Thracian tomb at Sveshtari** and the Muslim holy site of **Demir Baba Tekke** – both near Isperih – are the most worthwhile destinations.

The Sofia–Varna route also skirts the **Danubian Plain** (Dunavska ravnina), stretching from the northern foothills of the Balkan Range down to the banks of the river, which forms a natural boundary with Romania. Despite the name it's by no means uniformly flat, rather a rich agricultural area of rolling hills. The Central European ambience of **Ruse** and the nearby Rusenski Lom national park – home to the **rock monasteries of Ivanovo** and medieval **citadel of Cherven** – are the likely highlights of any trip across the plain. Travelling from the Danube towards the Black Sea coast you'll pass through the relatively unknown **Dobrudzha**, a rich, grain-producing plain which lies at the southernmost limits of the Eurasian Steppe. Although short on specific sights, its wide-open skies nevertheless exert a certain fascination.

THE WESTERN BALKAN RANGE

Travelling between Sofia and Vidin takes you across the western spur of the **Balkan Mountains**, an area of forested highlands scattered with tortuous rock formations. Although not as high as the Rila or Pirin ranges to the south, the peaks of northwest Bulgaria present some of the country's most rewarding walking and rambling areas. Practical maps of the area are, however, thin on the ground, and serious hikers will have to pick up local knowledge from the Bulgarians staying at the region's mountain chalets or *hizhi*. The largely rural, undeveloped character of the northwest marks it out as an ideal destination for off-the-beaten-track travel, although tourist accommodation is limited to the odd hotel, a couple of monasteries, and the aforementioned *hizhi*.

There are several routes across the mountains north of the capital: travelling by train, you'll pass through the magnificent **Iskâr Gorge** before reaching the train junction at Mezdra, and then heading via **Vratsa** towards Vidin and the Danube, with the mountains to your left. Much road traffic goes this way too, although an alternative route crosses the rugged terrain of Bulgaria's western borderlands. This takes you via the **Petrohan Pass** to the mountain resort of **Berkovitsa** before rejoining the main road northwards at the region's administrative centre, **Montana**. From here it's a straightforward trip across the plains to Vidin, although minor roads head westward to **Chiprovtsi**, a historic rug-weaving centre backed by sumptuous mountain scenery, and **Belogradchik**, whose spectacular rock formations demand a detour. For those who want to explore the area **by bus**, Vratsa, Montana and Vidin are the gateway towns serving Berkovitsa, Chiprovtsi and Belogradchik respectively. You can also achieve a great deal **by train** if you're prepared to study timetables carefully, with a branch line serving Montana and Berkovitsa leaving the main Sofia–Vidin route at **Boichinovtsi** north of Vratsa.

The Iskâr Gorge

The **Iskâr Gorge** is the most scenically impressive of the routes north. It's also within easy enough reach of Sofia to be a popular day-trip destination, although only the slow *pâtnicheski*, or "local", trains (most of which run early in the morning and late in the afternoon) stop at the smaller settlements along the gorge. Beware too that the gorge is almost totally devoid of tourist **accommodation** – Sofia and Vratsa are the most convenient places to stay, although the monasteries of Cherepish (see opposite) and Sedemte Prestola (see below) both offer basic rooms. The most breathtaking stretches of the gorge, where the river is squeezed beneath soaring crags, lie between **Gara Lakatnik** and **Mezdra**; it's feasible to stop off at one of the halts between these places, indulge in a spot of walking, and pick up another train later in the day.

Things begin to get interesting just beyond the town of **Novi Iskår**, 10km north of the capital, where the gorge burrows north into the Balkan massif, gradually becoming narrower and deeper, the road and railway competing for space above the river. Strewn with boulders and scored by gullies, it's archetypal partisan country. There's a monument near **Batuliya** village commemorating the 24 partisans who clashed with local police in May 1944, and a train halt called *Tompsân* after **Major Frank Thompson** (brother of left-wing English historian and veteran CND campaigner E P Thompson) who fought and died with them. A member of the British mission sent to observe the effectiveness of Bulgaria's antifascist fighters (and evaluate their suitability to receive Allied aid), Thompson was fondly remembered by the postwar Bulgarian regime, and his uniform used to be exhibited in Sofia's now defunct Museum of the Revolution.

Walks around Gara Lakatnik

GARA LAKATNIK (literally "Lakatnik Station") stands astride some promising Iskår Gorge walking trails, the most popular of which snake their way up the **Lakatnishki skali**, a precipitous knuckle of rock just north of the station on the west side of the valley. To get there, walk downhill from the station, cross the river, turn right onto the main road and walk straight on for about 1500m. Footpaths ascend the side of the cliff from beside a small (and sporadically open) roadside café-restaurant, working their way past two *dupki* or **caves** before emerging onto the grassy uplands at the top of the *skali*. **Temnata dupka** is the larger of the two caves here, extending for nearly 3km across four levels and including several lakes fed by a subterranean river. However, it's doubtful that anyone will be on hand to offer tours to casual visitors. An alternative route into the hills is to head south along the main road from the station, turning right after about 1km onto a minor road which heads up beside the Proboinitsa stream. After about 1500m, beyond a small bridge, a path heads up the small side valley to the right, passing several waterfalls and pools before leading on to the meadowy plateau above the *skali*. Keeping to the main Proboinitsa valley road, on the other hand, will bring you after 10km to the *Proboinitsa hizha*, base camp for assaults on the 1785-metre-high **Todorini Kukli**, from where paths descend to the Petrohan Pass (see p.147) on the other side. South of Gara Lakatnik, a more serviceable road heads for the pastoral highland village of **Lakatnik** itself, 8km away, and beyond that, the *Trâstena* chalet, again the start of numerous walking possibilities. Bear in mind, however, that the café and food store on the station platform at Gara Lakatnik are the only reliable places in the area to pick up **food** supplies.

Sedemte Prestola Monastery

Fourteen kilometres beyond Gara Lakatnik, a minor road leaves the Iskår valley at the village of **ELISEINA** to climb beside the Gabrovnitsa stream towards the mountain hamlet of **OSENOVLAG**, 23km beyond. About two-thirds of the way along, the road passes the **Monastery of Sedemte Prestola** (Seven Altars), a walled huddle of buildings surrounded by pine forests and crags. It's inside the dainty church (officially open daily 10–11am & 3–4pm, but often accessible outside these times at weekends) that the reason for the monastery's name becomes apparent, with the main altar at the head of the nave augmented by six side altars – low-ceilinged cubicles reached through arched doors on either side of the nave – each with its own small iconostasis and candle-lighting area. The wooded environs of the monastery present the perfect place for a short hike: cross the footbridge opposite the monastery gate to pick up a trail which leads up onto hay meadows and into the pines beyond. In theory the *Târstena hizha*, high above the village of Lakatnik to the west, is four hours' walk from here, although the path is badly marked.

There's only one **bus** a day from Eliseina train station to Osenovlag, passing the monastery on the way. The monastery has basic **rooms** (no phone; ②), but water supplies are intermittent and there's no food or drink.

Cherepish Monastery

More accessible than Sedemte Prestola for those dependent on public transport, **Cherepish Monastery** lies near the halt of the same name, midway between the villages of **ZVERINO** and **LYUTIBROD**. It's also accessible from the Sofia–Mezdra road, although the turn-off is difficult to spot; the nearest landmark to look out for is the *Han Cherna* roadside café 100m to the north, which is also the only source of **food** and drink in the area. If coming by train, alight at Cherepish halt, cross the rail tracks towards a large ochre seminary building, and bear left along an asphalt track until you reach a T-junction. The monastery is down the hill to the left. Founded in the fourteenth century, Cherepish was sacked by the Turks almost as soon as it was built, and most of the current buildings date (at least in part) from the seventeenth century, when the monastery was refounded by holy man and artist Pimen Zografski. Faded fragments of Pimen's work, notably his *Tree of Jesse*, can still be seen in the monastery **church**, although much better preserved are the frescos completed by Tryavna master Papa Vitan in 1836. His frieze of early Christian warrior saints (including George, Demetrius and other martyrdom-hungry Roman soldiers) reveal the nineteenth-century Bulgarian Orthodox church's taste for images of steely-eyed resistance and suffering. The intricate woodcarving of the iconostasis – with gryphons and ears of corn exquisitely rendered by Debâr masters – also stands out. There's a small **museum** outside the church displaying a few monastic vestments and icons, although opening times are unpredictable. Thousands of pilgrims descend on Cherepish for the Feast of the Assumption (*Sveta Bogoroditsa*) on August 15, when the monastery grounds are full of picnicking families. At such times the monastery's modest supply of **rooms** (no phone; ②) is likely to be fully booked.

Immediately northeast of Cherepish, the Iskâr Gorge ends with a final geological flourish nicknamed *Ritlite* or the "Cart Rails": three parallel ribs of fissured rock up to 198m high which you'll see a few miles before the road and rail track enter **MEZDRA**. A useful transport hub at the junction of the Sofia–Vidin and Sofia–Pleven–Varna lines, Mezdra has little else to offer.

Vratsa

Approaching from the south, arrival in **VRATSA** is presaged by the steaming pipelines and storage tanks of a vast chemical plant, which does much to detract from the undoubted beauty of the town's situation, standing at the base of a wall of mountains known as the **Vrachanska planina**. The town's main attraction for visitors is its beautiful rocky hinterland, starting with the **Vratsata** defile which ascends into the mountains just west of the town centre, although good **archeology** and **ethnographic museums** provide a respectable brace of worthwhile urban sights. Just south of Vratsa is **Mt Okolchitsa**, where **Hristo Botev**, one of the more romantic figures in Bulgaria's struggle for liberation (see p.386), met his death. An inspiring revolutionary leader as well as a poet known for his patriotic verses, Botev formed a *cheta* to lend assistance to the April Rising in 1876. Botev's men marched south into the Balkan Mountains from Kozlodui on the Danube, but were constantly harried by Ottoman forces. After days of running battles, Botev finally perished along with the remnants of his *cheta* on Okolchitsa on June 2.

Arrival and accommodation

Vratsa's **train and bus stations** stand together just east of the centre, from where the pedestrianized ribbon of bul. Nikolai Voivodov curves its way northwest, passing a vast open-air market, to meet the main thoroughfare, **bul. Hristo Botev**. For **accommodation**, the two-star, hundred-room *Hotel Hemus* (☎092/24150; ④) is conveniently located on the central square, **pl. Hristo Botev**, although its run-down ensuite rooms aren't as good value as those at the *Hotel Tourist*, a couple of blocks west of the centre on pl. Cherven (☎092/61528 or 62095), which has plain but acceptable ensuite doubles (③), or renovated doubles with cable TV (④). There are dorm beds available for $4 a night at the *Alpiiski*

SOFRONII VRACHANSKI (1739–1813)

Sofronii Vrachanski was born Stoiko Vladislavov in the central Bulgarian village of Kotel in 1739. He entered the priesthood in his home town and rose gradually through the ecclesiastical ranks, becoming *igumen*, or abbot, of Kapinovo Monastery near Veliko Târnovo in the 1780s. During these years he was one of the most enthusiastic copiers and promoters of Otets Paisii's seminal manuscript, the *Slav-Bulgarian History*, a key text in the awakening of Bulgarian national consciousness.

In accordance with the custom of the time, Sofronii had to bribe Greek church officials in order to be appointed bishop of Vratsa in 1794, an enterprise in which he was assisted financially by patriotic Bulgarian merchants. He was chased into exile by the local *kârdzhali*, who were then in alliance with the wayward Ottoman ruler of Vidin, Osman Pazvantoglu, and spent the rest of his life in Wallachia where he continued to work for the Bulgarian cause. A firm believer in Russia's messianic role as the protector of Balkan Christendom, Sofronii cultivated links with the St Petersburg court, and oversaw the emigration of thousands of Bulgarian families to Russian-occupied Bessarabia in 1808. The descendants of these "Bessarabian Bulgarians" still live there, occupying a coastal strip west of the Ukranian city of Odessa.

Sofronii is also remembered for his literary works, which include a translation of Aesop's *Fables* and the first autobiographical novel in Bulgarian, *The Life and Suffering of the Sinner Sofronii*, both of which assisted in the development of a standard written form of the Bulgarian language.

Dom (☎092/23006), 2km west of town in the Vratsata Gorge, although it has unpredictable opening times (sometimes summer-only) and is often fully booked by groups of rock climbers.

The Town

From the stations, turn left into bul. Hristo Botev and you'll pass a plaza built around the **Kula na meschiite**, a seventeenth-century fortified tower. Such towers were built as family dwellings by local feudal lords who wanted to intimidate their exploited subjects with a suitable symbol of invincibility. Shortly afterwards ul. Târgovska breaks off to the left, a side street blessed with a picturesque collection of pastel-coloured nineteenth-century town houses. At the end of the street stands a monument to **Sofronii Vrachanski**, local church leader and key figure in the Bulgarian Renaissance.

The Ethnographic Museum and complex

Immediately behind the Vrachanski statue is the **Ethnographic Museum** (9am–noon & 3–7pm) housed in a National Revival-period former girls' school, a fine half-timbered structure vaguely reminiscent of Tudor architecture. Inside is one of provincial Bulgaria's best collections of folk costumes and crafts, strong on local marriage customs: exhibits include the enigmatic *svatbeni bardeta* or "wedding pitchers", twelve earthenware jugs hanging from a two-metre-long wooden pole. One entire floor is devoted to brass band instruments, imported from Central Europe by village ensembles at the turn of the century; while, outside, a pavilion displays nineteenth-century carriages and carts (and a particularly ornate bright-blue ceremonial sled) built by the local Orazov factory, Bulgaria's leading coachmakers.

Next door to the museum is an **ethnographic complex**: a clutch of National Revival-style houses grouped around the *Vâznesenska* (Ascension) church, which itself contains a display of icons from the Vratsa area. A couple of the houses are open to the public (same times as museum); one displays the work of local jewellers, while the other features exhibits on Vratsa's **silk industry**. Silk was the region's major source of income a century ago, when each family would keep a tree for silkworms in the yard – a practice still continued in a few outlying villages. Examples of Vratsa-made fabrics are on show, alongside fading English-language posters offering handy hints on how to tend the worms.

The Historical Museum

Back on bul. Hristo Botev, it's a short stroll south to another seventeenth-century tower, the **Kula na Kurt Pashovtsi**, and another modern plaza, pl. Hristo Botev, home to the excellent **Historical Museum** (summer Tues–Sun 9am–1pm & 3–6pm; winter Tues–Fri 9am–noon & 2–5pm). Predictably, it harbours a "Botev Room" full of reminders of the warrior-poet's fateful march into Ottoman territory, but the real delights lie downstairs in the archeological section. Hordes of Neolithic and Bronze Age idols, including well-endowed fertility figures, point to the long history of civilization in the Vratsa area.

Pride of place, however, goes to **Thracian finds**, the most valuable of which come from *Mogilanskata mogila*, a large tumulus unearthed in 1965. Three tombs were found here, dating from the fourth century BC, the largest of which contained a chieftain accompanied by two young women, both of whom appear to have suffered violent deaths at the time of the burial – possibly consorts of the deceased (one of them was sufficiently bejewelled to be a princess) who were required to accompany him into the afterlife. Three horses, two of them harnessed to a ceremonial chariot, completed the burial party. The latter were provided with decorative horse armour, their silver buckles depicting swirling animals. The more elaborately dressed of the women sported a pair of exquisitely filigreed earrings and a **golden laurel wreath** of great delicacy, featuring eighty finely sculpted leaves grouped around little berries.

Eating and drinking

The numerous pavement **cafés** that line the central bul. Hristo Botev make Vratsa an invigorating place to be on a warm summer's day, although there's little to choose between them. If you don't fancy eating in the *Hotel Hemus*, *Klub Atlantik*, on the corner of ul. Botev and pl. Botev, is the town's nicest **restaurant**, with a pleasant outdoor garden in summer.

Around Vratsa: the Vratsata Gorge, Ledenika cave and Bozhiya most

Walk west from Vratsa's town centre past the *Tourist Hotel*, to pick up the asphalt road which heads between the stupendous limestone teeth that form the **Vratsata Gorge**. You only have to venture about 2km out of town to savour the gorge at its awesome best: sheer, ragged cliffs plunging towards grassy riverbanks where locals come to sunbathe, graze their goats, or wash carpets. There are a couple of café-restaurants in the gorge bottom, one of which is attatched to the *Alpiiski Dom*, a training base used by rock climbers who regard the Vratsata Gorge as the most challenging cliffscape in Bulgaria. A little way beyond the *Alpiiski Dom*, the left-hand fork of the road heads for the timelessly rustic village of **Zgorigrad**, while the right-hand fork zigzags its way uphill before emerging onto a goat- and sheep-nibbled alpine plateau, rich in wild flowers and herbs. It's an area of inestimable tranquillity and beauty, offering great views towards Mt Okolchitsa to the south. If you follow all the road's twists and turns from the valley bottom to the plateau, it's about 10km, but you're far better off opting for the various paths and short cuts which dive through fields and forests on the way up – using the pylons of a disused chair lift to guide you – and working your way back onto the road whenever the going gets too steep. Vratsa–Milanovo **buses** come up the road (check the times at Vratsa bus station), making a ride up followed by a walk down an attractive option. However you reach the top, you'll soon pick up an asphalt track heading north across the gently undulating plateau towards the **Ledenika cave** (daily: summer 8am–noon & 1.30–5.45pm; winter 9am–noon & 1.30–4.30pm; $3.50), 4km from the edge of the plateau and 16km from central Vratsa by road. The cave gets its name from the icicles that form here during the winter – *leden* means icy – and its largest chamber has been dubbed the "Great Temple". It's also a popular breeding ground for **bats**. There's an eighty-bed **hikers' chalet**, the *Hizha Ledenika* (☎092/24411; ②) near the mouth of the cave, and a couple of shacks selling drinks and snacks.

Another geological curiosity can be seen from the minor road heading northeast from Vratsa, just outside the village of **CHIREN**: a rock tunnel about 25m wide, 20m high and 100m long, which locals call **Bozhiya most** – "God's Bridge".

The Petrohan Pass and Berkovitsa

The road that heads northwest from Sofia, route 81, skirts round the western edges of the Balkan Range on the way to the mountain health resort of **Berkovitsa**. Few, if any, buses travel this way, so you'll be dependent either on your own transport or the vagaries of hitching – remember that if you're just interested in visiting Berkovitsa itself, you can reach it from Vratsa, Montana or Vidin by bus; and by train from Boichinovtsi, a train junction on the Sofia–Vidin line.

After about 65km the road from Sofia begins to ascend the Petrohanski prohod or **PETROHAN PASS**, 1446m above sea level, which sits between Mt Zelena Glava (literally "green-head") and the jagged **Todorini Kukli**. Deer, rabbits and roe deer reportedly abound here, and for the hardy souls who wish to stay, **accommodation** can be found at the *Petrohan* campsite (June–Sept) and the *Petrohan hizha* (☎096/25251; ②). From the pass the road zigzags down into the valley of the northward-flowing Bârziya, from where it's a short twenty-kilometre drive to Berkovitsa.

Berkovitsa and around

Surrounded by orchards, rest homes and hills, **BERKOVITSA** itself is a drab, dozy place which nowadays betrays little of its former status as a high-altitude health resort and favoured training camp of Bulgaria's wrestlers and weightlifters. However it's an important gateway to the highland area around Mt Kom, and contains a couple of worthwhile historic sights. In addition, Klisurski monastery (not one of the major foundations, but charmingly situated nevertheless) is easily visited from here.

Berkovitsa's few remaining nineteenth-century attractions lie between the modern town square and the River Berkovska. Hidden in a lush rose garden on ul. Cherkovna, the sunken **Church of Sveta Bogoroditsa** features icons by Dimitâr and Zahari Zograf and a carved wooden iconostasis on which exquisitely wrought angels blow trumpets and dragons attack lions. Three blocks east on ul. Berkovska reka is the **Ivan Vazov Museum** (Mon–Fri 8am–noon & 2–5pm; enquire at the ethnographic museum if shut), occupying the house where Bulgaria's "national writer" spent two years as the local magistrate. While the lower floor is taken up with the usual pictures and quotes, the upper floor features an exquisitely rendered Tryavna ceiling and the sitting rooms where Vazov and his landlord, Ivan Stoyanov, held court. Both are furnished in traditional Ottoman style, with comfy *minderi* (low bench-seats padded with cushions) surrounding a central *mangal* (lidded charcoal brazier). The **Ethnographic Museum**, just around the corner on ul. Poruchnik Grozhdanov (Mon–Fri 8am–noon & 2–5pm), harbours a display of local arts and crafts, including a room devoted to the yellow- and green-splashed pottery that used to be a Berkovitsa trade mark, but is nowadays made by just a few craftspeople.

Practicalities

Berkovitsa's **train station** is fifteen minutes' walk east of town at the end of ul. Atanas Kyorkchiev, while the **bus station** lies on the eastern fringe of the town centre on ul. Brezi. **Accommodation** is available at the *Han Tobo*, a small family-run place on ul. Nikolaevska (☎0953/2111; ②), offering neat, cosy rooms with

VAZOV IN BERKOVITSA

In 1878 the infant state of Bulgaria was desperately short of trained personnel, and a reasonable level of secondary education was often enough to secure a top government job. Thus it was that the 27-year-old poet **Ivan Vazov** (see p.254) was appointed magistrate in Berkovitsa, despite his complete lack of legal experience. Faced by a local populace accustomed to the partial justice of the Ottoman courts, Vazov was soon out of his depth. On one occasion he had to **sentence a dog to death** for savaging a chicken – an attempt to appease townsfolk who would have otherwise taken the law into their own hands. As a result, Vazov's reputation was rubbished by a gleeful Sofia press, and the government was forced to offer him an inferior post in Vidin. Seething with humiliation, Vazov resigned and left the Principality of Bulgaria for Eastern Rumelia – where he made his name as a journalist and writer.

What's remembered most about Vazov's stay in Berkovitsa is his mildly scandalous affair with a 19-year-old Turkish girl called **Zihra**. Local legends maintain that Zihra entered Vazov's house rolled up in a carpet, or was lowered over the wall in a basket, in order to avoid the prying eyes of gossip-mongers, although the reality is more prosaic. Zihra was initially married to a local Turkish *bey* and drunkard who fell into a river and drowned during the Russo-Turkish War of 1877. The wife of Vazov's landlord and colleague, Ivan Stoyanov, took pity on Zihra, engaging her as Vazov's housekeeper, and she tended the tubercular young writer through frequent bouts of ill health. He fell for her in a big way, referring to her as his first and greatest love, but unfortunately Zihra soon left him for the dashing Bulgarian officer Hristo Chavov.

shared facilities; or the old-style concrete high-rise *Ucheben Tsentâr Ashiklar*, ul. Ashiklar 16 (☎0953/3000 or 3120; ②), which has ensuite two- and three-bed rooms, as well as good-value top-floor apartments with TV and sitting room (③).

The best of several town-centre **cafés** is *Café Dame* just down from the main square on Aleksandrovska. For **restaurants** try *Han Tobo* (see previous page), which offers tasty Bulgarian staples and frequent live folk-pop, or *Krâsteva Kâshta*, an atmospheric nineteenth-century house on ul. Sheinovo.

There's a big Saturday-morning **market** next to the bus station, selling clothes, bric-a-brac and crafts.

The hills around Berkovitsa

You can explore the hilly terrain surrounding Berkovitsa by following any of the farm tracks leading out of town, although the most rewarding itineraries take you west towards the glowering ridge of the western Balkan Range. To get started, follow ul. Kiril i Metodii west from the main square, and past the sports grounds to the end of town, until it splits into right and left forks. The right fork winds its way round the near side of the *Mramor* marble factory before heading into the wooded valley of the Berkovska Reka, finishing up at the popular picnic spot of **Haidushki Vodopadi** ("*haidut* waterfalls"; 1hr 30min), a series of cataracts where the young river tumbles down a boulder-strewn valley floor. The left fork zigzags steeply up towards two hikers' **chalets** – confusingly, both are known as *Hizha Kom* – 12km away, useful starting points for assaults on the 2016m summit of **Mt Kom** itself (about 2hr from either *hizha*). Attempting to walk from Berkovitsa to Kom summit and back in one day is somewhat ambitious (unless you drive as far as the *hizhi*), and most people stay at least one night in one of the *hizhi* – the northernmost one of the pair (☎0953/4024; ②), nearest to Berkovitsa, is the newer and better equipped – where you can pick up advice on upward routes onto the mountain.

Klisurski Monastery

Ten kilometres southeast of Berkovitsa, just off the road to the dowdy (and eminently missable) spa town of Vârshets, **Klisurski Monastery** crouches beneath the pine-laden eastern slopes of Mt Todorini Kukli. Completely renovated in the 1990s, the monastery's galleried whitewashed buildings surround a courtyard and a small church, but it's the atmosphere of rural peace – rather than any architectural or historical pedigree – that's the real attraction here. The woods outside the monastery walls are worthy of exploration, although the numerous new tracks bulldozed by forestry workers have made it difficult to pick out the hiking route to Todorini Kukli (and onwards to the *Hizha Petrohan* on the other side) which once existed here.

Three daily **buses** from Berkovitsa to Vârshets go past the access road to the monastery, from where it's a pleasant 2.5km walk (bearing left after 200m) to the monastery itself. Catching a bus back can be more problematic: you'll have to enquire at Berkovitsa bus station about return services from Vârshets and make your own calculations as to when you need to be back on the main road ready to flag one down. Walking back to Berkovitsa along the road (2hr) is always an option if you can avoid the summer heat. There are tourist **beds** at the monastery (③) should you get stuck, and a couple of places outside the monastery gateway serving **food** and drink.

Montana, Chiprovtsi and around

Bulgarian towns with a revolutionary tradition tend to look drably modern or prettily archaic, and **MONTANA** – largely rebuilt in concrete – belongs to the former category. Originally called Kutlovitsa, the town was known as Mihailovgrad for much of the postwar period in memory of local revolutionary Hristo Mihailov, a leader of the Communist uprising of **September 1923**. Socialist historians always overestimated the importance of the revolt – a short-lived farce that never enjoyed popular support – but the way in which the right-wing Tsankov regime put the uprising down, massacring 30,000 Bulgarians within a couple of weeks, ensured that it was remembered as one of the most bloodily heroic episodes in Bulgarian history. After a local referendum in 1993 the town was renamed, ostensibly because a Roman settlement called Montana existed here in the first century AD.

Montana merits little more than a fleeting visit, to use its onward transport connections to more appealing destinations in the shadow of the mountains, such as Chiprovtsi and Lopushanski Monastery. If you've time to kill between buses – the terminal is diagonally opposite the train station – head through the fruit and veg market next to the bus station to reach a park where you'll find a small **history museum** (Mon–Fri 9am–1pm & 2–5pm), housing Chiprovtsi carpets and local costumes. Of the latter, several belong to the **Karakachani**, Greek-speaking nomadic herders common throughout the western Balkan Range until the 1950s, when a combination of settled lifestyles and intermarriage with local Bulgarians hastened their disappearance as a distinct group (although they're still very much in evidence in eastern Bulgaria; see p.000). There are plenty of **cafés** a block south of the train and bus stations on Montana's flowerbed-splashed main square, where the high-rise *Zhitomir* **hotel** (☎096/29186; ③) has comfortable but characterless ensuite rooms, and roomy apartments with TV and bath (④).

Chiprovtsi

Regular buses make the 25-kilometre journey west from Montana to the carpet-making village of **CHIPROVTSI**, nestling beneath the highest mountains of the northeast, their jagged peaks marking the frontier between Bulgaria and Serbia. Chiprovtsi was an important silver mining centre in the late middle ages, and Saxon miners were encouraged to settle here, bringing new technology, Catholicism and blond-haired, blue-eyed blood lines in their wake. Despite the Ottoman conquest, the village went on to become an important centre of Catholic learning, with local children being sent to Italy for training in the priesthood. Seventeenth-century statesmen **Peter Bogdan Bakshev** (Catholic Archbishop of Sofia) and **Peter Parchevich** (Archbishop of Marcianopolis – modern-day

---

CHIPROVTSI CARPETS

When the Ottoman authorities finally allowed people to resettle Chiprovtsi after the 1688 Uprising, carpet-weaving (an exclusively female occupation in Bulgaria) quickly became a key factor in the village's regeneration. Most Chiprovtsi carpets are **kilims** – double-sided woollen carpets hand-woven on a compact vertical loom known as a *stan*. They're famous for their colour-charged, stylized geometric designs, resembling more the paintings of Paul Klee than the products of some age-old peasant craft. Most characteristic of the Chiprovtsi designs is the *karakachka* ("black-eyed bride"), a geometrical form (usually red-on-black or black-on-red) which resembles a woman carrying two buckets of water. Although of eighteenth-century origin, it clearly harks back to pagan depictions of the earth mother. Other stylized forms favoured by successive generations of Chiprovtsi weavers include *lozite* ("vines"), *piletata* ("chickens"), and *saksiite* ("flowerpots") – each serving as a symbol of nature's bounty.

The kilims are still made today by individual weavers, either working at home or in the *Kipra* co-operative in the centre of the village. The craft has changed little over the last three and a half centuries, although the quality of the wool – nowadays coloured with chemical rather than vegetable dyes – may not be what it was. Certain kilim-related **customs** still prevail: it's common, for example, for a daughter or granddaughter to be swung hammock-style in a newly-completed kilim, to ensure that she, too, will grow up to be a skilled weaver.

At the time of writing, the only **retail outlet** for kilims in Chiprovtsi is the museum, where there's a wide choice of local wares, all tagged with set prices. The museum can also organize visits to the houses of individual weavers, and although they rarely have surplus kilims for sale, many will be quite happy to make a kilim to your specifications if you're staying in Bulgaria long enough (two to three months depending on the size) to collect it. A good Chiprovtsi kilim will last a lifetime if used as a floor covering, longer if it's employed as a wall hanging or drape. One word of warning: the "Chiprovtsi carpets" on sale in the Ethnographic Museum shop in Sofia are not actually made in Chiprovtsi, and are twice as expensive as the genuine articles you can pick up here.

Devnya) were born in Chiprovtsi and spent most of their lives trying to persuade the rulers of Europe to give the oppressed Balkan Slavs a helping hand. Neither lived to see the glorious failure that was the **Chiprovtsi Uprising of 1688**, when the Austrian army's successes against the Turks persuaded many in the Bulgarian northwest that the hour of their liberation was nigh. Unfortunately the advancing Austrians never got as far as Chiprovtsi, and Ottoman forces razed the village to the ground scattering its inhabitants. It wasn't until 1737 that their descendants were allowed back. Mining is still a mainstay of the local economy, giving the place a gruff, working-class feel, and the village's proximity to what was until 1989 a closed border zone means that tourism is still very much in its infancy. However Chiprovtsi is surrounded by some of the best scenery in the northwest, and for those prepared to rough it a bit, a short stay here has its rewards.

The village

Chiprovtsi lacks the historic buildings that would put it firmly on the tourist route, and it's really the surrounding bowl of pastured hills that give the village its visual appeal. Buses come to rest beside a modern flagstoned square, from where a lane ascends to the right to the National Revival-era **Church of the Resurrection** (*vâsnesenie Hristovo*), a sunken structure that harbours valuable icons but is rarely open. The ruins of a Catholic basilica can be traced in the grass outside. The next-door **museum** (Mon–Fri 9am–5pm, Sat–Sun 10am–4pm; if closed call at the museum administration office on the opposite side of the road) tells the story of the village in familiar words-and-pictures style. There are some interesting buckles, clasps and necklaces made by seventeenth-century silversmiths, and a whole room devoted to Chiprovtsi **carpets**, where museum staff are usually on hand to demonstrate the workings of a traditional *stan* or vertical loom.

Practicalities

State-run **buses** to Chiprovtsi depart from Montana's bus station, while privately-operated services use a stop on the main road just outside the station – although it's difficult to obtain timetable information about the latter. The destination boards of most state-run Chiprovtsi-bound buses are marked either "Martinovo" (the next village up the valley from Chiprovtsi) or "MOK" (an acronym denoting the local mining company).

The friendly and helpful museum administration office (same times as the museum; ☎09554/2168) acts as an unofficial tourist information centre, and will organize **accommodation** in their own self-contained apartment (②) or in private rooms in the village (②). There is currently no restaurant in Chiprovtsi, although there are numerous **cafés** round the main square, and a couple of late-opening food stores (*hranitelni stoki*). The best time to be in Chiprovtsi is during one of the Orthodox **religious holidays**, celebrated here (despite Chiprovtsi's Catholic past) with a verve and devotion which has largely disappeared from Bulgaria's main urban centres. Key dates are Ivanovden (St John's Day) on January 7, Gergyovden (St George's Day) on May 6, Petrovden (St Peter's Day) on June 29, and Ilinden (St Elijah's Day) on July 20. On each of these days, every *mahala* or neighbourhood cooks up a vat of *kurban-chorba* (stew made from a freshly-sacrificed sheep) ready for a communal feast. On December 6 the entire population heads for the ruined **Gushovski monastery** 4km south of the village for an outdoor mass and more communal feasting.

Chiprovski Monastery and the mountains

Having destroyed Chiprovtsi in the wake of the 1688 Uprising, the Ottomans also burned down the nearby **Chiprovski Monastery** as a token of their disapproval. About 6km east of town just off the Montana road (Montana–Chiprovtsi buses may drop you off here, but seem to have an aversion to picking passengers up), the most recent incarnation of this little-visited foundation dates mostly from the early nineteenth century, a clump of lumpy off-white outbuildings surrounding a dainty monastery church. The healing energies of the place are widely respected; prayers requesting cures for visitors' ailments are incanted daily at 10am, and the iconostasis is littered with votive offerings left by grateful believers – mostly cellophane-wrapped shirts and socks. This atmosphere of holiness extends to the accommodation policy: you can only **stay** at the monastery if the *igumen* (abbot) is convinced you have a spiritual need to do so.

West of Chiprovtsi, an imposing green-brown ridge known as the **Chiprovska planina** (Chiprovtsi mountains) marks the border with Serbia. Trails lead out of the village and up the Androvitsa and Ogosta valleys towards the fir-shrouded lower limbs of the ridge, although it's a good 6km before you hit the best of the hiking territory – so you need either a car or an early start to get the most out of the area. There's nothing to stop you exploring the mountains on your own, although bear in mind that hiking trails here are not yet properly marked or mapped, mists descend quickly, and that the summit of the ridge is a still-sensitive border. Expect to be shot at or arrested if you stray over to the wrong side. The sensible way to enjoy the region is to hire a local **guide** for about $25 a day plus expenses from the Chiprovtsi museum administration office: a typical one-day hike would involve jeep transport to one of the trail heads, followed by a lateral walk along the Bulgarian side of the ridge, with stunning views of Chiprovtsi and Montana laid out below.

Lopushanski Monastery and around

Ten kilometres due east of Chiprovtsi is **Lopushanski Monastery**, situated in one of the area's prettiest valleys, the Dâlgodelska ogosta. You'll find the monastery just beyond the village of **Georgi-Damyanovo**, lurking in a grove of pine trees – a tranquil location that provided Ivan Vazov with the peace and quiet he needed to complete several chapters of *Under the Yoke*. The monastery church is particularly noted for two icons by Samokov master Stanislav Dospevski, the *Virgin and Child* and *Christ Pantokrator* – both works showing an almost photographic realism. The monastery currently provides some of the best **accommodation** in the northwest region, with clean and simple rooms with shared facilities (③) and fancier quarters with ensuite shower and TV (④), all bookable through Odysseia-in in Sofia (see p.64 and p.50). There's also a traditional-style **restaurant** on the ground floor. It's an easy place to get to on public transport, with four daily Montana–Kopilovtsi **buses** passing the monastery entrance.

For a taste of the mountains, it's worth continuing west of the monastery to the village of **Kopilovtsi**, 17km upstream at the head of a northern branch of the valley. From here a badly potholed road continues a further 5km to **Kopren**, site of a few privately owned holiday villas and a (currently closed) rest home known as the Prophylactorium. Round the back of the Prophylactorium a track leads to the start of one of the nicest short walks in Bulgaria, the well-marked and well-maintained **Kopren ecotrail** (*ekopâteka "Kopren"*; 1hr 30min one way). The trail –

steep and boulder-strewn in parts – works its way up a wooded ravine, passing a waterfall and several smaller cataracts, before emerging onto a highland meadow ringed by looming peaks – the imposing 1964m **Mt Kopren**, marking the border with Serbia, is straight ahead.

Belogradchik and around

Lying in a bowl beneath the hills just east of the Serbian border, **BELOGRADCHIK** (literally "small white town") gives its name to Bulgaria's most spectacular rock formations, the **Belogradchishkite skali**, which cover an area of 90 square kilometres to the west. The limestone rocks greatly impressed French traveller Adolph Blanqui in 1841, who described them as an "undreamt landscape" rising to heights of 200m in shades of scarlet, buff and grey, with shapes suggestive of "animals, ships or houses, Egyptian obelisks" and "enormous stalagmites".

The towering rocks nearest the town form a natural fortress whose defensive potential has been exploited since ancient times. Begun by the Romans, continued by the Bulgars during the eighth century, and completed by the Turks a millennium later, the castle at Belogradchik used to command the eastern approaches to the Belogradchik Pass. Although no longer in use, the pass was for centuries the main trade route linking the lower Danube with the settlements of Serbia's Morava Valley. In Ottoman times the citadel and its garrison served to intimidate and control the local populace, and hundreds of Bulgarian insurgents were held here after the failed uprising of 1850. One particularly unsavoury tale relates that many of the prisoners were slaughtered when the Ottomans forced them to pass through a low doorway, only to have their heads lopped off by swordsmen lurking on the other side.

The Town and the rocks

Ruddy pinnacles of rock are immediately visible on arrival, glowering over the town from the hilltop around which Belogradchik is draped. The town's main street, lined with turn-of-the-century houses with spindly cast-iron balconies, winds up towards the summit, passing a small **art gallery** (Tues–Sun 8am–noon & 1.30–5pm) with modest exhibitions of local work, a **museum** (same times), strong on local folklore, and the almost derelict **Huseyn Pasha mosque**, its former glory recalled in the delicate green-and-purple abstract swirls adorning the main entrance. Before long you'll reach the entrance of the **citadel** (daily 8am–11.30pm & 1.30–5pm), three levels of fortifications representing different periods of occupation. The lowest two levels are Ottoman: solid, utilitarian blocks of stone enlivened here and there by the occasional floral-patterned relief. A steep climb between two enormous pillars of rock leads to the highest and oldest level, occupied by the medieval Bulgarian stronghold. The rocks themselves provided the perfect fortified enclosure, and apart from the tumbledown wall of a medieval reservoir there's little man-made to see. Enjoy instead the marvellous panorama of surrounding hills.

Another way of approaching the rocks begins at the opposite end of the main street, opposite the *Hotel Belogradchishkite skali*, where concrete steps lead down into a dry valley overlooked by some of the more spectacular rock formations. A path continues along the valley floor for several kilometres, providing views of a whole series of extravagantly weathered pillars, two of which are associated with misogynistic **legends**: the *Nun*, who was supposedly turned into stone for becoming pregnant by a knight; and the *Schoolgirl*, who was likewise afflicted after she was deserted by her husband.

The number of rock eagles and other hunting birds frequenting the Belogradchik area is said to be on the increase, although the only ones you're likely to catch sight of are the stuffed versions housed in the village's small **natural history museum** (*prirodonauchen muzei*; Mon–Fri 8am–noon & 2–5pm; ring the bell). To find it, take the road leading downhill from the *Hotel Belogradchishkite Skali* and look for a left turning into the woods.

Practicalities

Lying just off the main E79 between Montana and Vidin, Belogradchik is easily reached by **bus** from the latter. The town's **bus station** lies immediately below the main street. Trains on the Sofia–Vidin line stop at Oreshets station 10km to the east, from where there are regular buses.

The two-star *Belogradchishkite skali* **hotel** on the main square (☎0936/3151; ③) is run-down and sometimes lacks hot water, so you're better off heading for the *Hotel Tourist*, uphill from here past the sports stadium (☎0936/3382; ③), which has serviceable ensuite doubles, many with good views of the rocks. The road heading downhill from the *Belogradchishkite skali* leads to the enticingly wooded *Madona* **campsite** (May–Aug), where sanitary facilities and bungalows (②) are currently under construction. The café-**restaurant** of the *Hotel Tourist* has a terrace with spectacular views looking out towards the rocks. Hidden away in the residential streets opposite the access road to the *Hotel Tourist*, the *Mehana Madona* at Hristo Botev 26 has good home cooking and a vine-shaded courtyard.

The Magura Cave and Midzhur

Twenty kilometres northwest of Belogradchik lies the village of **RABISHA**, a couple of kilometres short of the much-publicized **Magura Cave** (Wed–Sun 9am–5pm; $2.50). As early as 2700 BC, the cave was occupied by hunters, traces of whom are now displayed in a small museum. It's best known, though, for its **rock paintings** executed in bat-droppings, which depict a giraffe, hunting scenes and a fertility rite. The female figures tend to be bigger than the male figures, suggesting that women enjoyed superior status in the cave society of the time. Some of the other chambers – with names like the "Hall of the Poplar" and the "Hall of the Fallen Pine" – contain interesting stalactite and stalagmite formations that give them their names. With Rabisha served by a single early-morning bus from Belogradchik, the cave can be difficult to get to without your own transport, though trips can be arranged from the *Hotel Tourist* in Belogradchik, if there's a group of you (they can also arrange to open the caves on Mondays and Tuesdays if you apply in advance). There's a **motel** just outside the cave entrance (bookable through the *Hotel Tourist* in in Belogradchik; ③), which also serves **food and drink**.

Twenty-five kilometres due south of Belogradchik is **MIDZHUR**, at 2168m the highest of a whole series of densely wooded hills that have only recently been made accessible to hikers. For decades they were considered off limits because of the supposedly sensitive nature of the border with Yugoslavia, and there's a corresponding lack of chalets or tourist facilities in the region. If you do fancy exploring, the foothill villages of **Gorni Lom** and **Chuprene** are the starting points for footpaths into the mountains, though the nearest **accommodation** is back in Belogradchik, where you can also hire guides from the *Hotel Tourist*.

THE DANUBIAN PLAIN

Stretching from the northern slopes of the Balkan Range to the Danube river, the **Danubian Plain** (*Dunavska ravnina*) is a more undulating region than its name would suggest, an agriculturally rich area crowded with maize fields, sunflowers and vineyards. The river itself forms Bulgaria's frontier with its northern neighbour, Romania, before wheeling away beyond Silistra to join the Black Sea far to the north. The shorelines possess different characters: the Bulgarian side is buttressed by steep bluffs and tabletop plateaus, while the opposite bank is low-lying and riven by shallow lakes called *baltas*, which merge first with marshes, then the Wallachian plain. Between the two lies a shoal of wooded islands that provide a haven for local birdlife, a population sustained by the river's rich stocks of fish.

In ancient times the Danube was one of Europe's most important **frontiers**, a natural barrier separating the riches of southern Europe from the barbarian tribes to the north. The Macedonian kings tried to make the Danube the northern boundary of their domains, with Alexander the Great campaigning against the Getae here in 335 BC, but their hold on the area was always superficial. The **Romans** were the first to turn the Danube into a permanent, fortified line of defence, building a series of garrison towns and administrative centres along its length. By the second century, thriving civilian towns such as Ratiaria, Oescus, Novae and Durostorum were beginning to emerge alongside the armed camps. By the fifth century, however, the frontier was being breached by raiders from the north, many of whom (including the *sklaveni*, ancestors of the Balkan slavs) increasingly chose to settle down south of the river once their plundering days were over. Justinian attempted to stem the tide in the sixth century, refortifying the old Roman sites and establishing new garrisons along the river, but Byzantine diplomacy subsequently concentrated on paying off the barbarians to keep them sweet rather than attempting to shut them out altogether.

With the decline of the lower Danube's strategic importance the settlements along its banks began to decay, only to revive when the last of the Bulgarian kings, the **Shishmanids**, fought a delaying action against the advancing Turks from Danubian strongholds such as Nikopol and **Vidin**. The Ottomans themselves were great fortress builders, erecting the eighteenth-century citadels of Ruse and Silistra in an attempt to strengthen the Danube frontier against the advance of Russian power.

During the nineteenth century, increased river transport brought the goods and culture of Central Europe down the valley, turning the towns along its banks into cosmopolitan outposts of Mitteleuropa. European fashions and styles often arrived here first before being transmitted to the rest of Bulgaria, turning towns such as **Ruse** and **Silistra** into centres of elegance and sophistication. With the development of the railways, however, the river trade went into decline, and nowadays most of Bulgaria's Danubian towns are quiet, provincial places, focusing their attention not on the river itself, but on the bigger cities inland. The only real exceptions are Vidin and most of all Ruse – an important cultural centre that commands the major road and train route to Bucharest and the north. Ruse is a good base from which to visit the valley of the **Rusenski Lom**, a hauntingly beautiful spot which harbours important medieval ruins, and several lesser sights along the river, such as the small port of **Svishtov** to the west, and the **Srebârna nature reserve**, just outside **Silistra**, to the east. Elsewhere along the river however, public transport is meagre, and tourist attractions few and far between. Heading along the riverbank from Vidin to Ruse for example is only a practical itinerary if you have a car: most bus links connect the Danubian towns with places inland rather than with each other, and reliable accommodation is practically nonexistent.

Travelling from the Danube towards the coast you'll pass through an extension of the Danubian Plain known as **the Dobrudzha**, a vast expanse of grain-producing flatland which extends from Silistra to the Black Sea. The region's administrative centre, the former Ottoman market town of **Dobrich**, provides the only potential stopoff en route.

Vidin

"One of those marvellous cities of eastern fairytale which, secure behind their fortress walls, is decorated with spires and cupolas and minarets piled one upon another in a fantastic medley of creeds, ages and styles." So **VIDIN** was rather fancifully described by Lovett Edwards in his book *Danube Stream* in 1941. Nowadays you'll find that the truth is more prosaic: Vidin's modern skyline leaves a lot to be desired, and although the great sweep of the fortress walls still dominates much of the riverfront, the spires and minarets characteristic of Edwards' day have largely gone, to be replaced by utilitarian housing projects. Ample reasons for visiting are, however, still provided by the showpiece medieval **citadel of Baba Vida**, presiding over luscious riverside parklands on the northern edge of town. Buses connect Vidin with the nearby Danubian towns of **Lom**, **Kozlodui** and **Oryahovo**, although there's little of touristic interest along this stretch of the river.

Some history

Vidin's potential as the guardhouse of the lower Danube was exploited by successive waves of Celts, Romans and Byzantines, but it was under the Bulgarian tsars and their Ottoman conquerors that the most frenzied fortress building took place. However, Vidin's relative isolation from major power centres like Târnovo and Constantinople made the place a breeding ground for semi-independent local kinglets, and the citadel they built was much coveted by neighbouring powers. In the fourteenth century it was the power base of **Mihail Shishman**, whom the nobles elected tsar rather than see Vidin secede from Bulgaria, and after 1371 it was the capital of an independent kingdom ruled by Mihail's grand-nephew **Ivan Stratsimir**. Vidin fought a rearguard action against Ottoman expansion in the Balkans, grudgingly accepting Turkish suzerainty in the 1390s – only to throw it off again as soon as help emerged from the West in the shape of the Crusade of 1396. The city was recaptured by Sultan Bayezid's army two years later.

In the late eighteenth century Vidin was the capital of **Osman Pazvantoglu**, a local ruler who rebelled against Sultan Selim III in 1794. Energetic, despotic and fond of inventing tortures, Pazvantoglu pillaged as far afield as Sofia in defiance

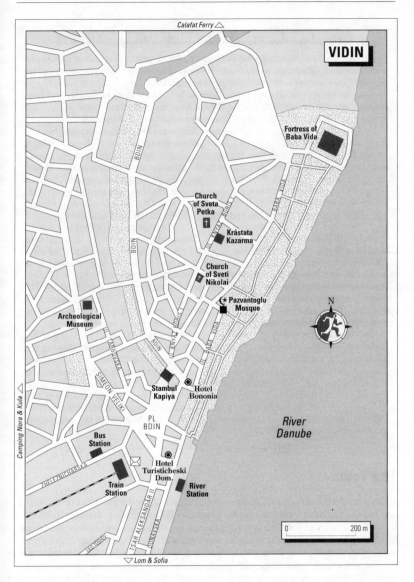

of the sultan, and strengthened Vidin's fortifications with the assistance of French engineers sent by Napoleon, who envisaged him as a potential lever for toppling the Ottoman Empire.

These days Vidin is comparatively quiet, but with the Romanian town of Calafat just across the river, and the Serbian border 30km northwest, the town still retains a little of its former cosmopolitan feel.

OSMAN PAZVANTOGLU AND THE KÂRDZHALI

By the early 1790s Ottoman-ruled northern Bulgaria was sliding slowly into chaos, with provincial Ottoman governors increasingly in revolt against a reforming sultan – Selim III – who they saw as a threat to their traditional powers. The provincial governors had begun to staff their private armies with a new class of dispossessed freebooters, mostly former imperial soldiers, known as **Kârdzhali**, who roamed the countryside in search of food and plunder, terrorizing Christian villages.

Foremost among the provincial power barons was **Osman Pazvantoglu**, born in Vidin in around 1758, the son of a local janissary executed in 1788 for leading a revolt. Osman himself was also sentenced to death for participating in the revolt, but managed to escape, re-emerging in the 1790s to harness the discontent whipped up by his father. Ruler of Vidin from 1794 onwards, Pazvantoglu attracted *Kârdzhali* from all over northern Bulgaria, not least because the town was seen as a safe zone where they could store their booty and sell it – with Pazvantoglu taking a percentage of the proceeds. The sultan laid **siege** to Vidin in 1795 and again in the winter of 1797–8, but the bulk of his troops simply melted away and joined the rebels. Pazvantoglu was popular with Islamic traditionalists who saw him as a bulwark against a Westernizing sultan, but he also took care to win the support of local Christians, cutting taxes and feudal impositions, and promising to treat all subjects as equals whatever their faith. For a time Pazvantoglu seemed capable of overthrowing the sultan and installing himself in Constantinople, but somehow failed to press home the advantage. Ultimately he was kept in check by the Russians, who feared that the autocratic structure of society in eastern Europe might suffer general collapse if truculent upstarts like Pazvantoglu were seen to get their way.

The **Serbian Uprising of 1804** spelled the end for Pazvantoglu. Many of his Bulgarian subjects were tempted to join their Serb neighbours, thus destroying the Muslim-Christian alliance which had thus far prevailed in Pazvantoglu's territory. January 1806 saw Pazvantoglu launch a vicious **pogrom** against Bulgarian priests and civil leaders in Vidin, fearful that they were about to launch a revolt of their own. Frequent outbreaks of plague gnawed away at the city's self-confidence, and Vidin was in steep decline by the time of Pazvantoglu's own death in February 1807. His uncharismatic successor, Idris Molla, was unable to prevent the gradual re-imposition of Ottoman control.

The Town

Vidin's modern heart stands at the southern end of the fortified old town, based around the flagstoned central square, **ploshtad Bdin**, which is dominated by customary examples of socialist urban planning: the high-rise style former headquarters of the Communist party vying for attention with the equally brutal modernism of the *obshtinski sâvet*, or town council building, next door. Somewhat less imposing are the structures lining the main downtown streets which radiate outwards from here – drab lumps of ochre and grey that reveal little of the town's former glory.

The only real interest in modern Vidin is the **Archeological Museum** (Tues–Sat 9am–noon & 1.30–5.30pm), housed in a pagoda-like nineteenth-century *konak* west of the main square at the end of ul. Târgovska. The display begins with prehistoric bone and stone tools found in the Mirizlivka cave near the village of Oreshets, but most space is devoted to Roman-period finds from the regional centre of Ratiaria, founded by Trajan in about 107 AD near the modern village of Archar, 25km southeast of Vidin. A floor mosaic on which a stag is chased by a wild cat, and a fine second-century marble sculpture of a pensive Hercules toying with his club, reveal something of the sophistication and comfort of life in this otherwise rather provincial outpost. Sarcophagi and gravestones from Ratiaria's necropolis litter the lawn outside. An adjoining section of the museum deals with the National Revival period, with particular reference to the local peasant uprising of 1850, centred on the towns of Gradets and Belogradchik.

The Old Town

On the northern side of the main square the borders of old Vidin are marked by the Stambul Kapiya or Istanbul Gate, a stocky portal in the Turkish style. Beyond it lies a pleasant turn-of-the-century residential district with an extensive riverside park to the east. On the edge of the park stands the Osman Pazvantoglu mosque, the only surviving mosque in the city – most of the others were knocked down in the 1970s and 1980s. To one side is the squat, domed kitabhane or Koranic library, currently pressed into service as an art gallery. Immediately opposite stands the modern Church of Sveti Nikolai, inside which Cyril, Methodius and other saints are rendered in colourful turn-of-the-century realist frescos, rather like illustrations in a children's encyclopedia. More interesting is the Church of Sveti Panteleimon, hidden round the back, an austere twelfth-century basilica made from heavy stone.

From Sveti Nikolai, ul. Baba Vida hugs the park's western flank, leading past an ensemble of sorry-looking buildings along the way: the peeling ochre plaster of the **banya** or town baths, and the shell of a derelict **synagogue**. Vidin was an important centre of Jewish culture until the late 1940s, when most local families emigrated to Israel. Parallel to Baba Vida to the west is ul. Knyaz Boris I, site of Pazvantoglu's **Krâstata Kazarma** (the "cross-shaped barracks"), now an ethnographic **museum** (usually Mon–Fri 9am–noon & 2–5pm; ring the bell and hope that a curator is around). Across the road, stranded behind railings in a patch of wasteland between two school playgrounds, is the seventeenth-century **Church of Sveta Petka**, an unassuming, sunken structure, traces of bright blue on the exterior giving some idea of its former appearance.

From the northern end of the riverside park stone ramparts run alongside the shoreline for over a kilometre, largely overgrown and deserted, eventually curving inland to protect the **Fortress of Baba Vida** (daily 9–11.30am & 1.30–5pm). Surrounded by huge walls and a deep, dried-out moat, the fortress dates from the thirteenth century, although the brutal, blockhouse appearance of its turrets and towers owes more to the continuous improvements carried out by the Turks and the Habsburgs, who briefly occupied the town in the sixteenth century. Once inside, you can scramble around an extensive network of courtyards and ramparts, and survey the Danube from gun positions overlooking the river. Further stretches of wall extend well to the west of the citadel, and crumbling gates stand surreally amid the modern housing estates.

Immediately below Baba Vida's walls lies the grandly named *gradski plazh* or **municipal beach**, a small stretch of pebbles on the river's edge with a grassy terrace for sunbathing above. North of Baba Vida paths lead beside concrete flood defences and a derelict rowing centre (*grebna baza*) towards an unspoiled **riverside meadow** some 2km beyond. Intermittently shaded with trees, it's popular with local bathers, amateur fishermen and grazing flocks.

CROSSING INTO ROMANIA

Roughly every hour a **car ferry service** (*feribot*) shuttles between Vidin's grandiosely named International Dock, 5km north of town, and the port of Calafat on the Romanian side of the River Danube (30min; $6, payable in leva). In theory services continue throughout the night, although timings are wholly unpredictable between around 8pm and 8am. Bus #1 runs from outside Vidin train station to the ferry dock, but timings are irregular. A taxi from the station to the dock will set you back about $5, more if coming in the opposite direction. A much more convenient option for **foot passengers** is the smaller ferry which leaves from Vidin's river station (*rechna gara*) 100m east of the train station, although there's currently only one daily service on Tues, Thur & Sat, and two daily on Mon, Wed & Fri.

Romanian visas cost about $25 at the frontier post (have US cash ready), and trains run from Calafat on to Craiova and Bucharest.

Practicalities

Most of the town's amenities lie in the modern centre a short distance from the main square: **bus** and **train** stations are a couple of blocks to the west, while the **river station** (*rechna gara*) is two blocks south, just off Tsar Aleksandar II, the main Sofia road. The cheapest of the town's **hotels** is the *Turisticheski Dom* on ul. Edelvais (☎094/22813), a downtown block offering dorm beds for $10 per person or doubles with ensuite facilities (③). Marginally more comfortable is the *Hotel Bononia*, beside the riverside gardens on pl. Bdin (☎094/23031; ③), which is a fairly dilapidated two-star, but with a few recently renovated rooms.

Daytime drinking and snacking is best in the **cafés** along ul. Târgovska, or in the riverside park, where there's a large open-air café at the *Telegraf Kapiya*, an Ottoman-era post office. The **restaurant** of the *Hotel Bononia* is the only decent place for a slap-up Bulgarian meal, although there's a tolerable pizzeria, the *Napoli*, on ul. Aleksandâr Batenberg between train and river stations.

Down the Danube: from Vidin to Ruse

The road heading east along the Danube from Vidin passes through a string of settlements which, despite an often dramatic history, lack the kind of attractions – save for the river itself – to warrant anything more than the briefest of halts. Given the social problems of Lom and the ailing nuclear power station at Kozlodui, any description of this part of the river is bound to read more like a catalogue of places to avoid rather than a recommended tourist itinerary, unless you have a taste for ancient history or riverine wildlife. Another reason for treating this route with caution is that bus transport along this stretch of the river is notoriously meagre; even if you succeed in getting as far as Oryahovo (see opposite), you'll probably then have to head inland to Pleven in order to make any further eastbound progress.

Thirty or so kilometres downriver from Vidin, the village of **Archar** was once the site of Ratiaria – the capital of Upper Moesia, from where the Emperor Trajan consolidated Roman rule over what's now the Romanian side of the Danube – though there's little to see beyond the relics now on show in Vidin's Archeological Museum (see p.164). A kilometre or two beyond the village of Dobri Dol look out for signs leading to Dobrodolski Monastery, home to the curious mid-nineteenth-century **Church of Sveta Troitsa**. A buff-coloured structure topped by an unusually tall drum, the exterior is unadorned save for a series of reliefs executed in a deliberately primitivist style, harking back to medieval, almost pre-Christian, Bulgarian models. A carving above the door shows a man fighting a dog-headed snake, flanked on either side by figures of the Archangel Michael and the builder of the church himself. Beyond here the road runs behind a wooded cliff more than 100m high, which continues in an unbroken line for about 20km. The river bank around **Orsoya**, 7km beyond Dobri Dol, is a well-known spot for watching waterfowl and wading birds.

During the last century this stretch of the Danube shore was chosen by the Turks to accommodate the *cherkezi* or **Circassians**, Muslim refugees from the Caucasus who had been expelled from their homelands by the armies of Imperial Russia. Used by the Ottomans to keep the local Bulgarians under control, many of them fled after the Liberation to escape reprisals, although a few small communities remain. Many of those who stayed were assimilated into Bulgaria's Turkish minority, with the result that surviving pockets of Circassians tend to be categorized (both by themselves and their Bulgarian neighbours) as Turks.

Lom and Kozlodui

The first major settlement east of Vidin is **LOM**, a town renowned throughout Bulgaria for the watermelons grown in the surrounding fields. Citizens of Sofia used to come up to Lom in order to stock up on the local produce – the kind of fresh fruit of which urban dwellers were often deprived – thus leading the locals to dub the train link between Lom and the capital as the *mazen vlak* – the "gravy train". Slightly closer to Sofia by train than Vidin, Lom has outstripped its western neighbour as the capital's port on the Danube, and it's correspondingly uglier and more industrialized as a result. In addition, the town's large **gypsy population** is one of the most downtrodden in Bulgaria, and gypsy demonstrations against local police harrassment have been a frequent occurrence in recent years (see p.409).

Forty kilometres east of Lom, **KOZLODUI**, the next place of any size, has a monument near the small harbour commemorating the "**landing of 1876**", when Hristo Botev (see p.258) launched his ill-fated raid on northern Bulgaria. More recently Kozlodui has become notorious as the site of Bulgaria's first and only **nuclear power station**, built with Soviet help in the 1970s. Throughout 1991 international observers became increasingly worried about the plant's safety, not least because the Soviet technicians who used to run it were being replaced by insufficiently qualified Bulgarian staff. Western companies, funded by the European Union, have been involved in overhauling the plant, but it is still considered one of the most dangerous installations in the former Eastern bloc. It's due to be decommissioned in 2020: in the meantime, beset by energy problems brought about by the sudden curtailment of cheap electricity supplies from the former Soviet Union, the Bulgarians have little choice but to keep Kozlodui going as best they can.

Oryahovo and Gigen

Another forty kilometres downriver from Kozlodui, **ORYAHOVO** slopes up a hillside overlooking a port used for the export of grain and grapes. In 1396, the Bulgarians holding Oryahovo's fortress, Rachova, surrendered willingly to the

Crusaders rather than fight for the Turks, but the French contingent in the crusading army pillaged and burned the town anyway, later justifying their action by claiming that they had had to take the town by force. Oryahovo is nowadays useful as a rail junction, with a couple of trains a day departing for **Cherven Bryag** on the Sofia–Pleven–Varna line. There's also a ferry connecting Oryahovo to Bechet on the Romanian side of the river, although the lack of public transport links at the latter make this a bad place to enter Romania, unless you're travelling by private car.

At the confluence of the Iskâr and the Danube beyond Baikal, the **ruins of Roman Oescus** can be found about 2km north of **GIGEN** village. Excavations

---

THE VLACHS

One minority living along Bulgaria's riverine border are the *Vlasi* or **Vlachs**, who speak a dialect of Romanian and are found in isolated villages throughout north Bulgaria, eastern Serbia, Macedonia and northern Greece.

Precise definitions of who is a Vlach and who isn't vary from area to area. To many Balkan Slavs, a Vlach is simply a Romanian-speaker who lives outside Romania. Elsewhere (notably in Croatia, Slovenia and the Czech and Slovak republics, the term "Vlach" is used to designate transhumant shepherds, without necessarily denoting a particular ethnic origin. The Vlachs of the Balkans are traditionally nomadic sheep farmers, pasturing their flocks on the lowlands during the winter and moving to the mountains in the summer. Nowadays, however, the attractions of urban life, and the restrictions on movement imposed by modern bureaucratic states (not least socialist ones), have meant that most Balkan Vlachs lead an increasingly sedentary lifestyle.

The origins of the Vlachs have been the cause of much inconclusive debate, but the fact that they speak a Latin tongue suggests that they are descended either from second- and third-century Roman settlers or from the native Balkan peoples – whether Dacians, Thracians, or Illyrians – who came into contact with these settlers and adopted their language. With the collapse of Roman and Byzantine power, hastened by the successive deluges of Slavs, Magyars and Turks, the Vlachs somehow ensured the survival of their tongue by retreating into highland regions and reverting to nomadism. The most enthusiastic proponents of this version of Vlach history are the Romanians, who point to the existence of the modern Romanian nation as proof that the ancient, Latinized population in the Balkans was able to retreat into the hills, only to re-emerge centuries later with its language and culture intact. Nationalist historians from other Balkan countries sometimes beg to differ, arguing that Vlachs are either ethnic Slavs or ethnic Greeks, learning Latin from their Roman or Byzantine masters, and somehow clinging on to the language due to the isolated nature of their lifestyle.

Bulgaria's Vlachs are found along the Danube and in the Dobrudzha, but during the Communist period they were encouraged to assimilate with the Slav majority, thus threatening the long-term survival of their language. The scattered nature of Vlach settlement, and the fact that many local gypsies declare themselves to be Vlach despite belonging to an altogether different ethnic group, make it difficult to ascertain exactly how many of them there are in the country. While the development of democracy has given other minority groups the opportunity to reaffirm their identity and culture, it's unlikely that Bulgaria's Vlachs have the cohesiveness to develop strong cultural organizations of their own.

have uncovered ramparts, foundation walls, drains and large paving-slabs that give a fair idea of the layout of the ancient town, though the site's rich yield of statuary and mosaics is now displayed in Pleven's history museum. Like other Danubian settlements, Oescus was razed by the Huns in the fifth century, rebuilt during the reign of Justinian and destroyed again by the Avars, so it's hardly surprising that nothing remains of the great bridge over the Danube built for the Emperor Constantine. Reportedly 1160m long, it was abandoned after less than forty years.

Nikopol and Belene

The road loops inland before arriving at **NIKOPOL**, 46km beyond, a sleepy backwater known primarily for the once-impregnable fortress founded in 629 by Emperor Heraclius I. Its capture by the Turks in 1393 frightened the Christian powers into organizing a crusade to retake the lower Danube. Feasting and pillaging their way south, the Crusaders treated the campaign as a sport, bringing "wines and festive provisions" instead of siege weapons. Unable to storm Nikopolis' 26 mighty towers, they instituted a blockade and began squabbling among themselves (the French, in particular, resented the fact that Sigismund of Hungary had been chosen by the pope to be supreme commander). Pigheadedness and disunity proved fatal on November 25, 1396, when Sultan Bayezid's army appeared on the neighbouring plateau. Against Sigismund's orders the French cavalry charged uphill after fleeing irregulars, only to be impaled on hidden stakes and then butchered by the Turkish cavalry. The Crusaders' defeat was shattering, and no further attempts were made to check Turkish expansion until the battle of Varna fifty years later, by which time the Ottomans were entrenched in the Balkans.

It's fairly easy to work your way up to the fortress from Nikopol's riverfront **bus station**, but there's little to see once you get there, save for earthen ramparts, and sombre views of abandoned Romanian factories on the opposite bank. Back in town, you'll find a couple of central **cafés**, and a smashed-up hotel which seems to have permanently closed its doors. Nikopol has **bus** links with the city of Pleven to the south, but not with its Danubian neighbours.

Beyond Nikopol the road cuts inland again, passing after 30km a left turn to **BELENE**, a small agricultural town standing opposite **Belene Island**, the river's largest, now notorious in Bulgaria for being the site of one of the country's biggest labour camps. Although political prisoners are no longer held here, Belene still functions as a high-security camp for dangerous criminals. More happily, Belene is a favoured nesting ground of **spoonbills** in May and June.

Svishtov

Twenty kilometres east of Belene, **SVISHTOV** is a long-established port and crafts town that grew up to the west of the former Roman city of Novae. A common crossing point for boats before the building of the bridge at Ruse downstream, Svishtov witnessed the arrival of the Russian liberators in 1877 and the invasion of Romania by German and Bulgarian forces in 1916.

Bus and **train** terminals both lie in a drab riverside area just below the bluff upon which Svishtov is built. Roads curl up into the hilltop town, passing a shabby overgrown park in the midst of which lurk remains of the medieval *kale*, or

BELENE LABOUR CAMP

Between Nikopol and Svishtov lies a cluster of green islands whose name is now notorious in Bulgaria – **Belene**, the site of an infamous labour camp. Established in 1947, together with a smaller women's camp which was soon closed, Belene held both political prisoners and dangerous criminals. The latter were reportedly favoured by the guards, who apparently permitted them to tyrannize the "politicals" according to Stalinist practice. During the 1950s when the purges were at their height, hundreds of Bulgarians perished here through a combination of malnutrition, overwork and brutality. Prisoners directed to woodcutting on neighbouring Bârzina Island had to chop 1120 cubic metres per day before receiving their rations, and inmates who violated camp rules (by scavenging for food, or addressing a guard as "comrade", for example) were used for target practice or marooned on rafts to freeze or suffer clouds of mosquitos.

Conditions improved somewhat during the 1960s following a limited amnesty, but Belene remained a savage place. During the 1970s many of the inmates were Pomaks, Slav Muslims from western Rhodopes who were being pressured to drop their Islamic-sounding names and adopt Bulgarian ones instead – those that resisted ended up in Belene. Ethnic Turks who objected to the revitalized name-changing campaign of the mid-1980s were sent here too. The camp was closed down swiftly after November 1989.

fortress. Just below the *kale*, the modern facade of the **Church of Sveti Dimitâr** obscures a ramshackle seventeenth-century nave, brightened by some colourfully naive nineteenth-century frescos.

Beyond lies the main square, where you'll find most of the amenities. Head right along Tsar Osvoboditel and right again into ul. Konstantinov to reach the **Church of Sveta Troitsa**, arguably the crowning achievement of National Revival architect Kolyo Ficheto. The curving lines of the roof are said to be a conscious imitation of the waves of the River Danube, while the octagonal bell tower is crowned with fanciful gothic pinnacles. Just beyond lies the former **house of Aleko Konstantinov** (daily 9am–noon & 1–5pm), a satirist remembered for creating *Bay Ganyu*, an itinerant peddler of rose oil and rugs who remains one of the most popular characters in Bulgarian fiction. Konstantinov was killed by mistake in 1897 by assassins aiming for his lawyer friend, and a jar holding his heart, complete with ragged bullet hole, is the museum's most striking exhibit.

There's little reason to stay in Svishtov, but if you need a **hotel**, head for the main square and the two-star *Hotel Dunav* (☎0631/22361; ③), which also has a good **restaurant**. A number of **cafés** are scattered around the main square and along Tsar Osvoboditel. There's just one bus a day from Svishtov to Ruse, the next major city along the Danube, with services heading south to Veliko Târnovo (see p.201) being much more frequent.

Ruse and around

"Everything I experienced later in life had already happened in **RUSE**", wrote Elias Canetti in the autobiographical *Tongue Set Free*, remembering his childhood home as an invigorating city of different races and creeds, whose cosmopolitan culture placed it firmly in the orbit of Mitteleuropa. Although the ethnic mix of Canetti's day has long since disappeared, travellers continue to be surprised by

Ruse's Central European elegance. Despite being blighted by the customary con-crete-and-steel overlay provided by Bulgaria's postwar urban planners, it's still a city of peaceful residential streets, where Art Nouveau-inspired ornamentation drips from delicate turn-of-the-century houses. Ruse bears a similarity to Bulgaria's other Danubian towns in lacking a riverfront of any great beauty, but a scattering of historic sights and the relaxed feel of its downtown streets more than compensate. An important cultural centre with an animated café life, the city also plays host to one of the liveliest evening *korsos* in Bulgaria. In addition, Ruse makes a good base for exploring the nearby **Rusenski Lom** national park, home to the dramatic **Rock Monastery of Ivanovo** and the ruined city of **Cherven**.

Some history

Apart from the fortress and a sprinkling of stately mosques (the former blown up by Marshal Kutuzov in the Russo-Turkish war of 1806–12, the latter demolished by post-Liberation Bulgarians), Ruse (Ruschuk to the Turks) was an unremark-able Ottoman provincial town until the enlightened governorship of **Midhat Pasha** (1864–68), who provided the town with schools, hospitals, factories and, most importantly, the British-financed Ruse–Varna rail line – Bulgaria's first. Until the construction of the more direct Belgrade–Sofia–Istanbul line in the 1880s, travellers flooded through Ruse on their way from Central Europe to Constantinople. A "European quarter" grew up rapidly along the river bank, although the speed at which the whole place was constructed gave it a rather tacky, boom-town appearance.

Trade received a further boost after the Liberation, and for many years Ruse had more inhabitants, consulates, factories, hotels and banks than Sofia. The city's eco-nomic and cultural wealth owed a lot to the merchant families – including Germans, Greeks and Armenians – who settled here. Most numerous, however, were the **Sephardic Jews** (of whom Elias Canetti was one, born here in 1905), descendants of those Jews given refuge in the Ottoman Empire after their expul-sion from Spain in 1492, and speaking Ladino, a mixture of archaic Spanish and Portuguese with numerous borrowings from the Turkish and Hebrew tongues.

Arrival and accommodation

Trolleybuses #1, #11, #12 and #18 head up ul. Borisova from the **train** and **bus** stations to the main square, **pl. Svoboda**. Dunav Tours, just southwest of the main square at pl. Han Kubrat 5 (Mon–Fri 9am–noon & 1.30–5.30pm; ☎223088), rents out **private rooms** (②) in central locations, and can also book rooms in Ivanovo (p.178) and Cherven (p.179). On the whole, Ruse's **hotels** are over-priced, the cheapest being the friendly but woefully run-down *Helleos*, Nikolaevska 1 (③), with tatty ensuite doubles. Centrally located alternatives are the ageing *Dunav*, pl. Svoboda 7 (☎082/226518 or 22031; ④), with comfortable ensuite rooms, and the more modern *Splendid*, Aleksandrovska 40 (☎082/235951, fax 238192; ⑤), with swish ensuite bathrooms, TV, and attentive staff. The latter is probably preferable to the high-rise *Riga*, Pridunavski 22 (☎082/22181; ⑤), whose main selling point is the riverside position.

Alternatively, you could rent a bungalow (②) or **camp** at the mosquito-prone *Ribarska koliba* (mid–May to mid–Oct; ☎082/224068), occupying a shady hillside site 6km west of town in the riverside Prista park – take bus #6 from ul. Nikolaevska.

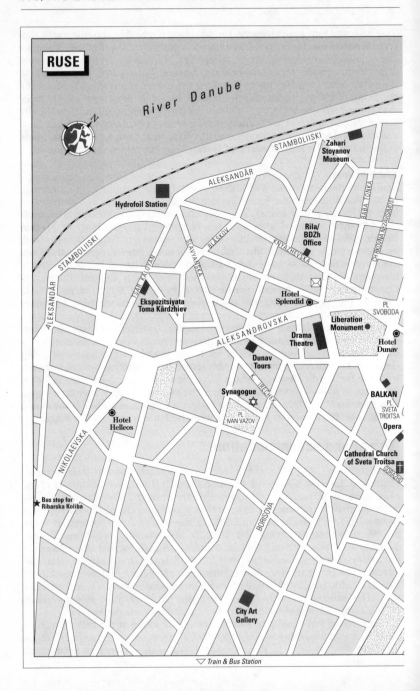

RUSE

River Danube

N

STAMBOLIISKI

Zahari Stoyanov Museum

ALEKSANDÄR

Hydrofoil Station

STAMBOLIISKI

ALEKSANDÄR

STAVANSKA

BLASKOV

KNYAZHEVSKA

BABA TONKA

CHKOVA NEZAVISIMOST

Rila/ BDZh Office

ISAB KALOTAN

Ekspozitsiyata Toma Kârdzhiev

Hotel Splendid

PL SVOBODA

ALEKSANDROVSKA

Liberation Monument

Drama Theatre

Hotel Dunav

Dunav Tours

K. IRECHEK

BALKAN

Synagogue

PL IVAN VAZOV

PL SVETA TROITSA

NIKOLAEVSKA

Hotel Helleos

Opera

Cathedral Church of Sveta Troitsa

GURKO

Bus stop for Ribarska Koliba

BORISOVA

City Art Gallery

▽ Train & Bus Station

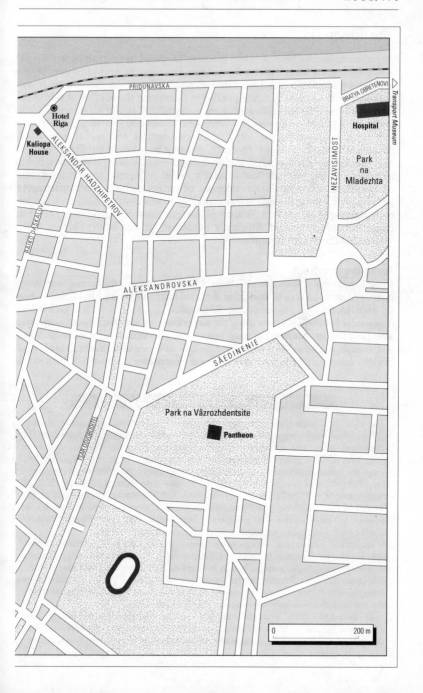

The Town

A spacious mixture of concrete and greenery bordered by open-air bookstalls and flower sellers, the central **pl. Svoboda** (Freedom Square) is watched over by one of Ruse's trademarks, the 1908 **Liberation Monument**, a classical pillar surmounted by an allegorical figure of Liberty. Occupying the southwest side of the square is Ruse's **Drama Theatre**, a once-magnificent neo-Renaissance pile currently lying gutted as a prelude to complete restoration. Skirting the northern side of the square is the city's main commercial and social artery, **ul. Aleksandrovska** – venue for shopping, drinking and aimless strolling. There's a food **market** and diverse street traders along the road's eastern stretches. North and south of pl. Svoboda lies a patchwork of residential streets lined with nineteenth-century bourgeois residences, nowadays divided up into apartments. Hidden away among them is one reminder of Ruse's cosmopolitan past, the former **synagogue** on pl. Ivan Vazov, which spent most of the postwar period as regional headquarters of Bulgaria's equivalent of the lottery before being returned to the Jewish community.

Along the riverfront

Ulitsa Knyazhevska leads downhill from pl. Svoboda towards the former merchants' quarter of town, an area of dust-laden stuccoed buildings where Elias Canetti's family used to have a warehouse, at Slavyanska 12. From here the cobbled ul. Aleksandâr Stamboliiski runs along the **waterfront** – a singularly unattractive area save for a few Art-Nouveauish town houses, the odd stretch of riverside parkland, and a couple of House-Museums where the bulk of Ruse's historic artefacts are kept. Slightly inland, the **Ekspozitsiyata Toma Kardzhiev** (Mon–Fri 9am–noon &

CHEMICAL EMISSIONS FROM GIURGIU

The citizens of Ruse played an important part in the democratizing tide of the late 1980s, when locals began to protest against the ecological damage caused by the **chemical plant** just across the river in Romanian **Giurgiu**. *Rusentsi* had been conscious of the regular chlorine gas emissions wafting over the river from Giurgiu – and the corresponding rise in respiratory complaints among the city's children – for over a decade. Cases of lung disease in Ruse rose from just 969 per 100,000 inhabitants in 1975 to 17,386 in 1985. In 1986, 150,000 people received out-patient treatment for respiratory problems, and almost 5000 were detained in hospital; on average ten days' work a year per person were lost to "Ruse lung" (toxic fibrosis), and four-fifths of Ruse's young men were unfit for military service.

Bulgaria's Communist rulers nevertheless tried to keep the problem quiet, unwilling to compromise their good relations with Ceaucescu's Romania. Protests first took place in 1987, and in March 1988 a Committee for the Protection of Ruse was formed in Sofia. Prominent Party members who took part in this initiative were subsequently removed from their posts – a purge that made public for the first time the growing disagreements among the ruling socialist elite.

In October 1991, a rumoured fire at the Giurgiu plant briefly sent Bulgarian–Romanian relations into crisis, but now that the plant has closed down, cross-border relations have returned to normal, and Ruse's air is once more relatively clean.

2–5pm), on the corner of Lyule Burgaz and Tsar Kaloyan, has changing exhibitions of historical interest.

Back on the riverfront, the **Zahari Stoyanov Museum**, Stamboliiski 15 (Mon–Fri 9am–noon & 2–5pm), commemorates the journalist, politician and author best known for his *Notes on the Bulgarian Uprisings*, a record of the author's own experiences during the 1870s. Inspired by the heroic suicide of Angel Kânchev (see p.220), the young Stoyanov joined the revolutionary movement and toured Bulgaria helping to set up clandestine patriotic cells. By the time of the April Rising of 1876 he was attached to the rebel group commanded by Georgi Benkovski, a leader of the Rising in the Koprivshtitsa area (see p.246). Stoyanov's subsequent account served to immortalize both Benkovski and many other leading personalities of April 1876, and helped enshrine the Rising as the crucial event in the nation's liberation. Zahari Stoyanov married the youngest daughter of Baba ("Granny") Tonka Obretenova, a formidable matriarch who was at the forefront of revolutionary activity in nineteenth-century Ruse, offering her home to the patriotic underground as a safe-house and arms dump, smuggling rifles through swamps, and leading Ruse's women in an armed assault on the town prison. She raised their children as fervent patriots, her five sons taking part in the April Rising, and their portraits fill one of the rooms here. The skull of Stefan Karadzha, preserved as a *memento mori* by Tonka after the illustrious *haidut* leader was hanged in Ruse in 1868 (he had in fact already died of wounds en route to the execution) is sometimes on display here, too.

As well as books and manuscripts recalling Stoyanov's work, the museum displays one of the suitcases Stoyanov was travelling with when he dropped dead in Paris in 1889, and exhibition space is devoted to another revolutionary, Panayot Hitov, who retired to Ruse with his Serbian wife. Guerrilla life in the forests is remembered with items such as Hitov's embroidered tobacco pouch, his secret money belt, and numerous antiquated pistols and shotguns. Finally, the house also contains a small ethnographic collection, featuring a dazzling array of ceremonial blouses embroidered by the unmarried girls of the region.

Further along the riverbank, opposite the *Hotel Riga*, lies a museum of nineteenth-century urban life which is popularly known as the **Kaliopa house** (*Kâshta na Kaliopa*; Mon–Fri 9am–noon & 2–5pm) after one of its former owners, the wife of the German consul. Beautifully restored, the house betrays the classic tastes of its wealthy inhabitants, who commissioned a painting of Cupid and Psyche on the stairs leading to the upstairs salons, where walls and ceilings decorated with Grecian urns awaited guests invited to the music recitals and literary evenings once held here.

A good ten minutes' walk further along the riverbank, the **Transport Museum**, at Bratya Obretenovi 1 (officially Mon–Fri 9am–noon & 2–5pm, although in practice hardly ever open), occupies the original station building and commemorates the establishment of the Ruse–Varna railway. The lines of historic locos and rolling stock parked outside include locomotive no 148, one of the initial set of steam engines built for the railway by a Manchester firm in 1866; and the sumptuous *Sultaniye* sleeping-carriage, used by Empress Eugenie of France in 1869 when on her way southwards to open the Suez Canal.

The Cathedral Church, the Pantheon and the City Art Gallery

A couple of blocks east of pl. Svoboda on ul. Gorazd is the **Cathedral Church of Sveta Troitsa**, dating from 1632 and twice rebuilt in successive centuries. The resulting building borrows liberally from Russian models, sporting a curious Baroque facade and a medieval Muscovite spire. Steps descend into an icon-rich subterranean nave, its stuccoed ceiling supported by trompe l'oeil marble-effect pillars crowned with Corinthian capitals.

Further east across bul. Tsar Osvoboditel, you'll find the **Park na Vâzrozhdentsite** (Park of the Men of the Revival), where the **Ruse Pantheon** (Mon–Fri 9am–noon & 2–5pm), a mausoleum devoted to nineteenth-century revolutionary heroes, squats on a flagstoned plaza. It's a grossly overstated building: a kind of high-tech Maya temple surmounted by half a giant ping-pong ball covered in gold. Inside, the marble graves of the great (including most of the Obretenov family) are watched over by four statues of grieving mothers. It all lacks the delicacy of the smaller, more tasteful nineteenth-century chapels – honouring, among others, Zahari Stoyanov – which lie under the trees of the surrounding park. North of here is **Park na Mladezhta**, or "Youth Park", where tree- and shrub-lined avenues provide a popular strolling area. Steps at the northern end of the park descend to the riverfront and the transport museum.

There's little incentive to stray too far south of the town centre, save for the **City Art Gallery**, at ul. Borisova 39 (Tues–Sun 8am–noon & 2–6pm), a largely parochial collection of local artists enlivened by a couple of eulogies to peasant toil from popular postwar painter Zlatyu Boyadzhiev. The only other attraction in this part of town is the **Kyuntukapu Gate**, sole remainder of the Turkish fortress, which lies just off Alei Osvobozhdenie, 300m west of the train station.

Eating, drinking and entertainment

Most of Ruse's eating venues are found on and around **pl. Svoboda** and the adjoining **ul. Aleksandrovska**, and there's not much point in straying beyond this area unless seeking out one of the more chic restaurants. For **picnic food**, head to the fresh fruit and veg stalls at the market on pl. Ivan Vazov. The best places for **drinking** are the pavement cafés scattered throughout the central area, although the trendy ones go in and out of fashion very quickly.

Restaurants

Ezeroto, ul. Petko Petkov. Popular open-air restaurant in a garden behind the *Hotel Dunav*, featuring live music and dancers most nights.

Happy Grill, pl. Svoboda. Dependable grills and chicken-and-chips-style dishes in a central location.

Hotel Riga, Pridunavska 22. Swishest place to eat in town offering live musical entertainment and top-notch Bulgarian cuisine. A three-course meal with drinks shouldn't cost much more than $15.

Leventa, near the TV tower just off bul. Gotse Delchev. A popular weekend venue in the southern outskirts of town, offering traditional Bulgarian and a few Central European dishes. Bus #17 or #18 from the train station.

Maksim, opposite the Pantheon. A wide range of traditional food, and a pleasant terrace overlooking the park.

Orbita, General Skobelev 21. Good-quality Bulgarian dishes in a nice old mansion, with plenty of outdoor seating.

Ribarska Koliba, just below the *Ribarska Koliba* campsite, 6km west of town on the Sofia road. Lively place serving fresh fish from the River Danube.

Music venues

Ruse's **opera**, on pl. Sveta Troitsa, is one of the finest in Bulgaria. Other types of classical music are showcased in the annual **March Music Weeks**, which attract some of the best ensembles, soloists and conductors in Europe. Tickets for all musical events can be bought from the **concert bureau**, ul. Aleksandrovska 61 (Mon–Fri 10am–1pm & 3–6pm). For regular **live jazz and rock** gigs, head for the *Sound Garden*, a lively bar on Episkop Bosilkov.

Listings

Airlines Balkan, pl. Sveta Troitsa (☎082/224161).

Airport 16km from town on the Razgrad/Varna road. Bus #101 from the train station.

Car rental Eurokontakt, bul. Gotse Delchev (☎082/626241).

Hospital Bratya Obretenovi, on the edge of Park na Mladezhta.

Pharmacies Main central pharmacies are at Aleksandrovska 26, Aleksandrovska 97 and Borisova 113. They take it in turns to be on duty at night.

Post office pl. Svoboda (Mon–Fri 7.30am–6.30pm, Sat 7.30am–6pm)

MOVING ON FROM RUSE

If you're **entering or leaving Bulgaria** via Ruse you'll first cross the three-kilometre-long **Dunav Most** or "Danube Bridge" (known as "Friendship Bridge" back in the days of socialist brotherhood), which spans the river on the outskirts of Ruse and Giurgiu. This ugly yet technically impressive structure was built by both countries (with Soviet assistance) between 1952 and 1954. The border is open 24 hours a day, and for those entering by road a **Tourist Service Office** on the Bulgarian side can book rooms in Bulgaria's more expensive hotels. Be warned that traffic on the bridge can be heavy, and waits can be unpredictably long when travelling in either direction. The Romanians charge all motorists a toll (currently about $5) for using the bridge. Both road and train travellers can buy Romanian visas (currently about $25) at the frontier. Drivers entering Bulgaria are subjected to a $2 "environment tax" levied by Ruse city council.

Travellers **leaving Bulgaria by train** have a choice of services and destinations. There are direct trains to **Sofia** and **Varna**, although those travelling south into the **Balkan Range** will probably have to change at Gorna Oryahovitsa. International connections are good, with three daily trains to **Giurgiu** on the Romanian side of the bridge, and a further three daily express trains that continue on to **Bucharest**. In addition, the *Bâlgariya Express*, which leaves Ruse at 5.30am, goes all the way to **St Petersburg**, calling at **Bucharest**, **Lviv** and **Vilnius** on the way; while the *Sofia Express* (leaving Ruse at 8.20pm) heads for **Moscow** via **Kiev**. There's also a daily train to **Istanbul** which leaves Ruse at 2.45pm and arrives 28 hours later, calling at **Veliko Târnovo** and **Stara Zagora** on the way.

International **tickets** can be bought in advance from the Rila bureau, at ul. Knyazhevska 39 (Mon–Fri 9am–noon & 1–5.30pm) or from the Rila counter at Ruse train station (opening times usually coordinated with train departures). If you need to buy tickets outside regular opening hours you can get them on the train itself, although prices are about fifty percent higher and payment can only be made in Bulgarian currency.

Privately run **Ruse-Sofia buses** pick up and drop off outside the train station.

Telephones at the post office (daily 7am–10pm).
Train ticket agents BDZh/Rila, ul. Knyazhevska 39 (Mon–Fri 9am–noon & 1–5.30pm).

The Rusenski Lom

Ruse is the obvious base from which to venture southwards into the **Rusenski Lom national park**, a steep-sided, canyon-like valley through which the River Rusenski Lom winds its way towards the Danube. The valley forms a picturesque setting for two sets of medieval Bulgarian ruins, the **rock monastery of Ivanovo** and the **citadel of Cherven**, from both of which a variety of tracks lead off the valley floor up into the gorge.

The Rock Monastery of Ivanovo

The most famous of the ruins in the Rusenski Lom valley belong to the so-called **Rock Monastery of Ivanovo** near Ivanovo village, 18km south of Ruse. Among the rocks on both banks of the river, the monastery is one of several hewn into the craggy gorge whose caves provided shelter for Stone Age tribes and medieval hermits alike. Monks first arrived at the gorge in the thirteenth century, a royal donation enabling one Yoakim of Târnovo to establish an extensive monastery complex dedicated to the Archangel Michael, its churches, cells and galleries cut from natural caves in the sheer cliff. At the time the main road linking Târnovo to the Danube ran through the gorge, providing the monastery with a steady stream of pilgrims.

Not all the monastery caves are open to the public, and it's a good idea to ring the office of the regional museum administration in Ruse (☎082/236015, 230123 or 238154) for precise information on what you can see. The fourteenth-century **Tsârkvata or "church" cave**, on the bank of the river nearest Ivanovo, is the most likely to be open (summer daily 9am–5pm; winter Wed–Sun 9am–4pm; $2), although you might have to wait some time for the cave's custodian to turn up. Inside are murals of scantily draped muscular figures depicting Christ's betrayal of Judas, followed by a grisly portrayal of the latter's suicide. *The Beheading of John the Baptist* betrays a similar lack of squeamishness, while the *Ascension* shows Christ enveloped by a star-like form, a typical representation of the Divine Light, as envisaged by the Hesychast monks (see p.216) of the time.

The caves on the far bank of the river are less likely to be open to visitors: the so-called **"Buried Church"** cave features a damaged mural of Tsar Asen presenting a model of the church to the Archangel, with a depiction of St Michael's miracles on the ceiling. Nearby is another, more derelict **rock church** decorated with a scene of the visions of St Peter of Alexandria. Along the same bank, the **Chapel of Gospodev Dol**, or "The Lord's Valley" (with portraits of its patron saints, Vlassius, Spiridon and Modestus), and the accurately named **Demolished Church**, both contain murals, variously faded by time.

To get to the monastery caves, turn left out of Ivanovo train station (served by five daily *pâtnicheski* trains from Ruse), and turn right after about 400m to pick up a road which winds south before descending into the gorge and heading upstream. After about 5km the road peters out and, beyond a small car park, paths zigzag uphill to the Tsârkvata; it's about a 75-minute walk from Ivanovo village. Carry straight on from the car park to pick up trails leading to the other caves and along the valley floor. You can in theory walk all the way to Cherven (see opposite) from here in about four hours, passing the confluence of the Beli and Cherni Lom rivers (take the right fork to follow the Cherni Lom) on the way.

You can rent **private rooms** (②) in Ivanovo's village houses, administered by the *obshtina* (village council offices), the large concrete building near the train station (☎098116/2253 or 2255). You're unlikely to find an English speaker, however, so you may prefer to book rooms here in advance through Dunav Tours in Ruse (see p.171), although you'll pay a few dollars extra in commission. There's nowhere to **eat** in Ivanovo, so it's wise to accept a half-board agreement if it's offered by your hosts.

Cherven

Fifteen kilometres south of Ivanovo, a fork in the gorge provides a niche for the **ruined citadel of Cherven**, clinging to the rock. Formerly known as the "City of churches" or "City of bishops", Cherven was founded in the sixth or seventh century when recurrent barbarian invasions compelled the inhabitants of Ruse to seek a more defensible site inland. The citadel was devastated by the Turks, but Cherven survived as the region's administrative centre for some time, with Ottoman governors and Orthodox bishops coexisting until the seventeenth century, when they both relocated to Ruse. Nowadays Cherven resembles a desolate and brutish version of Machu Picchu (albeit at a considerably lower altitude), with its meagre remains standing high above the valley on a rocky table flanked on three sides by unscalable cliffs. There are good views of the Cherni Lom gorge, with the red-rooved houses of **Cherven village** clinging to the limestone ridges above it. You can still make out the ground plans of Cherven's many churches, although the biggest of the town's structures was the fortified complex of the local *bolyarin*, Cherven's feudal lord. A still-discernible main street runs past his palace and on towards the rude dwellings of his underlings.

It can be difficult **getting to Cherven** without a private car. Sporadic buses to the village of Cherven may be running from Ruse's bus terminal; otherwise you'll have to take a *pâtnicheski* train to the Koshov halt, walk south for 1km, turn left, then walk the remaining 7km into Cherven village. The road winds its way through the village before arriving at a car park at the base of the citadel, 1km beyond. **Private rooms** (②) are available in the village, although it's advisable to book them through Dunav Tours in Ruse (see p.171) before setting out as there's no local accommodation office. There's a rudimentary **café** about 400m short of the citadel car park.

THE BRIDGE AT BYALA

Running roughly parallel to the Rusenski Lom valley to the west, the main E85 road from Ruse to Veliko Târnovo (see pp.201–211) forges south, through **Byala**, an eminently missable market town save for the **bridge over the River Yantra**. Lying 2km to the west of town just beside the E85, the bridge was built in 1867 by the National Revival's most prolific architect Kolyo Ficheto (see p.218), and originally rested on fourteen ornate piers – ten of which were subsequently washed away by floodwaters. The fluid, baroque forms of the remaining four are still intact, as are the reliefs of swans, nymphs and dragons that adorn the main body of the bridge.

Silistra and around

Regular buses continue east from Ruse to the last town on the Bulgarian stretches of the Danube, **SILISTRA**. It's also accessible by train, lying at the end of a branch line which leaves the Ruse–Varna line at Samuil. The site of Roman Durostorum and an important garrison town in Turkish times, Silistra is nowadays a sleepy border settlement lacking the vigour and comparative sophistication of Ruse. Economic activity in the town revolves around the port, main outlet for the grain of the Dobrudzhan Plain to the southeast. For the traveller, the nearby **nature reserve at Srebârna** provides the main reason to visit, but there's little to justify a stay of any length.

The Town

From the **train** and **bus** stations on the town's western outskirts, ul. Simeon Veliki winds its way eastwards through the town centre, arriving at a typically flagstoned and flowerbedded town square. A few steps beyond at G. Rakovski 24 is the **Archeological Museum** (Tues–Sun 8am–noon & 2–6pm), where a rich fund of material on life in Durostorum includes the epigraph-laden tombstones of the soldiers stationed here with the XI Legion. To the north, nineteenth-century residential houses occupy a grid of tree-shaded streets that separate central Silistra from the river. It's among these modest turn-of-the-century mansions, many with Art Nouveau details such as caryatids peering from upper storeys, that you get some impression of the elegance once enjoyed by the Danubian towns.

Occupying a hill 3km south of town (best reached by walking along ul. Izvorite from the centre) are the remains of the Turkish fortress of **Medzhitabiya**, another corner of the defensive quadrilateral built by the Ottomans, and one that was frequently attacked in the course of successive Russo–Turkish wars. The hilltop park also features a TV tower complete with revolving café, and there are expansive views of the Danube below, backed by the yellow and green hues of the Wallachian plain beyond.

The **border crossing** on Silistra's eastern fringes is relatively quiet, and with public transport on the Romanian side being virtually non-existent, is only really suitable for those with a car. The crossing is theoretically open 24 hours a day, although it may close up for a while if traffic is light.

Practicalities

Silistra's **accommodation** prospects are modest: the only place to stay in the centre of town is the *Zlatna Dobrudzha* hotel, on the corner of Simeon Veliki and Otets Paisii, (③), with plain but comfortable ensuite rooms. Offering a similar deal but with better views is the recently renovated *Orbita* (bookable through *Orbita* in Sofia ☎02/800102; ③), occupying a fine hillside site just below the Medzhitabiya fortress. It's a struggle to walk up there if you're heavily laden, but undoubtedly worth it.

The best of the **restaurants** is the *Starata Kâshta*, at Lyuben Karavelov 8, in residential streets between the archeological museum and the river. Housed in a National-Revival-style building, it has plenty of outdoor seating and a traditional Bulgarian menu. The restaurant of the *Zlatna Dobrudzha* hotel has reliable food and a large outdoor area at the back. The streets around the hotel have several **pavement cafés**, popular on summer evenings.

Lake Srebârna

Nineteenth-century Hungarian traveller Felix Kanitz called **Lake Srebârna**, 17km west of Silistra near the Danube shore, "the Eldorado of wading birds". An expanse of reedy marshland spreads around the lake itself, providing ninety species of wildfowl (including seventy different types of heron) with a secure habitat. The lake is also frequented by around eighty migratory species, and there's a fair likelihood of being able to see **egrets** in the summer and **pelicans** in the spring and early summer. In recent decades growing silt deposits have cut the lake off from the cleansing waters of the River Danube, causing Srebârna to stagnate. There's has been a consequent decline in the numbers of fish upon which the birds can feed, and local biologists reckon that the reserve's best days could be over – unless a lot of money is spent on new irrigation channels.

Just off the main Silistra–Ruse road, the reserve is approached from the villages of Srebârna to the west, or Popina to the northwest. Both are served by **bus #222** which leaves from the main road outside Silistra bus station every two hours or so between 7am and 9pm (ask in the bus station about exact timings). You could also catch one of the frequent Silistra–Ruse buses, and ask to be set down at the Srebârna stop on the main road – a walkable 2km away from Srebârna village itself. From here, it's really a question of wandering around the footpaths that surround the reserve, allowing yourself plenty of time to explore the enticingly reedy, wetland environment.

Dobrich and the Dobrudzha

Beyond Silistra the Danube swings north into Romania, leaving travellers with the choice of heading south across the Ludogorie hills towards Shumen (see p.226), or continuing east towards the Black Sea coast. The latter route takes you through the **Dobrudzha**, Bulgaria's main grain-producing region. Despite its agricultural wealth the Dobrudzhan Plain remains dully flat and heat-hazed, with few centres of much size or historical interest. The regional capital **Dobrich**, 50km short of the coast, is the only worthwhile stopoff, although with numerous onward bus connections to Albena (p.344) and Varna (p.326), it hardly merits a stay.

Dobrich (Tolbuhin)

Principal town of the eastern Dobrudzha, **DOBRICH** is an obvious place to break your journey if travelling between the Danube and the coast, or if heading towards the Romanian border at Kardam, 35km to the north. Between 1949 and 1990 it was named after the Soviet marshal who "liberated" the area in 1944, **Tolbuhin** (and it still appears as such on most postwar road signs and maps), but the town started life as **Hadzhioglu Bazardzhik**, supposedly named after itinerant merchant Hadzhi Oglu Bakal, who built the first house here in the sixteenth century. Circassians and Tatars formed the majority of the pre-Liberation population, and although many families fled south to avoid advancing Russian armies in 1877, the area retains a strong Muslim element. In the nineteenth century Dobrich was famous for its autumn horse fair, and horse-rearing remains an important part of the local economy. Several pockets of old Dobrich have been

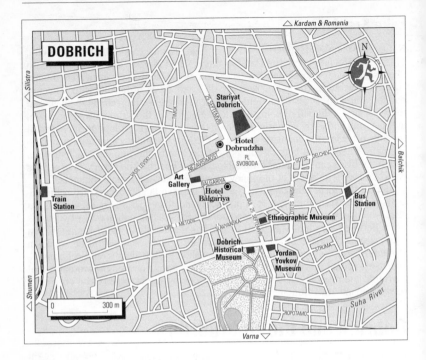

artfully preserved, and the town attracts a steady trickle of day-trippers from the package resorts of the nearby Black Sea coast.

The Town

Travelling through Dobrich in the 1870s, Felix Kanitz said that he knew of no other town in Bulgaria whose "Asiatic character . . . was so typical and unadulterated in appearance". Nowadays central Dobrich is resolutely modern, with stark concrete piles and plazas, although something of the nineteenth-century artisans' quarter has been rather antiseptically re-created in the **Stariyat Dobrich** (Old Dobrich) quarter just off the central pl. Svoboda. You can watch demonstrations of tradition-al crafts in some twenty workshops, including pottery, blacksmithing, woodcarving, bookbinding and jewellery. A hundred metres west of pl. Svoboda on bul. Bâlgariya is the **Regional Art Gallery** (daily 9am–12.30pm & 2–6.30pm), one of provincial Bulgaria's best collections. It's a good place to catch up on the leading quartet of twentieth-century Bulgarian painters – Vladimir Dimitrov-Maistor, Vasil Stoilov, Zlatyu Boyadzhiev and Dechko Uzunov – who tried to combine modernist styles of painting with indigenous Bulgarian traditions. Dimitrov-Maistor's portraits of peas-ant girls and Uzunov's Dobrudzha landscapes are both well represented; look out for the latter's *Dobrich in Springtime*, where ghostly peasant figures seem to rise out of the rich Dobrudzhan earth.

Bulevard 25 Septemvri heads south from pl. Svoboda towards an excellent **Ethnographic Museum** (daily 9am–noon & 2–6pm), where folk costumes, agricultural implements and weaving machines cram the rooms of a restored nineteenth-century merchant's house. The upstairs dining room and *chardak* – a south-facing verandah that the family used as a sitting room during the summer months – provide some idea of the elegant lifestyles enjoyed by those who grew rich on the Dobrudzhan wool trade a century ago.

Two more museums lie further south at the junction of 25 Septemvri and Otets Paisii. The **Yordan Yovkov Museum** (Mon–Fri 9am–noon & 2–5.30pm), a concrete-and-glass pavilion dominating the crossroads, is easiest to spot. Celebrating the Zheravna-born novelist and poet who spent many years in the Dobrudzha as

THE DOBRUDZHA IN HISTORY

"A wintry land deficient in cultivated grains and fruit", inhabited by a people "who are barbarous and lead a bestial existence" was how the third-century BC Thracian chieftain Dromichaetes described the **Dobrudzha** to his Macedonian captive Lysimachus, berating him for bothering to invade such a barren region in the first place.

Windswept in winter and parched in summer, the Dobrudzha has always had a reputation for harshness and inhospitability. Geographically speaking, it stretches from the mouth of the Danube in the north to the Gulf of Varna in the south, marking the southwestern extremity of the great **Eurasian steppelands** that once swept uninterruptedly round the north coast of the Black Sea and eastwards towards Central Asia and Mongolia. Successive generations of horseriding invaders have used the steppe as a corridor leading to the riches of southeastern Europe, and faced by such recurring dangers, Western civilization's hold on the region was always tenuous. Successive Macedonian, Roman, Byzantine and Bulgarian empires always found the Dobrudzha to be the most difficult part of the northern frontier to defend, and by the thirteenth century, when **Tatar bands** were beginning to roam the region with impunity, the area was well on the way to becoming a lawless desert.

Arab chronicler Ibn Battuta, crossing the Dobrudzha in the fourteenth century, was struck by its desolate appearance, describing it as "eighteen days of uninhabited wasteland, for eight days of which there is no water". By the time the Ottoman Sultan Mehmet I conquered the Dobrudzha in 1416, the region was so depopulated that he had to colonize it with **Turkish settlers** in order to provide the newly won province with inhabitants capable of defending it – with the result that the local ethnic mix still includes a fair proportion of Turks. These are intermingled with the Turkish-speaking **Dobrudzha Tatars**, descendants of Crimean Tatars who were expelled from the Russian Empire in the wake of the Crimean War.

By the beginning of the twentieth century, migrant Bulgarian peasants began to outnumber the other national groups in the area, but the ethnic balance of the region was altered yet again during the inter-war period, when the Dobrudzha became part of Romania. Eager to boost the Latin element among the population, the government encouraged the immigration of Romanian-speaking **Vlachs** (see p.168) from Macedonia. After regaining the territory in 1941, the Bulgarian authorities imported Slav colonists to redress the ethnic balance, but the existence of so many non-Bulgarian minorities in an area so crucial to the economy was a source of concern to the country's postwar Communist bosses. Special attention was paid to the Dobrudzha during the 1980s, when the controversial *Vâzroditelniyat protses* or Regeneration Process tried to force local Muslims to speak only the Bulgarian language in public and to adopt Bulgarian names. Nowadays you'll find inter-ethnic relations more relaxed, with the babble of Bulgarian and Turkic tongues heard on the streets of Dobrich reflecting the meeting of cultures from the Dobrudzha's turbulent past.

a schoolteacher, the museum's collection of sepia family portraits and Bulgarian language captions fails to communicate much about the man's work – renowned for conjuring up the lost world of nineteenth-century Bulgarian village life. Equally frustrating is the **Dobrich Historical Museum** in the park opposite (usually open Mon–Fri 9am–5pm; ring the bell and hope that there's a curator around), where a similar words-and-pictures display attempts to shed light on Dobrudzhan history. The region passed from Bulgarian to Romanian rule on numerous occasions between 1913 and 1945, and the endless black-and-white photographs showing armies of different hues marching in and out of Dobrich give some idea of the area's confused past. Beyond the museum several kilometres of partly wooded parkland spread south, providing the city with a verdant recreation area.

Practicalities

Dobrich's **train and bus** stations are on the western and eastern edges respectively of the downtown area – both involve a pretty straightforward ten-minute walk into the centre. Two high-rise **hotels** on the central pl. Svoboda, the two-star _Dobrudzha_ (☎058/24321; ④) and the four-star _Bâlgariya_ (☎058/25444; ⑤), complete with swimming pool and sauna, provide the main accommodation choices. The **restaurants** in the two hotels also represent your best bet for eating. Dobrich's pedestrianized centre is overrun with pavement **cafés** during the summer, when a certain joie-de-vivre fills the otherwise sterile flagstoned centre.

THE CENTRAL BALKAN RANGE

For more than a thousand years, the **Balkan Range** (in Bulgarian, the **Stara planina** or "Old Mountains") has been the cradle of the Bulgarian nation and the cockpit of its destiny. Sloping gently towards the Danubian Plain, the Balkan's fertile valleys supported the medieval capitals of Pliska and Preslav (mere ruins today) and Veliko Târnovo (still a thriving city), while steep ranges with defensible passes shielded them to the south. Much was destroyed during the Ottoman conquest, but the thread of culture was preserved by monasteries and the crafts centres that re-established themselves under the Turkish yoke.

The range's gentler slopes lie just **east of Sofia**, where small towns like **Etropole** and **Teteven** provide a measure of rural tranquillity lacking in the more touristed Balkan centres further east. First of these is **Lovech**, a well-preserved nineteenth-century town which lies within striking distance of **Troyan Monastery**, and, to the north, at the foot of the mountains, **Pleven**, site of a crucial battle in the Russo-Turkish War.

However, the best touring base in the central part of the range is **Veliko Târnovo**. A beautiful city in its own right, with a medieval citadel and several historic churches, Târnovo has good transport links with such villages, rich in vernacular architecture, as **Arbanasi**, **Elena**, **Tryavna** and **Etâra**. It also makes a good base for a whole cluster of monasteries: **Preobrazhenski**, **Dryanovo** and **Kilifarevo** are the big three, but numerous smaller foundations await further exploration.

The main urban centre in the east is **Shumen**, site of a fine medieval fortress and close to Bulgaria's first two capitals at **Pliska** and **Preslav**, and the enigmatic rock sculpture of the **Madara Horseman**. From here routes towards the

---

THE STARA PLANINA TOURIST ASSOCIATION

The **Stara Planina Tourist Association** co-ordinates the work of five tourist information offices in towns bordering on the central Balkan Range. The tourist offices
share information, and can book accommodation in any of the areas covered by the
association, making it possible to structure your itinerary in advance around the
towns where the offices are found. It's also worth noting that they rent out **mountain bikes** (stocks permitting) for $5 per day, and you're allowed to return the bikes
to any office within the scheme. You'll find details on addresses and opening times
of the tourist offices – in **Teteven**, **Troyan**, **Apriltsi**, **Tryavna** and **Gabrovo** – in the
relevant sections of the guide.

If you want information and advice on the region before you travel, contact the
Stara Planina Tourist Association, pl. Vâzrazhdane 2, 5300 Gabrovo (☎066/28483,
fax 36190).

Danube and the Dobrudzha pass through the Ludogorie hills, where the
Thracian tomb and **Dervish Tekke at Sveshtari** provide the chief attractions.

Towns in the western part of the central Balkan Range can be easily reached
by bus from Sofia. The **Sofia–Varna rail line**, skirting the mountains to the
north, is the fastest way of accessing places further afield. It passes through
Pleven, from whence buses depart to Lovech and Troyan; Gornya Orahovitsa,
with regular train and bus connections to Veliko Târnovo, Tryavna and Gabrovo;
and Shumen, before forging onwards to the coast. Once established in any of the
above places, you can explore neighbouring attractions using **local buses**.

East of Sofia

Travelling east by train, you completely bypass the foothills of the central Balkan
Range northeast of Sofia. However, the main Sofia–Veliko Târnovo–Varna highway (a gorge-defying dual carriageway for the first 60km or so) heads straight
across the westernmost shoulder of the range, passing a handful of worthwhile
villages and monasteries along the way. The market town of **Teteven** and nearby
village of **Ribaritsa** are the most attractive of the region's settlements if you need
a base from which to explore. Otherwise, most of the area's worthwhile sights are
accessible by bus from Sofia, or Lovech to the east.

Botevgrad, Pravets and Etropole

An hour's drive beyond Sofia the highway bypasses **BOTEVGRAD**, hardly worth
a detour unless you're aiming for the E79 to Vratsa, Montana and Vidin, which
heads north from here. Once a thriving market town, profiting from its position
at the northern end of the (no longer used) Baba Konak Pass, Botevgrad is nowadays a sterile modern place whose main claim to fame is the *Chavdar* factory –
makers of the buses that clatter their way across Bulgaria.

About 10km beyond the turn-off to Botevgrad, another minor road forks east to
PRAVETS, a previously unremarkable village whose status as the birthplace of
former dictator **Todor Zhivkov** made it into one of the most prosperous communities in Bulgaria. It's in places like Pravets that nostalgia for the certainties of the

TODOR ZHIVKOV

Born into a peasant family in 1911, **Todor Zhivkov** was a minor Communist functionary before emerging as Mayor of Sofia after World War II. The reasons for his rise are still the subject of much conjecture: his record of wartime service with the Chavdar partisan brigade is now known to be a fiction put about by servile biographers, and none of Bulgaria's party bosses regarded the affable and inoffensive Zhivkov as a serious political threat until it was too late. In 1954, within three years of joining the Politburo, he secured the post of First Secretary or Party Leader with the approval of Moscow, and elbowed aside the old Stalinist, Anton Yugov, to claim the premiership in 1962. He survived a coup in 1965 – a murky affair blamed on "ultra-leftists" at the time, but subsequently attributed to nationalist army officers.

Zhivkov was never a great ideologist: most of his political innovations were designed to wrongfoot opponents rather than introduce real social change. In foreign policy he slavishly followed the Soviet line, enthusiastically sending troops to help crush the Prague Spring in 1968. He tried to counterbalance this closeness to the USSR by pumping up Bulgarian nationalism at home, presenting Communist Bulgaria as the natural culmination of the national struggles of the past. Consistent with this policy were the extravagant celebrations marking 1300 years of the Bulgarian state in 1981, and persecution of Bulgaria's ethnic Turkish population in the years that ensued. It's for this abuse of Turkish human rights that the Zhivkov years will be long remembered in Turkey and the West. However Zhivkov also presided over a period of full employment and rising living standards – until the Bulgarian economy started going wrong in the early 1980s – and he's still spoken of with some affection by elderly Bulgarians bewildered by the economic changes of the 1990s.

When "reform Communists" ditched Zhivkov in November 1989, it suited them to make the erstwhile dictator the scapegoat for all that was wrong in Bulgarian society. He was accordingly arrested on a charge of "embezzling state funds" and sentenced to seven years' imprisonment – although he continued to lead a comfortable, if somewhat restricted, existence under house arrest in Sofia. He remained in combative spirits, giving interviews to anyone who would listen and accusing Mikhail Gorbachev of being the one who orchestrated his downfall. According to Zhivkov, a skilful self-publicist to the end, his own form of *perestroika* was much more logical and consistent than the "anarchy" brought forth by the former Soviet leader.

When Zhivkov died on August 5, 1998, fears that his funeral would provoke a wave of pro-Communist sentiment proved unfounded. The Bulgarian Socialist (ie: former Communist) Party did succeed in hijacking the event, turning it into an anti-government political meeting – rather ironic when one considers that they'd expelled Zhivkov from their ranks barely nine years before – but only 10,000 elderly mourners were there to listen.

Communist era is at its strongest. When Zhivkov made a much-publicized visit to his home town in May 1995 (despite being ostensibly under house arrest in Sofia at the time), he was given an emotional welcome by thousands of locals, many of whom were in tears. Although his modest childhood home is no longer open to the public, other aspects of the Zhivkov legacy will prove more lasting: most importantly, the **holiday complex and artificial lake** on the town's western outskirts. Complete with tennis courts, restaurants, boating, waterskiing facilities and fishing opportunities, this is a popular stopoff for travellers – fringed by the mountains of the Etropolska planina to the south, it's quite an idyllic spot. There's a **motel** (☎07133/2754; ③) and **campsite** by the lake, as well as the *Shatra restaurant*, a curious pagoda-like construction jutting out into the water, which, at the last visit, had a pair of storks nesting on the roof.

Etropole

Thirteen kilometres southeast of Pravets is **ETROPOLE**, a quiet agricultural town surrounded by subalpine pastures. The centre, a couple of blocks west of the bus station, harbours the usual eighteenth-century **clock tower** and a small **museum**, the latter containing memorabilia of Etropole's past as a wealthy mining town that attracted Saxon immigrants in the Middle Ages. The main draw, however, is the **monastery of Sveta Troitsa** 4km to the east above the village of **Ribaritsa**. Founded in 1158, the monastery was a well-known literary centre in the sixteenth and seventeenth centuries, when monks copied and distributed Bulgarian manuscripts. Nowadays it's a little-visited foundation populated by four nuns, with a grassy courtyard surrounding the four hexagonal towers of the monastery church.

Getting to the monastery is fairly easy. About five daily buses run from Etropole to Ribaritsa, but these are usually early in the morning or late in the afternoon. Alternatively, it's an hour's **walk**: turn right out of Etropole bus station into ul. Partizanska, walk to the end of the street where the Ribaritsa road forks right, then after 50m bear right onto a partly asphalted track which takes you over the hills to Ribaritsa itself – where a signposted lane climbs to the monastery. Following the lane beyond the monastery takes you uphill to an area of rolling pastures traversed by local sheperds – ideal for short hikes.

The fresh mountain air and numerous walking possibilities make Etropole well worth a **stay**. There's a three-star hotel, the *Etropole*, just above the bus station (☎0712/3616; ③), and a frugal but friendly establishment, the *Hotel Etropol*, on the main town square (☎0712/2018; ②).

Teteven and around

Back on the main highway, the next place of any importance is **YABLANITSA**, lynchpin of the local bus network and site of a turn-off for the Vit Valley, where the market town of Teteven and village of Ribaritsa provide access to some verdant pastures and craggy hills. Ten kilometres up the valley the road hits **GLOZHENE**, a drab industrialized village known chiefly for the nearby **monastery**, perched high above and practically invisible from the valley. It's a small monastery, housing a tiny nineteenth-century church enclosed by fortress-like living quarters with stone ground-floor walls and overhanging timber upper storeys. Track-suited monks will show you round a museum containing the church silver, and you can enjoy views of the surrounding countryside from the monastery's cliff-top eyrie. Most vehicles will balk at the gravelled roadway that winds up to the monastery from the village, and will opt for the longer, roundabout route, which takes you back along the Yablanitsa road for 8km before turning southwards to the village of Malâk Izvor, then eastwards on a gravel road to the monastery itself – a gorgeous rural ride by car or bike (available for rent from the tourist office in Teteven; see overleaf). If you fancy walking, a shorter route (for which you should allow 50 minutes) takes you south from Glozhene's central bus stop along the Teteven road, across a footbridge spanning the Vit, through the *Spartak* sports field, up a cobbled hillside path, then forking right up a wooded ravine.

Teteven

Surrounded by imposing mountains further up the valley, **TETEVEN** once inspired writer Ivan Vazov to declare that had he not come here, "I should regard myself as a stranger to my native land . . . Nowhere have I found a place so enchanting as this". An endorsement a shade too fulsome for modern Teteven, but the town is certainly appealing in a laid-back way. Teteven comes to life on Saturday mornings, when the town **market** attracts a deluge of visitors from surrounding villages – most notably the local Pomaks, easily recognizable by their *shalvari*, the brightly coloured trousers worn by the women.

Despite the undoubted prettiness of the pastel-coloured houses ranged above the **main square** (a couple of blocks south of the bus station), there's little in the way of specific sights, save for a small town **museum**, on the square itself (summer daily 9am–noon & 2–5pm; winter Mon–Fri 9am–noon & 2–5pm), housing a colourful display of local costumes and crafts, notably the town's characteristic *chergi* – hand-woven carpets or runners. Rich in yellows, blacks and reds, the typical Teteven *cherga* features a zigzag pattern (*krivolitsa*) made up of small triangles or rhomboids. Several women still weave in Teteven, using local wool dyed with the extracts of indigenous plants, and the tourist office (see below) can arrange visits. Sadly, there's nowhere to buy *chergi* in town, although individual weavers are always happy to take orders if you're going to be staying in Bulgaria for some time.

The Teteven **tourist office**, just south of the square (Mon–Fri 9am–1pm & 2–6pm; ☎0678/4217), offers local advice, sells maps, rents mountain bikes for $5 an hour, and can book accommodation in both Teteven and Ribaritsa further up the valley. They can also arrange hiking guides if you give them a couple of days' notice, and will provide information on the current status of **Sâeva Dupka**, a cave system 25km to the north of Teteven, which has been closed to the public for some years due to the theft of its lighting system. With the *Hotel Teteven* currently under reconstruction, the tourist office's **private rooms** (①) are the only accommodation in town. There are **cafés** aplenty around the main square, and a good **restaurant**, *Klasik*, 100m south along ul. Ivan Vazov.

Ribaritsa

Twelve kilometres beyond Teteven at the end of the valley lies **RIBARITSA**, a popular mountain village straddling the babbling river Vit – a popular location for bathing in summer. It is served by four daily buses from Teteven, and there's ample accommodation, mostly in the form of **private rooms** (②) booked through the tourist office in Teteven, although there are also several rest homes now open to all-comers. The centrally located *Voennen Pochiven Dom* ("Army Rest Home"; ☎0678/3540; ④) is one of the best **hotels** in the area, with a swimming pool, disco, bar and comfortable rooms. There's also a **campsite** with bungalows (②) at the western end of the village.

Walks from Ribaritsa head either southwest up the Kostina Valley (also cycleable if you rent a bike in Teteven), where, after 4km, you'll see a monument to **Georgi Benkovski**, the Koprivshtitsa-born revolutionary killed here in 1876; or south up the Zavodka Valley towards **Mt Vezhen** which, at 2198m above sea level, is the highest point in the Tetevenska planina. There's a hiker's **chalet**, *Hizha Vezhen* (also accessible by asphalt road) some two hours short of the summit. If you are hiking in the area, the 1:65 000 *Troyan Balkan* **map** (on sale at the Teteven tourist office) will prove an invaluable aid.

East of Ribaritsa, the main road climbs out of the Vit valley and crosses the hills towards Troyan (see p.196), some 40km away. Its another scenic route by car or bike (bikes rented at Teteven can be returned at the tourist office in Troyan), taking in heath-covered moorland and deep forest, although no buses pass this way.

The road to Pleven

Karstic limestone formations lurk underground throughout the region, and the river running beneath the **junction of the Pleven and Veliko Târnovo highways** emerges as the **Glavna Panega** spring near Zlatna Panega on the Pleven road (bear right just before the village), where it forms two lakes whose waters remain at an even temperature (10–12.5°C) whatever the season. The Roman legend of the fair but afflicted Panega, who was cured by bathing here, seems to have been the model for apocryphal stories relating to other spas – the "Virgin's Pass" near Kostenets, for example.

The last stage of the route to Pleven is pretty straightforward, and after passing through Cherven Bryag (the junction for trains to Oryahovo on the Danube), the E83 highway follows the same course as the Sofia–Pleven railway. Although trains don't stop there, motorists can visit **Lavrov Park** near the village of Gorni Dubnik en route. On October 24, 1877, during the War of Liberation, the Russians flung themselves upon the Turkish redoubt that stood here guarding the road to Plevna, inspired by the suicidal heroism of General Lavrov, their commander. There's now a small museum near the park entrance exhibiting the kind of plans beloved of wargamers, and a statue of a Bulgarian and a Soviet soldier entitled "Eternal Friendship". On the opposite side of the road, an ossuary contains the bones of Lavrov and his men.

Pleven

Sited where the foothills of the Balkan Range descend to meet the Danubian plain, the industrial city of **PLEVEN** is an important regional centre with an unusually high quotient of worthwhile urban sights. Many of these are monuments or museums honouring the **siege of Plevna** – probably the most decisive episode of the War of Liberation. When the Russians crossed the Danube at Svishtov in 1877, their flank was threatened by the Turkish forces entrenched at Plevna (as the town was then known), which resisted three assaults costing the Russians thousands of casualties. In response to Grand Duke Nicholas' pleas, Romanian reinforcements came with King Carol I, who personally led his troops into battle (the last European sovereign to do so) crying "This is the music that pleases me!" Russia's top generals, Skobelev and Totleben, then arrived to organize a professional siege, weakening the defenders by starvation and blasting each redoubt with artillery before the attackers made repeated bayonet charges, finally compelling the Turks to surrender on December 10. More than 40,000 Russians and Romanians and uncounted numbers of Turks and civilians died, but as a consequence of Plevna's fall northern Bulgaria was swiftly liberated. The defeat had a shattering effect on Ottoman morale, but garnered a great deal of public sympathy in the West, allowing the British and Austrian governments to adopt a much more openly anti-Russian line in the peace negotiations that followed. Pleven's other claim to fame is its extreme **climate**; Bulgaria's hottest

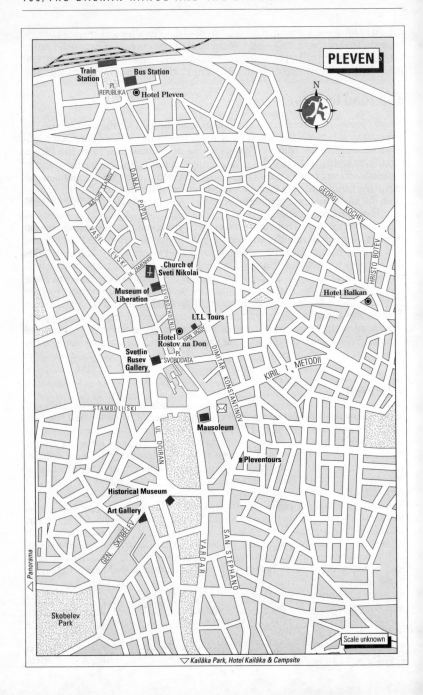

PLEVEN

Train Station

Bus Station

PL REPUBLIKA

Hotel Pleven

N

GEORGI KOCHEV

MARIA LUIZA

DANAIL POPOV

VASIL LEVSKI

UL ZAMENHOF

HRISTO BOTEV

Church of Sveti Nikolai

Museum of Liberation

SVOBODZENIE

I.T.L. Tours

IVAN VAZOV

Hotel Balkan

Hotel Rostov na Don

Svetlin Rusev Gallery

PL SVOBODATA

DIMITAR KONSTANTINOV

KIRIL I METODII

STAMBOLIISKI

Mausoleum

UL DOIRAN

Pleventours

Historical Museum

Art Gallery

GEN. SKOBELEV

VARDAR

SAN STEPHANO

Panorama

Skobelev Park

Scale unknown

▽ *Kailâka Park, Hotel Kailâka & Campsite*

summer temperatures are usually recorded here, and it's correspondingly cold in winter.

Easily reached from Sofia, Varna or Ruse by train, Pleven stands at the centre of an extensive local **bus network** that serves the smaller towns along the Danube to the north as well as Lovech and Troyan to the south.

Arrival and accommodation

Pleven's **bus** and **train** stations are at the northern end of town; to get to the centre, follow ul. Danail Popov (or take any bus) south until you hit ul. Zamenhof. From here, ul. Vasil Levski leads a short way to the main square, **pl. Svobodata**.

Most useful of the local **travel agencies** is ITL Tours, just off the square at Ivan Vazov 9 (Mon–Fri 8.30am–6.30pm; ☎ and fax 064/40183 or 36574), which organizes sightseeing trips of the city, runs excursions to places like Etåra (see p.225) and Veliko Târnovo (see p.201), and can book you into downtown **private rooms** for $10 per person. Pleventours, south of pl. Svobodata at San Stefano 3 (☎064/26329 or 24119), has a smaller supply of rooms for around the same price. Of the city's three high-rise **hotels**, the uninspiring *Pleven*, near the train and bus stations at pl. Republika 2 (☎064/30181; ④), and the gloomy *Rostov na Don*, just off pl. Svobodata at Slava Aleksiev 2 (☎064/23892; ④), are both acceptable but overpriced for their standard ensuite rooms with spartan shower unit. The much plusher *Balkan*, ul. Beshev 68 (☎064/22215; ⑤, but cheaper if booked in advance through ITL Tours), is an easily walkable 2km east of the centre, and has neat and comfortable rooms with bath, telephone and, in some cases, a TV. Also worth considering is the dowdy but pleasantly situated two-star *Kailâka* in the park of the same name (☎064/23515; ④), 5km out of the centre and served by bus from opposite the train station (bus route numbers are in the process of being reorganized, so ask before setting off). Further on into Kailâka park, about 7km south of town, is the *Kailâka* **campsite** (May–Sept).

If you're just passing through Pleven, there's a **left-luggage office** (*garderob*) in the train station (daily 6am–10pm with unpredictable lunch breaks).

The Town

South of the stations, ul. Zamenhof is a paved plaza containing the sunken **Church of Sveti Nikolai**. A nineteenth-century portrait of the saint himself presides over the doorway of this simple structure, believed to date from the 1300s. Inside is a collection of icons, including works by the Samokov masters Stanislav Dospevski and Zahari Zograf, although many of the most attractive are by anonymous artists from villages in the Pleven region. An eighteenth-century *Council of All the Saints* from the village of Koinare is particularly outstanding, with a cluster of golden haloes hovering above the heads of the holy ones. Beyond the church lies ul. Vasil Levski, Pleven's main downtown street. Follow this south and you'll pass the **Museum of Liberation** in the park between Vasil Levski and bul. Osvobozhdenie (Tues–Sat 9am–noon & 1–6pm), occupying the house where the Turkish commander, Osman Pasha, formally surrendered to Tsar Aleksandâr II. Here you'll see weaponry, mementos and plans lovingly detailing each phase of the battle.

A little further on is pl. Svobodata, the city's **main square**, a fountain-splashed expanse of flagstones, flowers and shrubs dominated by a Russo-Byzantine-style

mausoleum (daily 8am–noon & 2–6pm), built to commemorate the Russian soldiers who died at Pleven, although the number of Romanian names on the lists of the fallen makes it clear who saw the worst of the fighting. Garishly modernist grey-and-brown frescos swirl around inside, while marble necropolitan furniture adorns the crypt. On the opposite side of the square are the **old public baths**, a curious pseudo-Byzantine structure whose red- and-white striped facade could be easily mistaken for that of a church. It's now home to the **Svetlin Rusev gallery** (Tues–Sat: summer 11am–7pm; winter 10am–6pm), honouring the Pleven-born painter and former Politburo member. His florid figurative works look strangely conservative when compared to the postwar art of the West, and are easily outshone by the other pieces in the collection – notably a striking self-portrait by Vladimir Dimitrov-Maistor.

The Historical Museum

Follow paths through the park at the southern end of the square and you reach the **Historical Museum** or *Istoricheski muzei* (Wed–Sun 9am–noon & 1–5pm), housed in spacious former barracks at the foot of ul. Doiran. Natural history exhibits occupy the east wing, while the west wing has an enormous history collection, one of the nation's best, beginning with the pick of northern Bulgaria's archeological remains. A blackened square of earth turns out to be a **Neolithic dwelling** from the fourth millennium BC, excavated near the village of Telish to the west and transferred here in the condition in which it was found. It's surrounded by contemporaneous pottery, richly decorated with geometric shapes and animated squiggles.

BULGARIAN RAINMAKING RITUALS

The ethnographic section of Pleven's historical museum contains documentary evidence of many archaic folk practices once common throughout Bulgaria, and now on the verge of disappearing for good. Appropriately enough for a region famous for its long dry summers, pride of place goes to the **rainmaking rituals** which villagers hoped would bring an end to drought. Foremost among these was the parading of the **peperuda**, when a young girl (preferably an orphan, and always a virgin) was stripped bare by female helpers, clad in leaves and branches, and then taken round to every household in the village. The helpers would sing songs while the householder emptied a bucket of water over the *peperuda*, who responded by flapping her arms in imitation of a bird. The party then received a present of flour and beans from the householder before moving on.

Later the same day the villagers would emerge with a funeral bier bearing a **german** – a male doll endowed with an overlarge phallus (often represented by a red pepper). The *german* was then either buried near a well or thrown in the river. The doll was usually made of clay, although in the Pleven region it had to be fashioned from a broomstick stolen from the house of a pregnant woman. In some areas, the *german* could only be handled by chaste maidens, and had to spend the night prior to the ritual in the house of the girl chosen to play the *peperuda*.

The symbolic burial of the *german* seems to echo the fertility rites common to Indo-European peoples in ancient times, when, according to one branch of anthropological opinion, human sacrifices were made to mother earth in order to ensure good harvests.

More pottery comes from the **Roman town of Oescus**, near modern Gigen on the Danube, an important administrative centre and home to the Fifth Macedonian Legion. On show are numerous gravestones and a floor mosaic with abstract patterns swirling around a (small but discernable) scene from Menander's comedy *The Achaeans*. The medieval period is represented by finds from another Danube town, Nikopol, whose fortress had a reputation for invincibility under both Bulgarians and Ottomans.

In the **ethnographic section** you'll see the hooded cloaks worn by shepherds of the Danubian Plain, and a couple of blunt-ended boats carved from tree trunks used by fishermen on the river until very recently. Of particular interest are the reconstructions of local village houses, thatched-roofed dwellings built half above ground, half under, and surrounded by a stockade of twigs. Upstairs are seemingly endless halls filled with weapons and uniforms from the days of the siege, including the samovars presented by Russian officers to the Bulgarian families with whom they were billeted.

Skobelev park

Just to the southwest of the barracks, a lengthy processional stairway ascends towards **Skobelev park**, passing the city **art gallery** (Tues–Sat 9am–5pm) on the way. Inside are several more examples of Svetlin Rusev's work, and the inevitable idealized-peasant-girl canvas courtesy of Dimitrov-Maistor. At the top of the stairway is yet another Bulgarian-Soviet Friendship monument, followed by the gates of the park itself. The park is laid out on a hill formerly occupied by the **Isa Aga Redoubt**, the object of fierce fighting in 1877 and now restored and crowned with an obelisk commemorating the 405 troops who died capturing it. Numerous cannons are secreted within the greenery hereabouts, but the main focus of visitors' attention is the **Panorama** (Tues–Sat 9am–noon & 1.30–5.30pm; $2, English-language guide $3 extra), an enormous concrete funnel of a building housing a huge depiction of the early days of the siege, comprising three-dimensional figures set against a circular backdrop. Downstairs, a smaller diorama shows the Turkish commander Osman Pasha retreating over a bridge in the wake of the victorious Russian assault.

Kailâka park

Leaving central Pleven by either of the main southbound boulevards, San Stefano or Vardar, it's 2km to **Kailâka park**, laid out around the lush and rocky Tuhenitsa defile, and connected by regular buses to the town centre. Site of a Thracian settlement that the Romans took over and named Storgosia, it's here that the citizens of Pleven unwind at weekends, taking advantage of the park's swimming baths, watersports facilities, and open-air theatre. There's also the *Peshtera* restaurant in a cave at the foot of a limestone cliff – and below the baths a monument to the Jews who perished here in 1944 when the camp in which they were imprisoned burned down. (Although anti-Semitism has never been prevalent in Bulgaria, the government jailed the Salonikan Jews during the latter stages of the war to appease its Nazi allies.) Three kilometres upriver, a bronze statue of General Totleben (Russian hero of the 1877 seige) surmounts the **Totleben rampart** which separates two reservoirs: the lower reservoir is a popular bathing venue in summer. Trolleybuses #3 and #7 connect central Pleven with the northern entrance to the park. Another bus (currently #5, but be aware of potential changes) continues onwards to the reservoirs.

Eating and drinking

Pleven's **eating and drinking** venues are mostly found around pl. Svobodata and ul. Vasil Levski. The best of the **restaurants** are to be found in a small complex of National Revival-era houses just off the northern end of Vasil Levski near the junction with Naicho Tsanov; *Zlatna Guska* is a traditional-style *mehana* serving the usual range of Bulgarian grills, while *Bâlgarski koren,* just round the corner, is a step up in quality, and has a lovely courtyard built around a brace of fountains. *Plevensko Pivo*, between the centre and the train station on Danail Popov, has a more rough-and-ready culinary style but features live folk-pop music, as does the *Karadzheikata*, a large restaurant in the Kailâka park with ample outdoor seating.

Ulista Vasil Levski is the place to hang out in summertime, with a string of pavement cafés suitable for both daytime and night-time **drinking**. For late-night entertainment, it's worth checking out the open-air *Nelson* **disco**, about 2km into Kailâka park.

South of Pleven: Lovech and Troyan

Lying just off the main road and train routes, the towns of **Lovech** and **Troyan** are often missed out by those travelling east to west. However, they do sit on one of the important trans-Balkan routes linking Pleven, on the margins of the Danubian Plain, with the Valley of the Roses to the south. In terms of scenery or sheer excitement, this can't match crossing the more famous Shipka Pass (see p.264), but there are compensations. Lusher and less craggy than the mountains further east, the landscape has its own attractions, and **Troyan Monastery** merits a visit as much as any of the other ecclesiastical treasures of the Stara Planina. The small settlements around Troyan make good bases from which to explore the mountains, and the range of accommodation now available in the villages makes them infinitely preferable to the towns for an overnight stay; the tourist information office in Troyan (see p.196) can make bookings.

Plenty of buses ply the Pleven–Lovech–Troyan route, and Lovech is also accessible by train, lying at the end of a branchline which leaves the main Sofia–Varna line at the otherwise unimportant town of Levski.

Lovech

LOVECH lies an hour's drive to the south of Pleven, dunked between the rolling foothills of the Balkan Mountains. It divides precisely into two sections, the flag-stoned walkways and plazas of the modern centre contrasting sharply with the grey stone roofs and protruding *chardaks* of the nineteenth-century **Varosh**, or **old town**, now an architectural preservation area. An important strategic point since Thracian times, standing guard over the northern approaches to the Troyan Pass, Lovech has become famous in more recent times for having once been the headquarters of **Vasil Levski**, whose statue and museum are now major attractions.

Nowadays Lovech is notorious for having been the site of one of Bulgaria's largest postwar concentration camps, which the inmates dubbed **Slânchev bryag** (Sunny Beach) in a grimly ironic reference to the well-known Black Sea holiday resort. On a happier note, the town is home to the Liteks **football team**, whose rise from obscurity to the upper reaches of the league (they were champions in 1998) is one of the more positive stories to emerge from an otherwise stagnating sport.

The Town

Lovech's bustling centre is largely modern, an area of concrete and steel grouped around the pedestrianized **ul. Târgovska**. Heading south along here, you'll soon reach the older parts of town, coming first to the **Pokritya most** or "Covered Bridge", of which the locals are extremely proud. Spanning the River Osâm to link the new town with the old, it was originally designed by National Revival architect Kolyo Ficheto in 1874. The bridge burned down in 1925, and the present reincarnation is the result of successive renovations – the most recent of which resulted in the arcade of boutiques, craft shops and cafés that the bridge now holds. At the eastern end of the bridge is **pl. Todor Kirkov**, named after the local revolutionary killed on this spot by the Turks in 1876 after taking part in the April Rising in Tryavna. One block south, the National Revival-style facade of a kindergarten announces the boundary of the Varosh, which stretches up the flanks of the hill from here.

Most of the buildings in the Varosh are in fact modern constructions executed in traditional style, but an attempt has been made to preserve the atmosphere of the previous century in the narrow cobbled lanes that run up the hillside. One of them, ul. Marin Pop Lukanov, leads to a huddle of buildings occupied by the **Museum of Nineteenth-Century Life** (summer daily 8am–noon & 2–6pm; winter daily 8am–noon & 1–5pm). Bulgarians of the period obviously spent their lives close to the floor, eating their food from low wooden tables and sleeping on low beds. The changing lifestyles brought about by turn-of-the-century affluence are shown by the imported Viennese furniture that fills a couple of set-piece rooms, along with an enormous English iron bedstead. Below in the cellar are a *rakiya* still and a soap-making vessel in which fats were squeezed together and blended with natural perfumes.

Just up the hill from here, a modern concrete structure houses the **Vasil Levski Museum** (Tues–Sun 8am–noon & 2–6pm). Between 1869 and 1872, Levski was chiefly responsible for establishing a network of revolutionary cells in Bulgaria, which collected arms and recruits in preparation for a national uprising. The organization's largest base was in Lovech, where Levski usually stayed at the home of Nikola Sirkov, arriving and leaving in disguise. In 1870, the revolutionary committee in Lovech assumed leadership of the nationwide movement, becoming, in effect, the provisional government of the revolutionary underground. In 1872, however, the Turkish intelligence services managed to ensnare many local leaders, ultimately including Levski himself, who was betrayed and arrested at the neighbouring village of Kâkrina. Following interrogation and torture, he was hanged on a winter's morning in Sofia in 1873.

Despite the lack of captions in any language other than Bulgarian, several of the museum's exhibits are self-explanatory. A uniform of the First Bulgarian Legion recalls Levski's days in the 1860s fighting with fellow exiles in Serbia; there are copies of Levski's letters bearing the lion seal of the revolutionary committee; and the Lovech committee's original printing press – a wooden tray no bigger than a hand into which tiny lines of type were set – accompanied by the amazingly professional-looking documents thus produced. Levski's sabre and dagger lie downstairs, perched atop a shrine-like lump of stone.

Further up the hill, beyond the Uspenska church, steps ascend to the tall and heroic **Levski statue** on Stratesh hill, where townsfolk come to admire the view.

The partly reconstructed walls of a medieval Bulgarian **fortress** occupy the summit: Byzantine attempts to strangle the Second Bulgarian Kingdom at birth ended here in the 1190s, when they were forced to sign a peace treaty in Lovech castle recognizing Bulgarian independence.

Practicalities

Lovech's **train and bus stations** sit next door to each other on high ground west of the town centre (tickets for express buses to Sofia are sold from booths in the train station forecourt); from here a five-minute walk down ul. Zacho Shishkov will bring you towards the main ul. Târgovska. Hotel **accommodation** is uninspiring but plentiful: try the clean, comfortable and modern three-star *Lovech* (☎068/24716; ④), or the run-down but serviceable two-star *Hisarya* (☎068/23821; ③), both along ul. Târgovska in the modern town; alternatively, there's the more basic *Orbita* on pl. Todor Kirkov, on the other side of the river (☎068/23813; ②).

The *Varosha mehana* on ul. Poplukanov has a summer garden and is one of the most pleasant places to **eat and drink** in old Lovech; otherwise the restaurant of the *Hotel Lovech* offers the best choice in terms of standards and service, often accompanied by live folk-pop music. Cafés and snack bars are in plentiful supply around pl. Todor Kirkov, or along ul. Târgovska in the new town.

Troyan and around

The journey south from Lovech takes you through wooded hills to **TROYAN**, a ramshackle town ranged along the banks of the River Osâm. Though no great attraction in itself, Troyan has a relaxing, semi-rural feel, and provides transport connections to a host of places sheltering in folds of the Balkan mountains – **Troyan Monastery** and the hiker-friendly villages of **Cherni Osâm** and **Apriltsi** are the main places to aim for southeast of town, while subalpine settlements like Beli Osâm, **Chiflik** and **Shipkovo** lurk in side valleys to the west. All offer excellent walking opportunities, for which the 1:65 000 *Troyan Balkan* **map** (available from Troyan tourist office; see below) is indispensable.

The Town

Troyan's **bus station** lies a couple of blocks east of the town centre, where the inevitable flagstoned main square plays host to the **Museum of Folk Crafts and Applied Arts** (Tues–Sun 8am–noon & 1–5pm), a superbly organized display with English-language texts. Troyan became a major centre of ceramic production in the nineteenth century, and most of the souvenir pottery you'll see for sale around Bulgaria is still made here. Troyan wares are instantly recognizable from the *Troyanska kapka* ("Troyan droplet") design, achieved by allowing successive layers of colour to drip down the side of the vessel before glazing. Visits to local ceramicists, which usually involve an opportunity to purchase, can be organized through the tourist office. Other displays in the museum include copperware, woodcarving, textiles and folk costumes.

Troyan practicalities

Ulitsa Vasil Levski, the main street, heads north from the main square passing the **municipal tourist office** at no. 133 (Mon–Fri 9am–1pm & 2–5pm; ☎ & fax 0670/35064), which sells maps, rents bikes, hires out English-speaking hiking guides and arranges **accommodation** in small hotels and private rooms, although most of these are in the surrounding villages of Oreshak, Cherni Osâm, Chiflik and Shipkovo rather than in Troyan itself. Of the **hotels** in town, the *Nunki* (☎0670/22606 or 22160; ④) occupies an ensemble of National Revival-style build-ings by the bridge, diagonally opposite the tourist office. Its simple ensuite rooms come with characterful touches, such as wood-carved ceilings or Ottoman-style *minderi* (couches), and there are a couple of 2- to 3-person apartments ($60 a night) with fridge and satellite TV. More basic and prone to hot-water rationing is the run-down *Kâpina 1* (☎0670/22930; ③), occupying an enviable perch on the Kâpina hill above town to the east, which is eminently more preferable to the gone-to-seed and rather grisly *Kâpina 2* next door. The town's best **restaurants** are the *Starata Kâshta*, ten minutes south of the main square along ul. General Kartsov, which has a large selection of traditional dishes and a pleasant courtyard, and the standard but acceptable *Sechuan* Chinese restaurant on pl. Rakovski, across the river from the main square.

Shipkovo, Chiflik and the Troyan Pass

The main road heading south out of Troyan takes the high-mountain route over the Troyan Pass, but just after the end of town, two turn-offs give access to a cou-ple of attractive side valleys. The northern turning heads up the Râzhdavets val-ley, at the top of which sits the village of **SHIPKOVO**, sandwiched between steep wooded slopes with a small spa resort at its western end. Served by five buses a day from Troyan, it's an unassuming, family-oriented destination where people flock to use the open-air swimming pool in summer. There's a cluster of trade-union rest homes and hotels, all of which can be booked through the Troyan tourist office: your first choice should be the *Villa Borovets* (③), a cosy family-run place with ensuite rooms and cooking facilities. Beyond Shipkovo, the road winds its picturesque way over the hills towards Ribaritsa and Teteven (see p.188).

The middle turning follows the Beli Osâm River towards the village of **Beli Osâm**, an unspectacular place which stretches lazily along the roadside for sev-eral kilometres before fading imperceptibly into the attractive settlement of **CHI-FLIK** (five daily buses from Troyan), squeezed between narrowing valley walls. There are some very comfortable **private rooms** (②) here; look out for roadside signs advertising the *Ilian* or *Radoslava* houses, or contact the Troyan tourist office to book in advance. At the far end of Chiflik the road peters out beside a small complex of spa-related rest homes and another, much grander, open-air swimming pool, fed by mineral water which arrives ready-warmed from local springs. From the road end, a steadily worsening asphalt track continues for 4km towards the *Haidushka Pesen* **chalet** (you can drive part of the way but you'll have to walk the last bit), which is the starting point for the two-hour hike to the **Kozya Stena ridge** and, a little way beyond, the *Kozya Stena* **chalet**.

Continuing south along the main road, you'll begin to climb slowly through dense forests towards the **Troyan Pass**, past the fledgling ski-centre of **Beklemeto** just below the summit. A wonderful panorama appears as the road crosses the 1450m-high pass, with the Stryama Valley receding towards the Sredna Gora, and its highest peak Mt Bogdan (1714m), and the Plain of Thrace beyond leading to the bluish silhouette of the distant Rhodopes. At the foot of the mountains lies **Kârnare**, a nondescript town where you can catch regular buses or trains into the neighbouring **Valley of the Roses** (see Chapter Four). The pass is accessible via a daily Troyan-Plovdiv **bus** that currently leaves Troyan at 7am, returning from Plovdiv at 1.30pm (mid-April to mid-October only).

Troyan Monastery

Nine daily buses head east from Troyan up the Cherni Osâm valley, through the straggling village of **ORESHAK**, to Bulgaria's third-largest monastery. Perched on the west bank of the Cherni Osâm river and shaded by trees, the **Troyan Monastery** (*Troyanski manastir*; daily dawn to dusk; foreign visitors $1, Bulgarians free) was founded in the early fifteenth century, though its church, Sveta Bogoroditsa, wasn't built until 400 years later. It is the church, however, that is of most interest, principally because of its interior and exterior **frescos** by Zahari Zograf, Bulgaria's most outstanding exponent of nineteenth-century religious art. The highlight of his work is outside the church porch, a vivid series of scenes depicting the *Last Judgement*, including a suitably macabre figure of Death bundling unfortunates into the gaping mouth of hell. The theme is continued along the west side of the church's outer wall, with St Peter admitting the virtuous to the walled garden of paradise, and a marvellous scene revealing what the Orthodox Church really thought of rural Bulgaria's herbal remedy-wielding *vrachka* (wise woman). More of Zahari's work appears in the vestibule, where the archway leading into the nave is framed by pictures of horse-riding Russian warrior-Saints Gleb and Boris, and the artist even took the liberty of including a self-portrait (visible in a window niche on the north side of the nave), next to a picture of Hadzhi Filotei, the abbot who commissioned the work. Zahari's brother Dimitâr painted the icons which feature in the exquisite, Tryavna-produced **iconostasis**, with its intricately wrought walnut pillars topped by exotic birds of prey, each holding a snake in its beak. The only other object of note inside the church is the icon of the **three-handed Virgin** (so-called because She appears to be embracing the infant Jesus with more than two arms), which devoted pilgrims believe has the power to cure ailments and grant wishes.

Outside the church, on the third floor of the monastery living quarters, is a small **"hiding-place museum"** (open when there are sufficient visitors; $1), set up when the ubiquitous Vasil Levski encouraged the monks to start a branch of the revolutionary underground at Troyan. The table and food bowl used by the itinerant patriot stand beside the wooden cupboard in which he supposedly hid whenever agents of the sultan came calling. An adjacent room displays icons, archiepiscopal robes and church regalia, including the surviving doors of an eighteenth-century iconostasis from the previous monastery church.

A popular side-trip from the monastery is to walk to the much smaller (and rarely manned) **Monastery of Sveti Nikolai**, 30 minutes uphill on the other side of the valley. Cross the footbridge opposite Troyan Monastery's gate and bear right, picking up a track to the left when you see a small graveyard. From here a stony path zigzags uphill, offering a challengingly steep – but well shaded – climb. There's nothing to see at the tumbledown monastery itself, but its fragrant woodland setting makes the walk worthwhile.

Accommodation is available in the monastery itself from an office just inside the main gate, which offers dorm beds for $7 per person, or ensuite doubles (③), although there's a 10pm curfew. Things get busy during the days leading up to the monastery's main holy day, the Feast of the Assumption (*Golyama Bogoroditsa*) on August 15, but outside of this time you should have no problem getting a bed.

Food and drink is available from the stalls in the parking lot outside the monastery, or the *Manastirska Bara* restaurant opposite, which has a wooden verandah overlooking the river. Alternatively, Oreshak, the southern end of which begins just outside the monastery gates, has a couple of restaurants on or near its main street: the *Kaiser*, roughly halfway through the village, does a good barbeque in its courtyard, and the *Dobrudzhanska Sreshta*, signed off to the left if coming from the Troyan direction, offers good Bulgarian food in traditionally furnished rooms. It's also worth noting that Oreshak's **Fair of Arts and Crafts** (Tues–Sun 9am–5pm) sells pottery and textiles from all over Bulgaria of much better quality than those on sale at the touristy souvenir stalls outside the monastery itself.

Cherni Osâm

A couple of kilometres beyond the monastery, buses from Troyan come to rest in the village of **CHERNI OSÂM**, an unspoilt logging community which provides an excellent base from which to explore the upper reaches of the Cherni Osâm valley. It's the unusual venue for an extensive modern **Natural History Museum**, at the southern end of the village (daily 8am–noon & 2–5pm), which documents the local wildlife. Stuffed stags, bears, jackals and wolves feature prominently, some mounted on pedestals which revolve as a background tape plays the appropriate bark or growl.

There are a couple of friendly, family-run **pensions** (bookable through the tourist office in Troyan) just off the main street, the most comfortable of which is the *Spomen* (③), with snug ensuite rooms grouped around a central courtyard; filling breakfasts and dinner can be arranged for an extra fee. The more basic *Sherpa* (May–Oct only; ②, ③ with breakfast) is a converted family house with shared toilets outside in the courtyard, and the owner is an experienced hiker who can organize guided walks and picnics and offer guests advice on the best of the local trails. If you've got your own transport, you could consider staying in the hamlet of Stoynovsko, 3.5km south of Cherni Osâm, at the house of Lela Ruska (book through the tourist office in Troyan; ②–③), who offers traditional-style rooms, and an Eden-like back garden. For **eating and drinking**, the *Spomen* has a cosy bar and restaurant, currently the only place in the village where you can get an evening meal.

The most convenient starting point for forays into the mountains is **Yavorova Lâka**, 9km south of Cherni Osâm, where a fairly obvious trail ascends southwest beside the Malka Krayovitsa stream to the *Ambaritsa* **chalet** (2hr). From here, a path climbs steadily southwards to join the ridge of the main Balkan Range (1hr), just below the 2166m summit of **Mt Ambaritsa**.

Apriltsi

Four buses a day run east from Troyan to **APRILTSI**, a large village nestling in the Vidima valley. It covers a wide area, with the suburbs of **Vidima** and **Ostrets** spreading many kilometres into the side valleys which fork away from the centre of the village. Buses from Troyan terminate in Ostrets, 3km southeast of the centre, so it's best to ask the driver for "Apriltsi", ensuring that you'll be put down somewhere on the main street, ul. Vasil Levski, where you'll find the **tourist office** at no. 102 (Mon–Fri 8.30am–5pm; ☎ & fax 068958/3249). Here you can pick up hiking advice and maps, and book one of a number of **pensions** or private **rooms** (②–③), most of which offer half- or full-board for a few extra dollars. The family-run *Tihiya Kât* **hotel** in Ostrets (bookable through the tourist offices in Apriltsi or Troyan; ③) is probably the swankiest accommodation option, featuring a stylish open-air swimming pool.

The main trail-heads for **hikers** start 5km out from the centre, at the southern end of Vidima, where a right fork in the road leads to the head of the Stârna valley 6.5km away, while a left fork heads up the Lyava Vidima valley, passing the *Vidima* **chalet** after another 3km, then petering out 4km further on. Either spot serves as the jumping-off point for paths to the *Pleven* **chalet**, a steep one-hour climb further south. The forbidding terrain of the main Balkan Range lies immediately beyond, although you'll need a **guide** hired through the Apriltsi tourist office to make full use of it.

East towards Veliko Târnovo

If you have a car, it's relatively easy to cut northeast across country from the Troyan region to join the main E7772 highway towards Veliko Târnovo. Relying on public transport however, things are more complicated, and you may have to double back to Lovech or Pleven in order to pick up east-bound buses and trains. Most eastward road routes come together at **SEVLIEVO**, 40km east of Lovech, a small rural centre whose nineteenth-century buildings have largely escaped the mania for reconstruction and renovation lavished elsewhere. Ulista Skobelevska, the main street, bears a decrepit-looking **Church of the Prophet Elijah** with icons by Tryavna masters; next door, the **Historical Museum** at no. 10 (Tues–Sun 8am–noon & 2–6pm), housed in the former village schoolhouse, details the various craft industries that characterized town life before the Liberation. One of the more important trades was leatherworking, memories of which are preserved in the **Tabahana**, Tabashka 3 (Tues–Sun 8am–noon & 2–6pm), a nineteenth-century tannery decked out with original tools and animal skins. There's no reason **to stay overnight** in Sevlievo, but if you have to, try the central *Hotel Rositsa*, pl. Svoboda 1 (☎0675/3008; ③).

For those with plenty of time, a car, and a pathological desire to ride the backroads of Bulgaria, a couple of interesting sights lie hidden away to the south of Sevlievo. Minor roads lead to **Gradnitsa**, 15km to the southwest, where a medieval fortress tumbles down the slopes of Prechista hill on the south side of the village. Lower layers of the remaining walls are sixth-century Byzantine, but most of the remains date from the Second Kingdom. More intrepid travellers may consider a trip to **Batoshevo Monastery**, 27km to the south on the old road to Apriltsi, situated high above the west bank of the River Rositsa midway between the villages of Batoshevo and Stokite. Low, barn-like monastery buildings surround the Church of the Assumption, whose grey slate roof slopes down over a richly frescoed porch.

Vishovgrad

Northeast of Sevlievo lies one of the major white-wine-producing areas of Bulgaria, with low vineyard-cloaked hills feeding the wineries of towns like **Suhindol** and **Pavlikeni**. There are no real tourist centres here yet, save perhaps for the village of **VISHOVGRAD**, lying 15km north of the main Târnovo-bound E7772 on a minor road which cuts across country to Pavlikeni. If you're travelling by public transport, you'll have to approach the village from the north, catching a train to Pavlikeni (on the main Sofia–Varna line) and picking up a Vishovgrad bus from outside the station – most departures are timed to coincide with the arrival of trains from the Sofia direction. The village itself offers rural peace, and the chance to walk the 6km southeast to the **Emen Gorge**, where a wooden walkway leads past rushing waters to a small lake and a waterfall. Back in the village, the family-run **pension**, the *Dâlbok Zimnik* (book through Odysseia-in in Sofia; ☎02/989 0538; ③) offers bed-and-breakfast and advice on local walks. The best time to be in Vishovgrad is on **St Tryphon's Day** (*Trifon Zarezan*) on February 14, when the ritual pruning of the vines is celebrated with much drinking and feasting.

Veliko Târnovo

The precipitously perched houses of **VELIKO TÂRNOVO** seem poised to leap into the chasms that divide the city into its separate quarters. Medieval fortifications girdling the Tsarevets massif add melodrama to the scene, yet even more transfixing are the huddles of antique houses that the writer Ivan Vazov likened to frightened sheep, bound to the rocks by wild lilac and vines, forming picturesque reefs veined by steps and narrow streets. Le Corbusier raved about Târnovo's "organic" architecture, and even the dour Prussian Field Marshal Helmut Von Moltke was moved to remark that he had "never seen a town of more romantic location".

But for Bulgarians the city has a deeper significance. When the National Assembly met here to draft Bulgaria's first constitution in 1879, it consciously did so in the former capital of the Second Kingdom (1185–1396) whose medieval civilization was snuffed out by the Turks. Reclaiming this heritage was an integral part of the National Revival, and since independence (especially during the socialist era) archeologists have been keenly uncovering the past of Târnovo "the Great" – not only the medieval citadel of **Tsarevets** but also the churches of **Sveta Gora** and **Trapezitsa**. Nor is the city an isolated case, for in the hills and valleys **around Târnovo** are several monasteries and small towns founded during the Second Kingdom or in the aftermath of its collapse, which make great excursions from town.

Târnovo's convenience as a touring base is backed up by the city's **train and bus links** with towns like Dryanovo, Tryavna and Gabrovo to the south – all easy day-trips from here. In addition, the Bucharest–Istanbul express train travels through once a day in each direction, useful if you're travelling further afield.

TÂRNOVO'S UPRISINGS

Folk memories of Bulgaria's medieval greatness never really died out in Târnovo, and the Ottoman-ruled city has been host to three proudly remembered **uprisings**. The first came in 1598, when locals aided by Dubrovnik merchant Pavel Džordžic rose up in the mistaken belief that the Austrian Emperor Rudolf II had promised to send military help. The second, in 1688, came about when Polish victories against the Turks once again persuaded Târnovo's *charshiya* that foreign armies were preparing to ride to their aid. Local noble Rostislav Stratsimirovich, a direct descendant of Tsar Ivan Stratsimir, was delared Prince of Bulgaria, then forced to flee by the Ottomans, who set fire to the town in retribution. The third, known as **Velchova Zavera** or "Velcho's plot", came in 1835, when glass merchant Velcho Atanasov Dzhamdzhiyata hatched the hair-brained scheme of laying siege to the fortress of Varna in the hope of encouraging Russian intervention. Unsurprisingly, the conspirators were captured and hanged.

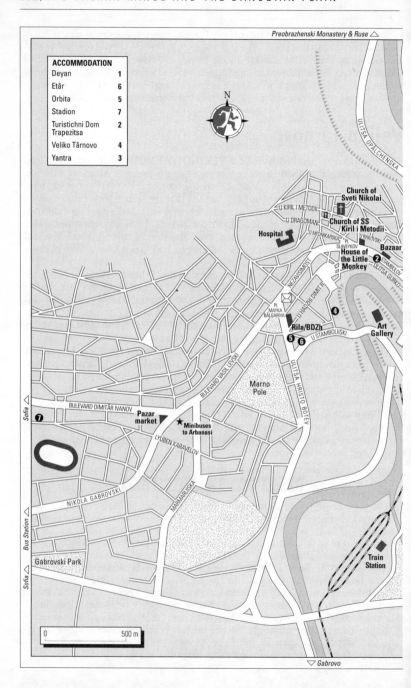

Preobrazhenski Monastery & Ruse △

ACCOMMODATION

Deyan	1
Etâr	6
Orbita	5
Stadion	7
Turistichni Dom Trapezitsa	2
Veliko Târnovo	4
Yantra	3

N

ULITSA OPÂLCHENSKA

Church of Sveti Nikolai

U. KIRIL I METODII

Church of SS Kiril i Metodii

U DRAGOMAN

U MEDNIKARSKA

U RAKOVSKI

Hospital

SLAVEYKOV

Bazaar

U STAMBOLOV

House of the Little Monkey

ULITSA GURKO

NEZAVISIMOST

PL. MAYKA BÂLGARIYA

U HADZHI DIMIT'R

Rila/BDZh

U STAMBOLIISKI

Art Gallery

ULITSA HRISTO BOTEV

BULEVARD VASIL LEVSKI

Marno Pole

△ Sofia

BULEVARD DIMITÂR IVANOV

Pazar market

★ Minibuses to Arbanasi

LYUBEN KARAVELOV

MARMARLIISKA

NIKOLA GABROVSKI

△ Bus Station

Gabrovski Park

△ Sofia

Train Station

| 0 | | 500 m |

▽ Gabrovo

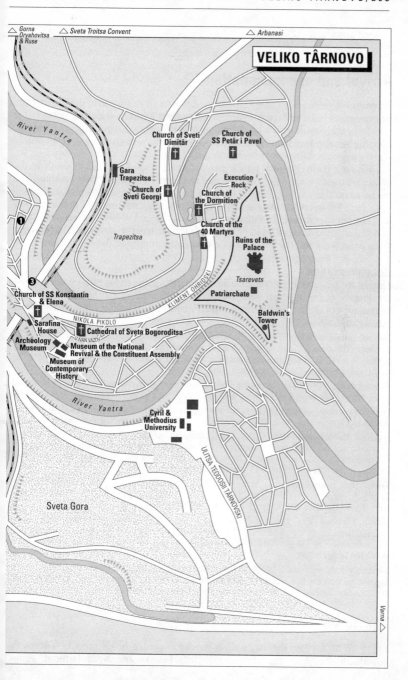

The **telephone area code** for Veliko Târnovo is ☎062.

Arrival and accommodation

All **trains** between Sofia and Varna stop at Gorna Oryahovitsa to the north, from where eight local trains a day cover the remaining 13km to Veliko Târnovo. In the middle of the day there's a large gap between services, so you can save time by hopping on the bus shuttle to Gorna Oryahovitsa's bus terminal, from where there's a connection every fifteen minutes (#10 or #14) to Veliko Târnovo.

Târnovo's **train station**, on the Stara Zagora–Ruse line, is 2km south of the centre – buses #4 and #13 (from the bus stop nearest to the station building) run to the main thoroughfare, bul. Levski. If you don't mind a fifteen-minute uphill walk, turn left out of the station yard and keep bearing left until you reach the centre. The **bus terminal** is southwest of town at the end of Nikola Gabrovski: take bus #12 or trolleybuses #1 and #21 to reach the centre. Privately operated bus services from Sofia and the coast pick up and drop off outside the *Hotel Etâr*.

Accommodation

Hotels are reasonably plentiful, if a little uninspiring: the city-centre establishments are largely of the modern concrete variety, and most of the smaller family-run places are out of town in Arbanasi, which makes an appealing rural alternative to staying in the city (see p.211).

Deyan, Yanaki Donchev 22 (☎30532). Small, privately run hotel offering simple rooms with shared bathrooms, but the situation – on a cobbled street in the quaint Varosh quarter of town – is ideal. Some rooms have good views of the Tsarevets massif, and there may be reductions for stays of more than three days. ③.

Etâr, ul. Ivailo 2 (☎626851). Imposing if slightly unkempt high-rise with good views of the old town, but slightly overpriced for what it offers. Rooms with shared facilities (③), ensuites (④).

Orbita, ul. Hristo Botev 15 (☎622041). Hostel-type accommodation on the third floor of a residential block in the new town. Most rooms have four beds and you will be expected to share. ②.

Stadion, Todor Balina 14 (☎620324). Unpretentious place next to the football stadium in the new town, a good 15-min walk from the central sights. Slightly run-down but still reasonable, rooms come with shared facilities (②) or ensuite bathrooms (④). There are a couple of two-to four-person apartments with TV and fridge ($60).

Turistichni Dom Trapezitsa, Stambolov 79 (☎22061). Unassuming but friendly hotel run by the Bulgarian Tourist Union on the old town's central thoroughfare. The rooms are basic with shared facilities, but fill up quickly with holidaying Bulgarians. ②.

Veliko Târnovo, Emil Popov 2 (☎630571, fax 639859). Elegant four-star concrete palace aspiring to an international business standard. Rooms come with the usual comforts, satellite TV, and sweeping views of the old town. There's also an indoor pool, sauna and gym. Breakfast included. ⑦.

Yantra, Velchova Zavera 1 (☎620391, fax 621807). Well-maintained three-star establishment in a central location, five minutes from Tsarevets hill. The rooms are ensuite with satellite TV, and those facing east have brilliant views of the fortress. Breakfast included. ④.

The Town

Lying on an incline, the city's drab **modern centre** holds most of Târnovo's downtown shopping area along boulevards **Levski** and **Nezavisimost**. From here you can proceed eastwards on foot and let yourself be drawn gradually into the **old town**. This is fascinating, not so much for its specific sights, of which there are relatively few, but for the feel of the place generally: there's always a fresh view of the city poised above the gorges or some new, unexpected detail.

Heading east along ul. Nezavisimost, you arrive at the small **pl. Pobornicheski** or "Combatants' Square", which has a monument to local rebel Bacho Kiro and other revolutionaries of 1876, whom the Turks hanged from gallows erected on what was then a rubbish tip. The **"House of the Little Monkey"** overlooking pl. Slaveikov at Vâstanicheska 14 gets its nickname from the grimacing statuette over the balcony, although the bay windows and deeply pointed brickwork are what make it so characteristic of Târnovo architecture. It was designed in 1849 by Bulgaria's leading nineteenth-century architect Nikolai Fichev or "Kolyo Ficheto" (see p.218), the first of many Târnovo buildings to bear his imprint. Like many of the town's old houses, it sits precariously above a limited groundspace, with orieled living quarters above what used to be a shop or warehouse.

The bazaar and the Varosh quarter

Various restored workshops and the facade of an old *caravanserai* make up the *Samovodska Charshiya* or **bazaar** at the junction of ul. Rakovski and pl. Georgi Kirkov. Aside from one surviving coppersmith and a weaver selling handmade *chergi* or rugs, most of the craftspeople who once had ateliers here have moved out to be replaced by clothes boutiques, but it's still highly photogenic, with its wrought-iron garnished facades and cobbled slopes. Starting from the square at the end of the bazaar, you can follow ul. Vâstanicheska up into the narrow streets of the peaceful old **Varosh quarter**, whose two nineteenth-century churches are verging on the decrepit. The **Church of Sveti Nikolai** has a carving on the bishop's throne which shows a lion (representing Bulgaria) in the coils of a snake (the Greek Church) being devoured by a dragon (Turkey), and up the hill from here the **Church of SS Kiril i Metodii** – with its belfry and dome by Kolyo Ficheto – still serves worshippers on ul. Kiril i Metodii.

Heading downhill from pl. Kirkov, you'll come upon **pl. Velchova Zavera**, where Velcho the glazier, Nikola the braid maker, Ivan the furrier and other conspirators were hanged for rebelling against the Turkish authorities in 1835.

The Sarafina House

Continuing from pl. Velchova Zavera along ul. Ivan Vazov you'll catch sight of the **Church of SS Konstantin i Elena** on the right (currently closed for restoration), skulking behind foliage at the bottom of a steep flight of steps. From here you can descend to what is perhaps the most characteristic of Târnovo's streets, **ul. General Gurko**, where the houses – mainly dating from Ottoman times – look stunningly picturesque, perched along the curve of the gorge. Don't miss the *Sarafinova Kâshta* or **Sarafina House** at no. 88 (Mon–Fri 9am–noon & 1–5.30pm), which is so contrived that only two floors are visible from General Gurko but a further three overhang the river. The interior is notable for the splendid octagonal vestibule with wrought-iron fixtures and a panelled rosette ceiling which, like the elegantly furnished rooms upstairs, reflects the taste of the architect and owner, the moneylender Dimo Sarafina. The emergence of bourgeois culture in nineteenth-century Târnovo is recalled in a collection of sepia family photographs displayed downstairs.

The Museum of the National Revival and the Constituent Assembly

Returning to Ivan Vazov and continuing southwards, you'll soon arrive at pl. Sâedinenie and a spacious blue and white building that houses the *Muzei "Vâzrazhdane i Ureditelno sâbranie"* – the **Museum of the National Revival and the Constituent Assembly** (Wed–Mon 8am–noon & 1–6pm). Designed by Kolyo Ficheto in 1872 as the *Konak* of the Turkish governor, Ali Bey (who mounted the trials of the rebels of 1876 here), the building subsequently hosted the first Bulgarian *sâbranie* (parliament), which spent two months in 1879 deliberating the country's first post-Liberation constitution – afterwards known as the "Târnovo Constitution". The union of Bulgaria and Eastern Roumelia (1885) was also signed here, and this hallowed building was exactly reconstructed (after being devastated by fire) in time to allow the proclamation of People's Power from the premises on September 9, 1944. Exhibits on the ground floor pay tribute to successive generations of Bulgarian patriots, telling the story (mostly through pictures and Bulgarian-only texts) of rebellion after rebellion against the Turks – notably the locally based uprisings of 1598 and 1686 (see box on p.201). Icons and devotional objects are grouped downstairs, including one sixteenth-century embroidered shroud depicting the Deposition of Christ; you can also see nineteenth-century Târnovo metalwork, weights and scales used by the money-lenders and tradesmen of the *charshiya*, and a big still for *rakiya*-brewing. On the first floor is the hall in which the Provisional Assembly sat, its timber-beamed ceiling supported by wooden pillars.

South to Tsarevets

Steps to the right of the National Revival Museum lead down to the **Archeology Museum** (Tues–Sun 8am–12pm & 1–6pm), with four dimly lit halls of finds labelled only in Bulgarian. The highlights of the collection are the columns and statue fragments culled from the Roman city of Nicopoils ad Istrum, 17km north of Târnovo, founded by Emperor Trajan in 107 to serve as an administrative centre for the Roman Empire's lower Danubian province, Moesia Inferior. Excavations at Nicopolis (just outside the modern village of Nikyup) are still going on, and the site can only be visited if you have permission from the Bulgarian Ministry of Culture. Elsewhere the museum's collection is pretty lacklustre, enlivened only by the grim-looking chain mail and helmets worn by the soldiers of the Second Kingdom. Around the corner and lower down the hill, a former Turkish **prison** now holds the **Museum of Contemporary History** (Mon–Fri 9am–noon & 1–5pm), which contains the personal effects of Târnovo-born politician Stefan Stambolov, an autocratic prime minister who was assassinated by disgruntled Macedonians in 1895, alongside military uniforms and pistols recalling the Balkan Wars. Above the square, the modern **Cathedral of Sveta Bogoroditsa** stands aloof on a terrace. From here, either ul. Ivan Vazov or Nikola Pikolo leads directly down to the entrance of Tsarevets, the medieval fortress.

Tsarevets

Approaching **Tsarevets** (daily 8am–dusk; $2) along the stone causeway that was erected after the original drawbridge collapsed beneath the *Bey*'s harem, you can appreciate how the *boyars* Petâr and Asen were emboldened enough by possession of this seemingly impregnable citadel to lead a rebellion against Byzantium in 1185. Petâr's proclamation of the Second Kingdom and his coronation occurred when Constantinople was already preoccupied by the Magyar and Seljuk Turk menace, and when a punitive Byzantine army was eventually sent in 1190 it was utterly defeated at the Tryavna Pass. Now restored, the ramparts and the Patriarchate (plus the ruins of the palace and various churches) convey something of Tsarevets's grandeur during the Second Kingdom, when travellers deemed Târnovo "second after Constantinople".

GATES AND TOWERS
Artisans and clerics serving the palace and the Patriarchate generally resided in the Asenova quarter below the hill, and entered Tsarevets via the **Asenova Gate** halfway along the western ramparts; foreign merchants, invited to settle here by Tsar Asen II, had their own entrance, the "Frankish" or **Frenkhisar Gate** near the southern end of the massif. Rapidly becoming a regional power, the Second Kingdom attacked and defeated the first Latin emperor of the East, Baldwin of Flanders, in 1205, the former emperor ending his days as a prisoner in the bastion overlooking the Frenkhisar Gate, thereafter known as **Baldwin's Tower**. No one knows exactly how Baldwin met his death. According to one fanciful legend, he resisted the advances of the Bulgarian queen, who promptly accused him of attempted rape and had him executed. Twenty years after Baldwin's capture, however, a hermit emerged in Flanders claiming to be the former emperor. Despite attracting a coterie of followers, the pretender was declared an imposter and put to death.

THE OLD PALACE AND THE PATRIARCHATE
The **ruins of the palace** seem insignificant compared to the ramparts, but contemporary chronicles and modern excavations suggest that the royal complex was once splendid and opulent. Delicate columns divided the 35-metre-long throne room into aisles, which were adorned with green serpentine, Egyptian porphyry and pink marble, and mosaics and murals depicting the rulers of three dynasties. The church of the Blessed Saviour or **Patriarchate**, built early in the thirteenth century and now unconvincingly restored, was, significantly, the only structure permitted to surpass the palace in height. Ribbed with red brick and inset with green and orange ceramics, the church contains florid modern frescos, which the visitor is invited to contemplate while curators switch on a backing tape of Orthodox choral music.

EXECUTION ROCK AND THE TERTERID DYNASTY
The **Lobna skala** (Execution Rock) at the sheer northern end of Tsarevets is associated with the dynasty that followed the brief reign of the swineherd **Ivailo** (1277–80). Proclaimed tsar after a popular anti-feudal revolt, Ivailo successfully organized resistance against invading Tatar hordes but neglected to guard against a coup by the *bolyari* (nobles), who had him flung off the rock. The **Terterid** dynasty which followed was chiefly concerned with its own survival and willing to suspect anyone – even the patriarch, Yoakim III, who was also executed – of collusion with the Tatars; it was only during the later, fourteenth-century reign of Todor Svetoslav that there was much progress or security.

However, Bulgarian culture – strongly influenced by that of Byzantium – revived during the Shishmanid dynasty (1323–93), and the enlightened rule of Ivan Aleksandâr and his son Ivan Shishman created the conditions whereby medieval Târnovo attained the zenith of its development. Trade with Genoa, Venice and Dubrovnik flourished; hospitals and hospices were maintained by the

---

THE SON ET LUMIÈRE

Occasionally on summer nights the entire Tsarevets massif is lit up by huge spotlights, and accompanied by a stirring musical soundtrack. Designed to tell the history of Tsarevets through the ages, the son et lumière is a stunning sight, especially when viewed from the terrace of open-air seating opposite the entrance to the fortress. Sadly, it's very difficult to find out when these performances are on, but if you do hear of one taking place, don't miss it. You could, of course, arrange your own personal performance in advance (☎36952, fax 27997), but you'd have to shell out in excess of $150 for the privilege.

---

public purse; students came from Serbia, Russia and Wallachia to study at the university; and Târnovo became one of the Balkans' main centres of painting and literature.

Nonetheless, by the late fourteenth century the Second Kingdom had fragmented into several semi-autonomous states, and the hegemony of the kingdom had been dissipated: individually, the states were no match for the expansionist Ottoman Turks, who besieged Târnovo for three months before capturing, plundering and burning the city in July 1393.

The Asenova quarter

To the west of Tsarevets on both banks of the Yantra lies the **Asenova quarter**, where chickens strut and children fish beside the river. During the Middle Ages this was the artisans' quarter, which it remained until 1913, when it was struck by an earthquake which levelled most of the medieval buildings and did great damage to the (much reconstructed) churches.

The **Church of the Forty Martyrs** (*Tsârkva na chetirideset mâchenitsi*; closed for long-term repairs), near the bridge is a barn-like edifice founded by Tsar Ivan Asen II to commemorate his victory over the Byzantine rulers of Epirus at Klokotnitsa on Forty Martyrs' Day in 1230. Subsequently much altered, to the extent that it has, apparently, baffled restorers, the church was the burial place of St Sava, founder of the Serbian Orthodox Church, and several Bulgarian tsars; the Bulgarians saw God's hand behind the collapse of the minaret built when the Turks impiously transformed this into a mosque. Among the pillars within stands Khan Omturag's Column, filched from another site, whose Greek inscription reads in part: "Man dies, even though he lives nobly, and another is born. Let the latest born, when he examines these records, remember him who made them. The name of the Prince is Omurtag, the Sublime Khan". Not to be outdone, Asen had another column inscribed with a list of his conquests from Adrianople to Durazzo (Durrës in Albania), whose inhabitants were spared "by my benevolence".

Further north, the early twentieth-century **Church of the Dormition** isn't intrinsically interesting, but stands on the site of the monastery of the Virgin of the Prisoners, where Tsar Ivan Aleksandâr confined his wife as a nun in order to marry the Jewess Sara. The **Church of SS Petâr i Pavel** (Easter–Sept unpredictable hours; $2), 200m beyond, is more remarkable: it contains several capitals in the old Bulgarian style (carved with vineleaves in openwork) and some well-preserved frescos of which the oldest – dating back to the fourteenth century – is the *Pietà* opposite the altar. On the south wall, opposite the entrance, the church's saints' namesakes are portrayed in a lively manner. The church was the site of the massacre of the *bolyari* in 1393 (only Patriarch Evtimii's intervention dissuaded the Turks from killing the entire population) and, much later, the place where the Ottoman-appointed Greek patriarch of Bulgaria was evicted by the citizenry.

On the other side of the river are two more restored churches, both currently closed for renovation. With its red-brick stripes and trefoil windows inlaid with orange plaques, the **Church of Sveti Dimitâr** is the best looking of the surviving medieval churches, although most of its original frescos were painted over during the sixteenth and seventeenth centuries. It was during the consecration of the church that the *bolyari* Petâr and Asen announced their rebellion against Byzantium, and Saint Demetrius (who, legend has it, came from Salonika to help the oppressed Bulgarians) became the patron saint of the Second Kingdom. The **Church of Sveti Georgi**, further to the south, is smaller but said to have better-preserved frescos.

Overhead rises the massif known as **Trapezitsa**, where the *bolyari* and leading clergy of the Second Kingdom built their mansions and some forty private churches, sixteen of which are currently being excavated. It's an area of great archeological importance, and although tracks onto the hilltop do exist, interlopers are discouraged.

THE BOGOMILS

Târnovo was the venue for a famous synod of the Bulgarian Church in 1211, which tried (unsuccessfully) to curb the growth of a notorious medieval heresy that plagued the Second Kingdom – **Bogomilism**. The movement is thought to have emerged from the teachings of a tenth-century priest named Bogomil (literally "beloved of God"), who inherited the concept of dualism from the earlier Manichaean and Paulician heresies. This held that the entire material world was the creation of the devil, and only the human soul was the province of God. Jesus was sent to earth to defeat Satan's reign on earth, but his mission failed; the fight with Satan's power therefore continued to be a daily war of attrition for all believers. The growth of the Bogomils coincided with the fall of the First Bulgarian Kingdom to the Byzantines, and the movement was strongly critical of the Bulgarian establishment, especially the clergy. Left-wing historians have been quick to emphasize Bogomilism's social impact, especially its appeal to the poor.

Our only real knowledge of the Bogomils, however, comes from the movement's enemies – critics like the monk Cosmas, who described them as "lamblike and gentle, and pale from hypocritical fasting", but really "ravening wolves" who "sowed the tares of their preaching" among "simple and uneducated men".

Cosmas was not the only person worried by the spread of the heresy throughout the Balkan peninsula. Byzantine chronicler Anna Comnena relates how her father Emperor Alexius I had the Bogomil leader Basil publicly burned in the Constantinople hippodrome somewhere around 1100. Despite repeated efforts to stamp it out, Bogomilism remained a powerful force throughout the Balkans, although once-fashionable theories that Bogomilism became the state religion of fifteenth-century Bosnia are nowadays questioned. Byzantine propaganda accused the Bogomils of all manner of unnatural practices, most common among which was sodomy – the adoption of the word "bugger" by the English language derives from confusion over the terms "Bogomil" and "Bulgar".

Sveta Gora

Sveta Gora (Holy Hill), on the south bank of the Yantra, used to be a centre of monastic scholasticism, and nowadays provides the site for the **Cyril and Methodius University**, which can be reached via a bridge to the south of Tsarevets, or on bus #15. The rocky spur, linked by footbridge to the *Hotel Veliko Târnovo*, is adorned with an obelisk commemorating the 800th anniversary of the foundation of the Asenid dynasty, but visitors are generally more interested in the contents of the large, copper-roofed **art gallery** nearby (Tues–Sun 10am–6pm), whose theme is "Târnovo through the eyes of diverse painters". A jumble of unchallenging townscapes and lionizations of medieval tsars for the most part, the collection is enlivened by a couple of naive exercises in mid-nineteenth-century portraiture by local artists Nikolai Pavlovich and Georgi Danchov.

Eating and drinking

Restaurants and **cafés** line the main strip – ul. Nezavisimost, ul. Stambolov and ul. Vazov – which leads through the town centre towards Tsarevets. While restaurants remain pretty stable, **drinking venues** change all the time, and your best bet is just to wander around pl. Slaveykov and pl. Mayka Bâlgaria until one takes your fancy. Of the more long-standing bars, try the studenty *Tequila Sunrise*, on Stefan Stambolov, or *Poltava*, on pl. Mayka Bâlgaria (entrance round the side from the cinema), which doubles as a terrace-café by day, and a disco by night.

The main **food market** is the open-air *Pazar*, on the corner of Vasil Levski and Nikola Gabrovski, and there's a 24-hour food shop with a good deli counter at ul. Vasil Levski 9.

Restaurants

Belite Brezi, Stefan Stambolov. Just off the main road, down a flight of steps near the church of SS Konstantin i Elena, this restaurant serves good Bulgarian food and hosts frequent live folk and pop music. The name means "silver birches", three of which provide dappled shade in the terrace at the back.

Elenite, Stefan Stambolov 34. An elegant place specializing in game dishes, although standard Bulgarian food is available as well. The rich, almost beefy taste of *gligan* (wild boar) is worth a taste if you've never tried it.

Gradina Pri Hadzhi Mihail, pl. Marno Pole. A rooftop garden restaurant just off bul. Levski, serving good-quality Bulgarian food, accompanied by music from nightclub-style crooners.

Hotel Yantra, pl. Velchova Zavera 1. Reliable food at reasonable prices, augmented by a view of the Tsarevets massif that takes some beating.

Lâv, Chitalishtna 3. Excellent restaurant decked out in cool modern rather than traditional Bulgarian style. Serves imaginative variations on Bulgarian cuisine, including a wide range of vegetable dishes.

Lovna Sreshta, Todor Balina 16. Another place offering (seasonally available) hunting dishes as well as a wide range of Bulgarian standards, just uphill from the *Hotel Stadion*. Big outdoor garden, and live folk/pop music.

Mehana Hadzhi Mincho, pl. Pobornicheski. Atmospheric, folk-style place just off ul. Stambolov. Good, cheap food and live folk/pop entertainment.

Starata Kâshta, Ljuben Karavelov 63. One of the best restaurants in the new part of town, just off the eastern end of ul. Nikola Gabrovski, offering the usual range of Bulgarian dishes.

Starata Mehana, Stefan Stambolov. Cosy place with good home cooking and a verandah perched above the Yantra valley. Down a flight of steps opposite the *Elenite*.

Voennen Klub, pl. Mayka Bâlgariya. The café-restaurant of the military club, with cheap but dependable grills and salads, and an extremely popular terrace overlooking the square.

Listings

Bus companies Express buses to Sofia and the coast are operated by Etâr Tours (information from the *Hotel Etâr*) and Group Travel, just round the side of the *Hotel Etâr*.

Hospital ul. Buzludzha 1 (☎23833).

Pharmacy 24hr pharmacy at Vasil Levski 29.

Post office Hristo Botev 1 (Mon–Fri 7.30am–7pm, Sat 8.30am–6pm).

Taxis Etâr Taxi ☎30029.

Telephones At the post office on Hristo Botev 1.

Train tickets Advance bookings and international tickets from Rila/BDZh, Hristo Botev 13 (Mon–Fri 8am–noon & 1–5pm).

North of Veliko Târnovo

The terrain **north of Târnovo** is a wild confusion of massifs sundered by the River Yantra and its tributaries, abounding in rocky shelves rendered almost inaccessible by forests and torrents. Nearly twenty monasteries were established here during the Second Kingdom, and several survived the Turkish invasion. These formed a symbiotic relationship with the later towns and villages founded by refugees after the sack of Târnovo. With a car it's feasible to visit the main sites within a day, but relying on public transport (or hiking), one expedition a day seems more realistic.

Arbanasi and around

Hiding high on a plateau 4km northeast of Târnovo, and overlooking Tsarevets and Trapezitsa to the south, **ARBANASI** is one of Bulgaria's most picturesque villages, resembling a cross between a *kasbah* and the kind of *pueblo* that Clint Eastwood rids of bandits. People vanish into their family strongholds for the siesta, and at high noon only chickens stalk the rutted streets.

The origins of Arbanasi have presented scholars with a characteristically Balkan ethnological puzzle. The village's name led most historians to assume that it was founded by Albanian refugees fleeing Turkish reprisals after a failed fifteenth-century uprising, although this is disputed by modern Bulgarian historians eager to establish the continuity of Slav settlement in the area. What's beyond doubt is that the people who lived here in the village's eighteenth-century heyday belonged to the Greek cultural orbit, speaking Greek and giving their children Greek names. The inhabitants grew rich on the proceeds of cattle-droving, drying meat for their own consumption and selling the fat to the local Muslims, who considered it a delicacy. The leather was loaded onto caravans and taken east, where it was exchanged for Asiatic luxury goods like silk and spices.

Arbanasi's merchants invested their wealth in the big, fortress-like stone houses for which the village is famed, but they also endowed churches, chapels and public drinking fountains, turning the village into a lively urban centre for the local Christian population, hidden from the eyes of Ottoman-dominated Târnovo below. The town was sacked three times in the nineteenth century by the *kârdzhali*, Turkish outlaws who menaced the townsfolk of the Balkans, and commerce became increasingly centred on Târnovo and other lowland towns, forcing Arbanasi's merchants to relocate their businesses. Mass emigration during the war-ravaged winter of 1877 further confirmed Arbanasi's decline. Nowadays a traditional rural population coexists with a post-Communist influx of pop singers, footballers and mafia types, taking advantage of Arbanasi's traditional high-walled architecture to preserve their privacy.

The village

Squatting on high ground just above Arbanasi's main square is the **Church of the Archangels Michael and Gabriel** (irregular opening hours) – the pair are depicted in a mural above the western portal. Dating from 1600, the church is a solid brick structure adorned with irregular lines of blind arcading, its gloomy interior illuminated by tiny, iron-grilled windows. Local schoolmaster Hristo was called on in the early eighteenth century to execute most of the frescos, including a panoramic *Nativity* scene in the apse, but look out also for the later *Virgin Horanta* painted jointly by itinerant masters Georgi of Bucharest and Mihail of Salonika.

A cobbled path leads south of the main square towards the asymmetrical, red-tiled roof of the **Church of Sveti Dimitâr**. The original church perished in the earthquake of 1913, and the pale, unweathered stones of its modern reconstruction make it look more like a suburban bungalow than a place of worship. Some of the interior frescos have been restored, and vibrant portraits of the two archangels preside over the adjoining chapel of Sveti Nestor. Richly carved Greek and Bulgarian headstones are propped up against the outer walls.

Returning to the village square and taking the main road west brings you to the finest of Arbanasi's mansions, the **Kostantsaliev House**. Like other dwellings erected after the conflagration that gutted Arbanasi in 1798, the ground floor (with servants' quarters and store-rooms) is built of stone and entered via a nail-studded gate, while the upper floor is made of wood. Many of the rooms have beautiful panelled ceilings and ornate plaster cornices bearing geometric or floral motifs. It's not hard to imagine the former owner, the Kokona Sultana (a relation of the *Bey*), greeting her guests on the wooden staircase that ascends to the reception hall, from which one door leads to the "winter room" or communal bedroom. The other opens onto a corridor leading to the dining room and the office of her merchant husband, furnished with a low table or *sofra*.

Beyond the house lies the **Kokona fountain**, built in 1786 on the orders of Mehmed Said Ali, author of its Arabic inscription: "He who looks upon me and drinks my water shall possess the light of the eyes and of the soul". Turn left at the fountain to reach the village's most beautifully decorated church, the **Church of the Nativity** (*Rozhdestvo Hristovo*). Like the others in Arbanasi it's outwardly plain, but inside you'll find richly coloured frescos dating from the seventeenth century. The main entrance leads into a long gallery, its ceiling supported by wooden beams decorated with geometric designs and Greek-language inscriptions. At the far end of the gallery, the chapel of St John the Baptist is richly decorated with images of martyred saints, and divided into separate areas for men and women to pray. The main body of the church, to the right of the gallery, is again divided into male and female sections. The latter is the smaller of the two, notable for a frieze of Greek philosophers along one wall, while the screen dividing the male and female portions bears an extravagantly imagined rendering of the Last Judgement. At the far end of the men's chamber, the gilded iconostasis contains scenes from the Book of Genesis (in which Eden contains a dream-like menagerie of exotic animals), and a boldly colourful *pietà*.

The monasteries of Sveta Bogoroditsa and Sveti Nikola

Tracks lead downhill from here to the **Monastery of Sveta Bogoroditsa** at the northwestern end of town, whose church presides over a tranquil courtyard frequented by the occasional nun. The church itself (ring the bell in the porch and someone will open it for you) is unremarkable, a product of successive destructions and rebuildings, although it does contain an image of the Virgin renowned for answering the prayers of the sick. It attracts pilgrims throughout the year, with most arriving on the Feast of the Assumption (*Golyama Bogoroditsa*) on August 15, when the icon's power is at its greatest.

To the west, another asphalt road descends towards the **Monastery of Sveti Nikola**, a predominantly modern-looking complex completely refurbished in the 1890s. There's not much to see here, but its tranquil atmosphere is worth savouring.

Petropavlovski Monastery

From Arbanasi, it's a 5km walk or drive northeast to the tenth-century **Petropavlovski Monastery** (the Monastery of Peter and Paul), a foundation built on the site of a Roman fort. The monastery occupies a hilltop site overlooking the town of Lyaskovets, with the gently undulating arable land of the Danubian Plain stretching out beyond. The church and outbuildings are largely unremarkable nineteenth-century affairs, with the restful courtyard garden and great views being the real attractions.

To get there, you can either walk or drive along the asphalt road heading uphill to the southeast from Arbanasi's main square, which takes you along a ridge providing views of Tsarevets; turn left after 3km, then right after another 2km, and the monastery is 200m downhill from here. Alternatively, you could catch the #14 Lyaskovets bus from opposite Veliko Târnovo's *pazar*, alighting at Lyaskovets town park (recognizable by a big white Communist-era memorial on your left). An asphalt track leads uphill to the monastery from here (50 min).

Arbanasi practicalities

Despite Arbanasi's proximity to Târnovo, both the gradient and the amount of traffic on the road make it an unappetizing, if not downright dangerous, walk – it's easier to take one of the minibuses that depart approximately every hour from opposite Veliko Târnovo's *Pazar*. A kiosk just downhill from Arbanasi's main square sells all-inclusive **tickets to the House-Museums and churches** ($2), which tend to be open from Tuesday to Sunday from 10am to noon and 2pm to 6pm – although be prepared for unpredictable closures.

Arbanasi has seen a rash of **hotel** building in recent years – starting from the western entrance to the village, the small, family-run *Konstantin i Elena* (☎062/600217; ③) offers simple ensuite doubles and a couple of apartments with TV ($55). Just off the main square, the spanking new *Bolyarska kâshta* (☎062/20484) has small ensuite doubles (③), larger doubles (④), and roomy apartments with bath ($60), all swankily furnished with TV, and breakfast included in the price. Just downhill from the square, the *Arbus* (☎062/28066; ④) is a traditional-style stone house with timber upper storeys, and ensuite rooms; breakfast included. Most luxurious of the bunch is the *Arbanasi Palace* (☎062/28060 or 30176, fax 23717; ⑦), a former Zhivkov family residence on the southern edge of the village commanding splendid views of the Tsarevets massif immediately below. A brief visit to the timber-ceilinged hotel bar will be sufficient to give you an idea of the former dictator's taste for opulence.

There are plenty of places to **eat and drink** in the village, especially around the main square. Both the *Arbus* and the *Bolyarska kåshta* hotels have good **restaurants**, and the *Mehana Lyulyaka*, diagonally opposite the *Bolyarska kåshta*, is also worth trying for a traditional Bulgarian meal.

Preobrazhenski Monastery and Sveta Troitsa convent

Four kilometres north of Târnovo, high in the crags above the main E85 road to Ruse, sits **Preobrazhenski Monastery**, the monastery of the Transfiguration (daily dawn to dusk). Founded in 1360 by Ivan Aleksandâr's Jewish wife who converted to Christianity, the monastery was abandoned during the Ottoman period, then re-founded in the 1820s by Târnovo guilds, who had to bribe the city's Greek bishop to get a Bulgarian abbot installed here. Dimitâr Sofyaliyata was commissioned as architect, but after being implicated in Velcho's Plot of 1835 and hung from the monastery gate, he was replaced by master-builder Kolyo Ficheto. Zahari Zograf was brought in to do the frescos, until he discovered that the monks were strict vegetarians, and refused to work unless he was given meat. The monks relented, issuing him a contract which euphemistically promised the artist food "suited to his delicate stomach".

Finished in the 1860s, the monastery almost looks old enough to be medieval, with a canopy of vines strung between the spartan cells. However Ficheto's elegantly proportioned, enclosed courtyard is sadly no more. Over the last decade repeated rock falls from the cliffs above have destroyed many of the monastery buildings (with more being demolished for safety reasons), although the central **Transfiguration church** still stands. Its south wall bears a remarkable painting of the *Wheel of Life* by Zograf, in which the stages of human existence correspond with allegorical representations of the four seasons. Rose- and green-hued **frescos** predominate in the porch, with an eye in a circle (traditional symbol of the Holy Ghost) being a recurrent motif, and evil-doers being thrust across a river of fire and strangled by demons in the *Last Judgement*. The upper naos (formerly reserved for married women) contains the obligatory homage to Russia's warrior saints Gleb and Boris, while the lower naos (where the men prayed) has saints surrounding Christ beneath the dome and submissive dragons flanking its crucifix.

Getting to the monastery is relatively easy: regular buses from Veliko Târnovo to Gorna Oryahovitsa pass by the turn-off, 4km north of town, from where a minor road zigzags 3km uphill through a lime forest.

Sveta Troitsa convent

More or less opposite Preobrazhenski on the other side of the valley, the **Sveta Troitsa** (Holy Trinty) **convent** (daily dawn to dusk) sits on a narrow shelf of rock, at the end of a partially asphalted road which begins in Veliko Târnovo's Trapezitsa quarter. The road is just about passable by car, although most people opt to walk – a journey of about ninety minutes. Founded as early as the eleventh century, Sveta Troitsa was a monastery rather than a nunnery during the Second

Kingdom, when Patriarch Evtimii established a school of translators here. The convent's delicate red-brick church (also built during the nineteenth century by Kolyo Ficheto) is difficult to get access to, but the charming, flower-bedecked courtyard overlooked by sheer cliffs, and the impressive surroundings, make the trip worthwhile.

To get to the convent, leave Veliko Târnovo on the Arbanasi road and take a left turn soon after passing the Church of Sveti Dimitâr. Ignore roads leading left towards Trapezitsa train station, but bear left after this, and carry straight on past several decaying factories. Pay no heed to the multicoloured hiking waymarks which tempt you uphill to the right. You could also walk to Sveta Troitsa from Arbanasi, although you'll probably need local knowledge and plenty of time to spare – markings are inadequate, and paths confusing.

South of Veliko Târnovo

The mill town of **Gabrovo** is the main urban centre south of Târnovo, although it's in the smaller towns and villages, where rural architecture and crafts have been best preserved – notably **Tryavna**, **Bozhentsi**, and the museum-village of **Etâra** – that the main attractions lie. Several historic **monasteries**, such as Kilifarevo, Dryanovo and Sokolski, are within easy striking distance of these places. Veliko Târnovo, Gabrovo and Tryavna are equally convenient as bases from which to explore the region, and even if you're reliant on **public transport** you'll find that you can reach several destinations in the space of one day-trip. Both Dryanovo and Tryavna are linked directly to Veliko Târnovo by train, although continuing to Gabrovo involves a change at Tsareva Livada. Buses, too, are plentiful, with hourly services linking the area's major towns. Less well served by public transport are the little-visited monasteries near the historic town of **Elena** to the southeast, although they present an easily digestible cluster of rustic sights to those with access to a car.

Travelling onwards to the Valley of the Roses (see Chapter Four) from here involves two of Bulgaria's most scenic mountain routes. The Veliko Târnovo–Tryavna rail-line winds its way southwards through the densely wooded **Tryavna Pass** (where Petâr and Asen defeated the Byzantine army in 1190, preserving the independence of the Second Kingdom), before joining the Sofia–Burgas line at Dâbovo. If travelling by road, the E85 heads towards the impressive **Shipka Pass** just above Gabrovo (the place to catch buses over the pass), then drops down towards Bulgaria's rose capital, Kazanlâk.

Kilifarevo Monastery and around

Twenty kilometres south of Veliko Târnovo, **Kilifarevo Monastery** was a favourite retreat for the tsars of the Second Kingdom. It was also the site of the famous college established by Teodosii Târnovski in 1350, which translated literary works from Greek and Hebrew into Slavonic script, making them legible to scholars far beyond Bulgaria. As many as 800 monks and novices from all over the Slav world were based here at any one time, and the School of Kilifarevo might have achieved parity with the great European universities had it not been burned by the Turks in 1393. Teodosii's successor Patriarch Eftimii was imprisoned by the Ottoman conquerors, but his right-hand man Grigorii Tsamblak fled to Russia

KILIFAREVO AND THE HESYCHASTS

In the fourteenth century, Kilifarevo was one of Balkan Christianity's most important centres, and played a crucial role in spreading one of Eastern Orthodoxy's most characteristic forms of mysticism: **hesychasm**. Taking their name from the Greek word *hesychia*, meaning "stillness", hesychasts believed that silent, solitary meditation, aided by highly ritualized forms of prayer, would eventually lead them to a revelation of the true nature of God. Central to hesychast thinking was the idea that the repetition of certain phrases (such as the mantra-like Jesus Prayer: "Lord Jesus Christ, Son of God, have mercy on me"), uttered while holding one's breath, would lead to the adept being filled with the "Divine Light"; the same light seen by the disciples of Jesus Christ when witnessing his Transfiguration on Mt Tabor. It was a popular doctrine, shrouding Christian belief in a seductive aura of mystery while at the same time holding out the possibility of true religious ecstasy to the really devout. Though the movement's critics found the possibility of seeing the Divine Light all a bit too fanciful, from the 1340s onwards hesychasm became the dominant form of monasticism in the Orthodox world. At a time when both Byzantium and Bulgaria seemed to be in decline and the threat of Ottoman Turkey was beginning to make itself felt, it seemed to offer a measure of spiritual purity and religious renewal.

The leading Bulgarian proponent of hesychasm was **St Theodosius of Târnovo** (Sveti Teodosii Târnovski), who trained at the Monastery of Paroria in the Strandzha mountains of southeastern Bulgaria before coming to Kilifarevo in 1350 to establish a monastic community of his own. One of the great ecclesiastics of the age, he cultivated links with leading churchmen throughout the Byzantine and Slav world, and played a key part in the Bulgarian state's supression of the Bogomil heresy (see p.209). Theodosius retired to Constantinople in the 1360s, but his pupil **Euthymius** went on to become patriarch of the Bulgarian Church, where he continued Theodosius' programme of spiritual renewal. Euthymius' main contribution was in the literary sphere, translating the writings of celebrated Byzantine mystics into Old Church Slavonic (the language developed by saints Cyril and Methodius in the ninth century before embarking on the conversion of the Slavs) then distributing them among the monasteries of Eastern Europe. Euthymius' mini Renaissance was cut short by the Turks, who subdued Bulgaria in 1393, but the fruits of his labours lived on to enrich the spiritual heritage of the Slavs. Today he is known to Bulgarians as **Patriarh Eftimii**, and streets throughout the country carry his name.

where he was able to carry on the Kilifarevo tradition, becoming Bishop of Moscow and a saint of the Russian Orthodox Church.

Now a nunnery, Kilifarevo was rebuilt during the nineteenth century around a principal church – dedicated to St Demetrius of Salonika – designed by Kolyo Ficheto. The main body of the church contains an iconostasis by Tryavna craftsmen, and a mesmerizing icon (on the opposite wall as you enter) of St John of Rila, painted by Ficheto's contemporary Krâstyu Zahariev. Outside, look out for a small but delicate relief of the Archangels Michael and Gabriel over the yoked south portal. Ficheto's church is tacked on to two older sixteenth-century structures which lie to the rear, the chapels of Sveti Teodosii and Sveto Rozhdestvo Bogorodichno (Birth of the Virgin). Both contain valuable frescos from the period, but are closed for long-term restoration.

The monastery lies just off the main Veliko Târnovo–Stara Zagora road, about 5km south of the village of Kilifarevo. The access road to the monastery is badly signed – look out for the truck stop used by TIR drivers just opposite. Some of the six daily Veliko Târnovo–Kilifarevo **buses** serve isolated villages south of Kilifarevo, and may take you near the monastery; otherwise, you'll have to walk from Kilifarevo village, saving yourself a dull and potentially hazardous trudge along the main road by turning left into the village of Natsovtsi after 3km, and following the river upstream to the monastery.

The monasteries of Plakovo and Kâpinovo

Seven kilometres to the east of Kilifarevo, in a wooded valley near the commune of Plakovo, lies another monastery, whose superior, Father Sergius, was involved in "Velcho's plot" (see p.217) and tortured to death by the Turks after its discovery. A plaque on the stone fountain in the courtyard of **Plakovo Monastery** commemorates him and his fellow conspirators. Some of the Târnovo–Kilifarevo buses continue on to Plakovo; check in Kilifarevo which ones.

Tracks continue 2km beyond Plakovo Monastery to the more impressive **Kâpinovo Monastery**, where the timber verandahs of the monks' cells overlook a courtyard shaded by vines. Sofronii Vrachanski was head monk here before being elevated to the bishopric of Vratsa in 1794, putting the monastery at the forefront of the revival of Bulgarian language and scholarship. The monastery church contains an unmissable *Day of Judgement* painted by Razgrad master Yovan Popovich in 1845, with lurid scenes of the dead emerging from their graves.

Elena

Like nearby Kotel and Koprivshtitsa, the nineteenth-century National Revival crafts town of **ELENA**, 40km southeast of Târnovo and served by five daily buses, lay far enough away from the centres of Ottoman power for Bulgarian crafts and culture to flourish. The Turks used the town's population to guard the local mountain passes, giving them a measure of autonomy in return, so painters and woodcarvers of nineteenth-century Elena were able to decorate the churches of the surrounding countryside, and patriotic local merchants could finance the restoration of nearby monasteries like Kâpinovo. Although Elena has not been renovated to the same extent as other National Revival towns, the core of nineteenth-century structures grouped around the hilltop church make a visit here more than worthwhile.

Beyond Elena, roads (but no public transport) head east through lonely highland villages towards the wooded **Kotel Pass**, on the far side of which lie the historic settlements of Kotel and Zheravna (see Chapter Four).

The Town

Heading downhill from the bus station then turning left into the main street, the first building of interest you come across is the **House-museum of Ilarion Makariopolski** (Mon–Fri 9am–noon & 2–5pm), located in a walled garden off to the right. Born Stoyan Mihailov in 1812, and later elevated to the Bulgarian bishopric of Constantinople (a post which brought him the honourific title *Makariopolski*), Ilarion was the leader of the Bulgarian church's battle against Greek control, who eventually persuaded the sultan to sanction an autonomous Bulgarian exarchate in 1870. The house is a lovely timber structure from the late eighteenth century, with vast verandahs overlooking the river on the first floor, where family and guests would sleep on warm summer nights. Chunky local carpets and a child's *lyulka* (hammock-like bed hung from the ceiling) provide a sense of period domesticity.

Beyond lies a bland town square, behind which the cobbled ul. Stoyan Mihailovski leads uphill to the **National Revival complex** (daily 9am–noon & 2–5pm), grouped around the mid-nineteenth-century church of Sveta Bogoroditsa. However the real star of the complex is the much smaller **Church of Sveti Nikola** slightly downhill, a sixteenth-century structure rebuilt in 1804 after being burned by marauding *Kârdzhali*. Blindingly colourful icons and frescos crowd a barrel-vaulted space; unremarkable in themselves perhaps, but together creating an overall impression of optimistic, ebullient spirituality. More devotional paintings are on display in the nearby **old school** (*Daskalolivnitsa*), including an 1873 *Last Judgement* displaying the hellish tortures beloved of Bulgarian artists of the period. At the bottom of the hill lies **Kâmburov han**, a former inn now taken up with displays of local trades and crafts. Characteristic of Elena are the fluffy *guberi* (fleecy rugs) in bright reds and greens, often featuring a tree-like central sumbol topped by a star. In the basement, loom vast wine vats and a *korab* – a long wooden trough in which the grapes were trodden.

Practicalities

One **ticket** covers all Elena's museums and can be bought at any of the sites ($1.75). Tourism in the town is in its infancy, and **accommodation** is limited to the modern but dowdy *Hotel Elena* on the main square (☎06151/3732, fax 3632; ③), which has simple ensuite doubles or two-person apartments with TV and fridge; or the nearby *turisticheska spalnya Dr Momchilov* at Stoyan Mihailovski 7 (☎06151/2517 or 4191), a traditional-style house offering rickety beds in spartan dorms ($3 per person), and one cosy two-person apartment (③). For **eating and drinking**, try any of the cafés around the main square, or the *Lovna Sreshta* **restaurant** just above, with the usual range of grills and traditional dishes.

Dryanovo and Dryanovski Monastery

Thirty kilometres southwest of Târnovo on the main road to Gabrovo, the drab town of **DRYANOVO** is only really of note for its proximity to Dryanovski Monastery, another 4km south. The town's only sights are down to local boy Nikolai Fichev, popularly known as **Kolyo Ficheto** (1800–1881), who is honoured with his own **museum** (Mon–Fri 8am–noon & 1–5pm), occupying a modern pavilion in the town centre. The most versatile of nineteenth-century Bulgaria's builders, he was responsible for town houses in Târnovo, bridges at Lovech and Byala, and numerous churches. Famous for the *Fichevska kobilitsa* (Fichev yoke), the wavy line which characterizes the roof-lines and pediments on all his best works, he often put double-headed eagles and lions on the eastern facade of his buildings, to symbolize the direction from which Bulgaria's liberation – in the shape of Russian power – was expected to come. The museum contains superb scale models of all Ficheto's key works, including the **church of Sveti Nikola**, the original of which (currently closed for restoration) lies 200m away on the road to Gabrovo.

Dryanovo's train and bus **stations** are both a couple of blocks east of the main thoroughfare, ul. Shipka, although most buses on the Târnovo–Dryanovo–Gabrovo route only stop on the main street.

Dryanovski Monastery

Set in a gorge beneath high crags, **Dryanovski Monastery** was chosen as the place from which to launch a local uprising in May 1876, while the fires of rebellion were still smouldering elsewhere after the suppression of the April Rising. Under the leadership of Bacho Kiro and the monk Hariton, several hundred rebels defended the monastery for almost a week against 10,000 Turkish troops rushed from Shumen, whose commander Pasha Faslâ offered to spare Kiro if he publicly repented – and hanged him when he refused.

The monastery was pretty much destroyed in 1876 and rebuilt with public donations soon after the Liberation. A fine ensemble of timbered buildings was the result, although once again it's the restful ambience rather than any single architectural feature that makes the place worthwhile. A small **museum**, (Mon–Fri 8.30am–4.45pm, Sat–Sun 9.30am–4.45pm) just off the monastery courtyard, displays old photographs of Bacho Kiro and company, as well as an ossuary containing rebel skulls. The museum basement concentrates on stone-age pottery and arrowheads discovered in the **Bacho Kiro cave** (April–Oct daily 8am–6pm; Nov–March Fri, Sat & Sun 9am–4pm; $1), 500m beyond the monastery at the end of an asphalt path. A small part of the cave interior is floodlit, and there are some interesting curtain-like stalagtite formations to admire, but nothing that justifies a special trip.

You can **walk** from Dryanovo to the monastery in about 45 minutes, or take one of the regular Dryanovo–Gabrovo **buses** which stop beside the monastery access road (marked by a big monument to the heroes of the April Rising), from where the monastery lies 1500m downhill. You can also get to the monastery by **train**, alighting at the first stop beyond Dryanovo, the Bacho Kiro halt, and walking the remaining 100m downhill (note that only *pâtnicheski* trains stop at the halt, which amounts to little more than a shed in the middle of the forest and is very easy to miss). You can stay at the monastery itself, where one modern **accommodation** block is run as a rest home by Dryanovo town council (☎0676/2314; ③), or in the *Momini Skali Hotel* (April–Dec only; ☎0676/2471 or 4471; ③) opposite the monastery gate, which has simple ensuite rooms with small balconies overlooking the burbling river, and roomier apartments ($40).

Tryavna

The old crafts centre of **TRYAVNA** may be a byword for icon painting and woodcarving and feature no fewer than 140 listed buildings, but it happily lacks the feel of a museum-town. Most of its visitors are Bulgarians rather than foreigners, and you're more likely to encounter art students sketching than bus parties jostling for a photo opportunity. For carless travellers, trains from Târnovo or regular buses from Gabrovo provide the best means of **getting there** (travelling by train from Gabrovo entails a change at Tsareva Livada, which makes it quicker to go by bus).

The town's narrow streets are evocative of the nineteenth century: although Tryavna was founded by refugees from Târnovo four hundred years ago, the oldest buildings all post-date the establishment of an official Guild of Master-builders and Woodcarvers in 1804. Often carved with birds and flowers, the wooden houses in the **old quarter** have an asymmetrical structure that disguises the essential similarity of their interiors. Traditionally, the large room containing the hooded *kamina* (hearth) was the centre of domestic life and led directly to the *chardak* or covered terrace; guests were received in a separate room and household goods stored in the ground-floor *odaya*.

Arrival, information and accommodation

Tryavna is pretty easy to find your way around: turn right out of either the **train** or **bus station**, both north of the centre, and by walking straight on you'll pass most of the town's sights along the way.

Tryavna's **tourist office**, just off the main square at Angel Kânchev 12 (Mon–Fri 8.30am–5pm; ☎0677/2247), sells maps, rents out bikes and organizes accommodation in **private rooms** (②–③) and local **hotels**. Of the latter, the three-star *Tryavna*, Angel Kânchev 46 (☎0677/2598, fax 2527; ④), is the biggest and most central, although its standard ensuite rooms don't have as much character as those at the cosy family-run *Tigâra*, just uphill at Gorov 7A (☎0677/2469; ③), also with ensuite rooms and breakfast. More comfortable than either but slightly further out is the *Brâshlyan*, ul. Panorama 6 (☎0677/3119 or 3019; ④), a mock National-Revival building on a hillside west of the centre, which also offers bungalows (③) in nearby woods.

The north end of town

Most of the northern end of town is modern, although the **birthplace of Angel Kânchev** at ul. Angel Kânchev 39 (Tues–Sat: summer 9am–1pm & 2–6pm; winter 8am–noon & 1–5pm) is a prime example of the nineteenth-century Tryavna housebuilder's art. Most of it was the work of Kânchev's father, Kâncho Angelov Popnikolov, his skilled handiwork revealed in details such as the wooden panels and fitted cupboards lining many of the rooms. Born in 1850, Kânchev's patriotism led him to join Belgrade's Artillery School at the age of seventeen, and later spurn a lucrative job offer to work for Bulgaria's liberation. Sent to assist Levski in constructing the revolutionary underground, Kânchev had completed two clandestine "tours" by 1872, when he was caught boarding a steamer at Ruse without a passport. Fearful of betraying secrets under torture, he shot himself, crying "Long live Bulgaria!" – in Levski's words, "the most honourable death for justice that should be considered sweetest for every proud Bulgarian of today".

BULGARIAN HOUSE-BUILDING RITUALS

There were a number of unusual **customs and rituals surrounding house building** in Bulgaria. It was considered unlucky to build a house near an empty well, an old watermill or a graveyard, and when doubts arose about a prospective site a bowl of water would be left there for bad omens (impurities or clouding) to appear overnight. Before the foundations were laid an animal was slaughtered on the site of the hearth or threshold, and the outlines of the walls were marked by dripping blood as an additional magical precaution. When the house was complete, blessings were shouted and the owners presented the builders with gifts before moving in themselves, preferably on a Monday, Thursday or Sunday at the time of a new moon. By custom, the eldest man would pour water over the threshold and scatter coins and wheat around the hearth in the hope of a future life "as smooth as water", prosperity and full barns. Once he had kindled the first fire with embers from the old family hearth, the woman of the family completed the occupation by breaking a loaf over the flames and hanging up a copper vessel.

Around the main square

Before long ul. Angel Kânchev hits **pl. Kapetan Dyado Nikola**, a set-piece square which retains most of its nineteenth-century character. Dominating the scene is the **clock tower**, a solid stone pillar topped by a half-timbered octagonal structure that supports a dainty wooden bell tower. The **Church of Archangel Michael** (daily 7am–noon & 3–6pm) stands to one side, a low-lying edifice sheltering under the shallow overhang of its slate roof, from which a slender minaret-like tower emerges. Inside, the iconostasis is wonderfully rich and dark, with twelve intricate tableaux surrounding the crucifix and a carved pulpit wound around one of the columns. At the rear of the church, originally founded by the *bolyari* Petâr and Asen to commemorate their successful twelfth-century rebellion against Byzantium, memorial photographs of the recently deceased are stuck into candelabras, part of the Orthodox forty-day mourning rite which Bulgarians also observe by putting up posters in the streets.

Immediately next door is the **Shkoloto** or old school (daily: summer 9am–6pm; winter 8am–noon & 1–5pm), its heavy wooden doors leading to a cobbled courtyard surrounded by a timber gallery draped with ivy. A downstairs gallery showcases the work of Tsvetan Dobrev, a local contemporary architect who presented the town with his watercolours – mostly documenting his travels in East European cities such as Berlin, Warsaw and Wroclav. On the first floor another gallery devotes itself to sentimental images of Bulgarian womanhood by modern Veliko Târnovo painter Nikola Kazakov, as well as several other collections, including an exhibition of the timepieces imported by wealthy Tryavna families of the last century.

Between the school and the church, an alley leads to **Raikova kâshta** at Prof. Raikov 1 (Tues–Sat: summer 9am–1pm & 2–6pm; winter 8am–noon & 1–5pm). Originally the home of scientist Pencho Raikov, the "father of Bulgarian chemistry", the house features exhibits on the domestic life of Tryavna's late nineteenth-century middle class, displaying the mass-produced furniture and crockery that had begun to penetrate Bulgaria from the West.

Along Ulitsa Slaveykov

A bridge leads from the square to the cobbled **ul. Slaveykov**, possibly the best-preserved National Revival-period street in all Bulgaria. Unusually for a Tryavna building, the **Daskalov House** at no. 27 (Wed–Sun: summer 8am–noon & 1.30–6pm; winter 8am–noon & 1–5pm) has a symmetrical plan with two wings joined by a curved verandah. The rooms inside are brightly carpeted, with arched windows and inbuilt *minder*, and also contain superb panelled ceilings – sun motifs made from walnut wood, with fretted rays inlaid within a frame decorated with floral and bird shapes. The two ceilings in the first-floor bedrooms are the result of an art contest arranged by the merchant Daskalov in 1808, pitting a master woodcarver against his apprentice. The apprentice, who produced the ceiling known as the "Burgas sun", was reckoned by Daskalov to be the winner. The ground floor holds a small museum of woodcarving, displaying the products of the State Woodcarving School, established in Tryavna in the 1920s to ensure the craft's survival.

Further along ul. Slaveykov are a couple more exhibitions of works donated by local artists: the **Totyu Gâbenski Picture Gallery** at no. 45, and the **Ivan Kolev Exhibition House** at no. 47 (both Mon–Fri 9am–noon & 1–5pm). The personal effects of the influential writer and teacher Petko Slaveykov (who taught the young Kânchev) and his son, the poet Pencho Slaveykov, are displayed in the **Slaveykov Museum** at no. 50 (Wed–Sun summer 8am–noon & 1.30–6pm; winter 8am–noon & 1–5pm) – Petko's residence for 26 years and Pencho's birthplace. Petko Slaveykov began a distinguished career in patriotism by editing Bulgarian newspapers in Constantinople, his texts fulminating against enemies of the people such as the Greek clergy and the native *chorbadzhii*. In the War of Liberation, he guided Russian troops over the Simitli Pass in Pirin Macedonia. Settling down to life as a teacher in Tryavna he presided over a precocious brood; quite apart from the poet Pencho, Petko's children included a future minister of education, a minister of justice, and a general in the Bulgarian army. As usual, captions are in Bulgarian only, but the house itself is worth seeing: the rooms are quite comfortable, but features such as the low table in the kitchen, and the simple, functional *minder* in the living room, point to a lifestyle rather more ascetic than that enjoyed by rich merchants like Daskalov.

By heading west from ul. Slaveykov, across the rail line and up ul. Breza, you'll reach a stairway which climbs to a church-like edifice housing the **Museum of Icon-painting and Woodcarving** (Tues–Sun 9am–5pm). Inside are numerous sumptuous products of the nineteenth-century **Trevnenska shkola** or "Tryavna School" – a guild with a distinctive style of cutting the wood back until acanthus leaves, birds and other favourite motifs were rendered in openwork like lace covering the surface of the iconostasis.

Eating and drinking

There are numerous small **restaurants, cafés** and **bars** along pl. Kapitan Dyado Nikola and along ul. Angel Kânchev. The *Balabanovata kâshta*, at Slaveykov 33, and *Staroto Shkolo*, behind the old school, are worth trying for good Bulgarian food in folksy surroundings, while the *Maestorât*, just off the main square at Kaleto 7, is an excellent traditional restaurant, regarded by locals as Tryavna's best.

Bozhentsi

Lying roughly between Gabrovo and Tryavna, **BOZHENTSI**'s cluster of two-storey houses with stone roofs and wooden verandahs gives some idea of the museum-village Tryavna could so easily have become. According to legend, Bozhentsi was founded by survivors of the fall of Târnovo, led by the noblewoman Bozhena and her nine sons. During the second half of the nineteenth century, Bozhentsi grew prosperous through the enterprise of its smiths, potters and weavers, and local merchants who traded as far afield as Hungary and Russia.

There are well over a hundred listed buildings in the village, but the main highlights are the **Kâshtata na Doncho Popa**, the early nineteenth-century home of a wool merchant; the **Baba Kostadinitsa House**, a much more humble dwelling which showcases the frugal lifestyle of the rural majority; and the various **workshops** used by village artisans (all daily: summer 8am–7pm; winter 8am–5pm).

Practicalities

Bozhentsi is an easy **day-trip** from Veliko Târnovo or Gabrovo. Privately owned minibuses run from Gabrovo's bus station during the summer, but timings are unpredictable. More regular are the Gabrovo–Tryavna buses that call at the *Torbalbuzh* stop about 2km downhill from Bozhentsi. If you're driving, you can approach Bozhentsi from the Dryanovo–Gabrovo road by turning south in the village of Kmetovtsi.

The **rooms** in Bozhentsi's old houses (③) fill up quickly, so it's wise to book in advance through the tourist office in Gabrovo (see below); alternatively, there's the *Parlopanovata Kâshta* (☎066910/229; ③), a 20-bed **pension** with ensuite rooms and a good **restaurant**. Five kilometres north of Bozhentsi in Kmetovtsi, the *Fenerite Hotel* (☎067193/367; ③) a restored nineteenth-century inn with galleried courtyard, offers ensuite rooms with satellite TV, and has a restaurant serving traditional Bulgarian fare.

Gabrovo and around

Long known for producing leatherwork and textiles that earned the town the sobriquet of the "Manchester of Bulgaria", **GABROVO** is the focal point for trips to Bozhentsi, or south to the ethnographic complex at **Etâra** and the nearby **Sokolski Monastery**. The town itself doesn't have a great range of things to do or places to stay, but it's a charmingly laid-back provincial place, and its efficient municipal tourist office is a good place to pick up information on the surrounding region. To the Bulgarians, Gabrovo is primarily known as the home of the **Dom na Humora i Satirata**, the House of Humour and Satire, opened on April Fool's Day 1974 in recognition of the position traditionally occupied by the town in Bulgarian humour. People in every country tell jokes about the supposed miserliness of a particular community, and in Bulgaria the butt of the gags has always been Gabrovo. A **Festival of Humour and Satire** takes place in May either every two or three years, depending on funds (contact the tourist office for details), comprising masked carnivals, folk music, animated cartoons, prizegiving and the ritual "cutting off the Gabrovnian cat's tail" (see box below).

The Town
Standing at the northern end of Gabrovo's thin, straggling town centre, the **Dom na Humora i Satirata** (Tues–Sun 9am–1pm & 2–6pm) will probably be your first port of call if arriving at the nearby bus or train stations. Inside is a massive collection of cartoons, humorous writings and photos, carnival masks and costumes drawn from scores of countries across the world. Exhibits are changed regularly,

---

TYPICAL GABROVO JOKES

The tight-fisted nature of the citizens of Gabrovo has long been a subject of mirth. According to such **jokes**, *gabrovtsi* invented the one-stotinka coin, gliding, short skirts, narrow trousers, and matchboxes with only one side for striking; they stop their clocks at night and carry their shoes to reduce wear and tear; let a cat down the chimney rather than hire a sweep; and dock the tails of these luckless creatures so they can shut the door a fraction sooner, conserving warmth. One *gabrovets* says to another, "Whenever I see you I immediately think of Stoyan". "Why?" "Because he owes me 60 leva, too." Another thinks, "Hmm, Pencho has been put on a strict diet . . . we can invite him to dinner". Two *gabrovtsi* have a wager on who can give least when the collection plate comes around; the first donates one stotinka, whereupon the other crosses himself piously and tells the sexton, "That was for both of us". And so on . . .

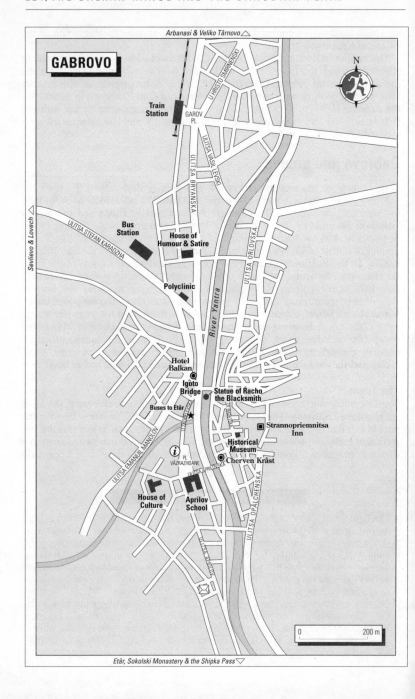

Arbanasi & Veliko Târnovo △

GABROVO

N

Train Station

GAROV PL

U.HRISTO SMIRNENSKI

ULITSA VASIL LEVSKI

ULITSA BRYANSKA

Sevlievo & Lovech △

ULITSA STEFAN KARADZHA

Bus Station

House of Humour & Satire

ULITSA ORLOVSKA

Polyclinic

River Yantra

Hotel Balkan

Igoto Bridge

Statue of Racho the Blacksmith

Buses to Etâr

Strannopriemnitsa Inn

ULITSA EMANUIL MANOLOV

(i)

PL VÂZRAZHDANE

Historical Museum

Cherven Krâst

ULITSA APRILOVSKA

House of Culture

Aprilov School

ULITSA OPALCHENSKA

ULI.KONIUV

0   200 m

Etâr, Sokolski Monastery & the Shipka Pass ▽

but cartoons involving ironic observations of human nature or worthy allusions to global political concerns – such as pollution – seem to be the order of the day.

As usual, the older quarters are the nicest parts of town, covering both banks of the River Yantra beyond the **Igoto Bridge**. A statue of Gabrovo's legendary sixteenth-century founder, Racho the Blacksmith, stands on a rock in midstream. The main downtown area is on the east bank grouped around ul. Radetska, although specific sights really boil down to the **Historical Museum** at ul. Genev 3 (Mon–Fri 9am–noon & 1.30–5.30pm). An absorbing archeological section displays the results of a dig carried out at nearby Gradishte in the 1920s, the site of both Thracian and medieval Bulgarian fortresses. Finds include functional Thracian pottery and a suit of medieval chain-mail armour.

Crossing the river by ul. Aprilovska brings you to the **Aprilov School**, founded by Odessa-based merchant Vasil Aprilov in 1835 and one of the first schools in the country to offer a secular education in the Bulgarian language. It used to house a museum of education, but was recently returned to its original function; plans are afoot to open part of the building to visitors in the future – ask the tourist office for details.

Practicalities

Gabrovo's tourist office, on pl. Vâzrazhdane, near the Aprilov school (Mon–Fri 8.30am–5pm; ☎ & fax 066/28483 or 29161), offers a whole range of advice on surrounding attractions and can book **rooms** and **pensions** in Bozhentsi, Etâra and other nearby villages – including Uzana, a small mountain resort 23km southwest. Accommodation in downtown Gabrovo boils down to the high-rise, three-star *Hotel Balkan*, ul. Emanil Manolov 14 (☎066/23474, fax 24619; ⑤), which has prim doubles with bath and cable TV, with breakfast included.

For **eating**, the *Stranopriemnitsa Inn*, on ul. Opâlchenska, serves traditional Bulgarian food in an attractive galleried courtyard, and sometimes features live folk music. The *Cherven krâst*, located behind a big white building with a red cross on it just over the bridge from the Aprilov School, has excellent food and service and a big summer garden complete with children's play area. Numerous pavement **cafés** bring Gabrovo to life during the summer months, especially in the tree-shaded environs of pl. Vâzrazhdane.

The Etâra complex

Since Racho the blacksmith set up his smithy beneath a large hornbeam (*gabâr*, hence the town's name), Gabrovo has been a **crafts** centre, gaining fresh impetus at the beginning of the nineteenth century when waterwheels were introduced from Transylvania. By 1870 the town had more than eight hundred workshops powered by water, making iron and wooden implements, clothing, wool and blankets sold beyond the frontiers of the Ottoman empire; today it produces textiles in quantities exceeded only by Sliven, and half the leather goods in Bulgaria. To preserve traditional skills, Gabrovo has established the museum-village of **ETÂRA** (daily: summer 8am–5.30pm; winter 8am–5pm; $3), 9km from town on the banks of the Sivek, a tributary of the Yantra.

Strung out along the valley bottom, the Etâr complex falls into three sections. Traditionally, crafts were inseparable from the *charshiya*, and a **reconstructed bazaar** of the type once common in Bulgarian towns forms the heart of the complex. Throughout much of the day artisans are at work here, hammering bells, throwing pots, sewing braid and sheepskin jackets and so on.

Even if your interest in crafts is minimal it's difficult not to admire the interiors of the old houses, which achieve great beauty through the skilful use of simple materials. Besides dwellings and workshops, the bazaar includes several places for grabbing a quick drink, and a bakery whence folks emerge clutching fresh *simitli* (glazed buns made of chick-pea flour), a Gabrovo speciality. Another section contains a **watermill** (*karadzheyka*) and **hydro-powered workshops** for cutting timber, fulling cloth, and making braid (*gaitan*), wine flagons (*bâklitsi*) and *gavanki* (round wooden boxes).

Etâr is an easy **day-trip** from Gabrovo – or even Veliko Târnovo. Take trolleybus #32 from central Gabrovo to the end of the line (the *Instrument* engineering works), where you change to bus #7. Should you want to **stay** longer, the *Hotel Korona*, Grigorovska 27 (☎066/43804; ④), is a friendly pension signposted off the main road just north of the complex, which also has space outside for **campers**. The larger *Strannopriemnitsa* hotel, near the entrance to the complex (☎066/42419 or 42026, fax 42023; ④), has ensuite doubles and includes breakfast. The *Strannopriemnitsa* **café/restaurant** is a touristy *mehana* at the other end of the complex, or there's a traditional-style café, in the middle of the complex, which serves Turkish coffee accompanied by white plum jam (*byalo sladko*).

Sokolski Monastery

An hour or so's walk southwest of Etâra (there's no public transport, although with a car you can drive there along the track that heads east from the complex), **Sokolski Monastery** perches on a crag above the village of Voditsi. During Ottoman times the monks offered succour to Bulgarian outlaws, putting up the *cheta*, or band, of local *haidut* Dyado Nikola in the 1850s, and providing the local rebels with an assembly point during the Rising of 1876. Nowadays it's a discreet, little-visited place, with rose bushes and privet shrubs laid out in a courtyard dominated by an octagonal stone fountain. The small church, dating from the monastery's foundation in 1832, lies at the bottom of a flight of steps to the right. The dome is supported by an unusually large drum of bright blue – also the dominant colour of the frescos inside (primitively painted by the original pastor, Pop Pavel, and his son Nikolai), which include a vivid *Dormition of the Virgin* above the main entrance.

Shumen

Lying midway between Veliko Târnovo and Varna, **SHUMEN** is the obvious base from which to explore the historical sites at Madara, Pliska and Preslav. The city itself has a fair share of ancient monuments and memorial houses, not least a spectacular **medieval fortress** that once guarded the road to Preslav. As Turkish Shumla, Shumen was one of the four heavily garrisoned citadel towns that formed the defensive quadrilateral protecting the northern frontier. Although the imposing Ottoman fortifications are no more, the thriving market town that existed within is still present in the shape of one surviving mosque, the **Tombul Dzhamiya**. Modern Shumen presents a good example of what state socialism brought to urban Bulgaria. Well-built, prestigious civic buildings line a showcase main boulevard, just seconds away from neglected, potholed side streets, where single-storey shacks rub shoulders with greying high rises.

Arrival and accommodation

Buses #1, #10 or #12 will take you from the **train** and **bus stations** in the east of the city, as far as the eastern end of the main drag, bul. Slavyanski. A ten-minute walk along this largely traffic-free street brings you, via pl. Osvobozhdenie which merges into pl. Bâlgariya, to pl. Oborishte, and the Madara-Intertours bureau (Mon–Fri 8.30am–6pm, Sat 9am–3pm), where you can get **private rooms** in centrally located apartments for about $8 per person, though these disappear fast in summer. Cheapest of the city's **hotels** is the *Orbita*, 2km west of the centre in the leafy Kyoshkove park (☎054/52398 or 58144; ③), with run-down but clean ensuite doubles and triples. Moving up in price, the disappointing high-rise *Madara*, pl. Bâlgariya 1 (☎054/57595; ⑤), has ensuite rooms, cable TV and breakfast, but is only slightly cheaper than the far superior *Hotel Shumen*, pl. Oborishte 1 (☎054/59141, fax 58009; ⑤), which offers a similar deal but with much higher levels of cleanliness and service, and an indoor pool and sauna. Local travel agency Aristour, Todor Ikonomov 5 (☎054/52509 or 59031, email *aristour@mbox.digsys.bg*), organizes trips to all the nearby historical sites, wine-tasting in Preslav, walking tours in the Shumen hills, and riding courses at the horse-breeding centre (see p.230).

The Town

Walking down **bul. Slavyanski**, with its blend of stately Central European and smart modern architecture, you'll see a modern red-brick building housing the **History Museum** (Mon–Fri 9am–5pm, Sat–Sun open by arrangement; ☎054/55487), and the pick of the region's archeological finds. A Bronze Age site at nearby Smyadovo yielded bone-carved idols of the fourth millennium BC, while the Thracian period is represented by silverware from two local burial sites, at Vârbitsa and Branichevo, and a reconstructed war chariot. Also here are many of the best medieval artefacts from Pliska and Preslav, the cultural achievements of the latter revealed in the abstract floral patterns adorning the capitals of stone pillars, and in the delicacy of a tenth-century gold necklace.

Along Tsar Osvoboditel

A hundred metres beyond the History Museum, ul. Layosh Koshut leads down to **Tsar Osvoboditel**, and what's left of Shumen's old quarter. Standing at no. 35 is the rarely open **Kossuth House-Museum** (officially Tues–Sat 9am–noon & 2–6pm, Sun 9am–noon), a warren of panelled rooms linked by creaking corridors, where the Magyar revolutionary Lajos Kossuth stayed for three months after fleeing Hungary in 1849, before the Turks interned him in Asia Minor. Ten minutes' walk to the east, at Enyu Markovski 42, is the **memorial house of Panaiot Volov** (officially Tues–Sun 8am–noon & 2–5pm), one of the leaders of the April Uprising who drowned while swimming across the River Yantra to escape Ottoman troops. The house preserves the humble shoemaker's quarters where Volov grew up, while an adjoining pavilion holds the obligatory words-and-pictures display detailing his revolutionary career.

A ten-minute walk west along Tsar Osvoboditel, the **House-Museum of Pancho Vladigerov** (Mon–Fri 9am–5pm), honours the Shumen-born pianist (1899–1978) who made his reputation as Bulgaria's leading composer with stirring patriotic works such as the opera *Tsar Kaloyan* (1936), and the little-performed tribute to the socialist takeover *September 9* (1949). The staff will play a tape of his

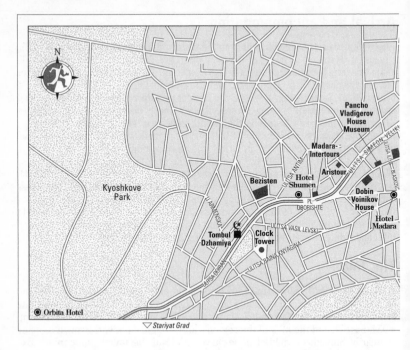

music as you examine the memorabilia on show, which include Vladigerov's raffish beret and suit, and some fine Chiprovtsi carpets. Further on at no. 87, the **Dobri Voinikov House** (Mon–Fri 9am–noon & 2–6pm) remembers the nineteenth-century author of the plays *Princess Raina* and *Civilisation Misunderstood*. There's little to see here save for a series of model stage sets, and photographs of early performers.

The Bezisten and the Tombul Dzhamiya

West of Tsar Osvoboditel the broad asphalt sweep of ul. Rakovski – subsequently ul. Doiran – cuts past two impressive relics of Ottoman Shumla. Sheltering beneath chestnut trees is the **Bezisten**, or covered market, built to cater for the needs of Dubrovnik merchants who established a trading post here in the sixteenth century. Constructed from heavy blocks of stone retrieved from the ruins of Pliska and Preslav, it's currently in need of renovation. Dominating the skyline to the west are the proud minaret and bulbous domes of Shumen's main sight, the **Tombul Dzhamiya** (daily 9am–noon & 2–5pm; $1). Built in 1744 on the initiative of Sherif Halil Pasha, a native of Shumen who rose to become deputy grand vizier in Constantinople, the complex aimed to meet both the spiritual and educational needs of the community. A *mektep*, or "primary school", occupied the east wing, while a *medrese* (Koranic school) and *kitaphane* (library) surrounded the cloistered courtyard to the east. This is dominated by the *shadirvan* or "fountain", an eclectic structure mixing Moorish arches with classical, Corinthian pillars. Inside the prayer hall, carpets cover the floor

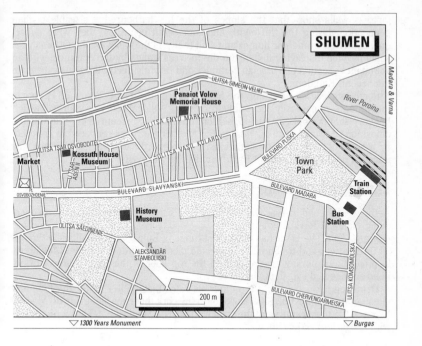

beneath a dome decorated with floral swirls and paintings of the great mosques of the Middle East. Upstairs, a balustraded balcony provides segregated accommodation for female members of the congregation. The mosque was converted into a museum during the Communist era, but has now reverted to its original role, for the benefit of Shumen's considerable Islamic community. The city is once more an important religious centre for the Muslims of northeast Bulgaria, with believers from far and wide annually descending on the Tombul Dzhamiya to celebrate *Kurban Bayram*, one of the major festivals of the Islamic calendar (see Basics, p.47).

The medieval fortress and the 1300 Years monument

Shumen is surrounded to the south and west by the **Shumensko plato national park**, a tableland of dense woodland. The most accessible part of it is the **Kyoshkove Park** at the western end of town (a 15-min walk beyond the Tombul Dzhamiya, or buses #1, #10 or #11 from the train station), where tracks lead up into the hills past the sites of World War II partisan bunkers.

Immediately above Kyoshkove (and reached by walking 2km uphill from the *Shumensko pivo* brewery at the entrance to the park) is the **Stariyat grad** or "medieval fortress" (daily: summer 7am–7pm; winter 8am–5pm; $1), whose monumental, part-reconstructed walls are reminiscent of Tsarevets in Veliko Târnovo. The Thracians were the first to fortify the site, followed swiftly by Romans, Byzantines and Bulgars, but it was during the Second Kingdom that the fortress developed its current monumental shape. Ruins of medieval houses outside the fortress walls show that the slopes of the hill harboured a sizeable civilian popu-lation during the thirteenth and fourteenth centuries; they were subsequently driven from their homes and sent to live in the valley by the Ottomans. A small pavilion displaying finds from the fortress stands by the entrance, with an abundant collection of Thracian ceramics and brightly decorated tableware from the Second Kingdom.

Roadways lead east through the forest towards the **1300 Years of Bulgaria** monument – more easily accessible from a processional concrete stairway which begins just above bul. Slavyanski, behind the History Museum. A bewildering juxtaposition of Khans, monks, *haiduti* and Mother Heroines rendered in concrete by a sculptor with Cubist inclinations, this extraordinary hilltop structure was unveiled on the nation-state's 1300th anniversary in 1981.

Eating and drinking

At the western end of Tsar Osvoboditel, there's a row of three **restaurants** occupying National Revival-style houses – *Popsheitanovata kâshta*, *Stariyat Bor* and *Osmarsa Izba*. The latter has the widest range of Bulgarian specialities, although all three offer good traditional cuisine and plenty of outdoor seating. Moving up in price, the panoramic restaurant on the top floor of the *Hotel Shumen* offers good service and excellent views.

Drinking takes place in the numerous cafés that shelter under the lime and chestnut trees along bul. Slavyanski, or in the park that runs alongside ul. Madara between the town centre and the train station. The *Shumen* hotel has a **nightclub** with discos and variety shows.

Around Shumen

The northeastern fringe of the Balkan Range is distinguished by three archeological sites, all easily accessible from Shumen. The ruins of **Pliska** are less interesting to look at than read about, but enough remains of **Preslav** to justify a visit if your taste inclines towards hunky masonry. As for the so-called **Madara Horseman**, the rockscapes all around make up for the eroded face of this unique and ancient bas-relief.

Fifteen kilometres northeast of the city, just beyond the village of Tsarev Brod, is the **Kabiyuk horse-breeding and riding centre**, founded by Ottoman governor Midhat Pasha in the 1860s to provide mounts for the Turkish army. Arabian, English thoroughbred and East Bulgarian (a cross-breed of domestic stock and both the above) horses are raised here, although if you want to view the stables and go on a short ride you'll have to arrange a visit through either Aristour (see p.227) or the *Hotel Shumen*.

Preslav

Founded by Khan Omurtag in 821, **VELIKI PRESLAV** acquired the prefix "Great" after it was made the capital of the First Kingdom, during the reign of Tsar Simeon (893–927) – although it began to eclipse the original capital, Pliska, at an earlier date. According to contemporary accounts, tenth-century Preslav was the most populous town in the Balkans, with extensive suburbs surrounding a walled inner town containing "large buildings of stone on both sides, decorated with wood". It also held a palace, a royal School of Translators, the Patriarchate and other "churches ornamented with stones, wood and paintings, marble and copper, silver and gold". Preslav's downfall began when it was captured by the Kievian prince, Svetoslav, causing the Byzantine Empire to respond by razing the town in 972, and although it later revived (the palace was occupied as late as the Asenid dynasty), Preslav never regained its former size and was subsequently surpassed by Târnovo. Eventually it was burned down by the Turks, who used the remains to construct their own buildings, including the Tombul Mosque in Shumen.

The Archeological Museum and the ruins

The **ruins of Preslav** are scattered over farmland to the south of the modern town. A signposted lane leads from Preslav's main square towards the site, which lies beyond the town park. Beyond the crest of a hill lurks a modern concrete bunker holding an **Archeological Museum** (daily: summer 9am–6pm; winter 9am–5pm), where plans and diagrams can be consulted before venturing out into the relic-strewn fields. The museum displays numerous examples of the ceramic tiles used to decorate the medieval town's buildings showing the swirling abstract patterns which characterized decorative arts during the First Kingdom. Prime pieces from Tsar Simeon's golden age include a valuable ceramic icon showing the bearded visage of St Theodore, and a golden necklace adorned with enamel plaques showing birds and floral designs.

Approaching the ruins from here you'll pass through the northern gate, first sign of the cyclopean **walls** which envelop the medieval city – reconstructed with modern breeze-blocks to something approximating their original height. To the west are the bare ruins of the **palace** where the tsar held court. Further west, the traces of a vast monastery complex lie raked across the hillside. Beyond the south portal on a hillock is the **Zlatna tsârkva** or "Golden Church", so called because the dome was said to be covered in gold leaf. Several arches, the bulk of its walls and twelve marble columns (some truncated) still remain, although you'll have to study the model in the archeological museum to appreciate its true grandeur.

Practicalities

Modern Preslav offers few inducements to spend longer than an afternoon, and regular bus services to Shumen happily mean that you don't need to. If you do get stuck, **accommodation** boils down to the standard two-star *Hotel Preslav* in the town square (☎0538/2508; ③), which is also the best place for **food and drink**.

The Madara Horseman

The most popular destination for excursions from Shumen is the village of **MADARA**, 10km to the east and served by frequent trains, where a range of cliffs show signs of human occupation dating back to the third century BC. The main road through the village leads up to Madara's most famous sight, the mysterious bas-relief known as the **Madara Horseman** (daily: summer 8am–7pm; winter 8am–5pm; $1.25). Carved into the rockface at a height of 95m, this is so eroded that details are only apparent by the light of a setting sun, but the carving is said to represent a horseman whose mount is trampling a lion with the assistance of a greyhound, while he holds the reins in one hand and a wine cup in the other.

THE PROTOBULGARIANS

Known to English-speaking historians as the **Bulgars**, and to the Bulgarians themselves as the *prabâlgari* or "**Protobulgarians**", the rulers who founded Pliska and Preslav, and who may have been responsible for commissioning the Madara Horseman, started out as Turkic nomads from the Eurasian steppe.

Originating in western Siberia, the Bulgars coalesced into three warlike tribes in the sixth century: the **Onogurs**, **Utigurs** and **Kutrigurs**. The latter were the first to descend on the Balkans, reaching the walls of Constantinople twice in the mid-500s AD before being pushed back by the armies of Emperor Justinian. For the next half century Byzantine diplomacy concentrated on keeping these three tribes at each other's throats, in an attempt to preserve the balance of power in the territories north and east of the Black Sea. Eventually, however, they began to cultivate the friendship of the Onogurs, who by this time ruled a swathe of steppe north of the Caucasus mountains – subsequently called **Old Great Bulgaria** by Byzantine chroniclers. The alliance was cemented in 619 with the baptism of the Onogur Khan Organa, together with his son Kubrat in Constantinople.

Nevertheless, things went awry when the Onogurs were driven from their lands by another Turkic tribe, the rapidly expanding Khazars. Kubrat's successor **Asparuh** led his people southwest to the Danube expecting hospitality from his Byzantine ally Emperor Constantine IV, who instead sent an army to prevent Asparuh from crossing the river. The Byzantine attempt failed, and by 681 Constantine was forced to recognize the existence of an **independent Bulgar state** ruled by Asparuh from his capital at Pliska.

The new kingdom was initially limited to the flatlands either side of the Danube, stretching from the Balkan Range in the south to the Carpathians in the north. However, the Bulgars began to expand beyond the Balkan Mountains and put down urban roots under Asparuh's successor, Khan **Tervel**, and the centuries-old culture of these Turkic-speaking steppe dwellers began to die out. An aristocratic elite ruling over a population of Thracians and Slavs (the latter, valued by the Bulgars as frontier settlers, became increasingly numerous), the Bulgars gradually lost their separate ethnic identity and became assimilated by their subjects. The process was confirmed by Tsar Boris's conversion to Christianity in 865 and the suppression of paganism that followed – many of the old Bulgar families, unwilling to break with the old faith, were simply wiped out.

Little is known about the beliefs and customs of the Bulgars. Byzantine chroniclers have provided us with a few scraps, telling us that they worshipped their ancestors, practised shamanism, sacrificed steppe wolves in times of trouble, and probably indulged in polygamy. Some Turkic-speaking Bulgars still exist, the so-called **Volga Bulgars** who survive in isolated pockets south of Kazan in Russia. They converted to Islam in the tenth century and enjoyed independent statehood until the thirteenth, when they were submerged beneath the advance of their fellow Muslims, the Tatars.

Various Greek inscriptions next to the carving provide ambiguous clues to its age: the oldest inscription, recording a debt owed by the Byzantine Emperor Justinian II to Khan Tervel, suggests that the Bulgars carved the horseman in the eighth century. However, some scholars believe it is far older than that. The figure, they argue, represents the nameless rider-god of the Thracians, and is of Thracian or Getae origin, the inscriptions merely evidence that it was later appropriated by Bulgarian rulers.

Around the Horseman

To the right of the relief, a path winds off towards the **Large Cave** (*Golyamata Peshtera*) beneath a giant overhang of rock. Beyond is a smaller cave, where flints, bones and pottery were discovered; while just above, you'll catch sight of the remnants of a fourteenth-century **rock monastery**, its crudely dug cells pitting the cliff face.

Not far away you'll find the source of the River Madara where Thracian period plaques and statues honouring the rider-god, Dionysus, Cybele and three water nymphs have been discovered; and remains of an early medieval **grain store** where enormous clay vessels were sunk into the ground to keep cool.

Early Bulgarian remains and the fortress

Most of the early Bulgarian finds are located to the left of the Horseman, where the barest outlines of eighth- and ninth-century churches and monastic complexes lie scattered at the foot of the cliff. Many of the churches were adapted from or built on top of earlier pagan structures – a sign that Madara was an important religious site from the earliest times. Paganism remained ingrained among the Bulgars long after Christianity became the official religion in 865, and although the precise nature of their beliefs remains shrouded in mystery, the discovery of the eighth-century **Old Bulgarian baths** points to the existence of water-based purification rituals.

A rough-hewn pathway works its way up the cliff face to the plateau above. Roughly 500m to the west lies a **ruined fortress** of fifth-century origin, although the remaining walls mostly date from the Second Kingdom. There are also two **tumuli** left by the Getae – who buried their dead in ceramic urns – 300m north of the fortress, but the real attraction is the **view from the plateau**. Roman ruins are scattered about at the foot of the massif, while the surrounding plain is cut off by the Balkans to the south and the Ludogorie hills to the north – where sharp eyes might be able to discern the ruins of Pliska (see below) amid the acacia groves.

Practicalities

It's pretty easy to see the site and return to Shumen in the space of a morning or afternoon, though there is rudimentary **accommodation** near the Horseman should you wish to stay. The *turisticheska spalnya* near the entrance to the Horseman complex is usually occupied by groups, but there should be bungalows for rent in the *Madara* campsite (May–Sept; ②), about 200m to the south. There's nowhere to **eat or drink** in Madara village save for the café and restaurant just outside the complex.

Pliska

Ten kilometres north of Madara, the ruins of **Pliska** are less well preserved than those in Preslav, but in its heyday during the First Bulgarian Kingdom (681–1018), Pliska was a sophisticated and important settlement, covering 23 square kilometres and protected by citadels on neighbouring hills. It was sacked by the Byzantine Emperor Nicephorus in the early 800s, but retained its status as the capital, and it was to Pliska that the disciples of Cyril and Methodius, Naum and Kliment, came in 885 to help spread the Slav alphabet. Pliska's days of glory were over by 900, after Tsar Boris I had come out of monastic retirement to stamp out a return to paganism sponsored by his son Vladimir – one of Boris' acts was to move the capital to Preslav in order to make a fresh start.

The ruins

The ruins (entered by a minor road which runs 3km eastwards from the village of Pliska) still occupy a considerable area, although most of the buildings have been reduced to low walls. As you can see from the reconstruction in the **museum** (daily 9am–5pm), Pliska originally had three lines of defences: a ditch, behind which was the outer town (with workshops and basic dwellings), a stone wall with four gates, surrounding the inner town, and finally a brick rampart around the so-called Little Palace. What remains of the former Royal Basilica (a few reconstructed walls and column fragments) lies a further 2km beyond the entrance to the ruins at the end of an asphalt track, an impressive but poignant sight stranded among corn and maize fields.

Practicalities

Unless you have a car, **getting to Pliska** from Shumen is time-consuming, and only really worth the effort if you have a strong enthusiasm for First-Kingdom remains. Regular buses travel from Shumen to the industrial town of Novi Pazar, 8km southeast of Pliska, from where four daily buses make their way to the village itself; from here it's still a 30–40 minute walk. There's nowhere to **eat or drink** in Pliska, so bring your own supplies.

The Ludogorie

North of Shumen, the low-lying **Ludogorie hills** separate the Balkan Range proper from the flatter terrain of the Danubian Plain and the Dobrudzha beyond. The region harbours a large Muslim population of Turkish and Tatar descent, although it's a predominantly rural area with few worthwhile urban centres. The main town, **Razgrad**, is of limited appeal, although quieter **Isperih**, further northeast, is the gateway to one of Bulgaria's most compelling off-the-beaten-track destinations, **Sveshtari** – famous for its **Thracian tombs** and the Muslim holy site of **Demir Baba Tekke**.

Razgrad is served by plenty of intercity **buses** from Shumen and Ruse, as well as Ruse–Varna **trains**. Isperih is more tricky to get to, with less frequent buses departing from Ruse, Razgrad, Shumen, Dobrich and Varna. It also lies on a branch line which leaves the Ruse–Varna rail route at Samuil. Services along this route are sparse, but there is at least one through train from Sofia to Isperih a day.

Razgrad

Situated midway between Shumen and Ruse, **RAZGRAD** sprawls messily around the banks of the Beli Lom. Since the Liberation in March 1878, the narrow lanes and artisans' stalls that characterized the town during Ottoman times have gradually succumbed to modern urban planning. Apart from a restored *Varosh* quarter north of the river, where a succession of whitewashed National Revival-style houses provide homes for various artists' and writers' unions, Razgrad remains fairly lacklustre, largely because its one great attraction – the seventeenth-century **Ibrahim Pasha mosque** – looks set to remain closed for renovation for many years to come. An imposing block of heavy masonry topped by a graceful dome and tapering minaret, it's a lasting tribute to the skills of its Albanian and Bulgarian builders – and to the Turkish governor Ibrahim, who commissioned it in 1614.

Razgrad's only other sight, lying east of town on the Shumen road, just beyond a large pharmaceutical factory, is the remains of **Abritus**, the fortified Roman town that guarded the road between the Danube and Odessos (now Varna) on the Black Sea. Part of the walls that once surrounded the town (originally standing 12–15m high) can be seen by the roadside, while near the site of the town's eastern gate stand the foundations of the so-called **Peristyle building**, a 23-room complex grouped around a columned courtyard, once used by shopkeepers and artisans. A small, irregularly open **museum** at the site displays pottery fragments and grave inscriptions, plus a collection of bronze tablets depicting the variety of deities – ranging from familiar Graeco-Roman figures such as Zeus and Hera to more exotic rider-gods and mother goddesses from the Middle East – worshipped by the cosmopolitan bunch of troops used to garrison the area. The museum's most valuable treasure – a gold drinking cup in the form of a winged horse – is worth too much to be displayed here, and remains locked in a strong-room.

Practicalities

Razgrad's **train station** lies 5km north of town: although all trains are met by buses into the centre, it's not the most convenient point of arrival. The **bus terminal** is on the eastern edge of town, within walking distance of both the Ibrahim Pasha mosque (about 15min west) and the ruins of Abritus (about 15min east). Razgrad has a couple of acceptable **hotels** if you get stranded: the modern two-star *Central*, ul. Beli Lom 40 (☎084/24225; ③), and the towering, ziggurat-like, three-star *Razgrad* on ul. Laipzig, above the main square (☎084/20751; ④). Plenty of **cafés** cluster around Razgrad's main square, but there's little to do after dark. Both the *Central* and *Razgrad* hotels have good **restaurants**; the latter also boasts a *disco*.

Isperih

Forty kilometres northeast of Razgrad, **ISPERIH** is a sleepy market town lying between gently undulating pastures. It has a pleasant town centre splashed with the usual pavement cafés, and an animated Friday-morning **market** which attracts villagers from all over the Ludogorie. However the town's importance to travellers is really as a jumping-off point for the historical sites around Sveshtari, 7km northwest (see below).

Head downhill from Isperih's **bus station** to reach the town centre, where you turn left then bear left past a small park to find the administrative building of the **town museum** (*gradski muzei*; Mon–Fri 9am–5pm; ☎0835/3500), where staff can book **private rooms** in nearby village houses (②). Most of these are in Malâk Porovets (served by infrequent buses), a rustic spot 8km northwest of town on the Ruse road. There's currently no regular display in the museum, although videos about the Sveshtari site are often shown in an affiliated building, and museum staff can advise you on the current state of affairs at the tomb (see below).

Sveshtari

The village of **SVESHTARI** is home to what is arguably the finest **Thracian tomb** yet discovered in Bulgaria. Found in 1982 in a mound of earth known locally as

Ginina Mogila, it is the largest of a group of 26 *mogili* (tumuli) lying about 2km beyond the western fringes of the village. The tomb is encased in a protective shell and is scheduled to be ready for visitors by summer 1999, though it's vital that you ring or call in at the museum in Isperih (see previous page) to check that it's open before making a special trip. The museum may even be able to provide you with a guide if you arrange things in advance. Two more tombs (for the time being known simply as **tomb #12** and **tomb #13**) have been discovered near Ginina Mogila, and a much larger mound (named **Omurtag** after the Bulgar Khan who was once thought to be buried here) is currently being excavated nearer to the village. Funds permitting, all of them will be opened to the public over the coming years.

Archeologists believe that as many as five necropolises were in use around Sveshtari, comprising more than 100 *mogili* in total. Some theories suggest that the configuration of the tombs either mirrors the constellations, or symbolizes the holy trinity of the Thracians, while ruins elsewhere in the vicinity have led many scholars to identify the Sveshtari neighbourhood with Dausdava, capital of the **Getae** (see below). Cracks in some of the tombs suggest that an earthquake hit the area sometime in the first century BC, possibly causing the abandonment of the city.

Getting to Sveshtari

It's too far to walk from Isperih to Sveshtari, so you'll have to either arrive by car (on leaving Isperih, follow signs to Tutrakan), or take your chances with the

---

THE GETAE

It's hoped that examination of the remains found in the Sveshtari tomb will shed new light on the civilization of **the Getae**, an important Thracian tribe who inhabited both banks of the lower Danube in classical times. Ancient authors disagreed on whether to classify the Getae as Thracians or as Dacians (who lived north of the Danube in what is now Romania), although it's safe to assume that all these groups came from the same ethnic roots.

Thucydides alluded to their skill as horsemen, and they proved more than a handful for successive invaders – from Darius' Persians in the fifth century BC to the Romans in the first. In 335 BC **Alexander the Great** chased the Getae north of the Danube and destroyed some of their settlements, but failed to subdue them. His successor, Lysimachus, was captured by Getae ruler Dromichaetes in 292 BC, only to be lectured on the value of peace and sent home. However, their period of greatest glory came in the first century BC, when King **Burebista** presided over a short-lived Danubian empire which exercised control of the whole western seaboard of the Black Sea – from what is now the Ukraine in the north to Apollonia (present-day Sozopol) in the south.

Evidence suggests that the Getae honoured·a trinity of deities comprising mother earth, sun and moon, and, indeed, items of treasure recovered from the Sveshtari tombs were often found positioned in symbolic groups of three. A sceptical Herodotus relates how the Getae worshipped a certain **Zalmoxis** (thought to be a north-Balkan version of Orpheus, see p.314), who hid himself in an underground chamber for several years before re-emerging, much to the surprise of his contemporaries, to proclaim that he had died and come back to life again. Herodotus also tells of how the Getae sent "messengers" to Zalmoxis by choosing a suitable courier, then tossing him onto a forest of upturned spear-points.

infrequent Isperih–Sveshtari buses. To **get to the tomb**, take a left turn out of Isperih, past the Omurtag Mogila on your left, and into a grove of trees – Ginina Mogila is over to the right. Continuing along the road brings you **to Demir Baba Tekke** (see below) after about 2km, then rejoins the Isperih–Ruse road just north of the village of Malâk Porovets.

The Thracian Tomb

The most striking aspect of the **Thracian tomb** is its small size – visiting it is a low-key, almost intimate, experience, and how much you get out of it will depend on your enthusiam for ancient remains. The tomb itself, thought to have been built in the late fourth or early third century BC, is entered via a corridor lined with well-cut slabs leading to three chambers united by a semi-cylindrical vault: the central one is occupied by two stone couches on which lie a Thracian king and his wife (five horses were buried in the antechamber to ensure them a mount in the afterlife). The ten stone caryatids and Doric semi-columns that line the tomb's walls show obvious Hellenistic influences, though their sturdy upraised arms and full skirts suggest aspects of the Thracian Mother Goddess. At one end of the chamber, you can discern faint traces of a wall painting depicting a mounted horseman – presumably the deceased – being offered a wreath by a female deity, another possible representation of the Mother Goddess.

Demir Baba Tekke

Beyond the tomb, the road continues through a wooded valley, past an (unsigned) parking and picnic area, where a path leads downhill towards **Demir Baba Tekke**, a sixteenth-century Muslim shrine built on the grave of semi-legendary holy man Demir Baba. The *tekke* itself is a simple structure, a seven-sided tomb-cum-temple topped by a dome, but is accorded an other-worldly grandeur by the limestone cliffs which rear up immediately behind. A neolithic settlement has been discovered by the **Pette Pârsta spring** at the foot of the cliffs, and the site was subsequently home to a Thracian sanctuary, so the place's importance as a spiritual centre predates the arrival of Islam in the fourteenth century.

The *tekke* is sacred to the **Aliani** (see box), a Muslim group whose rituals are open to the influence of the neighbouring Christian community, and both Aliani and Christian families visit the *tekke* on key holy days to picnic and dance to impromptu folk music. The most important dates are March 22 (*Chetirideset mâchenitsi* or Forty Martyrs' Day), May 6 (*Gergyovden* or St George's Day to the Christians; the spring festival of *Hidrelez* to the Aliani), August 2 (*Ilinden* or St Elijah's Day, adopted by the Aliani as a midsummer festival), and a hastily improvised autumnal date to mark the end of the harvest. People come here all year round to perform certain **rituals**: strips of cloth are tied to trees or the bars of the *tekke* windows to ward off evil, and items of female underwear are passed through a hole in a stone in the courtyard to ensure fertility. Inside the *tekke*, pilgrims lay presents (socks, handkerchiefs or small pieces of embroidery) on the tomb of Demir Baba, chant prayers and light candles.

Behind the *tekke*, a path leads up the side of the cliff to emerge on the plateau above, where the scant remains of Thracian stone circles and walled sanctuaries present further evidence that the territory around Sveshtari was of great religious significance to the ancient people.

THE ALIANI

Many of the Muslim communities of the Ludogorie are **Aliani** (known to the Turks as *Kizilbazi* or "red-heads"), a heterodox group who, like the Shiites, claim spiritual descent from Ali, the Prophet's son-in-law. Originally from Iran and Azerbaijan, the Aliani were distrusted by orthodox Sunni sultans, who had them forcibly resettled in the Balkans in order to serve the Ottoman empire as frontier troops. Mixing traditional Islamic beliefs with elements of sufi mysticism and pre–Islamic Iranian sun worship, the Aliani exerted a strong influence over dervish orders, notably the powerful Bektashi, a connection which helped protect the Aliani from outright persecution. The Aliani of northeastern Bulgaria shunned links with Sunni Muslims, but entered into a symbiotic relationship with their Christian Bulgarian neighbours, sharing customs, superstitions and rites. In the early fifteenth century, an Aliani leader from Silistra, Sheikh Bedredin Simavi, began preaching the equality of all the sultan's subjects, and led a combined Muslim-Christian revolt against the Ottoman feudal order. It took four years before the rebellion was stamped out.

Today the Aliani live in Sveshtari and several other villages between Isperih and the Danube. They don't have mosques in the traditional sense, preferring to meet for prayers in the house of a leading community member, and Aliani women don't wear the veil. They also have relaxed attitudes towards alcohol, and *rakiya* plays an important part in the rites conducted at Demir Baba.

Practicalities

The nearest **accommodation** to the tombs is in private rooms in the village of Malâk Porovets (booked through the museum in Isperih, see p.235), or at the modern *Ahinora* chálet, just up the road from the picnic area near Demir Baba (☎0835/4750), with dorm beds for $4 a night and a few doubles (②). There are a couple of **food stores** (*hranitelni stoki*) in Sveshtari village, but the only **restaurant** in the vicinity is the *Ahinora*'s ground-floor *mehana*.

travel details

Trains

Berkovitsa to: Boichinovtsi (7 daily; 1hr); Montana (7 daily; 45min).

Boichinovtsi to: Berkovitsa (7 daily; 1hr); Dimovo (6 daily; 2hr); Vidin (6 daily; 2hr 30min).

Dimovo to: Boichinovtsi (6 daily; 2hr).

Dobrich to: Kardam (3 daily; 1hr 15min); Varna (6 daily; 2hr).

Gabrovo to: Tsareva Livada (7 daily; 30min).

Gorna Oryahovitsa to: Pleven (14 daily; 1hr 30min); Ruse (6 daily; 2hr 30min); Shumen (5 daily; 1hr 30min); Sofia (6 daily; 4hr 30min); Târgovishte (5 daily; 2hr); Veliko Târnovo (6 daily; 30min).

Isperih to: Samuil (3 daily; 45min); Silistra (3 daily; 1hr 30min); Sofia (1 daily; 12hr).

Kardam to: Dobrich (3 daily; 1hr 15min).

Levski to: Lovech (6 daily; 1hr 30min); Pleven (7 daily; 30min).

Lovech to: Levski (6 daily; 1hr 30min).

Montana to: Berkovitsa (7 daily; 45min).

Pleven to: Gorna Oryahovitsa (14 daily; 1hr 30min); Levski (7 daily; 30min); Ruse (4 daily; 3hr 30min); Shumen (2 daily; 4hr 30min); Sofia (hourly; 3hr).

Ruse to: Gorna Oryahovitsa (6 daily; 2hr 30min); Ivanovo (3 daily; 30min); Pleven (4 daily; 3hr 30min); Samuil (5 daily; 1hr 30min); Sofia (5 daily; 7hr); Varna (3 daily; 3hr 30min).

Samuil to: Isperih (3 daily; 45min); Ruse (5 daily; 1hr 30min); Silistra (3 daily; 2hr 30min).

Shumen to: Gorna Oryahovitsa (5 daily; 1hr 30min); Pleven (2 daily; 4hr 30min).

Silistra to: Isperih (3 daily; 1hr 30min); Samuil (3 daily; 2hr 30min).

Sofia to: Cherepish (6 daily; 2hr); Eliseina (6 daily; 1hr 30min); Gorna Oryahovitsa (6 daily; 4hr 30min); Lakatnik (7 daily; 1hr); Lyutibrod (6 daily; 2hr); Pleven (hourly; 3hr); Ruse (5 daily; 7hr); Vidin (5 daily; 5–7hr); Zverino (8 daily; 1hr 30min).

Târgovishte to: Gorna Oryahovitsa (5 daily; 2hr).

Tryavna to: Tsareva Livada (5 daily; 15min).

Tsareva Livada to: Gabrovo (7 daily; 30min); Stara Zagora (2 daily; 2hr); Tryavna (5 daily; 15min); Tulovo (2 daily; 1hr 30min); Veliko Târnovo (8 daily; 50min).

Veliko Târnovo to: Dryanovo (6 daily; 30min); Gorna Oryahovitsa (6 daily; 30min); Tsareva Livada (8 daily; 50min).

Vidin to: Boichinovtsi (6 daily; 2hr 30min); Sofia (5 daily; 5–7hr).

Buses

Belogradchik to: Lom (4 daily; 1hr 30min); Montana (1 daily; 1hr 15min); Oreshets (4 daily; 30min); Rabisha (2 daily; 30min); Vidin (2 daily; 1hr 45min).

Berkovitsa to: Montana (3 daily; 30min); Vârshets (3 daily; 40min); Vratsa (1 daily; 1hr 30min).

Botevgrad to: Pleven (1 daily; 2hr); Sofia (hourly; 1hr).

Dobrich to: Albena (hourly; 40min); Balchik (6 daily; 1hr); Durankulak (3 daily; 2hr 30min); Isperih (2 daily; 2hr); Kavarna (7 daily; 1hr 30min); Ruse (2 daily; 4hr); Shumen (2 daily; 2hr 15min); Varna (hourly; 50min).

Elena to: Veliko Târnovo (4 daily; 1hr 15min).

Gabrovo to: Apriltsi (Sat & Sun only; 1 daily; 1hr 30min); Dryanovo (5 daily; 50min); Kazanlâk (6 daily; 2hr); Pleven (3 daily; 2hr); Sofia (2 daily; 4hr); Stara Zagora (5 daily; 2hr 40min); Troyan (1 daily; 2hr); Tryavna (2 daily; 50min); Veliko Târnovo (4 daily; 1hr).

Isperih to: Dobrich (2 daily; 2hr); Gorna Oryahovitsa (1 daily; 2hr 30min); Ruse (2 daily; 2hr); Shumen (2 daily; 1hr 30min).

Kozlodui to: Berkovitsa (1 daily; 3hr); Lom (2 daily; 1hr); Lovech (2 daily; 3hr); Pleven (2 daily; 3hr); Sofia (1 daily; 3hr); Vratsa (8 daily; 2hr 30min).

Lom to: Belogradchik (4 daily; 1hr 30min); Kozlodui (2 daily; 1hr); Oryahovo (2 daily; 2hr); Vidin (8 daily; 45min).

Lovech to: Kazanlâk (1 daily, 3hr); Pleven (hourly; 40min); Sevlievo (5 daily; 30min); Sofia (4 daily; 3hr); Teteven (4 daily; 2hr); Troyan (hourly; 1hr); Veliko Târnovo (1 daily; 2hr); Vratsa (1 daily; 2hr 30min).

Montana to: Belogradchik (1 daily; 1hr 15min); Berkovitsa (3 daily; 30min); Chiprovtsi (5 daily; 50min); Kopilovtsi (4 daily; 1hr 15min); Lopushanski Monastery (4 daily; 45min); Vârshets (1 daily; 1hr); Vidin (1 daily; 3hr); Vratsa (4 daily; 40min).

Novi Pazar to: Shumen (7 daily; 1hr).

Oryahovo to: Lom (2 daily; 2hr); Sofia (2 daily; 3hr); Vratsa (10 daily; 2hr 15min).

Pleven to: Belene (4 daily; 1hr 30min); Lovech (hourly; 40min); Oryahovo (2 daily; 2hr 30min); Nikopol (6 daily; 1hr 15min); Svishtov (3 daily; 1hr 15min); Teteven (2 daily; 2hr 30min); Vidin (1 daily; 4hr); Vratsa (1 daily; 2hr 15min).

Rabisha to: Belogradchik (5 daily; 30min).

Ruse to: Byala (2 daily; 1hr); Dobrich (2 daily; 4hr); Isperih (2 daily; 2hr); Pleven (1 daily; 2hr 30min); Razgrad (4 daily; 1hr 15min); Shumen (2 daily; 2hr 15min); Silistra (7 daily; 2hr 45min); Sofia (6 daily; 5hr); Svishtov (1 daily; 2hr); Varna (1 daily; 3hr 45min).

Sevlievo to: Lovech (5 daily; 30min).

Shumen to: Burgas (3 daily; 3hr); Dobrich (2 daily; 2hr 15min); Isperih (2 daily; 1hr 30min); Novi Pazar (7 daily; 1hr); Preslav (hourly; 30min); Razgrad (5 daily; 1hr); Ruse (2 daily; 2hr 15min); Silistra (4 daily; 3hr); Sliven (2 daily; 3hr); Varna (4 daily; 2hr).

Silistra to: Dobrich (4 daily; 2hr 15min); Ruse (7 daily; 2hr 45min); Shumen (4 daily; 3hr); Varna (5 daily; 3hr 30min).

Sofia *Avtogara Poduyane* to: Botevgrad (hourly; 1hr); Etropole (6 daily; 1hr 30min); Gabrovo (2 daily; 4hr); Kozlodui (1 daily; 3hr); Lovech (5 daily; 3hr); Oryahovo (2 daily; 3hr); Pravets (10 daily; 1hr); Teteven (2 daily; 2hr); Troyan (3 daily; 3hr).

Svishtov to: Ruse (1 daily; 2hr); Veliko Târnovo (4 daily; 2hr 45min).

Teteven to: Lovech (4 daily; 2hr); Pleven (2 daily; 2hr 30min); Ribaritsa (4 daily; 30min); Sofia (2 daily; 2hr).

Troyan to: Apriltsi (4 daily; 1hr); Cherni Osâm (9 daily; 30min); Chiflik (5 daily; 45min); Lovech (hourly; 1hr); Shipkovo (5 daily; 45min); Sofia (3 daily; 3hr).

Tryavna to: Gabrovo (hourly; 50min); Lovech (hourly; 1hr).

Veliko Târnovo to: Elena (4 daily; 1hr 15min); Gabrovo (4 daily; 1hr); Kazanlâk (2 daily; 2hr 30min); Kilifarevo (6 daily; 50min); Lovech (4 daily; 2hr); Sevlievo (4 daily; 1hr); Sofia (1 daily; 4hr); Svishtov (4 daily; 2hr 45min).

Vidin to: Belogradchik (2 daily; 1hr 45min); Kula (hourly; 45min); Lom (8 daily; 45min); Montana (1 daily; 3hr); Pleven (1 daily; 4hr).

Vratsa to: Berkovitsa (1 daily; 1hr 30min); Etropole (2 daily; 1hr); Kozlodui (8 daily; 2hr 30min); Lovech (1 daily; 2hr 30min); Mezdra (every 40min; 20min); Montana (4 daily; 40min); Oryahovo (10 daily; 2hr 15min); Pleven (1 daily; 2hr 15min).

Flights

Veliko Târnovo (Gorna Oryahovitsa airport) to: Sofia (2 daily; 45min).

THE SREDNA GORA AND THE VALLEY OF THE ROSES

T he most direct route between Sofia and the Black Sea coast cuts straight across central Bulgaria, between the mountains of the Balkan Range to the north, and the **Sredna Gora** to the south. Lining the valleys of the latter are some of Bulgaria's most historic villages, renowned for their folkloric and revolutionary traditions – above all, **Koprivshtitsa**, the starting point of the ill-fated April Rising of 1876, and the site of some of Bulgaria's finest nineteenth-century architecture. Nearby are the museums and memorials of **Panagyurishte**, another centre of the Rising, and the ancient Roman spa town of **Hisar**. The eastern stretches of the Sredna Gora are gentler and less dramatic, but the city of **Stara Zagora**, site of one of Bulgaria's greatest archeological treasures, the 7000-year-old Neolithic dwellings, provides an excuse to break your eastward journey.

Between the Sredna Gora and Balkan ranges lies the **Valley of the Roses** (really two valleys: the upper reaches of the Stryama and the upper reaches of the Tundzha), named after the rose plantations to which the area owes its wealth.

CYRILLIC PLACE NAMES			
GRADETS	ГРАДЕЦ	PANAGYURISHTE	ПАНАГЮРИЩЕ
HISAR	ХИСАР	SHIPKA PASS	ШИПЧЕНСКИЯ
ICHERA	ИЧЕРА		ПРОХОД
KALOFER	КАЛОФЕР	SINITE KAMÂNI	СИНИТЕ
KARANDILA	КАРАНДИЛА		КАМЬНИ
KARLOVO	КАРЛОВО	SLIVEN	СЛИВЕН
KATUNISHTE	КАТУНИЩЕ	SOPOT	СОПОТ
KAZANLÂK	КАЗАНЛЬК	SREDNOGORIE	СРЕДНОГОРИЕ
KLISURA	КЛИСУРА	STARA ZAGORA	СТАРА ЗАГОРА
KOPRIVSHTITSA	КОПРИВЩИЦА	STRELCHA	СТРЕЛЧА
KOTEL	КОТЕЛ	YAMBOL	ЯМБОЛ
MEDVEN	МЕДВЕН	ZHERAVNA	ЖЕРАВНА
NOVA ZAGORA	НОВА ЗАГОРА	ZLATITSA	ЗЛАТИЦА

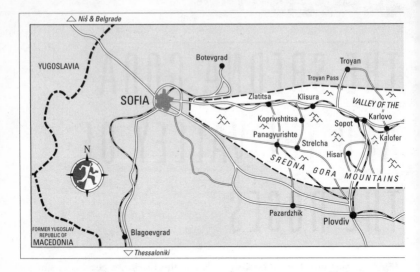

Though the valley is at its best when the rose crop is harvested in May, interest is provided throughout the year by the historic settlements lining the valley floor. Those most deserving of attention are **Karlovo**, the birthplace of the freedom fighter Vasil Levski and the best preserved of the valley's market towns, and the region's most convenient touring base **Kazanlâk**. Known for the Rose Festival, a folkloric bash which attracts visitors in early June, Kazanlâk also plays host to a unique collection of Thracian tombs, earning this part of the valley the title of Bulgaria's "Valley of the Kings". To the north of Kazanlâk lies the **Shipka Pass**, amidst some of the highest peaks of the Balkan Range, the site of a crucial battle during the Russo-Turkish War of 1877–78.

Midway between the valley and the Black Sea, **Sliven** is the starting point for excursions to the highland craft towns of **Kotel**, a carpet-weaving centre, and **Zheravna**, with its unique nineteenth-century rural architecture. Strictly speaking, both these places belong to the Balkan Range, but are included in this chapter because they're more easily visited by those travelling the Sofia–Black Sea route.

THE SREDNA GORA

. . . So, proudly you may gaze
Unto the Sredna Gora, the forest's single queen,
And hear the ring of swords, and all this song can mean . . .
Pencho Slaveykov, The Song of the Blood

The **Sredna Gora** or "Central Highlands" stretch from the Pancharevo defile outside Sofia almost as far as Yambol on the Thracian plain. With its forests of oak and beech and numerous caves and hot springs, the region was inhabited by humans as early as the fifth millennium BC. The Thracians subsequently left a hoard of gold treasure at **Panagyurishte** (since moved to the National History

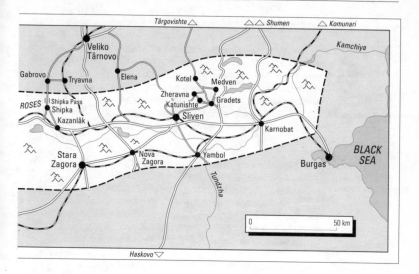

Museum in Sofia), and the Romans a crop of ruins at **Hisar**, but for Bulgarians, the Sredna Gora is best known as the "land of the April Rising", which started in **Koprivshtitsa**. For tourists, too, this town is the region's highlight, its peerless National Revival architecture and pastoral beauty making it a must-see.

Lying roughly midway between Sofia and Plovdiv, the Sredna Gora is a popular excursion from both towns. Without a car, Koprivshtitsa can only be reached on the main **train** line between Sofia and Burgas (a connecting bus meets services). Panagyurishte is served by buses from Sofia and trains from Plovdiv, while Hisar can be reached by bus from Karlovo in the Valley of the Roses, or by train from Plovdiv. However, **buses** running across the Sredna Gora range are few and far between, making travelling from Koprivshtitsa to Panagyurishte hugely inconvenient.

Koprivshtitsa

The small town of **KOPRIVSHTITSA** (pronounced "Kop*riv*shtitsa"), lying in the upper reaches of the Topolnitsa valley, is a lovely ensemble of half-timbered houses nestling amid wooded hills. It would be an oasis of pastoral calm were it not for the annual descent of summer visitors, drawn by the superb vernacular architecture and the desire to pay homage to a landmark in the nation's history. From the Place of the Scimitar Charge to the Street of the Counter Attack, there's hardly a part of town that isn't named after an episode or participant in the **April Rising of 1876**, when Bulgaria's yearnings for freedom from the Ottoman yoke finally boiled over (see p.246). It was Koprivshtitsa's role as a centre of commerce that provided the material basis for such an upsurge in national consciousness. Sheep and goat farming formed the backbone of the village's wealth, and the resulting wool (as well as byproducts, notably carpets and socks) was traded throughout the Levant. By the time of the Rising,

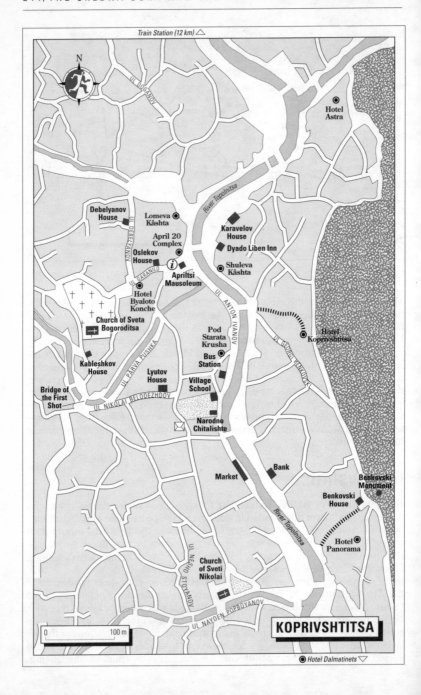

Train Station (12 km)

N

Hotel
Astra

River Topolnitsa

Debelyanov
House

Lomeva
Kâshta

Karavelov
House

April 20
Complex

Dyado Liben Inn

Oslekov
House

Shuleva
Kâshta

Apriltsi
Mausoleum

UL GARANILO

UL DEBELYANOV

UL ANTON IVANOV

Hotel
Byaloto
Konche

Church of Sveta
Bogoroditsa

Pod
Starata
Krusha

Hotel
Koprivshtitsa

UL PARVA PUSHKA

Bus
Station

UL GEORGI BENKOVSKI

Kableshkov
House

Lyutov
House

Village
School

Bridge of
the First
Shot

UL NIKOLAI BELODEZHDOV

Narodno
Chitalishte

Bank

Market

Benkovski
Monument

Benkovski
House

River Topolnitsa

Hotel
Panorama

UL NESHO STOYANOV

Church
of Sveti
Nikolai

KOPRIVSHTITSA

UL NAYDEN POPBOYANOV

0   100 m

Hotel Dalmatinets

Koprivshtitsa had a population of 12,000. After the Liberation, however, commercial life began to be centred on the lowland towns, and places like Koprivshtitsa ceased to develop – leaving it as a kind of fossil. Yet, despite its museum-town status, it remains a working agricultural community, with horse-drawn carts labouring through the narrow streets.

Koprivshtitsa also occupies an important place in the Bulgarian folk music calendar. The **Koprivshtitsa national music festival**, a huge gathering of musicians from all over the country, takes place on a hill outside the town every five years (the next one is due in August 2000). A smaller **regional festival** involving local folk groups is held annually (except when the big event takes place), usually on the weekend nearest to the Feast of the Assumption (*Sveta Bogoroditsa*), on August 15. Other traditional celebrations to look out for are **Iordanovden** (6 January), when the priest throws a wooden cross in the river and local lads dive in to retrieve it, and the feast of **Todorovden** (St Theodore's day, the first Saturday of Lent), which is celebrated with horse races on the meadow at the northern end of the village.

Arrival, information and accommodation

Train services stopping at the Koprivshtitsa halt are met by a bus that ferries you the 12km south to the town itself. The times of buses back to the train-halt are posted in the **bus station**, 200m south of the main square. There's a daily Sofia–Koprivshtitsa minibus from the bus park opposite the central station (currently leaving at 4pm), but bus connections with other towns are unreliable. There are usually several daily services from Srednogorie and one daily service from Panagyurishte, but don't stake your life on it. You can cash travellers' cheques at the **bank** opposite the market (Mon–Fri 8am–noon & 1.35–4.15pm).

Finding somewhere **to stay** in Koprivshtitsa is only likely to be difficult during the big five-yearly festival, when it's wise to reserve weeks ahead. At other times, **private rooms** (①–②) can be arranged by the **tourist information point** on the main square (opening times are unpredictable, so be prepared to ask around for rooms if it's closed). Many are in fine old houses, with friendly hosts who treat you to improvised music. Elswhere there are plenty of small **hotels** and pensions scattered throughout the village, most of which are welcoming, family-run affairs. Nearest the centre, a good bet is the *Byaloto Konche*, across the road from the Oslekov House (☎07184/2250; ③), with delightful low-ceilinged rooms in the National Revival style, and a communal *chardak* (porch) overlooking a grassy courtyard. Also very central, the *Shuleva Kâshta*, across the river from the main square (☎07184/2122; ③), has similarly atmospheric

THE APRIL RISING OF 1876

The **1870s** were troubled times in the Balkans, as a tired and corrupt **Ottoman Empire** tried to stem the tide of protest from subject nationalities longing for independence. In Bulgaria, the rise in education and literacy brought about by the National Revival had engendered an upsurge of national consciousness, and a generation of idealistic revolutionaries, such as Vasil Levski, Angel Kânchev, Lyuben Karavelov and Hristo Botev, succeeded in placing the idea of liberation in the forefront of Bulgarian minds.

Revolutionary strategy

In order to co-ordinate the struggle, various nationalist groups came together to form the Bucharest-based **Bulgarian Revolutionary Central Committee**, or **BRCK**. The network already established by Levski – who had travelled the country setting up revolutionary cells – was put at the BRCK's disposal. The death of Levski in 1873, and the failure of an uprising in Stara Zagora in 1875, persuaded many in the BRCK that the policy of fomenting armed insurrection had been a mistake. However several of the participants in the Stara Zagora uprising (future prime minister Stefan Stambolov among them) were determined to have another go. Encouraged by the Ottoman failure to put down a major revolt in Bosnia, and believing that Serbia and Russia were simply waiting for an excuse to declare war on Turkey, the veterans of Stara Zagora assumed control of the national movement and started planning another uprising.

Their **strategy** was based on the time-honoured guerrilla methods of the *haiduti*, Balkan outlaws who could survive for months in the mountains, harrying Turkish outposts and relying on the goodwill of the local populace for food and shelter. A series of *cheti*, or mobile armed groups, were formed to move through the countryside, avoiding heavily defended Ottoman positions, and gathering support where they could – eventually, it was hoped, snowballing into a popular revolt that would provoke foreign intervention. Bulgaria was divided into four regions (centred on Sliven, Vratsa, Plovdiv and Veliko Târnovo), each responsible for organizing its own military action. The organizers placed their emphasis on the mountain regions of Bulgaria, firstly because the ethnic makeup of the highlands was solidly Bulgarian, and secondly because they calculated (wrongly, as it turned out) that it would be difficult and time-consuming for the Ottoman authorities to send in reinforcements. The idea of the Rising caught the popular imagination, and preparations were impressive: village tailors secretly made uniforms for the insurgents, lead was melted down to make bullets, and rudimentary cannons were made from cherry trees .

The Rising begins

The Rising was scheduled for May 1, and on April 14 insurgent leaders were summoned to the Oborishte clearing, 25km southwest of Koprivshtitsa, to receive their final instructions. Unfortunately one of those present at the meeting, Nenko Terziiski, was a spy for the Ottoman authorities, who responded by sending a small unit to Koprivshtitsa to arrest local rebel leader **Todor Kableshkov**. Kableshkov

rooms in a suite of old buildings. Further afield in the northeastern quarter of the town, the *Astra*, Hadzhi Gencho 9 (☎07184/2364; ③), is a small family-run pension with comfortable rooms and shared facilities, while in the southeast, the *Panorama*, Georgi Benkovski 40 (☎07184/546747; ③), has attractive, modern had no choice but to launch the Rising ahead of schedule on April 20, capturing the Ottoman *Konak* and dispatching the famous **Bloody Letter**, written in the blood of the first dead Turk, informing the Panagyurishte leaders that fighting had already broken out.

A Bulgarian **provisional government** was declared in Panagyurishte, but the authorities reacted swiftly, and the Ottoman governor of Plovdiv dispatched irregular troops to suppress the Rising. These were made up of Pomaks, Bulgarian Muslims eager to settle private scores with their Christian neighbours, and *bashibazouks*, rapacious freebooters drawn from the Tatar and Circassian populations, only recently expelled from Russia and therefore hostile to Slavs in general. As the *bashibazouks* burned the neighbouring towns of Panagyurishte and Klisura, refugees flooded into Koprivshtitsa spreading panic, and the local *chorbadzhii* (rural middle class) attempted to disarm the insurgents. The rebels took to the hills, where rain played havoc with their homemade gunpowder, and eventually they were hunted down. Koprivshtitsa's *chorbadzhii* bribed the *bashibazouks* not to burn the village, which survived unscathed to be admired by subsequent generations as a symbol of heroism.

Elsewhere in Bulgaria, the premature launching of the Rising took most insurgents by surprise. The **Batak** area rose up on April 21, but was soon mercilessly crushed (see p.314). By the time the central Târnovo region began its action on April 28 it was already too late, and most of the leaders were arrested before any serious fighting took place. In a bizarre coda to the Rising, poet and revolutionary **Hristo Botev** (see p.258) collected emigrés living in Serbia and Romania, crossed the Danube in a hijacked Austrian steamboat on May 17, and tried to lend support to his (already defeated) countrymen by marching on Vratsa. They were wiped out on nearby Mount Okolchitsa.

The aftermath

Despite many individual acts of bravery the Rising failed to win mass support, largely because local civilians were too afraid of Turkish reprisals. The expected intervention of Serbia and Russia took too long to materialize: although the Serbs later fought a short war with Turkey in the summer of 1876 (in which many Bulgarian exiles participated), they were quickly routed. However, the savagery of **Ottoman reprisals** against civilians (see, p.314) in the aftermath of the Rising convinced the great powers of Europe that the Ottoman Empire could no longer be allowed a free hand to discipline its Balkan subjects. As news of the so-called "Bulgarian atrocities" spread, traditional allies like France and Britain lost the political will to shore up the Empire against its critics. This suited Russia, which was angling for the creation of a Bulgarian state to serve its own interests in the region.

Ordinary Russians were in any case outraged by the treatment of their fellow Slavs by the Ottomans, and pressed for war. The government of Sultan Abdulhamid spoke vaguely of introducing reforms, then drew back from real action, giving Russia the excuse it needed to attack. Tsar Aleksandâr II finally declared war on April 12, 1877, almost a year after the outbreak of the Rising. By the following January, the Ottomans were suing for peace, and Bulgarian independence was at last on the agenda.

---

ensuite rooms with lots of pine. Finally, the equally modern *Dalmatinets*, hidden away in the backstreets at the south end of town (☎07184/2904; ③), offers balconied rooms – some with ensuite facilities – and a cosy café-restaurant which serves breakfast and evening meals.

The Town

Koprivshtitsa straggles along either side of the River Topolnitsa, whose tributaries divide the town into five quarters (*mahala*) where stone bridges and the burble of water enhance the beauty of the **architecture**. More than 380 of the town's houses date from the National Revival era, the most elaborate from 1842 to 1870, when the symmetrical Plovdiv style took hold. Many have large wooden gates with separate doors for people and wagons; carved stone fountains and troughs adorn the cobbled lanes that wend between them. The total effect is both delicate and rugged, as red, blue and ochre-painted stucco counterpoints the natural tones of wood and stone.

The six house-museums open to the public can be visited in any order, but the most obvious starting point is from the **main square**, dominated by the stone **Apriltsi Mausoleum**, inscribed "Let us guard the national liberty for which the heroes of the rising of 1876 fell." A combined **ticket** valid for all the houses ($1) is available at the museum administration office on the main square, or at the Oslekov or Kableshkov houses.

The Oslekov House

One of the finest houses in Koprivshtitsa stands just uphill from the main square, on ul. Garanilo. The **Oslekov House** (Tues–Sun 8am–noon & 1.30–5.30pm) was built in 1856 for local tax collector and much-travelled entrepreneur, Nincho Oslekov. Its facade is upheld by pillars of cypress wood imported from Lebanon, and decorated with romanticized views of the cities visited by its owner, painted by the Samokov craftsman Kosta Zograf (brother of the icon-painter, Zahari Zograf). The upstairs rooms have lovely fretted wooden ceilings, especially in the Red Room, where one of the medallions on the walls shows the original, symmetrical plan of the house, never realized since Oslekov's neighbours refused to sell him the necessary land. You can imagine him brooding over the rebuff while reclining on the cushioned *minder*, taking solace from his pipes and hookah, in the room next door.

The Debelyanov House and the Church of Sveta Bogoroditsa

On a sidestreet leading north from ul. Garanilo stands the small **Debelyanov House** (Tues–Sun 8am–noon & 1.30–5.30pm), where the lyrical poet Dimcho Debelyanov was born in 1887. Painted royal blue with a white trim, its timbered upper floor contains a humdrum exposition of his tragically short career, with such personal items as his childhood cradle, and the suitcase of books that accompanied him to war. In the garden is a poignant statue of Dimcho's mother, vainly awaiting his return from the battlefields of Greece, where he was killed in 1916.

An identical statue broods over his **grave** in the local cemetery, at the top of ul. Garanilo, whose inscription is from one of his own poems: "Delaying in a gentle dream she becomes her own child." Also in the cemetery stands the **Church of Sveta Bogoroditsa**, built in 1817 on the site of an older church burnt down by the Turks, and partly sunken into the ground to comply with the Ottoman edict that no Christian building should be taller than the local mosque. The interior is rustic in its simplicity, aside from an elaborate iconostasis by Teteven craftsmen, containing several icons by Zahari Zograf.

The Kableshkov House

Leaving the churchyard by a gate on the far side and turning left, you'll come to the **Kableshkov House** (Tues–Sun 8am–noon & 1.30–5.30pm). Built by a local master-craftsman in 1845, its square plan and the combination of one curved and two square oriels on each side reflects the influence of the Plovdiv style. The ground floor preserves the simple living quarters of a reasonably prosperous *chorbadzhii* family, including a "women's work room" with a spinning wheel, and the room where Todor Kableshkov was born in 1854. Weapons used in the Rising are displayed on the top floor, whose circular vestibule has a wonderful ceiling with an abstract pattern based on the reflection of sunlight on rippling water. Kableshkov's decision to start the Rising ahead of schedule, after Turkish soldiers came to arrest him, was made at the "House of the Conspiracy" on a nearby street.

Kableshkov was later captured near Troyan, but managed to kill himself with a police revolver in Gabrovo, and is commemorated by a statue close to the **Bridge of the First Shot**, where the Rising began.

The Lyutov House and beyond

Cross the bridge and head up ul. Nikola Belodezhdov, and you'll come to the white **Lyutov House** (Mon–Thurs, Sat & Sun 8am–noon & 1.30–5.30pm), distinguished by its double staircase and yoke-shaped porch, with a lion signifying Bulgarian aspirations of freedom. Built by Plovdiv craftsmen in 1854, the house is famed for its wealth of murals: palaces, temples and travel scenes splashed across the walls and *alafranga*; wreaths, blossoms and nosegays in the Blue Room; and oval medallions adorning the ceilings. The basement houses an exhibition of *plâsti*, the locally made felt rugs which traditionally feature bold, sun-symbol designs.

Nearer the river stands a handsome pair of civic buildings, financed by local patriots. The former **Village School**, built in 1837, is now a conference and exhibition centre, while the nearby **Narodno chitalishte**, founded in 1869 as public reading rooms, played a big part in the National Revival, spreading literacy and nurturing a sense of national identity in towns and villages.

From Sredna to Byalo Kamâne

To see more of life in Koprivshtitsa, take a ramble through the Sredna (Middle) and Byalo Kamâne (White Rocks) quarters. Sredna withdraws from an outdoor **market** into a *kasbah*-like maze of reclusive houses and lanes where elders gossip and goats forage. With luck, you'll emerge at the **Church of Sveti Nikolai**, behind a high wall with a bell tower above the gateway. Despite the church's dedication, its iconostasis dwells on St Spiridion, whose life is told in ten medallions surrounding a figure of the saint. On the corner of the lane is a **fountain** donated by the Moravenovs, a leading family in the early eighteenth century.

Walk downstream and cross the river to reach Byalo Kamâne, a *mahala* of stolid timber buildings on a steep slope, where the **Benkovski House** (Mon & Wed–Sun 8am–noon & 1.30–5.30pm) recalls another revolutionary. Georgi Benkovski (1844–76) helped to rebuild the clandestine networks set up by Levski, after the latter's execution. A tailor by profession, he made the rebels' white uniforms and silk banner – embroidered with the Bulgarian Lion and the words *svoboda ili smârt* (Liberty or Death!). During the Rising his *cheta* wheeled south via Panagyurishte, trying to rally the locals, but was chased northwards and wiped out near Teteven. His career is covered in usual didactic style; among the texts is a quote from the Rising's chronicler, Stoyanov: "Koprivshtitsa was a republic for centuries, without senators, ministers or presidents; ten times more liberal than France, and a hundred times more democratic than America".

On the hillside above the house looms a striking **monument to Benkovski**, in the form of a Socialist superhero astride a leaping horse.

The Karavelov House

Returning towards the main square along the east bank of the Topolnitsa, you'll find, near the Freedom Bridge, the **Karavelov House** (Mon & Wed–Sun 8am–noon & 1.30–5.30pm), where Lyuben Karavelov was born. The son of a sheep merchant, his itinerant career was typical of the many patriots who spent years in exile trying to win support for the Bulgarian cause. Educated in Moscow, he was a strong believer in the need to attract Russian and Serbian help, and based himself in Belgrade. His enthusiasm for the idea of a Balkan Federation proved too radical for his hosts, who forced him to flee into Habsburg territory, where he was promptly jailed. Karavelov later found refuge in Bucharest, where he organized the BRCK and for ten years advocated armed struggle in the columns of the émigré newspapers *Svoboda* and *Nezavisimost*. After Levski's execution, however, he repudiated direct action in favour of change through reform and education, and was ousted from the leadership of the committee by Hristo Botev.

The house itself contains the usual items of nineteenth-century domestic life, plus the printing press on which Karavelov's newspapers were produced, brought to Bulgaria after the Liberation. An adjacent summer house contains the personal effects of his younger brother, Petko, a prominent liberal politician after the Liberation, and twice premier.

Eating and drinking

There's no shortage of places to **eat and drink** in Koprivshtitsa, with little to choose between the numerous establishments offering good, traditional Bulgarian food. Try *Lomeva Kâshta*, on the main road just north of the main square, with a folksy interior and outdoor seating in the courtyard, or *Pod Starata Krusha*, next to the bus station. The *Dyado Liben Inn*, across the river from the main square, occupies a lovely old house, with a restaurant upstairs and tables outside in the courtyard. The *April 20 Complex* on the main square harbours a café, restaurant, and the occasional lacklustre disco. For picnics, there's a fair range of fresh produce on sale at the **market** south of the bus station (daily except Sun).

Panagyurishte

After Koprivshtitsa, other towns in the Sredna Gora are an anti-climax, particularly **PANAGYURISHTE**, 39km southwest, whose memorials to the Rising hardly compare with Koprivshtitsa's magnificent houses. With a car, you could consider driving south across the mountains simply for the pleasure of the scenery en route – relying on meagre public transport however (one **bus** a day from Koprivshtitsa, several more from Pazardzhik to the south, and three **trains** daily from Plovdiv), it hardly seems worth it. Another drawback is that there's no tourist accommodation in town, so you risk being stranded without a bed after the last bus has left for Hisar or Sofia.

The Town

Despite its antiquity as a settlement, the existing town is predominantly modern, as Panagyurishte was set ablaze by the Turks for its participation in the April Rising.

The most obvious starting point is the austerely laid out main square, **pl. Pavel Bobekov** – named after a local insurgent and overlooked from a hillside to the east by the **Memorial to the April Rising**, a towering structure typical of the part-modernist, part Socialist Realist style that characterized Bulgaria's public monuments in the 1970s and 1980s. The memorial is reached by a processional stairway that runs past the **Church of Sveta Bogoroditsa**, partially burnt in the aftermath of the Rising. Patches of charred murals (immediately on the left as you enter) have been left *in situ* as a reminder of the conflagration. The rest of the interior was colourfully decorated by Samokov painters in the 1890s, covering the walls with a pictorial history of the life of the Virgin consisting of more than a hundred individual scenes – each inscribed with the name of the local benefactor who paid for it.

West of the main square, ul. Raina Knyaginya heads uphill into what remains of the old town. The two towers of the colonnaded, turquoise-coloured **Church of St George** precede the **Shtârbanova House** at no. 26, home to a prominent member of the local rebel government during the Rising. The house forms one part of a complex of buildings holding the town **museum** (Tues–Sun 8am–noon & 2–5.30pm), that bristles with antique militaria, including a cherry-tree cannon. Opposite the church, across a small square, ul. Oborishte leads to the **Raina Knyaginya House-Museum** at no. 5 (Tues–Sun 9am–noon & 2–5pm). As a girl, Knyaginya was the rebels' flag-bearer, mockingly nicknamed *knyaginya* (princess) by her Turkish captors. Tortured in Plovdiv, and then exiled to Russia, she returned to Bulgaria after the Liberation to become a schoolteacher in Veliko Târnovo. The house contains sepia family portraits alongside a "Liberty or Death" flag woven by Knyaginya herself in 1901, in memory of the one she had carried during the Rising. She is buried in the garden with her mother and father – the latter a casualty of the Rising.

Practicalities

Arriving in town by **bus**, head up the road beside the stream past a hospital to find the main square, on the right. The **train station** is a bit further southeast of the centre down ul. Shiskov. There is no **accommodation** in Panagyurishte, and no real reason to stay, while **eating** options are limited to a few cafés on the main square.

Hisar

Situated in the verdant foothills of the Sredna Gora, **HISAR** (sometimes written as "Hisarya"), 55km east of Panagyurishte, was one of the great watering-holes of antiquity. It was the **Romans** who founded the spa, building marble baths, aqueducts, temples and – after raids by the Goths in 251 – fortifications to protect the town, which they called Augusta. Subsequently an episcopal seat, it was devastated by Crusaders despite their appreciation of this "fair town", 150 years before its conquest by the Turks, who restored the baths in the sixteenth century and renamed the place Hisar ("the fortress"). Developed as a health resort for factory workers in Communist times, Hisar has been badly affected by the economic stagnation of the past decade, and the elegant tranquility once offered by its (now overgrown) parks and flowerbeds is long gone.

The Town

A couple of blocks south of the bus and train stations, a sizeable chunk of Hisar's history confronts visitors in the form of the damaged but still imposing **fortress**

walls, originally 2–3m thick and defended by 43 towers. The Roman builders employed the technique of *opus mixtum*, bonding stone and brick with red mortar – hence the sobriquet Kizil Kale (red fortress) which the Turks coined when they besieged the town in 1364.

The northern wall that runs along bul. Botev is bisected by a promenade, leading towards the massive **Kamilite Gate** in the south wall of the fortress, so called after the camels that once passed through it. En route to this you'll see a pseudo-Grecian colonnade and **fountain**, where visitors fill bottles with mineral water and have their portraits taken against a backdrop of crumbling *fin-de-siècle* buildings. A right turn at the Kamilite Gate, followed by a left turn up a flight of steps at the bottom of a hill, will bring you to a fourth-century **Roman tomb** (opening times vary) with frescoed walls and a mosaic floor. Stonework, coins and other finds are displayed in a small **History Museum**, at ul. Stamboliiski 8 (daily 8am–12 noon & 1–5pm; $1), one block east of the main drag.

Practicalities

Hisar's only habitable **hotels** are on the eastern fringes of town (from the bus and train stations, head left along bul. Botev for 500m before turning right just beyond the *Orfey* restaurant). The *Hisar* (☎0337/2781; ③) is just about acceptable, with simple if down-at-heel ensuite rooms, while the *Augusta* (☎0337/3821; ④) is in a different league altogether, offering rooms with TV and ensuite bathrooms fed by mineral water, and a range of spa treatments on site. Daytime **eating and drinking** centres around the numerous cafés on the main square, although at night you're probably better off sticking to the hotel restaurants.

THE VALLEY OF THE ROSES

Lying midway between Sofia and the coast, the **Valley of the Roses** (*Rozovata dolina*) is perhaps the most over-hyped region of Bulgaria. A sunbaked and dusty place for most of the summer, from mid-May to early June it's partially transformed by the blooms that give it its name. Even then, however, much of the rose-growing activity takes place around the villages on the margins of the valley, and if you're speeding through the region by road or rail you won't see a thing. Whatever the time of year its towns can seem unexciting – "ramshackle collections of unplastered cottages which might have dropped off a lorry," thought Leslie Gardiner, and he wasn't far wrong. One compensation of travelling through the valley is bewitching views of the imposing ridge of mountains to the north, which forms the backbone of the Balkan Range, or Stara Planina ("old mountain"). Access to the mountains is via the towns of **Klisura**, **Sopot**, **Karlovo** and **Kalofer**, all occupying honoured niches in Bulgarian history as the scene of heroic events or the birthplace of writers or national heroes, but have little that's worth seeing beyond memorial museums to local sons, captioned in Bulgarian only. The region's main town **Kazanlâk** is similarly bland, although it does feature some remarkable **Thracian tombs**, and hosts the Festival of Roses in early June. Within easy reach of the town to the north is the rugged **Shipka Pass**, heroically defended by Russian and Bulgarian troops during the 1878 War of Liberation.

Regular **trains** from Sofia to Karlovo or Burgas make it easy enough to travel through the valley (although express services don't stop at the smaller places en route, and there are few trains of any description between late morning and early

---

ROSES: BULGARIA'S GOLD

The **rose-growing area** between Klisura and Kazanlâk produces seventy percent of the world's attar – or extract – of roses. Considering that perfumiers pay more than $45 million a year for this, it's not surprising that roses are known as "Bulgaria's gold". Rose-growing began as a small cottage industry during the 1830s (supposedly started by a Turkish merchant impressed by the fragrance of the wild Shipka rose), and initially involved small domestic stills comprising a copper cauldron from which water-cooled pipes dripped the greenish-yellow rose oil. It became big business early in the twentieth century, but virtually ceased during World War II when Nazi Germany discouraged the industry in order to sell its own ersatz scents – since then Bulgaria's rose-growers have vastly expanded their operations.

Each acre planted with red *rosa damascena* or white *rosa alba* yields up to 1400 kilograms of blossom, or roughly three million rosebuds; between 3000 and 6000 kilos are required to make one litre of attar, leaving a residue of rosewater and pulp used to make medicaments, flavourings, *sladko* jam and *rosaliika* liqueur. The rose bushes (covering over 14,000 acres) are allowed to grow to head height, and are harvested during May between 3am and 8am before the sun rises and evaporates up to half of the oil. Nimble-fingered women and girls do most of the picking, while donkeys are employed to carry the petals away to the modern distilleries around Rozino, Kârnare and Kazanlâk. Kazanlâk also has a research institute where pesticides are tested and different breeds of rose developed; according to the director, its gardens contain every variety in the world.

---

evening). Coming down from the Balkan Range via the Troyan or Shipka Pass, you can pick up the valley route at Kârnare or Kazanlâk; Srednogorie and Karlovo are linked by buses or branch-rail lines to both the Sredna Gora and Plovdiv.

Towards Kazanlâk

Immediately beyond the halt for Koprivshtitsa, trains enter a long tunnel beneath the Koznitsa spur, emerging into the Stryama Valley, the upper part of the Valley of the Roses. Bleached and arid from the end of the rose harvest until the autumn, the valley looks surprisingly lush the rest of the year, when groves of fruit trees give way to pastures dotted with wild flowers, and the surrounding hills are covered by deep forests.

Despite its dramatic situation at the head of the valley, there's little reason to stop at **KLISURA**, although this small town "of tiles and flowers" is lauded for having been burned down during the April Rising, as described in Vazov's epic *Under the Yoke*. From here onwards it's roses all the way – at least during May – with fading posters from the Communist period exhorting the erstwhile collective farmers of **Rozino** – an isolated Turkish-speaking village – to produce more of the valuable blooms. The next small town, **Kârnare**, is the point of departure for Bulgaria's highest road, which winds north across the scenic Troyan Pass (see p.197).

Sopot

Further east along the valley, the nondescript town of **SOPOT** hardly justifies breaking your journey, but might be worth a brief excursion from neighbouring

Karlovo. Sopot's claim to fame is as the **birthplace of Ivan Vazov**, Bulgaria's "national" writer, a bronze statue of whom stands on the main square. A stone's throw to the west lies Vazov's birthplace, now preserved as a **museum** (Tues–Sun 8am–noon & 1–5.30pm). The buildings, grouped around a vine-shaded courtyard, suggest the comfortable home of a middle-class merchant – although the study of Vazov's father is frugal and most of the domestic utensils are functional, save for the imported porcelain in the guest room. Sopot's other main attraction is the boulder-strewn **pine forest** which stretches up the lower slopes of the Balkan Range immediately north of town. Crisscrossed by paths, it's an excellent place for tranquil woodland walks, and a welcome escape from the often heat-hazed valley below. To get there, head uphill from the Vazov museum as far as the church tower, behind which a flight of steps leads to the edge of the woods.

Sopot is easily reached from Karlovo, just 5km down the road. **Bus** #4 from Karlovo's main street (every 15–30min) drops you on the main square, where you may find the town's only **hotel**, the semi-derelict *Stara Planina* (☎03134/3075; ③) whose future is uncertain. Places to **eat and drink** are limited to the mundane cafés round the main square.

IVAN VAZOV (1850–1922)

Born into a Sopot merchant family, Ivan Vazov's youthful patriotism took him into exile in Romania as a teenager, where he met other Bulgarian revolutionaries (Hristo Botev and Stefan Stambolov among them), and began writing for émigré journals. On returning to Sopot he threw himself into revolutionary politics, but was forced to flee on the eve of the April Rising because of the threat of imminent arrest. Perhaps because he was unable to participate himself, the events of April 1876 inspired Vazov to write his best poetry.

After the Liberation the new state was desperately short of trained administrators, and Vazov, despite having no experience in the law, was appointed magistrate in **Berkovitsa** (see p.153). Unsurprisingly, this wasn't a great success and, threatened with demotion, a chastened Vazov withdrew to Sopot to lick his wounds. He soon relocated to Plovdiv, then the capital of Eastern Roumelia, where he became active in local politics and journalism. After the reunification of Eastern Rumelia and Bulgaria in 1886, Vazov fled to Odessa in order to escape the clutches of the anti-Russian Prime Minister, Stefan Stambolov, who distrusted Vazov's solidly Russophile sympathies. It was in Odessa that Vazov began work on **Under the Yoke** (*Pod Igoto*), his classic tale of small-town life before and during the April Rising.

Vazov returned to Bulgaria in 1889, and settled in Sofia, where episodes of *Under the Yoke* were published in the journal of the Ministry of Education. An immediate success, it made Vazov a national institution. After serving as Minister of Education (1897–99), he continued to write a stream of novels, articles and poems until his death in Sofia in 1922.

Under the Yoke remains the most admired of his works. Set in the imaginary town of Byala Cherkva (a thinly disguised version of Sopot), the novel follows the experiences of local patriots involved in the preparations for the April Rising, and culminates with their grisly deaths at the hands of the avenging Turks. Very much Bulgaria's "national novel", it was translated into English in 1893, and Sofia Press in Bulgaria published a new English translation in 1960. Both editions are exceedingly difficult to track down.

Karlovo and around

Set against a backdrop of lofty, arid crags and hollows descending to slopes partly covered with cypresses and fig trees, **KARLOVO** is the nicest town in the Valley of the Roses, despite its dreary suburbs. Hidden uphill, the charming old quarter, birthplace of the great revolutionary, Vasil Levski, is worthy of exploration.

Halfway between the train station and the centre of town, ul. Vasil Levski meets **pl. Vasil Levski**, an ensemble of nineteenth-century houses around a statue of Levski, grasping a pistol and accompanied by a small lion. Off to the south are the colonnaded basilica of the **Church of Sveti Nikola**, with its frescoed portico and elegant bell tower, and a **Town Museum** (Mon–Fri 9am–5pm, Sat & Sun 9am–noon & 1–5pm) in a former school, which contains a big folkloric collection.

Just uphill from there, cobbled alleys lead into a quarter full of nineteenth-century houses and spruced-up mansions. One of the most attractive (many are still inhabited and therefore not open to the public) is the tan-coloured **Hristo Pop Vasiliev House** on ul. Evstati Geshev, now a teachers' centre, whose orieled upper storeys and symmetrical appearance show the influence of Plovdiv styles. Another house, further along the same road, is painted all over with trompe l'oeil tiles. At the top of the street is the **Kurshum Dzhamiya** (Lead-roofed Mosque), dating from 1485, which has a spacious porch with cedarwood pillars, and a minaret shorn off just above roof level.

Further uphill lies **pl. 20 Yuli**, a split-level mix of *fin-de-siècle* and postwar edifices that forms the centre of the new town. Heading off past the cinema and a nineteenth-century clocktower, you'll see the **Vasil Levski House-Museum** (Mon–Fri 9am–5pm, Sat & Sun 9am–noon & 1–5pm), behind a low wall on the left. A simple quadrangle with a verandah, its living quarters are austere, the only ornamentation provided by a single shelf with pewter dishes arranged along it. Levski's mother worked as the *boyadzhiinitsa* (dyeing shed), which is today filled with earthenware pots and balls of coloured cord. Behind the house, an exhibition hall harbours photographs of Levski and his comrades in the First and Second Bulgarian Legions; among other slogans and texts is a list of the many pseudonyms that he used when travelling incognito.

Practicalities

From Karlovo's **train station** it's about 1km uphill to the centre; head straight across the park outside and up ul. Vasil Levski to reach the sights, or bear left to find the **bus station** – although some bus services, notably those to and from Plovdiv, stop outside the train station itself. You should be able to see all of Karlovo's sights (and make a short trip to Sopot into the bargain) in the space of a day, but if you wish to stay the night, you could try the family-run *Hemus Hotel*, two blocks north of the station, at ul. Levski 87 (☎0335/4597; ②), with paper-thin walls and rickety beds, or the uninspring but acceptable two-star *Rozova Dolina*, on the main square in the upper part of town (☎0335/3380; ③). A few cafés are clustered around the main square, although the *Vodopad*, north of the square at the end of ul. Vodopad, is the town's only decent **restaurant**, offering good Bulgarian fare and a leafy outdoor terrace.

The Stara Reka and the Balkan Range

Karlovo makes an excellent base from which to explore the imperious peaks of the **Balkan Range** to the north. The main route to the uplands, along the gorge

VASIL LEVSKI (1837–73)

Born **Vasil Ivanov Kunchov** and raised by a widowed mother, who supported them both by working as a dyer, Karlovo's most famous son briefly considered the priesthood and medicine before dedicating himself to the cause of Bulgaria's liberation. Like many patriots of the time, he chose exile, joining Rakovski's Bulgarian Legion in Belgrade, and after its disbandment sought refuge in Romania, where he and Hristo Botev spent one winter nearly starving to death in an abandoned windmill. He took part in Panaiot Hitov's notorious cross-border guerilla raid of 1867, and was given the name Levski (from the word *lâv*; lion) because of the courage with which he went into battle.

However the failure of such raids – infuriating the Turks but winning little sympathy from the local population – convinced Levski that Ottoman rule could only be overthrown by a revolutionary organization based within Bulgaria itself. He developed the idea that an elite group of committed activists, or "apostles", should travel the length and breadth of the country establishing a secret revolutionary network. Armed with funds from Bulgarian merchants in Bucharest, Levski set out on the first of his clandestine trips around Bulgaria in 1868, and over the next few years succeeded in establishing a virtual state-within-a-state dedicated to armed insurrection. In 1872, he was effectively appointed leader of the coming revolution by the newly formed Bulgarian Revolutionary Central Committe (BRCK) in Bucharest.

Towards the end of 1872, the revolutionary leader Dimitâr Obshti led an ill-advised attack on a postal wagon to raise funds for arms purchases. Ambushed by gendarmes, Obshti told the Ottoman authorities everything, in the hope that it would save him from the death sentence, but also because Levski distrusted him and had tried to freeze him out of the movement. Mass arrests followed, and Levski hurried to his headquarters in Lovech to try and destroy the organization's archives. Arrested at a nearby inn, Levski was executed the following February in Sofia, on the spot now marked by the Levski monument. The traitor Obshti preceded him to the gallows.

Although he became a national hero to subsequent generations, Levski may well have felt uncomfortable in the Bulgaria which came into being after his death. He was a convinced republican (hence the exploitation of his legacy by the equally antiroyalist Communists), and also a believer in racial harmony – he made it clear more than once that he was fighting against Ottoman power on behalf of all Bulgarians, and not just the Slavs.

of the **Stara Reka** ("old river"), begins immediately north of Karlovo town centre. The dramatic, steep-sided limestone defile has recently been declared a nature reserve, which means that the usual restrictions (don't pick plants and don't stray from marked paths) apply. The area features on the excellent 1:65 000 *Troyan Balkan* hiking map, though unfortunately it's not on sale anywhere in Karlovo; try and pick it up from Odysseia-in in Sofia (see p.21).

To get to the gorge, follow ul. Vodopad north from Karlovo's main square, passing an area of riverside parkland where locals splash around on hot summer days. At the top of ul. Vodopad you'll find a hydroelectric plant overlooked by a small waterfall; just before the plant, a waymarked path heads left up the hillside. It's a steep, winding track, but after about an hour a marvellous panorama of the gorge rewards your effort. From here, the path charts a course along the rocky walls of the gorge before arriving at the *Hizha Hubavets* chalet after another hour or so. Here the gorge splits from the main path; following the right fork, you'll ascend to the *Hizha Balkanski Rozi* chalet (1hr 30min) then the *Hizha Vasil Levski* chalet (1hr more), which lies just beneath the main ridge of the Balkan mountains. With a good map, walking experience and plenty of time to spare, you can ascend the ridge: dog-legging your way up to the 2035m **Kostenurkata** ("the tortoise") just above *Hizha Levski* takes around 1hr 30min; otherwise the main routes lead to the 2376m **Vrâh Botev** to the east (3hr), and the 2166m **Ambaritsa** to the west (2hr 30min). All these peaks provide access to lateral hikes along the ridge of the Balkan Range, or lengthy descents to the trailhead villages on the northern side of the Range, notably Apriltsi (see p.199) from the Vrâh Botev direction, or Cherni Osâm (see p.199) from Ambaritsa. Vrâh Botev is also accessible by car from Kalofer (see below).

Kalofer

Whether travellers heading east from Karlovo see vineyards, tobacco plants or roses depends on the season, but whatever the time of year you'll pass some of the grandest peaks in the Balkans. Crossing the Staga ridge, which joins the Sredna Gora to the Balkan Range, the road enters the small town of **KALOFER**, nestled in a lovely valley, and cut through by the River Tundzha. Like Karlovo, it has an attractive old quarter, and is indelibly associated with another revolutionary, **Hristo Botev**, whose ubiquitous portrait has become an icon.

A heroic-modernist **statue** of Botev overlooks the main square from the foothills of the highest peak in the Balkan range (2376m), which now bears his name, while Botev's exploits are detailed in a large modern **museum**, off to the right of the main square among the trees (Tues–Sun 8am–5.30pm). Inside is a didactic, Bulgarian-only words-and-pictures chronicle of Botev's life, centered around the printing press on which he published the nationalist newspaper *Zname*. Outside is the tiny cottage where Botev was born, an even simpler dwelling than Levski's childhood home. If asked, the curator will open up the school museum (same times) on the opposite side of the square, where you can peer at a couple of re-created nineteenth-century schoolrooms and ponder the conditions in which Botev and his father once taught.

If you have a car, you can also use Kalofer as a jumping-off point for excursions to **Vrâh Botev**, the Balkan Range's highest peak, which looms over the town from the northwest. An asphalt road (May–Oct) winds tortuously to the summit; it's a signed left turn as you enter Kalofer from the west.

Practicalities

As Kalofer's station is several kilometres outside town, all **trains** are met by a bus. There's also a direct **bus** service to Kalofer from Karlovo bus station every hour or so. **Rooms** and **meals** are available at the dilapidated but tolerable two-star *Hotel Roza* (☎093131/2234; ②), near the museum, or the marginally more atmospheric *Strannopriemnitsa Strazhata* (☎093131/2314; ③) on the opposite side of the stream near the bus stop, a small, simple place with four ensuite rooms.

Kazanlâk

Forty kilometres beyond Kalofer, **KAZANLÂK** is the capital of the rose-growing region, although you wouldn't necessarily realize that unless you pass through town during the first weekend of June, when the long-standing but fairly

HRISTO BOTEV (1848–1876)

Professional revolutionary, poet and idealist, Hristo Botev is perhaps the most romantic figure in Bulgaria's pantheon of heroes. After imbibing patriotism from his Kalofer schoolteacher father he became immersed in radical politics while a high-school student in Odessa. Devouring the texts of Russian revolutionaries like Herzen and Bakunin, Botev developed an enduring faith in republicanism, socialism, and the revolutionary potential of the masses. Thrown out of school for being a weak student, Botev returned home to serve as his father's assistant in Kalofer school, but had to leave town in 1867 after delivering a provocative speech on the Feast Day of Saints Cyril and Methodius. Ten years of exile in Romania followed, during which time he hung out with Vazov and other penniless Bulgarian outlaws in Braila, shared an abandoned windmill with Levski, and began writing for émigré newspapers. Landing a job as a schoolteacher in Izmail (a town on the northern bank of the Danube with a predominantly Bulgarian population), he renewed contacts with the Russian underground, but soon had to leave town under a cloud. According to fellow revolutionary and writer Zahari Stoyanov, Botev asked for voluntary contributions from his pupils' parents (again in order to finance a celebration of Saints Cyril and Methodius' Day), then ran off with the money. Apologists maintain that he hadn't been paid for three months, and this was his only way of getting even.

A trail-blazing career in émigré journalism followed: Botev launched his first paper in Braila in 1871, before moving to Bucharest to work on Lyuben Karavelov's titles *Svoboda* ("Freedom") and *Nezavisimost* ("Independence"). Another self-published periodical, *Budilnik* ("The Alarm"), came along in 1873, and in 1875 he became editor of the Bulgarian Revolutionary Central Committee (BRCK)'s official organ, *Zname* ("The Banner"). As an editor Botev combined caustic revolutionary prose with his own poems: eulogies to liberty, Levski and the legendary *haidut* Hadzhi Dimitâr among them. However Botev's firebrand rhetoric caused rifts within the BRCK. Attacking erstwhile mentor and BRCK president Lyuben Karavelov

lacklustre **Festival of Roses** (*Praznik na Rozata*) takes place. Involving folk music, dancing, and the appointment of a carnival queen, this is basically a tourist event – the rose harvest itself takes place in villages far from town at unsociably early hours of the morning. Nowadays Kazanlâk is enjoying a new lease of life as the centre of the *Dolinata na Trakiiskite Tsare* – the **Valley of the Thracian Kings**. Once an important area of Thracian settlement, the vicinity of Kazanlâk is dotted with countless burial mounds, many of which are still to be excavated. Enough of them have been opened to the public, however, to make the town an essential stopoff for anyone remotely interested in the Bulgarians' ancient antecedents. The most famous of the tombs lies just outside the town centre and contains unique paintings, although only a replica of the tomb is accessible to the public. Further groups of tombs lie in the surrounding countryside, and can be visited by prior arrangement with the local history museum (see below for details) – so forward planning is essential.

Although there's not a great choice of accommodation in Kazanlâk, the town's location at the centre of both north-south and east-west routes makes it a feasible day-trip destination from Plovdiv, Velito, Târnovo, or – at a pinch – Sofia. It also lies at the southern end of the **Shipka pass** road, one of Bulgaria's most spectacular cross-mountain routes.

for not being revolutionary enough, Botev took virtual control of the movement. After presiding over the failed Stara Zagora uprising of 1875, however, he retired to lick his wounds.

Plans to launch another new paper, *Nova Bâlgariya*, were cut short by the April Rising of 1876, when Botev – a man with no military experience whatsoever – agreed to lead a *cheta* or armed group across the Danube in support of the rebels. The plan was to march to the town of Vratsa in northwestern Bulgaria (see p.149), where weapons – purchased with money already sent to Bucharest by Vratsa community leaders – would be delivered to the locals and the banner of rebellion raised. Older, wiser revolutionaries disowned the project.

Biographers still disagree as to whether Botev's decision to take up arms was a coolly thought-out act of martyrdom or merely the emotional response of a man out of touch with reality. The idea of sacrificing blood for the motherland is a constant theme of Botev's poetry, so it's possible that he was reconciled from the outset to the idea of a glorious death. Whatever the motives, the expedition soon degenerated into farce. Launched several weeks after the Rising itself had been put down, it was doomed before it even started. Having hijacked the Austrian steamship Radetsky in order to cross the Danube on May 17 (see p.247) and landed at Kozlodui with two hundred men disguised as market gardeners, Botev's first speech on liberated "Bulgarian" soil had to be delivered in Romanian – the local inhabitants were all Vlachs. Botev's stirring oratory succeeded in recruiting a grand total of two people to the cause. Undeterred, and now the owner of a white horse confiscated from a local merchant, Botev led his men inland through an area where hostile Tatar and Circassian villages outnumbered those inhabited by Bulgarians. Even the latter were nonplussed by Botev's arrival: the insurrectionary network he expected to find here simply didn't exist. The Ottoman authorities, who had followed Botev's progress all the way from the Danube, had no trouble in neutralizing the *cheta*, killing most of its members and scattering the rest. Botev himself was cut down on Mt Okolchitsa near Vratsa on May 20.

Some history

The area around Kazanlâk has attracted successive waves of settlers and invaders, not least because of its strategic importance in controlling approaches to the Shipka Pass. In ancient times, the Tundzha Valley was the domain of the Thracian **Odrysae**, who exploited the vacuum left by the retreat of the Persians in the fifth century BC, to forge a powerful tribal state on the southern slopes of the Balkan Range. Their power was temporarily broken by Philip II of Macedon in 342 BC, but they re-emerged a generation later under **King Seuthes III**, an unruly vassal of Alexander the Great's successor Lysimachus, who built a new capital, Seuthopolis, 7km west of present-day Kazanlâk – now submerged beneath a reservoir. The river Tundzha is thought to have been navigable as far as Seuthopolis in ancient times, bringing trade, profits and Hellenistic culture to the Odrysae – who expressed their wealth in the solid, but exquisitely decorated **tombs** which abound in the region. Seuthopolis soon fell into decline however, and a deluge of **Celts** occurred around 280 BC, many of whom settled in the plain just east of Kazanlâk. There was a fortified medieval Bulgarian settlement at Krân, just to the northwest (where a village of the same name still exists), but the town of Kazanlâk itself is relatively modern, dating from the Ottoman occupation. Its name loosely translates as the "place of the copper cauldrons", a likely reference

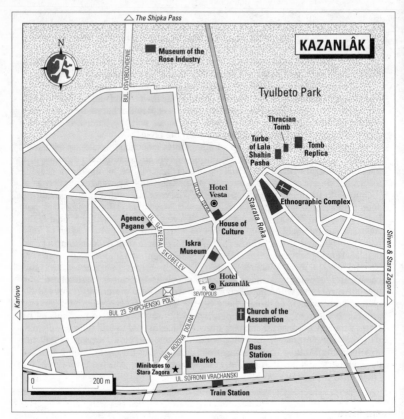

to the giant stills in which rose oil was prepared. By the turn of the century Kazanlâk's streets were filled with the shops and store-houses of the rose merchants – a breed of Balkan trader that has long since disappeared, squeezed out by social ownership and state control. Another legacy of the Communist era is the **arsenal factory** west of Kazanlâk, which – if you believe the locals – produces the best Kalashnikovs outside of the former Soviet Union.

Arrival and accommodation

Kazanlâk's **train** and **bus stations** are just south of the centre on ul. Sofronii Vrachanski, from where a five-minute walk up bul. Rozova Dolina will bring you to the town's main square, pl. Sevtopolis. Here you'll find the standard high-rise three-star *Hotel Kazanlâk* (☎0431/27828; ⑤), which has comfortable ensuite rooms and a covered swimming pool. Cheaper **accommodation** options are limited to the smaller, family-run *Hotel Vesta*, on ul. Iskra (☎0431/47740; ④), and the *Hadzhi Eminova Kâshta* in the ethnographic complex at Nikola Petkov 22 (booked through the Agence Pagane travel agency, see opposite; ③) which has four traditionally furnished ensuite rooms with TV. The *Krânsko Hanche* motel

(☎0431/24239; ④) and **campsite** (☎0431/24239; May–Oct), 4km north of town on the Shipka road, can be reached by bus #5 or #6. If you have the money and a car, *Hotel Sveti Georgi*, in the village of Enina 6km north of town (☎0431/25725; ⑤), has comfortable, balconied rooms, a walled garden and an outdoor pool – to get there, take the Shipka road and turn right after 2km. Of the local **travel agents**, Agence Pagane, ul. General Skobelev 24 (☎0431/26900, fax 22560), is the best bet for tours to Stara Zagora, Shipka and the mountains, and may be able to arrange trips to rose-picking villages during the season.

The Town

The hotels and civic buildings of Kazanlâk's main square – **pl. Sevtopolis** – present an uncompromisingly modern contrast to the remnants of the prewar town that straggle untidily westwards. The nineteenth-century **Church of the Assumption**, just off the square to the east, contains an exquisite iconostasis carved by Debâr craftsmen, while a host of finds from ancient Seuthopolis are displayed in the basement of the **Iskra Museum**, to the north of the square (daily 9am–5pm). Diagrams of the city's street plan show it to have been an ambitious undertaking, built from scratch on a grid pattern based on the theories of Hippodamus of Miletus, the doyen of Hellenistic town planners. Weapons, pottery, and coins minted by Seuthes III help to illustrate life in his capital, while the reconstructed floor plans of domestic houses reveal the bowl-like depressions that served as cult hearths, for appeals to tribal deities. Upstairs is a gallery exhibiting mediocre modern works and a collection of icons from local churches.

Ten minutes' walk northeast of the museum, on the far bank of the Starata Reka, ul. Knyaz Mirski runs off beside an **Ethnographic Complex**. Along here, several nineteenth-century houses have been restored to their former splendour, one of which serves as a **museum** (summer daily 9am–5pm; for winter hours enquire at the Iskra Museum), where period furnishings and an elegant walled garden recall the lifestyles of Kazanlâk's rose merchants. If the rose industry fires your imagination, you might want to trek out to the **Museum of the Rose Industry** (summer daily 9am–5pm; for winter hours, enquire at the Iskra Museum), 2km from the centre along the Shipka road – buses #5 or #6 pass by. Though there's relatively little information given in English, the museum successfully conveys an idea of how rose jam, toothpaste, eau-de-cologne, jelly and, of course, attar of roses are produced.

Tyulbeto Park and the Kazanlâk Tomb

On a hillside immediately north of the ethnographic complex, **Tyulbeto Park** is the site of two renowned funerary monuments. A stairway beyond the park gates ascends to the skeletal remains of the **Turbe of Lala Shahin Pasha**, conqueror of much of Bulgaria and first Ottoman governor of Rumelia. He fell in battle here, and it's thought that his entrails were interred on the spot before the rest of him was carried back to Bursa (probably embalmed in honey) to be buried in a much finer *turbe* closer to home.

Immediately behind the *turbe* is a protective structure built over the first of the **Thracian tombs** to be excavated, a late fourth- or early third-century BC burial chamber unearthed by chance in 1944 during the construction of an air-raid post. Its frescos are so delicate that only scholars with authorization from the Ministry of Culture may enter (and only then with a good reason), but the replica (summer daily 9am–5pm; for winter hours, enquire at the Iskra Museum), built 50m east along the path, is an atmospheric enough re-creation. Once inside, the domed burial chamber is approached through a narrow antechamber decorated by two bands of murals – one ornamented with plant and architectural motifs, the other displaying battle scenes. The floor and walls are stained a deep red, while in the cupola are the **paintings** for which the tomb is famed. They depict a procession of horses and servants approaching the chieftain for whom the tomb was built, who sits behind a low table laden with food. His wife, face downcast in mourning, reposes on an elaborate throne beside him, and the couple touch hands in a tender gesture of farewell. A bowl of fruit is offered to the deceased by a female figure to the right, who has been linked with both the Great Mother Goddess common to Thracian tribes, and the queen of the Underworld in the Greek pantheon, Persephone. Racing chariots wheel around the apex of the dome, a possible reference to the

THE THRACIAN WAY OF DEATH

The Bulgarian countryside is dotted with Thracian burial mounds, or *mogili*, the majority of which remain unexcavated. They were erected by a society that attatched great importance to the role of the tomb, both in providing the deceased with a fitting memorial and in giving the living a focal point for ancestor-worship and religious ritual. Some tombs were used as family mausoleums, and contain the bones of several generations. Principal tombs that are open to the public can be found near Kazanlâk and Sveshtari (see p.235); otherwise most Bulgarian museums contain Thracian burial finds of one sort or another.

According to **Herodotus**, deceased Thracian nobles were laid out for three days before a funeral feast of sacrificial animals which followed "a short period of wailing and mourning". After the corpse was buried or cremated, a "tumulus of soil" was raised, and various competitive games were organized, "the biggest prize being awarded for wrestling". Herodotus notes elsewhere that in those tribes where polygamy was practised, the wives of a dead warrior would compete for the honour of being buried with him. His assertion is partly borne out by the evidence of some of the excavated tumuli, where the bones of young females have been found lying near to those of the chieftain. In many cases, however, the deceased made do with the company of his favourite horse.

Modern archeological evidence points to a rich **funerary culture**, full of symbolic actions whose meaning can only be guessed at. Tombs were often regularly reopened so that sacrifices and other rituals could be carried out, suggesting that places of burial often fulfilled the same function as a temple. In some areas, the deceased was disinterred and moved to another location – either inside the tomb or elsewhere – pointing to ritual reburial as an important part of funerary practice. Each season of excavations reveals yet stranger rites: one of the Sveshtari tombs was found to contain half the skeleton of a large dog – the other half had for some reason been buried outside.

Indeed, hunting dogs may well have accompanied tribal chieftains into the **afterlife**, the existence of which Thracians took for granted – although it's not clear whether life beyond the grave was enjoyed by everybody, or merely an elite group of nobles and priest-kings. However Herodotus relates how certain tribes mourned the birth of children, and celebrated the death of their elders – as if the latter event represented release from the misery of the material world. Thracian beliefs about the immortality of the soul undoubtedly spread southward to Greece, where they contributed to the development of mystery cults such as **Orphism** (p.314).

games that often accompanied a Thracian funeral (see below). With its graceful composition and naturalistic details, the painting is a masterpiece of Hellenistic art, although opinions differ as to whether the frescos are the work of an itinerant Greek master or an inspired local.

The Valley of the Thracian Kings

The area northwest of Kazanlâk was a sacred place for the inhabitants of Seuthopolis, and they left a string of necropoli on either side of the road that runs along the Shipka Pass. Not all the 1500 **burial mounds** (*mogili*) in the vicinity contain the stone-built tombs of the wealthy, and it's not known which classes of Thracian society actually qualified for one: kings, priests, or noble families in general. It is clear, however, that the prevalence of tombs reflects the growing wealth and self-confidence of Odrysian society from the fifth century BC onwards. After years of intense archeological activity, a group of four tombs has now been opened to the public. However the Ministry of Culture looks set to limit further excavations, as the number of open tombs is outstripping the ability of the authorities to look after them adequately. **Visits to the tombs** must be arranged through the Iskra Museum (✆0431/26055 or 23741), at least three days in advance. The cost of $2–$5 per person per tomb (most people visit three or four to make the trip worthwhile) includes an English-speaking guide, but you'll need to pay extra for a driver if you don't have your own transport.

The nearest of the tombs to Kazanlâk on the south side of Shipka village is the fifth-century-BC **Mogila Ostrusha**, which contains a remarkable granite burial chamber in the form of a miniature Greek temple – indeed it may have served as a place of worship before being used as a tomb. The ceiling of the chamber was painted with a grid of small scenes, of which only one survives in recognizable form – a faded and tiny portrait of a red-haired girl, unique for the period.

The remaining tombs date from at least a century later than Ostrusha and, like the Kazanlâk tomb, are built in the form of a domed burial chamber approached through a narrow, corridor-like antechamber. Two are in the Shushmanets complex, an ensemble of six mounds on the eastern fringes of Shipka village. The burial chamber of the **Mogila Shushmanets** itself is characterized by a single doric column which supports the ceiling, while the nearby **Mogila Helvetsia**, named in honour of Switzerland, whose government paid for its excavation, boasts an elegant pointed-arch entrance. Finally, out beyond Shipka village on the Gabrovo road, the **Mogila Arsenalka** (so named because of its proximity to the Arsenal Kalashnikov factory) features an outer facade fashioned from blocks of porphyry granite quarried on the south side of the valley. Inside, the chamber is simple and undecorated but exudes harmony, with a stone bed for the deceased and a circular hearth on the floor for lighting sacrificial fires.

Eating and drinking

Central Kazanlâk doesn't have a great deal going for it in the eating and drinking stakes, with the **restaurant** of the *Hotel Kazanlâk* offering the best food – often accompanied by live music. Out on the Shipka road are two good restaurants serving traditional Bulgarian food: *Frank* at bul. Osvobozhdenie 3, and *Kâshtata* on the opposite side of the same street, which has a nice garden. **Cafés** around pl. Sevtopolis and ul. General Skobelev are lively on fine summer days, less so at other times of the year.

The Shipka Pass

For drama and majestic vistas, few routes in Bulgaria match crossing the **SHIPKA PASS**. Particularly at sunset, when the mountains darken and a chill wind disperses the tourists, you can feel something of the pass's potent historical significance. Ever since Alexander the Great drove back a force of Triballi here in 335 BC, control of Shipka has been an important strategic imperative.

When present-day Bulgarians think of Shipka, however, they recall the Russo-Turkish War, when 6000 Russians and Bulgarians resisted a 27,000-strong Ottoman force that had been dispatched northwards to break the siege of Plevna (modern-day Pleven) in August 1877. Snow exacerbated the hardships of Radetsky's ill-equipped Bulgarian volunteers (many of whom had been civilians in Gabrovo just days before), and despite the local women who brought supplies, the defenders' ammunition was exhausted by the third day of the **battle** and they resorted to throwing rocks, tree trunks and finally corpses at the Turks. The pass held, however, and in due time Plevna surrendered, whereupon the Russians reinforced Radetsky's army and ordered it to fight its way down the snowy mountainside to defeat the remaining 22,000 Ottoman troops outside Kazanlâk – which it did.

The **journey** across the mountains between Kazanlâk and Gabrovo takes about ninety minutes **by bus**, and it's wise to book seats when leaving either town – even if you're planning to stop halfway and then continue on or return by a later service (there are usually some empty seats by the time buses reach the pass). Most visitors head for three major destinations around Shipka: the scenery and war memorials of the **summit** itself; the neighbouring **Mt Buzludzha**, where renowned *haidut* Hadzhi Dimitâr bit the dust; and the **Shipka Memorial Church**, just 12km north of Kazanlâk.

The Shipka Memorial Church

From a stop near the corner of Sofronii Vrachanski and Rozova Dolina in Kazanlâk, you can catch bus #6 out to **Shipka** village, a rustic huddle of buildings a little way off the main road to the pass. From the wooded hillside rise the gold onion domes of the **Shipka Memorial Church** (daily 8.30am–4.30pm), built after the Liberation as a monument to both Russian and Bulgarian dead. Conceived by philanthropic Russian aristocrats and financed by public donations, the edifice was modelled on Muscovite churches of the seventeenth century.

The church is a vibrantly coloured confection of pinks and greens, topped off with a fifty-metre-high spire on the bell tower. Its **interior**, the work of Bulgarian artists under the direction of the Russian painter Pomerantsev, is perhaps the best example of the academic realist style that flourished in Bulgaria around the turn of the century. Folk-influenced floral and geometric patterns rich in primary colours weave their way around naturalistic depictions of Bulgarian saints and tsars. Many of them are dressed in Byzantine costume, a reminder of the pre-World War I days when Bulgaria's desire to extend its frontiers towards the former imperial capital was reflected in a passion for all things Byzantine.

At the western end of the church, murals portray great figures from Russian history, including the fourteenth-century ruler Dmitri Donskoi being blessed before going off to smite the Tatars, and an allegorical scene of Cyril and Methodius bringing literacy to the Slavs.

The pass

Though the **pass** itself has degenerated into a truck-stop, it's impossible not to be awed – and exhausted – by the final ascent of **Mt Stoletov**, whose summit the Bulgarians held during the battle, and which overlooks the pass. Visitors struggle up five hundred steps, past heroic bas-reliefs, to reach the towering stone **Freedom Monument**, erected in the 1890s, which commands a glorious panorama of the Sredna Gora and the Valley of the Roses (the monument itself can be seen from Kazanlâk). The tower contains a symbolic sarcophagus and a **museum** of weapons and paintings detailing each phase of the battle, but the real lure is the observation platform on the roof, affording superb views of the mountains. From here you can see the **Russian cemetery**, 300m to the northwest, which is the largest of the many concentrations of cannon and gravestones planted on the slopes of surrounding hills.

Accommodation at the Shipka Pass is limited to the humdrum two-star *Shipka Hotel* (☎066/29119; ②), which sometimes suffers water shortages. There's also a rather forlorn **campsite** (mid-May to Sept) with chalets, 800m down the road towards Gabrovo. Don't miss sampling the buffalo-milk yogurt, a local speciality sold at the pass.

Mt Buzludzha

From the pass a sideroad runs 12km east to **Mt Buzludzha**, topped by a bizarre structure resembling a spaceship come to earth, that counterpoints the monument at Shipka. It was on Mt Buzludzha that Hadzhi Dimitâr and his rebels died fighting the Turks on August 2, 1868, while the Bulgarian Socialist Party was founded on the same day in 1891, following a clandestine congress, also on the mountain – the **museum** within the "spaceship" covers both events. Alas, this gem of Communist kitsch can only be reached by car, as there are no longer any buses from Kazanlâk.

BEYOND THE VALLEY OF THE ROSES

East of Kazanlâk the Tundzha Valley broadens out, although it continues to be flanked by the wall of the Balkan Range and the lower, wooded hills of the Sredna Gora. Lurking on the far side of the latter is **Stara Zagora**, Bulgaria's sixth-largest city, with a population of 135,000. Home to one of the most important Neolithic sites in Europe, Stara Zagora warrants at least a brief detour, especially for those travelling southward from the Valley of the Roses towards Plovdiv, Haskovo, Kârdzhali or Turkey – all are easily accessible by train from here.

Another obvious stopoff on the way to the coast is **Sliven**, the most important town between the Valley of the Roses and the sea. Lying snug beneath the craggy Balkan Range, it is a good base from which to explore the **Blue Rocks** nearby or the historic craft villages in the mountains to the north; **Kotel**, with its clutch of interesting museums, and **Zheravna**, a captivating huddle of rustic architecture which is worth the effort required to get there.

Stara Zagora

STARA ZAGORA means "Old Town Behind the Mountain", an apt name for this settlement on the far flanks of the eastern Sredna Gora, at the crossroads of two Roman trade routes, and commanding a fertile area still noted for its wheat and fruit orchards. Under Ottoman rule Stara Zagora was one of the centres of the Bulgarian renaissance, and its school attracted such pupils as Levski, Botev and Raina Knyaginya. Burned down by the Turks in 1877 for welcoming the Russian army of General Gurko, and subsequently rebuilt on a strict grid-plan, today the city has an urbane, modern appearance, centring on leafy boulevards and lively cafés.

The Town

The heart of town is the **Pazarska** or **City Garden**, near the intersection of the main east–west and north–south thoroughfares, bul. Tsar Simeon Veliki and bul. Ruski. Toddlers, pensioners and lovers revel in its shady nooks and paths, while a kids' train and a row of booksellers run off towards the **Eski Dzhamiya** (Old Mosque). Built in 1409, this squat edifice has a seventeen-metre-wide dome that was considered a great architectural feat at the time. When it's open, you can see an Arabic inscription above the entrance to the prayer hall, which lauds the local worthy who paid for it, Emir Hamza Beg, as the "shadow of God on earth, glory of the state and of the Faith".

Diagonally across the Pazarska loom the old and new **Opera Houses**, home to the oldest and most prestigious provincial opera company in Bulgaria – it was here that the famous singer Boris Christoff first made his name. Across the way to the west, a sizeable restored portion of a **Roman theatre** is visible behind the town council building. To the north of here, on ul. Dimitâr Naumov, you can get a good idea of bourgeois life during the National Revival, at the **Museum of Nineteenth-Century Town Life**, housed in a distinctive sepia- and blue-painted mansion (Tues–Sun 10am–noon & 2–5pm).

Back on bul. Tsar Simeon Veliki, opposite the mosque, the **Art Gallery** (Tues–Sat 9am–noon & 2–6pm) displays work by local artists, and is worth a quick look on your way to the **Geo Milev House-Museum** (Tues–Sat 8am–noon), the home of the poet whose verses on the subject of the 1923 Uprising caused his untimely death. The museum contains several rooms re-creating his abode, a section on other local poets such as Ivan Hadzhihristov, and a nice café.

The Neolithic dwellings

Stara Zagora's chief attraction, the **Neolithic dwellings** (*Neolitni zhilishta*) were unearthed in 1969 during the construction of a hospital. Of the several dwellings excavated – the remains of a settlement destroyed by fire c. 5500 BC – two houses were preserved in the state in which the archeologists found them and covered by a custom-built pavilion, which is now a **museum** (Tues–Sat 9am–noon & 1–5pm). Inside, first impressions are of a moonscape of crumbling walls and pottery, but familiar domestic details become recognizable on closer inspection. English-language guided tours of the museum can be booked through the Regional Economic Development Agency (see below) for $10 (24 hours' notice needed).

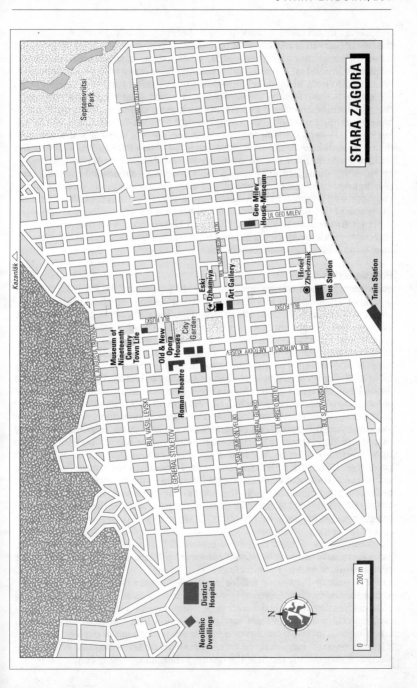

STARA ZAGORA

Kazanlâk

Septemvriitsi Park

UL GENERAL STILETOV

Geo Milev House-Museum
UL GEO MILEV

UL TSAR SIMEON VELIKI

Eski Dzhamiya

Art Gallery

Hotel Zheleznik

Bus Station

Train Station

BUL RUSKI

UL AUGUSTA TRAYANA

Museum of Nineteenth Century Town Life

Old & New Opera Houses

City Garden

BUL RUSKI

BUL MITROPOLIT METODIY KUSEV

Roman Theatre

BUL VASIL LEVSKI

BUL SAR SIMEON VELIKI

UL GENERAL GURKO

UL HRISTO BOTEV

BUL SAVANSKA

UL GENERAL STOLETOV

District Hospital

Neolithic Dwellings

N

200 m

0

Each family occupied a single-roomed dwelling, usually detached – although the two preserved here were built back-to-back, possibly the sign of an extended family. In one corner of the house stood a basic stove, in which bread was baked from flour ground on a nearby millstone. Another corner of the room was a cult area, used to keep idols of the household gods. A **gallery** in the basement holds the artefacts unearthed by the excavation, covering several millennia – the earliest ones include household implements such as sickles and spoons made out of bone – although most objects belong roughly between the sixth and fourth millennia BC. Pottery contemporaneous with the dwellings upstairs shows a high degree of sophistication, with diagonal lines and geometric patterns adorning the bulky vessels used for storing grain. An abundant collection of clay cult figures includes the ample forms of female fertility goddesses alongside various zoomorphic figures: cats, goats, hedgehogs, and an enigmatic pot in the shape of an animal body with a human head. A delicate child's bracelet from the fifth millennium BC is one of the oldest pieces of gold jewellery ever found.

To **get there**, walk west along ul. General Stoletov for fifteen minutes until you reach the district hospital (*okrâzhna bolnitsa*), then bear left to find the museum near some white houses around the back.

Practicalities

Stara Zagora's **train station** lies about five blocks south of the Pazarska, near the bottom of bul. Ruski; the **bus station** is further east on bul. Slavyanski – both are just ten minutes' walk from the centre. The Stara Zagora Regional Economic Development Agency, on ul. General Stoletov 127 (☎042/35007, fax 38075, email *office@szeda.bg*) doubles as a **tourist information centre**, and can act as an intermediary for non-English speaking travel agents, such as Mahiko (☎042/39559 or 37887), who arranges **accommodation in village houses** in the rustic settlement of Malka Vereia, 10km east of Stara Zagora (②; half- and full-board available on request). As far as central **hotels** are concerned, the main advantage of the old-style, two-star *Zheleznik*, on bul. Slavyanski (☎042/22158; ③), is its proximity to the bus depot. You'll find considerably more atmosphere, however, at the *Tangra*, Lyuben Karavelov 80 (☎042/600901 or 600902, fax 600903; ④), a lovely new private hotel about six blocks from the city centre offering clean, tiled ensuite rooms, with breakfast included, or at the more central *Dedov*, Tsar Simeon 162 (☎ & fax 042/862116 or 867022; ④), a small, friendly place whose rooms come with ensuite shower, TV and minibar. Moving up in price, modern comforts can be taken for granted at both the swanky new *Ezeroto*, Bratya Zhekovi 60 (☎042/600103 or 600104, fax 600409; ⑤), in the park between the train station and the centre, and the *Zagorka* (☎042/59021; ⑤), a large lakeside hotel 1km northeast of the centre.

For **eating**, the *Tangra*, *Dedov* and *Ezeroto* all have good restaurants, while the cafés and *sladkarnitsi* on Mitropolit Kusev are the best places in which to linger over a **drink** or an ice cream.

For details of the town's **folkloric events** throughout the year, contact the Economic Development Agency (see above). In particular, try and catch the local girls performing traditional Lazaruvane songs (see "Basics", p.43) in the town centre on the weekend of Palm Sunday, the **Trakia Pee** ("Thrace Sings") festival involving folk groups from throughout Thrace performing in outdoor venues in late May or early June, and the national **festival of Gypsy music** which takes place in Ayazmo Park, north of the centre, in late June or early July.

Sliven and the Blue Rocks

SLIVEN lies at the feet of craggy mountains that once sheltered so many bands of *haiduti* that Bulgarians called it the "town of the hundred *voivods*" after the number of their chieftains. The heyday of famous *haiduti* such as Hadzhi Dimitâr and Panayot Hitov coincided with the industrialization of Sliven, where Bulgaria's first textile factory was established in 1834 – its founder, Dobri Zhelyazkov (known as *Fabrikadzhiyata*, "the gaffer"), acquired parts and plans of looms by smuggling them back from Russia in bags of wool. The industry grew rapidly, and Sliven was soon likened to a "Bulgarian Manchester". Nowadays, Sliven makes a good stopoff between Sofia and Burgas on the coast – not so much for the town itself as for the nearby **Blue Rocks**.

The Town

A sprawl of apartments and red-roofed houses, Sliven converges on a leafy plaza where the high-rise *Hotel Sliven* and a modernistic theatre complex fail to provide

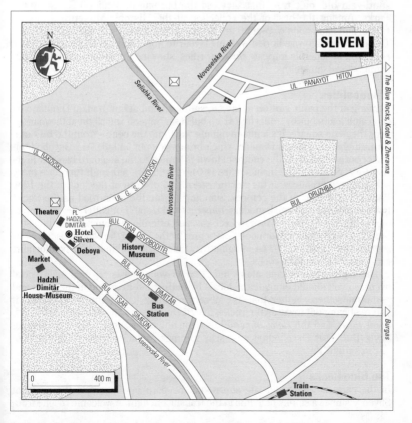

the focal point that the planners have evidently been groping for. The square is named **pl. Hadzhi Dimitâr** after Sliven's most famous son (1840–68), a statue of whom stands to the northeast of the hotel. To learn more about Dimitâr, head off past the **Deboya** or "Depot" – once an arsenal and then a *caravanserai* – through the covered **market** beside the River Asenovska .

Down a sideroad, the **Hadzhi Dimitâr House-Museum** (Mon–Sat 9am–noon & 2–5pm) honours the man who became Panaiot Hitov's standard-bearer by the age of twenty, later teaming up with Stefan Karadzha in Romania to form a *cheta* that made guerrilla raids into Bulgaria. Eventually Turkish troops caught up with them at Mt Buzludzha, where Dimitâr fell in battle, and Karadzha was clapped in irons and taken to be hanged in Ruse. The building itself used to be an inn, run by Dimitâr's father; today you can see everything set up as it was when he lived here. Frugal bedding on the floor denotes the guests' sleeping quarters: the family lived in the more comfortable rooms to the rear, dining on a balcony carpeted with rush mats.

Sliven's other sights can be found along two streets running eastwards from the main square. **Bulevard Tsar Osvoboditel** is an attractive pedestrian zone of shops and cafés, ending in a flourish of banks and fountains. Notice the **thousand-year-old oak tree** that survived the burning of medieval Sliven by the Turks. Among the best of the collection at the **History Museum** at no. 18 (Tues–Sun 9am–noon & 2–5pm) are funerary relics from Kaloyanovo – where a Thracian chieftain was buried with his favourite horse and Greek pottery – and a collection of superbly intricate *shishane* rifles, showing the artistry of nineteenth-century local gunsmiths.

Practicalities

Arriving at the **train station** at the far, southern end of bul. Hadzhi Dimitâr, you can catch a minibus or trolleybus #1 up bul. Tsar Simeon and alight at the market, near the main square. It's a fifteen-minute walk into the centre from the **bus station**, further up Hadzhi Dimitâr, which brings you out on bul. Tsar Osvoboditel.

Accommodation in the centre of town is limited to the standard two-star highrise *Hotel Sliven* on the main square (☎044/27065; ④), although there are more salubrious alternatives at the northeastern end of town at the foot of the Blue Rocks (bus #12 from the centre). Standing beside the main road as the Rocks hove into view is the swish modern *Imperia* (☎044/85071 or 83617, fax 80741; ⑤), owned by football player Yordan Lechkov, and offering ensuite rooms with satellite TV, as well as an indoor pool. Further on by the foot of the chairlift is the *Hotel Alpina* (☎044/89215; ④), an imaginative chalet-style building with comfortable rooms and views of the rocks.

The nightly promenade along bul. Tsar Osvoboditel is Sliven's main social event, so you should emulate the locals by **eating** and **drinking** in the cafés and restaurants there, rather than the deserted dining hall of the *Hotel Sliven*. If you're staying out towards the rocks, the *Bistro Briz* has an outdoor terrace with good views, and the *Hotel Imperia* has a top-notch restaurant too. Café-hopping along Bul. Tsar Osvoboditel on warm summer evenings is about the limit of Sliven's **nightlife**.

The Blue Rocks

In the early morning and late afternoon, the porphyry massif to the north of Sliven assumes a smoky blue hue in the translucent light. A welcome respite from the town, the appropriately named **Blue Rocks** (*Sinite Kamâni*) feature scree slopes swathed in wiry trees and shrubs, with a profusion of streams and butterflies; the crags above are eyries for birds of prey, braved by climbers.

To **get there**, catch bus #12 from the corner of pl. Hadzhi Dimitâr and ul. Rakovski to the stop after the bus park. From here, a sideroad leads up past the *Hotel Alpina* to the lower terminal of a **chairlift** (*lifta*). In theory the lift operates daily from 8am to 6pm in summer, and from 8am to 4pm in winter, with short breaks for maintenance in spring and autumn. However there are often long breaks for lunch, and staff may wait for enough customers to turn up before switching it on.

The best-known feature of the Blue Rocks can actually be reached on foot, by slogging uphill to the fifth pylon of the chairlift and then bearing left. A jagged arch nearly 8m tall, the **Ring** (*Halkata*) is associated with several legends. Ancient mariners supposedly moored their boats here during the Flood, while fairy tales have it that a girl passing through will turn into a boy (or vice versa), and a couple doing so will fall in love forever.

The chairlift gets you to the summit in twenty minutes, giving wonderful views only slightly marred by the TV tower on **Mt Tyulbeto** (if you miss the chairlift back down, it takes an hour to scramble down the mountainside, following a path below the lift). Once at the top, head right up the steps from the terminal and across the road into the woods, where a trail soon emerges at the *Pobeda* **chalet** (①), which has dorm beds and a café. More comfortable rooms and hiking maps are available at the *Karandila* **hotel**, 750m down the road from the top of the chairlift (☎044/82021; ②), an excellent base for walking and a popular food-and-drink stopoff for day trippers. You can also get to the Karandila area by car by following the Kotel road from Sliven and taking a signed left turn 15km out of town.

Around Sliven

Like Koprivshtitsa in the Sredna Gora or Elena in the Balkan Range, **Kotel** and **Zheravna** were important centres of Bulgarian culture during the nineteenth century, whose contribution to the National Revival was way out of proportion to their small size. Located in the hilly sheep-rearing terrain northeast of Sliven, they're both picturesque highland settlements with their fair share of traditional wooden architecture. Nearby, the villages of **Katunishte** and **Medven** are well-known for retaining considerable numbers of nineteenth-century houses, although tourism in both places is minimal. Indeed, given the region's undoubted charms it's surprising how stagnant tourism has become here, though accommodation (albeit limited) does exist, and if an off-beat village holiday is what you're after, Zheravna, in particular, is as good as they get.

THE KARAKACHANI FESTIVAL

This Karandila area becomes especially animated on the third weekend of August, when there's a festival celebrating the music and culture of the **Karakachani**, a minority community who live scattered throughout the Sliven and Kotel area. Although today's Karakachani no longer lead the nomadic pastoral lives of their forefathers, they retain a distinct identity, speaking a dialect of Greek and bringing out their dazzling white-smocked costumes on feast days.

It's worth making the effort for the scenery alone, with the road from Sliven zigzagging over the Blue Rocks massif and down into pine-clad valleys where Gypsies camp among the wildflowers and herds of sheep block the roads. It's an enchanting, almost time-warped corner of Europe which still follows a pastoral way of life, with many of the villages along the route preserving rickety examples of nineteenth-century village architecture, although rural poverty and depopulation has given the whole region a careworn feel.

Getting around the region by **public transport** isn't difficult providing you start from Sliven, from where there are seven daily buses to Kotel, three to Zheravna. You can treat either place as a day-trip from Sliven, but not both: despite their proximity to each other, Kotel and Zheravna are connected by just one bus a day.

Kotel

Founded by sixteenth-century migrants from the Ottoman-dominated plains, **KOTEL** was one of those remote towns where Bulgarian customs and crafts survived centuries of Turkish rule, to re-emerge with new vigour during the National Revival. This was in part due to the special privileges awarded the town by the Ottoman authorities, who employed *Kotlentsi* to defend the nearby mountain passes against brigands and allowed them to carry arms in return. Uniquely in Ottoman-occupied Bulgaria, the locals were allowed to build fortifications around the town in 1800 to deter attacks by the *Kârdzhali*, outlaws who sacked nearby Zheravna instead. Such was the extent of Kotel's autonomy that not only were

KOTEL CARPETS

Alongside Chiprovtsi (see p.156), Kotel is Bulgaria's major carpet-weaving centre. Manufactured here since the seventeenth century on vertical looms, Kotel carpets come in the form of either **kilims** (carpets with a complex design and a distinct border round the edges) or **chergi** (carpets with simpler designs, often just stripes of different colours). *Chergi* are often long, thin affairs used as runners, although they may be stitched together to form a larger floor covering. They're invariably made from sheep's wool nowadays, although rough goat's wool carpets were popular in the past. Also made here are the tufted woollen **rugs** known variously as *guberi*, *kitenitsi* or *postelki* and traditionally used as blankets.

Kotel **designs** are very distinctive, and always feature four colours; black, red, blue and green. Kilims usually have lozenge- or diamond-shaped geometric patterns, many of which symbolize the stars, sun, moon, or more abstract ideas like the struggle between good and evil – shown by juxtaposing triangles of different colours. Kilims featuring the design known as *tablite* (literally "the trays") were traditionally made for the weaver's first-born granddaughter; those featuring *krâsti* ("crosses") were made for a grandchild's christening.

There's little in the way of a retail **market** for carpets in Kotel itself. The Carpet Exhibition (see opposite) has a small range of pieces for sale, and can arrange visits to see weavers at work. If you're staying in Bulgaria for more than a month or two, you can order a rug from a weaver, pay a deposit, and pick it up later. When buying from individuals, however, all prices are subject to negotiation, so it pays to check prices at the Carpet Exhibition first to get an idea of the going rate per square metre. As a general rule, anything bought in Kotel is about half the price of carpets bought in Sofia or the Black Sea coast.

Turks forbidden from settling here, they weren't even allowed to enter the town on horseback. Kotel's main source of income was from **sheep**- and **goat-breeding**, with local herdsmen crisscrossing the eastern Balkan Range seeking pastures. Herders often spent up to three years away from home at a stretch, and were engaged to local girls *in absentia* to prevent them from settling down elsewhere.

Though much of old Kotel was destroyed by fire in 1894, one quarter survived to become the subject of modern-day preservation orders. The local industry is **carpetmaking**, with weavers still producing handmade kilims and *chergi*, either at home or in the factory just outside town. Kotel is also the site of Bulgaria's foremost **folk music school** (*muzikalno uchilishte*), where talented youngsters from all over the country come to study traditional instruments – you may get to see a performance if you visit the town as part of a tour group.

The Town

From Kotel's bus station, flights of steps ascend to a plaza dominated by the **Pantheon of Georgi Sava Rakovski** (Mon–Fri 9am–5pm). A gigantic stone cube with glass panels, it supposedly holds the bones of Rakovski, a Kotel-born revolutionary, and a **museum** (Tues–Sun 9am–5pm) devoted to him and other local patriots – notably church leaders Sofronii Vrachanski and Neofit Bozveli – as well as educationalist Petâr Beron, who wrote the first Bulgarian-language school primer in 1824. Arranged in subterranean halls lined with *faux* grey marble, the museum is more like the sepulchral vault of an ancestor-worshipping cult than a tourist attraction, with the embalmed heart of Petâr Beron usually on display.

Follow ul. Izvorska from the plaza down past the sombre **Church of the Trinity**, and you'll enter the Galata quarter of squat, vine-covered wooden houses and steep, cobbled alleys, where the **Carpet Exhibition** (Mon–Sat 8.30am–noon & 1.30–6pm), housed in a old schoolhouse, displays an incandescent collection of antique and modern kilims, and tapestries based on medieval frescos. From the fountain opposite, ul. Shipka runs uphill to an **Ethnographic Museum** (Mon–Fri 9am–6pm), which occupies the house of a nineteenth-century seed merchant. Although well off by Kotel standards, the family of two adults and six kids all slept in the same room (on a floor softened with layered carpets), with the baby slung from the ceiling in a hammock-like cot.

Carrying straight on along ul. Izvorska from the Carpet Exhibition, you'll come to the lovely **Izvorite Park**, named after nearby springs. There are so many that settlers likened them to a bubbling cauldron (*kotel*) – hence the name of the town.

Practicalities

There are plans to develop the **private room** market in Kotel, but don't expect it to be flourishing by the time you arrive: the staff at the Carpet Exhibition – or any of the museums – will know if there are any local landladies with tourist beds to spare. Otherwise, **accommodation** is limited to the dilapidated, water-shortage-prone *Hotel Kotel*, at the upper end of ul. Izvorska (☎0453/2762; ③), or the next-door *Motel Izvorite*, which has spartan rooms with shared facilities (①) and a couple of extremely cosy apartments with ensuite shower and TV (③) – it's worth getting hold of the latter if you can. **Eating and drinking** options are poor, too: choose between the unexciting *Diaveda* restaurant on the main square, a couple of nearby cafés, or buying your own supplies from the foodstores (*hranitelni stoki*) along the main street. There's sometimes a late **disco-bar** at the *Hotel Kotel*.

GEORGI SAVA RAKOVSKI (1821–67)

Of all the patriots produced by nineteenth-century Kotel, **Georgi Sava Rakovski** is the most fondly remembered. In many ways he was the father of the national liberation movement, taking the Bulgarian tradition of *haidutstvo*, or banditry, and turning it into revolutionary doctrine. Born into a leading Kotel family and educated in Odessa, Rakovski first appeared on the political stage in 1841, when the Bucharest authorities sentenced him to death for trying to invade Ottoman territory with a guerilla band. He escaped to resume his career as an underground agitator, heading for Belgrade in 1860 where he formed the Bulgarian Legion, enabling young exiles to gain battle experience by fighting alongside Serbia in the latter's struggle against the Turks. He was also an indefatigable publicist, launching émigré newspapers and penning the epic poem *Gorski pâtnik* ("Woodland wanderer"), a paean to the idealized Balkan outlaw of popular legend.

Increasingly influential in émigré circles, Rakovski's big idea was to send compact groups of armed men into Ottoman territory to gather support from the local populace, and instigate a mass uprising. The bigger the uprising, the better the chance of winning sympathy from the great powers. In 1867 a trial run of Rakovski's theory took place, with *cheti* led by Panaiot Hitov and Filip Totyu heading into occupied Bulgarian territory. The action achieved little, however, and Rakovski died a broken man in October of the same year. Rakovski's successors continued to use his insurrectionary blueprint to tragic effect, with guerilla leaders like Stefan Karadzha, Hadzhi Dimitâr and Hristo Botev marching off to instant martyrdom. Only Ottoman over-reaction to the April Rising of 1876 saw the fulfilment of the final part of Rakovski's plan – intervention by brother Russia and defeat for the Turks.

The return of Rakovski's bones from Bucharest in 1897 was the occasion of national rejoicing, although rumour has it that the whole thing was funded by Macedonian insurgents who smuggled gold ingots across the border inside Rakovski's coffin. Initially Rakovski's remains were kept in the church of Sveta Nedelya in Sofia (see p.71), but were scattered by a bomb explosion in 1925, and no one knows who the bones purporting to be his in Kotel really belong to.

Zheravna

ZHERAVNA huddles on a ridge 6km off the main road between Sliven and Kotel, surrounded by steep pastures and maize fields. Its spacious wooden houses date from as early as the seventeenth century, when the village earned its living from sheep-breeding and diverse crafts, and the cobbled alleys still reverberate to the tinkle of goat bells and the rumble of donkey-drawn carts. With a clutch of museum-houses open to visitors, it offers a good mix of day-tripper-oriented tourism and rural peace.

Buses from Sliven arrive at the bottom of the village by the small market. Heading uphill from here you'll soon come upon the village's main street, which ascends gently past the best of the houses. Built by itinerant Tryavna craftsmen in the mid-1700s, the **Sava Filaretov House**, home of a local educationalist, is a triumph of the woodcarver's art, squatting beneath a vast overhanging roof supported by spindly pillars decorated with zigzags and sun symbols. Inside, the main living and sleeping room is a picture of domestic harmony with ornate fitted cupboards stuffed with rugs, while the *minsofa*, or guest room, has the strangest of domed ceilings. The first-floor verandah boasts a *guber*-carpeted platform where the family would have slept on warm summer nights. A little further up the road is the **Rusi Chorbadzhii House**, a typical example of a nineteenth-century merchant's home, with more kilim-rich wooden interiors. Signposted high up on the northwestern side of the village is the **Yovkov House**, where writer Yordan Yovkov (1880–1937) spent the first years of his life before moving to the Dobrudzha, with his parents and their flocks of sheep. Yovkov remained a regular visitor to his native village, and tales of nineteenth-century Zheravna life form the core of his best-known short story collection, *Legends of the Stara Planina*. Also in the upper part of the village, you'll find the **church of Sveti Nikolai**, whose frivolous birthday-cake interior features a painted icon screen and leafy-capitalled columns. Lining the porch outside are stacks of eighteenth-century gravestones, carved with crosses, sun symbols and vividly depicted dragons.

Should you feel like staying the night, traditionally furnished **rooms** are available at the *Zlatna Oresha* complex (☎994535/273; ③), a rambling ensemble of wooden houses linked by a maze of cobbled paths at the top of the village near the church. There's a **restaurant** and café in the complex itself, or try the cosy, traditional *Mehana Krincha* in the warren of alleyways just to the west.

MUSEUM-HOUSE OPENING HOURS

Zheravna's museum-houses and church keep irregular hours, but there's usually at least one of them open on any given day of the week. Sometimes opening times are staggered, with the Filaretov House, for example, opening in the morning, and the Rusi Chorbadzhii House in the afternoon. Expect to pay $1 to $1.50 for each of them.

Katunishte and Medven

Six kilometres southeast of Zheravna, and accessible by an asphalt road which arcs towards Gradets on the main Sliven to Kotel road, **KATUNISHTE** is another village which harbours a rich ensemble of century-old wooden houses. It's an evocative spot, stretched along a babbling stream amidst woodland and wheatfields, but is immeasurably poorer than its neighbour, in a worse state of preservation, and has no museum-houses to visit.

In a similar state, **MEDVEN** lies slightly further afield in a lovely hill-encircled bowl, some 8km northeast of Gradets. Central Medven looks like a typically depressed post-Communist village, but the outer *mahali* (quarters or suburbs), where geese and turkeys stalk the cobbled alleys, seem to have come straight out of the last century. A left turn in the centre of the village brings you to the most atmospheric of the old quarters, where there's a small **museum-house** honouring local boy-made-good **Zahari Stoyanov** (Wed–Sun 8am–noon & 1–5pm), whose eyewitness account of the 1876 insurrection, *Notes on the Bulgarian Uprisings*, became a classic piece of reportage. There's not much to see save for the author's coat, favourite ashtray (a curious affair in the form of a partridge), and the suitcase he was using when he suddenly dropped dead in a Paris hotel in 1889. Served by a meagre two **buses** a week from Sliven, Medven is hardly worth the effort unless you have your own transport. **Food** and **drink** is available from the *Byalata Lastovitsa Mehana* just off the central square, on the way to the Stoyanov house.

travel details

Trains

Hisar to: Plovdiv (2 daily; 1hr).

Karlovo to: Burgas (5 daily; 4–6hr); Kalofer (7 daily; 20min); Kazanlâk (8 daily; 45min–1hr 15min); Plovdiv (9 daily; 1hr 45min); Sliven (4 daily; 2–3hr); Sofia (6 daily; 2–3hr).

Kazanlâk to: Burgas (5 daily; 3hr); Sliven (5 daily; 1hr 30min); Sofia (6 daily; 3–4hr); Varna (2 daily; 4–6hr 30min).

Koprivshtitsa to: Burgas (3 daily; 5hr); Karlovo (9 daily; 1hr); Sofia (8 daily; 1hr 30min–2hr 30min).

Panagyurishte to: Plovdiv (3 daily; 2hr).

Sliven to: Burgas (5 daily; 1hr 45min); Varna (1 daily; 3hr 30min).

Sofia to: Karlovo (10 daily; 2hr 30min–3hr 30min); Kazanlâk (6 daily; 3hr 30min); Koprivshtitsa (6 daily; 1hr 30min–2hr 30min).

Stara Zagora to: Burgas (3 daily; 2hr 30min–3hr 30min); Plovdiv (4 daily; 1hr 30min–2hr); Tulovo (5 daily; 30min); Varna (1 daily; 4hr).

Buses

Hisar to: Karlovo (10 daily; 35min); Panagyurishte (2 daily; 1hr 30min); Pazardzhik (1 daily; 2hr); Plovdiv (hourly; 1hr).

Karlovo to: Hisar (10 daily; 35min); Kalofer (hourly; 30min); Klisura (7 daily; 50min); Plovdiv (hourly; 1hr 15min); Sopot (every 15–30min; 15min); Troyan (April–Oct 1 daily; 2hr 30min).

Kazanlâk to: Gabrovo (6 daily; 2hr 15min); Lovech (2 daily; 2hr 30min); Sofia (1 daily; 3hr 30min); Stara Zagora (8 daily; 45min).

Kotel to: Burgas (1 daily; 4hr); Plovdiv (1 daily; 3hr); Sliven (7 daily; 1hr 30min); Zheravna (1 daily; 30min).

Panagyurishte to: Hisar (2 daily; 1hr 30min); Karlovo (2 daily; 2hr 15min); Koprivshtitsa (1 daily; 45min); Pazardzhik (12 daily; 45min); Plovdiv (3 daily; 2hr); Sofia (3 daily; 2hr).

Sliven to: Burgas (2 daily; 3hr); Haskovo (1 daily; 4hr); Katunishte (3 daily; 1hr 15min); Kotel (7 daily; 1hr 30min); Medven (every Tues & Sat; 1hr 30min); Shumen (2 daily; 3hr); Stara Zagora (3 daily; 1hr 45min); Veliko Târnovo (1 daily; 4hr); Zheravna (3 daily; 1hr 15min).

Sofia *Avtogara Yug* to: Panagyurishte (3 daily; 2hr).

Bus Park opposite the train station to: Kazanlâk (1 daily; 3hr 30min); Koprivshtitsa (1 daily; 1hr 30min).

Stara Zagora to: Harmanli (8 daily; 2hr); Haskovo (5 daily; 1hr 15min); Kazanlâk (8 daily; 45min); Sliven (3 daily; 1hr 45min).

Zheravna to: Sliven (3 daily; 1hr 45min).

CHAPTER FIVE

THE RHODOPES AND THE PLAIN OF THRACE

F ew parts of Bulgaria are as closely associated with antiquity as **the Rhodopes and the Plain of Thrace**. If the Balkan Range was the cradle of the Bulgar state, then the fertile plain between the Sredna Gora and the Rhodope Mountains was the heartland of the Thracians and the magnet that drew conquerors like Philip of Macedon and the Romans, whose legacy still remains in the graceful ruins of **Plovdiv**. Bulgaria's second city, and a fair rival to the capital in most respects, Plovdiv never fails to charm with its old quarter – a wonderful melange of Renaissance mansions, mosques and classical remains, spread over

CYRILLIC PLACE NAMES

ARDINO	АРДИНО	MADZHAROVO	МАДЖАРОВО
ASENOVGRAD	АСЕНОВГРАД	MANASTIR	МАНАСТИР
BACHKOVO	БАЧКОВО	MEZEK	МЕЗЕК
BATAK	БАТАК	MOGILITSA	МОГИИЛИЦА
BELITE BREZI	БЕЛИТЕ БРЕЗИ	MOMCHILOVTSI	МОМЧИЛОВЦИ
BORISLAVTSI	БОРИСЛАВЦИ	MOSTOVO	МОСТОВО
CHEPELARE	ЧЕПЕЛАРЕ	MUGLA	МУГЛА
DEVIN	ДЕВИН	NARECHENSKI	НАРЕЧЕНСКИ
DOLEN	ДОЛЕН	BANI	БАНИ
DORKOVO	ДОРКОВО	PAMPOROVO	ПАМПОРОВО
DOSPAT	ДОСПАТ	PAZARDZHIK	ПАЗАРДЖИК
HARMANLI	ХАРМАНЛИ	PESHTERA	ПЕЩЕРА
HASKOVO	ХАСКОВО	PLOVDIV	ПЛОВДИВ
IHTIMAN	ИХТИМАН	PODKOVA	ПОДКОВА
IVAILOVGRAD	ИВАЙЛОВГРАД	RUDOZEM	РУДОЗЕМ
KAPITAN	КАПИТАН	SEPTEMVRI	СЕПТЕМВРИ
ANDREEVO	АНДРЕЕВО	SHIROKA LÂKA	ШИРОКА ЛЬКА
KÂRDZHALI	КЪРДЖАЛИ	SMOLYAN	СМОЛЯН
KOSTENETS	КОСТЕНЕЦ	SVILENGRAD	СВИЛЕНГРАД
KRÂSTOVA	КРЪСТОВА ГОРА	VODENICHARSKO	ВОДЕНИЧАРСКО
GORA		YAGODINA	ЯГОДИНА
KRUMOVGRAD	КРУМОВГРАД	ZABÂRDO	ЗАБЬРДО
LÂKI	ЛЬКИ	ZLATOGRAD	ЗЛАТОГРАД
MADAN	МАДАН		

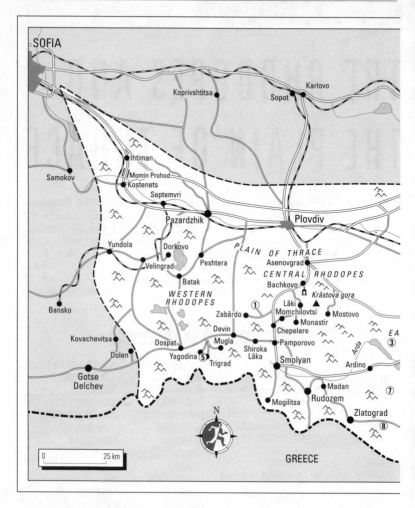

three hills. The whole region is full of memories of the Turks, whose descendants still inhabit the area around **Kârdzhali**, while the mosques and bridges built by their forebears constitute the chief sights of **Pazardzhik**, **Haskovo**, **Harmanli** and **Svilengrad**, strung out along the route between Sofia and Istanbul, nowadays busy with convoys of Turkish *gastarbeiter* bound for Germany.

The Rhodope Mountains to the south of the plain harbour **Bachkovo Monastery** and small towns such as **Shiroka Lâka** and **Batak**, whose fortified houses testify to the insecurity of life in the old days, when bandits and Muslim zealots marauded through the hills. **Pamporovo**, Bulgaria's premier ski resort, attracts thousands of tourists, but otherwise foreigners rarely venture into the Rhodopes, where poor roads and a relative lack of tourist facilities

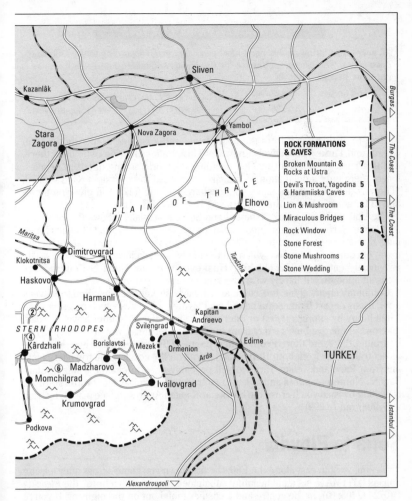

ROCK FORMATIONS & CAVES

Broken Mountain & Rocks at Ustra	7
Devil's Throat, Yagodina & Haramiiska Caves	5
Lion & Mushroom	8
Miraculous Bridges	1
Rock Window	3
Stone Forest	6
Stone Mushrooms	2
Stone Wedding	4

form an effective deterrent. This is a shame, because the scenery in Bulgaria's southern margins can be truly stupendous, ranging from rugged gorges to dense pine forests and alpine pasturelands, with the stunning caves around the **Trigrad Gorge**, and the wonderful hikes around the pilgrimage site of **Krâstova Gora** being two of the highlights.

THE PLAIN OF THRACE

Watered by the Maritsa and numerous tributaries descending from the Balkans and the Rhodopes, the **Plain of Thrace** (*Trakiiskata nizina*) has been a fertile, productive land since antiquity. The ancient Greeks called it Upper or Northern

---

ACCOMMODATION PRICE CODES

All **accommodation** in this book has been categorized according to the following price codes. The prices quoted are for the cheapest double room in high season. For more details, see p.30.

| ① $9 and under | ③ $18–36 | ⑤ $60–90 | ⑦ $120–150 |
| ② $9–18 | ④ $36–60 | ⑥ $90–120 | ⑧ $150 and over |

Thrace, to distinguish it from the lush plains on the far side of the Rhodopes in Greece and Turkey, collectively known as Thrace after the tribes who lived there. A Bulgarian legend has it that God, dividing the world among different peoples, forgot them until a delegation of Bulgars mentioned the oversight. God replied, "There is nothing left, but since you are hard-working folk I will give you a portion of Paradise". And so the Bulgars received part of Thrace.

The E80, which now links Istanbul and Sofia, essentially follows the course of the Roman Serdica–Constantinople road, past towns ruled by the Ottomans for so long that foreigners used to call this "European Turkey". The most important town, of course, is **Plovdiv**, which quite simply overshadows all the others. The provincial centres of **Pazardzhik**, **Haskovo**, **Harmanli** and **Svilengrad** are pleasant enough, but hardly warrant extensive investigation.

Communications along this route are all fairly straightforward. Roughly every hour, trains depart **from Sofia** bound for Plovdiv – a journey which takes two and a half hours by express (*bârz*) or intercity services. If you'd rather travel by road, take one of the five buses a day from the Novotel terminal, which do the journey in around the same time. **From other parts of Bulgaria**, there is at least one direct train a day from both Burgas and Varna on the coast; while travellers coming from Ruse and Veliko Târnovo will probably need to change trains at Stara Zagora. Numerous buses and at least two trains a day link Plovdiv with **Istanbul**: travelling by road you'll cross the border at Kapitan Andreevo (see p.300), by train at Svilengrad (p.299).

Sofia to Plovdiv

Travelling west to east along the E80, the first town you come across after leaving Sofia is **IHTIMAN**, set amid beautiful subalpine scenery, with a **hotel**, the *Eledzhik* (☎0724/2405; ③), in the centre and a costlier motel out on the highway. If you're on a direct bus, you'll follow the dual carriageway almost as far as Plovdiv, bypassing the towns below, but if you're taking the Sofia–Plovdiv rail line, or driving along the old E80, you'll wind your way in a leisurely fashion through the hills that precede the Maritsa Valley, before entering **KOSTENETS**, a small town encroaching on **Momin Prohod**, or the "Maiden's Pass". This gets its name from the daughter of a rich merchant of Philippopolis, whose long-standing paralysis vanished when she bathed here in the **mineral springs**, whose mildly radioactive waters are still used today to treat diabetes, ulcers, rheumatism and skin diseases. **BELOVO**, the next town, is a stop for most express trains, and has a **campsite** (May–Sept) and a mineral swimming pool 5km to the east beside the highway. From the next proper town, **SEMPTEMVRI**, you can catch a **narrow-gauge train** to Velingrad in the western Rhodopes (see p.315) and Bansko in the Pirin Mountains (see p.124).

Pazardzhik

A market town founded by Crimean Tatars during the reign of Sultan Bayezid II, **PAZARDZHIK** was the site of the third-largest fair in the Ottoman Empire, capable of stabling 3000 horses and 2000 camels in its *caravanserai*, and until the late nineteenth century commercially more important than Sofia. Many of the Bulgarian artisans who began settling here towards the end of the sixteenth century adopted Islam, and Pazardzhik remained a predominantly Turkish and Muslim town until the 1960s, when large numbers of gypsies were settled here to dilute their influence. Bulgarians from elsewhere stigmatize Pazardzhik as full of criminals, and its motorists as the worst drivers in the country. This sinister reputation is enhanced by the fact that a local craftsman specializes in making miniature guns disguised as cigarette lighters, ideal for assasination at close range and undetectable by scanning. Though visitors need have no fear of such James Bond weaponry, **pickpockets** are a definite hazard here.

The Town

Although the town has long since lost the appearance of an Ottoman bazaar, Pazardzhik's mercantile traditions live on in one of Bulgaria's liveliest daily street markets, lining the alleys of the pedestrianized downtown area just east of the main square, **Cherven ploshtad**. Directly behind the square, at Georgi Kirkov 34, is the **City Museum and Art Gallery** (Tues–Sun 9am–noon & 2–6pm), an uninspiring collection largely concentrating on Thracian oddments.

A short distance south of the square, the pink stone **Cathedral of Sveta Bogoroditsa** is an example of the National Revival style applied to church architecture, partly sunk beneath street level to comply with the Ottoman restrictions on Christian places of worship. Its walnut iconostasis is perhaps the finest product of the nineteenth-century School of Debâr (in western Macedonia), whose craftsmen endeavoured to show the psychological relationships between human figures rather than fill the icon screen with plant and zoomorphic motifs in the manner of the Samokov woodcarvers.

Zahari Zograf aside, Bulgaria's most famous nineteenth-century painter was probably **Stanislav Dospevski** (1826–76), whose former house and studio opposite the cathedral is now a **museum** (Mon–Fri 9am–noon & 2–5pm). Born in Pazardzhik and educated at the Academy of Fine Art in St Petersburg, Dospevski drew extensively during visits to Odessa and Constantinople, but is best remembered for his icons, portraits and murals, several of which decorate the walls of the house. A participant in the April Rising, he was flung into the dungeons of Constantinople and died before Bulgaria's Liberation.

Most of Pazardzhik's surviving nineteenth-century houses lie near the Dospevski museum, where squat pastel-coloured structures huddle along either side of a stream, or among the tree-lined residential streets just west of the cathedral. Here, at Kiril i Metodii 4, is an **Ethnographic Museum** (Tues–Sun 9am–noon & 2–6pm), which has the usual selection of costumes and crafts from the National Revival period. Another block west is the rather dilapidated walled **Church of SS Konstantin i Elena**, with faded murals of the saints above the portal.

Finally, on the far side of the park north of the centre, is the **Kurshum dzhamiya**, or "Bullet Mosque", so-called because of its pointed dome. Built in 1667, it is larger and grander than the mosques in Plovdiv and Haskovo, but sadly derelict.

Practicalities

Pazardzhik's **train station** lies about 5km south of the centre, and all arrivals are met by buses into town. The **bus terminal**, a couple of blocks north of the town centre, is a more convenient point of entry.

With regular buses to **Plovdiv**, **Batak** in the Rhodopes and **Panagyurishte** in the Sredna Gora, Pazardzhik is the kind of place to spend an afternoon before moving on. If you do wish to **stay**, however, try the standard two-star *Hotel Trakiya*, on the main square (☎034/26006; ③), the smaller *Riva*, ul. G. Tsvetanov 21 (☎034/20334; ③), a quiet pension in the backstreets near the bus station, or the *Elbrus*, pl. Olimpiiski 2 (☎034/26530; ③), which features a late-night **bar** and **disco**.

Beyond Pazardzhik

The road **between Pazardzhik and Plovdiv** runs straight as an arrow across the widening plain beside the River Maritsa, flanked by acres of trees bearing apples, plums and pears. Bulgarians say that traditionally passers-by may pick fruit from roadside orchards providing they eat it on the spot, but removing any constitutes theft in the eyes of the law. About 20km before Plovdiv, just off the road, an annual **Rockers' Festival** takes place each June, where quiffs, leather jackets, classic 1950s' and 1960s' cars and bikes are the order of the day; for details, contact Todor on ☎0799/33300. A couple of kilometres before Plovdiv, the road passes the *Trakiya campsite*, before entering the city's northern suburbs.

Plovdiv

Lucian the Greek called **PLOVDIV** "the biggest and most beautiful of all towns" in Thrace; he might have added "and Bulgaria", for the country's second-largest city (with a population of 360,000) is one of its most attractive and vibrant centres. Certainly, there's plenty to see: the old town embodies Plovdiv's long and varied history – Thracian fortifications utilized by Macedonian masons, overlaid with Byzantine walls, and by great timber-framed mansions erected during the Bulgarian renaissance, looking down on the Ottoman mosques and artisans' dwellings of the lower town. But Plovdiv isn't merely a parade of antiquities: the city's arts festivals and trade fairs rival Sofia's in number, and its restaurants and promenade compare favourably with those of the capital.

Some history

An ancient Thracian site, rebuilt and renamed by Philip II of Macedonia in 342 BC, classical **Philippopolis** was initially little more than a military outpost designed to keep a watchful eye over the troublesome natives. It was a rough frontier town that the Macedonians deliberately colonized with criminals and outcasts; the Roman writer Pliny later identified it with Poneropolis, the semi-legendary "City of Thieves". Under Roman rule urban culture developed apace, with the town's position on the Belgrade–Constantinople highway bringing both economic wealth and a strategic role in the defence of Thrace.

Plovdiv was sacked by the Huns in 447, and by the seventh century, with the Danube frontier increasingly breached by barbarians, the city was in decline. With the arrival of the Bulgars, Byzantine control over the area became increasingly tenuous. "Once upon a time", lamented Byzantine chronicler Anna Comnena in the

---

THE PLOVDIV FAIR

A trade centre of long standing, **Plovdiv** became Bulgaria's principal marketplace during the 1870s, when the railway between Europe and Istanbul was completed and the great annual fair held at Uzundzhovo since the sixteenth century was moved here. Plovdiv's first international trade fair (1892) was a rather homespun affair – a man from Aitos proposed to show his hunting dogs, while Bohemia exhibited bee-hives – but since 1933 the event has gone from strength to strength, and nowadays claims to be the largest of its kind in the Balkans. There are actually two annual **fairs**: the spring event, devoted to consumer goods in early May, and the larger autumn industrial fair, during the second half of September. Both are held at the complex on the north bank of the river. Members of the public are free to come along, and there's a special bus service laid on between the train station and the fairground.

---

twelfth century, "Philippopolis must have been a large and beautiful city, but after the Tauri and Scyths [Slavs] enslaved the inhabitants . . . it was reduced to the condition in which we saw it". In Comnena's time Philippopolis was a notorious hotbed of heretics, a situation usually blamed on local Armenians, who migrated to Thrace en masse in the eighth and tenth centuries, bringing with them the dualistic doctrines of Manichaeanism and Paulicianism. Although these heresies eventually fizzled out, Plovdiv's Armenian population has endured to this day.

The Byzantine town was further damaged by the Bulgarian Tsar Kaloyan in 1206, and it was a rather run-down place that the Turks inherited in the fourteenth century, renaming it Filibe. It soon recovered as a commercial centre, with a thriving Muslim quarter, complete with bazaars and mosques, growing up at the base of the hill where Plovdiv's Christian communities continued to live. Many of the latter were rising members of a rich mercantile class by the mid-nineteenth century, and they expressed their affluence in the construction of opulent town houses that showcased the very best of native arts and crafts. Plovdiv's urban elite also patronized Bulgarian culture, and had the Great Powers of Europe not broken up the infant state of Bulgaria at the Congress of Berlin in 1878, Plovdiv would probably have been designated as its capital. In the event, it became instead the main city of **Eastern Rumelia**, an Ottoman province administered by a Christian governor-general. Much of the Christian population naturally wanted union with the rest of Bulgaria, which was finally attained in 1885.

Plovdiv has continued to rival Sofia as a cultural and business centre ever since, not least because of the **international trade fairs** held here in May and September. With its longstanding liberal-bourgeois tradition, Plovdiv is politically the "bluest" city in Bulgaria, a stronghold of the conservative SDS since the demise of Communism, whose proximity to Turkey and Greece has ensured that private enterprise has flourished here more than anywhere else in the country.

Arrival, orientation and information

Trains arrive at the central train station (*tsentralna gara*) to the south of central Plovdiv, near the two intercity **bus terminals**: Rodopi, serving the mountain resorts of the south, is just on the other side of the train tracks (accessible via the underground walkway from the station), while Avtogara Yug, serving the southeast, is one block east of the train station. A brisk ten-minute walk north of

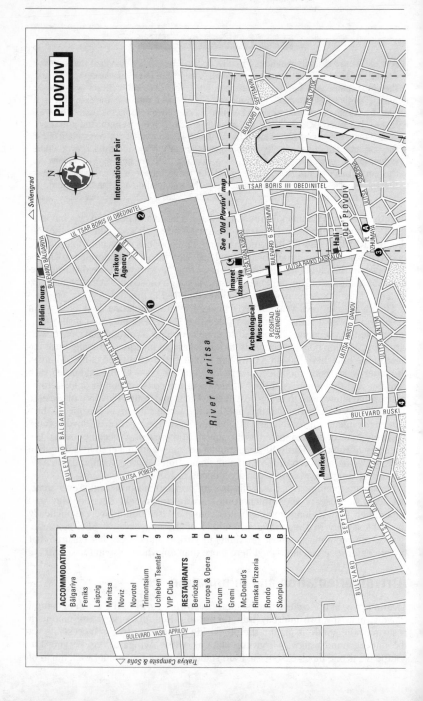

PLOVDIV

△ Svilengrad

International Fair

N

BULEVARD 6 SEPTEMVRI
ULITSA PTICK

UL TSAR BORIS III OBEDINITEL

See "Old Plovdiv" map

UL TSAR BORIS III OBEDINITEL

OLD PLOVDIV

Traikov Agency

Paldin Tours

BULEVARD BÅLGARIYA

ULITSA OBReshte

ULITSA BÅLGARIYA

BULEVARD BÅLGARIYA

River Maritsa

ULITSA NAIKUBRAT

BULEVARD 6 SEPTEMVRI

Imaret dzamiya

PL DZHUMAYA

Hali

ULITSA RAIKO DASKALOV

Archeological Museum

PLOSHTAD SAEDINENIE

ULITSA HRISTO DANOV

ULITSA ANTIM

ULITSA POBEDA

BULEVARD RUSKI

Market

SEPTEMVRI

6 BULEVARD

ULITSA 6 SEPTEMVRI

BULEVARD VASIL APRILOV

▽ Trakiya Campsite & Sofia

ACCOMMODATION	
Bålgariya	5
Feniks	6
Laipzig	8
Maritsa	2
Noviz	4
Novotel	1
Trimontsium	7
Ucheben Tsentår	9
VIP Club	3

RESTAURANTS	
Beriozka	H
Europa & Opera	D
Forum	E
Gremi	F
McDonald's	C
Rimska Pizzeria	A
Rondo	G
Skorpio	B

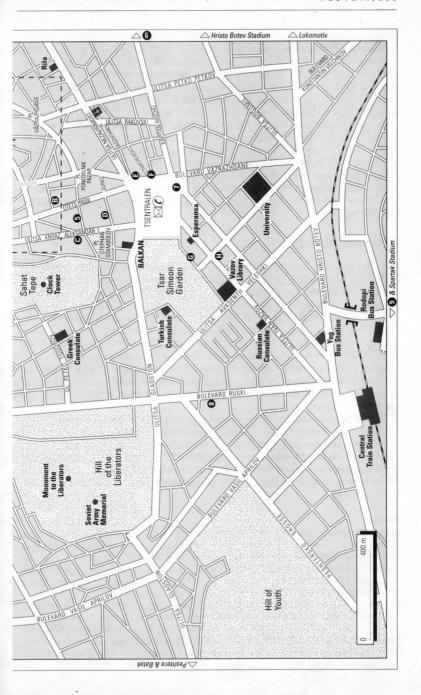

the station, along ul. Ivan Vazov – or three stops on buses #2 or #102 – brings you to **ploshtad Tsentralen**, immediately north of which is the modern town centre.

Though most of Plovdiv's sights are near enough to be explored on foot, the city is divided into two distinct parts, quite different from each other in atmosphere: the nineteenth-century **Stariyat grad** or "old town", covering the easternmost of Plovdiv's three hills; and the **lower town** – predominantly modern with a scattering of Turkish and Roman relics – which spreads across the plain below.

In the absence of a tourist office you'll have to get **information** from hotel receptionists (try the *Trimontsium* or *Bâlgariya* first) or private agencies such as Pâldin Tours 91, on bul. Bâlgariya 106 (daily 9am–5.30pm; ☎032/555120) – take bus #2 or #102 from the station and alight once you've crossed the river. The Esperansa agency (see below) is nearer and also gives out information, but only if you speak Bulgarian. While all the agencies dispense free brochures, for up-to-date **maps** such as the *Plovdiv City Guide* you'll have to search the bookstalls on the streets.

Accommodation

The only time you might have trouble finding somewhere to stay is during the trade fairs, when all the better hotels and private rooms are taken; if you're particular about where you stay, reserve a month ahead. The most convenient source of **private rooms** is Esperansa, at ul. Ivan Vazov 14 (daily 11am–5pm; ☎032/260653), which charges $8 for a single and $12 for a double room in the centre. For motorists coming from Sofia or Turkey it's easier to use the Traikov Agency, on the north side of the river at ul. Ibar 31 (Mon–Fri 9am–5pm; ☎ & fax 032/653014), which charges similar rates and also rents flats with kitchens ($20 a night). Pâldin Tours (see above) charges $13 for a single and $17 for a double, but has the advantage of English-speaking staff. Alternatively, you could go direct to a landlady like Mrs Malcheva, ul. Rakovski 25, 5th floor (☎032/236660), and negotiate your own rates.

Plovdiv's **hotels** are almost as expensive as Sofia's and hike their **prices** by up to 100 percent during the fairs. They're also a highly variable bunch so it pays to be choosy – as it does with **hostels**. Unless otherwise stated, all the hotels below are marked on the Plovdiv map on pp.284-285 The city's three **campsites** are some way from town along the Sofia–Plovdiv–Istanbul E80 highway – too far away for those who want to be at the centre of things; all three charge around $6 per tent per night.

Hotels

Bâlgariya, Patriarh Evtimii 13 (☎032/626064, fax 631214). Clean and friendly but a bit shabby, this two-star hotel's chief virtue is being right in the heart of things, just off Knyaz Aleksandâr I, which makes the street-facing rooms rather noisy. ④.

Feniks, Kapitan Raicho 79 (☎032/224729). Though signposted as a hotel, it's really just some rooms with TV and a bathroom on the third floor of a block of flats, and it costs more than a room from Esperansa. ③.

Hebros, ul. Konstantin Stoilov 51 (☎032/260252); see map on p.290. A gorgeous, opulently furnished National Revival house in Old Plovdiv that was formerly reserved for the *nomenklatura* but now takes anyone. There aren't many rooms so it's essential to reserve. ⑤.

Laipzig, bul. Ruski 20 (☎032/632250, fax 451096). Like the *Bâlgariya* but with nicer decor, and TV and fridges in the singles. It's also cheaper, and handy for the station, but almost 1km west of the centre. ④.

Maritsa, ul. Tsar Boris III Obedinitel (☎ & fax 032/552727). Beside the international fairgrounds on the north bank of the Maritsa (bus #2 or #102 from the station), this modern business hotel has a casino, massage parlour and laundry service. ④.

Noviz, bul. Ruski 55 (☎032/631281, fax 633770, email *novizinc@plovdiv.ttm.bg*). Small, new and stylish, with air-conditioning, cable TV, minibar and fridge in all the rooms; there's also a sauna, fitness centre, massage room and solarium. A 15-minute walk from pl. Dzhumaya. ④.

Novotel, Zlatyu Boyadzhiev 2 (☎032/652505, fax 551979). Plovdiv's plushest hotel, on the north bank of the Maritsa, with air-conditioning, an indoor pool, tennis courts, car rental and other facilities. ⑥.

Park-Hotel Sankt Peterburg, bul. Bålgariya 97 (☎032/55391, fax 551830). Don't be deceived by the four-star status of this soulless, bug-ridden high-rise, miles from anywhere. It's a landmark in the city, but as sleazy as they come, with a nightclub on the top floor. ⑤.

Trimontsium, ul. Kapitan Raicho 2 (☎032/624186, fax 628821). Vintage Stalinist-style hotel with atmospheric rooms, brass chandeliers and acres of red carpet, though it lacks the standards of service that you'd expect for this price. ⑤.

VIP Club, Knyaz Aleksandâr I 1 (☎032/626623). Large air-conditioned rooms with all mod cons above a flash 24-hour cocktail bar overlooking pl. Dzhumaya. Noisy but comfortable. ④.

Hostels

Turisticheski Dom, ul. Petko Slaveykov 5 (☎032/633211). A cut-price version of the *Hotel Hebros*, in an atmospheric National Revival house in Old Plovdiv (see map on p.290). Simply furnished but clean, its doubles and dorm-beds costs about $10 per person per night. Reservations advisable.

Ucheben Tsentâr, ul. Konstantin Nunkov 13A (☎032/722847). A fairly spartan, seven-storey postgrad students hostel, 15 minutes' walk from the train station; cross the tracks, go on past the stadium and turn into the fourth street on the right. With dorm-beds costing around $10 per night, you're better off opting for a private room nearer the centre.

Campsites

Chaya, 15km east of Plovdiv just off the E80 to Istanbul, on the banks of the River Chepelarska. Open mid-April to mid-Oct.

Maritsa, 10km west of town, well signed from the main road from Sofia. Open April–Nov.

Trakiya, on Plovdiv's western outskirts. Most convenient of the sites, though somewhat unkempt; take bus #4 from bul. Vâzrazhdane or bus #23 from the station. Open April–Nov.

Modern Plovdiv

Modern Plovdiv revolves around **ploshtad Tsentralen**, an arid concrete plaza dominated by the post and telephone office and the ponderously Stalinist **Hotel Trimontsium,** whose restaurant-garden with its brass lamps has a Thirties ambience. Remnants of a **Roman forum** were discovered during the development of the area – you can explore this marble-paved, once-colonnaded square by descending into a sunken area in front of the hotel. Just east of here is ul. Kapitan Raicho, a leafy residential street enlivened by a daily open-air clothes market.

The **Tsar Simeon Garden** to the west of Tsentralen marks the tail end of the evening *korso*, an animated **promenade** in which hundreds of people stroll down Plovdiv's main street, **ulitsa Knyaz Aleksandâr I**. Pedestrianized and lined with shops and café-bars with outdoor tables, the street was named after the ideologue Vasil Kolarov in Communist times, but now rejoices in its prewar title, once more. The **City Art Gallery**, at no.15 (Mon–Sat 9.30am–noon & 1–5pm), is one of

Bulgaria's better collections, with some fine nineteenth-century portraits including one deeply reverent, almost iconic, *Portrait of Bishop Sofronii of Vratsa*, painted in 1812 by an unknown artist. Also look out for Tsanko Lavrenov's pictures of nineteenth-century Plovdiv, painted in the 1930s and 1940s and suffused with a dreamlike nostalgia.

Ploshtad Dzhumaya and beyond

Further north, Knyaz Aleksandâr I gives onto **ploshtad Dzhumaya**, where Plovdiv's history and social life coexist in an amiable confusion of monuments, cafés and stalls, around a concrete pit exposing the **ruins of a Roman stadium**. This is but a paltry fragment of the original, horseshoe-shaped arena where the Alexandrine Games were held during the second and third centuries: as many as 30,000 spectators watched chariot races, wrestling, athletics and other events from the marble stands that once lined the slopes of the neighbouring heights.

A more impressive structure is the **Dzhumaya dzhamiya** or "Friday mosque", with its diamond-patterned minaret and lead-sheathed domes. Its thick walls and the configuration of the prayer hall (divided by four columns into nine squares) are typical of the so-called "popular mosques" of the fourteenth and fifteenth centuries, although it's believed that the Dzhumaya might actually date back to the reign of Sultan Murad II (1359–85). Unfortunately, it is only open for noon prayers on Friday and festivals (the Imaret mosque serves for everyday use), so you'll have to time your visit carefully if you want to see the fountain, floral motifs, and medallions bearing Koranic texts that adorn its interior.

Northeast of the mosque lies the old *charshiya*, or **bazaar quarter**, where narrow streets still bear the names of the trades that used to operate from here: ul. Zhelezarska was the preserve of the ironmongers, and Abadzhiiska, that of the weavers and cloth merchants. The name *abadzhiya* derives from *abas*, the coarse woollen cloth that the Plovdiv merchants bought from Rhodopi shepherds before exporting it throughout the Levant. In Ottoman times Plovdiv's commercial district stretched from here northwards to the River Maritsa, and in the sixteenth century the Arab traveller Chelebi counted 880 shops raised "storey above storey". Today, the municipal market hall or **Hali** stands empty, but ul. Raiko Daskalov is full of shops, banks and kebab joints, with stalls selling books as far north as the pedestrian subway beneath bul. 6 Septemvri, and clothes stalls right across the **footbridge** to the north bank of the Maritsa, making it almost as lively as it must have been in Chelebi's day.

Imaret dzhamiya and the Archeological Museum

Just south of the river, two further relics of Turkish rule are enjoying a new lease on life. The **Turkish baths** near pl. Hebros were allowed to rot for decades but are currently being restored and are expected to start taking clients again in 1999, while Plovdiv's Muslim community has already repaired and reopened the **Imaret dzhamiya**, on ul. Han Krubat (daily from noon–1pm), whose prayer hall contains honeycomb squinches, traces of Arabesque frescos, and the tomb of Gazi Shahabedin Pasha. The mosque was built on Sultan Bajazet's orders in 1444, and got its name from the pilgrims' hostel (*imaret*) that once stood nearby. Zigzag brickwork gives the minaret a corkscrew twist, jazzing up the ponderous bulk of the building, which a frieze of "sawtoothed" bricks and a row of keel arches with tie beams fails to do.

Further west, on pl. Sâedinenie, the **Archeological Museum** (Tues–Sun 9am–12.30pm & 1.30–5.30pm) contains ample evidence of Thracian culture from excavations of tribal burial grounds at Duvanli, 20km north of Plovdiv. Austere local earthenware stands in contrast to a series of exquisitely decorated pots imported by Thracian warlords from Greece, while abundant weaponry (including a bronze helmet found near the village of Brestovitsa) attests to the belicosity of Thracian society. Life in Roman Trimontsium is well documented, with a range of bronze and terracotta artefacts; the medieval period is represented by a twelfth-century Byzantine coin hoard found near Asenovgrad and the vibrant, expressive pottery of the Second Kingdom, decorated with multicoloured swirls and coils punctuated by the occasional bird or animal figure. Unfortunately, you may find some of the exhibits packed up, awaiting the museum's move into new, larger premises in the Hali sometime in 1999.

Old Plovdiv

With its cobbled, hilly streets and orieled mansions, Plovdiv's old quarter (most of which is designated as an "Architectural-Historical Reserve") is a painter's dream and a cartographer's nightmare. Attempting to follow – let alone describe – an itinerary is impractical given the topography and the numerous **approaches**, each leading to a different point in the quarter. Glimpses of ornate facades or interiors tempt visitors to stray down the occasional alleyway or into a courtyard – and generally speaking, that's by far the best way to see the area.

Along ulitsa Sâborna

Most people approach the old town from pl. Dzhumaya, from which ul. Sâborna gently draws you upward into Old Plovdiv. A flight of steps to the right leads to the **Danov House** (Mon–Fri 9am–noon & 1.30–6pm), the former domicile of Bulgaria's first large-scale publisher and now home to a museum of printing. Danov was one of those who regarded distribution of the printed word as a patriotic duty: a crucial step in the peoples' struggle against five centuries of Ottoman rule. Besides printing books he opened Bulgaria's first bookshops in Plovdiv and

---

OLD PLOVDIV'S NATIONAL REVIVAL ARCHITECTURE

Blackened **fortress walls** dating from Byzantine times can be seen lurking beyond several streets, sometimes incorporated into the dozens of **National Revival-style houses** that are Plovdiv's speciality. Typically, these rest upon an incline and expand with each storey by means of timber-framed oriels – cleverly resolving the problem posed by the scarcity of ground space and the nineteenth-century merchants who demanded roomy interiors. The most prominent oriel on the facade usually denotes the grand reception room inside, while the sides of the upper storeys sometimes feature blind oriels containing kitchen niches or cupboards. Outside and inside, the walls are frequently decorated with niches, floral motifs or false columns painted in the style known as *alafranga*, executed by itinerant artists. The rich merchants who lived here also sponsored many of the artistic developments that made up the Bulgarian National Revival, and much of Plovdiv's cultural role is reflected in the numerous small art galleries and concert venues that crowd into the houses.

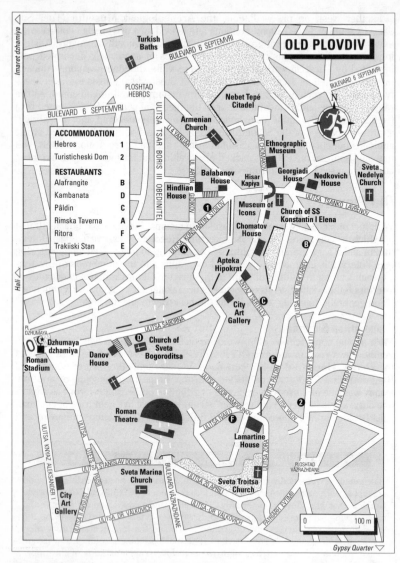

OLD PLOVDIV

ACCOMMODATION

Hebros	1
Turisticheski Dom	2

RESTAURANTS

Alafrangite	B
Kambanata	D
Pâldin	C
Rimska Taverna	A
Ritora	F
Trakiiski Stan	E

Ruse, made globes, thermometers and weighing scales for schools, and founded Plovdiv's first daily newspaper, *Maritsa*, in 1878 – a title resurrected after the changes of November 1989.

Perched on a bluff just beyond, the imposing **Church of Sveta Bogoroditsa** is decorated with frescos of Orthodox monks and saints, and contains some icons by the Samokov master Stanislav Dospevski. Also worth seeing are the furnishings and medallions in a nineteenth-century **Apteka Hipokrat** (daily 9am–5pm)

Suvraki revellers, Koprivshtitsa

Old houses, Sozopol

Roman walls, Hisar

Bachkovo monastery

The Last Judgement (fresco at Bachkovo)

Rose petals ready for distilling

Rock church at Ivanovo

National Revival architecture in Plovdiv

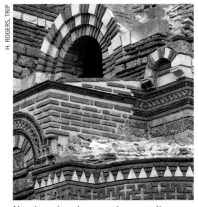

Nesebar church; note the swastikas

Freedom Monument at the Shipka Pass

Beachfront bar, Varna

Fishing boats at Ahtopol

that's been preserved as a pharmacy museum, uphill just past a branch of the **City Art Gallery** (opening times vary).

Further along ul. Sâborna, the spacious **Chomatov House** (daily 9am–noon & 1–5pm) is now a gallery devoted to the work of Zlatyu Boyadzhiev, one of post-war Bulgaria's best-loved painters. Works like *Pernik Miners* show a genuine sympathy for the struggles of working people and won Boyadzhiev the favour of the Party. After a stroke paralysed his right hand, he turned to painting with his left and produced earthier, more mystical pictures like *Dve svadbi* (Two Weddings) and *Orfei* (Orpheus). At weekends the key to the gallery is held at the Balabanov House (see below).

Just beyond here, at no. 22, the **Museum of Icons** (Tues–Sun 9.30am–12.30pm & 2–6pm) is rich in fifteenth- and sixteenth-century, specimens rescued from the region's churches, while next door is the walled **Church of SS Konstantin i Elena** (daily 8am–noon & 1.30–6pm). The frivolous floral patterns adorning its porch give way to a riotously colourful interior, with the brightly painted geometric designs of the ceiling held aloft by pillars topped with Corinthian capitals. Scenes from the gospels cover the surrounding walls, and there's a fine gilt iconostasis by Debâr master Ivan Pashkula, partly decorated by Zahari Zograf.

Upon leaving the church you can turn left at the **crossroads** to reach the Balabanov and Hindlian houses; go straight uphill past the Ethographic Museum towards the Nebet Tepe Citadel; or turn right and pass under the Hisar Kapiya – as described in the following sections.

Around Nebet Tepe

Turn left at the crossroads then head downhill, and you'll come to the maroon-coloured **Balabanov House**, on the corner of Konstantin Stoilov and 4 Yanuari (daily 9am–12.30pm & 1–5.30pm). Once the home of merchant Luka Balabanov, it's now a venue for modern art shows and contains some fine ceilings and a large scale-model of Old Plovdiv. More impressive, however, is the pale blue **Hindlian House** (daily: summer 9am–5.15pm; winter 9am–noon), further downhill at ul. Artin Gidikov 4. The Hindlians were Armenian merchants who travelled as far as Alexandria, St Petersburg and Venice, hence the cityscapes painted in niches upstairs, where the salon contains a wall fountain that once gushed rosewater. An eclectic collection of furniture from other homes fills much of the house, including two Biedermeier-period sitting rooms packed with trinkets from Vienna. Downstairs, the family bathroom resembles a miniature *hammam*, with a marble floor and fountain. Many of Plovdiv's surviving Armenian families still live nearby, sustaining their identity through an **Armenian church**, school and cultural centre, with a monument in the yard recalling the Plovdiv Armenians who died for "Mother Bulgaria" in the Balkan Wars and World War I.

Back at the crossroads, take Ulitsa Dr. Chomakov northwards to the summit of the hill on which the old town is built, and you'll pass Plovdiv's most photographed building, the **Kuyumdzhioglu House**, named after the Greek merchant who commissioned it in 1847. It was built by Hadzhi Georgi of Constantinople, who combined Baroque and native folk motifs in the richly decorated facade, painted black with a yellow trim, its undulating pediment copying the line of the *kobilitsa* or carrying yoke. Now an **Ethnographic Museum** (Tues–Sun 9am–noon & 2–5pm), the mansion's lower rooms display sumptuous paste jewellery and traditional Rhodopi folk costumes, a rose-still and a splendid oil painting of Plovdiv streetlife during the nineteenth century. Upstairs is a grand reception hall with a rosette-and-sunburst ceiling, and two rooms furnished with objects reflecting the *chorbadzhii's* taste for Viennese and French Baroque. During June and September, **chamber music** can be heard in the courtyard.

At the top of Dr. Chomakov, beyond some derelict nineteenth-century houses, lies the ruined **Nebet Tepe Citadel**, covered in punky graffiti. Although it's difficult to discern precise features among the pits and rubble, the site is archeologically rich. Fortified by the Thracian Odrysae tribe as early as the fifth century BC, the hilltop and the settlement of Eumolpios, below, were the beginnings of modern Plovdiv, captured by Philip II of Macedonia in 342 BC. Philip ordered the former to be rebuilt in tandem with the new town – modestly named Philippopolis – which his son, Alexander the Great, abandoned in search of new conquests in Asia. Over the following centuries, the inhabitants must have often resorted to the secret **tunnel** linking Nebet Tepe with the river bank, as the town and citadel were sacked by Romans, Slavs, Bulgars, Byzantium and the Ottoman Empire, to name but a few.

From Hisar Kapiya to the Roman theatre

Turn east at the crossroads, around the corner from the Church of Konstantin i Elena, and you'll pass under the gloomy-looking **Hisar Kapiya** or "fortress gate", which has been rebuilt countless times since Philip II of Macedonia had it raised to form the citadel's eastern portal. Beyond the gate, it's the structure rather than ornamentation that makes the **Georgiadi House**, on ul. Tsanko Lavrenov (Mon & Wed–Sun 8.45am–noon & 2–5pm), so remarkable: the architect has combined "box" oriels with bay windows on a monumental scale. Built for a rich Turk in 1846–48, the mansion contains a gallery where musicians once played, plus various salons now occupied by the **Museum of National Liberation**. Pride of place is given to replicas of the bell that tolled and a cannon that fired during the April Rising, when the *bashibazouks* (see p.425) hung Plovdiv's streets with corpses that the population were forbidden to bury. For her relief-work, Britain's Lady Strangord has a street named after her and her picture in the museum; Disraeli, on the other hand, is execrated for condoning the atrocities and ensuring that one-third of newly liberated Bulgaria was returned to the Turks in the form of Eastern Roumelia. The next-door **Nedkovich House** (Mon–Fri 9am–noon & 1–6.30pm) is renowned for the wood-carved ceiling of the enormous first-floor salon, which contains another collection of nineteenth-century furnishings.

The alleys running downhill behind the Georgiadi and Nedkovich houses lead to several **craft workshops** and many humbler dwellings that have yet to be renovated despite their obvious architectural merits. Looking particularly folorn is the **Church of Sveta Nedelya**, a three-aisled basilica said to contain a delicately carved wooden iconostasis and bishop's throne, and finally undergoing repairs. Descend further still and you'll find yourself in Plovdiv's inner-city **Gypsy quarter** (there are others on the outskirts), a shantytown of one-storey dwellings between the old town and bul. Nezavisimost, where wedding bands play outdoors.

Most visitors, however, head south from here along Kiril Nektariev, one of old Plovdiv's best roads: few facades can match that of the house at no. 15, embellished with swags, medallions and intricate tracery in a vivid shade of blue. Follow Nektariev to the end (the far end of the road is known as Ulitsa Pâldin), and you'll arrive at the Mavrudi House at the corner of Knyaz Tseretelov and Todor

Samodumov, a large buff-coloured mansion with dozens of windows and sturdy ribs supporting the oriels. Popularly referred to as the **Lamartine House** after the French poet who stayed in 1833, writing *Voyage en l'Orient* and recovering from the cholera that killed his daughter in Constantinople, it now contains a small **museum** (in deference to the families that still live there, opening times are limited to Sun, Mon & Tues 9am–noon). There's little to see save for a few pictures of the poet and the places he visited on his travels, accompanied by a few lines of appropriate text, but it's worth peeping inside merely to admire the unusual circular lobby of the house itself.

Ulitsa Tsar Ivailo continues south from here to the **Roman theatre** (daily 9am–5pm), whose stands provide a wonderful view of the distant Rhodopes, and a splendid venue for **concerts and plays**. These imposing ruins are practically the only remains of an acropolis which the Romans built when they raised Trimontium from the position of a vassal town to that of provincial capital during the second century. The acropolis, like the residential districts below, was devastated by Kiva's Goths in 251, and later used as building material when the town revived. From here, paths descend to bul. Vâzrazhdane, at the point where it enters the tunnel beneath the hill, beside which stands the walled **Church of Sveta Marina** (entered from ul. Dospevski or Dr Vâlkovich), with boldly coloured murals beneath its porch and beguiling devils, storks and other creatures peeping out from the wooden foliage of its intricate iconostasis.

Southwest of Old Plovdiv

As well as the three hills covered by the old town, there are three more heights ranged across the southwestern quarter of Plovdiv. The one nearest to the centre, **Sahat Tepe**, provides a great view of the city, and the site for what some believe is the oldest **clock tower** in Eastern Europe, restored by the Turks in 1809, with an inscription enjoining visitors to "look upon" it "and admire!" From here one can gaze levelly across to the giant **Soviet Army Memorial** nicknamed "Alyosha" (which Plovdiv's SDS Mayor wanted to remove but couldn't afford to) on the **Hill of the Liberators**, which also has a pyramidal monument to the liberators of 1878 on a lower peak, where a Thracian temple dedicated to Apollo once stood. Further to the southwest lies the **Hill of Youth**, the largest and most park-like of the three.

Eating

Plovdiv is full of kiosks and cafés selling coffee, *hamburgeri*, sandwiches and other **snack food**, especially along Otets Paisii and Knyaz Aleksandâr I, where you'll also find a *Macdonald's* (the first to open in Bulgaria) at no. 42. For fresh fruit and veg, there's an outdoor **market**, known as the Polnedelnik pazar, on pl. Vâzrazhdane, to the east of Otets Paisii, and a larger one near the junction of bulevards Ruski and 6 Septemvri, west of pl. Sâedinenie.

The choice for evening **meals** is equally wide. Some of the most stylish places are in the National Revival-style houses of Old Plovdiv. They are expensive by native standards, but still affordable to most visitors, if you don't mind splashing out $10–20 for a slap-up meal. Sadly, the food and service at the *Hotel Trimontsium* doesn't match the grandeur of its terraced courtyard nor its nightly folklore floorshow; standards (and prices) at the *Novotel* are far higher.

Modern Plovdiv

Beriozka, Ivan Vazov 25. Housed in the centre for Bulgarian Friendship behind the *Vesta* cinema, this good-value restaurant has a few Russian specialities but concentrates on Bulgarian grilled-meat standards.

Europa, General Gurko 17. Quiet garden restaurant with moderately priced dishes, off ul. Knyaz Aleksandâr I.

Forum, bul. Vâzrazhdane, off pl. Tsentralen. A flashy but reasonably priced place with a kids' playground and naff music, serving regular Bulgarian food and catering to families. Daily 24hr.

Gremi, bul. Vâzrazhdane. Next door to the *Forum*, this lively restaurant on several levels of a turn-of-the-century house with a palm-filled garden serves good mixed grills and fish, at moderate prices. Daily 24hr.

Opera, General Gurko 19. An inexpensive garden restaurant next door to the *Europa*, serving a wide range of pizzas and the usual Balkan grills. Daily noon–midnight.

Rimska Pizzeria, pl. Dzhumaya. Popular eatery offering good value authentic pizzas, with outdoor seating just behind the Dzhumaya mosque. Daily noon–11pm.

Rondo, Veliko Târnovo 9. Upmarket restaurant in a nineteenth-century town house on the south side of the Tsar Simeon Garden. Try the delicious *kombinirana salata*. Daily noon–midnight.

Skorpio, Dr. Vâlkovich 4. Inexpensive air-conditioned eatery off the main drag, serving soups, omelettes and grills. Daily 24hr.

Old Plovdiv

Alafrangite, Kiril Nektariev 17. A tourist trap in elegant surroundings, with a summer garden. Overpriced Bulgarian nosh and surly service. Daily noon–midnight.

Kambanata, ul. Sâborna. Modern air-conditioned restaurant built into a cellar beneath the Church of Sveta Bogoroditsa. The menu features snails and other oddities, besides all the usual native dishes. Daily noon–midnight.

Pâldin, Knyaz Tseretelev 3. Most exclusive of the restaurants in the old town, with a wide choice of traditional Bulgarian dishes. A three-course meal with drinks costs about $20. Daily noon–11pm.

Rimska Taverna, Konstantin Stoilov 16. Reasonably priced restaurant serving well-cooked Bulgarian dishes, including grilled shark and other seafood. Daily 10am–midnight.

Ritora, ul. Tsar Ivailo. Another classic venue for Bulgarian cuisine in an old house near the Roman theatre, rated by many as superior to the *Pâldin*, but with similar prices. Daily noon–midnight.

Trakiiski stan, ul. Pâldin 7. Another beautifully refurbished National Revival interior. Often overrun with tour groups enjoying folklore performances, and average, but overpriced Bulgarian food. Daily noon–10pm.

Drinking

As elsewhere in Bulgaria, you can snatch a quick **coffee** or **fruit juice** almost anywhere in the downtown area from breakfast time till after midnight – and the same goes for drinking alcohol, whether you're talking beer, vodka or cocktails. **Cocktail bars** deserve a special mention as the haunt of nouveaux riches and fashionable youth; the one on the corner of Otets Paissi and Dr. Vâlkovich is lively all day, while those at Knyaz Aleksandâr I 36 and the *VIP Club* (see p.287) are mainly for nightbirds.

Arkite, corner of bul. Vâzrazhdane and Kapitan Raicho. Pleasant outdoor drinking venue with beer garden atmosphere. Also serves basic grilled food.

Big Ben, Knyaz Aleksandâr I 29. A place to lounge in wicker chairs and watch the *korso*. Does good ice creams and crummy pizzas.

Panorama, ul. Sâborna 53. A quiet daytime drinking spot in the old town, that also serves ice cream sundaes. If full, try the *Saga* or *Blansh* immediately next door.

Sinyata kâshta, ul. Slaveikov 25. Cosy bar housed in a National Revival mansion. Good place to drink or enjoy a quiet evening meal.

Vladi, Pâldin 6. Family-run bar in an old house in the *Stariyat grad*, with a pleasant garden at the back.

Entertainment and nightlife

Plovdiv takes its culture seriously, and hosts a comprehensive programme of music all year round. Unfortunately, there's no centralized office where you can find out what's on and events are simply publicized by banners or posters – invariably in Bulgarian only. **Classical concerts** take place at the Plovdiv Philharmonic Orchestra's concert hall on the south side of pl. Tsentralen, while the *Mesalitinov Theatre* at Aleksandrovska 36 is the best venue for **drama**.

There's a busy schedule of festivals too. During the first half of January, the **Winter Festival of Symphony Music** allows the Philharmonic Orchestra to flex its muscles; international virtuosi participate in the prestigious **Festival of Chamber Music**, held in the courtyard of the Ethnographic Museum in June every odd-numbered year (native ensembles play on until September, and during even-numbered years); and **Trakiisko Lyato** (Thracian Summer) in August features pop and classical music, as well as **folk dancing** ensembles from as far away as Egypt, performing in the spectacular surroundings of the Roman theatre – which is also used for staging **opera** and **drama** in May and September (coinciding with the fairs).

Although students organize their own **discos** (including Greek, Turkish and Macedonian events for their respective contingents), the venues change so often that they're strictly by word of mouth and not readily accessible to visitors, leaving you with a choice of two permanent venues. *Florida* on Avksenii Veleshki near the southwest corner of the Tsar Simeon Garden plays techno and pop and attracts all kinds, while *B52*, directly opposite the entrance to the fairgrounds, is a glitzier place aimed at nouveau riches. Over the summer there are also three discos in a building near the rowing lake (*grebnata baza*) in Loven Park, 5km west of the centre, which is a popular hangout. One plays techno, another pop and rap, and the third Turkish, Gypsy and Arabic music. You can get there on bus #5 or #15 but will need to take a taxi back.

Listings

Airlines BALKAN, ul. Gladston 4 (Mon–Fri 8am–1pm & 2–6.30pm, Sat 8am–noon ☎ 032/633081).

Books and newspapers There's a foreign-language bookshop (Mon–Fri 9am–6pm, Sat 9.30am–1.30pm) outside the Vazov Library on ul. Vaptsarov. A stall on the pl. Tsentralen sells foreign newspapers.

Buses Seats on international buses can be booked through MATPU in the pedestrian subway in front of *Hotel Trimontsium* (Mon–Fri 9am–6pm, Sat 9am–noon), or at Diligence Express, Knyaz Aleksandâr I 49 (Mon–Fri 9am–6pm, Sat 9am–noon).

Car rental Available at the *Novotel*, Zlatyu Boyadzhiev 2 (☎032/652505), and *Maritsa*, ul. Tsar Boris III Obedinitel (☎032/652877), hotels.

Car repairs Autoservis, near the *Trakiya* campsite (see p.287).

Consulates Greece, Preslav 10 (☎032/232003); Russia, Ivan Vazov 20 (☎032/224767); Turkey, Filip Makedonski 10 (☎032/239010).

Dentists Knyaz Aleksandâr I 1, 3rd floor (☎032/267043).

Emergencies Ambulance ☎150; police ☎032/232410.

Filling stations out along the Svilengrad and Sofia highways.

Football Plovdiv has three first-division teams: Botev, Lokomotiv and Spartak. Botev, currently the city's premier outfit, play at the Hristo Botev stadium east of the centre on bul. Iztochen (trolleybus #3 from the station), and have a hard core of supporters who model themselves on Real Madrid's "Ultras". The Lokomotiv stadium is farther south off bul. Sankt Peterburg, and best reached by taxi, while the decrepit Spartak ground is just south of the central station on the other side of the tracks. Tickets cost about $1.50.

Money exchange The 24-hour exchange beside *McDonald's* only takes US$ and DM. You can cash travellers' cheques at the *Novotel* (see p.287), or Bulbank (Mon–Fri 9am–4.30pm) on pl. Stefan Stambolov, which also has an ATM , accepting Visa, Plus and Electron cards.

Pharmacies Dzhumayata, on ul. Sâborna, behind the Dzhumaya mosque, is open 24 hours a day.

Post office Pl. Tsentralen 1 (Mon–Sat 7am–7pm & Sun 7–11am).

Telephones At the post office on Pl. Tsentralen 1 (daily 6am–11pm).

Train tickets Domestic and international bookings from BDZh/Rila, Nezavisimost 29 (Mon–Fri 8.30am–noon & 1–5pm).

Plovdiv to the Turkish border

There are good reasons why so many visitors travel between Plovdiv and Turkey non-stop. The settlements along the way are mainly workaday places lacking in specific attractions, and there are more facilities for travellers along the E80 than there are off the highway. Bulgarians have become accustomed to the sight of foreigners speeding through their country en route to Turkey or Greece, so travellers shouldn't be surprised if the hand of friendship isn't always extended. In the past, stories abounded of the police hassling travellers with transit visas who strayed off the highway, hitting them with petty fines for "safety violations" or demanding that they change money into non-convertible leva. Nowadays, cases

---

MOVING ON FROM PLOVDIV

From Plovdiv there are frequent trains to **Sofia** plus four daily expresses to **Burgas** and two to **Varna**. Reaching **central or northern Bulgaria** often entails a change of trains at Stara Zagora, but direct services run to Karlovo, Asenovgrad, Panagyurishte and Hisar.

Travelling to **Turkey** from Plovdiv, the Balkan Express runs daily trains to Istanbul throughout the year (8hr 30min), while an additional service, the Istanbul Express, operates between May and September. If travelling to **Greece**, there's a connecting service to Thessaloniki at Svilengrad (12hr). You can buy tickets at the Railway Bookings office on bul. Nezavisimost (see "Listings", above).

Both MATPU and Diligence Express (see "Listings", on previous page) offer daily **buses** to Thessaloniki (14hr), and Athens (23–26hr), and daily services to Istanbul (except on Fri; 4–5hr). Fewer services run to Izmir (3 weekly on Mon, Wed & Sun; 8–10hr), Xanti (Mon & Fri; 12–14hr) and Ohrid (July & August only 1 daily; 10–11hr). Both companies charge about $45 to Athens, $20 to Istanbul.

such as these seem to be the exception rather than the rule, but officials at the border still have a well-deserved reputation for venality.

Travelling **by road** you'll pass **Klokotnitsa** village, just west of Dimitrovgrad, the site of Ivan Asen's victory (1230) over Theodor Comnenus, the usurper of Byzantium, that forced the empire to recognize Ivan as "Tsar of the Bulgarians and Greeks" and accept the betrothal of his daughter to Baldwin, the teenage emperor of Byzantium. Approaching the border **by train** means a brief encounter with Dimitrovgrad – full of power stations and reeking chemical factories – before speeding on to Svilengrad and the Turkish border or catching a bus or train south to Haskovo and Kârdzhali.

Haskovo

Little visited by tourists except as a stopover en route to Turkey, **HASKOVO**, 78km southeast of Plovdiv, has slightly more to offer than first meets the eye, hosting festivals throughout the year and serving as a springboard for visiting the nature reserve at Madzharovo (see p.320). Aside from that, its appeal lies in the faintly raffish mixture of Turkish and Bulgarian culture, symbolized by the oldest mosque in the Balkans and a smattering of National Revival buildings. The town was founded in around 1395 and named Haskoy by the Turks, who predominated here for the next five hundred years until the development of the tobacco industry and the Balkan War of 1912 swelled the number of Bulgarians, who now form the majority. Relations betweeen the two are good, however, with Socialists, conservatives and the Muslim DPS working together on the city council.

The Town

Civic and social life revolves around **pl. Svoboda**, a T-shaped junction of flagstones and flowerbeds centred on a memorial to the dead of successive wars. The **History Museum**, on the junction's southern arm (Mon–Fri 9am–noon & 2–6pm), contains a fine collection of pre-Ottoman artefacts – especially Roman, Byzantine and medieval **coins** – but passes over five centuries of Turkish rule in relative silence; the tobacco workers' strike of 1927 gets more attention.

A block or so south towards the river, a graceful minaret rises above the **Eski dzhamiya** (Old mosque), whose facade has been recently replastered so that it's hard to believe that this was the first mosque erected on the Balkan peninsula, immediately after the Ottoman conquest. Even during the 1980s, when mosques elsewhere in Bulgaria were locked and derelict, Haskovo's remained in use, its prayer hall covered in carpets and its *imam* unfazed by foreign visitors, who are nowadays more welcome than ever.

Follow bul. Bâlgariya beside the River Haskovska (or take bus #1, #12 or #101) to find the **Church of Sveta Bogoroditsa**, a simple basilica of heavy brick filled with fussy woodcarving, and an **exhibition of icons** (Tues, Sat & Sun 9am–noon & 2–6pm) next door. By crossing over the road bridge and heading back towards the centre along Tsar Osvoboditel you can also visit the **Paskalevata Kâshta**, on the corner of Episkop Sofroni (Tues, Sat & Sun 9am–noon & 2–6pm). This period-furnished house was the birthplace of Aleksandâr Paskaliev, a pioneer of Bulgarian publishing.

The wooded **Park Kenana** to the north of town is a favourite place for recreation, with tennis courts, restaurants and cafés; catch bus #2 or #102 from pl.

Spartak, on the north bank of the bend in the river. On the last weekend in May special buses are laid on to take people to the **Gathering of Beautiful Trakiya**, a festival of folk groups from the southeastern Rhodopes and Aegean Thrace. Two other events for music lovers are the three-day **Jazz Festival** in late September or early October, and the festival of **Symphonic Music** named after the violinist Nedyalka Simeonova, at the end of October. While the festival of **Young Poets** (late March/early April) celebrates new poetic talent, the **Haskovo Fair** (around September 8) is a trade fair with some sports events to enliven things.

Practicalities

From the **bus station** on bul. Sâedinenie, ten minutes east of the centre along ul. San Stefano, there are hourly buses to Kârdzhali, five a day to Svilengrad and three to Sofia, but the most useful are the daily buses to Madzharovo (9am & 3.20pm) and Borislavtsi (Sun–Fri at 3.20pm) – enabling one to reach the nature reserve there (see p.320) – and the private Artour buses to Plovdiv, Harmanli, Burgas and other destinations. The **train station**, 1.5km further out along bul. Sâedinenie (bus #5, #12 or #13), is of less use.

The three-star *Aida*, on pl. Svoboda (☎038/25164; ③), is the plushest of Haskovo's **hotels** and far better value than the dismal *Rodopi* (☎038/35988; ③) at bul. Bâlgariya 39. Cheaper options include the *Mini-Hotel Cuba* at bul. Sv. Sv. Kiril i Metodi 80 (②) in the modern suburb of Kuba (bus #5 from pl. Spartak), or the seedy *Zodiak* (☎038/62644; ②) above a kebab shop on bul. Osvobozhdenie (bus #4 or #6). If you've got your own transport, the *Motel Klokotnitsa*, 5km west of town on the E80 (☎038/25387; ③), is a good bet, as is the agreeable *Yoniko Hotel* (☎038/2194; ④) in the small spa resort of Haskovski Mineralni Bani, 20km from town (also accessible by bus).

There's no shortage of places **to eat and drink** around pl. Svoboda, where the *Aida-tours* restaurant by the *Hotel Aida* is patronized by local VIPs and has a singer most nights and a floorshow at weekends. Another place that's highly rated is the *Gurkovata Kâshta*, in an old house in the Bulgarian quarter with a garden and private rooms, which can be reached from the Church of Sv. Bogoroditsa by heading up ul. Berkovski and turning right into General Gurko. Both charge around $10 for a three-course meal, and stay open until midnight.

An ATM in the *Hotel Aida* allows **cash** withdrawals on Visa, Cirrus and Eurocard.

Harmanli

Founded by the Turks in the sixteenth century, **HARMANLI**, 33km east of Haskovo, gets its name from the threshing mills (*harman*) that once abounded on the surrounding plain, nowadays given over to growing cotton, mulberries (for silkworms) and tobacco. It's a tiny, sleepy place that seems to ignore the E80 and the outside world, where dry fountains and riverbeds speak of a desolation measured out over coffee and worry-beads. The shell of the *Hotel Hebros* guides strangers from the bus station to the central square, near Harmanli's only "sights", both of which date from the 1500s. To one side of the hotel stands the chunky ruined wall of an Ottoman **caravanserai**, while behind the supermarket is the hump-backed **Gurbav Bridge**, with its flowery dedication in Arabic:

As a token of his gratitude to God the Grand Vizier ordered an arch like a rainbow to be built over the River Harmanli . . . and alleviated rich and poor alike from their sorrows. The world is a bridge which is crossed by both king and pauper. When I saw the completion of this bridge, in praying to God, I spoke this inscription.

From midway across the bridge you can see a discarded statue of Lenin, languishing behind the police station.

Practicalities

Harmanli's centrally located **bus terminal** is preferable as a point of arrival to the **train station**, some way out to the southeast and connected to town by bus. While the *Hotel Hebros* is under refurbishment, the only **accommodation** in town is the family-run *Algera*, on ul. Arda (☎0373/5193; ①) by the E80, 1km from the centre in the direction of Svilengrad. Motorists have an alternative in the pleasant *Izvorât na Belonogata* **motel** (☎0373/5091; ③) 4km further on, which takes its name from the PR Slaveykov poem "The spring of the maiden with snow-white feet", a reference to a nearby fountain, said to have been built by a vizier of Constantinople to win the heart of a Bulgarian woman.

Svilengrad and the borders

Despite its proximity to two busy border crossings, **SVILENGRAD** seems almost as dozy as Harmanli. There's little specific to see save the sixteenth-century **Mustafa Pasha Bridge** – known to the locals as *Stariya Most* – which links the town with village-like suburbs on the far bank of the River Maritsa. This 295-metre-long structure of Karabag stone supported by thirteen arches is an even finer achievement than Harmanli's similar Gurbav Bridge. By **staying** in the fancy *Hotel Svilengrad*, on the main square (☎0379/260935; ③), or tracking down the so-called *English Pub*, you can also see local *bortsi* (mafiosi) and smugglers at play. Humbler traders stick to mini-hotels (①) like the two on ul. Levski, around the corner from the *Svilengrad*.

Worth a visit if you have a car are a couple of antiquities near the village of **MEZEK**, 10km southwest of town, reached by turning off near the truck park for the Greek border crossing. Just before the village, a road to the left leads past an army base (ask the guard for permission) to a **Thracian tomb**, left open to the elements. You'll need a torch to examine the fine masonry in the corridor (21m long and corbel-roofed, like the stairway in the Great Pyramid) and circular funerary chamber (where bronze artefacts were found, from the fourth century BC). About 1km beyond Mezek, the ruined **Neutzikon fortress** (or *Kaleto*) is the best preserved of the many fortresses raised to guard against Byzantine incursions during the eleventh and twelfth centuries. Both languish in a so-called *granichna zona*, or **border zone**, which used to be strictly off-limits in Communist times and is still patrolled by border police, nowadays engaged in keeping refugees out rather than Bulgarians in. You'll be expected to produce your passport and a valid reason for being here if you're stopped.

Crossing into Greece or Turkey

Svilengrad's **train station** is 5km west of town, with irregular buses to and from the centre, so travellers heading for Turkey should either stay aboard the train from Plovdiv and skip Svilengrad entirely, or be sure to leave plenty of time to get to the station to catch a train to Istanbul around midnight. Trains to Alexandroupoli in Greece run daily, but only during June and July, while the 24-hour **road crossing into Greece**, 2km nearer town than the station, is used almost exclusively by truckers.

Far more traffic crosses the **Turkish border** at **KAPITAN ANDREEVO**, 15km beyond Svilengrad (three buses daily), where vehicles entering Bulgaria are liable to rigorous examinations. Inside Turkey (where motorists and train passengers undergo customs at Kapikule), it's pretty easy to catch a *dolmus* (shared taxi) to **Edirne**, 19km east, which should drop you in the centre near the town's splendid mosque; the bus station is 3km to the southeast and the train station 2km further out.

THE RHODOPES

According to Thracian mythology, the mortal lovers Hem and Rhodopis dared call themselves after the divine Zeus and Hera, who duly punished the couple by turning them into mountains separated by the River Maritsa – him the Balkans and she **the Rhodopes**. Straddling Greece and Bulgaria, the Rhodopes are the land where panpipes, Orpheus and the Orphic Cult originated, a region rich in gems and ores, but otherwise not fit for much beyond raising sheep and growing tobacco. Unlike the rest of Bulgaria, whole communities converted to Islam after the conquest, and of the numerous Turks who settled here many outstayed the empire's collapse – their descendants now constitute Bulgaria's largest ethnic minority. While hydro-electric schemes and tourism have pushed the Rhodopes into the twentieth century, the region is still, as Leslie Gardiner noted in the 1960s, a weird mixture of opposites: "donkeys and turbo-generators, Alpine flowers and tropical foliage, bikinis in winter and thick Turkish woollens in summer".

While the ski resort of **Pamporovo** and the **Bachkovo Monastery** are well known to foreigners, the region's scenic highlands and picturesque villages have only been "discovered" quite recently. Of all Bulgaria's mountain ranges, this is the best for **walking** (the central and western Rhodopes especially), **caving** (around **Trigrad**), **birdwatching** (near **Madzharovo**) and other special interests. The Rhodopes are also the home of some fantastic folk music and **festivals** (mostly in August) at **Rozhen**, **Mugla**, **Dorkovo**, Madzharovo and **Shiroka Lâka**. The last is deservedly renowned for its traditional architecture though it is far from the only village in the range with stone houses and bridges, nor even the finest example of the genre, an accolade which belongs to the Agushevi Konak at **Mogilitsa**, near the regional capital, **Smolyan**. The eastern Rhodopes are less rewarding, although **Kârdzhali** can serve as a base for exploring the weird rock formations in the region, and its museum has a fine collection of folk costumes, gemstones and historic artefacts.

Should you wish to join an **organized hiking tour** in the region, contact the Sofia-based adventure tourism agency Odysseiya-In (see p.000), whose Rhodopes itinerary includes Mostovo, Krâstova gora, Manastir, Rozhen, Progled and Trigrad, and can be extended into the Pirin and Rila mountains if desired. Tours booked abroad through a foreign operator are likely to be handled by SunShine Tours, also based in Sofia (see p.50).

The legacy of its history is far from abstract here, as Bulgarians recall five centuries of oppression epitomized by the massacre at **Batak** in 1876, while the Pomak (Slav Muslim) and ethnic Turkish inhabitants of the Rhodopes have living memories of the "name-changing campaign" and "Great Excursion" of the late 1980s, when more than 200,000 of them fled to Turkey (most later returned). Though it's partly due to the state's efforts to hide what was happening in the region that the Rhodopes remained *terra incognita* for so long, even in olden times roadbuilders were sometimes attacked by villagers, who preferred to be as remote as possible – as the Turks living between **Krumovgrad** and **Ivailovgrad** still do.

Tourist facilities and public transport vary from good to non-existent, and the recent growth in **private hotels** is still currently confined to a few areas. While a car provides greater flexibility, there's enough transport and accommodation for you to be able to visit almost all of the region's attractions, given sufficient time. Even with a **car**, one averages only 40km per hour, due to the poor terrain and the roads. **Buses** from Plovdiv run to Bachkovo, Pamporovo and Smolyan in the central Rhodopes; Velingrad to the west, and Kârdzhali to the east; while Madzharovo can be reached from Haskovo. With the exception of the scenic narrow-gauge line linking Septemvri on the plain with Bansko in the Pirin Mountains, the limited **train** service in the Rhodopes is of little use.

The central Rhodopes

The northernmost spurs of the Rhodopes rear up from the plain barely 10km south of Plovdiv, with numerous minor roads running up the narrow valleys of the streams that gush down to feed the Maritsa. The main route south, however, into the **central Rhodopes** starts beyond the town of **Asenovgrad**, and follows the ruggedly beautiful valley of the River Chepelarska past the historic **Bachkovo Monastery** up to the ski resorts of **Chepelare** and **Pamporovo**, before descending to **Smolyan**. This road is well served by bus, unlike those in other parts of the highlands, where you need a car to get around or enough time to go walking. The scenery in this region is magnificent and there are enough villages offering accommodation to support all kinds of hikes around **Mostovo**, **Manastir**, **Momchilovtsi** and **Progled**.

Asenovgrad

Half-hourly buses speed across the dusty plain between Plovdiv and **ASENOV-GRAD** 20km south, a light and breezy town built around a large park. Train and bus terminals lie on the northern outskirts, from where it's a short walk through a park and across the river to a modern town square. Two church spires are visible on the hill immediately above: the resplendently ochre-coloured Sveti Dimitâr on the left and the smaller Sveta Troitsa on the right. More interesting, however, is the town's main shopping thoroughfare running south from the square, where a small **Historical Museum** (Mon–Sat 9am–noon & 2–5pm) holds local Neolithic and Thracian finds – including a fine bronze helmet and the iron wheel rims of a Thracian chariot.

It was the Thracians who first fortified a crag overlooking the entrance to the Chepelarska gorge, which can be reached by a side-road 2.5km south of town. If it seems a hard slog, remember that the thirteenth-century **Church of Sveta Bogoroditsa** just below the summit was rebuilt by a disabled man who walked every day to work on his self-appointed task. Higher uphill are the **remains of a medieval fortress** founded during the eleventh century and enlarged after Asen II's victory over the Byzantine Empire in 1230, half of which slid down the hill some years ago. From this derived Asenovgrad's medieval name, Stanimaka – "protector of the mountain pass".

If you want **to stay**, you could try the two-star *Hotel Asenovets* on the main square (☎0331/23288; ③), though you'd do better to take one of the regular buses up the valley towards Bachkovo, Chepelare or Smolyan.

Towards Bachkovo

Just beyond Asenovgrad the road enters the impressive **Chepelarska gorge**, its river nowadays harnessed to produce electricity. Heavy trucks bound for the mines around Ardino are another sign that modernization has come to the Rhodopes, though goatherds with their flocks and mule-trains bearing packs are still a common sight. The area immediately south of Asenovgrad is a popular weekend picnic spot, with pebble-strewn riverside beaches, trails into the forested hills, and numerous roadside cafés.

Throughout the centuries of Ottoman rule, the Rhodopes was the region most consistently infested with outlaws: *haiduks*, whom the Bulgars now romantically view as precursors of the patriotic *cheti*, but also bandits of Turkish origin known as *kârdzhalii*, who spread terror among the villages. The last wave of armed resistance to authority occurred in 1947–49, when anti-Communist partisans operated in the hills around Asenovgrad.

Bachkovo Monastery and around

Nine kilometres south of Asenovgrad, the village of **Bachkovo**, with its stone houses overgrown with flowers, gives no indication of what to expect 1.5km further up the road at **BACHKOVO MONASTERY** (*Bachkovski manastir*; daily 6.30am– 9pm). Gardiner's description of it as "a mixed bag of buildings – chapels, ossuaries, cloisters, cells – daubed with frescos more naive than artistic" doesn't do justice to Bulgaria's second largest monastery, which, like Rila, has been declared a world monument by UNESCO. It was founded in 1083 by two Georgians in the service of the Byzantine Empire, one of whom, Grigoriy Pakuryani, renounced the governorship of Smolyan and Adrianople to devote the remainder of his life to meditation.

You enter the monastery through a small iron-plated door which opens onto a cobbled courtyard surrounded by wooden galleries. The wall of the refectory on the left is covered with **frescos** providing a narrative of the monastery's history: they show Bachkovo roughly as it appears today, but watched by God's eye and a celestial Madonna and child, with pilgrims proceeding to a hill in the vicinity to place icons. Other frescos depict the slaying of the dragon: a powerful archetype in ancient European and Chinese cosmology, appropriated by Christianity to be vanquished by St George and symbolize the demise of paganism. It can also be read as an allusion to the Turks who laid waste to Bachkovo in the early sixteenth century, and the patient restoration of the monastery by the Bulgarians.

Though it's not immediately apparent, the monastery consists of two separate courtyards connected via the wing containing the seventeeth-century **refectory** (*trapeznitsa*), whose vaulted hall is decorated with a *Tree of Isaiah* and a *Procession of the Miraculous Icon* executed by pupils of Zahari Zograf. Unfortunately it's not open regularly and neither is the **museum**, a jumble of carved spoons, broken teapots, ecclesiastical hats and filigreed crosses. If the gate into the second courtyard is open, you can view one of Bachkovo's churches, **Sveti Nikolai**, whose porch features a fine *Last Judgement*, which includes portraits of the artist Zograf and two colleagues in the upper left-hand corner. Alas, it too may be inaccessible due to ongoing repairs.

The oldest building in the monastery is its principal church, **Sveta Bogoroditsa**, built in 1604. Frescos in the porch of its bell tower depict the horrors in store for sinners: among the scenes of retribution, a *boyar* (a medieval nobleman) is tormented on his deathbed by a devil brandishing a female doll-figure (presumably representative of past infidelities), while women watch in terror. The entrance is more cheerful, with the Holy Trinity painted on strips set at angles in a frame, so that one sees God or Christ flanking a dove, depending on which side you approach from, like a medieval hologram. On the right of the nave as you enter is a fourteenth-century Georgian **icon of the Virgin** which legend claims to be an authentic portrait of Mary, painted by the Apostle Luke. The icon plays a central role in celebrations of the name-day of the Assumption of the Virgin (August 15), and a ritual procession to a chapel in the nearby hills 25 days after the Orthodox Easter (see below).

Walks around the monastery

If you want to make more of your visit, there's a pleasant thirty-minute walk to a shrine near the spot where Bachkovo's treasures were once hidden from the Turks – a deed commemorated by an annual procession of believers bearing an icon. The path begins opposite the monastery gates and passes by the **church of Sveta Troitsa**, which contains early medieval frescos and life-size portraits of Tsar Ivan Aleksandâr (1331–71) and his family who endowed the monastery, but is kept locked to protect them from looters. Don't be led astray by the red arrows near the picnic-meadow, fifteen minutes or so further on. Instead take the path straight ahead across the meadow, which leads shortly to a sign marking the **Chervenata Stena nature reserve** of Balkan plant species, and a chapel built beside a stream, on the far side of which, rock-cut steps lead to a cave chapel and a stone-built one – the three are collectively known as **Ayazmoto**.

Although the **trail** continues upwards via dramatic waterfall basins (traversable only in summer on ladders made of branches) and punishing switchbacks (known as the "Forty Legs"), the *Martsiganitsa* chalet that was once the objective for hikers has now been demolished – though it's still marked on maps – leaving anyone who completes this strenuous but exhilarating 3–4 hour hike with no option but to follow another, easier path back down to the road a few kilometres past the monastery in the direction of **Narechenski Bani**. This small resort with open-air mineral baths, makes a good base for exploring some more delightful trails into the foothills, which abound in butterflies, insects, fungi and rare herbs; if you're lucky, you might even see a spotted eagle.

Practicalities

An easy day-trip from Plovdiv, the monastery can be reached by any of the five or so daily **buses** to Chepelare or Smolyan, as well as on hourly services from Asenovgrad to Bachkovo, which run past the monastery drive. It's hard to find

HIKING AROUND KRÂSTOVA GORA AND MOSTOVO

South of Bachkovo, there are some superb **hikes** amidst stunning mountain scenery, which can be tackled by arranging for a driver to drop you at one location and pick you up elsewhere – a strategy which can also be applied to longer hikes involving an overnight stay at the *Svoboda* chalet or Manastir (see opposite). Such **buses** as exist in the region centre on the ugly mining village of Lâki, 24km south of Bachkovo, with one a day from Plovdiv and two from Asenovgrad, plus local services to Belitsa (two daily) and Borovo (Tues, Wed & Thurs only). All the walks described below are covered by the two *BTS* **maps** of the Rhodopes, #3 and #5.

One of the most rewarding walks in the area is to the summit of **KRÂSTOVA GORA** (Hill of the Cross), a place of pilgrimage for centuries until the Communists suppressed it, but now revived. Its holiness derives from a fragment of the True Cross which was sent for safekeeping to Bachkovo after the fall of Constantinople, and transferred to a monastery here after Bulgaria was invaded by the Turks. Although the relic was lost when the monastery was ravaged, people came to pray and claimed to have seen a gleaming cross in the sky. The spring below the peak was also said to have medicinal properties. After the Ottoman yoke was lifted a **cross** was erected on the summit weighing ninety-nine kilos (three times the age of Christ when he was crucified) and the **Sveta Troitsa** church was built with stones from the original monastery. Legend has it that if a pregnant woman enters the church she can choose the sex of her child. The other church and the chapels lining the way to the summit were only built a few years ago. Traditionally, pilgrims spend the eve of *Krâstovden* (September 14) camped out on the mountain, before greeting the sunrise with a special liturgy devoted to health; in 1998, 20,000 people attended. People also come at Easter, Christmas and New Year (despite the snow), and you'll encounter a few souls on any day of the year.

Although Krâstova gora is accessible by a dirt road from the village of Borovo, off the road to Lâki, a much nicer approach is to walk there from **MOSTOVO**, on the other side of the hills. The village's name derives from a natural rock bridge (*most*) in the gorge below, where the river vanishes underground – you can see it before entering Mostovo, then pick up the **trail to Krâstova gora** near the top of the village, on ul. Hristo Smirnenski. Initially a steep goat track that divides after 45 minutes, the path to Krâstova gora is clearly signposted and walkable in just over an hour – providing you turn right upon emerging from the woods. By turning left instead you'll be on the trail to Velichki Vrâh, passing an ex-Party hunting lodge en route to the **Karadzhov Kâmak** (1hr 30min) – colossal rocks dimpled with giant "fingerprints". A further hour brings you to a clearing where the trail starts descending; an hour and forty minutes later you face a brief, taxing ascent of a ridge called the **Rhodopskoto Konche** (Rhodope Horse), before reaching a forestry road down to Perleza, a good place to be met if you're not up to carrying on to the *Svododa* chalet (a further two hours).

out the exact times of buses returning (there's usually one every hour until about 5pm), so you may be in for a wait, though minibuses between Smolyan and Plovdiv sometimes pick up passengers here.

In the vicinity of the monastery are three **restaurants** (*Vodopad* is the best) and various snack stalls. You can stay in the monastery's guest "cells" for $6 a night, but there's no hot water. Otherwise the nearest **accommodation** is back in Asenovgrad, or 14km farther on in Narechenski Bani, which also has two decent hiking chalets, a year-round campsite 3km upriver, plenty of private rooms (ask around at the bus station), and two local tavernas serving delicious traditional food.

Hikes around Manastir

About 40km south of Bachkovo, **Manastir**, 1500m above sea level, is the highest village in Bulgaria and (they say) the Balkan peninsula – and if that wasn't enough, is also the birthplace of Petâr Stoyanov, Bulgaria's current president, though he's not liked here since most of the local mines closed down, and his relatives don't invite him back any more. With its steeply terraced houses, potato and tobacco plots, stacks of firewood and scampering goats, Manastir makes a a good base for hiking and gives a feel for rural life in the Rhodopes. The easiest way to get there is on the daily **bus** (at 5.30pm) from **Lâki**, 20km north.

One of the best hikes from Manastir is to **Progled**, a trip which can be done in 5–6 hours, but is far nicer stretched out with an overnight stay at a hiking chalet or Momchilovtsi; you'll need map #4 in the *BTS* Rhodopi series. The trail begins behind Manastir, blue and white markers starting at a fountain five minutes' walk uphill, whence it's fifteen minutes to a flat, stony track where you bear right into the woods after 500m to find an old Roman road. Another twenty minutes brings you to a junction of trails, a blue one to the *Svoboda* and a red one to the *Prepsa* chalets. The latter passes a beautiful clearing of fallen pines and purple thistles and is easy going all the way, so that you arrive at *Prepsa* two and a half hours after setting out, in the mood to press on to *Svoboda* (2hr) or westwards to Haidushki Polyani (35min) and the *Momchil Yunak* chalet (1hr more).

Haidushki Polyani (Outlaws' Meadows) is a trade union resort where you can sink a beer before examining an obelisk in the woods, on the spot where leaders of the Macedonian revolutionary movement decided to launch the 1903 Ilinden uprising. The partisan figures on the obverse side typify the Communist Party's efforts to identify itself with past liberation movements. Sporadic red and white markers indicate the trail from here to *Momchil Yunak*, a primitive chalet near an ex-Party villa that's now an exclusive hotel. From here it's 20 minutes' walk to the main road, where by heading left you'll soon reach the turn-off for **Momchilovtsi** – a further 6km uphill. If you're heading to **Progled**, simply stay on the main road, and follow it downhill for 11km.

Practicalities

There's no shortage of places **to stay** in any of the villages mentioned above. In **MANASTIR**, you best bet is with the Angelov family (☎030528/289), who charge $10 a night including breakfast – if you're lucky you'll be served a delicious home-baked *Rodopska banitsa* (a kind of soufflé). The bar-grill on the square can rustle up surprisingly good **meals** and sometimes has music and dancing.

MOMCHILOVTSI, set on a steep slope with gorgeous views in all directions, abounds in family hotels – some with carved wooden ceilings and open fires – such as *Antonia Kaneva's*, ul. Elitsa 2 (☎0323/249; ④); *Shipkata*, Stamboliiski 22 (☎0323/510; ③); *Igrev*, Sv. Sv. Kiril i Metodi 9 (☎923/804; ③); or *Rodopchanka* (☎0323/863; ③), Byalo More 40. You can also book accommodation through the local **tourist office** (irregular hours; ☎03023/2212, fax 03023/2823), which holds the key to a small museum of local history and handicrafts. The tourist office or your hotel owner can usually arrange rides to Pamporovo or Smolyan (14km), and the observatory or the festival at Rozhen (7km).

THE ROZHEN OBSERVATORY AND FESTIVAL

Visible for miles around, the lofty white dome of **Rozhen Observatory** contains a mammoth optical telescope manufactured at the Zeiss works in East Germany, which has scanned the cosmos since the 1970s. The site was chosen beacause of the clear skies and absence of background light; besides the main telescope, there are three smaller ones on other hilltops. As they only work at night, people who take the trouble to fix a **visit** (Thurs 2–4pm; ☎921/356 or 357) are denied the thrill of stargazing but may still enjoy the telescope and its vintage early 1960s' computer hardware, which are mainly used for checking astronomical maps.

The Rozhen peak near the observatory is the setting for the largest folklore festival in the Rhodopes – the **Rozhenski Sâbor** – where almost every village is represented by dancers, singers or musicians. It's usually held on the last weekend in August, but check with the tourist office in Smolyan to be sure (see p.308). One or two buses a day from Plovdiv cross the Rozhen Pass en route to Smolyan (and vice versa), running past the slip road to the observatory, or you can walk here from Progled in an hour cross-country (or a couple of hours along the road).

In **PROGLED**, a nice village just off the main road between Chepelare and Pamporovo, accommodation is available at the hostel behind the church or at the nameless, comfortable hotel (③) in a large white house with a satellite dish, farther uphill. The village also boasts a surprisingly classy restaurant, the *Progledski Hanche*, which is open 24 hours.

Chepelare and Zabârdo

The small mountain town of **CHEPELARE**, 6km north of Progled, is popular with Bulgarians who want somewhere quiet to relax and enjoy the fresh air and scenery, and are unfazed by such blots on the landscape as a timber mill or the Orion ski factory – the only one in Bulgaria. Aside from its **ski run** – at over 5km, the longest in the Rhodopes – the only specific attraction is the well sign-posted **Speleological Museum**, (officially Tues–Sat 9am–5pm, but hours variable) that whets your appetite to visit the local caves; some "cave pearls" from the Yagodina Cave (see p.313) are its most prized exhibit.

Chepelare has many new family **hotels** that compare favourably with the older complexes at Pamporovo (see opposite). *Skior 19*, ul. Sportna 1 (☎03051/3681; ③), and *Kiryakov-B*, ul. Zora 2 (☎03051/3069; ③), are both owned by former skiing champions, while the *Trifonov* (☎03051/3552; ③) and *Kostovski* (☎03051/3063; ③) guest houses have suites and cable TV. The best **restaurants** in which to enjoy Rhodopi specialities, and a roaring log fire, are the *Gergana* and *Gorski Kât*, both moderately priced.

In a valley off the main road, 28km northwest of Chepelare, **ZABÂRDO** is the best-known **weaving** village in the Rhodopes, and home to the colouful rugs and blankets that abound in the region. Here, you can buy a *kozek* (the local word for a rug) from individual weavers, and watch them at their work. Unusually for what is a predominantly Pomak village, Zabârdo has a **folk music festival** on the Day of the Assumption (August 15). With a car, you can also visit from here the so-called **Miraculous Bridges** (*Chudnite Mostove*), rock formations resembling bridges, created when an earthquake destroyed an old cave. Near the second bridge is the entrance to the Icy Cave, which remains below freezing even in summer (you can't go inside). The bridges are sited in another side valley, accessible by a fork in the road to Zabârdo.

Pamporovo

PAMPOROVO the "Gem of the Rhodopes" currently looks rather tarnished, with many of its hotels showing their age. That said, it remains a user-friendly ski resort where mild weather and good snow-cover make **skiing** conditions near perfect from mid-December to mid-April, with a range of classes and pistes to suit everyone from absolute beginners to the pros – and remarkably cheap, for those on package holidays. Over summer it is marketed as a mountains-and-lakes resort – though **hikers** would do better elsewhere – but in May and from September until the start of the skiing season Pamporovo is pretty folorn, with only a few hotels and facilities open.

Buses drop you at the junction of the Plovdiv to Smolyan road and the slip road to the main complex of hotels. The beginners' slopes are just below the outlying *Malina* chalet complex, reached by bus or a thirty-minute walk from the centre of the resort. **Equipment** can be rented there, at the bus depot, or at the Studenets way-station (accesible by chair lift from *Malina* or the bus station). Chair lifts also run from Ardashlar (just below *Malina*) and from Studenets to the 1926-metre-high summit of Mount Snezhanka, starting-point of many of the **ski runs**. Advanced skiers can take a drag lift from Studenets up the side of "The Wall", the most difficult and demanding run at Pamporovo.

The **TV Tower** on Mount Snezhanka (daily 9am–4.30pm) has a café and an observation gallery giving a marvellous view of the Rhodope Mountains and, on clear days, parts of the Pirin and Rila, too – and makes a useful landmark for hikers. Twenty minutes' walk from here, the **Orpheus Rocks** (*Orfeevi Skali*) overlook a superb panorama of the mountains surrounding the Smolyan Valley.

Practicalities

As independent travellers are charged considerably more for rooms, tuition and equipment than people on **package holidays** (and might find that everything's booked up anyway), would-be skiers are strongly advised to take one of the cheap deals offered by foreign tour operators (see p.5), plus the optional "ski pack" which covers all rentals and lift rides. If you do just turn up on spec, the *Rozhen* (☎921/323; ③), *Panorama* (☎921/321; ③), *Orpheus* (☎921/315; ③) and *Snezhanka* (☎921/316; ③) hotels, and the *Malina* complex (☎921/388; ④), have the cheapest **beds** (the latter's chalets have recently been equipped with under-floor heating and satellite TV), and the tourist office in the *Perelik* hotel (Mon–Fri 9am–5pm, Sat 9am–noon; ☎921/405) will probably ring around and help with bookings if requested. You could also stay in Chepelare (see opposite) or down the valley in Smolyan (see overleaf), from where there are regular buses up to the pistes of Pamporovo during the winter season.

The tourist office offers a variety of excursions and **activities**, such as snow-boarding, and the facilities at the *Perelik*, which include a swimming pool, sauna and gym, are available to non-residents for a fee. Traditional Rhodope dishes like spit-roasted lamb (*cheverme*), stuffed vine leaves (*sarmi*), white bean stew (*Smolenski bob*) and a local variation on the cheese-filled *banitsa* are on offer at "folk-style" **restaurants** such as the *Chevermeto* and *Malina* – and *Vodenitsata* in the village of Stoykite, 7km to the west – all of which feature music and dancing.

Otherwise **entertainment** consists of the usual aprés-ski parties and bar crawls, and discos in the *Prepsa* and *Perelik* till the small hours.

Smolyan

A conglomerate of three villages (Smolyan, Raikovo and Ustovo) that straggles for 10km along the banks of the River Cherna, **SMOLYAN**, the administrative and cultural capital of the central and western Rhodopes, embodies Communism's attempt to mould the mixed Christian–Pomak agrarian population of Bulgaria's southern margins into the urbanized citizens of a modern socialist state. Situated 1000m above sea level, it's the highest town in Bulgaria, with a population of almost 40,000. Attractively squeezed between pine-clad peaks, the modern housing estates perched above the centre have maintained something of the region's traditional highland architecture, giving the whole place a rural feel, underscored by the goats and piles of logs in the backstreets.

Arrival and accommodation

Smolyan has two bus stations, at opposite ends of town. Coming from Sofia, Plovdiv or anywhere north or west you'll probably **arrive** at *Avtogara zapad* on ul. Minyorska, just downhill from the upper end of bul. Bâlgariya, which runs down into the centre. You can walk it in ten minutes or wait for a bus #3, which runs from one end of Smolyan to the other via the modern centre, terminating at *Avtogara iztok* in Ustovo, the station that serves Kârdzhali and other points east. However, some buses from Plovdiv that bypass Pamporovo and come via the Rozhen Pass arrive at Ustovo, while private buses from Sofia drop passengers outside the *Hotel Smolyan*, smack in the centre.

Beside the hotel, the helpful **tourist information centre** (☎0301/24643, fax 0301/24631, email *tic-smo@mbox.digsys.bg*) can arrange **private rooms** and advise on trips and activities in the Smolyan region. One thing they lack is a map of town, making it difficult to locate any of the outlying **hotels**. The most central are the cosy *Sportna 17*, signposted midway down bul. Bâlgariya (☎0301/38392; ②); *Babylon*, farther uphill on ul. Kolo Shismanov (☎0301/32668; ③); and the large three-star *Hotel Smolyan* at the bottom of bul. Bâlgariya (☎0301/23293; ③). Alternatively, you could base yourself in the picturesque mountainside suburb of **Smolyanski ezera**, where several small lakes surrounded by crags and forests provide a setting for the *Hotel Ezerata* (☎0301/32272; ③) and the all-year *Panorama* **campsite** (☎0301/32303) – accessible by bus #4 from *Avtogara zapad*.

The Town

A four-lane boulevard carrying so little traffic that its overhead walkway is redundant runs through the **civic centre**, passing a silver-domed **planetarium** whose shows (10am, 11am, 3pm & 4pm, except Mon) include footage from Rozhen Observatory. The post office, the town hall, the Rhodope Drama Theatre and other public buildings, are all massed on the hillside.

Steps behind the post office lead up to Smolyan's **Ethnographic Museum** and **Art Gallery** (both Tues–Sun 9am–noon & 1–5pm). Though not labelled in English, the museum has a superb collection of artefacts from Thracian times onwards, including "secret" Christian gravestones resembling Muslim ones but carved with crosses underneath, gorgeous silver jewellery and festive apparal, and colourful carpets (*chergi*) and tufted goat's-hair rugs (*halishta*) – still manufactured

MOVING ON FROM SMOLYAN

Chances are you'll be catching a **bus** out of *Avtogara zapad*, which not only serves Plovdiv but Lâki (see p.305), Mogilitsa (see below), and Devin in the western Rhodopes. Except for the 5.30am service via the Rozhen Pass, all buses to Plovdiv pass through Pamporovo and Chepelare. If you're heading towards Kârdzhali, you can take a state bus from *Avtogara iztok*, or a private one from the separate terminal a block or so uphill. There are also **minibuses** from *zapad* to Plovdiv and *iztok* to Kârdzhali.

around Smolyan. Best of all are the grotesque *Kukeri* costumes, worn by celebrants at New Year in the Rhodope and Pirin regions. Another room on the top floor is devoted to photos and models of traditional architecture in villages such as Shiroka Lâka and Mogilitsa – especially the Agushev Konak (see below). The **art gallery** across the way is likewise worth a visit, with Rhodope landscapes by Dechko Uzunov and Vasil Barakov, Nensko Balanski's iconic *Woman with a Cup of Coffee*, and temporary exhibitons of graphics or photography.

The older quarters of town contain a few more sights such as a sixteenth-century **mosque** that's visible on the way in from Pamporovo; the National Revival-style **Pangalov House** on ul. Veliko Târnovo (no longer open, alas); the churches of **Sv. Nedelya** and **Sv. Todor Stratilat** in Raikovo; and **Ustovo**, which still resembles the village it once was, sited higgledy-piggledy on the hillsides around the confluence of the Cherna (Black) and Byala (White) rivers.

Practicalities

Bulevard Bâlgariya is lined with **restaurants** and pavement **cafés**, from *Taverna Tatiana* on the corner of ul. Minyorska, with its fountains, leafy plants and live music most nights, down past two pizzerias, the *Vassilius* and *Venus* bars and the *Kafe-Aperitiv*, at no. 41, that does a great *gyuvech*, to the plush restaurant and lacklustre terrace of the *Hotel Smolyan*. The town's hottest nightspot is the *Top Stars* **disco** at Bâlgariya 71.

Banks are also concentrated along bul. Bâlgariya, with OBB (Mon–Fri 8.30am–5.30pm) giving credit card advances, the Central Cooperative Bank (Mon–Fri 8.30am–noon & 1–4.30pm) changing travellers' cheques, and the Post Bank (Mon–Fri 9am–4pm) other kinds of cheques. Aside from Pamporovo, this is the only place in the Rhodopes where you can avail yourself of these services. The **post office** (Mon–Fri 7.30am–6pm, Sat 8am–11pm) has an express mail service, and the **telephone office** (daily 7am–10pm) is just around the corner.

Mogilitsa and the Agushev Konak

Having seen the model of the Agushev Konak in Smolyan's museum, you may want to check out the original in the village of **MOGILITSA**, 26km south of town. You can do this in a day by taking the 12.40pm bus from *Avtogara zapad* terminal to Arda (the next village up the valley), which stops in Mogilitsa en route, then catching the 3.30pm bus back to Smolyan. Alternatively, you could catch the later Arda bus (5.40pm), stay at the *Loven Kât Hizha* (☎936/219; ②) and visit the Konak next day. The *Hizha* (which has a taverna with live music) is at the far end of the village, up the road past the mosque and a café with a satellite dish.

The **Agushev Konak** (Wed–Sun 9am–noon & 1–5.30pm) is a splendid example of the fortified manor houses built by rich Rhodope merchants in Ottoman times, when villages like Mogilitsa owned vast herds of sheep and were far wealthier than today. As the largest sheep-owners in the region, the Agushevs could afford to build a winter residence in Mogilitsa (1812–42) and a summer one in the hills (which hasn't survived). Divided into three compounds (for Agushev's household and the families of his eldest sons), the complex is visually unified by its thick slate tiles and pinacled chimneys, with latticed screens designed to preserve the privacy of the women's quarters (it has 86 doors and 221 windows altogether). Though quite plainly furnished the interior has some remarkable features, such as an enormous hall with platforms for seating guests and a salon with a secret door into another room, where a bodyguard or a spy could hide during meetings. Aromatic box-shrubs were planted outside the sliding screens of the summer rooms to deter flies; built-in wardrobes in the bedrooms acted as insulators against the cold; and a dumbwaiter in the hut reserved for strangers allowed them to be served meals without compromising the security of the household.

The western Rhodopes

Despite its average altitude being only 1000m, the **western Rhodopes** offer some of the finest **walking** in Bulgaria. Their perfectly proportioned gorges and crags are covered by aromatic pines and spruces, with lizards and bluebirds flashing among the rocks, as hawks and eagles soar overhead. Around **Trigrad** there are some fabulous caves such as the Devil's Throat, as well as the annual bagpipe festival at nearby **Mugla** in early August. The picturesque village of **Shiroka Lâka** makes a popular excursion from Pamporovo or a sleepy hill towns of **Devin** and **Dospat**. From Dospat you can head north to the historic town of **Batak** and on to the spa resorts of **Velingrad** and **Yundola** – which can also be reached by bus from Plovdiv, or on the narrow-gauge railway running between Septemvri and the Pirin mountain town of Bansko.

Travelling through the region you're struck by the degrees of separation between its Christian and **Pomak** (Slav Muslim) inhabitants, with some villages exclusively one, others a mixture of both. Broadly speaking the area is Christian as far west as Devin but the majority of villages thereon are Pomak. While a mosque or a church is an obvious sign, many Pomak villages weren't allowed to build mosques during Communist times and have only begun to do so recently. Most feature a boxy prayer hall and a white pencil-minaret in the Ottoman style. Although Pomak women cover their heads and bodies, this stipulation is variously interpreted in different villages: some wear a headscarf (*zabradka*) and a long dress or pantaloons (*shalvari*), with others sporting a white wimple and a dun-coloured smock, or even a half-veil (*feredzhe*).

Shiroka Lâka and Devin

SHIROKA LÂKA is a popular destination for coach parties from Pamporovo, wanting to see a genuine Rhodope village. With its humpbacked bridges and asymmetrical slate-roofed houses built into the mountainside, this remarkably unspoilt settlement of 2000 people could have been lifted off a picture-postcard. The advantage of coming on a tour is that you get to see a performance by the students of

> Local **legend** has it that the area between Shiroka Låka and Devin was the last refuge of the **Russian royal family**, who are said to have escaped the massacre at Ekaterinburg, fled south across the Urals, the Caspian and the Black Sea, and finally settled in a remote Rhodope village where the tsar, tsarina and tsarevitch died, and the four grand duchesses lived on as peasants. It remains to be seen if the legend will survive now that the Romanovs' remains have been found at Ekaterinburg and ceremonially reburied in St Petersburg.

the **School of Folk Instruments and Music** – something you might miss should you turn up on spec – and also stand a chance of visiting the **Sugurov House** or the **Kalamdzhi House** (containing the local Ethnographic Museum), which tend to remain shut until a tour bus arrives. You may have more luck with the walled **Church of the Assumption** at the western end of the village, where worshippers are greeted by a sobering fresco of a funeral procession surrounded by prancing demons. Essentially, however, Shiroka Låka is a place to stroll around the cobbled lanes and enjoy picnics in the surrounding meadows – unless you happen to be around for the first weekend of March, when there's a *Kukeri* **carnival** of dancers in weird costumes.

Though there's no **accommodation** *per se* in Shiroka Låka, Mrs Botuvska has a double room to let ($6) in her ramshackle house in the highest lane to the right near the eastern end of the village; alternatively, you may find somewhere better by asking around. The sole **restaurant** in the village is meant for coach parties and regarded as expensive by locals, but its folk-pop band does a fair job of competing with the *Night Club* **disco** on the main square, where the village youths go to drink themselves sick.

Thirty-four kilometres west of Shiroka Låka, **DEVIN** is a pleasant enough town in a bowl between rugged mountain ranges, but there's little to do other than enjoy the warm pool (Mon–Fri 9am–noon & 2–7pm, Sat & Sun 9am–5pm) and baths (Tues–Sat only same hours) at the **spa** to the left of the bridge beyond the bus station. There's a big military garrison here, and the presence of a firing range in the surrounding hills ensures that hiking possibilities are limited. Aside from a mosque and a church, the only official "sight" is a display of Rhodope folklore in the rarely opened **museum** on the main square (officially Mon–Fri 10am–noon & 2–5pm). Beyond the square, along ul. Rodopi, is the *Manolov* (☎0341/2674; ④), the best of Devin's **hotels**, while the *Churinski* (☎0341/4141; ②), uphill to the right from the army base, is a decent budget option.

Two **buses** a day leave Smolyan's *Avtogara zapad* terminal for Devin, passing through Shiroka Låka en route, from where up to seven local services a day also go to Devin. From Devin, a single daily bus (at 7.30pm) heads westwards to Dospat (see p.313).

Trigrad and around

The star attraction in the southwestern Rhodopes is the locality of **Trigrad**, with its awesome **gorge** and **caves**. Getting there without a car can be a challenge, as the only bus to Trigrad (from Devin; Mon–Sat) leaves unpredictably, if at all. Hitching is an option: quite a lot of traffic runs the 9km along the main Devin to Dospat road to Teshel, from where you could walk to Trigrad (10km) or **Yagodina** (8km), along minor roads, both of which run through gorges noted for their caves. Once there, you could easily **hike** round all the sites in the area within 2–3 days. The region is covered by **map** #2 in the *BTS* Rhodopes series.

Trigrad

The **TRIGRAD GORGE** (*Trigradsko zhdrelo*) is one of the most spectacular vistas in Bulgaria, its sheer walls overhanging the foaming River Trigradska, which disappears into a stupendous cave called the **Devil's Throat** (*Dyavolsko Gârlo*), accessible via a 150-metre-long tunnel at ground level (daily 9am–6pm; hourly tours). The thunder of water is audible long before you sight a huge waterfall that vanishes into the bowels of the earth; objects swept into the cave are never seen again. As big as two cathedrals, the cave is traversed by crudely built stairways that can cut visitors fumbling for handholds in the gloom, as bats flit around the shaft of light entering through a mossy fissure overhead. On leaving, you can walk uphill to a viewing platform above the void where the Trigradska goes underground – in legend, the entrance to the underworld used by Orpheus (see box on p.314) – or scramble down beside the mouth of the road tunnel to find a placid pool at the bottom of the gorge, where the river reappears.

Fifteen minutes' walk beyond the Devil's Throat lies the sprawling village of **TRIGRAD**, whose mosque and tiny church reflect the relative size of its Muslim and Christian communities – and their closeness. The village was wealthy during Turkish times (when one landowner alone had 12,000 sheep), but is nowadays remarkable only for its bikers, who zoom about on vintage Czech and East German machines. The best place **to stay** in the village is at the unsigned *Silivriak Hotel*, on the highest street to the right above the main square (☎03040/220; ②). It's run by the custodian of the Devil's Throat cave, Kostadin ("Kotse") Hadzhesky, one of Bulgaria's foremost cavers and the person to ask about serious speleology. The only other accommodation option is the less appealing *Trigradskite skali* chalet (①), just beyond the end of the gorge, before you reach the village.

Yagodina

The road to Yagodina runs through the longer, but less precipitous **Buzhnov Gorge**, past the mouth of a side-canyon that's great for hiking and caving. Only

---

HIKING TO MUGLA

On the first Sunday in August, musicians from all over the region get together to blow their *gaidi*, at **MUGLA's** annual **bagpipe festival**. A speciality of the Rhodopes, the huge, deep-voiced *kaba gaida* accompanies singing or plays dance music, alone or in concert with other bagpipes, and Mugla's festival is a rare chance to hear the awesome sound of *Sto kaba gaidi* – one hundred of them playing together.

Mugla can be reached by a side road starting between Teshel and Gzhovren (the last village before the Trigrad Gorge), or by **hiking from Trigrad** (4–5hr). The trail from Trigrad begins as a dirt track by the farm buildings across the bridge between the chalet and the village. It soon leads to a karst plateau where you bear right along a path onto a ridge with drinking fountains to rejoin the track and follow it as far as a highland meadow, where a cart track to the left and then a forest path provide a short-cut to a sharp bend in the dirt track. Here you turn right and follow it down to a tarmac road in the Lividitsa Valley, running past the lakeside beauty spot of Livadite. Follow the pylons beyond the final lake till you reach a fork in the trail, and head right uphill to arrive in Mugla thirty minutes later.

2km long and 2–4m wide, the **Haidushki dol** (Outlaws' Ravine) ascends in cascades to its watershed between two peaks connected by a natural rock bridge called the **Devil's Bridge**, after a legend that only he can cross it. This wild karst terrain abounds in caves – 102 have been found so far – which are mostly only accessible to cavers. However, Kotse (see opposite) can arrange a trip to the **Haramiiska Cave** ($15 per person) that needs more nerve than skill, where you crawl into one chamber before being lowered 42m in a harness into another cavern – an awesome but safe experience, as the guides take every precaution.

The **Yagodina Cave** (*Yagodinska Peshtera*), 2km up the road, is an established attraction, with 45-minute tours (Tues–Sun 9am–6pm) covering 1km of the 10km labyrinth, the largest cave-system in Bulgaria. You'll need warm, waterproof clothing, as the temperature is 6°C and water drips constantly, enlarging the stalactites at a rate of one centimetre every fifty to a hundred years. Don't miss the **cave pearls** formed by drops falling on tiny pebbles, gradually coating them with a lustrous shell; and the **Devil's Face** on the wall, which bears an uncanny resemblance to Old Nick. Look out also for the **Newlyweds** formation, where 21 weddings have taken place between Bulgarian caving enthusiasts, who also host an annual Speleologists party in the cave on January 1.

While the lowest of the cave's three levels was flooded 300,000 years ago, the uppermost later served as a **Prehistoric Cave-dwelling**, where excavations have unearthed Stone and Bronze Age kilns, potsherds and grindstones that can be seen *in situ* after finishing the tour of the lower cave. It's thought that groups of 20–30 people lived here, using several hearths as the direction of the draught varied with the seasons, blowing in the mouth of the cave or out of a hole at the back. As the lecture is in Bulgarian you're unlikely to learn much, but if you do speak the lingo, the lecturer, Sergei Tentchev, another famous caver, is a mine of information.

Head down the road past the entrance to the lower cave, cross a wooden bridge and then a concrete one to regain the road to Yagodina, which is all uphill but has a path that cuts the walk to under an hour. Hikers refresh themselves at a *cheshma* inscribed with a paen to water by Saint-Exupéry, before entering **YAGODINA**, a purely Pomak village with a smart new mosque. Visitors can **stay** at the *Iglika* chalet (①) in the hills, or hike to Trigrad (1hr 45min) and sleep there. To get to Trigrad, continue straight ahead on entering the village, past the post office, till you see a barn. The path beside it joins a track that soon reaches the junction of many paths; the one to the right that disappears behind a rock leads to a wide highland meadow, where you pick up a trail near the left-hand scarecrow, which, after an uphill slog, levels out in the woods. Turn left when you come to a broad path and you'll start descending the heights above Trigrad, to enter the village near the *Silivriak Hotel*.

Dospat

One daily bus (Mon–Sat at 7.30pm) connects Devin with **DOSPAT**, 40km west. You'll pass through lots of Pomak villages en route before descending into this small town once noted for its folk costumes and festivities but now known for its reservoir and clean mountain air. Downhill from the bus station is a small square with a mosque, where a right turn takes you towards the jade-green **reservoir**, distantly overlooked by a nice **hotel**, the *Tihiyat Kât* (☎03045/2082; ②). To reach it, head uphill from the bus station and fork left – it's at the far end.

Dospat is a turning point, where you can either head north along the desolate route to Batak (see overleaf), or **continue westwards** past the turn-offs for

THE ORPHIC MYSTERIES

The **legend of Orpheus** originated in ancient Thrace, where he was supposedly born of a Muse (perhaps Calliope, patron of epic poetry) and King Oeagrus of the Odrysae tribe (Apollo in other versions of the story). His mastery of the lyre moved animals and trees to dance, and with his songs – which had previously enabled the Argonauts to resist the Sirens' lure – Orpheus tried to regain his dead wife, Eurydice, from the underworld. His music charmed Charon, the ferryman, and Cerebus, the guardian of the River Styx, and finally Hades himself, who agreed to return Eurydice on the condition that neither of them looked back as they departed – but emerging into the sunlight of the overworld, Orpheus turned to smile at Eurydice and so lost her forever. Thereafter, Orpheus roamed the Rhodopes singing mournfully until he was torn apart by "the women of Thrace" (whom Aeschylus identifies as followers of Dionysus having a Bacchic orgy). His head continued singing as it floated down the River Mesta to Lesbos, where it began to prophesy until its fame eclipsed that of the Oracle at Delphi.

Despite having its origins in Thracian religion, the myth of Orpheus had a bigger effect in Greece, where an **Orphic cult** rich in mysticism was well established by the fifth century BC. Itinerant priests offering initiation into the Orphic mysteries traversed the Greek world, and Orphic communities arose in southern Italy and Sicily. Original texts codifying Orphism's basic tenets have been lost, although later Hellenistic writers held that initiates were vegetarians and that they regarded the material world as evil (describing the body as a "prison", according to Plato), and the spiritual world as divine. Little is known about the cult's practices, but it's thought that the ritual involved the mimed – or actual – dismemberment of a person representing Dionysus, who was then "reborn" as a free soul after death. Another theory has it that the cult's true, secret purpose was to bestow upon its adherents longevity, or even physical immortality.

Dolen and Kovachevitsa, towards Gotse Delchev in the Mesta Valley and the Pirin Mountains beyond (see p.118–135). This route passes through some of the loveliest countryside in Bulgaria, with an ever-changing panorama of gorges, forests and meadows dotted with a succession of highland villages, where tobacco farming is the main source of income, which amply compensates for the awfulness of the road. Be warned, though, that **buses** from Dospat to Gotse Delchev or Batak only leave on Mondays, Wednesdays and Fridays, at 7.30am. The Batak bus is signposted for Pazardzhik, as it terminates there.

Batak

The highlands to the north of Dospat are as thickly wooded and thinly populated as any in the Rhodopes, with not a single village on the road to Batak, only hunting lodges and a hikers' chalet (①) beside the Vasil Kolarov Reservoir. In such a lonely, peaceful setting, it's hard to imagine that **BATAK** was once a byword for infamy that reverberated across Europe – the Srebrenica of its day. During the April Rising of 1876 the Turks unleashed *bashibazouks* and Pomaks from other settlements to rape, pillage and slaughter the populace. Five thousand people – nearly the entire population – were hacked to death or burnt alive, an act for which the Pomak commander responsible was decorated. Britain's Prime Minister Disraeli cynically dismissed the **atrocities** to justify the continuing alliance with Turkey, until the weight of reports by foreign diplomats and JA

MacGahan of *The Daily News* became impossible to ignore. Yet only a sustained campaign by trade unions, Gladstone and public figures like Victor Hugo and Oscar Wilde prevented Britain's support of Turkey in the Russo-Turkish War of 1877–78. Although the defeated Turks were obliged to concede an independent Bulgaria under the Treaty of San Stefano, Disraeli ensured at the Congress of Berlin that Macedonia and Thrace were returned to the Ottomans, and the half of Bulgaria south of the Balkan range became the Turkish protectorate of Eastern Roumelia – in return for which Turkey rewarded Britain with Cyprus.

The Town

As a bloody milestone on the road to liberation the massacre is still commemorated in April, and the town echoes with memories of the dead. One wall of the **museum** on the main square (Tues–Sun 8am–noon & 2–6pm) is inscribed with a seemingly endless roll-call of those who died, and sepia photographs show old women who survived sitting beside piles of skulls and bones – some set out on a table to form the words *Ustanak ot 1876*: (Rising of 1876). Display cabinets are filled with press reports and denunciations of the Turks and those who seemed to lend them support – including Turgenev's attack on Disraeli and Queen Victoria, *Croquet at Windsor*. A burnt tree trunk commemorates local rebel leader Trendafil Kerelov, who was lashed to it before it was set alight. Exhibits upstairs relate to Batak's contribution to the Balkan and World wars, including documents from the nearby partisan camp of Tehran – so-named in honour of the Allies' summit in 1943 – and a gruesome photograph of heads left on a wall in the village.

Immediately opposite the museum lies the low, roughly hewn **Church of Sveta Nedelya** (enquire at the museum if it's closed), where MacGahan found naked corpses piled one metre deep. Its bare interior contains stark reminders of the violence: the bloodstains on the walls have never been expunged; signs point to bullet holes in the walls; a glass case holds one of the heavy woodsmen's axes used to bludgeon the *Batachani* into submission; while in a sunken chamber at the end of the church lie the bones of the massacred.

After all this you may not have much stomach for further sightseeing, though there's a small **Ethnographic Museum** (opened on request; ask at the museum) one block north of the church; and an **art gallery** (Wed–Sun 2–6pm) occupying a National Revival-style house east of the main square on ul. Apriltsi.

Practicalities

Batak's **bus station** is at the eastern end of the main street, **ul. Apriltsi**. Head west along here to reach the main square, past the murky and unwelcoming *Tekstil Hotel* (②). Much better **accommodation** possibilities, however, exist around the Batak Reservoir (*Yazovir Batak*), about 6km from town, whose bleak station is the only blot on this beauty spot. Here you'll find the tourist complex of *Tsigov Chark*, (④), with a **campsite** attached (June–Oct), and the *Orbita Hotel* (☎03542/3794; ③); Velingrad buses pass by.

Velingrad and around

With its diverse springs, excellent climate and leafy parks, **VELINGRAD** is one of Bulgaria's most popular spa towns, although those not intent on taking a cure will find little else to do here. It consists of three former Pomak villages originally named Kamenitsa, Lâdzhene and Chepino – lumped together in 1948 and renamed after local partisan heroine Vela Peeva. Both the train and bus stations are a few minutes' walk east of the modern centre, which in turn lies just to the east of **Lâdzhene**, where Velingrad's oldest baths, the **Velyova banya** (founded in the sixteenth century, although the buildings are modern), stand in a park beside the Yundola road. Just to the north of the centre is **Kamenitsa**, fringed by wooded parks that harbour the town's open-air baths, most of the modern spa facilities, and a small Ottoman-period *hammam*, the **Kremâchna banya** or "Flint Baths".

Velingrad's third cluster of baths lies 2km south of the centre in the **Chepino** quarter (bus #1 from the centre), where mineral water flows free from taps in the streets. Above Chepino to the south lies the Kleptuza spring, waters from which flow down to the **Kleptuza lake**, just east of Chepino: with pedalos, rowing boats and lakeside walkways, this is the most popular of Velingrad's resort areas.

Practicalities

Private **rooms** are allegedly on offer from a desk in the unkempt two-star *Hotel Zdravets*, on the modern town's central square (☎0359/2682; ③), although staff may refuse to find you one if the hotel isn't full: a much better option is the three-star *Velina* in Chepino (☎0359/3412; ④). Velingrad's main square has no shortage of places to **eat** and **drink**, and the restaurant of the *Zdravets* hosts live music most nights, while in Chepino the scene revolves around the lake, and there's a good restaurant and café-bar in the *Velina*.

There are two **buses** a day to Plovdiv and regular services to Yundola and Batak, but travellers are more likely to be interested in the three or four daily **trains** to Bansko in the Pirin range (see p.124). The narrow-gauge line switchbacks through glorious pine forests and sub-alpine meadows, calling at Avramovi Kolibi, the highest station on the Balkan peninsula, before descending to the logging town of Yakoruda and skirting the southern flanks of the Rila Mountains en route to Razlog (see p.124) and Bansko.

Yundola and Dorkovo

A 16km bus ride to the northwest of Velingrad, **YUNDOLA** is another small health resort 1390m above sea level, set amid rounded hills and copses of trees. It used to be a popular rest-home for trade unionists and Young Pioneers, but is chiefly remarkable for its inhabitants' longevity. The prevalence of **centenarians** in Bulgaria is ascribed to features of life in the highlands, where "Nature takes years off the weak and adds them to the strong" – as Leslie Gardiner was told. Human longevity is supposedly extended by pure air, climatic extremes, a lack of stress, and a spartan diet with little meat and plenty of yoghurt.

GOATS IN THE RHODOPES

Goats are still the basis for life in many Rhodope communities. Every family owns several, which are entrusted to the village goatherd, or *manzardzhiya*. Their milk is drunk or turned into yoghurt and cheese, which together with salted goat's meat (*pastârma*) forms the villagers' wintertime staple; goats' hair is woven into rugs which can last for eighty years; and their skin can be made into everything from wine-sacks and sandals to bagpipes (*gaidi*). During the Ottoman occupation, when Bulgarians were forbidden to carry arms, goats' horns served as daggers, and many of the country's most famous *haiduks* (including the female outlaw Rumena Voivoda) started their careers as goatherds.

The village of **DORKOVO**, 14km northeast of Velingrad, is notable only for its annual **folklore festival**, on the first Sunday in August, which aims to represent the blend of three cultures – Christian, Pomak and Vlach – that characterizes the Chepino Valley. There's a strong Macedonian element, as most of the villagers are descended from Macedonians who came here as refugees after the Congress of Berlin. Before then Dorkovo was a Pomak village, but many of the inhabitants fled after 1877, fearing reprisals for their participation in the slaughter at Batak. Buses to Batak can take you as far as the turn-off for Kostandovo, halfway there – you'll have to walk or hitch the remaining 7km.

The eastern Rhodopes

The **eastern Rhodopes** were the Ottomans' first conquest and their last foothold in Bulgaria before the Balkan Wars of 1912–13, and to this day many of the inhabitants are of ethnic Turkish origin. Geographically it is distinguished by 2500 hamlets and villages (far more than in either the central or the western Rhodopes) and comparatively low highlands (the average altitude is 329m). Traditionally, this was the poorest, least developed region of Bulgaria – a condition that only began to be remedied after dams and non-ferrous metal plants were established in the 1950s, and which seems likely to relapse as these industries collapse today.

From a tourist's viewpoint the chief attractions are **birdwatching** at the nature reserve on the River Arda near **Madzharovo**, and the variety of strange **rock formations** in the Kârdzhali region. However, as the reserve is only accessible by bus from Haskovo and the widely scattered rocks can only be reached by car, anyone coming from Smolyan and reliant on buses is limited to **hiking** around **Belite Brezi** or a visit to **Kârdzhali**, a town whose past is more intriguing than its present.

Heading east from Smolyan to Kârdzhali

Fairly regular buses run from Smolyan to Kârdzhali, passing Pomak and Turkish villages and the entrance to the **Arda Gorge** (a lovely spot for walking and picnicking if you have your own transport), en route to the mainly Turkish mining town of **ARDINO**. A few kilometres further on, the *Belite Brezi* hotel (②) and campsite is the starting-point for many fine **hikes**, including a seven-hour trail to the 90-metre-high **Ardino waterfall** on the River Arda. From there, it's only another hour or so walk to the **Devil's Bridge** (*Dyavolskiyat Most*), one of the humpbacked bridges built by the Turks on the Arda's tributaries along the route from Plovdiv to the Aegean. Though you wouldn't think so from its meagre source near Mogilitsa, the Arda is vital to the region, flowing through serpentine gorges to feed the reservoirs and power stations near Kârdzhali, Madzharovo and Ivailovgrad.

Another road from Smolyan approaches Kârdzhali by way of Momchilgrad, running closer to the Greek border, through the mining centres of **MADAN** (from the Arabic word for "ore") and **ZLATOGRAD** (Gold Town). Like **RUDOZEM**, nearer Smolyan, they did well under Communism, but the 1990s have seen the mining industry crippled by spiralling energy costs and the collapse of the leva and the price of non-ferrous metals on the world market. With the remaining mines due to close in 1999 things can only get worse, and plans to kick-start trade with Greece by opening a new border crossing near Rudozem have so far come to nothing.

Kârdzhali and around

Founded by a Turkish general, Kârdzhi Ali, **KÂRDZHALI** was one of the last towns to remain in Ottoman hands, and when it was captured by the Bulgarian army in 1912 it had fewer than 3000 inhabitants. Old photos and paintings of the town depict a maze of lanes thronged with hawkers in fezzes, veils and pantaloons, mingling with Bulgarian peasants, brigands and Turkish officers – quite unlike today's city of mid-rise blocks. Sadly, only a trace of this exoticism lingers in the bazaar quarter, and there are precious few reasons to visit the town. However, for those with a car, it can be a base for trips to numerous **rock formations** – the nearest is 4km from town – or a stopover en route to the nature reserve at Madzharovo.

The Town

Kârdzhali is particularly difficult to find your way around, since the only **map** available for scrutiny (in the *Hotel Arzepos*; see below) is years out of date, and many of the street names have changed. **Arriving** at the train or bus station in the southern part of town, catch any bus along the broad sweep of bul. Republikanska into the centre, where the **municipal garden** (*Gradska gradina*) with its elegant floral arrangements, makes a useful focal point. North of here is the commercial quarter, where butchers, fruit sellers and artisans ply their trades in shacks beside a **mosque** whose Ottoman minaret is all that distinguishes it from dwellings in the area. The nearby riverside offers a view of the suburbs on the far bank of the Arda, connected by a bridge to bul. Availo, which cuts across town from east to west.

The town's most interesting sight is the **Historical Museum**, on a nameless street some four blocks east of bul. Republikanska (Tues–Fri 9am–noon & 2–5pm). Housed in a vast edifice designed by a Russian architect living in Istanbul, and resembling a hybrid of a Stalinist barracks and the mosques of Tashkent, it was intended (but never used) as an Islamic seminary. The ground-floor history section includes a reconstruction of a 6000-year-old dwelling-workshop, copies of the marble wall panels from the Armira Roman Villa and genuine zoomorphic swastikas carved from nephrite. Even better is the superb collection of costumes, crafts and ritual objects in the ethnographic section on the top floor. Notice the loaves of bread shaped like snakes, supposedly to avert the risk of being bitten by vipers. There are also halls devoted to the gemstones, minerals, flora and fauna of the eastern Rhodopes, including photos of some of the nearby strange rock formations (see opposite).

Practicalities

The three-star, high-rise *Hotel Arzepos* (☎0361/28825; ③), near the riverside, is Kârdzhali's most luxurious accommodation (and can arrange a car with a driver to visit the nearby rocks; see opposite), though a cheaper option is the perfectly decent *Ustra* (☎0361/20468; ②) tucked away behind a café on the right near the far, eastern end of the crossways boulevard. Good local **food** can be sampled at the *Rusalka* restaurant in the municipal garden, or the restaurant in the *Arzepos*, which is noted for regional specialities such as mutton, sausages (*suzdurma*), *baklava* and figs, along with Armira wine from the Ivailovgrad district.

From Kârdzhali, there are hourly **trains** to Haskovo, as well as **buses** to Plovdiv (hourly, on the hour), Sofia (2–4 daily), Varna and Ahtopol on the Black

Sea coast (Mon, Sat & Thurs only), and several Turkish cities including Istanbul. All the buses leave from the station near the bridge into town on the way in from Momchilgrad.

Rock formations in the Kârdzhali region

Most of the odd **rock formations** in the Kârdzhali region originated in the volcanic eruptions that raised the land from the sea forty million years ago, and whose ashes solidified into the porous golden-coloured rock known as tufa, which is easily eroded – the same process that created the "fairy chimneys" of Cappadocia in Turkey. Kârdzhali's formations are far smaller, but diverse enough to appeal to geologists or anyone with more than a passing interest in such things. As all except one are near out-of-the-way villages, you'll need a **car** and **map** #6 in the *BTS* Rhodopi series (which doesn't show all of the sites, but identifies the localities).

The nearest rock formation to Kârdzhali is marked on maps as the *Piramidite* (Pyramids) but known to locals as the **Stone Wedding** (*Vkamenenata Svatba*), after a legend that a wedding party was turned to stone by the gods to punish the bridegroom's mother for envying his bride's beauty. The clusters of pink and red-tinged tufa do indeed resemble a procession frozen in mid-motion, but the villagers of Zimzelen, just uphill, have no qualms about using clefts in the rock as goat pens. This is the only formation within walking distance of Kârdzhali (about 1hr) – take the road uphill past the Bulgarian and Turkish cemeteries, then follow the surfaced fork and the rocks are visible at a distance – though it's easier to take a taxi than risk getting lost.

Further afield, the **Stone Mushrooms** (*Kamenite Gâbi*) stand about 2.5m high, their brown-spotted stalks and pink caps with green undersides coloured by traces of manganese and other minerals. Legend has it that they represent the heads of four sisters decapitated by Turkish brigands for stabbing their chief when he tried to rape them. A large dark rock nearby is known as the Murderer. The mushrooms are located near Beli Plast, 20km north of Kârdzhali, along the minor road to Haskovo (not the E-85).

Spectacularly suspended in the air by two green tufa columns (a third has been destroyed) and a limestone "bridge", the **Rock Window** (*Skalen Prozorets*) stands 10m high, 15m long, 7m wide and 1.5m thick. It's situated between the hamlets of Zrânche and Krushka just beyond Kostino, about 15km northwest of Kârdzhali.

Just outside the village of Tatul, roughly 20km northeast of Momchilgrad, the **Stone Forest** (*Vkamenenata Gora*) consists of a dozen charred-looking stumps up to 1.5m high and 4m in diameter, which are marked with rings and may actually be prehistoric trees, covered in lava.

The ridge of the **Broken Mountain** (*Yanuk Tepe*) looks like someone has taken a cleaver to it, terminating midway in a precipitous drop with rilolite columns strewn around – the result of a landslide late last century, near Vodenicharsko. Nearby, the fantastic **Rocks at Ustra** (*Skalite na Ustra*), huge purple pillars in the form of prisms, cones or stairways, perch on the hillside above Ustren. Both formations are in the vicinity of the small town of Dzhebel, 21km southwest of Kârdzhali.

The **Mushroom** (*Gâbata*) and the **Lion** (*Lâvât*) are examples of two kinds of tufa formation in the vicinity of Benkovski, on the road to Zlatograd. Shaped like a giant puffball mushroom, with a stalk that narrows at the bottom and a brown, flattened cap 3m in diameter, the Mushroom lies 1.5km southwest of Benkovski. The Lion – which resembles a lion's head and gets its texture and colour from particles of gritstone – is in the same area, but closer to the village of Kitna (or Kitka).

The Madzharovo nature reserve

For birdwatchers, the chief attraction of the eastern Rhodopes is the **nature reserve** on the River Arda, established in 1994 under the Bulgarian-Swiss Biodiversity Conservation Programme. The gorges of the Arda are one of the few breeding grounds in Europe for four different **vultures** (the Egyptian, Griffon, Black and White-headed), and the habitat of eight kinds of **falcons**, as well as black storks, bee-eaters and other species. Falcons catch mice, lizards, hamsters, snakes, butterflies and birds, while the vultures feed only on carrion, cleansing the environment of pathogenic micro-organisms.

> For information on other birdwatching sites, contact the **Bulgarian Society for the Protection of Birds** (BDZP), 1172 Sofia, PO Box 114, kv. "Dianabad" bl. 42, et. 5 apt. 34 (☎ & fax 02/689 413).

Guided tours of their feeding sites are arranged through the **Nature Information Centre** (daily Mon–Fri 9am–5pm, Sat & Sun 11am–5pm; ☎03720/280 or 304, email *bspicer@main.infotel.bg*) off the road by the bridge across the River Arda, near Madzharovo. Besides photos of the birds, mammals and flowers within the nature reserve (named in Bulgarian and Latin), there are three cosy double bedrooms (②) for the use of visitors, which should be reserved well in advance, through the information centre. If the birdwatchers' chalet is full and you don't fancy staying in a block of flats in nearby **Madzharovo**, 3km west, you can rent private rooms ($10 per person) in the agreeable village of **Borislavtsi** on the opposite bank of the Arda, 6km from the birdwatching centre and 4km from the nearest feeding site. Talk to Ivo or Mitko Nicolov at the *Café Nico* (☎993759/372), who can also arrange transport or nature walks in the vicinity.

Buses from Haskovo (see p.297) are the only means of reaching the reserve without a car. There are two services daily to Madzharovo (9am & 3.20pm), and one taking a different route to Borislavtsi (3.20pm except Sat). While there are no buses from Krumovgrad to Madzharovo, there are two (6.30am & 12.30pm) from Krumovgrad to Studen Kladenets, a village set in a lunar landscape 30km upriver from Madzharovo, where the ravines of the Vâlchi Dol are home to another **vulture colony**, though there is no visitors centre nor anywhere to stay here.

MADZHAROVO'S THRACIAN FESTIVAL

The inhabitants of the small dreary town of Madzharovo are known as "Thracians" by the Bulgarians, due to their being descended from refugees from Aegean Thrace who fled during the Greek civil war of 1945. The town's **Thracian Festival**, which takes place in the first week of September, is a lively affair involving two days of dancing, wrestling and fireworks.

From Momchilgrad to Ivailovgrad

The only reason for travelling this far East is to experience the most **Turkish region** of Bulgaria. In Momchilgrad and Krumovgrad you'll hear more Turkish spoken than Bulgarian (which isn't even *understood* by some people), and satellite dishes, trade and transport are oriented towards Turkey. People have redder skins, broader faces and stockier physiques than the inhabitants of the western Rhodopes – as sure a sign of their Turkish ancestry as their names (written in Turkish, rather than Cyrillic on the tombstones). While being able to speak Turkish will help, people are generally reserved towards outsiders due to the region's long history as an embattled borderland and the vicissitudes of ethnic–state relations (see "Bulgaria's Muslim Minorities" in Contexts) having inculcated habits of clannishness and isolation.

The **landscape** is characterized by eroded, deforested expanses which, seen by moonlight, resemble deserts or lunar surfaces. With its dry sandy soil and Mediterranean climate, it has always needed irrigation to produce crops, and the minerals in the mountains – zinc, lead, gold and silver – made mining more profitable than agriculture until the Turks introduced the cultivation of tobacco, which is still the main crop. They chiefly grow an aromatic strain called *dzhebel basma*, a name deriving from *djebel*, the Arabic word for hill. Though there are daily **buses** from Kârdzhali to Krumovgrad, and to Ivailovgrad on Tuesdays, Wednesdays and Fridays, this is really a journey to do by **car**, despite the awful road.

MOMCHILGRAD, 15km south of Kârdzhali, marks the start of the highlands, encrusted with **ruined fortresses** built by both Bulgaria and Byzantium, when the area was contested by the two empires. More recently, it was here that the worst violence of the "name-changing campaign" occurred, when about forty people died in clashes between protestors and the Militia in the winter of 1984–85. The succession of Muslim villages over the next 30km culminates in an elegant, isolated **mosque** before the road descends to **KRUMOVGRAD**, a larger town with some cafés for a pit stop and the *Ahriga Hotel* (②) should you need to spend the night before catching a bus to Istanbul (ask at Özavar Turizm), Studen Kladenets (see opposite), Haskovo (8am & 2pm) or Plovdiv (6am).

Beyond Krumovgrad lies splendid open rolling countryside, planted with wheat and dotted with copses where livestock graze around waterholes, but eerily devoid of human settlements so far as you can see. There are, in fact, dozens of Turkish hamlets in the hills that are so small and isolated that none of the children go to school, which explains why the Ivailovgrad region has the highest illiteracy rate in Bulgaria (60 percent). Fifty-nine kilometres east of Krumovgrad, **IVAILOVGRAD** marks a return to the Slav, Christian areas of settlement, and boasted the impressive remains of the **Armira Roman Villa** until it was looted in 1996. By way of compensation, motorists can visit the Thracian tomb at Mezek as a detour off the road to Svilengrad (see p.299), though be sure that all your documents are in order, as there's a **checkpoint** at the hydroelectric dam on the Arda Reservoir. Despite its proximity to Greece and Turkey, there's nowhere to cross the **frontier** until you reach Svilengrad.

travel details

Trains

Asenovgrad to: Plovdiv (16 daily; 25min).

Dimitrovgrad to: Harmanli (5 daily; 1hr); Haskovo (6 daily; 30min); Kârdzhali (3 daily; 2hr); Momchilgrad (3 daily; 2hr 15min–2hr 45min); Plovdiv (4 daily; 1hr–1hr 30min); Podkova (3 daily; 3hr 30min).

Harmanli to: Dimitrovgrad (5 daily; 1hr); Plovdiv (5 daily; 2hr–3hr 30min); Simeonovgrad (6 daily; 15min); Svilengrad (6 daily; 30min).

Haskovo to: Dimitrovgrad (6 daily; 30min); Kârdzhali (6 daily; 1hr–1hr 45min); Momchilgrad (6 daily; 2hr–3hr 15min); Stara Zagora (3 daily; 1hr 30min–2hr 30min).

Kârdzhali to: Dimitrovgrad (5 daily; 2hr); Haskovo (6 daily; 1hr–1hr 45min); Momchilgrad (9 daily; 30min); Podkova (3 daily; 50min); Stara Zagora (3 daily; 3hr–4hr).

Momchilgrad to: Dimitrovgrad (3 daily; 2hr 15min–2hr 45min); Haskovo (4 daily; 2hr–3hr 15min); Kârdzhali (5 daily; 30min); Plovdiv (1 daily; 5hr); Podkova (5 daily; 20min); Stara Zagora (1 daily; 2hr 15min–4hr 30min).

Pazardzhik to: Plovdiv (20 daily; 30–45min).

Plovdiv to: Asenovgrad (16 daily; 25min); Burgas (3 daily; 3hr 45min); Dimitrovgrad (4 daily; 1hr–1hr 30min); Harmanli (5 daily; 2hr–3hr 15min); Hisar (2 daily; 1hr); Karlovo (5 daily; 1hr 45min); Momchilgrad (1 daily; 5hr); Panagyurishte (2 daily; 1hr 45min); Pazardzhik (20 daily; 30–45min); Septemvri (3 daily; 45min–1hr); Sofia (20 daily; 2hr–3hr 30min); Svilengrad (4 daily; 2hr); Varna (2 daily; 6hr); Yambol (1 daily; 1hr).

Podkova to: Dimitrovgrad (3 daily; 3hr 30min); Kârdzhali (3 daily; 50min); Momchilgrad (5 daily; 20min).

Septemvri to: Bansko (3 daily; 5hr); Plovdiv (3 daily; 45min–1hr); Sofia (8 daily; 1hr 30min–2hr 15min); Velingrad (3–4 daily; 1hr 30min).

Svilengrad to: Harmanli (6 daily; 30min).

International trains

Plovdiv to: Istanbul (1 daily; 8hr 30min).

Svilengrad to: Athens (1 daily; 23hr); Istanbul (2 daily; 7hr); Thessaloniki (1 daily; 12hr).

Buses

Asenovgrad to: Bachkovo (4–6 daily; 30min); Lâki (2 daily; 45min); Plovdiv (hourly; 30min).

Bachkovo to: Asenovgrad (4–6 daily 2hr; 30min).

Batak to: Pazardzhik (7 daily; 1hr 20min); Velingrad (5 daily; 1hr).

Devin to: Dospat (1 daily; 1hr); Plovdiv (2 daily; 2hr 15min); Nastan (9 daily; 15min); Smolyan (2–4 daily; 2hr 30min); Trigrad (1 daily except Sun; 30min).

Dimitrovgrad to: Haskovo (every 30min; 25min).

Dospat to: Batak (3 weekly Mon, Wed & Fri; 1hr 30min); Devin (1 daily; 1hr); Gotse Delchev (1 Mon, Wed & Fri; 1hr); Pazardzhik (1 Mon, Wed & Fri; 3hr); Plovdiv (2 daily; 3hr 15min); Smolyan (1 daily; 3hr).

Harmanli to: Haskovo (14 daily; 40min); Ivailovgrad (2 daily; 2–3hr); Sofia (2 daily; 5hr); Stara Zagora (1 daily; 1hr); Svilengrad (7 daily; 45min).

Haskovo to: Borislavtsi (1 daily except Sat; 3hr 40min); Dimitrovgrad (every 30min; 25min); Harmanli (14 daily; 40min); Ivailovgrad (2 daily; 3hr); Kârdzhali (12 daily; 50min); Krumovgrad (1 daily; 4hr); Madzharovo (2 daily; 2hr) Plovdiv (8 daily; 1hr 30min); Sofia (3 daily; 4–5hr); Svilengrad (5 daily; 1hr 20min).

Ivailovgrad to: Haskovo (2 daily; 3hr); Kârdzhali (2 daily on Tues, Wed & Fri; 3hr).

Kârdzhali to: Ahtopol (June–Sept 1 daily: 4hr); Haskovo (12 daily; 50min); Ivailovgrad (2 daily on Tues, Wed & Fri; 3hr); Krumovgrad (6 daily; 30min); Plovdiv (hourly; 2hr 30min); Varna (June–Sept 1 daily; 5hr); Sofia (5–7 daily; 5–6hr).

Krumovgrad to: Kârdzhali (6 daily; 30min); Plovdiv (2 daily; 3hr); Sofia (1 daily; 8hr); Stara Zagora (1 daily; 4–5hr); Studen Kladenets (2 daily; 2hr).

Lâki to: Asenovgrad (2 daily; 45min); Belitsa (2 daily; 15min); Manastir (1 daily; 30min); Plovdiv (1 daily; 1hr 15min); Smolyan (1 daily; 1hr 15min).

Madzharovo to: Haskovo (2 daily; 2hr).

Manastir to Lâki (1 daily; 30min).

Pamporovo to: Plovdiv (6 daily; 2hr 30min); Smolyan (hourly; 30min).

Pazardzhik to: Batak (7 daily; 1hr 20min); Dospat (1 daily; 3hr); Gotse Delchev (2 daily; 4hr); Panagyurishte (every 45min; 1hr 30min); Peshtera

(5 daily; 35min); Plovdiv (18 daily; 40min); Septemvri (5 daily; 30min).

Plovdiv *Avtogara Yug* to: Asenovgrad (hourly; 30min); Blagoevgrad (1 daily; 4hr); Dupnitsa (3 weekly on Mon, Wed & Fri; 5hr); Haskovo (10 daily; 1hr 30min); Kyustendil (Mon & Fri; 4–5hr); Pazardzhik (18 daily; 40min); Sliven (1 daily; 3hr 15min); Smolyan (6 daily; 3hr); Sofia (1 daily; 2hr); Velingrad (2 daily; 1hr 15min).

Avtogara Rodopi to: Devin (1–4 daily; 2hr 15min); Dospat (1–2 daily; 3hr 15min); Gotse Delchev (1 daily; 6hr 30mn) Haskovo (8 daily; 1hr 30min); Kârdzhali (hourly; 2hr 30min); Krumovrad (2 daily; 3hr); Madan (5 daily; 3hr 30min); Pamporovo (6 daily; 2hr 30min); Rudozem (4 daily; 2hr); Smolyan (6 daily; 3hr); Sofia (5 daily; 2hr); Zlatograd (3 daily; 4hr).

Shiroka Lâka to: Devin (5–7 daily; 2hr); Smolyan (2–4 daily; 45min).

Septemvri to: Pazardzhik (5 daily; 30min).

Smolyan *Avtogara iztok* to: Madan (8 daily; 30min); Kârdzhali (5 daily; 3hr); Plovdiv via Rozhen Pass (1 daily; 4hr); Rudozem (hourly; 20min); Zlatograd (hourly; 1hr)

Avtogara zapad to: Ardino (hourly; 2hr); Devin (2–4 daily; 2hr 30min); Dospat (1 daily; 3hr); Lâki (1 daily; 1hr 15min); Mogilitsa (2 daily; 1hr); Momchilovtsi (1 daily; 3hr); Pamporovo (6 daily; 30min); Plovdiv (6 daily; 3hr), via Rozhen Pass (1 daily; 4hr); Shiroka Lâka (2–4 daily; 45min).

Svilengrad to: Dimitrovgrad (1 on Sun; 2hr); Harmanli (7 daily; 45min); Haskovo (5 daily; 1hr 30min); Kapitan Andreevo (3 daily; 20min).

Velingrad to: Batak (5 daily; 1hr); Blagoevgrad (2 daily; 3hr); Yundola (every 45min; 30min).

International buses

Kârdzhali to: Edirne (2–3 daily; 5–8hr); Istanbul (2–3 daily; 12–15hr).

Krumovgrad to: Istanbul (1 daily except Fri; 6–8hr).

Plovdiv to: Athens (1 daily; 23–26hr); Istanbul (1–2 daily except Fri; 4–5hr); Izmir (3 weekly on Mon, Wed & Sun; 8–10hr); Ohrid (July–Aug 1 daily; 10–11hr); Thessaloniki (1–2 daily; 14hr); Xanti (2 weekly on Mon & Fri; 12–14hr).

CHAPTER SIX

THE BLACK SEA COAST

The Bulgarian **Black Sea coast** has quietened down a bit since the Seventies and Eighties, when it served as the playground for the entire Eastern bloc, but it is still a magnet for hundreds of thousands of Bulgarians and foreign visitors. The vast tourist complexes built to attract West European package tourists still do good business, Bulgarians are taking more holidays here than ever before, and the Russians, Poles, Germans and Czechs who descended on Bulgaria's seaside towns in the Communist era are beginning to return. Private enterprise has taken off here quicker than anywhere else in Bulgaria, and the wealth of bars, restaurants and seaside landladies offering rooms lends the area a vibrant quality that much of inland Bulgaria lacks.

Many continue to think of the Bulgarian coast in terms of its big package-oriented complexes, the largest of which have discouragingly ersatz names like **Sunny Beach** and **Golden Sands** and are correspondingly characterless once you arrive. Newer resorts like **Albena** have a more varied range of hotels and activities, and the most recent "holiday villages" such as **Elenite** compare favourably with villa settlements in the Mediterranean. Holidays in such places are cheap and beaches are clean, but none of these purpose-built resorts reveals much of what the Black Sea is really about – and they are sited sufficiently far away from centres of population to prevent you from finding out for yourself. Independent travellers should stick to the main seaside towns, where **private rooms** are plentiful, family-run **guesthouses** are on the increase, and out-of-town **beaches** are easy to reach on foot or by bus. The ideal base for exploring the northern coast is the riviera town of **Varna**, which, after Sofia and Plovdiv, is Bulgaria's most animated metropolis. North of Varna crumbling rock formations and imposing cliffs characterize the coast around **Balchik** and **Kaliakra**, while to the south lie quieter seaside backwaters and the **Longoza**, a dense riverine forest that lines the lower banks of the **River Kamchiya**.

Controlling access to the southern half of the Black Sea coast is the rough-edged trawler port of **Burgas**, far outshone by the historic peninsula towns immediately north and south – old Greek fishing villages like **Sozopol** and **Nesebâr**, the latter noted for its ruined Byzantine churches, and swarming with visitors in the summer. The coast beyond Sozopol and the Turkish border offers a succession of glorious white sand **beaches** and a wide variety of flora and fauna, ranging from the near-tropical forest around the **River Ropotamo** to wildfowl-infested marshes. Numerous local museums recall the Greek settlers who colonized the area six centuries before the birth of Christ.

The Black Sea coast is governed by the **seasons**. The tourist season runs from late May to late September, and is at its height in August, when transport and accommodation are overburdened. It's difficult to find private rooms at this time, but you shouldn't find yourself stranded without a bed for the night if you

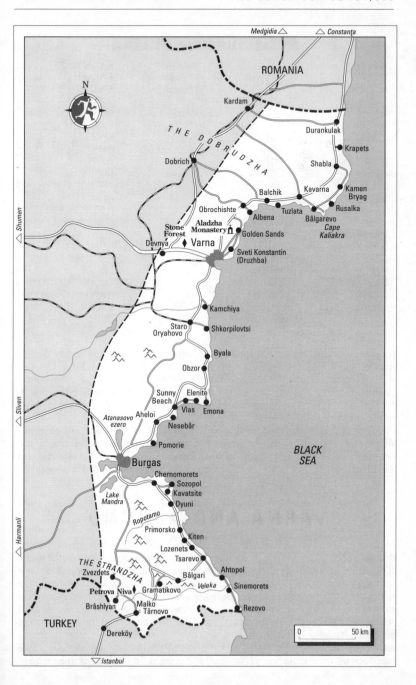

CYRILLIC PLACE NAMES			
AHELOI	АХЕЛОЙ	KAMCHIYA	КАМЧИЯ
AHTOPOL	АХТОПОЛ	KAVARNA	КАВАРНА
ALADZHA	АЛАДЖА	KAVATSITE	КАВАЦИТЕ
MONASTERY	МАНАСТИР	KITEN	КИТЕН
ALBENA	АЛБЕНА	MALKO	МАЛКО ТЪРНОВО
ARKUTINO	АРКУТИНО	TÂRNOVO	
ASPARUHOVO	АСПАРУХОВО	NESEBÂR	НЕСЕБЪР
BALCHIK	БАЛЧИК	OBROCHISHTE	ОБРОЧИЩЕ
BRÂSHLYAN	БРЪШЛЯН	OBZOR	ОБЗОР
BURGAS	БУРГАС	POMORIE	ПОМОРИЕ
BYALA	БЯЛА	RUSALKA	РУСАЛКА
CAPE KALIAKRA	НОС КАЛИАКРА	SHABLA	ШАБЛА
CHERNOMORETS	ЧЕРНОМОРЕЦ	SHKORPILOVTSI	ШКОРПИЛОВЦИ
DEVNYA	ДЕВНЯ	SINEMORETS	СИНЕМОРЕЦ
DRUZHBA	ДРУЖБА	SOZOPOL	СОЗОПОЛ
DURANKULAK	ДУРАНКУЛАК	STONE FOREST	ПОБИТИ КАМЪНИ
DYUNI	ДЮНИ	SUNNY BEACH	СЛЬНЧЕВ БРЯГ
ELENITE	ЕЛЕНИТЕ	SVETI	СВЕТИ
EVKSINOGRAD	ЕВКСИНОГРАД	KONSTANTIN	КОНСТАНТИН
GALATA	ГАЛАТА	TSAREVO	ЦАРЕВО
GOLDEN SANDS	ЗЛАТНИ	VARNA	ВАРНА
	ПЯСЪЦИ	ZORA	ЗОРА

persistently ask around; solo travellers, however, may be asked to pay double rates or share with a stranger, as owners are loath to lose money. From October to April the coast can be freezing cold, and a number of hotels close down entirely. Outside Varna and Burgas, many museums and tourist attractions open only during the summer, and hours become erratic as tourist numbers begin to slacken off in September.

However you travel, your likely **point of arrival** on the coast will be either Varna or Burgas, from where **buses** can take you to the smaller towns and resorts. It's also possible to travel **on from Bulgaria** to destinations elsewhere in the Black Sea regions, with buses and ferry trips to Istanbul, and seasonal bus services to Odessa and Kiev.

VARNA AND AROUND

Back in the days when **VARNA** was a cholera-ravaged Ottoman garrison town, British troops passed through on their way to the Crimean War; one of them, Major General J R Hume, described the town as "no paradise . . . a wretched place with very few shops". Until recently many foreign visitors may have said the same, but over the past few years Bulgaria's third city has struggled more than most to Westernize. Signs of change are everywhere: old state-owned shops stand empty, while the streets around them sprout fashion boutiques, exchange bureaux, Japanese car showrooms, video-rental stores, and fast-food outlets staffed by mini-skirted waitresses. Crop-haired youths practise skateboarding manoeuvres in the main square, or stroll along the main boulevards in a range of pseudo-designer summer threads more reminiscent of west coast USA than some far-flung eastern outpost of Europe.

Varna still has its problems – loss-making **shipyards** southwest of the centre give the place a hard industrial edge – and most of the consumer goods on sale in the town centre are well beyond the means of those who inhabit the high-rise suburbs. Nevertheless, the self-confident riviera-town swagger of the place comes as a breath of fresh air after the more austere appearance of much of inland Bulgaria. It rivals Sofia and Plovdiv in providing a wide range of sights and **museums**, from the outstanding treasures in the Archeology Museum to the off-the-wall ghoulishness of the Museum of Medical History. Of its cultural attractions, most notable is the annual **Varnensko Lyato** (Varna Summer): a summer-long festival of classical music, folklore and jazz, which attracts world-class performers.

As well as being a **beach resort** in its own right, Varna offers access to the purpose-built tourist complexes of **Sveti Konstantin** (formerly "Druzhba") – now swallowed up by Varna's suburbs – **Sunny Day**, **Golden Sands** and **Albena** to the north. Also within easy reach are quieter seaside villages like **Kranevo**, and popular day-trip destinations such as the nature reserve at **Kamchiya**, the rock monastery of **Aladzha**, and Queen Marie of Romania's former palace at **Balchik**.

Some history

Highly skilled gold- and coppersmiths lived around the Gulf of Varna 6000 years ago, and their Thracian descendants littered the interior with burial mounds, but Varna's importance as a port really dates from 585 BC, when a mixed bag of Apollonians and Milesians established the Greek city-state of **Odyssos**. The town's best years came in the second and third centuries when it was the Roman province of Moesia's main outlet to the sea, a bustling place where Greek and Thracian cultures met and mingled. Devastated by the Avars in 586 AD, and repopulated by Slavs (who were probably responsible for renaming it *Varna*, or "Black One"), it nevertheless remained the region's biggest port and an important staging-post for the Byzantine fleet on its way to the Danube. Declining somewhat under the Turks, Varna recovered as an important trading centre in the nineteenth century, when a population of Bulgarians, Greeks, Turks and Gagauz (Turkic-speaking Christians, see p.342) made it one of the coast's more cosmopolitan centres. To the Turks, Varna was the key to the security of the western Black Sea, and the town's military role is still reflected in the students of Varna's Naval Academy, who stride around town in uniforms belted with ceremonial daggers.

Arrival, information and city transport

Varna's **train station** is just south of the centre, a ten-minute walk up ul. Tsar Simeon into town. The **bus terminal** is 2km northwest on bul. Vl. Varnenchik; take bus #1, #22, or #41 from here to reach the streets surrounding the central **Cathedral of the Assumption** (an area known as *Tsentar* or "centre" on bus destination boards), a few paces north of the main downtown area. Varna **airport** on the city's western outskirts is served by bus #409, which passes through central Varna before continuing on past Sveti Konstantin to Golden Sands.

Central Varna is easy to explore on foot, although **local buses and trolley-buses** come in handy if you're heading for the suburbs or the seaside resorts to the north – most stop either in front of or behind the Cathedral. **Tickets** are

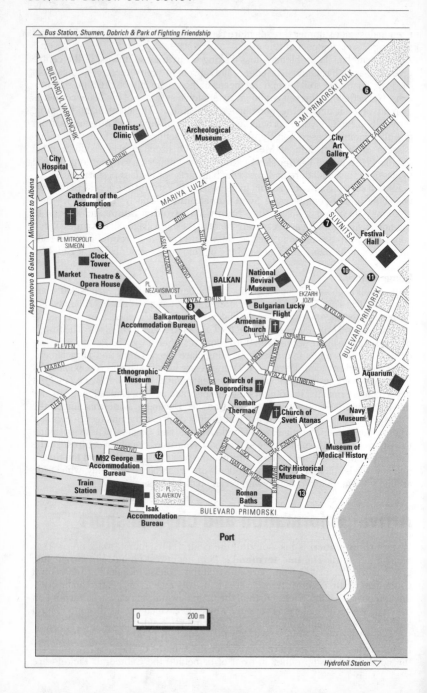

BULEVARD VL VARNENCHIK

Dentists' Clinic

Archeological Museum

8-MI PRIMORSKI POLK

6

City Art Gallery

LYUBEN KARAVELOV

City Hospital

KNYAZ BORIS

SADOVI

Cathedral of the Assumption

8

MARIYA LUIZA

MARKO BALGARANOV

SLIVNITSA

7

Festival Hall

PL MITROPOLIT SIMEON

IVDIN

SHIPKA

ASEN ZLATAROV

VOYNIKOV

KNYAZ BORIS

TSAR

Clock Tower

Market

Theatre & Opera House

PL NEZAVISIMOST

KNYAZ BORIS I

BALKAN

National Revival Museum

PL EKZARH IOZIF

10

11

BULEVARD PRIMORSKI

9

Balkantourist Accommodation Bureau

Bulgarian Lucky Flight

Armenian Church

M KOLONI

PLEVEN

PANAGYURISHTE

MURNA

PRESLAV

HAN

ASPARUH

ODRIN

Asparuhovo & Galata △ Minibuses to Albena

LI MARKO

DEBAR

Ethnographic Museum

TSAR SIMEON

DMITRIAR BRAZAKI

Church of Sveta Bogoroditsa

Roman Thermae

KLIMENT

KNYAZ AL BATENBERG

SAN STEFANO

Aquarium

Navy Museum

Church of Sveti Atanas

GABROVO

12

M92 George Accommodation Bureau

Train Station

PL SLAVEIKOV

HAN DIMITUR

HAN OMURTAG

PLISKA

YANTRA

GRAF IGNATIYAV

Museum of Medical History

City Historical Museum

13

Isak Accommodation Bureau

Roman Baths

BULEVARD PRIMORSKI

Port

0   200 m

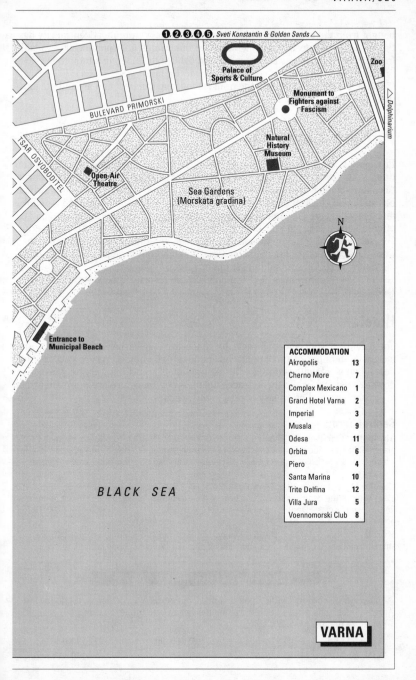

❶, ❷, ❸, ❹, ❺, *Sveti Konstantin & Golden Sands* △

Palace of
Sports & Culture

Zoo

△ *Dolphinarium*

Monument to
Fighters against
Fascism

BULEVARD PRIMORSKI

Natural
History
Museum

TSAR OSVOBODITEL

Open-Air
Theatre

Sea Gardens
(Morskata gradina)

N

Entrance to
Municipal Beach

ACCOMMODATION

Akropolis	**13**
Cherno More	**7**
Complex Mexicano	**1**
Grand Hotel Varna	**2**
Imperial	**3**
Musala	**9**
Odesa	**11**
Orbita	**6**
Piero	**4**
Santa Marina	**10**
Trite Delfina	**12**
Villa Jura	**5**
Voennomorski Club	**8**

BLACK SEA

VARNA

bought from the conductor, with a flat fare of 20¢ covering most central city destinations. Up-to-date **maps** which include bus routes are sporadically available from street stalls. Buses run from around 6.30am to 11.30pm; although services to the northern beach resorts stop at around 10pm.

Taxis leave from in front of the train station, and can be found around the junction of bul. Knyaz Boris I and Slivnitsa.

Accommodation

Providing you can dodge the old ladies offering accommodation at the train station, your best bet is to head for the Varnenski Bryag/Balkantourist Accommodation Bureau at Musala 3 (Mon–Fri 8.30am–12.30pm & 1–6pm), which has an ample stock of **private rooms** for around $12 a single and $16 a double, many of which are reasonably central – although in the peak season you may be offered something quite far out. Other private room bureaux worth considering are Isak, inside the station beside the main exit, and M92George, across the road from the station at ul. Tsar Simeon 36b, although both have unpredictable opening hours, especially outside the summer season.

The nearest **campsites** lie 20km north in the resort complex of Golden Sands (see p.343), which is linked to the city by buses #9, #109 and #409.

Hotels

You'll find no shortage of **hotels** to chose from in Varna, largely due to the increasing number of small pensions and family-run hotels. Where you stay will depend on what you want to do: the central hotels are within walking distance of downtown sights, while those places northeast of the centre are more suburban in atmsophere and offer easy access to the beaches.

Central Varna

Akropolis, Tsar Ivan Shishman 13 (☎052/603108, fax 603107). Spotless new motel-style place behind a residential block just east of the train station, offering roomy ensuite doubles which will sleep three if neccessary. Breakfast is available in the hotel café for an extra charge. ④.

Cherno More, bul. Slivnitsa 33 (☎052/232111, fax 236311). Modern, multi-storey, three-star place bang in the centre of town. The best of the downtown hotels, but still short of international business class. Doubles with shower (⑤), with bath (⑥), or posh suites for $200. Buffet breakfast.

Musala, Musala 3 (☎052/223925). Dingy, with spartan furnishings, ancient carpets and shared facilities. Acceptable for a short stay if all other budget options are full. ③.

ACCOMMODATION PRICE CODES

All **accommodation** in this book has been categorized according to the following price codes. The prices quoted are for the cheapest double room in high season. For more details, see p.30.

| ① $9 and under | ③ $18–36 | ⑤ $60–90 | ⑦ $120–150 |
| ② $9–18 | ④ $36–60 | ⑥ $90–120 | ⑧ $150 and over |

Odesa, bul. Primorski 4 (☎052/228381, fax 253883). Nondescript but perfectly located three-star place just next to the Sea Gardens, offering ensuite doubles (some slightly decrepit, others recently renovated) with cable TV. Breakfast included. ④.

Orbita, Tsar Osvoboditel 25 (☎052/225162, fax 259288). Average postwar high-rise, a little lacking in character but the ensuite rooms have TV and it's within walking distance of the central sights. ④ .

Santa Marina, ul. Baba Rada 28 (☎052/603826 or 603827, fax 603825). Bright, modern, clean downtown hotel hidden away in residential streets behind hotels *Cherno More* and *Odesa*. All rooms have satellite TV and telephone, and breakfast is included. ④.

Trite Delfina, ul. Gabrovo 27 (☎052/600911). Small pension in the backstreets near the train station. Friendly, with clean ensuite rooms, but fills up quickly. ③.

Voennomorski Klub, bul. Varnenchik 2 (☎052/238312). Hotel on the top two floors of the Bulgarian navy club, whose rooms are arranged around a communal sitting area with socialist-era furnishings and potted plants. Slightly grotty but perfectly clean ensuite doubles (③), and comfy two-room apartments (④).

Northeast of the centre

Complex Mexicano, Sveti Konstantin (☎052/362978, fax 362730). Motel-style complex on the southwestern edge of the Sveti Konstantin resort, consisting of wooden ensuite chalets each with TV. There's a (sometimes noisy) Mexican restaurant on site, hence the name. To get there, take bus #8 from in front of the Cathedral, get off at the police checkpoint at the entrance to the Sveti Konstantin resort, and head right for 300m. Turn left, then take a right into an area of residential houses and newish hotel developments. ③.

Grand Hotel Varna, Sveti Konstantin (☎052/861491). Large five-star hotel in the middle of the Sveti Konstantin resort. Superior to the *Cherno More* in town, but not as good as the *Imperial* (see below). It boasts saunas, indoor sports facilities, a casino and swanky nightclub on site. ⑥.

Imperial, Riviera (☎052/855591). Bastion of luxury in the *Riviera* holiday complex on the southern fringes of Golden Sands, once reserved for top party functionaries. It's the region's best hotel, although you'll have a 20km taxi ride into town. ⑧.

Piero, Sveti Konstantin (☎052/362424 or 361445, fax 362409). Very cosy pension tucked away on the southwest fringe of Sveti Konstantin. Three ensuite doubles with TV and telephone (③), and three two- to four-person apartments ($40 per apartment) with nice big bathrooms. Breakfast included. Directions as for Complex Mexicano.

Villa Jura, Sveti Nikola 59 (☎052/826023). Cosy pension in a villa 5km out of town in the suburb of Sveti Nikola (still known to many locals by its Communist-era name, Pochivka). The hotel has a nice garden café, and is within walking distance of the eastern end of Sea Gardens. Take bus #8 or #9 from in front of the Cathedral to the Sveti Nikola/Pochivka stop. ④.

The Town

Varna's social life revolves around **pl. Nezavisimost**, where the opera house and theatre provide the backdrop for a collection of restaurants and cafés. The square is the starting point of Varna's evening promenade, which flows eastward from here along bul. Knyaz Boris I. To the north of pl. Nezavisimost, Varna's main lateral boulevard (bul. Mariya Luiza to the east; bul. Hristo Botev to the west) cuts through pl. Mitropolit Simeon, an important traffic intersection dominated by the domed **Cathedral of the Assumption**. Constructed in 1886 along the lines of St Petersburg's Cathedral, this contains a splendid iconostasis and bishop's throne carved by craftsmen from Debâr in Macedonia, and murals painted after World War II. South of the cathedral in the city gardens stands the **Old Clock Tower**, a fairly unremarkable structure paid for by the city guilds in the 1880s, whose silhouette serves as something of a trademark for the city.

In general, however, the downtown area is a place in which to stroll and enjoy the vigour of emergent enterprise culture rather than visit specific sights. Most of the latter are to the south and east, among the residential streets between the centre and the port, although the otherwise undistinguished bul. Mariya Luiza is home to the biggest of the city's museums.

The Archeological Museum

The **Archeological Museum** (Tues–Sun 10am–5pm) occupies Varna's former girls' high school on the corner of Mariya Luiza and Slivnitsa. There's a display of nineteenth-century icons upstairs, but it's the archeological collection, scattered throughout innumerable halls on the ground floor, which commands most attention.

The Chalcolithic necropolis
Bulgaria's claim to be one of the cradles of European culture was bolstered by the discovery of a **Chalcolithic** (the era when Neolithic man began to smelt copper) necropolis on the outskirts of town in 1972. Dating from the fourth millennium BC, the necropolis was unusual in that it contained many graves in which effigies, rather than human dead, were buried – probably to ensure the continuing health of the living. The gold trinkets with which these symbolic corpses were adorned are displayed extensively in the museum: baubles, bracelets, and pendants in the shape of animals. Many pieces are simply executed; others display an incredible degree of skill considering that they were made as long as 6000 years ago. They're possibly the oldest examples of gold jewellery ever discovered, and have led many to assume that metalworking techniques were developed in Bulgaria independently of the other *loci* of civilization in the Near East.

Greek, Thracian and Bulgarian artefacts
No less impressive than the Chalcolithic collection is the third-century BC jewellery from Greek Odyssos. On one earring a magnifying lens reveals a perfectly shaped Hermes-like deity surrounded by a golden shell – to the naked eye the details of the tiny figure are imperceptible. However, most space is devoted to Bulgaria's finest assemblage of Roman-period **funerary sculpture**. Prominent Greek and Roman citizens were honoured with a tombstone depicting scenes of funeral feasts, usually showing the deceased reclining on a couch surrounded by wife and kids. Townsfolk of Thracian origin preferred a grave plaque decorated with a relief of the so-called **Thracian horseman** (see opposite), the rider god whose worship became universal among the natives from the Hellenistic era onwards. Bulgarian gold and silver from the fourteenth century introduces a collection of medieval weaponry and ecclesiastical art, while the National Revival and revolutionary periods are represented by the usual banners and manifestos.

The City Art Gallery

A couple of hundred metres to the east of the history museum on Lyuben Karavelov is the **City Art Gallery** (Tues–Sun 10am–6pm), whose ground floor hosts high-profile temporary exhibitions. Visitors to the permanent collection on

THE THRACIAN HORSEMAN

Even the smallest of Bulgaria's historical museums devotes at least some space to a display of stone tablets portraying the principal deity of Thrace during the Roman era, the **Thracian horseman** (*Trakiiski konnik*; sometimes also translated as the "Thracian rider" or the "Thracian hero").

In ancient times, in the lands bordering the Black Sea, the **cult of horse and rider** was common among the Thracians and the plain-dwelling Scythian nomads to the north, as well as Asiatic peoples across the Bosphorus to the east. The horse was regarded as an animal capable of reaching the underworld and communicating with the dead, while the rider was deemed a protector of both nature and the souls of the departed. An early manifestation of the rider cult is included in Homer's *Iliad*, in which an archetypal horseman figure, the Thracian King **Rhesus**, has his prized herd of horses stolen by wily Greeks Odysseus and Diomedes.

Stone tablets bearing reliefs of a spear-wielding horseman, often accompanied by a hunting dog, began appearing in Thrace in the third century BC, and soon became universal throughout the eastern Balkans. Tablets were placed in sanctuaries and sacred caves, often those linked with deities associated with health or the protection of nature like Asclepius and Apollo; and they were increasingly used as **funerary monuments**, implying that bereaved families were eager to identify the deceased with the person of the rider god himself. The stylized iconography of the Thracian horseman probably found its way into the subsequent Christian art of the Balkans; with the familiar, spear-wielding, mounted hero re-emerging in medieval icons of **St Demetrius** and **St George**.

the first floor are greeted by a row of seventeenth-century diplomats painted by Flemish portraitist Anselmus von Hulme; beyond these are several rooms of contemporary art. Beside a few lionizations of the Bulgarian peasantry courtesy of Vladimir Dimitrov-Maistor (see p.103) and Stoyan Venev, most room is taken up with works by previous winners of the Varna Graphics Biennale, held in the summer during odd-numbered years.

From bulevard Knyaz Boris I to the sea

Many of Varna's attractions are to be found amid the crumbling turn-of-the-century buildings which lie between **bul. Knyaz Boris I** and the **port**, where the commercial bustle of the city centre gives way to quiet residential streets lined with chestnut trees. Huddled among the town houses are several excellent museums, a couple of churches, and the best of Varna's Roman remains. Careful map-reading is often required to find them, but it's worth the effort.

The National Revival Museum

Just north of bul. Knyaz Boris I, at the southern end of ul. 27 Yuli, stands the **National Revival Museum** (Mon–Fri 10am–5pm), occupying the former Church of Archangel Michael and the premises of Varna's first Bulgarian school. Both school and church were established here in the 1860s, much to the chagrin of the local Greeks, who formed the majority in this part of town and were accustomed to controlling educational and ecclesiastical affairs. A preserved schoolroom includes the balustraded pulpit from which the teacher surveyed his pupils, the latter sitting in wooden pews and using sand trays to write in. Discipline was ensured by placing older boys at the end of each row of pews to supervise the younger ones. The former girls' classroom upstairs holds photographs and texts telling the history of nineteenth-century Varna, with lithographs celebrating the the town's occupation by Russian forces in 1877.

The Armenian church and the Church of Sveta Bogoroditsa

South of the National Revival Museum is pl. Ekzarh Iosif, where elderly *Varnentsi* gather for an evening chat, and locals bring jerry cans and flagons to collect the hot mineral water gushing from a public fountain. Just beyond, at the junction of Han Krum and Kliment, is a small nineteenth-century **Armenian church**, squeezed into the corner of a schoolyard. Serving a local population of about 3000, the church contains naive, child-like icons covered in Armenian script. Outside, a small tablet commemorates the genocide of 1915, when up to one and a half million Armenians lost their lives at the hands of the Ottomans – suggesting a shared history of suffering in which both Armenians and Bulgarians can find common cause.

Of more historical value, however, are the intricately carved iconostasis and bishop's throne of the seventeenth-century **Church of Sveta Bogoroditsa** at Han Krum 19, a partly sunken church whose tower was added later once Ottoman restrictions had been removed.

The Roman thermae and the Church of Sveti Atanas

Across the road from the Church of Sveta Bogoroditsa stands a vast tower of crumbling red brick, once the western wall of the **Roman thermae** (Tues–Sun 10am–5pm), a sizeable complex thought to have been built in the late second or early third century – coins found on the site bear the visage of the then emperor, Septimus Severus. Scrambling among the ruins, it's possible to imagine the ritualized progress of the bathers from the *apodyterium*, or changing room, through the rising temperatures of the *frigidarium*, *tepidarium* and *caldarium*; and then back again. The daily visit to the baths was an important part of social life, and bathers would circulate and exchange gossip in a large central hall, the solid walls of which cut through the middle of the ruins.

The adjacent **Church of Sveti Atanas** (Tues–Sun 10am–12.30pm, and around the time of the evening service at roughly 6–7pm) is a classic example of National Revival architecture. An arcaded porch precedes a sumptuous interior, with a rich, gilt iconostasis, carved wooden ceiling, and painted marble-effect pillars. The icons on display here contain many of their original Greek inscriptions, which is unusual in that in most churches they were scratched off once the Bulgarians took control.

The Ethnographic Museum

A ten-minute walk west from here brings you to one of Bulgaria's finest museums, the **Ethnographic Museum** (Tues–Sun 10am–5pm) occupying an old house on ul. Panagyurishte. The one fault of this attractively arranged collection is that it concentrates exclusively on Bulgarian ethnography, despite the fact that Varna was a predominantly Greek, Turkish and Gagauz town until the Liberation.

Downstairs lie reminders of the region's traditional trades and occupations: among them a variety of fishing nets, wine barrels, wattle-and-daub beehives and a nineteenth-century *yamurluk* or hooded cloak, as worn by the shepherds who roamed the hills of the interior. On the first floor, there's a fine display of **regional costumes**, showing great diversity of styles, largely because the area inland of

Varna was a crossroads of migrating peoples. One distinct local group were the *chenge*, represented here by a wedding scene from the village of Asparuhovo, 50km west of Varna. Costumed mannequins are grouped around a ceremonial wooden wedding sledge, with the bride surrounded by men in black hats wreathed with flowers and accompanied by the slightly menacing figure of the village match-maker holding aloft a cockerel. Items relating to regional folk beliefs include the embroidered **masks** worn during *Kukeri* (spring) and *Survakari* (New Year) rites, and a couple of the **New Year camels** paraded through the streets in some areas – approximations of the humped beast made from sheepskin and mounted on skis. Also on display are a variety of **ritual loaves** baked to mark specific occasions: the *Kravai* for New Year or St John's Day; the "Pony" (*Konche*) for Todorovden (the feast day of St Theodore, patron of horse-breeding); or the *Proshtupalnik* – shaped like a baby's foot – to celebrate a child's first steps.

The City Historical Museum

Bearing southeast from the Enthographic Museum along Han Ormurtag will bring you to ul. 8 noemvri and the relaunched **City Historical Museum**, at no. 5 (Tues–Sat 10am–5pm). Ancient sepia photographs showing a skyline bristling with (now demolished) minarets are among many reminders of the town's past, where exhibits emphasize the transformation of Varna from Balkan backwater to comfortable bourgeois European town. On the basement floor original copies of French fashion mag *Marie Claire* lie strewn over a reconstructed tailor's work-shop of the 1940s, while upstairs lie further re-created interiors, including that of an inter-war photographer's studio – complete with cumbersome, ancient camera. Varna's development as a seaside resort in the 1920s is documented in numerous photographs, including pictures of the annual **beauty contests** – a competition which *Varnentsi* claim the dubious honour of inventing. Initially contestants were dubbed "Sea Hyenas" (perhaps because of their long, stripy bathing suits), and as costumes got skimpier during the 1920s they were renamed "Sea Nymphs".

A few paces further south are the overgrown remains of more **Roman baths**, this time dating from the late fourth century, and far less extensive than the better-preserved *thermae* on Han Krum.

The Museum of Medical History

Considerably more interesting is the **Museum of Medical History**, ul. Paraskeva Nikolau 7 (Mon–Fri 10am–4pm with an unpredictable lunch break), sheltered within the sandy-coloured nineteenth-century building that once housed Varna's first public hospital. Inside a words-and-pictures display adopts a patriotic tone, attempting to show how the medieval Bulgarian state inherited the medical wisdom of the ancients and transmitted it to the rest of Europe – only to have their standards of public hygiene ruined by the Turks, who made everybody live in smelly, unsanitary cities. However, the early Bulgarians were not without their forays into perversity. An array of tenth-century **skulls** on the ground floor reveal that one in three of the local population had been subjected to a symbolic form of trepanation (the practice of drilling holes in the skull) – in which the bone had been scratched and dented but not actually pierced. Archeologists presume that this had some kind of ritual purpose – but quite what, no one knows.

Less macabre but equally disconcerting are the ferocious-looking early twentieth-century surgical instruments on display upstairs, along with a reconstructed turn-of-the-century dentist's consulting room and antiquated x-ray machines.

The Sea Gardens

The massed flowerbeds of Varna's *Morskata Gradina,* or **Sea Gardens**, were laid out at the end of the nineteenth century by Czech horticulturalist Anton Novak (invited here by those other Bohemian Bulgarophiles the Skorpil brothers; who supposedly modelled them on the Baroque palace gardens of Belvedere and Schönbrunn in Vienna. The park's tree-lined pathways are patrolled from dawn to dusk by young families and courting couples, and you'll occasionally come across chained **dancing bears** resting in the shade, brought here by their Gypsy owners to be photographed alongside tourists in return for a few leva.

The Navy Museum and the Aquarium

At the western end of the park, the gunboat responsible for the Bulgarian navy's only victory lies honourably embedded outside the **Navy Museum** (9am–noon & 1.30–5pm). The boat in question, the *Drâzhki* (Intrepid), sank the Turkish cruiser *Hamidie* off Cape Kaliakra during the First Balkan War of 1912. Since Bulgaria's navy was reduced to a rump by the Neuilly Treaty of 1919, and later collaborated with Hitler's *Kriegsmarine*, there's little else for it to take pride in, and the exhibits inside trace seapower and commerce on the Black Sea and the lower Danube back to its earliest days, devoting special attention to the Russian Black Sea Fleet's campaign against the Ottomans in 1877–78.

Just beyond is the **Aquarium** (Mon 2–5pm, Tues–Fri 9am–5pm), a small collection of fresh- and seawater creatures whose habits are – frustratingly – explained in German texts only. Most interesting specimens are the sea-needles, who reproduce when the female of the species deposits her eggs in a pouch on the male, who is expected to do the brooding; the Black Sea turbot, a denizen of the sea bed which assumes the colour of rocks to disguise itself against predators; and the freshwater sturgeon, which can grow to a length of 9m in the wild. Those confined to the bubbling tanks here are significantly smaller, but still magnificent enough to be the star attractions.

A little way to the east, pathways descend to Varna's *Morski bani* or municipal **beach**, where bathers can look out at the shoals of tankers and cargo vessels anchored in the bay. The beach stretches northwards for a couple of kilometres, lined with a succession of outdoor bars and restaurants which remain buzzing well into the early hours. At the far end of the beach, steaming mineral water spews out of the hillside, collecting in a pool often used by elderly bathers well into winter.

The Natural History Museum, the Zoo and the Dolphinarium

Back in the park, tree-lined avenues stretch eastwards towards an angular **Monument to Fighters against Fascism**, to the south of which lurks an unassuming **Natural History Museum** (Tues–Sun 10am–5pm), providing a useful introduction to the coast's flora and fauna, if you can make out the Bulgarian captions. Live specimens prowl their spartan quarters in a small **Zoo** just beyond (daily 8am–5pm) featuring camels, lions, Shetland ponies and wolves – the latter being the most animated of a generally sorry-looking bunch. A little further on is the **Dolphinarium**, (shows at 11am & 3pm Tues–Sun; $7). On the other side of bul. Primorski looms the ultra-modern **Palace of Sports and Culture**, venue for concerts and indoor sports such as wrestling and basketball.

The Park of Fighting Friendship

Among the housing estates that mark the city's northwestern margins lies the bizarrely named **Park of Fighting Friendship** (bus #22 from the Cathedral), where a granite monument tops a Thracian tumulus marking the site of the **Battle of Varna**. An army of 30,000 Crusaders made their way here in November 1444, intending to meet a fleet of Venetian and Genoese ships before sailing on to Constantinople. Unbeknown to them Sultan Murad II had bought off the boat captains and taken command of the fleet for himself, landing on the Varna shore with an army of 120,000. During the subsequent clash King Ladislas III of Poland and Hungary (known to the Bulgarians as Vladislav Varnenchik) recklessly led a charge to capture Sultan Murad in his tent, but was cut down in the attempt. His army wavered, forcing János Hunyadi to order an inglorious retreat, marking the end of Christendom's last attempt to check the Ottoman advance.

A small **museum** (daily 9am–5pm) built into the mound displays medieval armour and tributes to the various East European races that made up Ladislas' army.

The northern suburbs and Evksinograd

Varna's northeastern suburbs have always been favoured by city folk as a place to relax; the villas and holiday cottages of the more affluent cling to vine-covered hillsides overlooking the sea, or nestle in small gardens rich in fruit. The one specific sight in the region is **Evksinograd Palace**, former residence of monarchs Aleksandâr and Ferdinand. Less interesting to visit but worthy of mention is the village of **VINITSA** 10km northeast of town (bus #31 from opposite the Cathedral), still inhabited by one of the Black Sea's more elusive and mysterious minorities, the **Gagauz** (see p.342). Three kilometres up the hill from the beaches of Sveti Konstantin, Vinitsa is a relatively unspoilt village with plenty of private rooms, although there is no *kvartirno byuro* so you'll have to ask around.

Evksinograd Palace

Built under the name of Sandrovo by Prince Aleksandâr Batenberg in 1882, and renamed (combining the Greek word *euxine* – "hospitable" – with the Slavonic *grad* – "town" or "fortress") by his successor Ferdinand, **Evksinograd Palace** is nowadays notorious for being the former holiday home of the Bulgarian Politburo. It still belongs to the state, and members of the government spend their holidays here, but the construction of a new hotel (the *Sandrovo*) in the palace grounds seems designed to place Evksinograd on the international conference circuit.

You can't visit the palace itself, but there are sometimes guided tours of the grounds on offer to tourists staying at Sveti Konstantin or Golden Sands (independent travellers can enquire about tour availability from the reception desk of the *Sandrovo Hotel* beside the entrance; ☎052/861241). These lead past the **vineyards** where Bulgaria's most sought-after wines and brandies are produced, and descend towards the seafront through the **botanical gardens** layed out for Ferdinand by French horticulturalists at the turn of the century. The Communist Party hierarchy built themselves a deluxe **beach complex** in the woods overlooking the shore, complete with state-of-the-art health clinic and sports hall – the latter including a bowling alley. Each member of the Politburo had his own beach house, linked by secret tunnel to a central command bunker – in the unlikely event of being taken unawares by the apocalypse while bathing. Party Secretary Todor Zhivkov's beach house was, of course, bigger than the rest, isolated from those of his comrades on the other side of the headland.

The entrance to the palace lies on the main coast road running north out of Varna (bus #7 or #8 from in front of the Cathedral).

Sveti Konstantin (Druzhba)

Immediately beyond Evksinograd, suburban Varna fades imperceptibly into the first of the great tourist complexes built in the postwar drive to develop the coast. Originally named "Druzhba" ("friendship"), **SVETI KONSTANTIN** (bus #8 from in front of the Cathedral) first admitted Western tourists in 1955, and has since served as a prototype for others. The elite trade union rest-homes which used to grace the northern end of Sveti Konstantin are now hotels operating under the banner of the **Sunny Day** (*Slânchev Den*) resort, which has its own beach, but to all intents and purposes is still part of Sveti Konstantin. Taken together, Sveti Konstantin and Sunny Day are still quite small compared with the mega-resorts of Golden Sands and Albena further north, so there's less in the way of things to do – although the centre of Varna is only 12km away.

The resort has a parklike cosiness, with an abundance of oaks and cypresses, and a number of small beaches and coves. On the downside, it is extraordinarily badly lit at night, and is overrun by stray dogs living off restaurant hand-outs. The emergence of several small family-run hotels on the western fringes of the resort has meant that there's more scope for independent travellers here than previously, and the Swedish-built *Grand Hotel Varna* in the centre of Sveti Konstantin is still one of the city's better business hotels (see p.331). Food and drink in the resort's numerous café-restaurants tends towards the bland, and is more expensive than in central Varna.

The Stone Forest

Roughly 18km due west of Varna on either side of the Devnya road, the desolate scrubland is interrupted by scores of curious stone columns standing as high as 7m, known as *pobiti kamâni* or "standing stones", usually translated as the **Stone Forest**. These strange, snake-haunted formations were created around fifty million years ago when fragments of two chalk strata gradually bonded together in the intervening sand layer, by a process analogous to stalactite formation. Nowadays this is a popular spot for picnics and leisurely hikes. **Getting there** is difficult unless you have your own transport: the region is best accessed by travelling west out of Varna along the old main road to Devnya, ignoring the Devnya-bound A2 motorway which runs parallel to the north.

Eating and drinking

The majority of Varna's places to eat and drink are along the route of the evening *korso*, which stretches **east from pl. Nezavisimost** along bul. Knyaz Boris I, before turning down Slivnitsa towards the Sea Gardens. There are plenty of **cafés** and **restaurants** lining the route, although the Varna restaurant scene changes so rapidly that it's sometimes difficult to provide precise recommendations. In general the places along this main strip are more expensive than elsewhere in Bulgaria, but not prohibitively so. On the whole restaurants in Varna tend to open daily from noon until 11pm or midnight, unless otherwise stated below.

The **snack bars** around pl. Nezavisimost and along Knyaz Boris I are the best places to grab **breakfast**; while a succession of *sladkarnitsi* along Knyaz Boris I sell pastries, *banitsa*, small pizzas and other snacks throughout the day. If the local fast food doesn't appeal, there's a *Pizza Hut* at Knyaz Boris I 62; and *Macdonald's* on pl. Nezavisimost.

For **evening drinking**, most of central Varna's cafés serve alcohol well into the night, and a string of outdoor **bars** and grilled-fish restaurants lines the municipal beach, accessible via pathways that lead down from the Sea Gardens. Few of these establishments have names, and it's best simply to wander along until you see a place that takes your fancy.

Restaurants

Bistro Rimska Terma, 8 noemvri. Modern, chic place just downhill from the thermae, with excellent Bulgarian cuisine and friendly service; the prices are high but deservedly so.

Happy Bar and Grill, pl. Nezavisimost. A range of chicken-and-chips-style dishes as well as a few Bulgarian regulars. Reliable food, breezy service and modest prices. There's another branch (dubbed somewhat misleadingly "Happy English Pub") near the train station at the bottom of ul. Drâzhki.

Lubovta e Ludost, Slivnitsa. Upscale restaurant on the first floor of the Festival Hall. Good food and attentive service, but pricier than average.

Odessa, bul. Primorski 4. On the terrace of the hotel of the same name. Mediocre, overpriced food, but the floorshow – Russian-language pop singers, cheesy disco dancing, and belly-dancing – is entertaining.

Paraklisa, corner of Paraskeva Nikolau and bul. Primorski. The best and most imaginative traditional Bulgarian food in Varna, served up in the courtyard of an old chapel. It's more expensive than most, but worth the extra cost.

Panorama, top floor of the *Cherno More* hotel. Excellent food in elegant surroundings, with live chamber music or jazz most nights.

Staviko, ul. 8-mi noemvri 11. Good-quality Bulgarian standards in a convenient location behind the Roman baths, near the entrance to the church of Sveti Atanas. There's a roof terrace, and occasional live music in the basement dining hall.

Cafés and bars

Davidoff, Knyaz Boris I 46. The best of the café-bars on the main strip, with comfy wicker chairs and excellent (if pricey) ice creams. There are other branches on pl. Nezavisimost and Slivnitsa.

Grâtski Dvor, Knyaz Boris I 57. Elegant outdoor garden café serving luxuriant creamy coffees and good ice-cream.

Kipos, bul. Mariya Luiza 46. No more than a shed serving drinks in a suburban garden, this is a nice place to get away from the main tourist trail and drink in the company of locals. Closes around 10pm.

Look, Knyaz Boris I 60. Trendy hangout, frequented by Varna's youth and student population.

Planeta, pl. Garov. 24hr café in a pavilion just outside the train station – useful when catching late or early trains.

Titanic, Ivan Vazov 39. Elegant café-bar, with a small restaurant upstairs.

Nightlife and entertainment

Those looking for a taste of seaside hedonism, Bulgarian style, should head for the big warehouse-style techno club, *Comics*, just west of the Cathedral on ul. Hristo Samsarov, which is open all year round; or the summer-only discos

---

VAMPIRES AND VAMPIRE HUNTERS

The ugly, industrial town of **Devnya**, 30km west of Varna, is now known only for its highly noxious chemical industry, but during the last century its reputation was widespread as Bulgaria's **vampire capital**. Reports brought back from the Black Sea region by nineteenth-century travellers reveal that belief in vampires was widespread among the Bulgarian peasantry of the time. Travelling in the 1880s, the Czech Balkanologist Konstantin Jireček found a wealth of vampire lore in the isolated rural communities west of Varna, with inexplicable illnesses among humans, and particularly sheep – the region's main source of income – being attributed to a visitation by some bloodthirsty demon, and local wise men (known as *vampirdzhiya* or *dzhadzhiya*) being paid handsomely by villagers to drive the fiends away. According to Jireček, the vampire hunters of Devnya were considered the best in eastern Bulgaria.

The belief was that people became vampires if proper burial customs were not observed or if certain portentious events happened before their death: for example, a shadow passing across their body, or a dog or cat jumping across their path. After burial, an invisible spirit would rise up from the grave each night, feeding off local flocks and bringing listlessness and ill health to the human population. Vampires could also assume solid form, often living among humans for many years, getting married and having children before being detected. To chase the vampires away, a *dzhadzhiya* would be summoned to walk among the flocks, holding an icon aloft. The icon also came in handy when trying to identify the resting place of the vampire. If it began to tremble when held above a particular grave, it meant that the culprit had been found. The best way to **deal with a vampire** was to exhume the body, stab it through the heart with a hawthorn branch, then burn it with kindling taken from the same shrub. If the vampire was in spirit form, it could be driven into a bottle which was then thrown onto a fire.

The beliefs noted by Jireček were by no means isolated cases. The British travellers St Clair and Brophy, who lived in a village south of Varna in the 1860s, wrote of a boy forbidden from marrying his sweetheart because locals earnestly believed that he was of vampire descent. They also relate how peasants in a neighbouring village burned a man alive for vampirism, because he was fond of nocturnal walks and was "found to have only one nostril".

According to Jireček, the best vampire hunters were thought to be descended from *vâlkodlatsi*, literally **werewolves**, who resulted from the sexual union of a vampire and a young maiden, and were the only living beings who could see vampire spirits. The *vâlkodlatsi*'s vampire-hunting descendants were also thought to have another supernatural power: the ability to detect buried treasure. In an area full of ancient Thracian, Roman and Byzantine remains, it's not difficult to see why the idea of hidden hordes of goblets and coins – all waiting to be unearthed by the lucky peasant – exerted such a hold on the popular imagination.

Another associated piece of local lore concerns the Lake of Varna (a fjord-like inlet stretching west from the city), which used to be known as Vampire Lake. According to popular belief, the lake required an annual **human sacrifice**, the last recorded instance of which was in 1933, when one Ana Konstantinova went swimming there despite warnings, and was duly sucked underwater.

below the Sea Gardens beside the main town beach. Other rave events and occasional gigs take place, but the venues change with alarming frequency, so you'll need to rely on local knowledge, or have a go at deciphering the fly-posters.

The **Opera House**, on pl. Nezavisimost (box office: Mon–Fri 10.30am–1pm & 2–7.30pm), is Varna's main cultural institution, although it closes in July & August. Many other major events, including orchestral concerts, take place in the open-air theatre (*Leten teatâr*) in the Sea Gardens; the modern Festival Hall (*Festivalen kompleks*) on Slivnitsa 2; or, on occasion, the Palace of Sport and Culture out on bul. Primorski. All the above are pressed into service during the annual **Varnensko lyato** or "Varna Summer" of symphonic, operatic and chamber music (mid-June to September), which attracts some of the world's finest orchestras and companies. The Varna Summer also comprises the Varna jazz festival, and an international film festival (both usually in August). A complete schedule and advance tickets are available from the ground floor of the Festival Hall itself.

The **cinema** in the Festival Hall shows the best range of first-run and cult films, most of which are shown in their original language, with Bulgarian subtitles. For children, there's a **puppet theatre** at ul. Dragoman 6, although it takes a summer break in July and August.

Listings

Airlines Aeroflot, bul. Mariya Luiza 40; Balkan, Shipka 2 (☎052/331451).

Car rental Avis, at the airport (☎052/650832); Hertz, at the airport (☎052/650210).

Car repairs Try the big city-centre depots at bul. Vl. Varnenchik 262 (☎052/449885), and Vl. Varnenchik 184 (☎052/441252), although they may only have parts for East European models. The repair shop beside the filling station in Sveti Konstantin (☎052/861377) deals with Fiat, Lada and Zastava.

Dentist Dental polyclinic at bul. Sâborni 24.

Hospitals bul Sâborni 40. In emergencies call ☎150.

Pharmacies Sanita, bul. Vladislav Varnenchik 12, is open 24hrs.

Post office The main post office is at bul. Sâborni 36 (Mon–Sat 7.30am–7pm, Sun 8am–noon).

Telephones At the main post office (see above).

MOVING ON FROM VARNA

A number of **international buses** leave Varna: the ticket office at the bus station provides information and tickets on daily services to Istanbul, as well as seasonal departures (probably weekly in summer) to Odessa and Kiev. Istanbul-bound buses are also run by Nisikli, at Hristo Botev 3 (☎052/222761). Domestic and international **train bookings** can be made from BDZh/Rila, ul. Vaptsarov 11 (Mon–Fri 8am–6.30pm, Sat 8am–3pm).

For international **airline tickets** try Balkantourist-Bulgarian Lucky Flight, ul. Koloni 2 (☎052/226291).

Agencies dealing with **boat trips** to Istanbul come and go, but the English-speaking staff at Varnenski Bryag (see p.330), or any of the big hotels, should be able to tell you when, and if, the boats are running, and where to get tickets.

North of Varna

When people think of the coastline north of Varna they normally think of sprawling tourist complexes like **Golden Sands** (Zlatni pyasâtsi) and **Albena**, and, indeed, the first 50km of the E87's northward progress can seem like an endless procession of high-rise hotels and dusty building sites. Once you get away from the main road, however, even the biggest of the resorts can be quite peaceful and relaxing, making good use of the sandy beaches lining the shore and the forests which form their immediate hinterland. Golden Sands is near enough to Varna to be on the urban bus network, while Albena is served by regular minibuses from a stop 200m west of Varna's Cathedral.

Beyond Albena the atmosphere changes, with the less crowded towns and villages of the Dobrudzhan littoral perched above an increasingly rocky coast, which culminates in the dramatic cliffs of **Cape Kaliakra**. Although all the settlements along this stretch of the water make good **day-trips by bus** from Varna, the picturesque town of **Balchik** is the most likely base to appeal to the non-package tour crowd.

THE GAGAUZ

Bulgaria's Black Sea shore hosts several communities of **Gagauz**, a Turkish-speaking Christian people whose origins remain the subject of much controversy. Turkish sources maintain that they are descended from the **Seljuk Turks** of Sultan Izzedin Kaykaus, who came to the area in 1261 and soon converted to Christianity under pressure from their Bulgarian neighbours. This is disputed by Bulgarian ethnologists, who suggest that they are descended from the original **Bulgars**, the Turkic nomads who descended on the Balkans in the eighth century. Perhaps the most likely theory is that they are descended from the **Cumans**, another Turkic tribe who started moving into eastern Bulgaria in the twelfth century, and formed the backbone of the short-lived fourteenth-century coastal empire of Balik and Dobrotitsa, which was centred on the towns of Balchik and Kavarna (see p.347).

Although many Gagauz were Islamicized and assimilated by their Turkish conquerors during the Ottoman era, enough of them remained Christian to ensure their continued existence as a distinct community. Many of them **emigrated to Bessarabia**, where they could practise their Christian faith more freely than they could under the Ottomans. They still retain a strong presence in the former Soviet republic of Moldova, where the Gagauz lands around the provincial town of Komrat enjoy autonomous status. Those Gagauz who remained in Bulgaria found themselves increasingly torn by the **national struggles** of the nineteenth century, when many identified themselves with Varna's Greek population in order to distinguish themselves both from their Turk overlords and from the Bulgarian peasants who were increasingly moving into the city. Most Gagauz joined the Greeks in opposing the opening of Bulgarian-language schools and churches, and therefore received little sympathy from the Bulgarians after the Liberation. Unlike the Greeks, however, the Gagauz had no other national homeland to emigrate to, and despite their small numbers, they still retain a distinctive presence in Vinitsa, Kichevo, and a succession of villages strung out over the hills north of Varna. Older Gagauz still speak a dialect of Turkish among themselves, but a literary version of the Gagauz tongue never developed in Bulgaria, and knowledge of the language is slowly dying out among the young.

Golden Sands (Zlatni pyasâtsi)

Tourists generally baulk at pronouncing Zlatni pyasâtsi, so most Bulgarians along the coast will understand if you say "Goldstrand" or **GOLDEN SANDS** instead. It's a polyglot place: of all the nationalities here, Germans predominate, and two members of the 2nd of June terrorist group were actually arrested here in 1978 after being recognized by a West German prison warder who, like them, was on holiday. The resort's myriad hotels occupy a wooded, landscaped strip behind Zlatni pyasâtsi's greatest asset, its **beach**: a soft, pale golden expanse 4km long, sloping gently into an undertow-less sea.

Golden Sands also offers a wide range of bars, restaurants and discos; and **activities** such as scuba diving, waterskiing and paraskiing are offered by kiosks along the beach. The strolling areas behind the beach feature well-tended gardens, outdoor pools, and plenty of sports facilities for children. A group of hotels at the southern end of the resort operate seperately under the name of the Riviera Holiday Club, site of the *Imperial* hotel (see p.331).

Practicalities

Independent travellers are charged much more for hotel **rooms** than those who have booked a package holiday, but if you do fancy the idea of spending the odd night here then your first port of call should be the **accommodation bureau** (*byuro za nastanyavane*) in the administration building on the main E87 highway, which runs along the upper, western fringe of the resort (☎052/855681, *www. goldensands.bg*). They can fix you up with rooms in a two-star hotel for about $30 per person, or in a three-star place for $40 per person, as well as checking vacancies at the resort's *Panorama* campsite.

There are several ways of getting here **by bus from Varna**: #9 from in front of the Cathedral to the Riviera Holiday Club; #109 from the train station or in front of the Cathedral to the administration building, or #409 from the airport to the administration building.

Aladzha Monastery

In the Hanchuka Forest, 4km southwest of Golden Sands, dozens of cells and chambers hewn into a cliff comprise what remains of **Aladzha Monastery** (Tues–Sun 9am–5pm). The caves to the west were occupied during the Stone Age by people whom Strabo called "pygmies", and served as a place of refuge during the Dark Ages. A Christian church may have existed here as early as the fifth century, though the monastery itself was probably established during the thirteenth century, in the same way as the Ivanovo rock monasteries.

Aladzha's monks were *hesychasts*, striving to attain union with God by maintaining physical immobility and total silence. However, they did get round to painting several exquisite murals in the chapels, which can be seen at the end of the first and second galleries. Nowadays they're scrappy and faded, although in olden times they were sufficiently impressive to earn the monastery its name – *Aladzha* means "multi-coloured" in Turkish.

A **museum** at the entrance displays models of how the monastery used to look when occupied, alongside ornaments, weapons and other artefacts dating from around 5000 BC, discovered in a Chalcolithic necropolis on the western outskirts of Varna in 1972. You might enjoy poking around the various catacombs and surrounding woods – the latter a place of many **legends**. Its mythical guardian, Rim Papa, is said to awake from a cotton-lined burrow every year to ask whether the trees still grow and women and cows still give birth, and go back to sleep upon being answered in the affirmative.

The best way **to get to the monastey** is to walk from Golden Sands: it's about 3km uphill from the resort (signed from the crossroads near the main adminis-tration building), along an asphalt road – not too unpleasant providing you avoid the midday heat.

Kranevo

Just beyond the northern end of Golden Sands, **KRANEVO** is a rapidly expand-ing village sitting at the southern tip of a glorious curve of beach which extends onwards towards the mega-resort of Albena, some 4km distant. Kranevo's grow-ing number of private rooms and family-run hotels make it a useful budget alter-native to its more package-oriented neighbour: you can in any case walk along the sands to Albena if you fancy using the facilities there. The main E87 coastal road forges through the eastern fringes of Kranevo, and it's here that Varna–Albena and Varna–Balchik buses pick up and drop off. A 1km walk downhill brings you to what passes for the village centre, a parade of hastily-constructed cafés and restaurants leading down towards the **beach**.

Rooms are available from the Ekrene-96 bureau in the centre (open June–August daily approx 8am–dusk; be prepared to ask around outside these times), with prices ranging from $7 to $15 per person depending on proximity to the shore. Two of the best **hotels** are the *Stefan*, on the main road near the south-ern entrance to the village (☎05722/4202; ③), some of whose neat rooms have balconies looking down towards the bay; and the *Apolon*, further along the same road (☎05722/2330; ③), which offers comfy, characterful ensuite rooms with TV and telephone. Both have good **restaurants**, although there are plenty of places offering grilled fish in the village centre. Food and drink in Kranevo is signifi-cantly cheaper than in neighbouring Albena up the road.

Albena and around

The step-pyramid architecture of **ALBENA**'s hotels marks it out as one of the more architecturally inventive of Bulgaria's purpose-built resorts; it's also the most efficiently run, the cleanest, and by far the most expensive. It's undoubted-ly a beautiful place, with well-tended flowerbeds and lawns lying behind an invit-ing expanse of beach, and the range of activities on offer here is second to none. Bordering the resort to the south is an area of swamp-like semi-submerged forest known as the **Balta**; access to this alluring landscape is via the asphalted track to the *Gorski Kât* restaurant.

Albena is bypassed by the main road, but well served by minibuses from Varna (departing from a stop 200m west of the Cathedral) and buses from Balchik (see p.346). Arriving at the terminal at the eastern end of the resort, walk down the main road for about ten minutes to reach the **tourist bureau** on the right-hand side of the road (☎05722/62152). Here you can get rooms in any of the resort's forty **hotels**, with prices ranging from $30 per person in the two-star places, to $45 per person in the best of the beachside establishments, most of which are patronized by Western tour groups, with standards of comfort and service to match. Albena also has a good **campsite** (off the entrance road to the left) with well shaded areas for tents, and ensuite four-person bungalows ($13 per person), some of which have self-catering facilities ($25 per person). If you're keen to stay in Albena, it's worth ringing the resort's marketing department (☎05722/62051 & 62090, fax 63647, *www.albena.bg*) in advance – independent travellers will be given a significant reduction on the walk-in rates quoted above.

Food and drink in Albena are probably the most expensive in Bulgaria and, unless you periodically escape to neighbouring Kranevo or Balchik (see overleaf), this may not prove the inexpensive holiday destination you anticipated. There are plenty of alfresco restaurants, bars and cafés along the resort's main thorough-fares and beside the beach, though individual recommendations are impossible, as things change from one season to the next.

Albena boasts at least five **sailing and windsurfing** schools strung out along the beach, offering boat and board rental from about $5 per hour, as well as week-long courses (around $100 for fourteen hours' tuition). There's also a **scuba-diving** centre, with prices starting at $20 for an introductory session, and $100 for a week-long course. The resort's **riding** centre is currently the best in Bulgaria, with twelve hours of tuition costing around $90, and a variety of rides (ranging from one-hour "gallops" to day-long picnics) laid on for all abilities.

The Tekke at Obrochishte

Beyond the vast roundabout marking the western fringe of Albena, the E87 heads eastwards along the coast, although most traffic takes the inland route through the village of **Obrochishte**, overlooked from a hillside by the partially ruined Dervish monastery of **Ak Yazula Baba Tekke**. This sixteenth-century foundation consists of two seven-sided structures roughly 50m apart, with the smaller of the two, on the right, containing the still-intact *turbe* or **tomb** of Ak Yazula Baba himself. A fourteenth-century holy man who subsequently became an object of veneration for local Muslims, Yazula Baba attracted Dervish communities to the area and, although the latter have long-since departed, the Tekke is still a power-ful draw for both Muslims and Christians alike. Bulgarians believe it to be the last resting place both of St Athanasius (patron saint of lost sheep), and of the coun-try's first Christian ruler, Knyaz Boris I, and pious shepherds used to sacrifice hundreds of sheep here on St George's Day – hence the name Obrochishte, which means "place of sacrifice". Even today local Muslims and Christians observe common holidays and join in each other's rites, assembling here to eat a sacrificial meal (followed inevitably by drinking and dancing) on four important dates of the year: Atanasovden (St Athanasius's Day, 19 Jan), Gergyovden (St George's Day, 6 May), Kurban Bayram and Sheker Bayram (both moveable Muslim feasts, see p.47 for details). Unfortunately it's rare to find the *turbe* open outside these dates, although pilgrims can still thrust their hands through a spe-cial opening in the building to acquire good fortune from the head of the saint buried within. Visitors also hang clothes or strips of cloth on neighbouring trees to ensure good health and protection from evil. The roofless ruin to the left of the *turbe* is the old Dervish *imaret* or refectory, where people gather on the four main holy days to cook vast cauldrons of meat.

Only 3km from the Albena roundabout, Obrochishte is an easy walk from the resort itself: an asphalt path runs parallel to the road on the left-hand side. Otherwise, hourly Albena–Dobrich buses pass through the village.

Balchik

Occupying a succession of sandy cliffs and crumbling sugarloaf hills, **BALCHIK**'s whitewashed cottages hover precipitously above a series of ravines running down to the sea. It's the kind of scene beloved of artists, and Balchik-inspired seascapes are a regular sight in provincial galleries throughout Bulgaria. Founded by the Milesians in the sixth century BC and named Krounoi (The Springs), the town was a valued haven for Greek merchants attempting to pass the treacherous waters around Cape Kaliakra, as well as an important centre for viniculture – hence its later name, Dionysopolis, honouring the god of the vine. By the sixth century AD, the harbour had silted up, and the Turks were subsequently to dub the town Balchik, or "town of clay".

Despite being popular with Bulgarians who take advantage of the numerous private rooms and inexpensive hotels, Balchik doesn't see many foreign tourists, largely because it lacks a really good beach. Inmates of Albena (see p.344) are, however, bussed into town during the day to stroll around the streets and visit Balchik's main attraction: the **summer palace of Queen Marie of Romania**, a memory of the inter-war years when Balchik was ruled from Bucharest.

The Town

Assuming that you arrive at the **bus station**, any exploration of Balchik should begin with the **Ethnographic Complex** at Hristo Botev 4 (Mon–Fri 9am–noon, plus some afternoons if enough tourists are around): head uphill from the bus station and take a left when you see the whitewashed church bell tower. The complex consists of a reconstructed nineteenth-century school house and the Church of Sveti Nikola, built in 1845 by local National Revival architect Koyu Raichov. The iconostasis is decorated with pictures by itinerant artists from Galichnik in western Macedonia, and there's a splendid gold-suffused portrait of the saint himself, patron of seafarers, on the left side of the nave as you enter.

Heading downhill from the bus station you'll soon come across the **History Museum** on pl. Nezavisimost (Mon–Fri 8am–noon & 1.30–5.30pm), which contains marble and bronze statuary from Dionysopolis, including a torso of the deity himself. Opposite is a small **Ethnographic Museum** (Mon–Fri 8am–noon & 1.30–5.30pm) displaying traditional local costumes and reconstructed nineteenth-century peasant interiors. From here the main thoroughfare, ul. Cherno More, winds down to the port, passing on the way a flight of steps leading up to an **art gallery** at ul. Otets Paisii 4 (Mon–Fri 8am–noon & 1–4.30pm), which features icons from local churches. At the bottom of the hill, a small whitewashed mosque stands inland from the port, where looming grain silos blight a lively seafront square.

From here an esplanade stretches westwards past the misshapen concrete lumps that form Balchik's sea defences. There are a few areas of sand (shipped in every spring to create an artificial beach), although most bathers prefer to position themselves on the various piers and jetties protruding into the bay.

The palace of Queen Marie

Two kilometres west of town, ranged on a hillside overlooking the sea, is the **Quiet Nest**, summer residence of Queen Marie of Romania. Kent-born Marie, a granddaughter of Queen Victoria, ordered the construction of a series of follies here, presided over by a whimsical-looking villa topped by a minaret (the reconciliation of her Christian and Muslim subjects was one of Marie's pet projects, inspired either by her adherence to the Baha'i faith or by her Turkish lover). The surrounding **botanical gardens** (summer daily 8am–5pm; winter hours unpredictable; $5), home to more than six hundred varieties of trees, shrubs and cacti, are dotted with pavilions now used as rest homes by the Union of Bulgarian Artists. Descending towards the sea just behind the villa are six terraces – one for each of Marie's children, the sixth one (truncated by the cliff) symbolizing Mircea who died of typhus at the age of two. To the east of the villa are several set-piece follies, including a water mill, a rose garden, a Roman bath, and a small chapel, where naively executed frescos include a picture of Marie herself in Byzantine garb. The queen left instructions for her heart to be buried within the chapel in a jewelled casket – the latter was hurriedly removed from Balchik in 1940, when Bulgaria regained the southern Dobrudzha.

You can see the Quiet Nest's minaret clearly from Balchik's seafront esplanade: unfortunately, the gardens are not accessible from here, its lower gates locked to discourage bathers from picnicking in the grounds. Head instead for the northern entrance, just off the Balchik–Albena road – best reached by following ul. Primorski westwards from the port, or taking the Balchik–Albena bus (every 30min from Balchik's port area; ask to be put down at *dvoretsa*, "the palace").

Practicalities

Balchik's **bus station** (where minibuses for Varna line up waiting for passengers) is on the high ground above the town centre, just over 1km from the seafront. From here ul. Cherno More winds down the hill to the town centre and the port, to the east of which lies the main **beach**. Albena–Balchik buses pick up and drop off by the port. The ensemble of whitewashed buildings set back from the port, known locally as the *bazar*, houses a couple of local agencies, Balchik Tours and Briz, who rent out **private rooms** graded according to their distance from the sea; expect to pay $7 per person for something 1km away, slightly more for something central. Otherwise, the best **hotels** are the *Jupiter*, just above the beach at ul. Timok 1 (☎0579/2354, fax 2605; ④), offering clean, modern ensuite rooms, and the *Byala Kâshta*, five minutes west of the port at Geo Milev 18 (☎0579/3951; ④), which has lovely pine-floored rooms with sea views, satellite TV and breakfast included.

Opportunities for **eating and drinking** in Balchik tend to be concentrated on the seafront path west of the port, where several outdoor restaurants and cafés serve grilled fish, coffee and spirits until late: the restaurant of the *Byala Kâshta* hotel is one of the best of these. There are a couple more cafés and a touristy *mehana* in the *bazar*.

Kavarna and Cape Kaliakra

Eighteen kilometres along the coast from Balchik, **KAVARNA** was probably founded by the Mesembrians in order to challenge the importance of the harbour at nearby Krounoi. A predominantly Greek and Gagauz town in the nineteenth century, Kavarna was burned to the ground by marauding Circassians (Turkic Muslims from the Caucasus) in July 1877, and at least 1000 of its townsfolk murdered. Nowadays it's a quiet place, lying a couple of kilometres inland from the seafront, where there's a small beach resort, the **Morska zvezda**, and a port used for the export of Dobrudzhan grain. It's a good spot from which to explore the coastal cliffs just to the east which culminate in the dramatic **Cape Kaliakra**.

Kavarna

Ulitsa Chernomorska heads from the **bus station** into the town centre, where steps behind the *Dobrotitsa* hotel descend to a fourteenth-century Turkish *hammam* containing the town **museum** (summer Tues–Sun 8am–noon & 1–6pm; winter Tues–Fri 8am–noon & 2–6pm). Exhibits within tell of the local noble Balik, who set up an independent principality based on Kavarna in the 1340s, extending his power southwards as far as the River Kamchiya. His son Dobrotitsa wrested independence from his nominal suzerains the Bulgarian tsars, and severed links with the Târnovo patriarchate, accepting the writ of Constantinople instead. A couple of blocks west of here lies an **Ethnographic Museum** (May–Sept Mon–Fri 8am–noon & 2–6pm; Oct–April Mon–Fri 8am–noon & 1–5pm), housed in a former schoolhouse, its classrooms now decorated in the style of a typical small-town family home of the nineteenth century. Among the oddities on display is a mirror framed by fine lacy curtains: the curtains were drawn for forty days in the event of a death in the family.

As for accommodation, the *Dobrotitsa*, at ul. Chernomorska 22 (☎0570/2191 or 2585; ③), is a fairly standard two-star **hotel**, offering plain ensuite rooms, while the *Morska zvezda* **campsite**, on the beach, 2km away, has a wide range of bungalows for about $3 per person; buses leave from just outside the bus station every thirty minutes. For **food and drink**, your best bet is one of the rough-and-ready grilled fish joints near the beach, or the any of the cafés along ul. Chernomorska.

Cape Kaliakra

Bulgarians make much of the "Beautiful Headland" – as **CAPE KALIAKRA** ($1 admission if the kiosk on the road to the cape is manned), a reddish crag rearing 70m above the sea, was dubbed during the Middle Ages. Along the shore are ruined fortifications raised as early as the fourth century BC (according to Strabo) and subsequently enlarged by the Roman and Byzantine empires, which reached their zenith during the fourth century when the *bolyari* Balik and Dobrotitsa ordered shafts dug through the rock so that the garrison could be supplied by sea. Legend has it that during the Ottoman conquest forty women tied their hair together and jumped from the rocks rather than be raped by the Turks, and other bodies have been washed up after naval battles off the cape. The headland is covered in evocative ruins, mostly dating from the Middle Ages, and a **museum** in one of the caves (mid-May to mid-Oct daily 10am–7pm) commemorates Russian Admiral Ushkov's defeat of the Turkish fleet in 1791 and the sinking of the Ottoman gunboat *Hamidie* by the Bulgarian navy in 1912. There's also some delicately wrought Middle Ages jewellery on display, and gaming dice used by thirteenth-century soldiers. The cave is said by Muslims to contain the grave of **Sari Saltuk**, a mythical Turkish hero who, in the style of St George, came here to kill a seven-headed dragon and thereby free two of the sultan's daughters. Christians claim that it is the last resting place of St Nicholas, who saves seafarers from shipwreck and guides fishermen towards their prey.

You can occasionally see **dolphins** frolicking off the coast here, although monk seals, once frequent visitors to Kaliakra, haven't been spotted hereabouts since 1970.

Getting to the cape is not entirely straightforward; tourists staying at Albena and Golden Sands can get to Kaliakra on organized bus trips, but otherwise you'll need your own transport or an appetite for walking. Served by six buses a day from Kavarna, the Gagauz village of **Bâlgarevo**, 6km short of Kaliakra, is the closest you can get by public transport. From here it's a straightforward one-hour walk across a coastal heath, covered in prickly shrubs and wild flowers. However, the asphalted track is unshaded, and the going can be tough at the height of summer. Luckily there's a **café-restaurant** in a cave next to Kaliakra's museum, but no **accommodation**.

Rusalka and the coastal steppe

From **Bâlgarevo**, midway between Kavarna and Cape Kaliakra, a minor road runs northeast to the one-horse settlement of **Sveti Nikola**, where a right turn leads sharply downhill to Taouk Liman, the Bay of Birds, better known as the **Rusalka Holiday Village**. A villa complex accompanied by the usual bars and restaurants, Rusalka is a quieter alternative to the bigger resorts to the south, a temptingly isolated place whose brace of shingle beaches is framed by moody, crumbling cliffs. Originally, the resort was divided into a Bulgarian-only northern half, and a southern half reserved for the French tour operator Club Mediterranée. There's no such distinction anymore, although the southern half still tends to have the better facilities, and – unusually for the Bulgarian coast – French-speaking staff. Rusalka is a small enough resort to have an intimate, family feel, with plenty of supervised activities to keep young children busy, while older holidaymakers can enjoy scuba diving, windsurfing, tennis or horseriding. There's also an imaginatively conceived **underwater museum**; really a collection of ancient anchors positioned a few metres offshore, which can be visited in the company of a guide from the resort's scuba-diving school. **Accommodation** in Rusalka's villas (☎0570/3016 or 3105, fax 2586) is relatively expensive: $50 per person in the "French" half, and $25 per person in the Bulgarian half, but all food and most activities are included in the price. There are no bus services to Rusalka, although taxi transfers from Varna can be arranged if you ring in advance.

Rusalka stands in the middle of one of the last surviving stretches of uncultivated **steppe** in Europe, a thin coastal ribbon rich in wild grasses, herbs, insects and bird life. Carpeted by wild flowers in May, the steppe is taken over by hardier, though no less alluring, thistles as the summer progresses. Group walks and jeep safaris, led by expert guides in the local flora and fauna, are sometimes on offer from Rusalka; otherwise it's a question of just heading north or south out of the resort and seeing where you end up. Resist the temptation to pick any plants; most are protected by law. The steppe can also be accessed from the village of **Kamen Bryag**, 5km up the coast from Sveti Nikola, although you'll need your own transport to get there. A track leads east out of the village onto a heath-covered clifftop, where you're bound to come across one of the many family graves hewn out of the rock here, remnants of a second-to-fifth-century **necropolis** thought to be the work of Sarmatians – a northern Black Sea tribe who travelled down from the Crimea before intermarrying with local stock and disappearing for ever. Work your way south from here to find a path leading down to the ruins of a late-Roman fortress and a grass-tufted clifftop meadow known as **Yailata**, a sublime spot from which to survey the northern coastline.

Around Shabla, and the Durankulak border crossing

The majority of buses heading north from Kavarna take the main E87 road further inland and aim for **SHABLA**, a small farming town made up of the neat, whitewashed one-storey houses so typical of the Dobrudzha. In summer local minibuses offer a shuttle service from here to the seafront, 5km northeast of town, where the *Dobrudzha* campsite offers bungalows for rent at about $3 per person. There are a couple of beach bars and a restaurant serving grilled fish, but this relatively little-visited part of the coast seems a world away from the packed beaches of Varna, Golden Sands and Albena. Immediately north of the campsite are two lakes shrouded in bullrushes, the **Shablensko ezero** and the **Ezerechko ezero**, frequented by many varieties of birds, principally ibises, herons and grebes. Beyond here an enticing landscape of deserted beaches and crumbling ochre cliffs carries on for kilometres. It's excellent walking territory, although there's an official government residence just north of the *Dobrudzha* campsite and plain-clothes security police often descend from nowhere to check ID.

Served by a single daily bus from Shabla, the seaside village of **KRAPETS**, 10km north of Shabla, is a sleepy place known for its dunes and bird life. Locked in rural solitude, it's an ideal place to get away from it all, and there's a beachside campsite, the *Krapets*, with bungalows (②), signposted off the main E87 just outside the village. However, the main reason to venture this far is to cross **the border** 6km north of **DURANKULAK**, another rural community famous for being the epicentre of the 1900 peasant rebellion against the *desyaták*, a crippling tax imposed on agricultural produce by the Radoslavov regime. Six kilometres east of town is a fish-rich lake, and a **campsite**, the *Kosmos*, offering bungalows (②).

Crossing the frontier involves catching one of the three daily buses from Shabla to Durankulak before completing the remaining 6km of the journey on foot or by taxi. The 24-hour border post is relatively quiet, but you should still allow a couple of hours if crossing the frontier by car, less if you're on foot. Romanian entry visas are sold here for about $35, and taxi drivers on the other side will take you to the resort town of **Mangalia,** 10km away, where you can link up with the Romanian public transport system.

South of Varna

Although there's no direct rail link along the coast it is possible to travel from Varna to Burgas by train: a time-consuming inland journey, usually involving at least one change. It's far better, however, to take one of the regular buses running **south of Varna** along the E87 highway, a road that winds its way across the coastal hills, occasionally offering glimpses of the sea. Ultimately you hit the mega-resort of Sunny Beach some 100km to the south, but the towns you pass along the way are among the quietest of the Black Sea coast. They're seldom visited by anybody but Bulgarians, and are visibly suffering from the decline in the cheap-and-cheerful Eastern European tourism of the Communist era. You'll find a scattering of campsites, and plenty of families offering **rooms**, but the *kvartirno byuro* that used to handle them will probably have closed down – be prepared to ask around.

Kamchiya

South of Lake Varna the highway swings inland to climb the Momino plateau, and you won't catch sight of the sea again for another 55km unless you take one of the minor roads which branch off towards the coast. The first of these, approximately 25km out from Varna just beyond the village of Bliznatsi, descends to the mouth of the **Kamchiya**, a slow-moving silt-laden soup of a river where a small resort sits beside the wooded estuary. The main attraction is the **Kamchiya nature reserve** slightly upstream, an area of marshy forest and luxuriant vegetation known as the Longoza, which covers about thirty square kilometres. The waters are rich in pike and carp, and wild pigs run free in the woods. In high season **boat trips** commence from the river's mouth, although the Longoza's elusive pelicans, kingfishers and waterfowl tend to make themselves scarce when they hear the tourists coming.

Only two buses a day run from Varna to Kamchiya, making it just about feasible as a day-trip. There's a lovely **beach** just north of the estuary, with a few food-and-drink shacks, and a couple of run-down, little-used hotels (③).

Shkorpilovtsi

Further south a minor road leaves the E87 at Staro Oryahovo for **SHKOR-PILOVTSI**, 8km away on the coast. A modest resort with a dune beach and two campsites, *Izgrev* and *Horizont*, the town was named after the Czech Skorpil brothers who "founded" Bulgarian archeology in the late nineteenth century. Karel and Herman Skorpil came to Varna in 1882 and immediately began sorting out and cataloguing the region's antiquities, a collection that formed the basis of the Varna History Museum (see p.335). They were pioneers in the field of medieval Bulgarian archeology too, and Karel was honoured by being buried among the ruins of the medieval capital Pliska (see p.233).

Byala, Obzor and beyond

Seven kilometres beyond Staro Oryahovo, the highway veers eastwards, passing vineyards whose grapes are made into Dimyat **wine** at **BYALA**, a small town facing Cape Atanas. There are plenty of private rooms here, and a sprinkling of largely Bulgarian tourists, but it's something of a backwater nevertheless, and you're not likely to want to stay for long. South of this, the last wooded foothills of the Balkan range descend to meet a six-kilometre-long **beach** backed by the *Luna*, *Prostor* and *Slântse* campsites, where buses will halt on request before entering the small resort of **OBZOR**. Broken columns in a large park to the left of Obzor's main square show that the town, the *Naulochos* of the ancients, was once graced by a Temple of Jupiter, but its principal asset nowadays is the aforementioned beach to the north. Much more animated than Byala, Obzor is popular with Bulgarians and East Europeans, and is well served with family-run cafés and restaurants. Private **rooms** are usually available from a *kvartirno byuro* on the main street, but this may be closed outside the peak season.

Heading south, the road turns inland once more, ascending the ridge of a mountain that slopes down to **Nos Emine**, Bulgaria's stormiest cape. On the way you'll pass through **Banya**, a pleasant highland village presiding over a carpet of vineyards. From here a slow climb through dense forest leads to the *Lovno Hanche*, a popular roadside **restaurant**, after which the main road descends for a magnificent view of Nesebâr, the southern coastline and the distant Strandzha massif.

Sunny Beach and around

Slânchev Bryag – called Sonnenstrand by the Germans and **SUNNY BEACH** by the Brits – is Bulgaria's largest, and least atmospheric, coastal resort. It's a vast, only partly shaded expanse of hotels interspersed with restaurants, snack bars and other places to spend money, and on (rare) rainy days its soullessness quickly becomes apparent. That said, Sunny Beach does possess all the essentials for a lazy holiday, not least its six-kilometre-long expanse of fine sand sloping gently into the sea. Numerous restaurants, nightclubs and discos provide a wide range of nightlife, but Sunny Beach's principal drawback is its sheer size: it's impossible to explore the resort's facilities without shuttling up and down the main strip by bus, and the faceless gridiron-style layout of the place soon induces feelings of disorientation and alienation. Many of the resort's individual hotels (especially those favoured by Western package groups) have been tastefully refurbished, although the overall infrastructure – the roads, pavements and stretches of park – remain uncared for. Independent travellers would be better off staying in nearby Nesebâr, a perfectly viable base from which to make use of Sunny Beach's enviable stretch of sand.

Though Varna–Burgas buses pass through Sunny Beach, most people approach the resort from Burgas, from where there are bus services every twenty minutes. You'll be dropped at the "centre", where an accommodation office in the central administration building (055422256, fax 22921) will assign hotel rooms (④–⑤), should you wish to stay.

Sveti Vlas and Elenite

Hourly buses head from Sunny Beach to **SVETI VLAS**, 6km away on the northern shoulder of the bay. Increasingly popular as an elite vacation venue for Bulgarians, the village is currently groaning under the weight of over-hasty development. New hotels abound, and there's the makings of a good beach, 1km away from the village across untidy scrubland, but until Sveti Vlas shakes off its dust-laden, building-site image, it's probably best avoided.

Buses continue northwards to the **ELENITE HOLIDAY VILLAGE**, 6km further up the coast, a predominantly package destination divided into two villa colonies sharing restaurants, bars and discos. It's a well-run, well-looked after resort with a good beach, good sporting facilities, and childcare provision in a central kindergarten, although it can seem rather isolated if you're after more than just a beach holiday. A central reception desk (☎0554/82423, fax 85147) allocates rooms, although costs are high for independent travellers, with prices of around $70 per person per day in the high season – meals, daytime drinks and entertainment are all included, though. The villas themselves come with cable TV, fridge and kitchenette (although the choice of food in the local store is limited, making the idea of self-catering unappealing).

Nesebâr

Three kilometres south of Sunny Beach, a slender isthmus connects the old town of **NESEBÂR** (ancient Mesembria) with the mainland, ensuring a constant stream of visitors to what was once undoubtedly a beautiful spot. Harbouring the best of the coast's nineteenth-century **wooden architecture**, as well as a unique collection of medieval **churches**, it's easy to see why Nesebâr has become the most publicized of Bulgaria's Black Sea attractions. At the height of summer the town can be a little oppressive, with tourists and vendors thronging the narrow streets, but a willingness to put up with the crowds is rewarded by Nesebâr's many fine sights.

A thriving port in **Greek and Roman** times, Nesebâr really came into its own with the onset of the **Byzantine** era, when it became the obvious stopover for

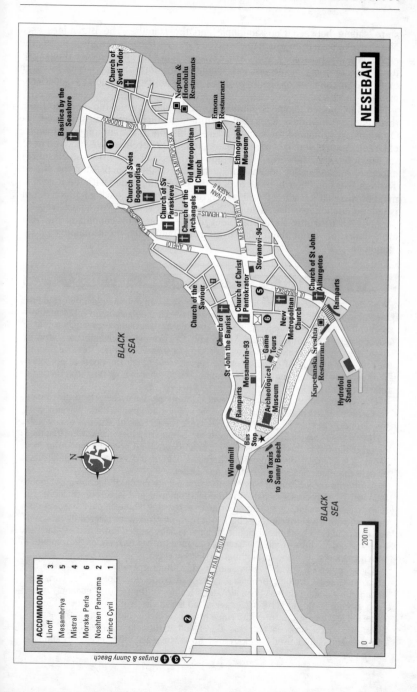

NESEBÂR

ACCOMMODATION

Linoff	3
Mesambriya	5
Mistral	4
Morska Perla	6
Noshten Panorama	2
Prince Cyril	1

Burgas & Sunny Beach

BLACK SEA

BLACK SEA

Basilica by the Seashore

Church of Sveti Todor

Neptun & Honolulu Restaurants

Emona Restaurant

Church of Sveta Bogoroditsa

Old Metropolitan Church

Ethnographic Museum

Church of Sv Paraskeva

Church of the Archangels

ULITSA MITROPOLSKA

UL VASIL TODOROV

UL IVAN ASEN II

UL HEMUS

UL MESEMBRIYA

Church of the Saviour

Church of Christ Pantokrator

Stoyanovi-94

Church of St John Aliturgetos

UL AHELOI

Ramparts

Church of St John the Baptist

New Metropolitan Church

Mesambria-93

Gama Tours

Archeological Museum

Kapetanska Sreshta Restaurant

Hydrofoil Station

Ramparts

UL RIBARSKA

Bus Stop

Windmill

Sea Taxis to Sunny Beach

ULITSA HAN KRUM

N

200 m

0

ships sailing between Constantinople and the Danube. The Byzantines used Nesebâr as a base from which to assail the **First Bulgarian Kingdom** during the eighth century, provoking Khan Krum to seize it in 812. The bellicose Bulgar captured tons of booty in the process, including the formula for "Greek Fire", an explosive mixture which the Byzantines relied on for their military superiority over the "barbarians".

Nesebâr passed from Byzantine to Bulgarian ownership several times throughout the Middle Ages, but continued to thrive regardless. Under the Ottomans, it remained the seat of a Greek bishopric and an important centre of Greek culture, which is why so many medieval churches have survived here. In the long run, however, Varna and Burgas were to grow at Nesebâr's expense, hastening its decline into a humble fishing port. After the Russo-Turkish War of 1828, when the bulk of the population sided with the Russians, most of Nesebâr's leading families emigrated to Odessa, leaving a much diminished population earning a living by building caïques. Nowadays Nesebâr depends on **tourism**: its fishing fleet unable to employ enough of the 7000 inhabitants, of whom about 3000 live on the peninsula, the remainder on the mainland.

THE BLACK SEA GREEKS I: ANCIENT COLONISTS

Why the ancient Greeks ever bothered to venture north into the Black Sea remains the subject of much conjecture. Initially they called it the *Axeinos*, or "inhospitable", sea; and heroic legends exemplified by the tale of the **Argonauts** suggest that it was perceived as a hostile place where only the bravest of adventurers dared to tread. By the sixth century BC, however, Greeks from Asia Minor were beginning to establish a string of colonies in the region, first along the coast of northern Turkey, subsequently moving on to the shores of what is now Bulgaria, Romania and Ukraine.

Overpopulation and political upheaval at home obviously helped to precipitate this sudden burst of outward migration, but opportunities for trade played a part too. Pioneers in colonizing the Black Sea were the Greeks of **Miletus** (a city-state on the Aegean coast of Turkey), although some Bulgarian historians argue that they merely followed in the footsteps of their neighbours the Carians: a race from Asia Minor (closely related to Bulgaria's Thracians) who had developed mercantile contacts in the Black Sea several generations earlier.

Apollonia (now Sozopol) was Miletus' first colony on the Bulgarian coast, soon followed by **Odyssos** (Varna), **Anchialos** (Pomorie) and **Krounoi** (Balchik). In many cases the colonists settled on or near an existing Thracian port: this was certainly so with **Mesemvria** (Nesebâr), where the natives were ejected by newcomers from the Greek mainland city of Megara. Having settled down and established a network of maritime trade, the Greeks renamed the sea *Euxinos*, or "hospitable" – which remained its name throughout the Classical era.

These colonies couldn't have survived without friendly contacts with the Thracians, and a mutually beneficial system of **trade** developed. The Thracians obtained wine and salt (salt-pans are still a feature of the regional economy, especially around Pomorie) in return for grain and livestock – which the Greeks then re-exported at a tidy profit. **Intermarriage** must have been common from the earliest days, and cities such as Odyssos developed a thriving hybrid culture where colonists and natives lived cheek-by-jowl, observing each other's customs and paying homage to each other's gods.

Arrival, information and accommodation

Getting to Nesebâr is easy: buses run every twenty minutes from Sunny Beach, and every forty minutes from Burgas, 35km down the coast. There are also regular minibuses from Burgas, and infrequent "water taxis" from Sunny Beach.

Private rooms (②), many of them in fine old houses, are available from several agencies in town; three of the longest-established being Mesambria-93, on ul. Mesambria; Gama Tours, ul. Mena 11; and Stoyanovi-94, in an alleyway opposite the *Hotel Mesambriya*. The bland *Hotel Mesambriya* itself, ul. Ribarska (☎0554/43255; ④), is fully booked by groups over summer, but might have off-season vacancies, although you'll probable find better-value rooms and classier service in the increasing number of family-run **hotels** around town. The *Morska Perla*, Tsar Simeon 4 (☎0554/45606; ③), is a modern three-storey block in the old town most of whose neat ensuite rooms have a small balcony; while the *Prince Cyril*, in the warren of streets towards the end of the peninsula at Slavyanska 9 (☎0554/42215; ④), has pine-furnished ensuite rooms with cable TV, fridge and telephone, as well as four-person apartments for $50. Back across the causeway in the new town, *Noshten Panorama* on the corner of Vasil Levski and Han Krum (☎0554/84236; ③) has small rooms with TV, but no ensuite bathrooms, while the more imposing *Mistral*, Han Krum 22 (☎0554/42593, fax 42933; ④ including breakfast), has comfier ensuite rooms and an on-site sauna and gym. The *Linoff*, Hristo Botev 24 (☎0554/87351; ④), also has clean, modern ensuite rooms with TV and fridge.

The Town

Approaching the peninsula you'll pass a wooden **windmill** of the type once found by the dozen in every coastal town. Ahead loom the massive **ramparts** that protected Nesebâr in antiquity; blocks from the Greek fortifications of the fourth century BC serve as foundations for the masonry and brick walls of Roman and Byzantine times. Just inside the gateway, an **Archeological Museum** (Mon–Fri 9am–7pm, Sat & Sun 9am–1.30pm & 2–7pm) displays votive statues, coins and other evidence of Nesebâr's classical past (captioned in English), plus a collection of icons from the eighteenth and nineteenth centuries downstairs. One Greek inscription from ancient Mesembria records a peace treaty between the city and the local Thracian ruler Sadala, giving him the right to parade around town in a golden laurel wreath on the occasion of the annual festival of Dionysus.

A rash of shops and cafés along ul. Mesembriya masks the transition into the **old town**, a maze of cobbled lanes and wooden houses juxtaposed with many of Nesebâr's antique churches. The Muskoyanin House, at ul. Mesembriya 34, contains an **Ethnographic Museum** (daily 9am–noon & 2–6pm), with a disappointing lack of information on the fate of Black Sea Greeks (see opposite and p.366). However, it's worth visiting to see the cunningly asymmetrical interior of the house, whose cosy wooden living-quarters overhang a sturdy ground floor of undressed masonry.

Nesebâr's churches

Though usually termed "Byzantine" by foreign art historians, Nesebâr's **churches** are understandably regarded by the locals as masterpieces of Bulgarian culture. Most of them are the result of three waves of building that corresponded to the era of Byzantine rule and the First and Second Bulgarian Kingdoms (which naturally drew upon Byzantine traditions). As they date from a period when control of the town changed hands frequently, and the ethnicity of the people who built them is hard to discern, it's probably fairest to regard them as products of a great Orthodox civilization – both Slav and Greek – which flourished in the Balkans during the late Middle Ages.

You first encounter an example from the reign of Tsar Ivan Aleksandâr (1331–71), who was responsible for several of Nesebâr's churches. A chunky, ruddy-hued structure of stone and brick, the **Church of Christ Pantokrator**, on ul. Mesembriya, is notable for its exterior decoration, with blind niches, turquoise ceramic inlays and red brick motifs – all redolent of late Byzantine architecture. An unusual feature is the frieze of swastikas (at that time a symbol of the sun and continual change) on the apses. Currently used as an art gallery, the church is usually accessible during the daytime.

Just downhill from here, on ul. Mitropolska, lies the **Church of St John the Baptist** whose plain, undressed stone exterior dates it as a tenth- or eleventh-century creation. Also converted into an art gallery, its interior retains some fragmentary frescos; one, from the seventeenth century, depicts St Marina pulling a devil from the sea before braining it with a hammer – possibly representing local merchants' hopes that their patron saint would deal with the Cossack pirates who raided Nesebâr in those days.

Better-preserved frescos can be seen in the early seventeenth-century **Church of the Saviour** (*Sveti Spas*; Mon–Fri 9.30am–1.30pm & 2–5.30pm, Sat–Sun 9.30am–1.30pm; $1), whose dull exterior conceals colourful frescos commissioned by local merchants of the time – evidence that a thriving and wealthy culture existed in Nesebâr even at the height of the Ottoman occupation. Scenes from the lives of Christ and the Virgin predominate, defaced by centuries-old graffiti of sailing vessels – an art form common to Nesebâr's churches, and executed by those praying for safety on the seas. One of the prettiest parts of town lies beyond, its cobbled alleys overhung by half-timbered houses carved with sunsigns, fish and other symbols. Here you'll find the **Church of the Archangels Michael and Gabriel**, featuring a chequered pattern of brick and stone on its blind niches, and the half-restored **Church of Sveta Paraskeva**, studded with green ceramics. Both date from the same period as the Christ Pantokrator church. Further northeast is the comparatively ugly, nineteenth-century **Church of Sveta Bogoroditsa**, heated by a long, protruding stovepipe.

The historic centre of town is now a small plaza occupied by picture-sellers, surrounding a pit containing the ruined **Old Metropolitan Church** (*Starata Mitropoliya*), built in the fifth or sixth century. It was here that bishops officiated during Nesebâr's heyday as a city-state, when Byzantine nobles demonstrated their wealth and piety by endowing more than forty ecclesiastical edifices. Several were concentrated at the northern tip of the peninsula, where the **Basilica by the Seashore** proved to be so vulnerable to raids by pirates that a fortified keep was added. Both are now in ruins, as is the old windmill in the vicinity, while the thirteenth-century **Church of Sveti Todor** nearby has become a gallery.

To wrap up Nesebâr's churches in some kind of chronological order, head back along ul. Mesembriya, then turn left down ul. Ribarska to find the **New Metropolitan Church**, known as Sveti Stefan (daily 9am–1pm & 2–6pm; $1). Founded in the tenth or eleventh century during the First Kingdom, the church was enlarged under the Second Kingdom, then supplanted the Old Metropolitan Church in the fifteenth century. Most of the frescos that you see today were added in the sixteenth and seventeenth centuries. So alike are the faces of the seven

FISHING IN THE BLACK SEA

The harbours of old peninsula towns like Nesebâr, Pomorie and Sozopol remain clogged with the small boats that traditionally provided most local families with a livelihood – **fishing**. Although the numbers of full-time fishermen are in decline, most families still have access to a boat and augment their income by fishing in the coastal waters.

The working year is dictated by the seasonal migrations of fish. Most activity takes place in the spring and autumn, when shoals of *skumrii* (mackerel) and *palamudi* (brown-striped tunny fish) pass along the Black Sea coast on their way between the waters of the Crimea and their wintering grounds in the Sea of Marmara and the Aegean. The *hamsiya*, or Black Sea anchovy, also makes fleeting appearances off the Bulgarian coast during its extensive circuits of the Black Sea, but the rest of the time people hunt *barbun* (mullet), *safrid* (scad), *kalkan* (turbot) and *tsatsa* (sprat) – piles of the latter, deep-fried and crispy, are a staple of coastal snack bars.

In recent decades it's become increasingly difficult to make a living from fishing, due to the **depletion** of the Black Sea's stocks. Those with small fishing operations feel particularly threatened by the big state-owned fleets operating out of Burgas, and are agitating for a complete ban on trawling in coastal waters. Such a ban would help preserve the small-town economy of places like Pomorie and Sozopol, but may not be enough to save the Black Sea's fish.

handmaidens who accompany the Virgin to the Temple (on the southwest pillar) that legend has it that the unknown artist was infatuated with his model. The patron who financed the church's enlargement is given pride of place among the *Forty Martyrs* on the west wall. Also note the bases of the marble columns, which originally formed the capitals of pillars in a pagan temple, and the opulently carved eighteenth-century bishop's throne, one of the best of its kind in Bulgaria.

It's fitting to end with the ruined **Church of St John Aliturgetos**, in splendid isolation by the shore, at the bottom of ul. Ribarska. Though never consecrated, St John's represents the zenith of Bulgarian–Byzantine church architecture, achieved during the Second Kingdom. Its exterior decoration is strikingly varied, employing limestone, red bricks, crosses, mussel shells and ceramic plaques, with a representation of a human figure in limestone blocks embedded in the north wall.

Eating and drinking

There's a surfeit of **places to eat** on the peninsula, from harbourside kiosks selling mackerel, mussels and other snacks, to dozens of restaurants trying to attract tourists with full English breakfasts and roast-beef lunches. The *Kapetanska sreshta* theme restaurant – with waiters in maritime shirts and a band playing Slavic sea shanties – goes way overboard. For seafood and sea breezes, you can try any number of restaurants with sea-facing terraces along the southern side of the peninsula: *Neptun*, towards the far end of town, is reasonably reliable, while *Plakamo*, just down from the New Metropolitan Church at Ivan Aleksandâr 8, is family-run and relatively sheltered. Over on the mainland, the *Noshten Panorama* hotel has a top-floor restaurant with good views of the coast. The long-established *Café Rumi*, on ul. Ivan Asen II, still serves the best cake and ice cream in town, while the *Bar Burgas*, ul. Mena 10, is the place for an intimate evening drink.

Pomorie

Continuing south from Nesebâr, beyond **Aheloi**, the road passes the salt-pans surrounding Lake Pomorie, one of Bulgaria's main sources of salt, and renowned for its therapeutic **mud baths**. Sited upon a peninsula beside the lake, **POMORIE** (pronounced "Pah-mor-ye") would probably resemble Nesebâr if it hadn't been gutted by fire in 1906 and rebuilt in concrete during the 1950s. Pomorie's ancient precursor, Anchialos, was founded by the Apollonians, became rich through the export of salt and wine, and found favour in the Roman era as an exclusive health resort. The lakeside sanatorium remains important to the local economy, as does another speciality of long standing, the locally produced aromatic dry *Pomoriiski Dimyat* **wine**. Apart from an abundance of private rooms and an underused stretch of beach, however, there's little in modern Pomorie to justify a stopover.

The Town

Pomorie's **bus station** is separated from the centre by a three-kilometre stretch of grotty industrial suburbs, best avoided by catching bus #1 (every 20–30 minutes). This runs past the **Monastery of St George**, whose domed belfry is visible to the right. A medieval foundation re-established by the Ottoman governor Selim Bey (who reputedly converted to Christianity after being cured of illness by a miraculous spring), the monastery now occupies a rather functional

---

MIHAIL CANTACUZENE (1515–1587)

Descended from a leading Byzantine family, **Mihail Cantacuzene** (dubbed Zeytanoglu – son of the devil – by the Turks) was typical of the noble-born Greeks who maintained their wealth and prestige by serving the Ottoman regime. He was a leading spokesman for the Empire's Orthodox Christian subjects, and cultivated influential friends at court – notably the Grand Vizier, Mehmed Pasha Sokolović, himself a Balkan Christian who had converted to Islam as a teenager. Appointed governor of the Black Sea salt pans by Sultan Suleiman the Magnificent, Cantacuzene built a palace in Anhialo (modern-day **Pomorie**) and ruled in the style of an independent prince, surrounded by a legion of former slaves whose freedom had been bought with his own money. After the defeat of the Ottoman navy at Lepanto in 1571, Cantacuzene won favour with Suleiman's successor Selim II by re-equipping the fleet with new ships.

The accession of Murad III in 1574 spelt the beginning of the end for Cantacuzene. The new sultan was jealous of the power concentrated in Sokolović's hands, and was determined to do away with the Grand Vizier's coterie of rich friends. In 1576, Murad had Cantacuzene imprisoned in Constantinople's Yedikule fortress and he was only released on payment of a huge ransom. Cantacuzene then began trading furs with the Russians, hoping that his growing contacts with the court of Ivan the Terrible would give him protection against Murad's enmity. The latter, however, saw a potential Russian–Cantacuzene alliance as a danger to the security of his northern borders, and had Cantacuzene hanged from the portals of his palace in Anhialo in 1576. It took two galleys to transport the contents of Cantacuzene's palace to Constantinople, where they were auctioned on the quayside. Cantacuzene's sons managed to escape, and their descendants went on to pursue illustrious, and often outrageously corrupt, careers at the courts of Moldavia and Wallachia.

ATANASOVSKO EZERO

Midway between Pomorie and Burgas the road passes **Atanasovsko ezero**, a ten-kilometre-long stretch of shallow inland water frequented by herons in the spring. The lake serves as the midway point on the "Via Pontica" – the route used by birds migrating between Scandinavia and Africa.

array of nineteenth-century buildings, brought to life by the shrubs and pot-plants that fill the courtyard. The seaside town proper centres on a lively pedestrianized zone, with a fishing port one block to the south, and the small eighteenth-century **Church of the Transfiguration** lying at the eastern end of the peninsula. Pomorie's **beach** occupies a 4km-long sand bar which stretches north from the tip of the peninsula, and seperates the town's famous salt pans from the open sea. You won't find much here apart from a few huts selling drinks and snacks, although the underdeveloped nature of the place may come as a welcome change after Sunny Beach.

Practicalities
Private rooms (②) can be rented from the numerous accommodation bureaux on the way into town. Tiva, about 200m east of the bus station, Marini, and Happy Beach, both on the main road into town, Knyaz Boris I, are all worth trying. Pomorie's best **hotel** is the *Palace* on Knyaz Boris I (③ including breakfast), with modern, neat ensuite rooms, and a couple of four-person apartments ($50) complete with kitchenette and enormous fridge. The nearest **campsites** are the *Evropa*, 2km along the Burgas road, where there's another popular stretch of sandy beach; and *Kâmping Aheloi*, occupying an isolated coastal spot just south of the town of Aheloi on the road to Nesebâr (Burgas–Nesebâr buses drop off by the entrance). There's no shortage of **restaurants and bars** in the pedestrianized zone in the centre of town.

BURGAS AND AROUND

Most guidebooks dismiss **BURGAS** as a polluted dump whose only asset is its good transport connections with more desirable destinations further south. Though the city's suburbs are certainly dreary, the centre is surprisingly pleasant and tourist-friendly, due to recent efforts to improve its seedy image. As the site of an oil refinery and associated chemical plants, Burgas is far more industrial than any of its neighbours on the coast, and its deep harbour is home to Bulgaria's oceanic fishing fleet. The presence of visiting ships and passing tourists gives the town a certain cosmopolitanism – especially in late August, during the **folk festival** – but nothing to compare with the cultural life of Varna.

Road traffic southwards is borne by a thin finger of land that separates the gulf itself from the land-locked Burgasko ezero to the west. The latter was long used as a dumping ground by the oil refinery and chemicals plant that blights its northern banks (see below), and has nothing of the natural beauty of **Mandrensko ezero** (Lake Mandra), lying beside the main E87 road 10km south of Burgas. Surrounded by reeds, the lake is a good place to observe wildfowl, especially **spoonbills**, which nest here in May and June.

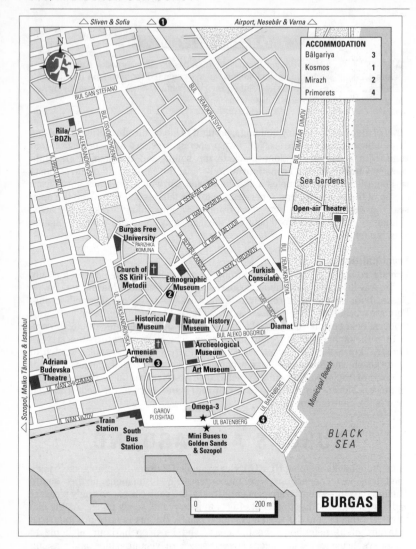

△ *Sliven & Sofia*   △ **①**   *Airport, Nesebâr & Varna* △

ACCOMMODATION

Bâlgariya	**3**
Kosmos	**1**
Mirazh	**2**
Primorets	**4**

BUL SAN STEFANO

BUL DEMOKRATSIYA

BUL OSVOBOZHDENIE

BUL ALEKSANDROVSKA

Rila/
BDZh

Sea Gardens

Open-air Theatre

UL GENERAL GURKO

UL HAN ASPARUH

Burgas Free
University
PARIZHKA
KOMUNA

UPRAVA KANSKA

UL KIRIL METODII

Church of
SS Kiril i
Metodii

Ethnographic
Museum
②

UL ASEN DIMANOV

Turkish
Consulate

BUL DEMOKRATSIYA

UL ALEKSANDROVSKA

Historical
Museum

Natural History
Museum

BUL ALEKO BOGORIDI

Diamat

Armenian
Church **③**

Archeological
Museum

Adriana
Budevska
Theatre

Art Museum

UL IVAN SHISHMAN

UL BATENBERG

GAROV
PLOSHTAD

Omega-3

★

④

UL IVAN VAZOV

UL BATENBERG

Train
Station

South
Bus
Station

★

Mini Buses to
Golden Sands
& Sozopol

Municipal Beach

BLACK
SEA

△ *Sozopol, Malko Târnovo & Istanbul*

0 _____ 200 m

BURGAS

Arrival and accommodation

Both the **train** station and the main **bus** station (*Avtogara Yug*) are just south of the centre on Garov ploshtad. The half-hourly bus #15 from the airport ends up here too, and it's the best place to pick up a taxi. There's a left luggage office behind the bus station. An additional bus station, *Avtogara Zapad*, lies 3km northwest of the centre (buses #4 and #9 go the nearest), although you're only likely to use it if you're travelling to or from Malko Târnovo.

Private rooms in downtown apartment blocks are available from Diamat, Tsar Simeon 15, for $4 per head, while the town's **hotels** tend to be overpriced for what they are. The cheapest is the *Mirazh*, Lermontov 48 (☎088/921019; ③), which offers basic rooms in a downtown block, while the other downtown options are the newly refurbished *Primorets*, at the bottom end of the Sea Gardens at pl. Aleksandâr Batenberg 2 (☎056/842772 or 842045, fax 842934; ⑤), and the imposing but dated *Bâlgariya* on ul. Aleksandrovska (☎056/45336; ⑤). Your best bet if you're here on business is the *Kosmos*, a high-rise building 3km north of the centre on bul. Demokratsiya (☎056/35901; ⑦), which has refurbished rooms with modern amenities. The nearest **campsite** is *Kraimorie*, 14km south of town and 2km off the coastal road: any bus heading south can drop you at the turn-off.

The Town

Burgas' best feature is **ul. Aleksandrovska**, the long boulevard that scythes north–south through town. The upper part is sedate, shaded by trees and largely residential, while the lower end of the avenue is brash and colourful, lined with cafés and thronged with people. Everyone comes here to stroll in the evening and gypsies importune tourists with dancing bears. Midway along is a spacious plaza whose marble Soviet war memorial has been outclassed by the gleaming white

---

POLLUTION IN THE GULF OF BURGAS

Arriving at Burgas you'll see both the best and the worst of what the coast has to offer: while glorious beaches and wildlife-infested lakes lie a few kilometres away both north and south, the city itself is one of the **most polluted** in Bulgaria.

The **Black Sea** as a whole is in a sorry state. Rivers such as the Don, Dniestr, Dniepr and Danube carry the waste products of a vast industrial hinterland into a sea which is largely closed – only the Bosphorus to the south provides an outlet for the accumulated gunk. The depths of the Black Sea have always been low on oxygen, leaving only a thin upper layer of water capable of sustaining life. Twentieth-century pollution is rendering this layer thinner than ever, and intensive fishing threatens to reduce even further the stock of marine animals this once-rich body of water contained. **Dolphins**, previously a common sight off the Bulgarian shore, are increasingly rare: the fish they used to feed off are gone.

Burgas' problems are compounded by the presence of a vast chemicals plant, **Neftohim**, on the western outskirts of town (you're sure to pass it if entering or leaving the city by train). Neftohim's waste products used to be diluted in a series of water tanks before being released into the gulf, but during the Communist period few paid attention to the kind of toxins which were allowed to seep into the sea this way. Nowadays emissions of this kind are more closely monitored and stiff fines imposed on transgressors, but the Gulf of Burgas remains pretty ugly. The tankers and cargo ships frequenting the port here all shed a little oil from time to time, and the currents in the gulf tend to circulate within the bay itself instead of diluting these concentrations of waste in the open sea. Naturally enough, few people patronize Burgas' municipal **beaches** these days, but neighbouring resorts don't seem to have been affected by the city's environmental problems. Coastal waters around Nesebâr to the north or Sozopol to the south are remarkably pure, and you shouldn't have any qualms about bathing there.

stone and bronzed glass of **Burgas Free University**, Bulgaria's first privately funded fee-paying college, offering courses in marketing.

The other axis of social life in Burgas is **bul. Aleko Bogoridi**, which turns off by the towering *Hotel Bâlgariya*, in the direction of the Sea Gardens to the east. Narrower than ul. Aleksandrovska, but likewise full of shops and cafés, it runs past the small **Armenian Church** of St Hach, a modern structure with an odd-looking bell tower, ministering to the needs of the town's few hundred Armenian residents. A third of the way along bul. Bogoridi is an **Archeological Museum** (Tues–Sat 9am–noon & 2–5pm) crammed with Roman-period votive tablets depicting the Thracian rider god. Classical-era burial finds include the gold jewellery of a Thracian priestess, and a second-century BC wooden sarcophagus complete with the deceased's sandals and burial shroud. One block south of the museum at ul. Vodenicharov 22, a Moorish-style former synagogue contains an **Art Museum** (Mon–Sat 9am–noon & 2–6pm), with a fine display of eighteenth- and nineteenth-century icons on the top floor.

North of bul. Bogoridi, residential streets huddle around the **Church of SS Kiril i Metodii**, built between 1894 and 1905. The saints are depicted in peeling murals above the entrance, framed by Art Nouveau stained glass. A couple of minutes walk east, the **Ethnographic Museum**, at ul. Slavyanska 19 (officially Mon–Sat 8am–noon & 1–5pm), exhibits regional textiles and fearsome *Kukeri* costumes, but often only opens when tour groups are on hand. Just south of here, the **Natural History Museum**, at ul. Konstantin Fotinov 30 (Mon–Fri 9am–noon & 1.30–5pm), has the usual display of stuffed animals, while the **Historical Museum** round the corner, at Lermontov 31 (Mon–Fri 9am–noon & 1.30–5pm), holds sepia pictures of old Burgas and Bulgarian-only texts detailing the region's history.

Bulevard Bogoridi ends near the **Sea Gardens**, a terraced park overlooking the sea, faced by Italianate villas, from which steps descend to the city's **beach**.

Eating, drinking and entertainment

Restaurants and **cafés** vie for custom along ul. Aleksandrovska, where you can eat seafood in one place, cakes in another, and enjoy a post-prandial drink somewhere else, all the while sitting outdoors, observing the *korso*. Most promenaders are dressed to the hilt, be they window-shopping or flirting. For a change of scene, try the *National*, near the *Hotel Primorets* on ul. Filip Kutev, a three-tier restaurant with an excellent *mehana* on the ground floor, plusher dining room upstairs, and a

---

MOVING ON FROM BURGAS

Burgas is the transport hub for the whole coastline from Nesebâr down to Ahtopol. If you miss one of the **buses** to Sozopol, Nesebâr or Sunny Beach, private **minibuses** depart in-between times from the eastern side of Garov ploshtad. Inland-bound travellers can buy **tickets** for international and domestic **trains** from Rila/BDZh, ul. Aleksandrovska 106 (Mon–Fri 8am–12.30pm & 1–8pm). Desks in the hotels *Bâlgariya* and *Kosmos* sell tickets for express **buses to Sofia.** Numerous centrally located travel agents – try Omega-3 on Garov ploshtad – handle reservations for buses **to Istanbul**. Travellers heading for Turkey should be able to get a visa at the border-crossing; in case of any difficulty, there's a **Turkish Consulate**, north of the Sea Gardens at bul. Demokratsiya 38 (Mon–Fri 9am–1pm & 2.30–5pm; ☎056/42718 or 47010).

Greek taverna in the basement; or *Mehana Stefano*, Konstantin Fotinov 26A, a busy downtown restaurant in a covered courtyard. Further afield, *Korab Burgas* offers fine food in a beached ship at the northern end of the Sea Gardens.

The town's biggest **disco** is the *Cosmopolitan*, decked out to look like the interior of a spaceship, beneath the Adriana Budevska Theatre. Some of the best music can be heard at the annual **International Folk Festival** in the last week of August, which takes place in the open-air theatre in the Sea Gardens.

Sozopol

There are only two settlements of any size on the south side of Burgas bay: **Kraimorie**, a naval town serving a big base on the nearby peninsula of Aitia, and **Chernomorets**, a small beach resort with a neatly manicured park, numerous private rooms and a campsite, the *Gradina*, located on the beach to the south. Both towns are served by hourly buses on the Burgas–Sozopol route, but it's better to press on to the small fishing port of **SOZOPOL**, the favoured resort of Bulgaria's literary and artistic set since the beginning of this century, and popular with package tourists since the 1970s.

An engaging huddle of nineteenth-century houses on a rocky headland, backed up by two fine **beaches**, scores of bars and restaurants, and a lively **promenade**, Sozopol is fast overtaking Nesebâr as the coast's prime attraction. Slightly incongruously, its harbour also serves as one of Bulgaria's chief naval bases, with ranks of gunboats anchored off the neighbouring island of Sveti Kirik.

For the first ten days of September, Sozopol hosts the **Apollonia Arts Festival**, comprising classical music, jazz, theatre and poetry, and frequent open-air pop concerts take place throughout the summer. Be warned that finding **accommodation** can be difficult in August, when the tourist season is at its height.

Some history

Stone anchors in the local archeological museum suggest that traders from the Aegean visited Sozopol harbour as early as the twelfth century BC, although the identity of these early seafarers remains the subject of much conjecture. More certain is the town's status as the first of the **Greek colonies** along the coast, founded around 610 BC by a party of adventurers from Miletus. They named the town **Apollonia Pontica** after Apollo, the patron of seafarers and colonizers, and prospered by trading Greek textiles and wine for Thracian honey, grain and copper. Apollonia's major customer was Athens, and the decline of the latter in the fourth century BC ended the town's brief reign as a minor maritime power.

Having spent several centuries existing quite happily on the fringes of more powerful Thracian and Macedonian states, the Apollonians flirted with various anti-Roman alliances in the first century BC in order to try and stave off the inevitable advance of Latin power. In 72 BC, their attachment to the Black Sea empire-builder **Mithridates of Pontus** was punished by the Roman general Marcus Lucullus, who sacked the town and carried off the treasured statue of Apollo that had graced its harbour.

Apollonia disappeared from the records of chroniclers during the latter stages of the Roman Empire, re-emerging in 431 as **Sozopolis**, the "City of Salvation". Under the Byzantines the town soon developed a reputation for the good life, and rebellious nobles and troublesome bishops were "retired" here by emperors

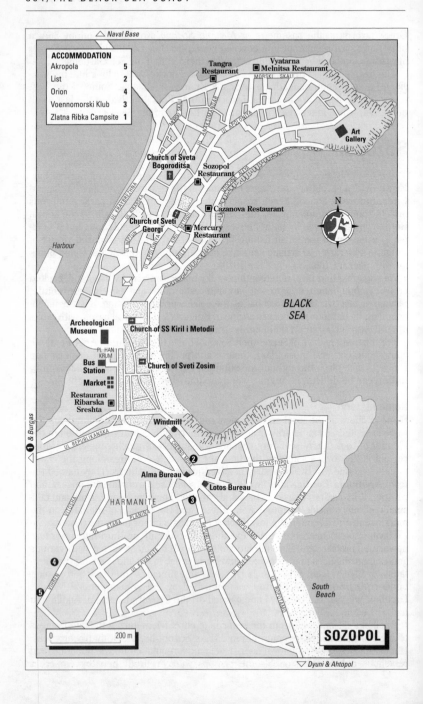

△ Naval Base

ACCOMMODATION

Akropola	5
List	2
Orion	4
Voennomorski Klub	3
Zlatna Ribka Campsite	1

Tangra Restaurant

Vyatarna Melnitsa Restaurant

MORSKI SKALI

Art Gallery

Church of Sveta Bogoroditsa

Sozopol Restaurant

Cazanova Restaurant

Church of Sveti Georgi

Mercury Restaurant

Harbour

N

BLACK SEA

Archeological Museum

Church of SS Kiril i Metodii

PL. HAN KRUM

Bus Station

Market

Church of Sveti Zosim

Restaurant Ribarska Sreshta

Windmill

& Burgas

UL. REPUBLIKANSKA

Alma Bureau

UL. CHERNO MORE

Lotos Bureau

UL. SEVASTOPOL

HARMANITE

UL. STARA PLANINA

VITOSHA

UL. REPUBLIKANSKA

UL. ROPOTAMO

UL. KAVARNITE

UL. ODESA

South Beach

UL. ROPOTAMO

0   200 m

SOZOPOL

▽ Dyuni & Ahtopol

unwilling to see their peers too harshly punished. However, marauding armies returned during the fourteenth and fifteenth centuries, and following the Turkish invasion Sozopol sunk into anonymity, replaced by Burgas as the area's major port.

Arrival and accommodation

Just 35km south of Burgas, Sozopol is easily accessible by **bus**. Arriving at the bus station on pl. Han Krum, you may be approached by locals offering **private rooms**. Alternatively, you can book through several local agents; Lotos, Ropotamo 1, and Alma, diagonally opposite, are both pretty reliable, with rooms ranging from old houses on the peninsula, to the more spacious chalet-style buildings of Harmanite (②–③).

The new part of town also has some good small **hotels**: *List*, Cherno More 5 (☎05514/235, fax 55; ④), is the nearest to the seafront, and has TV, minibar and air-conditioning in all rooms. Further uphill, the *Orion*, Vihren 28 (☎0489/79096; ③), has small but comfortable ensuite rooms with TV and balconies – some with quite spectacular views – as well as several four-person apartments for $40–50. The nearby *Akropola*, Vihren 6 (☎05514/260) has a couple of simple, clean apartments, each with kitchenette ($40). All three may well close out of season, in which case the *Voennomorski klub* or Navy Club, ul. Republikanska (☎05514/245307; ③), is a reliable, year-round source of cheap if unexciting ensuite rooms. The *Zlatna Ribka* **campsite** 3km north of town is one of the south coast's best, situated on a part-sandy, part-rocky coastline – the bus from Burgas passes the site on its way into town.

The Town

Sozopol divides into two parts: the **old town** on the peninsula, and the modern, **Harmanite** district on the mainland (whose name means "The Windmills"). There are two **beaches** with a small admission charge: one nestling within the curve of a sheltered bay where the peninsula joins Harmanite; the other further south, beyond a headland. Walking between the two entails a foray into the backstreets of Harmanite, uphill from a solitary wooden **windmill** which now serves as a bar.

The touristic hub of Sozopol is a cobbled **concourse** between the peninsula and Harmanite, flanked by souvenir stalls and portrait artists, always thronged with strollers and bombarded by a cacophany of rock and pop. Alongside runs a shady municipal **park**, carpeted with cottony wads of blossom during early summer; east of this is the beach. Sheltering among the trees is the pale sandstone **Chapel of Sveti Zosim**, honouring the patron saint of seafarers, the Christian Church's answer to Apollo. The **Church of SS Kiril i Metodii**, further north, is used as a concert hall during the Apollonia Festival.

The Archeological Museum

On the other side of the concourse from the church, Sozopol's municipal library forms the backdrop for a temporary **amphitheatre**, erected for use during the Apollonia Festival and serving as a concert venue throughout the summer. Hidden around the side of the library, the **Archeological Museum** (summer Mon–Fri 8am–4.30pm, Sat & Sun 10am–2pm; winter closed on Sat & Sun) displays rows of amphorae dredged up from ancient wrecks on the seabed, and what

THE BLACK SEA GREEKS II: THE MODERN ERA

Occasionally you still come across elderly residents of Sozopol speaking **Greek** among themselves – a reminder that the Greek population of the coast remained an important feature of local life well into this century. The Greeks of the coastal towns had maintained some degree of wealth and influence under Turkish rule, and thus seemed poised to take advantage of the upsurge in commerce that occurred in Ottoman lands in the wake of the Crimean War. However, the decline of Turkish power and the rise of **modern national movements** had a detrimental effect on the cosmopolitan culture of the Black Sea towns, whose ethnic groups squabbled among themselves rather than unite to challenge the moribund Ottoman Empire. The Greeks, inspired by the existence of an independent Greek state from 1830 on, came under the influence of the **Megáli Idhéa** (Great Idea) of liberating all the Hellenes within Turkish territory and forging a new Byzantine empire.

The idea that the Black Sea towns formed an integral part of the Hellenic world was anathema to the **Bulgarians**. Increasingly numerous in the coastal towns due to migration from the countryside, they saw the Greeks – who controlled the Church, education, and most local trade – as agents of the ruling Ottoman elite. The Ottomans played one group off against the other, eventually acquiescing to Bulgarian demands for the establishment of a Bulgarian Orthodox Church independent of Greek control – a move that infuriated the Greeks.

With the foundation of a Bulgarian state after 1878, mistrust between the two groups faded into the background, only to re-emerge in 1906 when the Greek patriarchate in Constantinople tried to appoint a new bishop of Varna without the prior agreement of the Bulgarian government. The new bishop, Neophytos, was prevented from disembarking at Varna's harbour by a hostile crowd, and a donkey in priest's robes was paraded through the streets. Things took an uglier turn in Pomorie, where the local Greeks were rumoured to be arming themselves to prevent a Bulgarian takeover of their churches. Greek-owned shops and houses were put to the torch, and many Hellenic families fled to Greece.

After World War I both governments agreed to settle their differences with an exchange of populations. According to the **Mollov-Kafandaris Agreement** of 1924, Black Sea Greeks would quit the coastal towns to be replaced by ethnic Bulgarians from Aegean Macedonia and southern Thrace. Greeks in Sozopol, Pomorie, Nesebâr and elsewhere had to choose between declaring themselves to be Bulgarians and adopting Slav names, or leaving. The poorer Greek families stayed behind because they lacked the resources to contemplate uprooting themselves and starting afresh, and their descendants were largely assimilated by the Bulgarian majority over the next seventy years. Despite the population exchange, the atmosphere of the coastal towns didn't change that much – most of the new arrivals tended to be vine-growers and fisherfolk, very much like those who moved out, and locals still joke that the incoming Bulgarians from southern Thrace usually spoke better Greek than the Hellenes they were replacing.

The bitterness that used to characterize relations between Greeks and Bulgarians on the coast has these days largely disappeared, especially now that the straitjacket of Communist educational policy – which trumpeted Bulgarian achievements at the expense of everyone else's – has been cast aside. Many Bulgarian families on the coast can dredge up a Greek ancestor or two – nowadays the subject of fond reminiscences rather than ethnic angst.

is arguably Bulgaria's best collection of Greek vases, including twelve Attic *kraters* with vibrant red-figure depictions of mythical scenes. At least five of them show Dionysus, god of wine and lustful celebration, a reminder that each *krater* was originally used for the mixing of wine and water during feasts. The Thracians who lived inland – and mined the copper so profitably shipped overseas by the Greeks – are remembered in an extensive collection of weaponry and functional pottery.

The Old Town

The **old town** begins beyond the post office, where three cobbled roads thrust into a labyrinth of alleys and vine-shaded houses and tourists are ambushed by old ladies brandishing lace tablecloths for sale. The best examples of traditional architecture lie towards the head of the peninsula along ulitsas Apoloniya and Kiril i Metodii. In winter, boats and fishing tackle are kept inside the stone lower storeys; families occupy the creaking wooden rooms upstairs, which extend so far out that they threaten to touch the houses on the other side of the street. Their eaves are sometimes carved with suns or fish, for good luck.

Several shed-like *paraklisi* or **chapels** can be found scattered throughout the old town, usually bare inside save for a picture of the saint to whom they're dedicated. Despite its central location, it's hard to find the **Church of Sveta Bogoroditsa** (July–August only; check hours at the Archeological Museum), hidden within a walled courtyard on ul. Anaksimandâr. Inside the subterranean nave are a finely carved iconostasis and bishop's throne – both executed by anonymous local masters in the early 1800s – and a wooden screen behind which female worshippers were required to stand.

Sozopol's former high school at the far end of ul. Kiril i Metodii now contains an **Art Gallery** (Tues–Sun 8am–noon & 2–6pm), although most of the works on the ground floor look like the daubs dashed off by holidaying artists between drinking bouts at the local *mehana*. Things are more interesting upstairs, where works by local marine artists Aleksandâr Mutafov and Yani Chrisoupolis document pre-World War II Sozopol and the working lives of its fisherfolk.

Eating, drinking and nightlife

There are dozens of **cafés** and snack stalls along the concourse leading to the old town, and beside both beaches, while most of the residents of Harmanite seem to be converting their garages and front gardens into *café-aperitif* **bars**. As for **restaurants**, places come and go and standards are variable, so some trial and error is inevitable. Sozopol offers the widest and freshest selection of fish on the coast, although you can't always tell whether your fillet has been recently grilled, or merely heated up in a microwave, and sea views can be enjoyed at the numerous places along Morski Skali or Istochna Aleya, the path along the eastern side of the peninsula. The *Sozopol*, at ul. Apoloniya 46, and the *Vyatarna Melnitsa* on Morski Skali are both touristy folk-style places with outdoor seating and easy-listening live music, while the *Tangra*, at Morski Skali 25, is as good a place as any to enjoy standard Bulgarian fare. For something slightly more upmarket, the *Cazanova*, on Istocha Aleya, is an Italian-influenced joint built into an overhanging portion of coastal cliff. In the uphill part of Harmanite, the restaurant of the *Hotel Orion* has an inviting east-facing terrace. Many of the above restaurants are seasonal; somewhere that's open all year round is the *Ribarska Sreshta* just south of the bus station, an unpretentious place with decent grilled fish.

Aside from flirting and promenading in the old town or attending a **concert** in the amphitheatre, nightlife consists of a couple of **discos** full of teenage Bulgarians, open from 10pm till dawn: venues tend to change, although they're usually to be found in Harmanite near the south beach.

South of Sozopol

South of Sozopol, the coast offers some of Bulgaria's most glorious stretches of **sandy beaches**. A whole string of semi-deserted beaches are punctuated by areas of coastal wetland, notably the lush woodlands around the estuary of the **River Ropotamo**, while the sandy soil of the coastal hills provides a tenuous base for prickly conifers. Hugging the Turkish border just west of the coast are the mountains of the **Strandzha**, covered by Bulgaria's deepest and least-explored **forests**.

Other than the **Dyuni Holiday Village**, the resorts along this stretch of the Black Sea were largely frequented by Eastern bloc tourists in the past, and now depend on Bulgarians for custom. If you don't mind the absence of other foreigners or the lack of nightlife, quiet seaside towns like **Primorsko**, **Kiten** and **Ahtopol** offer inexpensive lodgings and proximity to a beach (the size and quality of which vary). Beyond Ahtopol a lonely coast road continues to **Sinemorets**, a middle-of-nowhere village whose stunning beaches deserve a place on the itinerary of every self-respecting Black Sea traveller.

Those with private **transport** can cruise the area and pick their ideal bathing spot; travellers reliant on local buses will have to time things carefully. There are six buses a day between Sozopol and Tsarevo, calling at Kavatsite, Dyuni, Ropotamo, Primorsko and Kiten; two of them continue on to Ahtopol. In high season, services fill up quickly and drivers won't stop to pick up travellers at roadside halts if the vehicle is already packed. In addition, private **minibuses** zoom down the stretch of coast between Burgas and Tsarevo, although they're unlikely to call in at Sozopol en route.

Kavatsite and Dyuni

Four kilometres down the coast from Sozopol, the highway descends towards a long sandy bay backed by three campsites. At the northern end of the bay on the right-hand side of the road is the *Smokinite* **hotel** (☎05514/471, fax 293; ③), a slightly down-at-heel concrete holiday complex offering fairly standard ensuite rooms, a few alfresco restaurants and an outdoor swimming pool. Immediately beyond lies **KAVATSITE**, a vast wooded campsite with an abundance of bungalows (②), the odd restaurant, and direct access to a huge sweep of sandy beach. The southern reaches of Kavatsite run straight into the more dilapidated *Smokinya* site (enquire at Kavatsite reception about its bungalows; ①). At the southern end of the bay, the bungalow-less *Kâmping Veselie* is the most basic of the trio, occupying a wild, dune-punctuated stretch of beach popular with nudists. Coastal bus services will drop off at the entrance to Kavatsite on request, as will the hourly open-sided tourist buses that run between Sozopol and Dyuni in season.

The once-stylish **DYUNI HOLIDAY VILLAGE**, 4km beyond Kavatsite, was one of the last tourist complexes built on the coast. The resort is divided into a seaside **marina** and two hillside colonies – **Club Pelican**, a hotel complex built around an attractive open-air pool, and **Alepu**, an ensemble of self-catering villas. Accommodation in either is of a reasonable standard, but the surrounding lawns, parklands and walkways have become woefully neglected in recent years. Food and drink in Dyuni is twice as expensive as elsewhere on the south coast, and independent travellers would be better off staying in Sozopol or Kavatsite (from where you can walk to Dyuni along a roadside path). If you do want to stay, there's a *kvartirno byuro* above the marina – on the left as you head south along the coastal road (☎05514/466).

Aside from the water sports on offer at the marina, Dyuni's chief attraction is the marvellous sandy **beach** that extends southwards for 3km, protecting an inland plain of marsh and reed and **Lake Alepu**, a lagoon surrounded by dunes and sand lilies. The area is vastly popular with beach-hoppers, although it has a tendency to become increasingly litter-strewn as the season progresses – unfortunately, only those portions of the beach within the orbit of Dyuni are regularly cleaned.

Arkutino and the River Ropotamo

Four kilometres south of Dyuni, **ARKUTINO** (the name refers to an area rather than a precise settlement) is the site of a (currently closed) motel and an inviting moonscape of shifting, scrub-covered coastal **dunes**. From here several unmarked walking trails run south along the coast, picking their way over shrub-carpeted clifftops before emerging at the estuary of the Ropotamo river, where there's an attractive stretch of near-deserted sand which can only be reached on foot. On the opposite side of the main road from the motel, there's a small area of coastal swamp accessed by wooden walkways (uncertain opening times; $2), allowing glimpses of **giant waterlilies** that bloom in the late summer.

The River Ropotamo

A few kilometres south of Arkutino, the highway crosses the **River Ropotamo**, whose estuary has been designated a **nature reserve**. Local tourist agencies imbue the Ropotamo with the mystique of the Florida Everglades, especially its **waterlilies**, although the reality can be something of a letdown. Boat trips (departures depend on the volume of custom; $4) usually cover the stretch from the highway to the estuary, missing the best of the flora and fauna. This lies beyond the waterlily lake along the banks upriver, which are lined with oaks, beech, willows and creeping lianas. The river attracts fishermen with its abundance of whitefish, barbel, grey mullet and carp; dragonflies, small black turtles and (non-poisonous) watersnakes are also found here. To the south of the river mouth rises **Cape Maslen**, where the sea has hollowed out caves that are sometimes frequented by **seals**.

The easiest way to see the river is to book an **excursion** with one of the many travel agents in Sozopol ($10–15 per person). Otherwise, Sozopol–Tsarevo **buses** stop at the bridge from where boats take off, but drivers seem reluctant to pick up passengers here – so be prepared to hitch back.

Primorsko, Kiten and Tsarevo

On the other side of the cape, the peninsula village of **PRIMORSKO** commands the northern approaches to another glorious curve of a **beach**, running along the bay to the south. It's a dusty place blighted by uncontrolled holiday-house construction, but its popularity as an inexpensive resort for Bulgarians and Czechs gives the place an appealing vigour. Most of the accommodation is in **private rooms** (available from a *kvartirno byuro* on the main square where Sozopol–Tsarevo buses stop), although there are a couple of smallish **hotels** in the grid of streets that form the village centre. The *Flamingo*, 3 Mart 8, at the eastern end of the peninsula (☎05561/3031; ③), is small but modern and comfortable, while the *Lilyana*, nearer the square at Lilyana 8 (☎05561/2626; ③ including breakfast), is a Spanish-style villa containing smart rooms with TV. Paths lead downhill from the square to the beach, where you'll find a small cluster of bars and grilled-fish **restaurants**.

Slightly quieter is the less developed, dune-backed beach on the northern side of the village, a kilometre-long stretch of sand that culminates in the private bathing area of the exclusive **Hotel Perla** (booked through Intertravel in Sofia ☎02/881401, fax 880870; ⑧), former holiday home of communist leader Todor Zhivkov. It was here that Bulgaria's post-1989 "socialist" rulers invited the tycoon Robert Maxwell, who entertained his hosts with tales of how he would turn the Black Sea coast into the California of the Balkans. Nowadays the guests here can hunt boar and stag in Zhivkov's former game preserve, or use the covered swimming pool, although the rooms, decked out in ponderous Socialist-era furniture, hardly merit the price of $100 per person.

Two kilometres south of Primorsko lies the grandly titled **International Youth Centre**, a hotel complex that originally bore the name of Georgi Dimitrov and was intended as a holiday camp for Eastern bloc students. With the demise of fellow socialist regimes, the centre lost its *raison d'être*, and fell into stagnation for a few years before pulling itself together as a private venture. Despite commanding direct access to the southern end of Primorsko beach, the resort remains strangely lifeless, with a couple of uninspring **hotels** (☎05561/2045; or through *Orbita* in Sofia ☎02/800102, fax 988 5814; ③) and a neighbouring **bungalow** settlement (②).

Kiten and Lozenets

Barely a kilometre beyond the Youth Centre, the coast road runs into **KITEN**, another peninsula village girdled with beaches, the attractive and sheltered **Atliman bay** to the north garnering more bathers than the slightly scruffier, wind-whipped expanse of sand to the south. It's a low-key, family-oriented (and almost exclusively Bulgarian) resort, full of trade union-owned rest homes. Although hotels in all but name, many of these establishments still cater for those employed by a particular factory or company, and only open their doors to outsiders if occupancy is low. However most private houses in the village offer **rooms**, though the tourist service kiosk in the bus station only seems to open at peak times, so you may have to ask around. In addition, there's a growing number of small family-run **hotels**: the *Globus*, just east of the bus station in the village centre (☎ & fax 05561/2281; ③), has simple ensuite doubles and triples, optional breakfast for an extra $2, and one four-person apartment with sitting room and TV ($40). Of the two **campsites**, the *Atliman* at the northern entrance to the village is preferable to the unkempt *Kiten* to the south. With virtually every garage and garden in Kiten transformed into a rudimentary café or restaurant, you're unlikely to have any problem finding somewhere to **eat** or **drink**.

There's little to detain you in **LOZENETS**, the next town down the coast, although the well-run *Oasis* **campsite** (signed off the main road just to the south) is one of the best in the area, and has ensuite bungalows (②).

Tsarevo (Michurin)

A century ago, tsars Ferdinand and Boris used to enjoy bathing near the Greek-populated village of Vasiliko, now known as **TSAREVO**. In 1948 the Communists renamed it "Michurin" (in honour of the Soviet plant-breeder), by which name it is still known to many of the locals, despite having officially reverted to its prewar title. The shabbiest town on the south coast by far, there's little to write home about: an untidy main street runs downhill to a park, with the harbour to the south and a small beach on the other side of the rocky promontory. Unless you fancy **camping** at the *Arapya* site, 5km north of town, an appealingly isolated spot with a good beach, you'd do best to press on to more enticing Ahtopol and Sinemorets further south. If you get stuck in Tsarevo, ask locals at the bus station about **rooms**; otherwise they're available from the sporadically open Horizont tourist bureau on the flagstoned square just uphill.

The far south

Beyond Tsarevo the E87 swings inland towards the Strandzha and the frontier crossing at Malko Târnovo (see p.373), while a well-surfaced minor road continues along an increasingly rocky coastline before reaching the next town of any size, **Ahtopol**. Occasionally forced inland, the road dives between coastal hills, where herders watch over grazing sheep and pigs. Eight kilometres beyond Tsarevo the road passes through **VARVARA**, a sleepy village built around a small shingle cove. There's little here save for a couple of central snack bars, but the village's **private rooms** (there's no *kvartirno byuro*, so you'll have to ask around) are increasingly popular with urban Bulgarians eager for a taste of seaside rusticity. The beach at Ahtopol is just about walkable from here, and there are plenty of grassy clifftops to explore in the vicinity.

Ahtopol

Surrounded by a girdle of trade-union rest homes, **AHTOPOL** is a tranquil, sea-battered little place whose peninsular position echoes that of Sozopol and Nesebâr. From the bus station, situated at the western end of town, the main street leads down towards a small fishing harbour. Just above is a **museum** (Tues–Sun; irregular hours) which recalls the original Greek settlement of Agathopolis, and a flight of steps leading into the rather bland town centre. At the head of the peninsula, surrounded by well-tended flowers, stands the **Hram Vâsnesenie Gospodne** (Chapel of the Ascension), a low, unadorned structure with vivid nineteenth-century frescos behind its icon screen.

The peninsula has several tiny shingle **beaches** separated by rocky headlands, with a much larger sandy one to the north, beyond the rest-home colony. A bureau next to the bus station rents out plentiful **rooms** (①), a much better bet than the three dilapidated **hotels** (③) on the clifftop road. You'll find **cafés** and a **market** on the street across the park from the bus station.

Sinemorets

From Ahtopol the coast road heads south through a forest thick with Strandzha oak, before dropping down to cross the reed–shrouded **River Veleka**. On the opposite bank stands the windswept hilltop settlement of **SINEMORETS**, a village that until 1989 was out-of-bounds to outsiders due to its proximity to the

Turkish border. Since then it's been discovered by beach-hoppers, and wealthy city dwellers building seaside villas and second homes. It's a strange mixture of bucolic village and building site, the kind of place where expensive cars trundle down the dirt tracks that serve as streets, and imported drinks are doled out from hastily erected shacks. Sinemorets's new-found fame rests on its two **beaches**: the south beach, accessible by a track which leads eastwards through the village towards the headland before veering south, is a dazzling expanse of fine white sand bordered by rocky promontories. It's the kind of place that attracts younger, liberal-leaning Bulgarians – bathing nude here will hardly raise an eyebrow. More spectacular still is the beach to the north, a kilometre-long sand bar that slows the progress of the River Veleka towards the sea. Framed by low green hills, it's one of the most beautiful spots on the Black Sea coast.

There are three daily buses from Ahtopol to Sinemorets, although it's possible to walk the 6km that seperates the two if you're not weighed down with luggage. Almost all the houses in Sinemorets offer **rooms** – just ask around or knock on a few doors. There are several hotels currently under construction: the *Blue Shark* (☎05563/783; ③) is a well-regarded family **pension** that's already up and running. Otherwise, you can **camp rough** among the trees and wild raspberry bushes backing the south beach.

From Sinemorets it's another 10km south to the village of **Rezovo** on the Turkish border, though it's *not* possible to cross the frontier here.

The Strandzha

The interior west of the south coast is dominated by the wooded **Strandzha**, a region of plateaux and hills interrupted by rift valleys, and watered by the Ropotamo and Veleka rivers. It's a captivating area of untouched forests, thick with beech, alder, elm and the ubiquitous Strandzha oak, and would be perfect hiking territory were it not for the fact that distinct paths are rare and good maps of the area nonexistent. Private **rooms** are available in the region's main town, **Malko Târnovo**, as well as in the nearby villages of Brâshlyan, Kosti and Gramatikovo. They're all booked through the **Strandzha National Park Administration** in Malko Târnovo (☎05952/2229), so this should be your first port of call if you want to stay in the area. Otherwise, tourist accommodation is hard to find.

The most direct route into the region **from Burgas** is via a minor road (served by four buses a day from Burgas' *Avtogara Zapad*) which works its way over the western shoulder of the Strandzha massif before arriving at Malko Târnovo, 10km short of the Turkish border. **From the south coast**, the main E87 highway dives inland from Tsarevo towards Malko Târnovo, passing some of the region's most picturesque villages on the way – although this route is only served by three buses a week from Burgas' *Avtogara Yug*. If you want to explore the Strandzha in depth, you definitely need your own transport.

South from Burgas

Immediately south of Burgas the main inland route to Malko Târnovo begins to ascend through wooded hills, passing a sequence of rustic, half-abandoned villages. Fifty-three kilometres out of town, at the village of **ZVEZDETS**, a minor road forks left towards **Petrova Niva**, a hilltop overlooking the river Veleka, which serves as a popular spot for picnics and short hikes. Bulgarian insurgents met here in 1903 to launch the **Preobrazhenie Uprising** against the Turks (so called because it was launched on *Preobrazhenie* – Transfiguration – an important Orthodox holy day falling on August 6). The event is still marked by an annual *sâbor* or "gathering" on the weekend nearest to *Preobrazhenie*, which involves folk music, feasting and dancing.

Continuing along the main route from Zvezdets, a right turn after 10km leads to the tiny village of **BRÂSHLYAN** (all Malko Târnovo buses from Burgas–Zapad call in here), site of the Strandzha's best-preserved ensemble of traditional peasant houses. None of them are open to the public, and the village hasn't received the kind of funding awarded to other heritage sites such as Koprivshtitsa and Zheravna, but it's a charming spot imbued with rural calm. The village is centred on the sunken church of **Sveti Dimitâr**, built, according to Ottoman restrictions, behind a wall high enough to render it inoffensive to any passing Muslim. Call in at the mayor's office (*kmetstvo*), opposite, to obtain the key for the restored **church school** (*kiliino uchilishte*) next door, a small room where the better-off village children once sat on goatskin rugs and wrote on wax tablets, erasing their work by holding the tablets up to the heat of the nearby fireplace. There's a small **ethnographic collection** inside the *kmetstvo*, showing the woollen cloaks once worn by Brâshlyan's menfolk – predominantly herders who wintered their flocks on the shores of the Aegean to the south. There's nowhere to eat and drink in Brâshlyan, but there are **rooms** in an old village house bookable through the National Park Administration in Malko Târnovo, 15km further south.

Inland from Tsarevo

The other main route into the region, the E87, heads inland from Tsarevo, winding its way slowly over the hills. The first village of any note is **BÂLGARI**, renowned for the still-practised custom of *nestinarstvo* or **fire dancing**. Traditionally associated with the feast day of saints Konstantin and Elena (which falls on May 21 in most parts of Bulgaria, but is celebrated here on June 4, or the nearest weekend), the ritual involves initiates falling into a trance and dancing on hot embers, to furious bagpipe and drum accompaniment. The secret lies in the low thermal conductivity of the embers, whose heat is transmitted slowly enough for the walkers to avoid injury by moving at a fast pace. Preparations for the fire-dancing last all day, with icons of the saints paraded round the village, and the inevitable sacrifice of sheep prior to communal feasting.

From Bâlgari, a minor road heads off towards **KOSTI**, another bucolic spot lying 7km south, on the banks of the River Veleka. There's a wealth of (unmarked) hiking paths heading up and down the river, with the most inviting being the eight-hour trek downstream to Sinemorets (see p.371). There are a few **rooms** in Kosti, again bookable through the National Park Administration in Malko Târnovo.

Back on the main road, **GRAMATIKOVO** lies midway between Bâlgari and Malko Târnovo, offering a smattering of traditional buildings, and a few more of the National Park Administration's rooms.

Malko Târnovo and the border

All roads in the Strandzha lead to **MALKO TÂRNOVO**, a former copper-mining town lying in a bowl surrounded by hills. It's a down-at-heel place where tourism was never encouraged in the past due to the proximity of the border. A small collection of National Revival buildings huddles above the main square, four of which together serve as a **town museum**, including ethnographic and icon collections. Opening times are erratic, but someone may open the collections up if you call in at the Strandzha National Park Administration (*Upravlenie na naroden park Strandzha*; Mon–Fri 9am–5pm; ☎05952/2229), in an anonymous office block just off the main square at Yanko Maslinkov 1. This is also the place at which to book **private rooms**, which are infinitely preferable to the run-down **motel**, the *Strandzha* (③), which lies midway between Malko Târnovo and the border. There are a couple of **cafés** around the main square, and a **restaurant**, *Club 21*, just off it.

Travelling on from Malko Târnovo **by car**, traffic at the frontier is pretty light, but clearing Bulgarian customs can still involve lengthy queuing. Things can be even more time-consuming on the Turkish side, where you'll have to wait behind files of bus passengers in order to buy an entry visa, which will cost about $16 (£10).

It's impossible to predict how long it will take to cross the border **by bus**. Malko Târnovo is overrun with Bulgarians, Romanians and Ukrainians on the way to Istanbul (many carrying holdalls stuffed with goods they hope to sell on Turkish markets), and their baggage gets a thorough going-over by officials on both sides. Bus passengers will probably be stuck here all night, but the wait is worthwhile – the descent into Turkey through the scrub-covered southern slopes of the Strandzha is highly scenic.

travel details

Trains

Burgas to: Karnobat (12 daily; 45min–1hr 30min); Kazanlâk (4 daily; 3hr 15min); Plovdiv (3 daily; 4hr 30min); Sofia (4 daily; 6hr 30min); Stara Zagora (4 daily; 3hr).

Varna to: Dobrich (6 daily; 2hr 45min); Karnobat (7 daily; 3hr–3hr 30min); Plovdiv (2 daily; 6–7hr); Ruse (2 daily; 4hr); Sofia (5 daily; 8–9hr).

Buses

In addition to the services below there are regular **minibuses** (which set off when there are enough passengers) linking Varna with Albena, Balchik and Burgas; and Burgas with Sunny Beach, Sozopol, Kiten and Tsarevo.

Ahtopol to: Burgas (4 daily; 2hr 15min); Sinemorets (3 daily; 15min); Sozopol (3 daily; 1hr 30min); Tsarevo (5 daily; 20min).

Albena to: Balchik (every 20min; 30min); Dobrich (hourly; 40min); Golden Sands (every 15–30min; 30min).

Balchik to: Albena (every 20min; 30min); Dobrich (6 daily; 1hr); Durankulak (Sat & Sun only 1 daily; 1hr 20min); Kavarna (6 daily; 30min); Shabla (4 daily; 1hr); Varna (6 daily; 1hr 30min).

Burgas (Avtogara Yug) to: Ahtopol (4 daily; 2hr 15min); Malko Târnovo (Tues, Sat & Sun only 1 daily; 3hr 30min); Nesebâr (every 40min; 50min); Obzor (1 daily; 1hr); Pomorie (every 30min; 20min); Primorsko (2 daily; 1hr 20min); Ruse (1 daily; 4hr); Sofia (4 daily; 6hr 30min); Sozopol (hourly; 50min); Sunny Beach (hourly; 45min); Tsarevo (6 daily; 2hr); Varna (4 daily; 3hr).

Burgas (Avtogara Zapad) to: Malko Târnovo (4 daily; 2hr).

Durankulak to: Balchik (3 daily; 1hr 20min); Kavarna (3 daily; 50min); Shabla (5 daily; 20min).

Dyuni to: Kavatsite (hourly; 15–30min); Sozopol (hourly; 15–30min).

Golden Sands to: Albena (every 15–30min; 30min); Sveti Konstantin (every 10–30min; 20–25min); Varna (every 10–30min; 30min).

Kavarna to: Balchik (6 daily; 30min); Bâlgarevo (6 daily; 20min); Dobrich (7 daily; 1hr 30min); Durankulak (3 daily; 50min); Shabla (8 daily; 30min); Varna (6 daily; 2hr).

Kavatsite to: Dyuni (hourly; 15–30min); Sozopol (hourly; 15–30min).

Malko Târnovo to: Brâshlyan (4 daily; 20min); Burgas Avtogara Yug (Tues, Sat & Sun only 1 daily; 3hr 30min); Burgas Avtogara Zapad (4 daily; 2hr); Tsarevo (1 daily; 1hr 30min).

Nesebâr to: Burgas (every 40min; 50min); Pomorie (every 40min; 30min); Sunny Beach (every 15–20min; 15min).

Obzor to: Burgas (1 daily; 1hr); Sunny Beach (1 daily; 25min); Varna (7 daily; 1hr 30min).

Pomorie to: Burgas (every 30min; 20min); Nesebâr (every 40min; 30min); Sunny Beach (every 40min; 30min).

Shabla to: Balchik (4 daily; 1hr); Durankulak (3 daily; 20min); Kavarna (8 daily; 30min); Krapets (1 daily; 15min).

Sofia *opposite Central Station* to: Burgas (4 daily; 6hr 30min); Sozopol (1 daily; 7hr 15min); Varna (5 daily; 8–9hr).

Sozopol to: Ahtopol (2 daily; 1hr 30min); Burgas (hourly; 50min); Dyuni (hourly; 20min); Kavatsite (hourly; 15min); Kiten (6 daily; 45min); Primorsko (6 daily; 30min); Sofia (1 daily; 7hr 15min); Tsarevo (6 daily; 1hr 10min).

Sunny Beach to: Burgas (hourly; 45min); Elenite (8 daily; 20min); Nesebâr (every 15–20min; 15min); Obzor (1 daily; 25min); Pomorie (every 40min; 30min); Sveti Vlas (8 daily; 10min); Varna (7 daily; 2hr 10min).

Sveti Konstantin (Druzhba) to: Golden Sands (every 10–30min; 20–25min); Varna (every 10–30min; 25min).

Tsarevo to: Ahtopol (5 daily; 20min); Burgas (via Sozopol 6 daily; via Yasnya Polyana 3 daily; 2hr 30min); Kiten (8 daily; 20min); Malko Târnovo (1 daily; 1hr 30min); Sinemorets (3 daily; 15min).

Varna to: Balchik (6 daily; 1hr 30min); Burgas (4 daily; 3hr); Byala (6 daily; 1hr 20min); Dobrich (10 daily; 50min); Golden Sands (every 10–30min; 20min); Kamchiya (2 daily; 50min); Kavarna (6 daily; 2hr); Obzor (4 daily; 1hr 30min); Ruse (2 daily; 4hr); Shabla (4 daily; 2hr 30min); Shumen (4 daily; 2hr); Silistra (4 daily; 3hr); Sunny Beach (4 daily; 2hr 10min); Sveti Konstantin (every 10–30min; 25min); Veliko Târnovo (4 daily; 4hr).

Flights

Burgas to: Sofia (1–2 daily; 1hr).

Varna to: Sofia (2 daily; 1hr).

International trains (mid-June to mid-Sept only)

Varna to: Buzau (6 weekly; 12hr); Istanbul (2 weekly on Wed & Fri; 8hr); Kiev (6 weekly; 30–36hr); Minsk (4 weekly; 24hr); Moscow (4 weekly; 51hr).

International buses

Burgas to: Istanbul (1 daily; 12hr).

Varna to: Istanbul (1 daily; 14hr); Krasnodar (1 weekly; 60hr); Odessa (1 weekly; 24hr); Rostov-on-Don (1 weekly; 48hr); Skopje (3 weekly; 13hr).

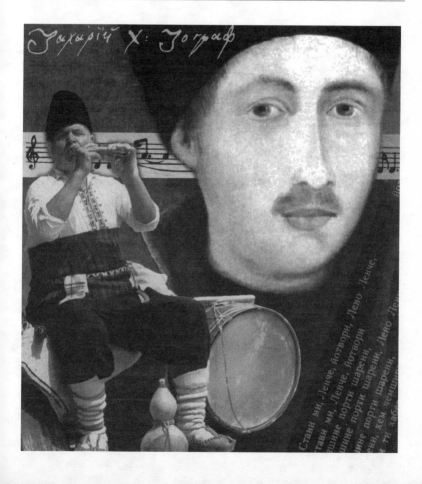

THE HISTORICAL FRAMEWORK

National history is a serious business in a country that was virtually effaced for five hundred years – when this part of the Ottoman Empire was referred to by Westerners as "European Turkey". Since the Liberation in 1877–78, successive regimes have tried to inculcate a sense of national pride among their citizens, emphasizing historical continuity between the modern state and the medieval Bulgarian empires of the past.

NEOLITHIC BEGINNINGS

Despite several Palaeolithic finds in the caves of the Balkan Mountains, the early inhabitants of the Bulgarian lands don't really enter the limelight of history until the sixth millennium BC, when the Balkans were a major centre of the so-called **Neolithic Revolution**. This came about when Stone Age hunters began to be replaced by a more settled, agricultural population – probably the result of a wave of migration from the Near East. This sudden flowering of organized urban culture is best observed at the recently excavated Neolithic village at **Stara Zagora** (see p.266), famous for its decorated pottery, clay figurines and fertility symbols. By the fourth millennium BC mining and metallurgy took off in a big way: copper and gold objects found in the

Chalcolithic necropolis near **Varna** (see p.327) show that the Balkan peoples were developing smelting techniques independently of the civilizations of the Near East.

Chalcolithic culture went into decline at the end of the fourth millennium BC, a process hastened by a worsening of the climate. Civilization in the Bulgarian lands was revitalized by the arrival of newcomers from Central Europe, bringing with them the metalworking techniques of the **Bronze Age**. By the end of the second millennium BC these migrant groups, together with the original tribes of the eastern Balkans, were coalescing into an ethnic and linguistic group subsequently known to history as the **Thracians**.

THE THRACIANS

Ruled by a powerful warrior aristocracy rich in gold treasures, the ancient Thracians inhabited an area extending over most of modern Bulgaria, northern Greece and European Turkey. Close ethnic links with their neighbours in both the Danube basin to the north and in Asia Minor to the east placed them at the centre of an extensive Balkan–Asian culture. Despite their subsequent absorption by a whole host of invaders and their eventual assimilation by the Slavs, the Thracians are regarded as one of the **bedrock peoples** of the Balkans whose ethnic stock (though much diluted) has endured – and the present-day Bulgarians are proud to claim them as ancestors. We're largely dependent on ancient Greek authors – notably Herodotus, Xenophon and Strabo – for knowledge of the Thracian world. Herodotus, in a famous passage you'll see quoted in museums throughout Bulgaria, claimed that the Thracian population was "greater than that of any country in the world except India", and would have been a force to be reckoned with had it not been for their tribal disunity.

Although the Thracians were admired for skills such as archery and horsemanship, many of their **customs** seemed slightly barbaric to their southerly neighbours. Certain tribes practised polygamy, others allowed their young women unlimited sexual freedom before marriage, while tattoos for both males and females were *de rigueur* in most areas. Strabo relates how one group of Thracians was nicknamed the *Capnobatae* (literally the "smoke treaders"), suggesting that they burned hemp seeds indoors and got high on the fumes. Dope-crazed hopheads or not, the Thracians practised an ecstatic, **orgiastic religion**, honouring deities closely linked with the Greek god Dionysus. Themes of death, rebirth and renewal figured highly in their religious rites, providing a corpus of belief from which the Greeks borrowed freely – most notably in the case of the legendary Thracian priest-king **Orpheus**.

GREEKS, PERSIANS AND MACEDONIANS

Certain Thracian tribes developed close links with the **Greek colonists** who began settling the Black Sea coast from the seventh century onwards. The Greek presence turned the Black Sea into an extension of the Mediterranean world, and while bounteous harvests of wheat and fish were shipped southwards to the Aegean to feed cities like Athens, exquisite sculpture and pottery came in the other direction, enriching the culture of the eastern Balkans.

The **Persians** invaded the area in the late sixth century BC, disrupting the lively system of trade that linked the Black Sea Greeks with the Thracians inland. However, their departure allowed the emergence of powerful Thracian tribal kingdoms such as that of the **Odrysae**, which brought stability to the region in the mid-fifth century BC and allowed Greek–Thracian mercantile contacts to flourish anew.

The Odrysae briefly threatened to become the nucleus of a powerful Balkan empire, but this role was taken up a century later by the neighbouring **Macedonians** under Philip II – who invaded Thrace and founded Philippopolis (present-day **Plovdiv**). It took Philip and his son Alexander the Great (who marched to the Danube in 335 BC) a lot of time and men to subdue the Balkans, but their empire (under Alexander's successors the Antigonids) proved lasting. It was during this period that the Thracian interior was opened up fully to the ideas, goods and culture of the Hellenistic world, and the **tombs** of local Thracian rulers (most notably those at **Kazanlâk**; see p.263) were sumptuously kitted out with Greek-inspired frescos and luxurious furnishings.

ROME AND BYZANTIUM

The **Romans** became the dominant power in the region after their defeat of Macedonia in 168 BC, but it took almost two centuries for the empire to subdue the Thracians, who were in constant revolt. It wasn't until about 50 AD that the conquerors were finally able to carve out secure administrative units, creating the province of **Thrace** to the south of the Balkan range and **Moesia** to the north. Using slave labour, the Romans built garrisons, towns, roads and bridges across their domain, and conscripted many Thracians into their legions.

Military strongholds and neighbouring civilian settlements sprang up along the **Danube frontier** (relics of which can today be seen in the museums of Vidin, Pleven and Sofia), while prosperous new towns like **Nicopolis ad Istrum** (near Veliko Târnovo; see p.201) commanded the trade routes inland. Many of the old Greek towns along the coast continued to thrive, and although they now hosted a population of mixed Greek and Thracian descent, Greek language and culture remained dominant throughout the region.

From the third century onwards the empire's contraction and decline was hastened by recurrent invasions of the Danubian provinces by the Goths (238–48), Visigoths (378), Huns (447) and other so-called **barbarians** – civilization in Moesia and Thrace suffered greatly as a result. However, the division of the empire into two parts, with **Byzantium** inheriting the mantle of Rome in the east, meant that the authorities in nearby Constantinople could (for a while at least) concentrate their military resources more effectively here.

Both the Danubian frontier and the stronghold of Thrace were reinforced by Emperor **Justinian** in the sixth century, allowing urban life in the region a brief reprieve. Both Philippopolis (Plovdiv) and **Serdica** (Sofia) flourished during his reign. Even under Justinian, however, the **sklaveni** (ancestors of the Balkan Slavs) found a way of breaching the empire's defences, and indulged in big looting trips into Thrace in the 540s. By the seventh century, increasing numbers of Avars and **Slavs** were crossing the river with impunity, leaving the Byzantines with little choice but to allow them to settle and employ them as irregular frontier troops.

SLAVS AND BULGARS

The **Slavs** who migrated into the Balkan peninsula from the late fifth century onwards were one of the indigenous races of Europe, the distant forebears of the Russians, Poles, Czechs,

Slovaks, Slovenes, Croats and Serbs – and, of course, the Bulgarians. Many of them came in the wake of the Avars, a warlike Central Asian people who briefly forged a Central European empire in the sixth century and press-ganged the Slavs into their all-conquering armies. However they got here, the Slavs who settled south of the Danube soon began to outnumber any remaining Thracians in the area and established a linguistic and cultural hegemony over the region.

The Slavs were later to fuse with a new wave of migrants, the warlike **Bulgars**. These mounted nomads, possibly originating deep in Central Asia, swept down towards the Balkans after being driven out of "Old Great Bulgaria" – a swathe of territories over which they briefly ruled lying between the Caspian and the Black Seas. They were a Turkic people, ethno-linguistically akin to the Huns, Avars and Khazars. Under pressure from the latter, the Bulgars began a great **migration** into southeastern Europe, where the largest group (some 250,000 strong) led by **Khan Asparuh** reached the Danube delta around 680 and shortly afterwards entered what would soon become Bulgaria.

THE FIRST BULGARIAN KINGDOM

Theophanes the Confessor records that in 681 the Byzantine emperor Constantine IV was forced to recognize the independence of a "new and vulgar people" north of the Balkan range. Asparuh's new **Bulgar Khanate**, subsequently known as the *Pârvo Bâlgarsko Tsarstvo* – the **First Bulgarian Kingdom** – was centred at **Pliska** and ruled over a Danubian state that stretched from the Carpathians in the north to the Balkan Range in the south. Although the Khanate was very much reliant on Slav strength, the Bulgars – whose society was geared to movement and war – definitely provided the impetus for its expansion over the next 150 years.

THE KHANATE – AND THE GROWTH OF CHRISTIANITY

The Khanate's growth was greatest during the reign of **Khan Krum** "the Terrible" (803–14), who collected goblets fashioned from the skulls of foes, and pushed his boundaries as far as the Rila Mountains in the west and the Rhodopes in the south. Finally, having conquered all that he could, **Khan Omurtag** (816–31) signed a thirty-year treaty with the Byzantine Empire, and in the ensuing peace the Bulgar state was increasingly opened up to Byzantine culture. The most obvious manifestation of this process was the decision of **Khan Boris** (852–89) to adopt Orthodox **Christianity** as the official state religion in 865. The move was a pragmatic one, recognizing that a rapprochement with Byzantium was in the First Kingdom's long-term diplomatic interests, but Boris' son **Simeon** feared that the Orthodox Church could be used as a vehicle for Byzantine interests in Bulgaria: he therefore established a separate **Bulgarian Patriarchate**, thus ensuring the Bulgars full ecclesiastical autonomy.

The **majority Slav population** over which the Bulgars ruled was largely Christianized well before 865, and Boris' decision to adopt the new religion bolstered the growing influence of the Slavs in the Bulgar state. Many Bulgar nobles agitated for a return to **paganism**, and their defeat only served to confirm the gradual eclipse of the Turkic culture of the original Bulgars – although the name of the former ruling class has been perpetuated in the name **Bulgaria**.

LANGUAGE AND THE CYRILLIC ALPHABET

The position of Slavs in the Bulgarian Kingdom was also enhanced by the decision to adopt the **Slav tongue** (rather than Greek) as the official language of the Bulgarian Church. The Byzantines themselves were eager to promote this, as they thought that their missionaries, armed with a Slavonic translation of the gospels, would be able to go forth and convert the entire population of Central and Eastern Europe. Thessaloniki-based missionaries **Cyril and Methodius** began the job of creating an alphabet suited to the needs of the Slav language, initially opting for a rune-like script subsequently known as Glagolitic. However, the task was completed by their disciples **Kliment** and **Naum**, who named the script (still used in varying forms by the modern Bulgarians, Serbs, Ukrainians and Russians) **Cyrillic** in honour of their mentor.

ZENITH AND DECLINE

Armed with the Cyrillic alphabet, Bulgaria became the main centre of **Slavonic culture** in Europe. The "golden age" of literature and arts coincided with the reign of **Tsar Simeon** (893–927), whose defeat of the Byzantine army at Aheloi in 917 allowed the annexation of sizable chunks of Macedonia and Thrace, and the haughty claim to be "Tsar of all the Bulgarians and Byzantines".

But the tsars' perennial exactions and wars bred discontent with the feudal order. Thus arose the **Bogomils**, a sect whose "heretical" doctrines amounted to a rejection of Church and state, which took fright wherever Bogomilism appeared in the Balkans, and in France and Italy where like-minded movements emerged during the twelfth and thirteenth centuries.

Besides such conflicts, the reigns of Petâr I (927–69) and Boris II (969–71) were also marked by increasingly violent conflicts between the nobility, or **bolyari**. Byzantium, too, posed a constant threat, and an invasion by Prince Svyatoslav of Kiev gave the Byzantines the pretext they needed to launch a full-scale onslaught. Bulgaria was reduced to a rump, known as the **Western Kingdom**, governed from Ohrid in Macedonia. **Tsar Samuil** was partly successful in restoring the old kingdom until the Byzantine emperor Basil Bulgaroctonos – the "**Bulgar-Slayer**" – defeated his army at Strumitsa in 1014 and blinded the 14,000 prisoners taken. Samuel died of horror after seeing the maimed horde fumbling its way into Ohrid.

Following Ohrid's capture in 1018 the whole of Bulgaria fell under **Byzantine domination**. As a result, the Orthodox Church was largely Hellenized, and Bulgarian architecture and art were increasingly influenced by Byzantine styles. The authorities in Constantinople visited savage repression upon heretics like the Bogomils, and retaliated violently to various eleventh-century rebellions. However, their power didn't extend to protecting the local populace against marauding **Magyars** and **Pechenegs**, who plundered south of the Danube in the eleventh and twelfth centuries.

THE SECOND KINGDOM

In 1185 the *bolyari* Petâr and Asen led a successful popular uprising against Byzantium, proclaiming the **Second Kingdom** in Veliko Târnovo, henceforth its capital. Byzantine forces under Emperor Isaac Angelus confidently expected to be able to crush the rebel state at birth, but after two attempts in 1187 and 1190,

were finally forced to accept Bulgarian independence. Asen's brother and successor **Tsar Kaloyan** (1197–1207) extended Bulgaria's borders further, recapturing Varna and parts of Macedonia and Thrace from Byzantium. However, it was the **fall of Constantinople** to the **Crusaders** in 1204 that gave the Second Kingdom the chance it needed to consolidate and grow. Exiled Byzantine aristocrats, having established statelets in Epirus and Nicaea, proceeded to make war on both each other and the Crusaders' self-styled **Latin Empire of the East**. Tsar Kaloyan sought to exploit this fragmentation of Byzantine power in the Balkans, dreaming of one day setting up a Slav–Greek empire of his own.

Kaloyan succesfully negotiated **union with the Catholic church** in 1204 in the hope that the Pope would support Bulgarian expansion, although at grass roots level Bulgaria's church remained Orthodox in all but name. Widely admired in his own time (the name *Kaloyan* was derived from the Greek for "John the Handsome"), Kaloyan was also mercilessly cruel, notoriously razing Plovdiv to the ground and flaying its leading citizens alive in 1205, and hostile chroniclers were subsequently to dub him *Skiloyan* – "John the Dog".

Kaloyan inflicted a stunning defeat on the Latin rulers of Constantinople in 1205, capturing Emperor Baldwin and holding him prisoner in Târnovo (see p.207). Before he could take advantage of this success however, Kaloyan was murdered in a palace coup – as were almost all of Bulgaria's thirteenth-century tsars. A period of anarchy ensued under Tsar Boril before **Ivan Asen II** (1218–41) could restore order and continue the expansion of Bulgaria's frontiers. His victory over Theodore Comnenus of Epirus at **Klokotnitsa** in 1230 won him territories from the Adriatic to the Aegean, and ushered in an era of prestige and prosperity that marks the zenith of medieval Bulgaria's development. Ivan Asen also brought an end to the union with Rome, allowing a vibrantly Orthodox, Bulgaro-Byzantine culture to flourish.

THE MONGOLS

This period of plenty was cut short by an unexpected disaster. After 1240 **Mongol hordes**, fresh from their campaigns in Central Europe, withdrew through Serbia and Bulgaria, desolating the countryside. The ensuing chaos provided the Byzantines with an opportunity to win back some of the ground they had lost in the plain of Thrace.

One batch of Mongols – subsequently known as the **Tatars** – settled in southern Russia and the Crimea, from whence they mounted continuous raids on the lands bordering on the Black Sea. The presence of this powerful and unpredictable warrior-state on its northeastern borders considerably weakened Bulgaria's freedom of manoeuvre – perpetually threatened by enemies on both sides, the Second Kingdom increasingly had to compromise with its neighbours in order to avoid their wrath.

THE LATE THIRTEENTH CENTURY

The latter half of the thirteenth century saw a return to internecine feuding and punitive taxation, producing a **peasant rebellion** that led to the crowning of **Ivailo the Swineherd**, whose brief reign (1277–80) was largely devoted to fighting off the Tatars. Referred to as "the Cabbage" by Byzantine historians eager to accentuate his humble origins, Ivailo was a messianic figure who mobilized a hitherto docile peasantry by claiming to have been inspired by miraculous visions. Despite early successes against the Tatars, Ivailo was incapable of meeting the aspirations generated by his rebellion, and the Bulgarian nobility mounted a counter-coup. Ivailo fled to the court of the Tatar khan Nogai expecting to secure an alliance that would return him to power, but was instead put to death.

He was replaced by the first of the **Terterids**, a dynasty whose only remarkable tsar, Todor Svetoslav (1300–21), succeeded in making peace with the Tatar khans. By threatening to secede from the kingdom, the feudal ruler of Vidin, **Mihail Shishman**, managed to have himself crowned tsar in 1323, inaugurating the new **Shishmanid dynasty**. However, Mihail was fatally wounded at the battle of Velbâzhd (modern Kyustendil) in 1330, when the Bulgarian army was smashed by that of **Serbia** – by now the ascendant power in the Balkans.

IVAN ALEKSANDÂR – AND THE TURKISH CONQUEST

During the reign of Mihail's successor, **Ivan Aleksandâr** (1331–71), Bulgaria almost regained the prosperity and level of civilization attained during Asen II's time, with literature, sculpture and painting displaying a harmonious fusion of Bulgarian and Byzantine styles. However, the rest of the fourteenth century was a confused story of disintegration and decline. Over-powerful *bolyari* asserted their autonomy from Tsar **Ivan Shishman** (1371–96), weakening the central authority of the kingdom just when it was needed to organize resistance to a new threat: the **Ottoman Turks**.

Possessing a disciplined war machine and superior numbers, the Turks proved unstoppable; mutual distrust between Balkan and Byzantine rulers prevented any meaningful concerted action against the invaders, and the defeat of a powerful Serbian army at **Kosovo** in 1389 effectively sealed the fate of the whole Balkan peninsula. Most of Bulgaria had been overrun by 1393 and the anti-Turkish **crusades** of 1394 and 1444 failed to reverse the situation. With the fall of Constantinople, last bastion of the Balkan Orthodox world, in 1453, any remaining hope of outside help against the Turks disappeared for good.

"UNDER THE YOKE"

It's estimated that almost half of Bulgaria's population was massacred or enslaved and transported to another part of the empire within a few years of the Turkish conquest, whose long-term effects were equally profound. The **Ottoman Empire** not only isolated Bulgaria from the European Renaissance, but imposed and maintained a harsher system of **feudalism** than had previously existed. Muslim colonists occupied the most fertile land and prosperous towns, while the surviving Bulgarians – mainly peasants – became serfs of the Turkish *Spahis* (land-holding knights), who gouged them for their own profit and for numerous state taxes. In northern Bulgaria and the Rhodopes some Bulgarians succumbed to forced **Islamicization** and, as converts (*pomaks*), gained rights denied to the Christian *Rayah* or "Herd", notably exemption from the hated **blood tax** or *devshirme*, whereby the oldest boys were taken from their families and indoctrinated before joining the elite Ottoman janissary corps.

The Turks looted monasteries and subordinated the native **Orthodox Church** to the Patriarchate of Constantinople, which imposed Greek bishops and ignorant, grasping clergy on the faithful. Worst of all was the perpetual insecurity, for Bulgarians were raped and robbed by Turkish troops or "visiting" dignitaries, cheated by tax collectors and Greek merchants, and had no way of getting **justice** through the Ottoman courts.

Ottoman power in Bulgaria was repeatedly challenged by popular **rebellions**, which tended to break out whenever Turkish armies were beaten back by those of their European neighbours. Austrian and Moldavian advances encouraged an uprising in Târnovo in 1598, and the successful Austrian and Polish campaigns of the 1680s led to widespread revolt throughout northern Bulgaria. For the most part, however, life under Ottoman rule settled down to something approaching normality in the seventeenth and eighteenth centuries. Highland settlements such as Koprivshtitsa, Elena and Kotel were accorded privileges and allowed to accumulate wealth through trade, merchants sank their money into the renewal of churches, and the *devshirme* system gradually withered away. It was only with the disintegration of Ottoman provincial government in the late eighteenth century, and the emergence of the rapacious Turkish bandits known as the **Kârdzhali**, that the idea of Turkish rule as something fundamentally unjust and corrupt once again gripped the popular imagination. The partiality of the Ottoman legal system was one reason why many Bulgarians took to the forests to became **haiduti**, or outlaws.

Meanwhile, spiritual and artistic values predating the conquest were nurtured in the monasteries, which restored contact with **Russia** after the sixteenth century. Having rid itself of Tatar domination, re-enshrined Orthodoxy, and started to expel the Turks from Caucasia, Russia came to be viewed as the great hope of the subject Christians of the Balkans.

THE NATIONAL REVIVAL

The role of Bulgaria's monasteries in preserving ancient traditions ensured that memories of the medieval empire never died out altogether. Interest in Bulgaria's past began to express itself with the publication (outside Ottoman territory) of a *History of Bulgaria*, written by Peter Bogdan Bakshev, seventeenth-century Catholic bishop of Sofia, and a *History of the Serbs and the Bulgarians*, written by Hristofor Zhefarovich a century later. However, neither of these had the impact of **Paisii of Hilendar**'s *Slav-Bulgarian History*, written in 1762. Circulated in manuscript form (because the Greeks who controlled the Church wouldn't countenance the printing of Bulgarian-language texts), Paisii's work inspired a generation of nationalists, and became the spiritual cornerstone of the Bulgarian renaissance, the **National Revival**.

The material base for such an upsurge in national feeling was provided by the economic changes of the nineteenth century. Bulgaria was increasingly supplying the Ottoman Empire with wool, cloth and foodstuffs, giving rise to a prosperous **mercantile and artisan class** based in the towns and villages of both the Balkan Mountains and the Sredna Gora. Economic development speeded up after the Crimean War, when Turkey's French and British allies demanded that the Ottoman Empire should be opened up to Western European trade.

Bulgaria's cultural reawakening expressed itself in protests against the **Greek Church**, which controlled all ecclesiastical affairs in the country and ran most of the schools. The Greeks opposed Bulgarian efforts to establish churches and schools of their own, and **riots**, in which the local Greek priest was chased out of town, were a common feature of mid-nineteenth-century life.

Community leaders had to bargain hard with the Ottoman authorities in order to gain concessions on the issue of Bulgarian-language schooling, but by the 1840s Bulgarian **education** was beginning to take off. The growing middle class endowed schools offering a modern, secular education; in addition, there were *chitalishta* or "reading rooms" – cultural centres that offered courses for adults. The campaign for church autonomy was rewarded in 1870, when a decree from the sultan permitted the foundation of the **Bulgarian Exarchate** – a semi-independent institution nominally subject to the Greek Orthodox Patriarch of Constantinople, but capable of enforcing use of the Bulgarian language in churches and church schools. This emboldened the Bulgarians to extend their struggle further into the political sphere.

Whereas their elders had sought reforms, "second generation" nationalists increasingly pursued Bulgarian independence through armed struggle, and émigrés in the Serbian capital Belgrade, led by **G S Rakovski**, began organizing a **Bulgarian Legion** in 1861. Its members fought alongside Serbia in its wars with the Ottoman Empire, while other Bulgarian exiles formed *cheti* or armed groups that raided Turkish-controlled territory from sanctuaries in Serbia and Wallachia.

THE REVOLUTIONARY UNDERGROUND

The *cheti* received little support from the Bulgarian peasantry, however, and their unpopularity convinced **Vasil Levski** and the Bucharest-based **Bulgarian Revolutionary Central Committee (BRCK)** that a mass uprising could only be inspired by an indigenous **revolutionary underground**, which they set about creating. Levski himself led the way, travelling the length and breadth of the country in order to establish clandestine revolutionary cells: Levski and the other agents charged with setting up the BRCK network were henceforth known as **apostles** due to the almost evangelical nature of their work. Levski himself was captured and executed in 1873, a setback that nevertheless provided the liberation struggle with its first great martyr, inspiring idealistic and patriotic youngsters everywhere to rally to the cause.

THE APRIL RISING

The culmination of the BRCK's organizational efforts was the **April Rising of 1876**, which after exhaustive (but, as it turned out, insufficient) preparation was launched in the Balkan Mountains and the Sredna Gora – a heroic attempt answered by savage Ottoman reprisals, which took an estimated 29,000 Bulgarian lives.

THE "EASTERN QUESTION"

Despite these valiant efforts, the fate of Bulgaria didn't really rest with the Bulgarians themselves. The gradual stagnation of Ottoman power in Europe had raised the problem – dubbed the "**Eastern Question**" by contemporary politicians and journalists – of who would profit from the empire's demise. The main contenders in the area were Austria–Hungary and tsarist Russia, the latter nursing a long-standing ambition to extend its influence as far south as Constantinople and thereby gain control of the Bosphorus. Both the French and the British were horrified by the prospect, and tended to support Turkey in order to frustrate Russian expansion. The British establishment was notoriously

hostile to any Bulgarian aspirations that involved Russian backing, with Queen Victoria herself remarking that the Bulgarian people "hardly deserved the name of real Christians". In the cynical environment of Great Power diplomacy, the aspirations of the nationalities languishing under Ottoman rule counted for little.

The Russians exploited the ideology of **Pan-Slavism** – the belief that Slav peoples everywhere should be freed from foreign domination and united under the authoritarian guidance of the Russians – in order to stir up anti-Ottoman sentiment in the Balkans and exert control over the liberation movements thus produced. It was therefore taken for granted by Russia's opponents that any future Bulgarian state would merely be a vehicle for the Balkan ambitions of its big Slav brother. However, the Western powers found it difficult to give the Turks their unqualified support: public opinion in the West was often deeply sympathetic to the demands of the Ottoman Empire's Christian subjects – of which Russia fancied itself to be the protector.

Russian troops had temporarily expelled the Ottomans from parts of Bulgaria during the 1810–11 and 1828–29 **Russo-Turkish wars**, but were consistently unwilling to provoke the Western powers by pressing their advantage in the region too far. Britain and France had even laid siege to Russia's Black Sea ports in the **Crimean War** of 1854–56 in order to demonstrate their support for the Ottoman Empire – which they hoped would survive in its present form if only they could persuade it to introduce "reforms".

THE CONSTANTINOPLE CONFERENCE

In 1876, however, the **massacres** that followed the April Rising sent a wave of revulsion throughout Europe, and the Russian army prepared to teach the Turks a lesson. The British and French, faced by an angry public enraged by tales of Ottoman **atrocities** against Bulgarian civilians, were no longer in a position to back the Turks. The British tried to diffuse the situation by bringing the Turks to the negotiating table, but after assenting to the **Constantinople Conference** in November 1876, the Ottoman government rejected its draft proposals for an autonomous Bulgarian province.

The Russians were initially cautious about embarking on a war with Turkey because they feared an armed response from Austria. By the time the Constantinople Conference broke up, however, the Russians had reached a secret agreement with the Austrians; promising them Russian support for their claim to Bosnia-Hercegovina if they remained neutral in any Russo-Turkish conflict. Free to act, the Russian Tsar Alexander II (subsequently known to Bulgarians as **Tsar Osvoboditel** – the "Tsar-Liberator") declared war on Turkey in April 1877.

THE WAR OF LIBERATION

Romanians and Bulgarian volunteers fought alongside the Russians in the 1877–78 **War of Liberation**, which would have been a total rout had the Turks not fought belated rearguard actions at the siege of Plevna (modern-day Pleven) and the battle of the Shipka Pass.

The defeated Turks signed the **Treaty of San Stefano** in March 1878, recognizing an independent Bulgaria incorporating much of Macedonia and Thrace. This so-called "**Big Bulgaria**" was too much for the Western powers to swallow, and was promptly broken up by the speedily summoned **Congress of Berlin** (July 1878). The outcome of the Congress reflected the desire of British prime minister Benjamin Disraeli to "keep the Russians out of Turkey, not to create an ideal existence for Turkish Christians". Macedonia and southern Thrace were returned to the Turks, and the rest of Bulgaria was split into two chunks: land south of the Balkan Mountains became **Eastern Roumelia**, an autonomous province of the Ottoman Empire; while land to the north became an independent **Principality of Bulgaria** owing nominal suzerainty to the Turks and paying annual tribute to the sultan.

FROM INDEPENDENCE TO WORLD WAR II

In the immediate post-Liberation years, attempts to build a stable **democracy** in the principality were hampered by continuing Great Power interest in Balkan affairs. The Russians still regarded Bulgaria as a potential instrument of Tsarist policy, provoking tension between pro- and anti-Russian elements within the country itself.

Russian advisers were responsible for drafting an autocratic constitution for the fledgling state, but this was rejected by the Constituent Assembly which met at Târnovo in 1879.

Dominated by the Liberal Party (in which many leading lights of the liberation struggle were gathered), the Assembly drew up the so-called **Târnovo Constitution**, which envisaged a single chamber parliament elected by universal male suffrage. This went down badly with Bulgaria's newly chosen prince, the autocratically minded Alexander Battenberg (Aleksandâr Batenberg to the Bulgarians) – a German aristocrat who had served with the Russian army during the War of Liberation. The prince suspended the constitution and convened a special assembly in the Danubian town of Svishtov – which he blackmailed into voting him emergency powers by threatening to abdicate if they refused. To the new Russian Tsar, Alexander III (Alexander II had been murdered in March 1881), however, the German-speaking prince was a living reminder of Russia's humiliation at the Congress of Berlin. Eager to forge alliances with those in Bulgaria who were suspicious of Russian influence, Aleksandâr accepted a return to democratic government in 1883.

UNIFICATION – AND THE SERBO-BULGARIAN WAR

Many of the Liberal politicians who fled Aleksandâr's so-called **personal regime** ended up in Eastern Roumelia, which since 1878 had been ruled by local governor-generals eager to advance the Bulgarian cause in the region, despite its continuing status as a province of the Ottoman Empire. Growing popular agitation for **unification with Bulgaria** culminated in an uprising within Eastern Roumelia and the declaration of union in September 1885; a *fait accompli* that Turkey accepted after much sabre-rattling.

Serbia, offended that changes of Balkan borders could be made without its permission, and afraid that Bulgarian unification would be followed by territorial gains elsewhere, launched a punitive attack on Bulgaria – in the ensuing **Serbo-Bulgarian war of 1885** a ramshackle Bulgarian army successfully routed the Serbs at Slivnitsa.

INTERNATIONAL INTRIGUE

More serious, however, was the displeasure expressed by Russia at Bulgaria's failure to consult its big Slav cousin on the issue of unification. In a **turn-around of international attitudes**, Bulgarian expansion was now opposed by the Russians, because they were constrained by an agreement with Germany and Austria promising to preserve the status quo in the Balkans. The British, slowly becoming aware that Bulgaria wasn't necessarily the subservient Russian creature they had feared it to be, responded to Bulgarian unification with glee. The Russians withdrew their advisers and troops from Bulgaria, expecting the principality to collapse. When this didn't happen, pro-Russian officers in the Bulgarian army deposed Prince Aleksandâr and spirited him out of the country in 1886, before themselves falling victim to a counter-coup organized by leading Liberal politician **Stefan Stambolov**. Stambolov secured Aleksandâr's return, but the fawning way in which Aleksandâr attempted a reconciliation with the Russian Tsar enraged Stambolov, and the prince's position became so untenable that in September 1886 he was forced to abdicate. The Russians prepared to mount a takeover of Bulgaria but misjudged local opinion, parliamentary elections producing an anti-Russian, pro-Stambolov majority. Acting as the head of a **Council of Regents**, Stambolov attempted to sever the Russian connection entirely by realigning Bulgaria's foreign policy with Austria and Germany, and inviting the Habsburgs' favourite German toff **Ferdinand of Saxe-Coburg Gotha** to become the new monarch.

Stambolov, however, had to initiate a repressive regime in order to get these changes accepted by the country, and an **uprising by Russophile army officers** in 1887 was mercilessly supressed. Stambolov's **dictatorship** lasted until he was ditched by former protégé Ferdinand in 1894. Ferdinand sought a rapprochement with Russia, and set about creating a more **absolutist monarchy**. Stambolov, the only politician with the stature to challenge the court, was killed by Macedonian terrorists – possibly with Ferdinand's connivance – in 1895.

THE BALKAN WARS

By the turn of the century, growing turmoil in the Ottoman Empire left the Great Powers of Europe increasingly unable to control events in the region – however desperate they were to do so – giving the small states of the Balkans more room for independent action. Ferdinand exploited the chaos created by the **Young Turk** revolution in July 1908 to declare Bulgaria's full independence from Ottoman suzerainty, crowning himself **tsar** in the same year. Political crisis in the Ottoman lands meant that the future of **Macedonia and southern Thrace** was once more back on the agenda, and Bulgaria and its neighbours began discussing ways of driving the Turks from the area for good.

The **First Balkan War** of 1912 gave Bulgaria the chance it had been waiting for to try and reclaim some of the territories taken away by the Congress of Berlin. In alliance with Serbia and Greece, Bulgaria launched an attack on Turkey, coming within a whisker of capturing Istanbul. Bulgarian forces were so confident of capturing the city that Ferdinand ordered his state carriage to be sent to the front line so that he could enter the city in triumph – ultimately, bad weather and a cholera outbreak saved the Turks from defeat. Bulgarian troops succeeded in occupying the Pirin region of eastern Macedonia, but found that the Serbs and the Greeks had beaten them to the rest. Unable to agree on an equitable division of the spoils, the former allies fell out, Greece and Serbia defeating Bulgaria in the **Second Balkan War** of 1913.

Bulgaria was forced to renounce claims on the bulk of Macedonia and surrender the southern Dobrudzha to Romania, but still managed to finish the Balkan Wars with a positive balance. Allowed to keep the Pirin, it also obtained Thracian lands in the south, including access to the Aegean Sea at the port of Dedeagach (now the Greek town of Alexandroupolis).

WORLD WAR I

Following the outbreak of **World War I**, much of Bulgarian opinion sided with the Entente Powers of Britain, France and Russia, largely due to ties of Slavic kinship with the Russians and a common dislike of the Turks. However, the Entente's commitments to Bulgaria's major Balkan rival, Serbia, dissuaded Bulgaria from joining the alliance. Instead, German promises to restore **Macedonia** persuaded King Ferdinand and prime minister Radoslavov to enter the war on the side of the Central Powers.

Hoping to gain large amounts of territory at very little human cost, Bulgaria waited until September 1915 before joining the action, with Radoslavov confidently boasting to his compatriots that it would all be over by Christmas. Three years of agony ensued: anti-war politicians like the leader of the Agrarian Party, Stamboliiski, were jailed; and countless thousands of Bulgarians were dispatched to die in the trenches and mountains of Macedonia.

1918–1944

With the country bled white, Bulgaria's army collapsed beneath the Allied offensive along the Salonika front in September 1918. Deserting soldiers hoisted red flags and converged on Sofia, soon to proclaim the **"Radomir Republic"**, while the cabinet declared an **armistice** and released **Aleksandâr Stamboliiski**, hoping to avert a revolution. Though the mutineers were swiftly crushed, Ferdinand was forced to abdicate in favour of his son, **Boris III**, leaving Stamboliiski's **Bulgarian Agrarian National Union** or **BZNS** the most powerful force in the country.

The Agrarians emerged as the largest party in the 1919 election – the general desire for radical change was reflected in the fact that the Communists came second – and Stamboliiski became prime minister of a country whose wartime allegiance the Allies punished by the **Treaty of Neuilly** (1919). Under its terms, Bulgaria was bound to pay crippling war reparations, Romania reoccupied the southern Dobrudzha, Yugoslavia claimed most of Macedonia, while southwestern Thrace – and with it, access to the Aegean – went to Greece.

Unlike previous governments, the **Agrarians** favoured the countryside rather than the towns, exalting "peasant power" to the dismay of Bulgaria's traditional elite. The bourgeoisie became alarmed by Stamboliiski's dictatorial radicalism, and nationalists everywhere were outraged by his attempts to build peaceful relations with neighbouring Yugoslavia – a policy that entailed renouncing Bulgarian claims on Macedonia. Bulgaria had been flooded with Macedonian refugees since the end of the war, many of whom owed their allegiance to the **Internal Macedonian Revolutionary Organization**, or **IMRO** – a group committed to liberating Macedonia from Yugoslav control and therefore implacably opposed to Stamboliiski's new direction in foreign policy.

THE 1923 COUP

In June 1923, right-wing military officers supported by IMRO gunmen staged a bloody **coup d'état** against the Agrarians, assassinating Stamboliiski in the process. The reactionary **"Democratic Concord"** coalition under Aleksandâr Tsankov assumed power, which it monopolized until 1931. Having failed to come to Stamboliiski's aid in June, the **Communists** staged a hastily planned **uprising** in September 1923, provoking the army and police to savage repression and anti-Communist terror. The Communist Party was banned, and many of its leaders who fled to the Soviet Union later perished during the Stalinist *Ezhovshchina*, or "Great Purge".

THE 1930S

The Thirties were a time of stagnation and political unrest, epitomized by the murderous feuds within the IMRO. The June 1931 election brought to power a left-of-centre coalition, the "People's Bloc", but faced by the constraints of the **Great Depression**, the new government was unable to carry out its radical social programme. Economic slump provoked an increase in political extremism, which mirrored the growth of authoritarianism elsewhere in Europe. The Communists re-emerged in the shape of a front organization, the **Bulgarian Workers' Party**, banned by the government in 1932; while Aleksandâr Tsankov made up for the demise of the Democratic Concord by forming the Hitler-inspired **National Socialist Movement**.

Disintegration of the body politic encouraged the **Military League** to assume power in May 1934 in a coup inspired by the ideas of **Zveno** (Link), another elitist organization whose programme included the customary hotch-potch of militant left- and right-wing ideologies. Parliament was dissolved, all parties were abolished and the IMRO was brought to heel: Bulgaria was "depoliticized". But in government the League proved as faction-ridden and ineffectual as its civilian predecessors, and after November 1935 **Tsar Boris III** established his own **dictatorship**, periodically erecting a parliamentary facade.

WORLD WAR II

Nazi Germany's economic penetration of the Balkans during the late 1930s provided the Third Reich with considerable influence over Bulgaria and its neighbours, and despite the country's declaration of neutrality on the outbreak of **World War II**, Bulgaria inexorably succumbed to the Reich, which required it as a "land bridge" across which German troops could cross in order to mount the invasion of Greece. In return for Hitler's offer of Macedonia, Boris committed Bulgaria to the Axis in March 1941, although he baulked at declaring war on the Soviet Union due to Bulgaria's traditionally good relations with the Russian people (it was long believed that Boris' death, following a visit to Berlin, was the result of Nazi poisoning, although a team of pathologists examining the tsar's heart in 1991 finally put an end to these rumours).

Many Bulgarian Communists exiled in Moscow returned home to foment resistance, but Bulgaria's wartime **partisan movement** was a relatively small affair. However, the Communists did manage to infiltrate and manipulate other opposition groups, combining them into the **Fatherland Front** (*Ochestven Front*) in 1942. Events moved towards a climax with the Red Army's advance and Romania's escape from the Axis in August 1944. On September 8 the USSR declared war and crossed the Danube; that night, junior officers acting with the connivance of the minister of defence, Gregoriev, seized strategic points in Sofia, while partisan brigades swept down from the hills. This virtually bloodless putsch was repeated across Bulgaria the next day, making September 9 **Liberation Day**.

THE PEOPLE'S REPUBLIC

After September 9, the **Bulgarian Communist Party** emerged from two decades of clandestine existence to become the leading political force in the country. Initially their radicalism was hidden behind the ostensibly moderate **Fatherland Front government** fronted by political veteran Kimon Georgiev, principal architect of the 1934 coup. However, the Communist Party's domination of the Front was never in doubt. Manipulating the Ministries of Justice and the Interior to cow right-wing collaborators, and driving the left and centre parties into opposition by repeated provocations, the Party increased its membership from 15,000 to 250,000 in six months. Dominant in government, they then staged a referendum on the **monarchy**, abolished it, and proclaimed the **People's Republic** on September 15, 1946.

Now controlled by **Georgi Dimitrov**, **Vasil Kolarov** and **Anton Yugov**, the state apparatus

was turned against the opposition. Many of the political parties left outside the Communist-controlled Fatherland Front had boycotted Bulgaria's first postwar elections in 1945, convinced that the presence of the Red Army on Bulgarian soil would intimidate voters into backing the Front.

A more organized campaign was mounted for the general elections of October 1946, producing a parliament that included a small but vociferous number of anti-Communist MPs. The opposition centred around the Agrarian party or **BZNS**, heir to the popular radical tradition of Stamboliiski, and leaders of peasant resistance to enforced collectivization of the countryside. The Communists claimed that they were traitors sabotaging the economic recovery of the nation: hundreds of BZNS party workers were purged and their leader, **Nikola Petkov**, was hanged for "treason" after a show trial in 1947. Other parties outside the Front were snuffed out at the same time. The same year, Bulgaria acquired the new "Dimitrov" **Constitution** (modelled on the USSR's) and the **nationalization** of 2273 enterprises struck the "bourgeoisie" a mortal blow.

The following year saw a power struggle within the Party, largely over **economic links with the Soviet Union** and **relations with Tito's Yugoslavia**. The Tito-Stalin row of 1948 and Yugoslavia's subsequent expulsion from the Soviet camp gave Communist leaders everywhere the chance they needed to get rid of comrades who they found troublesome. Moscow-trained cadres targeted "homegrown" Communists – that is those who had chosen to remain in the country during the inter-war years rather than flee to the USSR – in an attempt to settle old scores.

Some of the more patriotic Bulgarian Communists criticized the terms of Bulgaro-Soviet trade (80 percent of Bulgaria's tobacco crop was purchased at below market prices and then undersold abroad), leaving themselves open to accusations of nationalism at a time when blind loyalty to the Soviet Union was the order of the day – as good a reason as any to launch a purge of "Titoists". Ten ministers, six Politburo members (including **Traicho Kostov**, shot after renouncing his "confession" to having been a fascist spy since 1942) and 92,500 lesser Party members were arrested or dismissed in the purge of 1948–49, while the nation was paralysed by **police terror**. Stalinism pervaded

Bulgaria, and for his total sycophancy the Party leader who succeeded Dimitrov, **Vâlko Chervenkov**, was dubbed "little Stalin".

THE ERA OF "SOCIALIST CONSTRUCTION"

With opposition both outside and inside the Party effectively crushed, the government could embark on the transformation of Bulgaria into a modern industrial state. Average Bulgarians, however, gained little from the first **Five-Year Plan**, though this gave a great boost to heavy industrial production (up 120 percent from 1949 to 1955). While factories mushroomed, workers were expected to meet ever-rising production targets, and consumer goods and foodstuffs grew increasingly scarce. Agricultural production remained at roughly its 1939 level, despite an increase in the population and Bulgaria's acquisition of the grain-producing southern Dobrudzha. Unlike elsewhere in Eastern Europe, there were few large estates to be expropriated – on the contrary, economists bemoaned the mass of smallholdings and the individualism of their owners.

Following the **death of Stalin** (1953), Moscow gradually withdrew support from hardliners in the satellite states, and advocates of less spartan policies replaced them. In Bulgaria, Chervenkov lost the position of Party Secretary (1954) and prime minister (1956) to **Todor Zhivkov** and Anton Yugov. The separation of these offices reflected the Kremlin's new policy of "collective" leadership, and Bulgaria's dutiful purge of "Anti-Party" elements in 1957 followed their example by avoiding bloodshed. China, however, seems to have inspired Zhivkov's sudden announcement of the "**Big Leap Forward**" in October 1958, whereby the economy aimed to fulfil the Five-Year Plan in three years, and smallholdings were pooled into 3290 **collective farms**. Industrial dislocation was considerable, but the effect on agriculture was mitigated by the private plots that peasants were allowed to retain – unlike in China, where famine followed Mao's Great Leap Forward.

THE ZHIVKOV ERA

For much of the **Zhivkov era**, Bulgarian conformity to Soviet wishes became a cliché of East European politics, with the country jokingly referred to – even by Bulgarians themselves – as the sixteenth republic of the USSR. However, this pliability did have its advantages: Bulgaria obtained cut-price Soviet oil, electricity and raw materials, and was relieved of the duty of hosting significant Soviet garrisons.

With access to education and employment consistently denied to people who failed to conform, most Bulgarians had no choice but to grudgingly accept rigid Party control of public life, although this passivity was made easier to bear by the Communist system's achievements in the social sphere. Given adequate food, guaranteed work, schooling and medical care, and the prospect of an apartment in the future, people were generally prepared to tolerate low wages, shortages of consumer goods and the lack of many liberal freedoms.

The West's image of Bulgaria under Zhivkov was almost wholly negative, coloured by the country's slavish adherence to Soviet foreign policy, and the fearsome reputation of the *Dârhavna Sigurnost* or **DS**, the state security police. The assassination of dissident writer **Georgi Markov**, who was killed after being stabbed by a poison-tipped umbrella on London's Waterloo Bridge in 1978, gave the Bulgarian security services a reputation for subterfuge and cruelty. Subsequent allegations that the DS had abetted a **plot to kill the pope** in 1981 suggested that Bulgaria did the kind of dirty work with which not even the KGB would wish to soil its hands.

However, it was the Party's manipulation of **nationalism** that seemed to Western eyes to be the most distasteful aspect of the regime. On the surface, attempts by the Party to present socialist Bulgaria as a homogeneous national state, the logical culmination of centuries of struggles for freedom, seemed to start off innocently enough. Vast amounts of money were spent on the monuments and festivities celebrating the **1300th anniversary of the founding of the Bulgarian state** in 1983, and resources were channelled into the restoration of historical monuments associated with Bulgaria's past greatness.

However, there wasn't much room in Zhivkov's Bulgaria for people of different ethnic origin. Ever since the 1950s smaller minorities like the Vlachs (see p.168) and Islamicized Gypsies had been encouraged to drop their traditional names and adopt Bulgarian ones. The campaign moved on to the **pomaks** (Muslim Bulgarians) in the 1970s, and to the million-strong **Turkish minority** in the 1980s. Those who refused to Bulgaricize their names were refused work, housing, or worse still, sent to concentration camps such as Belene and Lovech. Opposition to the **name-changing campaign** sparked violence in 1984, and led to a mass exodus of Bulgarian Turks in summer 1989, provoking outrage from human rights groups across the world. All this led to a further deterioration of relations between Bulgaria and the outside world – even Bulgaria's socialist allies were increasingly embarrassed to be associated with it.

THE DEMISE OF THE COMMUNIST REGIME

Bulgaria's socialist economy was beginning to stall well before the emergence of **perestroika** in the Soviet Union began to raise fundamental questions about the continuing viability of the whole system. Summer droughts in 1984 and 1985 had harmed agriculture and reduced hydroelectric power (which usually accounts for much of Bulgaria's needs) at a time when Soviet oil supplies were cut back, causing widespread energy shortages. Prices skyrocketed with hardly any corresponding wage increases, and for the first time in many years a note of testiness entered Bulgaro-Soviet relations.

As Gorbachev increasingly toyed with the idea of wide-reaching democratic reform in the USSR, the hard-line leaders of his Soviet bloc allies became more and more of an embarrassment. Zhivkov was particularly unpopular with the new Soviet leadership, not least because they found his anti-Turkish policies repugnant. Aware of this, high-ranking Bulgarian officials began jostling for position in preparation for the day when they could (perhaps with Gorbachev's backing) oust their aging leader. However, they had to wait until the end of the decade for their opportunity to do so, by which time they were almost as discredited as he was.

THE JULY CONCEPTIONS

The Bulgarian Communist Party's initial reaction to Gorbachev's innovations was predictably cautious, and it wasn't until July 1987 that Zhivkov announced the **July Conceptions**, an attempt to give the Party a patina of perestroika-esque credibility. Although it promised decentralization of state-run businesses and democratization of party structures, it was difficult to find examples of these fine-sounding commitments ever being carried out.

By January 1988 Bulgarians were being allowed to form private firms providing that they employed no more than ten people, and the government increasingly advocated a departure from rigid state planning and a tentative move towards **market economics**. Enthusiasm for political change continued to be lukewarm, however, and for some time Bulgarians moved in a strange political limbo, where talk of glasnost and perestroika was officially sanctioned, but any practical application of them merely invited the usual hassles from the security police.

PROTEST

Ecological protesters from the city of **Ruse** were the first independent citizens to organize themselves into pressure groups outside Party control in spring 1988. Encouraged by their example, intellectuals in Sofia formed the **Club for the Support of Glasnost and Perestroika** in November of the same year, an organization that united both dissidents and moderate Party members, but the Club's supporters were subjected to petty harassment, denied meeting space and forbidden to use photocopiers.

The Communist Party itself was split between those around Zhivkov who favoured caution, and those eager to rush ahead with political change. Throughout 1989 opposition organizations like **Podkrepa**, the new independent trade union federation formed in February 1989, and **Ecoglasnost**, a green pressure group (which did much to unite disparate strands of the opposition around a cause which they could all share), were allowed to operate after a fashion, but their members never knew from one day to the next what the precise limits to their political freedom were. As the year progressed Zhivkov attempted to win support by stoking up nationalist fervour, with renewed repression of Bulgaria's Turks. The resulting **mass exodus** of Bulgarian Muslims into neighbouring Turkey merely served to convince many in the country that the Communist regime had finally lost all legitimacy to rule.

THE FALL OF ZHIVKOV

In October 1989 Sofia's police were still beating up members of Ecoglasnost with impunity on the capital's streets, but in the end the forces of conservatism were overtaken by events. On **November 10, 1989** (the day after the Berlin

Wall came down) reformers within the Party seized their chance and called a meeting of the Central Committee, which forced Zhivkov's resignation. The former dictator was arrested on charges of inciting racial hatred and, soon afterwards, embezzling state funds; new Party leader **Petâr Mladenov** promised free elections, market reforms, and an end to the corruption and gangsterism of the past. Opposition leaders took advantage of the new atmosphere to form the **SDS** or *Sâyuz na demokratichnite sili* (Union of Democratic Forces) on December 7, an impressive assemblage of dissidents, greens and human rights activists which non-Communist Bulgarians everywhere pressed forward to join.

POST-COMMUNIST BULGARIA: A SLOW START

The reformist wing of the Bulgarian Communist Party had obviously thought that by ditching Zhivkov and committing themselves to the idea of a multi-party system, they stood a good chance of being perceived as the authors of democratic change, thereby winning back the trust of the populace. Initially, however, their strategy ran into trouble. Throughout December 1989 the Bulgarian parliament was regularly under siege from protesters demanding a speeding up of democratic reforms, most notably the abandonment of the Communist Party's **leading role** in society, hitherto enshrined in the constitution. The Party was also under pressure from its own hardliners, who tried to sabotage democratization by organizing **nationalist demonstrations and strikes** throughout the country in protest at the government's retreat from Todor Zhivkov's anti-Turkish policies.

In 1990 the dismantling of Communist power structures began in earnest. Separation of party and state was symbolized when Petâr Mladenov became state president and relinquished the Party chairmanship to **Aleksandâr Lilov**, previously the victim of one of Zhivkov's purges. Former hardliners were removed from government, Mladenov's protégé **Andrei Lukanov** became prime minister, and the Party itself changed its name to the **Bulgarian Socialist Party (BSP)**.

Multi-party elections were called for **June 1990**, too early for either the BSP or the opposition SDS to establish themselves as credible

democratic movements. The BSP, despite verbal commitments to democratic socialism, still included far too many dyed-in-the-wool Communists for people to take its new identity seriously; while the SDS, a loose coalition of newly formed parties and citizens' pressure groups, could agree on little save for a hatred of Communism and a desire to speed up market reforms.

Public uncertainty over the economic changes proposed by the SDS played into the hands of the BSP, which garnered 45 percent of the vote and an absolute majority in the *Veliko Narodno Sâbranie* or **Constituent Assembly**. Much of this success was attributed to the conservative nature of the Bulgarian countryside, where the Socialist Party machine was far more effective in reaching potential voters than its cash-starved opponents. The other main beneficiary of the poll was the **Movement for Rights and Freedoms** – *Dvizhenieto za prava i svobodi* or **DPS**. Formed to protect Bulgaria's Muslims, the DPS gained solid support from the country's Turks and *pomaks*, giving it 23 MPs in the new chamber. However, Bulgaria's urban population had voted en masse for the SDS, and many suspected that the BSP's majority had been artificially inflated by **vote rigging**.

THE SUMMER OF 1990 – AND AFTER

The SDS leadership was split on the issue of whether to accept the election result or stage some kind of protest, but the potentially volatile nature of Bulgarian society persuaded them to refrain from anything that might provoke violence. Nevertheless, **discontent** smouldered on throughout June, with regular street demonstrations in the capital, and student-manned **barricades** going up outside Sofia University. Frustration at the BSP's victory boiled over with the discovery of an old **video tape** that showed President Mladenov threatening to use tanks against opposition demonstrators in Sofia the previous December. Mass meetings called for his resignation, a demand echoed by Socialist Party members themselves after an expert panel of video-watchers pronounced the recording to be genuine.

Mladenov bowed to pressure and resigned on July 7, but this only encouraged further demonstrations by opposition groups dissatisfied with the slow pace of change. In Sofia, university lecturers and students established the "**City of Truth**" – a tent settlement near the mausoleum of Communist Bulgaria's founder, Georgi Dimitrov – to demand a removal of all former Communist MPs and a speeding-up of the criminal proceedings against Todor Zhivkov. Similar "cities" soon sprang up in provincial capitals. In the meantime, **conservative forces** egged on by hardline Communists continued to protest against the new freedom accorded to Bulgaria's ethnic Turks, outraged by the thought that national unity might be compromised by the presence of Turkish deputies in parliament.

By the time the Constituent Assembly convened in Veliko Târnovo in mid-July, political authority within the country was in a serious state of disintegration, prompting dark rumours of a return to hardline government with possible help from the military. The Assembly's first and most urgent task was to elect a new president who could somehow hold the country together. Despite their parliamentary majority, BSP MPs realized that they would provoke serious divisions in the country if they opted for one of their own candidates, but they were initially unwilling to accept anyone put forward by the opposition. After more than a month of deadlock, however, the Assembly awarded the presidency to the leader of the SDS, **Zhelyu Zhelev**, a respected dissident academic who had been sent into internal exile by the former regime for writing a book entitled *What is Fascism* – a work that embarrassed Bulgaria's erstwhile rulers by demonstrating the similarity between both left- and right-wing forms of totalitarianism.

Zhelev faced a potentially dangerous breakdown in public order almost immediately upon his election. A decision by parliament ordering the removal of Communist symbols from all public buildings was interpreted by the Sofia mob as an invitation to **set fire** to the Socialist (Communist) **Party headquarters** – where a big red star was prominently displayed – on August 26. Socialist Party bosses exploited the situation by accusing the opposition of unleashing the forces of "neo-fascism", and it was rumoured that Podkrepa-leader and SDS-ally Konstantin Trenchev had encouraged the violence. Zhelev established his presidential impartiality by swiftly denouncing the vandals, and things began to calm down. The "Cities of Truth" were dismantled by opposition activists as a sign that the tactics of political confronta-

tion had, for the time being, been abandoned.

Plummeting confidence in the socialist system had, however, produced a crisis in the Bulgarian **economy**. The cabinet of BSP prime minister Andrei Lukanov courted the likes of Robert Maxwell in an attempt to attract foreign investment into the country, but unwillingness to adopt necessary market reforms soon led to the government's collapse. Made nervous by a nationwide wave of **strikes** and **student protests**, the socialist-dominated Assembly consented to the formation of a **coalition government** in December 1990. Led by non-party lawyer Dimitâr Popov and including SDS members in the key ministries of industry and finance, the new administration was charged with the task of speeding up the transition to capitalism and preparing the ground for **new elections**. Stiff medicine was applied to the Bulgarian economy with the **liberation of prices** in February 1991. Subsequent massive inflation and high interest rates caused bankruptcies, growing unemployment, and widespread **social misery**.

OCTOBER 1991 AND AFTER

As the **elections of October 1991** approached, Bulgarian society appeared to be as divided as at any time in its history. The most visible results of post-Zhivkov change – rising prices, declining social services, and the ostentation of those who grew fat on the proceeds of private enterprise – were an affront to people on fixed incomes, especially pensioners and employees of ailing state firms. The BSP tapped these resentments by proposing a slowed-down model of economic reform and the retention of some measure of state planning. More ominously, the BSP increasingly posed as the party of **discipline and order** to Bulgarians left bewildered by collapsing public morals (a huge rise in crime had accompanied the decay of the Communist system); and exploited the nationalist sentiments of those disquieted by the sudden appearance of Bulgaria's Muslims as important players on the political scene. By emphasizing the need for **national unity**, the socialists seemed to be offering a return to the certainties of the past. For the SDS and other non-socialists, however, Bulgaria's salvation depended on a further **purge of Communist influence**, and the wholesale adoption of a **free market** – whatever the social cost.

There was clearly an anti-socialist majority in the country, but **political infighting** threatened to destroy the opposition's chances of victory. Dismayed by the motley collection of right-wingers, monarchists and messianic capitalists increasingly drawn into the fringes of the SDS, Social Democrat and Green splinter groups left to form mini-SDS coalitions of their own. The presence of two **Agrarian parties** (the *Unified BZNS* and the *BZNS-Nikola Petkov*, both of which claimed descent from the *BZNS* originally created by the great Agrarian leader Aleksandâr Stamboliiski) split the anti-socialist vote even further.

In the end the election was a **close-run thing**. The SDS received 34 percent of the vote and 110 seats in the new 240-seat Assembly; the BSP 33 percent and 106 seats; the DPS 7.5 percent and 24 seats. All other parties failed to exceed the 4 percent barrier necessary for representation in parliament. Despite the narrow margin of victory, the result was hailed as a turning-point in Bulgarian history by the BSP's opponents – but claims that Bulgarian socialism had been finally laid to rest proved to be premature.

The new government of prime minister **Filip Dimitrov** initiated a crash programme of economic reform, removing barriers to foreign investment, speeding up the **privatization** of state-run firms, and establishing the ground rules for *restitutsiya* or "**restitution**" – the process by which property and land nationalized by the Communists could be reclaimed by its former owners. Public spending was slashed and wages in the state sector were held down, producing much social hardship and polarizing the country even further. The winter of 1991/92 was characterized by extensive **power cuts**, after former Soviet republics began to demand hard currency for the electricity they used to supply so cheaply.

The first challenge to the post-socialist order came in the **presidential elections** of January 1992, when Zhelyu Zhelev only narrowly beat off the challenge of BSP-sponsored candidate Velko Vâlkanov. As well as pointing to declining living standards, Vâlkanov had exploited growing unease about alleged "Turkish" influence in Bulgarian affairs resulting from the DPs' central position in political life.

President Zhelev was also being targeted by the anti-Communist coalition that had brought him to power. Zhelev was keen to heal the rifts in Bulgarian society by encouraging a smooth and painless transition from socialism to capitalism, and right-wing members of the SDS, emboldened by their grip on government, were frustrated by Zhelev's oppositon to wholesale change. The president became embroiled in a niggardly power struggle with former protégé Filip Dimitrov, and the latter began to remove Zhelev's allies from top government posts.

Disillusionment with Zhelev led to a reawakening of interest in a return to **monarchy**. Many Bulgarians believed that **Simeon**, the Madrid-based son of Tsar Boris III, would be an ideal figurehead capable of healing some of Bulgarian society's wounds: having lived in exile for the last 45 years, Simeon was entirely uncompromised by any involvement in contemporary Bulgarian politics. There was also a strong legalistic argument in his favour: the referendum that had abolished the monarchy in 1946 had been rigged by the Communists and was therefore – according to some – null and void.

Throughout 1992 the economic reform programme had done little to improve living standards for the bulk of the population. In order to demonstrate that Bulgaria's economic collapse was the fault of the outgoing regime rather than the ruling SDS, the government developed a new taste for **anti-Communist witch hunts**. Throughout the summer the SDS newspaper *Demokratsiya* ran daily articles detailing the activities of former Communist functionaries, who allegedly emptied state coffers in order to provide themselves with country villas, luxury cars, and expense-account trips abroad.

August 1992 saw the court appearances of Todor Zhivkov, as well as former prime ministers Georgi Atanasov and Andrei Lukanov, to answer charges of **embezzlement** – Zhivkov himself was sentenced to a seven-year prison term, which he was allowed to serve under house arrest. Dossiers on their more serious misdemeanours – responsibility for concentration camps, repression of ethnic Turks, and so on – soon got bogged down in legalistic wrangling.

Failure to win an **outright majority** in October 1991 had left the SDS dependent on the support of the predominantly Turkish DPS in order to remain in government. However, the SDS's drift to the right put this relationship under increasing strain. Ultimately, the Dimitrov government's reluctance to give aid to the economically depressed tobacco-producing regions of the south – where much of the DPS's bedrock support comes from – led to a split.

Without DPS support Dimitrov lost a parliamentary vote of confidence in December 1992, and President Zhelev called upon economist Lyuben Berov to form an administration of non-party technocrats. Although Berov promised to continue the market reforms of the SDS while trying to limit their more socially harmful consequences, it was clear that Bulgaria's push towards capitalism had been put on hold.

Despite successfully renegotiating Bulgaria's foreign debt repayments with major international creditors, the Berov government did little to tackle the problems dominating the minds of most Bulgarians: declining living standards, mass unemployment and rising crime. Supported unenthusiastically by a parliamentary majority comprising the DPS, breakaway members of the SDS, and all but the extreme left of the BSP, the Berov cabinet limped on until September 1994 when it was replaced by another caretaker administration headed by presidential protégée Reneta Indzhova.

TOWARDS THE WINTER OF DISCONTENT

The SDS suffered a humiliating defeat in the parliamentary **elections of December 1994**, which gave the rejuvenated BSP an absolute majority in the National Assembly. Led by the young and popular Zhan Videnov, the BSP was by now an odd grouping of genuine social democrats, old-style Communists, and out-and-out careerists, supported by industrial workers, pensioners and rural Bulgarians bewildered by the changes of the last few years. The BSP continued the cautious policies of the Berov government, indexing pensions and industrial wages to the rate of inflation and devaluing the lev in the hope of kickstarting Bulgaria's moribund economy with an export boom.

Privatization of Bulgaria's state-owned industries moved at a snail's pace, prompting the government's critics to claim that most big enterprises were being run down prior to being sold off cheaply to former Communist functionaries. Indeed, the relationship between Bulgaria's emerging business class and the old political elite raised a few eyebrows. Considerable popular resentment was directed towards members of the old regime who were able to build up sizeable reserves of hard currency in foreign bank acounts in the late 1980s, and then return to buy into the country's economy.

The BSP's dominance of Bulgarian politics was confirmed by the local elections of November 1995, when 80 percent of Bulgaria's towns and cities elected socialist councils. Sofia, Plovdiv, Stara Zagora and Varna were the only major urban areas to remain in SDS hands.

Ultimately, though, the Videnov administration was brought down by its own economic incompetence. Market reforms ground to a standstill, and all levels of the economy became infected with corruption – often with government connivance. BSP elder statesman Andrei Lukanov – who had himself become a byword for shady dealings – was gunned down by mystery assailants in October 1996 for threatening to blow the whistle on government corruption. As **winter 1996** approached, foreign investors fled the country, the lev plummeted against the dollar, and food shortages re-emerged. With the government unable to meet its foreign debt repayments, and unwilling to introduce the economic austerity programme demanded of it by the IMF, Videnov resigned in December, ushering in a period of acute instability.

The BSP had already lost the initiative following the presidential elections of November 1996, when Zhelev had been replaced by the SDS lawyer **Petâr Stoyanov**. However they still tried to cling to parliamentary power, refusing to yield to opposition demands for fresh elections. With the economy getting worse, a wave of anti-government demonstrations swept the country, and with SDS-inspired crowds mounting an assault on parliament in mid-January 1997, the BSP finally threw in the towel. A caretaker administration under Stefan Sofianski (the popular SDS mayor of Sofia) took over, and a general election called for the beginning of April. The SDS won by a landslide, with suave technocrat **Ivan Kostov** becoming prime minister.

INTO THE NEW MILLENNIUM

Bulgaria's **economy**, however, has been left in such bad shape by the departing administration that the new government has had little choice but to swallow the medicine offered by the IMF – now the real power in Bulgarian affairs. A programme of economic austerity and speedy privatization is in place, with inflation being kept in check by pegging the lev to the Deutschmark. While restoring public confidence in the government, these measures haven't yet resulted in an improvement in the living standards of the majority of the Bulgarians, who continue to eke out a living on meagre wages.

Western investors, however, have been encouraged by the new government's **anti-corruption drives**, although the big business interests under investigation have tended to be those linked to the BSP rather than the SDS. With Bulgarian political parties still lacking a solid class base, however, it seems likely that the country's leaders will continue to cultivate the backing of powerful business cliques and post-Communist clan networks in order to stay in power, thereby hampering the development of a smoothly functioning liberal state.

BULGARIA'S POSITION IN THE WORLD

Before the removal of **Cold War certainties**, Bulgaria's priorities were close links with the USSR and the maintenance of strong defences against nearby NATO countries Turkey and Greece. After November 1989 Bulgaria was free to develop relations with its Balkan neighbours regardless of ideological constraints, but the situation was complicated both by worsening conditions in Yugoslavia and political infighting at home.

In the immediate post-Communist period, the SDS, along with most Bulgarians, understandably sought **closer relations with the USA and Western Europe**, convinced that financial and moral support from the leading capitalist nations would ease Bulgaria's transition to democracy. Most importantly, it was thought that Bulgaria's position in the Balkans – with a chaotic situation in Yugoslavia to the west and two quarrelsome NATO members, Turkey and Greece, to the south – would oblige the

Western powers to give top priority to the cultivation of a stable Bulgaria. In the event, Western policy in the Balkans remained confused, and Western investment in the Bulgarian economy never lived up to expectations.

With the BSP victory of 1994, attitudes to foreign policy became more conservative, and traditional links with Russia were renewed, only for the pendulum to swing back after January 1997. Fondness for Russia and suspicion of the West, however, remains a powerful emotional draw – not least because of the prominent, and often unpopular, role played by the IMF in Bulgaria's domestic affairs.

The **war in Yugoslavia** disrupted much of Bulgaria's trade with the rest of Europe, and despite improved links with Turkey and Greece, Bulgaria has become increasingly isolated economically. The SDS government elected in April 1997 considered membership of NATO and the EU as central planks of its long-term programme, but little progress has been made on either front. There's a growing fear that, while Poland, the Czech Republic and Hungary are being prepared for future incorporation into the trade structures of the European Union, Bulgaria (along with Albania and Serbia) has been relegated to the second division of post-Communist states, with little immediate prospect of promotion.

Bulgaria's frustration with Europe is compounded by the fact that most ordinary Bulgarians now find it very difficult to travel to the West. Member states of the European Union, fearing a flood of economic migrants from Eastern Europe, have tightened up border controls considerably. Not only do Bulgarian citizens need a visa (bought, of course, in hard currency) to enter the EU, but also need to provide exhaustive details of their travelling itinerary, together with proof that they have enough money to afford the trip. For many, the concept of "Europe" is as distant now as it was during the era of the Iron Curtain.

THE MACEDONIAN QUESTION

The name "Macedonia" is a geographical term of long standing, applied to an area that has always been populated by a variety of races and cultures. For centuries an area of discord between Balkan peoples, it's currently divided between three states – Bulgaria, Greece, and the Former Yugoslav Republic of Macedonia (FYROM) – each of which has deep-seated historical reasons for regarding the Macedonian name and the Macedonian heritage as something exclusively its own. Bulgaria has gone to war over Macedonia three times this century, only to end up on the losing side on each occasion. As a symbol of the nation's unfulfilled destiny in the Balkans, Macedonia continues to occupy an important place in the Bulgarian psyche.

HISTORICAL MACEDONIA

The original **kingdom of Macedonia**, which reached its zenith in the fourth century BC under Philip II and Alexander the Great, was governed by Greek-speaking kings and inhabited – from what historians can gather – by a predominantly Greek-speaking population. Its early borders spread from Mt Olympus in the south to the upper Vardar basin in the north, and it was this core area that provided the basis for the subsequent **Roman province of Macedonia**, although the region was carved up into different administrative units during the Byzantine period. The name Macedonia faded from people's consciousness during the Middle Ages, only to be resurrected from the Renaissance onwards by West European geographers and diplomats eager to give the area a convenient geographical label. The ethnic composition of the area was in any case constantly changing (in ancient times Greeks lived cheek-by-jowl with Thracians and Illyrians, and from the sixth century onwards they were increasingly joined by **Slavonic tribes**), so there was never really any ethnic or political continuity between the Macedonia of the ancients and the Macedonia of the modern era.

Under **Ottoman rule** Macedonia was known officially as the "**Three Provinces**", with administrative centres at Thessaloniki, Skopje and Monastir (present-day Bitola in the Former Yugoslav Republic of Macedonia). Turn-of-the-century Macedonia was one of the most cosmopolitan regions of the empire, peopled by Slavs, Greeks, Turks, Albanians and Jews. Cities like Thessaloniki were centres of **revolutionary intrigue**, rocked not only by the increasing national consciousness of the subject peoples of the empire, but also by Turkish reform movements that hoped to liberalize the archaic institutions of the Ottoman state.

In the late nineteenth century the newly independent **nation-states** of Greece, Serbia and Bulgaria each coveted Macedonian territory, but their claims were complicated by the confused ethnic map of the area. The races who lived here didn't inhabit clearly defined geographical units: towns with predominantly Greek or Turkish populations were often surrounded by exclusively Slav or Albanian rural areas. To make matters worse, people were also divided along **religious lines**. Local Slavs who had converted to Islam in the fifteenth century (known hereabouts as *pomaks*, *torbeshes* or *poturs*, they're still very much in evidence) often identified with Macedonia's Turks and Albanians more strongly than with the Christian Slavs. It's not surprising, therefore, that the Greek, Albanian and Slav **armed bands** that roamed the countryside in the early years of this century were often implacably opposed to each other – each fighting for a "Free Macedonia" that would exclude the national aspirations of its rivals.

Education was one way in which the struggle for the allegiances of the Macedonian people was waged. By raising money to establish schools in the area, Bulgarian, Serb and Greek cultural societies could impose modern **literary languages** on people whose patchwork of regional dialects had hitherto confused their sense of ethnic belonging. Macedonia's Slavs, who were concentrated in the north of the region, but also formed substantial communities in the south along the Aegean seaboard, spoke a language grammatically very close to Bulgarian, but local dialects often shaded into neighbouring Serbian. Both states were eager to claim the Macedonian Slavs as their own; provoking the formation of the Bulgarian **SS Cyril and Methodius Society** and the Serbian

MACEDONIA

SERBIA

Sofia

Shar Mts

Kyustendil

BULGARIA

Skopje

Blagoevgrad (Gorna Dzhumaya)

Pirin Mountains

Veles

R. Struma

Debar

REPUBLIC OF MACEDONIA

Gotse Delchev

R Vardar

Strumitsa

Melnik

Ohrid

Bitola (Monastir)

Petrich

ALBANIA

Dhrama

Serres

N

Thessaloniki

0   100 m

Mt Olympus

GREECE

– – – Modern State borders

☐ The historic region of Macedonia

Society of St Sava in the 1880s, both of which intended to carry out educational work throughout the province and win local hearts and minds.

THE BULGARIAN CLAIM

It's axiomatic to Bulgarian thinking that the Slavs who inhabit Macedonia are, in fact, Bulgarians. They speak the same language (or at the very least, a dialect exceedingly close to it), and are descended from tribes that came to the Balkans at around the same time.

In the medieval period Macedonia was closely linked to Bulgaria, thus bolstering the latter's **historical claims** to the area. Northern Macedonia was conquered by the Bulgar Khans in the ninth century, and remained within the orbit of the First Bulgarian Kingdom until 1218, when the western Macedonian town of **Ohrid** – by that time the Bulgarian capital – finally fell to the Byzantines.

Under the Second Bulgarian Kingdom (1185–1396) things were more confused, with the emergent power of **Serbia** increasingly extending its influence in the area in the 1300s. The central Macedonian town of Skopje was briefly the capital of the greatest of medieval Serbia's rulers, **Tsar Dušan**. The feudal principalities into which Macedonia fragmented immediately before the **Ottoman conquest** are claimed by both Serbian and Bulgarian historians as their own; and the Macedonian-based **Krali Marko**, a semi-legendary figure who fought vainly to stem the Turkish advance, is a popular figure in the folk literature of both countries – an example of how modern ideas of ethnicity don't always conform to the complex racial mix which prevailed over much of medieval Europe.

Under Turkish rule links between Bulgaria and Macedonia remained strong. The needs of Bulgaria's Christian population were served by the **Archbishopric of Ohrid**, a town which became synonymous with Bulgarian spirituality and learning, until the Church was eventually placed under the jurisdiction of Constantinople in 1767.

During Bulgaria's nineteenth-century **National Revival**, Bulgarians and Macedonians shared a common upsurge in Orthodox culture and art. Woodcarvers from **Debâr** in west Macedonia, an area famed for its craft traditions, worked in churches throughout Bulgaria. Bulgaria's struggle to free ecclesiastical affairs from the control of the Greek Patriarchate was accompanied by assumptions that any future

Bulgarian Church would extend to cover the Orthodox Slavs of Macedonia as well. When the Ottoman authorities acquiesced to the creation of an autonomous **Bulgarian Exarchate** in 1870 they included within it much of central Macedonia, and promised that it would have jurisdiction over any other areas where at least two-thirds of the population voted to join. Those around Skopje, Ohrid and Bitola did so – a move regarded by the Bulgarians as an implicit recognition of their claims to the region.

Bulgarian designs on Macedonia found a powerful sponsor in the shape of **tsarist Russia**. After the Russo-Turkish War of 1877–78 the Ottomans agreed to the creation of an independent Bulgarian state, which included the lion's share of Macedonia, at the **Treaty of San Stefano**. This didn't just antagonize the many non-Slav nations who lived within the borders of this so-called "Big Bulgaria" – it also struck fear into the hearts of the European Great Powers, who saw the new country as a vehicle for Russian ambitions in the Balkans. The subsequent **Berlin Congress** promptly returned Macedonia to the Turkish Empire, on the condition that the Ottoman authorities carried out a vague programme of "reforms". The Bulgarians have always regarded the Berlin Congress as a cynical move to frustrate their legitimate national aspirations, and the desire to regain control of Macedonia has been a recurring theme in Bulgarian politics ever since.

MACEDONIAN REVOLUTIONARY POLITICS: THE IMRO

Whatever the peoples of Macedonia felt about the idea of being incorporated into a "Big Bulgaria", most of them were pretty unhappy to find themselves once again languishing within the borders of the decaying Ottoman Empire. The ensuing frustration helped to fuel a growing **Macedonian separatist movement**, characterized by a plethora of clandestine groups who specialized in terrorist action and political assassination. Most influential of these was the *Vâtreshnata Makedonska revolutsiyonna organizatsiya* or **Internal Macedonian Revolutionary Organization** – more commonly known by the acronym of *VMRO* or **IMRO** – founded by schoolteachers **Gotse Delchev** and **Dame Gruev** in Thessaloniki in 1893.

Inspired by Bulgarian freedom fighters like Vasil Levski and Hristo Botev, and adopting the "Liberty or Death" slogan beloved of Bulgarian

insurgents, the IMRO clearly saw themselves as the inheritors of the **Bulgarian revolutionary tradition**. Although the IMRO's early leaders undoubtedly considered themselves to be ethnically Bulgarian, none of them thought that Macedonia's interests would be served by straightforward incorporation into Bulgaria.

Delchev, a committed republican, was disillusioned by post-Liberation Bulgaria's degeneration into monarchical dictatorship, and saw the creation of an **autonomous Macedonia** within some future **Balkan federation** as the best possible antidote to the wave of authoritarianism currently sweeping the infant nation-states of the region. Together with other IMRO leaders, Delchev also judged the development of a specifically Macedonian political identity to be the best way of winning support from Europe's Great Powers – who were for once united in their suspicion of Bulgarian expansionism in the area.

Delchev and Gruev therefore set about creating a clandestine organization within Macedonia itself in order to ensure the movement's independence from Bulgarian government interference. However, many of the **Macedonian emigrants** who found refuge in Sofia after the Berlin Congress began to look towards the Bulgarian state as their most likely means of liberation. In the 1880s and 1890s up to a third of Bulgaria's army oficers and civil servants were from Macedonia, and links between government circles and Macedonian émigré organizations were strong. Most influential of the Macedonian organizations within Bulgaria was the **Supreme Macedonian Committee** (whose members came to be known as the *vârhovisti*, or **Supremists**), a Sofia-based group that worked closely with the Bulgarian court. Jealous of the IMRO's influence within Macedonia itself, the Supremists set out to gain control of the Macedonian freedom movement for themselves.

Supporters of both IMRO and the Supremists began to infiltrate each other's organizations, and Macedonian activists became increasingly **split** – between those who saw Macedonia as an entity in its own right and those who favoured its incorporation into Bulgaria. These two strands in the Macedonian revolutionary tradition were exploited by future Bulgarian and Yugoslav governments, each eager to secure historical legitimacy for their diametrically opposed policies in the region.

THE ILINDEN UPRISING

IMRO leaders particularly resented incursions by Supremist-sponsored armed bands into Ottoman territory. Ill-starred adventures such as the **occupation of Melnik** in 1896 and the attempted **uprising** in **Gorna Dzhumaya** (now Blagoevgrad) in 1902 merely served to provoke Ottoman repression and hamper the work of the underground IMRO network within Macedonia. Eager to demonstrate their independence from the Sofia-based Supremists, and fearful that a reform programme forced on Turkey by the Great Powers might take the limelight away from the revolutionary movement, the IMRO opted to launch a premature and hurriedly planned uprising. Leaders like Delchev were against the idea, but eventually had to go along with the argument that the IMRO needed to do something in order to regain the initiative in the anti-Ottoman struggle.

Named **Ilinden** (St Elijah's Day) after the day on which it was launched – August 2, 1903 – the uprising was centred on the town of Krushevo high in the mountains southwest of Skopje. Intended as a beacon of hope to the surrounding populace, the so-called **Krushevo Republic** fell in a matter of weeks.

Fierce Ottoman reprisals followed, and surviving IMRO members retreated into despair and impotence. Gotse Delchev had been killed three months before the uprising in a chance run-in with police, and Dame Gruev fell three years later in an isolated guerrilla action. The IMRO itself was increasingly divided into left- and right-wing factions. The left, led by **Yane Sandanski** (after whom one of Bulgaria's Pirin towns is named), argued that the movement had to stop being an exclusively Slav organization and seek alliances with Macedonia's other ethnic groups, while the right sought better relations with the Bulgarian government. Sandanski, who ordered the murder of one of IMRO's most flamboyant leaders Boris Sarafov, found his ideas rejected by the majority, and was himself assassinated by IMRO rivals in 1915. With the bitter failure of Ilinden still hanging over the IMRO, power increasingly passed into the hands of the right wing of the organization.

FROM THE BALKAN WARS TO WORLD WAR II

In the aftermath of Ilinden, Serbian organizations had taken advantage of IMRO's failure by flooding the area with cultural workers and priests. The government in Sofia increasingly sought a rapprochement with Serbia in order to preserve what was left of Bulgarian influence in Macedonia. Planning a joint attack on Turkey, the two states agreed in March 1912 to split Macedonia between them, with Bulgaria being promised the west-central portion around Bitola and Ohrid. Greece joined the alliance soon afterwards, and in the **First Balkan War** of 1912, Greek and Serbian troops occupied most of Macedonia, while the bulk of the Bulgarian army was tied up fighting the Turks in the east. The Serbs were particularly unwilling to give up any portion of land thus acquired: the creation of an independent state of Albania had frustrated Serbian dreams of westward expansion, and so Macedonia – renamed "**South Serbia**" by government propagandists – became a legitimate target of Serbia's imperialist ambitions.

Bulgaria protested, but its attempt to drive its erstwhile allies from the region in the **Second Balkan War** of 1913 ended in defeat. The subsequent carve-up of the historic province created divisions that endure to this day. The Bulgarians were allowed to keep the eastern part, known as **Pirin Macedonia**; while **Aegean Macedonia**, comprising the port of Thessaloniki and its hinterland, fell to Greece; the Serbs grabbed **Vardar Macedonia** to the north and west, including the towns of Skopje, Bitola and Ohrid. Each of the three states regarded their newly acquired inhabitants respectively as Bulgarians, Greeks or Serbs – expressions of any other ethnic identity were either ignored or suppressed.

After a brief period of Bulgarian occupation during World War I, predominantly Slav-populated Vardar Macedonia ended up in a Serb-dominated **Yugoslav state** that had no place for a separate Macedonian identity. Serbian administrators, priests and schoolteachers descended on the region to run local affairs, and Serbian settlers were encouraged to settle on land vacated by emigrating Turks. In Greek-controlled Aegean Macedonia, many Slav communities moved north into Bulgaria during the inter-war years, thus consolidating Greek ethnic dominance of the region.

Bulgaria found itself **diplomatically isolated** after 1918, and therefore unable to press any claim to the Macedonian territories of which it felt unjustly deprived. However, a resurgent IMRO, sustained by the refugees who poured into

Bulgaria to escape Serbian rule in Vardar Macedonia, put pressure on politicians to take a tough line on the Macedonian question. The presence of such a vociferous (and heavily armed) Macedonian lobby, with strong clandestine networks in both Sofia and the Pirin town of Petrich, was a serious threat to internal stability at a time when Bulgarian governments were eager to build bridges with their Balkan neighbours.

IMRO IN THE INTER-WAR YEARS

Years of guerrilla struggle in the Balkans had turned IMRO into a disciplined revolutionary force, and armed bands continued to harry the Yugoslav authorities in Vardar Macedonia from their sanctuaries in the Pirin. The organization also carried out **terrorist attacks** in Bulgaria itself, occupying Kyustendil in 1922 in protest against the government's pro-Yugoslav policies, and threatening the lives of political opponents. Bulgarian nationalists initially thought that they could use IMRO as a private army, enlisting their support to topple the Stamboliiski regime in 1923. However, successive governments regarded IMRO as an obstacle to good relations with Yugoslavia and Greece and worked to neutralize its influence.

In Moscow the newly established Communist International, or **Comintern**, saw the IMRO as a potential partner, imagining that the creation of a revolutionary situation in Macedonia would be a prelude to the toppling of reactionary regimes throughout the Balkans. Discussions in Moscow and Vienna in 1924 led to the **May Manifesto**, a document calling for co-operation between IMRO and the Comintern signed by IMRO leaders **Todor Aleksandrov**, **Aleksandâr Protogerov** and **Petâr Chaulev**.

Communist strategy for the Balkans, however, envisaged the creation of a free Macedonia – not its incorporation in an enlarged Bulgarian monarchist state – and therefore ran counter to the wishes of many of IMRO's right-wing, pro-Bulgarian activists. Aleksandrov and Protogerov bowed to pressure by disowning the *Manifesto*, launching a purge of "socialist" elements from the organization, and expelling Chaulev. However, Aleksandrov was still regarded as a traitor by more reactionary IMRO colleagues, who had him assassinated in August 1924.

Confined to "exile" in Pirin Macedonia and unable to find a proper role for itself, the IMRO spiralled downwards into **self-destruction**. In July 1928 veteran leader Protogerov was shot on the instructions of fellow Central Committee member **Ivan Mihailov**, a particularly ugly piece of internecine strife from which the organization never recovered. Mihailov ran IMRO like a mafia boss, liquidating opponents and funding arms purchases by trading in opium grown in the valleys of the Pirin Mountains.

By the 1930s IMRO had become completely ineffectual as a Macedonian liberation movement. Its last great act of wanton terrorism came in 1934, when – in a plot hatched with Croatian fascists – Yugoslav **King Alexander** was shot dead in Marseille by Macedonian Vlado Chernozemski. As far as the Bulgarian government was concerned, IMRO was by now simply a **criminal organization** that needed to be eliminated – a task carried out the same year when troops were sent into the Petrich region to destroy the IMRO network.

The demise of IMRO meant that, for much of the inter-war period, the denizens of Vardar Macedonia were left without any effective political leadership, and had to endure **Serbian repression** alone. This led many young intellectuals in Vardar Macedonia to find solace in the ideology of **Macedonism** – which held that the Macedonian Slavs should not aspire to inclusion in the Bulgarian nation, but should aim for separate statehood within something approximating to Gotse Delchev's original idea of a Balkan confederation. Many saw Macedonism as an ideology invented by the Serbs in order to break the unity of Bulgarians and Macedonians, but it did attract some notable adherents: former IMRO member Dimitâr Vlahov, who had been involved in the preparation of the *May Manifesto* in 1924, emerged at the head of pro-Comintern "**United IMRO**" which agitated for the formation of an autonomous Macedonia separate from Bulgaria. Vlahov's organization was never very popular within Macedonia itself, but it helped to keep autonomist traditions alive – something that Yugoslavia's Communists were subsequently to exploit.

THE SOCIALIST REPUBLIC OF MACEDONIA

With the outbreak of **World War II** Bulgaria was invited to occupy Macedonia in return for supporting the Axis powers. Having endured two decades of heavy-handed Serbian rule, the locals greeted the Bulgarian army with open arms, but the imposition of a military government – often staffed by officials with little knowledge of the area – soon led to disillusionment.

Eager to exploit the rumbling discontent, Yugoslav Communist and partisan leader **Josip Broz Tito** sent his able sidekick **Svetozar Vukmanović Tempo** southwards to help organize a Macedonian resistance movement, which would act in concert with the Yugoslav partisan army. Not all the local Communists agreed with Tito's avowed aim of creating a Macedonian Republic within a federal Yugoslavia, and a purge of "Bulgarophiles" – who included Macedonian party boss Metodije Šatorov Šarlo – had to be carried out.

The success of Yugoslavia's partisans in combatting Nazi aggression gave them an enormous amount of prestige among fellow Communists after the war, and their Bulgarian comrades were very much the junior partners in an unequal relationship. Tito hoped that the creation of a Macedonian Republic would be a good way of enticing Bulgaria into a Balkan Federation that he himself could then dominate.

The Bulgarian leadership felt obliged to open negotiations on the subject of a **merger between the two countries**, not least because the idea had the backing of Stalin, although they were suspicious of Tito's ambitions. Most importantly, they feared that any Macedonian component of a future federation would seek to remove the Pirin region from Bulgarian control, thus weakening their own power and importance. For the time being, however, the laws of Communist solidarity decreed that such reservations had to remain unvoiced: Bulgaria recognized the right of the Macedonians to have their own republic, and *de facto* recognized the existence of a Macedonian nationality – something that all previous Bulgarian governments had refused to do.

Plans for Bulgarian–Yugoslav union ultimately came to nothing, and Bulgaria retained the Pirin region, but the inhabitants of the Pirin were from 1945 onwards accorded the status of a **national minority**, and positively encouraged to declare themselves as Macedonians – not Bulgarians – in state **censuses**.

Greece's rulers, on the other hand, were horrified by the creation of the Yugoslav Republic of Macedonia. The government in Athens feared that the Greek Communists, currently waging a guerrilla war in the north of the country, had come to a secret agreement to turn over parts of Aegean Macedonia to the Yugoslavs in the event of a Communist victory. It became apparent that the Greek Communists were themselves divided on the issue, and such plans came to nothing. However, the Greeks have accused Yugoslav Macedonia of harbouring **territorial pretentions towards Aegean Macedonia** ever since.

FORMING A MACEDONIAN NATION

Having established the Socialist Republic of Macedonia, and having won from the Bulgarians an admission that such a state had the right to exist, the Yugoslav authorities set about building a Macedonian **national identity**. Most important was the creation of an official **written language**, which was based on a dialect far enough removed from literary Bulgarian to be just about credible as a separate tongue.

Leaders of the original, autonomist IMRO – most notably Gotse Delchev – were elevated to the status of national heroes in order to provide the new republic with **historical legitimacy**. The Macedonian Empire of Alexander the Great was claimed as the state's ancient precursor, and pro-regime academics argued that although Alexander may have been Greek-speaking, he belonged to a distinct Macedonian race whose bloodlines had been preserved through intermarriage with the Slavs.

Although Yugoslavia's federal constitution permitted the republics a certain degree of autonomy, Tito's League of Communists ensured that manifestations of national feeling were never allowed to get out of hand. Macedonians who advocated outright independence or, worse still, expressed overly warm feelings towards neighbouring Bulgaria, were swiftly silenced. In **1967**, however, the Communist authorities supported the local clergy in the establishment of an autonomous **Macedonian Orthodox Church** (ecclesiastical affairs in the republic had hitherto been under Serbian jurisdiction). This was a typical example of Tito's management of Yugoslavia's nationality problems: throwing a concession or two to the Macedonians was a good way to prevent the Republic of Serbia from becoming too cocky.

In Bulgaria, worsening relations with Yugoslavia following the **Tito-Stalin split of 1948** produced a turn-around in official policy towards the Pirin Macedonians. Initially they continued to be classed as an ethnic group in their own right, with the Bulgarians demonstrating to Yugoslavian Macedonians that they would be treated with sympathy should they ever choose to rebel against the benighted Tito regime. By the early 1960s, however, Bulgaria's rulers were increasingly keen to emphasize the ethnic homogeneity of the Bulgarian nation. The authorities henceforth refused to issue personal identity documents to inhabitants of the Pirin region who failed to declare themselves as Bulgarians, and the version of history taught in schools once again drove home the message that the true boundaries of the Bulgarian people extended from the Black Sea in the east to Ohrid in the west.

In Yugoslav Macedonia, the change in Bulgarian attitudes assisted the process of nation-building. By playing on people's fears of Bulgaria as an expansionist power, the authorities succeeded in uniting people around a sense of regional Macedonian pride.

THE 1990S

With the collapse of Communism throughout Eastern Europe and the disintegration of the Yugoslav state, the unresolved ethnic problems of the Balkans were once more up for grabs. Initially, however, the Yugoslav Republic of Macedonia entered **the 1990s** as one of the most conservative forces in the region. Home to a Communist bureaucracy that owed its existence to the regime in Belgrade, and too poor to be viable as an independent state, Macedonia joined Serbia in opposing the reformist and secessionist doctrines emanating from northerly, Westernized republics like Slovenia and Croatia. A gradual **change of heart** occurred when it became clear that the Serbian struggle to preserve the Yugoslav state would inevitably lead to Serb domination of those parts of the federation that chose to remain. Throughout 1990, **fear of Serbia** was the prime factor in mobilizing Macedonian national sentiment.

Several nationalist parties were formed to contest the republic's first democratic elections, timetabled for November 1990. Prominent among these was the **VMRO-DPMNE**, led by 25-year-old poet Ljupčo Georgievski, which claimed descent from the original IMRO of Gruev and Delchev. Together with an allied nationalist group, the *Macedonian Action Party* or **MAAK**, *VMRO-DPMNE* called for the reunification of all Macedonian peoples – an open challenge to the governments of Bulgaria and

Greece. Even during the Communist period, the authorities in Yugoslav Macedonia had protested at the treatment of Macedonian minorities in neighbouring states, but had refrained from jeopardizing inter-Balkan relations by pressing these complaints too far. Now that these resentments were out in the open, the emergence of a boisterous democratic Macedonian state threatened to become a destabilizing influence on the region.

VMRO's popularity forced the adoption of a nationalist agenda upon other parties, including the Macedonian League of Communists or **SKM**, which had thrown its former leadership overboard and adopted a social democratic programme. The *SKM* was able to form a coalition government after the elections of November 1990, but the emergence of the *VMRO-DPMNE* as the strongest party in the *sobranie* or Assembly forced the government to adopt a nationalistic line. The Assembly issued a declaration of Macedonian **sovereignty** in January 1991, to be followed by a full declaration of **independence** in April 1992 once the collapse of Yugoslavia had become an unavoidable reality. Bulgaria recognized the infant state at once, but objections by **Greece** prevented the European Community and other Western powers from doing the same.

The ostensible reason for Greek intransigence was the **name** of the republic: seeing as much of northern Greece went under the same title – and had done so since before the days of Alexander the Great – how, insisted the Greeks, could a foreign state call itself "Macedonia" and thereby usurp the rich heritage that went with it? Lurking behind this objection lay Greek concern over the future of remaining pockets of Slavs (the so-called "**Slavophone Greeks**") who still lived in Aegean Macedonia. The presence of a newly independent Macedonian state threatened to reawaken demands for minority rights in northern Greece, perhaps calling into question the unitary nature of the Greek state. The Greeks invited their northern neighbours to rename their state Vardar Macedonia or Skopje-Macedonia, but despite EC mediation no compromise was reached. Certain **symbols** adopted by the republic led to increased Greek disquiet. A picture of the **White Tower**, a famous landmark in Thessaloniki, found its way into Skopje's official publicity literature; while a **sun motif** previously associated with the empire of Philip II and Alexander became the centrepiece of the Macedonian flag. Both cases suggested that the Republic of Macedonia nursed territorial pretensions far beyond its current borders, although this was strenuously denied by the authorities in Skopje.

Consigned to the **limbo** of independence without international recognition, Macedonia spent most of the early 1990s teetering on the brink of economic collapse. Observers argued that any prolongation of this state of affairs would lead to the republic's disintegration from the inside, possibly provoking intervention from neighbouring powers.

The biggest potential threat to the republic's stability, however, comes from the presence of a large **Albanian minority** in western Macedonia. Though ethnic Albanian MPs occupy a quarter of the seats in the Macedonian Assembly, many members of the Albanian community feel that they're not getting a fair deal from the infant state. Attempts to set up an independent Albanian-language university in the west-Macedonian town of Tetovo were suppressed by the authorities in 1994, and tensions between the communities remain high.

In the meantime, instability in the adjacent Serbian province of Kosovo – also predominantly Albanian – has tended to push the Albanians of Macedonia into rethinking their options. Their loyalty to the Macedonian state is now compromised by the desire to be unified with their Albanian kin in Kosovo and the state of Albania itself. The worst scenario for Balkan politics would be the destabilization of Macedonia through an upsurge of Albanian feeling, dragging neighbouring countries such as Serbia, Bulgaria and Greece into the conflict.

On the positive side, Macedonia's relations with the outside world are gradually beginning to be normalized. Official diplomatic **recognition** came in 1993; although the republic was forced to adopt the rather clumsy title of the **Former Yugoslav Republic of Macedonia** in order to avoid inflaming Greek sentiment. A Greek trade blockade of Macedonia initiated in early 1993 was called off two years later when the Macedonians promised to change the design of their national flag.

BULGARIAN RESPONSES

Despite **recognizing the Republic of Macedonia** and offering it economic and political support, the Bulgarian government continued to stress that it couldn't recognize the existence of a Macedonian nation. Such a stance is largely popular in Bulgaria itself, with all but a tiny minority of the inhabitants of the Pirin region regarding themselves as Bulgarians first, Macedonians second.

Indeed the removal of totalitarian restrictions has failed to produce any great outpouring of Macedonian consciousness. April 1990 saw the emergence of the *Obedinenata makedonska organizatsiya* (United Macedonian Organization) or **OMO-Ilinden**, which called for recognition of Macedonian nationhood and autonomy for the Pirin region. Ilinden was accused of receiving funding from Skopje, and a clause in the Bulgarian constitution that forbade ethnic-based parties ensured that the organization was driven underground.

While OMO-Ilinden has never enjoyed a membership of more than a few hundred, the *VMRO-Sâyuz na makedonskite druzhestva*, or **IMRO-Union of Macedonian Societies**, has emerged to become one of the most influential organizations in southwestern Bulgaria. Claiming descent from the original IMRO, the VMRO-SMD is generally sympathetic towards the infant republic of Macedonia, but refuses to believe that the Macedonians themselves are anything other than Bulgarians.

THE PRESENT

Bulgarian-Macedonian relations in the mid-to-late 1990s were hampered by two main areas of dispute. Firstly, the Bulgarian inability to recognize the Macedonian language meant that many political and business agreements went unsigned, as no-one could agree what language they should be written in. Secondly, the political power enjoyed by the fomer Communists (many of whom had built their careers on anti-Bulgarian rhetoric) in Skopje ensured that Sofia-bashing remained a recurring theme in Macedonian political life. Defeat for the former Communists in the Macedonian elections of October 1998, and the appointment of VMRO-DPMNE's Ljupčo Georgievski as prime minister, opened the way for closer Bulgarian-Macedonian relations, although it's too early to say what form they may take in the future.

BULGARIA'S MINORITIES

Despite a proud Slavonic heritage forged through centuries of national struggle, Bulgaria is far from being an ethnically homogeneous state. As well as Vlachs, Armenians, Jews and Karakachani, the country contains about a million Muslims (many of whom are ethnic Turks), and more than half a million Gypsies.

BULGARIA'S MUSLIMS

Bearing in mind that Islam is associated with the Ottoman Empire, under which Bulgarian Christians languished for five hundred years, it's not surprising that Bulgaria's Muslims have on occasion been regarded as a threat to national unity and have suffered state repression as a result.

During the 1980s Todor Zhivkov's Communist regime attempted to **forcibly integrate** Muslims into mainstream Bulgarian life by pressing them to abandon their traditional culture and **adopt Slavonic names** – attracting widespread international outrage in the process. Democratic changes after November 1989 brought an end to such blatant abuses of human rights, but the question of inter-ethnic relations remains a touchy subject for all concerned.

ORIGINS

Some sources estimate that Muslims constituted up to a third of Bulgaria's population on the eve of the Liberation. Many of them fled in the wake of the Ottoman collapse, but the descendants of those who stayed are scattered throughout the country. Today, the heaviest concentrations of Muslims are found **near the Turkish border** around Kârdzhali, Harmanli and Haskovo; near the towns of Shumen, Razgrad, Târgovishte and Isperih **in the Rhodope mountains**; **northwest of the Balkan Range**; between Burgas and Varna **on the Black Sea coast**; and north of Varna in the **Dobrudzha**.

During the 1980s Bulgarian historians argued that almost all of the surviving Muslims were descended from **ethnic Bulgarians** who adopted the religion, and in many cases the language, of their Ottoman conquerors in the fifteenth century. That said, however, it is known that a constant stream of **settlers** came from Asia to Europe in the wake of the Ottoman advance, and it's impossible to believe that their blood lines are not in some way preserved in the Muslim communities of the Balkans.

Many of Bulgaria's 700,000-strong **Turkish population** are likely to be descended from **Yörük tribespeople**, nomadic sheep-rearers from central Anatolia who were introduced to the Balkans by the Turkish sultan in order to guard the frontiers of his European domains. These newcomers put down roots throughout Bulgaria, especially in lowland regions where the native Christian population was either wiped out or put to flight.

Tatars had been frequenting the Dobrudzha and the Black Sea coast since the thirteenth century, and their Islamic religion and Turkic language made them natural allies of Bulgaria's Ottoman conquerors. Their numbers were augmented in the nineteenth century by refugees fleeing from Turkey's wars with Tsarist Russia. Large numbers of Crimean Tatars were settled here in the 1850s, but they found it hard to adapt to a sedentary lifestyle, continued to practise nomadism, and in lean years pillaged Christian and Muslim farmers alike. Similarly unruly were the **Circassians**, also refugees from the Tsarist empire, who were given lands along the southern banks of the Danube. The Circassians were recruited as irregulars by the local Ottoman gendarmes, and soon earned a reputation among the local Bulgarians for arbitrary cruelty. Both Tatars and Circassians were gradually assimilated by the more numerous Turks, and soon lost many of their specific racial characteristics – nowadays, Dobrudzhan Tatars are usually referred to as Turks by the local Bulgarian population.

Some fifteenth-century Bulgarians **renounced Christianity** in favour of Islam. It's unclear whether these conversions were forced, or whether landholding peasants willingly adopted Muslim ways in order to retain their privileges under a new regime. In many cases village priests went over to Islam and took their flock with them, despairing at the way in which Balkan Christianity had collapsed so quickly. Subsequently known as **pomaks** (derived from the word *pomagach*, or "helper" – they were viewed as collaborators by their Christian neighbours), about 300,000 of these Slavic Muslims still live in compact communities throughout the western Rhodopes. Under the Ottoman Empire, *pomak* irregulars were often used by the authorities to police the local Christians. It was a *pomak* leader from Dospat, Ahmed Aga Barutanliyata, who was allegedly responsible for the **Batak** massacre in 1876 (see p.314).

MUSLIMS UNDER THE MODERN BULGARIAN STATE

Muslims tended to occupy a privileged position under Turkish rule, and fear of Bulgarian reprisals caused many of them to flee during the War of Liberation in 1877. The Bulgarian government undertook to preserve the religious rights of Muslims that remained, paying for the upkeep of mosques and providing Turkish-language teaching in some schools. Isolated cases of **revenge** did occur, with ethnic Turks being burned out of their villages by irate Slavs, but few of these incidents are documented.

During the **inter-war years** Muslims were left largely unmolested by the state, although several Turkish settlements were awarded Bulgarian names in the 1930s – the northwestern town of Târgovishte, *Eski Dzhumaya* until 1934, is one example. Local government officials habitually doled out Slavonic names to ethnic Turks when registering births, although there was no consistent, government-sponsored campaign to do so.

The Soviet-inspired **constitution of 1947** paid lip service to minority rights, although Bulgaria's Communist bosses seemed eager to facilitate **emigration** of Muslims to Turkey during the immediate postwar years. Around 155,000 Turks departed between 1949 and 1951, and were followed by a second wave in the late Sixties. The early years of the **Zhivkov regime** were characterized by attempts to encourage Turks to join the Party and participate in Bulgarian political life. In 1964, Todor Zhivkov made a much-publicized speech calling for an improvement of Turkish-language schooling and a widening of minority cultural activities, but with hindsight this appeared to be the swan song of Bulgaria's enlightened nationality policy rather than the herald of some new dawn.

TURNING MUSLIMS INTO BULGARIANS

Educational facilities for ethnic Turks were being wound down by the late 1960s, marking a radical change in the government's attitude towards Bulgaria's minorities. From now on the emphasis was to be on outright **assimilation**. Bulgaria's atheist leaders were frustrated by the way in which Turks and *pomaks* clung to religious traditions – of all the country's inhabitants, the Muslims were the most impervious to the propaganda of secular education – and began to wonder whether they could ever be turned into loyal citizens of the socialist state.

To make matters worse, Muslim fertility was increasing at a time when the Bulgarian birth rate was in decline. Anxieties about Bulgaria's changing demography were coupled with the Party's growing exploitation of **nationalism**. The Zhivkov regime was eager to camouflage its subservience to the Soviet Union by posing as the guardian of patriotic values, and the ideology of the integral nation-state – in which there was little room for ethnic minorities – began to brush aside the proletarian internationalism of Marx and Lenin.

The *pomaks* were the first to experience the effects of the **name-changing campaign**, which aimed to coerce the bearers of traditional Islamic names into adopting Bulgarian alternatives. Beginning in 1971, official ceremonies took place in villages throughout the western Rhodopes, in which *pomaks* were awarded fresh identity papers bearing their new Bulgarified names. The vast majority had little choice but to accept them without complaint, as any dissent was harshly dealt with. Riots in Pazardzhik, in which two Communist Party officials were reportedly killed by an angry mob, resulted in mass arrests and deportations. Opposition to the campaign in the Gotse Delchev region led to a military clampdown, accompanied – it is alleged – by public hangings of *pomak* leaders.

The unexpected strength of resistance probably led to a lull in name changing over the next decade, but **the winter of 1984** saw the full force of the campaign directed against Bulgaria's ethnic Turks. This time the campaign was accompanied by a full-scale attack on Muslim traditions. Mosques were closed down or demolished, local religious leaders were replaced with Party stooges, circumcision was discouraged, and use of the Turkish language in public places was forbidden. The speed and ferocity of the campaign was surprising, but it was part of the Communist mentality to believe that wholesale social change could be achieved through administrative decisions from above. The Party leadership had been shaken by events elsewhere in the Balkans – in Yugoslavia, the emergence of Muslim Albanian sentiment in Kosovo posed a threat to that state's continued existence – and Zhivkov obviously wanted to deprive Bulgarian Turks of their ethnic identity before they developed separatist aspirations of their own.

The campaign, going under the sanitized name of the *Vâzroditelniyat protses* or "**Regeneration Process**", was presented to the Bulgarian public as another glorious chapter in the country's progress towards national rebirth. Sycophantic academics were employed to argue that the Turkish minority had in fact been Bulgarians all along: forcibly Islamicized in the fifteenth century, they were merely fulfilling their destiny by adopting Bulgarian names and returning to the fold. Repressive aspects of the campaign were often conducted under the smokescreen of social progress. Well-intentioned Bulgarians were led to support the measures against the Turks when it was argued that Muslim women, denied access to educational and career opportunities by the bonds of patriarchal society, would benefit from forced assimilation.

The campaign met with **fierce resistance** from the Turks themselves. Numerous demonstrations in towns in the Kârdzhali district ended with security forces firing on angry crowds; and eight civilians were shot dead during one peaceful protest in Momchilgrad in December 1984. Such events soon attracted the attention of human rights organizations abroad, but the regime turned a deaf ear to foreign criticism. The government turned the crisis to its own advantage, garnering domestic support by accusing Amnesty International and the Western press of participating in a plot to destabilize socialist Bulgaria.

SUMMER 1989: THE "GREAT EXCURSION"

With the Zhivkov regime increasingly relying on nationalist excesses in order to detract attention from the Communist system's failings, anti-Turkish policies were stepped up in the **spring of 1989**. This time the action moved on to Bulgaria's northwest, where strikes and demonstrations in the Razgrad area gave vent to Muslim anger.

Growing numbers of Turks sought to emigrate rather than change their names, and the Turkish government declared its willingness to accept as many Bulgarian Muslims as wanted to leave. Sofia called Turkey's bluff by issuing passports to any Muslims requesting them, and by June 1989 the Bulgarian–Turkish border was jammed with people trying to leave, many taking their entire worldly possessions with them. Official sources claimed that the crowds gathering at the frontier were "tourists (*ekskurziyanti*)" taking advantage of the new freedom of travel, unintentionally providing the phrase by which 1989's exodus of Turks came to be known – the *golyama ekskurziya* or "**Great Excursion**".

Between May and August up to 300,000 Turks and *pomaks* crossed the border. Initially Turkey promised to provide sanctuary to Bulgaria's entire Muslim population if necessary, but by August the flood of refugees was placing impossible strains on the Turkish economy. There was insufficient accommodation or work for the newcomers, many of whom were housed in tent cities along the border, and the special treatment accorded to them (however meagre it may have been) was resented by local people. Many *ekskurziyanti* were beginning to return home after a couple of months, dismayed by Turkey's inability to provide them with a life better than the one they had left. Turkey had in any case **closed the border** by the end of August, unable to take any more.

The Great Excursion was beginning to have serious consequences for Bulgarian society. Whole areas had been depopulated, and entire towns and villages deprived of highly trained professional people like teachers and doctors. Most importantly, the economically vital **tobacco crop**, traditionally concentrated in areas of Muslim settlement, lay unharvested in the fields. Urban Bulgarians were organized into work brigades and sent to the countryside to save the crop – for many of them, this was their first experience of the havoc wrought by Todor Zhivkov's nationality policies.

Inspired by the progress of glasnost in the Soviet Union, Bulgarian intellectuals were increasingly eager to join persecuted Turks in denouncing the totalitarian nature of the state, and organizations like the **Independent Committee for the Defence of Human Rights** brought leaders of both groups together for the first time. Sharing a common hatred of

Communism, Bulgaria's ethnic Turks and urban liberals seemed to be at the start of a fruitful political friendship when the Zhivkov regime came to an end on November 10, 1989.

THE POST-ZHIVKOV ERA

Conservative fears that rapidly emerging democratic forces would sell the country out to the Turks initially provoked a nationalist backlash. When new Party leader **Petâr Mladenov** admitted that the name-changing campaign had been a big mistake, hardliners tried to undermine him by organizing protest strikes and demonstrations in mixed-race towns like Haskovo and Kârdzhali, where Bulgarian-Turkish relations were sensitive. A big nationalist demonstration in Sofia on December 7 called for a referendum on the issue of whether Bulgaria's Muslims should be permitted to have their old names back.

Muslims themselves responded to the demise of totalitarianism by reclaiming their culture. *Pomaks* took to the streets of Gotse Delchev to demand the right to wear *shalvari*, the baggy trousers banned during the dark days of the name-changing campaign; nowadays traditional dress is worn with pride, even by Westernized younger women, in many parts of the Rhodopes. The Turkish language – and Turkish music – were loudly flaunted in those areas where ethnic Turks lived; and attendance at the local mosque once more became *de rigueur* for respectable members of the community.

Nationalist unrest flared again in July 1990, when protestors tried to prevent newly elected Turkish MPs from taking their seats in the Grand National Assembly in Veliko Târnovo. Originally, ethnic Turk leaders had joined the main opposition coalition, the SDS, but personality clashes within the movement had persuaded them to form a political party of their own in early 1990. Named the "Movement for Rights and Freedoms" – *Dvizhenieto za prava i svobodi* or **DPS** – the party was led by **Ahmed Dogan**, a former university lecturer imprisoned by the Zhivkov regime for his opposition to the name-changing campaign.

The DPS made every effort to present itself as a multi-racial human rights organization, although it was clear that most of its supporters were Turks and *pomaks*. Bulgaria's Muslims voted en bloc for the DPS in June 1990, leaving its critics to claim that the

Movement would lead to the ghettoization of the country's minorities, not their rehabilitation into national life. Others feared that the DPS' monopolistic hold over the Muslim population, especially in the Kârdzhali area where ethnic Turks form a majority, would lead to demands for regional autonomy and, eventually, outright secession. The BSP, increasingly the natural home for conservative forces within the country, portrayed the DPS as an exclusively Turkish national party which owed its allegiance to Ankara rather than Sofia. The DPS' dominance over Bulgarian Muslims would also lead, they argued, to the gradual Turkification of Bulgaria's *pomaks*, who would slowly lose their Slavonic roots.

THE 1990S

As the **elections of October 1991** approached it became clear that neither of Bulgaria's main parties – the SDS and the BSP – were capable of winning an outright majority, and the DPS would in all likelihood hold the balance of power. The BSP knew that an SDS–DPS coalition was the likely outcome of such a situation, and began to play on public fears of a "Turk-dominated" parliament in an attempt to win support.

The BSP's eagerness to pose as the "keep the Turks out" party led to a dangerous polarization of attitudes in areas with a sizeable Turkish population. In cities such as Shumen and Razgrad, Muslims and Bulgarians voted en masse for the DPS and the BSP respectively; and people like the SDS, who tried to play down the national issue, were totally squeezed out.

The election **result** confirmed the BSP's worst fears, with DPS deputies agreeing to support an SDS administration committed to market reforms and "de-Communization", but in the end, the alliance between ethnic Turks and other anti-Communists was short lived. Economic policy proved to be the cause of disagreement, with the DPS withdrawing its support from the SDS administration in October 1992, after the government had refused to provide sufficient aid to Bulgaria's ailing tobacco industry. The DPS was responsible for nominating Bulgaria's next government, the non-party administration of Professor Lyuben Berov, but Berov's cabinet relied on the DPS' erstwhile enemy the BSP for support as well – a sign that the entrenched political differences of 1990 and 1991 could be quietly overlooked once the balance of power in the National Assembly changed.

The **elections of December 1994** confirmed the DPS' status as the only effective Muslim political force in the country, and an important political player on the national stage, but with the BSP securing an outright majority in the Assembly, the DPS no longer held the balance of power. The DPS entered a coalition of centre parties (led by former president Zhelyu Zhelev) just before the **elections of April 1997**, a sign that while remaining instinctively anti-BSP in nature, it couldn't bring itself to wholeheartedly support the ultra-capitalist line offered by the SDS. The DPS nevertheless retained its bedrock support in the Turkish areas of the country, and party leader Ahmed Dogan enhanced his reputation as one of the key political figures of the post-Communist era.

Conditions for Bulgaria's Muslims have radically improved since November 1989, even though many in the country – including politicians on both left and right – feel threatened by the sudden reappearance of Muslim influence at the very heart of Bulgarian politics, and regard the Muslim minorities as potentially disloyal to the Bulgarian nation-state. The DPS remains the target of considerable resentment, if only because there's a widespread popular belief that Muslims are given preferential treatment in areas under DPS control. However, the fact that Bulgaria's Muslims are entitled to political representation is now largely taken for granted, and a return to the anti-Muslim policies of the past is unlikely.

THE GYPSIES

One of Bulgaria's minorities with no political muscle and largely ignored and abused by their neighbours, are the **gypsies** (*Roma* in their native tongue; *Tsigani* in Bulgarian). Descended from a low-caste Indian tribe, they made their way into Eastern Europe in the late middle ages, and, although many urban gypsies converted to Islam and adopted Turkish as their mother tongue during the sixteenth and seventeenth centuries, on the whole they have remained remarkably isolated from the communities around them. Intermarriage with other groups is rare, and they still tend to live in their own *mahala* or quarter of town – usually run-down suburbs which have become virtual no-go areas

for the local Bulgarians. These gypsy **ghettos** exist in every major Bulgarian city, with some of the biggest being in Sliven, Lom and Sofia – where they are known colloquially as "Cambodia" and "Abyssinia". In Kazanlâk and Plovdiv, large roadside screens have been erected in order to prevent passing travellers from seeing into the gypsy *mahalas*.

According to the 1992 census there were 313,000 gypsies in Bulgaria, although this figure doesn't take account of the many gypsies who, in the hope of avoiding racial discrimination, declared themselves as Bulgarians or Turks. Unlike the Turks however, gypsies have never developed political organizations capable of defending their interests. This is largely because they lack a common sense of identity, and think of themselves as members of specific gypsy **tribes** rather than a larger unified whole. These tribes are named after the trades with which they were once associated, and remain a valuable badge of identity for gypsies even if the trades themselves are no longer practised. Predominant among these are the *kardarashi* (coppersmiths), *kalaidzhii* (tinners), *ursari* (bear tamers) and *kalburdzhii* (sieve-makers). Originally they would travel the country selling their wares, or working in the supply train of the Ottoman army, although **nomadism** had largely died out by the time of the Liberation, and was in any case outlawed by the Communists. Very few gypsies practise nomadism nowadays, although *ursari* still move from town to town with their animals between spring and autumn.

After World War II most gypsies joined the industrial workforce or were employed as **labourers** on collective farms. The economic stagnation of the 1980s and 1990s hit the gypsy community especially hard, and high unemployment has been one of the features of gypsy life during the last decade, increasing their isolation from other sections of Bulgarian society. This background of non-integration and social deprivation, coupled with the fact that only fifty percent of gypsy children regularly attend school, helps to explain why gypsies tend to be blamed for the **increase in crime** which has taken place in Bulgaria since 1989. Indeed, some tribes regard pickpocketing as a legitimate trade, and the involvement of gypsies in petty crime and theft has increased over the past two decades – in 1986, ten percent of crimes in Bulgaria were attributed to gypsies; by 1994 the figure had risen to 37 percent – but this shouldn't hide the fact that most criminal acts in the country are still committed by non-gypsies.

Increasingly cut off from the mainstream of national life, Bulgaria's gypsies face an uncertain future, and the political elite's failure to engage with gypsy grievances can only serve to store up social problems for the millennium.

BOOKS

There is more writing on Bulgaria than you might initially imagine – though, as a rule, it appears more in books on the Balkans as a whole than forming the central subject of either travel writing or fiction. Sadly, much of it is no longer in print. What follows is a collection of books on or about the country either currently in print or out of print (o/p) and available in larger libraries or specialist secondhand bookstores.

TRAVEL BOOKS AND GENERAL ACCOUNTS

Randall Baker, *Summer in the Balkans* (UK & US, Kumarian Press, 1995). An American academic goes off on various study visits to Slovenia, Romania and Bulgaria in the years following the fall of Communism and meets several interesting people on the way. A harmless account, which lacks bite.

Frank Cox, *Bulgaria* (UK, A & C Black, 1915; o/p). The *Morning Post's* Bulgaria correspondent during the Balkan Wars, Cox was impressed by a well-organized country that seemed to have imposed order on this hitherto chaotic corner of southeastern Europe. He found Sofia rather staid though, commenting that "the system of partial seclusion of the womenfolk kills all social life, and the absence of a feminine element in the restaurants and other places of social resort deprives them of all convivial charm".

Lovett Fielding Edwards, *Danube Stream* (UK, Muller, 1939; o/p). This book on the Danube and its influence on southeastern Europe is chiefly interesting for its account of life amongst the polyglot boatpeople. Includes descriptions of Vidin, Lom and Ruse, but otherwise only marginally relevant to Bulgaria.

Leslie Gardiner, *Curtain Calls* (UK, Duckworth, 1976; US, Biblio Distribution Centre, 1976). The last six chapters deal with Gardiner's experiences in Bulgaria – including a slow-burning flirtation with his *Balkantourist* guide, Radka – recounted in an amusing style.

A. L .Haskell, *Heroes and Roses* (UK, Dartman, Longman & Todd, 1966; o/p). Potted biographies of Bulgarian revolutionaries, sections on the arts, and chunks of travelese, combined with diatribes against pop music and other things that this pompous ballet critic dislikes most.

Jeremy James, *Vagabond* (UK, Pelham, 1991). Recounting a voyage on horseback from Bulgaria to Western Europe in 1990, James' book offers a convincing picture of rural life in the Balkans of today. The author seems especially at home in gypsy culture – a milieu that other travellers rarely get to grips with.

Stowers Johnson, *Gay Bulgaria* (UK, Hale, 1964; o/p). More earnest than Newman and prosier than Savas, Johnson voyaged by Dormobile across Bulgaria just before the country became a tourist destination, which constitutes the book's main attraction.

Claudio Magris, *Danube* (UK, Collins Harvill, 1989; US, Farrar, Straus & Giroux, 1989). This highly praised account of the Danubian countries interweaves history, reportage and high-brow literary anecdotes in an ambitious attempt to illuminate their cultural and spiritual backgrounds. Only one section is devoted to Bulgaria, naturally enough, but the rest is a fascinating read.

Bernard Newman, *The Blue Danube* (UK, Jenkins, 1935; o/p); *Bulgarian Background* (UK, Robert Hale, 1961; o/p). The latter is marginally more lively – and contains a lot more about Bulgaria – than Newman's earlier book, relating his epic bicycle ride alongside the Danube. Solid stuff, but hardly riveting.

S.G.B. St Claire and Charles A. Brophy, *Residence in Bulgaria* (UK, 1869; o/p). These two former British army officers lived in a village south of Varna in the late 1860s, returning to write a book on a country "which although but five or six days distant from England, is as little known as the interior of Africa". Their account is largely pro-Ottoman and anti-Bulgarian, although their characterization of the Bulgarians as a surly bunch who overcharge foreigners will be familiar to those holidaying on the Black Sea coast today. Worth tracking down for the folkloric anecdotes alone.

James A. Samuelson. *Bulgaria Past and Present* (UK, 1888, o/p). A British barrister recalls his travels through what was still a semi-wild, war-ravaged country. Good on the changing face of post-Liberation Sofia.

George Savas, *Donkey Serenade* (UK, Faber, 1940; o/p). Savas did his travelling on foot along the backroads of Bulgaria, accompanied by the roguish ex-IMRO fighter Vasil. Rather twee, but includes a couple of fine Bulgarian poems and the odd notable vignette.

Philip Ward, *Sofia: Portrait of a City* (UK & US, Oleander, 1992). A guide to the Bulgarian capital interspersed with potted history and character sketches, this book is a little too lightweight to get to grips with Sofia's urban character. The same author's *Bulgaria: A Travel Guide* (UK, Oleander, 1989; US, Pelican, 1990) is chatty if somewhat dated, with numerous historical and cultural digressions.

Giles Whittel, *Lambada Country* (UK, Chapmans, 1992). Whittel travelled from the Baltic to the Aegean by bicycle in 1990, and offers an impressionistic account of a region in transition. Concentrating on chance encounters and cultural ephemera (the title refers to the kind of imported popular music he encountered en route) rather than political analysis, it's a light read, short on real insights.

GUIDE BOOKS

Peter Carney and Meri Anastassova, *Bulgaria: the Mountain Resorts* (Bulgaria, PMC, 1998). Useful guide to the highland regions, written by a Sofia-based team and full of insightful nuggets. On sale from bookshops and kiosks in Bulgaria, as are the same authors' *Bulgaria: Sofia and Plovdiv* and *Bulgaria: the Black Sea Coast*.

Julian Perry, *The Mountains of Bulgaria* (UK, Cordée, 1995). No-nonsense practical guide to trekking routes in the Balkan, Rila, Pirin and Rhodope ranges, written by an experienced trek leader. A good investment if you're planning a major hiking expedition.

HISTORY, POLITICS AND SOCIOLOGY

Amnesty International, *Bulgaria: Imprisonment of Ethnic Turks* (1986). Reports on the forced "assimilation" of Bulgaria's largest minority group, using documentary, eye-witness and hearsay evidence.

Christo Anastasoff, *The Bulgarians* (UK, Exposition Press, 1977; o/p). Academic essays on diverse aspects of Bulgarian history. The diplomacy, religious schisms and Byzantine feuds of centuries are minutely dissected.

J.D. Bell, *Peasants in Power* (UK & US, Princeton UP, 1977; o/p). Before, during and after World War I, the Agrarians were the largest radical opposition party in Bulgaria and were the "Greens" of southeastern Europe. Bell discourses on the brief period of Agrarian government and their charismatic leader, Stamboliiski, in a scholarly but uninspiring manner.

Stephen Constant, *Foxy Ferdinand* (UK, Sidgwick & Jackson, 1979; US, Franklin Watts, 1980). Readable and impeccably researched biography of Bulgaria's unlamented tsar, who privately referred to his subjects as *mes bufles* – "my buffalos". Deals candidly with Ferdinand's bisexuality – a subject that contemporary Bulgarian historians still shy away from.

R.J. Crampton, *A Short History of Modern Bulgaria* (UK & US, Cambridge University Press, 1987). Probably the definitive work on the subject: an informed, well-balanced and easy-to-read account widely available from bookshops and public libraries. Especially good on the intrigues of Bulgarian political life after the Liberation.

Stanley Evans, *A Short History of Bulgaria* (UK, Lawrence & Wishart, 1960; o/p). Slightly turgid and inevitably dated, but a useful general history, including coverage of the periods before the collapse of the Second Kingdom and after unification.

Isabel Fonseca, *Bury Me Standing* (UK, Vintage, 1995; US, Knopf, 1995). Part travelogue, part social enquiry, presenting a sympathetic description of contemporary gypsy life in Eastern Europe. The one chapter on Bulgaria concentrates on the town of Sliven, where gypsies and ethnic Bulgarians are more integrated than anywhere else in the country.

Stephane Groueff, *Crown of Thorns* (UK, Madison, 1987; US, University Press of America, 1987). Boris III, Ferdinand's successor (see above), is the subject of this slavish work – complete with endorsements by William

Buckley and other right-wing fanatics – written by an émigré whose dad served Boris.

R.F. Hoddinott, *The Thracians* (UK & US, Thames & Hudson, 1981). Thorough introduction to the Bulgarians' ancient antecedents, although descriptions of archeological evidence sometimes seem a bit too technical for the lay reader.

Elizabeth Kwasnik, *Bulgaria: Tradition and Beauty* (UK, Liverpool Museum, 1989; o/p). The catalogue to an exhibition that toured several provincial museums in the UK, with essays on carpet-weaving, traditional costumes and rural celebrations, accompanied by excellent colour pictures.

D.M. Lang, *The Bulgarians* (UK, Thames & Hudson, 1976). Traces the Bulgars from Central Asia until the Ottoman conquest, neatly complementing Macdermott's history. Illustrated.

Mercia Macdermott, *A History of Bulgaria, 1393–1885* (UK, Allen & Unwin, 1962); *The Apostle of Freedom* (UK, Allen & Unwin, 1967); *Freedom or Death* (UK, Journeyman Press, 1979); and *For Freedom and Perfection* (UK, Journeyman Press, 1988). Written sympathetically and with obvious enjoyment – all in all, probably the best histories of Bulgaria in the English language. The last three are biographies of famous nineteenth-century revolutionaries – Vasil Levski, Gotse Delchev and Yane Sandanski – which, despite being tinged with hero worship, are impeccably researched and eminently readable.

Georgi Markov, *The Truth that Killed* (UK, Weidenfeld, 1983; o/p). Disillusioned by constraints on his literary career in Sofia, Georgi Markov defected for a new life in England, where he began broadcasting for the BBC World Service. Both autobiographical and a sermon à la Solzhenitsyn, this book apparently so enraged the Politburo that they ordered his murder. Jabbed with a poison-tipped umbrella on Waterloo Bridge, Markov died of a rare fever a few days later. Essential reading.

Dimitri Obolensky, *The Byzantine Commonwealth* (UK, Weidenfeld; US Nicolson). Classic work on the spread of Christianity and Byzantine culture in the Balkans during the Middle Ages; it's particularly good on the medieval Bulgarian church.

Duncan M. Perry, *Stefan Stambolov and the Emergence of Modern Bulgaria* (US, Duke University, 1993). A political rather than personal biography of the most talented and charismatic of Bulgaria's post-Liberation politicians, which makes a good introduction to the period as a whole. The same author's *The Politics of Terror: the Macedonian Revolutionary Movements 1893–1903* (US, Duke University, 1988), is a thorough and readable account of the genesis of the IMRO.

Hugh Poulton, *The Balkans: Minorities and States in Conflict* (UK, Minority Rights Group, 1991; o/p; US, Paul & Co, 1991; o/p). Exhaustively researched compendium on the national minorities of Bulgaria and its neighbours.

Steven Runciman, *History of the First Bulgarian Empire* (UK, Bell, 1930; o/p). Though long out of print, this is the classic account of the rise and fall of Bulgaria's first medieval kingdom, by a respected scholar of Byzantine and Balkan history.

Claire Stirling, *Time of the Assassins* (UK, Angus Robertson, 1984; o/p; US, Henry Holt). *Readers' Digest* bankrolled Stirling's hunt for the "Bulgarian Connection" whereby Mehmet Ali Agca's attempted murder of the pope in 1981 was stage-managed by the KGB, and her tendentious account is couched in the *Digest's* breathless right-wing house style. Similar assertions are made in *The Plot to Kill the Pope* by **Paul Henze** (US, Simon & Schuster, 1983; o/p). In an earlier book, *The Terror Network* (UK, Holt & Reinhardt, 1981; US, Weidenfeld & Nicholson, 1981; o/p), Stirling accused Bulgaria of smuggling arms and narcotics into Turkey.

E.P. Thompson, *Beyond the Frontier* (UK, Merlin, 1997). Heartfelt account of the allied mission to aid Bulgarian partisans in World War II, led by the author's brother Major Frank Thompson.

FICTION AND POETRY

Ivan Davidikov (trans Ewald Osers), *Fires of the Sunflower* (UK, Forest, 1988; US, Dufour, 1986). Representative range of works by well-respected contemporary lyric poet.

Blaga Dimitrova (trans Brenda Walker and Belin Tonchev), *The Last Rock Eagle* (UK, Forest Books, 1992). Bulgaria's most popular contemporary poet, Blaga Dimitrova was a prominent anti-Communist in the late 1980s, and served briefly as vice president in 1992–93.

Nikolai Haitov, *Wild Tales* (UK, Peter Owen, 1989; US, Dufour, 1979). Short stories set in the rural communities of the Rhodope Mountains, from a popular contemporary Bulgarian author.

Lyubomir Levchev (trans Ewald Osers), *Stolen Fire* (UK, Forest 1986; US, Dufour, 1986). Levchev was a Central Committee member and president of the Writers' Union under the old regime, but despite occasional flashes of ideological content most of his work is unashamedly personal and emotional.

Geo Milev (trans Ewald Osers), *Roads to Freedom* (UK, Forest, 1988). Milev's death at the hands of the reactionary Tsankov regime in 1925 made him into one of socialist Bulgaria's favourite left-wing martyrs, but it's often forgotten that he was a ground-breaking modernist poet who borrowed from expressionism and other Western styles.

John Naughton (ed), *The Traveller's Literary Companion to East and Central Europe* (UK, In Print, 1995). The Bulgarian section of this book, written by Sofia-based critic Belin Tonchev, contains an excellent overview of Bulgarian literary history, accompanied by extracts from the works of major Bulgarian authors.

Viktor Paskov, *A Ballad for Georg Henig* (UK, Peter Owen, 1990; US, Dufour, 1990). Acclaimed Bulgarian novel of the 1980s, recounting in mildly Kafkaesque manner the story of an elderly Sofia violin maker who has somehow managed to be overlooked on all official state records.

Yordan Yovkov (trans John Burnip), *The Inn at Antimovo and Legends of the Stara Planina* (UK, Slavika, 1989; US, Slavika, 1990). Twentieth-century novelist Yovkov was born in Zheravna in the eastern Stara Planina (the Balkan Range), and this collection of short stories recalls the atmosphere of small-town life under the Ottoman occupation.

Young Poets of a New Bulgaria (UK, Forest, 1990; US, Dufour, 1990). A collection of more than twenty poets, mixing those who did well under the old regime with those who suffered for their anti-Communist convictions. Other anthologies published by Forest/Dufour are *Poets of Bulgaria* (1988) and *The Devil's Dozen* (1992), a collection of women poets, including work by Blaga Dimitrova.

BULGARIA IN WESTERN LITERATURE

Julian Barnes, *The Porcupine* (UK, Cape, 1992; US, Knopf, 1992). Political satire centring on the trial of deposed Communist dictator Stoyo Petkanov – a fictional character based on Bulgaria's Todor Zhivkov. A telling account of how democratic revolutions can soon degenerate into cynicism and disillusionment.

Malcolm Bradbury, *Rates of Exchange* (UK, Secker & Warburg, 1983; US, Knopf, 1983; o/p). Comic novel recounting the misadventures of an English academic sent by the British Council to lecture in the imaginary Communist state of Slaka, loosely based on Bulgaria. As a Westerner's view of the absurdities of life under Communism, it's extremely funny. The same author's *Why Come to Slaka?* (UK, Secker & Warburg, 1986; US, Penguin, 1991; o/p) was a less successful send-up of the kind of propagandist tourist literature published by Balkan states before 1989 – although anyone with experience of Bulgaria in those days will find it curiously familiar.

Robert Littel, *October Circle* (UK, Faber, 1993; US, Houghton Mifflin, 1976; o/p). Cold War thriller concerning a group of young Bulgarian Communists who fall foul of the regime in the aftermath of the Warsaw Pact's 1968 invasion of Czechoslovakia. Breezy, undemanding, and with plenty of local colour.

CUISINE

Dan Philpott, *The Wine and Food of Bulgaria* (UK, Mitchell Beazley, 1989; o/p). Marrying coffee-table values with practical, easy-to-follow recipes: an essential buy if you want to tell your *kebapche* from your *kavarma*.

BULGARIAN MUSIC

Until very recently all aspects of Bulgarian musical life, from musicological research to composition and teaching to recording and broadcasting, were under the control of the state. Although this helped to preserve the music and encourage certain developments, it also introduced distortions and affected the natural growth of the music. This has led to the paradoxical situation that the beautiful recordings of the Women's Choir of RTV Bulgaria, sold in the UK under the title of "Le Mystère des Voix Bulgares", were thought of here as folk music, when they are in fact postwar pieces by the country's leading modern composers. On the other hand, the band of Ibraim (Ivo) Papazov is seen as that of a unique Balkan jazz genius – when he is actually the most remarkable representative of a movement that managed to flourish *outside* official encouragement or censorship. Both are products of the postwar era and examples of growth from village roots, yet are utterly different in aesthetic and ideology.

OPEN THROAT

There is something about Bulgarian music that at once proclaims itself: both its matter and manner are powerfully individual. To the Western ear one of the most immediately recognizable characteristics is the vocal timbre of such singers as Nadka Karadzhova, Yanka Rupkina and Konya Stojanova, a rich, direct and stirring sound, referred to in the West as "**open-throated**". In fact the throat is extremely constricted and the sound is forced out, which accounts for its focus and strength

and which allows the complex yet clean ornamentation that is such a striking feature of this style of singing. The only songs that the villagers dignified with the name of "folk songs" are the slow, heavily ornamented solo songs that are particularly the province of women. These used to be sung at the social events called *sedyanki*, evenings when unmarried women would gather together to sew and embroider, gossip and compare fiancés, or at the table on the occasion of various parties of one sort or another. Songs for dancing, or for various rites, were seen as being "practical" or "useful", and weren't felt quite worthy of being called music. The ornamentation, although subtly varied with each performance, was always considered a vital part of the tune, and the only time you will ever hear a song without such decoration is when the singer is too old to manage it.

Much Bulgarian music, both sung and played, was performed with no harmony, or with (at most) a simple drone like that of a bagpipe. Nonetheless, in some districts a most extraordinary system of **polyphonic performance** grew up. In the Shop area near Sofia, women in the villages of Plana, Bistritsa and others sing in two- and three-part harmony, though not a harmony that Western ears readily recognize, as it is full of dissonances and tone clusters and decorated with whoops, vibrati and slides. The singers themselves say that they try to sing "as bells sound". In the Pirin district, in the southwest, the villagers sometimes sing two different two-voiced songs with two different texts simultaneously, resulting in a four-part texture. This polyphonic style of performance is normally the domain of women, although in Pirin men also sing in harmony, but with a different repertoire and in a rather different and simpler style.

The **rhythmic complexity** of Bulgarian music is also striking, and for the Hungarian composer and collector of folk songs **Bela Bartok** (1881–1945), the discovery of these irregular rhythms was a revelation. The most widespread is probably the *Ruchenitsa* dance, three beats arranged as 2 2 3, closely followed by the *Kopanitsa* (2 2 3 2 2). More complex patterns like 2 2 2 2 3 2 2 (*Bucimis*) or 3 2 2 3 2 2 2 2 3 2 2 (*Sedi Donka*, also known as *Plovdivsko Horo*) are also common. These patterns, foreign to us, are ingrained in the Bulgarian people, who snap their fingers in such rhythms while waiting for a bus or hanging around on the corner of the street.

Though Bulgaria is a small country, there are several clearly defined regional styles: the earthy, almost plodding dances from Dobrudzha, in the northeast, are quite different in character from the lightning-fast dances of the Shop people, while the long heart-rending songs from the Thracian plain contrast with the sweet and pure melodies from the northeast. In the remote mountains of the Rhodopes, in the south, you can still hear the distant sound of a shepherd playing the bagpipe to his flock of a summer evening, and in the villages or small towns of the valleys groups of people sing slow, broad songs to the accompaniment of the deep *kaba gaida*, a large, deep-voiced bagpipe.

RITUAL MUSIC

The yearly round of peasant life was defined by the rhythm of the seasons, sowing and harvest, and many of the **ancient rituals** intended to ensure fertility and good luck still survive, though more as a folk tradition than in the belief that they will produce any kind of magical effect. All these customs, such as *Koleduvane*, which normally involves groups of young men going in procession around the village and asking for gifts from the householders; *Laduvane* at New Year; and *Lazaruvane* on St Lazarus' Day in spring (the most important holiday for the young women, when they take their turn to sing and dance through the streets) have particular songs and dances connected with them. The songs are usually simple, repetitive and very old. The most startling of these rites, *nestinarstvo* – from the villages of Bulgari, Kondolovo and Rezovo in Strandzha – has died out in its original form, when its exponents would fall into a trance and dance on hot coals to the sound of bagpipe and drum to mark the climax of the feast of saints Konstantin and Elena, but it's sometimes presented at festivals and folklore shows. The wild stirring music remains the same.

These days the two most important rites of passage in Bulgarian life, be they in the country or in the town, are **getting married** and **leaving home** to do military service. Both occasions are marked by music. Every aspect of a wedding – the arrival of the groom's party, the leading out of the bride to meet it, the procession to the church and so on – has a particular melody or song associated with it. The songs sung at the bride's house the night before the wedding are by no means joyful celebrations of marriage: on the contrary, they are the saddest songs in the whole body of Bulgarian music, because the bride is leaving home, never to return to her parents' house.

Parties to see the young men off to the army are more cheerful. In the town the family of the recruit hires a restaurant and a band, normally some combination of accordion, violin, electric guitar, clarinet/saxophone and drum kit, which plays a haphazard mix of folk, pop and other melodies, and the guests eat, drink and dance. In the country the feast is often held in the evening and outdoors. In the village of Mirkovo the guests are entertained by a little band of two clarinets, trumpet and accordion, who play the slow melodies called *na trapeza* (at the table) while the guests eat. Later the young soon-to-be soldier is led round and presented with gifts of money, flowers or shirts. (**Shirts** in fact play a great role in Bulgarian folk life. At weddings each member of the party wears a handkerchief pinned to their breast, but the more important relatives are permitted an entire shirt, sometimes still in its cellophane wrapping).

After all the food has gone, the band strikes up a set of local dance tunes, and everyone rushes to join in a *horo* whose leader capers and leaps while flourishing an enormous flag on a long pole. Dancing is very popular, especially among villagers; and at the end of a festival or similar event, if the band starts to play a bit for pleasure you can see people – from grannies to young children – literally racing across the grass to join the circle.

In most of the country the bands for weddings and so on are made up of modern, factory-made **instruments** often amplified, but around the town of Yambol in the Strandzha area, in the east, many people prefer the old folk instruments and if they can afford it, will even hire a band from Sofia to come and play them.

BANDS AND INSTRUMENTS

Traditional bands almost invariably consist of *gaida* (bagpipe), *kaval* (end-blown flute), *gadulka* (a bowed stringed instrument) and *tambura* (a strummed stringed instrument), sometimes with the addition of the large drum, the *tapan*. They always were common throughout the country, but when after World War II the state founded its own ensembles for folk songs and dances, these instruments were the ones chosen to make up the huge orchestras thought necessary to accompany them. As a result they have undergone certain developments and refinements to aid reliability of tuning and tone, while some players have brought their skill to a quite unbelievable peak of virtuosity.

The **gaida** is maybe the most famous of all these instruments, although it's fairly simply made: a chanter for the melody, a drone and a mouth-tube for blowing, all attached into a small goatskin that acts as a reservoir for air. It's capable of a partly chromatic scale of just over an octave, and in the hands of a master such as Kostadin Varimezov or Nikola Atanasov the wild sound has an astonishing turn of speed and rhythmic force. These players also have the ability to use the possibilities that the *gaida* has for rich ornamentation to perform beautiful versions of slow songs and other *na trapeza* melodies. In the Rhodopes the huge, deep-voiced *kaba gaida* accompanies singing or plays dance music, sometimes alone and sometimes in groups of two, three, four or even more. There is one group called rather literally *Sto kaba gaidi* (One Hundred *kaba gaidi*), and although this could be thought excessive the sound is undeniably impressive.

Like the *gaida*, the **kaval** was originally a shepherds' instrument, and some of its melodies, or rather freely extemporized meditations on certain motifs which are specific to it, go by such names as "Taking the herd to water", "At noon", "The lost lamb". The modern *kaval* is made of three wooden tubes fitted together, the topmost of which has a bevelled edge that the player blows against on the slant to produce a note. The middle tube has eight finger holes and the last has four more holes that affect the tone and the tuning. They are sometimes called **Devil's holes**: the story goes that the Devil was so jealous of the playing of a young shepherd that he stole his *kaval* while he was sleeping and bored the extra holes to ruin it. Of course, they only made the instrument sound sweeter and the Devil was, as usual in folk tales, discomfited once more.

The school of *kaval*-playing led by Nikola Ganchev and Stoyan Velichkov that has grown up since the war is extremely refined and capable of all manner of nuances of sound. The sound is sweet and clear (the folk say "honeyed"), the low (*kaba*) register is rich and buzzing, and in the last ten years or so someone (possibly Nikola Kostov) invented a new technique called *kato klarinet* (clarinet style) where the instrument is played as though it were a trumpet, producing a sound very like the low register of the clarinet.

The **gadulka** is a relative of the *rebec*, with a pear-shaped body held upright on the knee, tucked into the belt or cradled in a strap hung round the player's neck. It has three, sometimes four bowed strings, and as many as nine sympathetic strings that resonate when the instrument is played, producing an unearthly shimmering resonance behind the melody. The *gadulka* is unbelievably hard to play – there are no frets and no fingerboard, the top string has to be stopped by fingernails and the whole thing keeps wriggling out of your grasp like a live fish. This makes the *gadulka* players' habit of showing off by playing virtuoso selections from the popular classics both startling and irritating. Mihail Marinov and Atanas Vulchev are among the older players of note, and Nikolai Petrov is one of the younger generation.

The **tambura** is a member of the lute family, with a flat-backed pear-shaped body and a long fretted neck. Its original form, found in Pirin and in the central Rhodopes, had two courses of strings, one of which usually provided a drone while the melody was played on the other. These days the common form of the instrument has four courses tuned like the top four strings of a guitar, and in groups it both strums chords and plays melodies.

Around the end of the nineteenth century factory-made instruments like the accordion, clarinet and violin appeared in the country and were soon used to play dance music and to accompany songs. Modern **accordion style** was pretty much defined by **Boris Karloff** (no relation to the horror-movie star) who wrote a number of elegant tunes – *Krivo Horo* in particular – that have become standards. More modern accordionists worthy of note are the Gypsy Ibro Lolov (sometimes known as Ivo as a result of the programme of Bulgarianization of names of Turkish origin under the Zhivkov regime; see p.390), Traicho Sinapov and Kosta Kolev, also well known as a composer, arranger and conductor who plays in a very unique style which contrasts in its restraint and care with the high-speed acrobatics of some of the younger players. By far the most brilliant of these is the young **Petar Ralchev**, a Thracian, who unlike some of the speed-merchants combines new ideas with a lot of taste and, more importantly, a lot of soul.

STATE CONTROL

The extent to which music was controlled by the former Communist government and how far the musicians themselves were able to escape this control is an integral part of the development of music in Bulgaria. In the early Fifties the Communists set up the **State Ensemble for Folk Songs and Dances** under the leadership of **Philip Kutev** (sometimes spelt Koutev), an extraordinarily talented composer whose style of writing and arranging became the model for a whole network of professional and amateur groups across the country. His great gift was the ability to take the sounds of village singers, drone-based and full of close dissonances but essentially harmonically static, and from this forge a musical language that answered the aesthetic demands of Western European concepts of form and harmony without losing touch with the particularly Bulgarian feeling of the original tunes. If you compare his work with the attempts of earlier arrangers to force the tunes into a harmonic system which they really didn't fit, his success is as obvious as their failure. This is what you hear on the "Le Mystère des Voix Bulgares" recordings, and from the Trio Bulgarka and the instrumental group Balkana.

It is impossible to over-estimate the tight grip that the state had on every aspect of life, and this is as true of music as of anything else. What began as a praiseworthy attempt to preserve and enrich folklore became a straitjacket to which all musicians had to conform or else stop working as musicians. It reached even such ridiculous extremes as prescribing a certain percentage of Russian songs to be played in the course of an evening's entertainment in a restaurant, say, to demonstrate the eternal friendship of the Bulgarian and Soviet peoples. And you couldn't ignore this insanity, because there were people around whose job it was to make sure that you were complying. One musician told with rage how he had had to audition all his new songs and dances to a committee

that he called "The Committee of Pensioners" before he was permitted to perform them on the radio. If they were "not Bulgarian enough" then permission was refused. Even if it was granted, then the style of performance had to be acceptable. "Once they told me that I was playing too fast, and that Bulgarian music is not played so fast. This was a tune that I myself had written, it was I that was playing it, and I am a Bulgarian musician. How should they tell me the way to play my own song? But they could. I tell you, Bulgarian music used to be behind closed shutters – but now the shutters have been opened."

This doesn't mean that the people working in the field of folklore were all apparatchiks or that they failed to produce beautiful music. The network of regional professional ensembles fed by a stream of talent trained in special schools set up to teach folk instruments and folk singing meant that time, money and opportunity were available for people to develop the approved language in their own way, and many composers – among them **Kosta Kolev** and Stefan Mutafchiev and Nikolai Stoikov with the "Trakiya" ensemble in Plovdiv – created their own individual styles. The mass-production of cheap folk instruments under the Communist regime, and the encouragement shown to amateurs, also managed to keep music alive in the villages. Unfortunately, this was at the cost of alienating many people, particularly young city-dwellers, by insisting on such propagandist drivel as "Mladata Traktoristka" (The young girl tractor-driver) and referring to them as "contemporary developments in folk creativity".

Another crucial factor in the growth and encouragement of Bulgarian music is the series of regional competitions and festivals held around the country. The **Koprivshtitsa festival** (see p.245), is particularly important, not merely because of its size (there are literally thousands of performers bussed in from all over the country) but because it is the only one devoted to amateur performers. Practically the only recordings of genuine village music that the state record company *Balkanton* has ever released were made here: *Koprivshtitsa '76* and the double album *Koprivshtitsa '86*, among the most beautiful and valuable recordings of Bulgarian songs and dances ever made.

WEDDING BANDS

The **wedding bands** are a fascinating example of the formerly "underground" folk music that is currently an extremely important part of Bulgarian musical life. Unlike the musicians mentioned above, who were approved by the state (though none the worse for that), they existed outside the framework of official music making, hired to play at weddings, the seeing off of recruits and various village festivities. Because they did not have to conform to the Communist idealization of the people and the people's music in order to record or get on the radio, they were free to experiment with new instrumentation, fusing folk instruments such as the *gaida* and *kaval* with electric guitar, synthesizer and kit drums, rock and jazz rhythms, and foreign tunes. As the recording industry in Bulgaria didn't allow the formation of a commercial style like that of the Yugoslav folk-based pop music, they simply took those songs straight across, learning them from radio broadcasts picked up from over the frontier (or from pirate cassette tapes) and performing them to a public that responded to their directness and energy. It was only in the mid-1980s that officialdom realized the existence of this music, and through the efforts of some quite brave and far-seeing musicologists was persuaded to recognize them as worthy of public support and recording. A tri-yearly festival was set up in the town of **Stambolovo** (hence their alternative name *Stambolovski orkestri*) which presented them in perhaps a somewhat bowdlerized form – they were subjected to the "assistance" of approved musical directors – but the *Balkanton* record *Stambolovo '88* gives a very good impression of the amazing revelation of this kind of previously unsuspected music.

Ivo Papazov is the best known of these musicians in the West, thanks to the work of Hannibal Records, who managed to record him with his electric band after a long struggle with the bureaucracy. His flirtations with jazz following his work in the late Seventies and early Eighties with the Plovdiv Jazz-Folk Ensemble are maybe less successful than his startling transformations of traditional Thracian music, but some of his most intriguing achievements lie in the performance of **Turkish music**. He is of Turkish origin, and even in the period just prior to the fall of the Zhivkov regime when the very existence of a Turkish minority in Bulgaria was denied, you could get home-made recordings of Papazov playing Turkish melodies with a typical small band of the type common today in Istanbul. Now that under the new government *Balkanton* has released tapes and records of "Turkish Music from Bulgaria" he should be producing some interesting music. His second Hannibal release, *Balkanology*, begins with a Turkish dance and also includes Macedonian and Greek material.

There are many other modern bands of this type, often gypsy, now using the new freedom in all kinds of ways. The bands Sever, Juzhni Vetar, Vievska Grupa, Shoumen and Trakiiski Solisti all have fresh and startling ways of interpreting their traditional music. Some have made commercial recordings, others are still only to be heard live or on poor-quality home-made tapes sold in the markets of the small towns where they live.

NEW SOUNDS

It is not only the *Stambolovski orkestri* who have been pushing back the boundaries. Some of the bands that play purely traditional instruments have been experimenting. Black Crown records in the UK has recently released a record of the band Loznitsa called *Moods*, featuring both the old master of the *gaida* **Nikola Atanasov** and the incredible young *kaval* player Georgi Zhelyazkov: it's a good representation of the new trend. Particularly worth investigating is the work of the *kaval* player **Teodosii Spasov** who has not only recorded a very beautiful and practically avant-garde folk album, *Dâlâg Pât* (The Long Road) in collaboration with composer Stefan Mutafchiev, but also played to great acclaim with the well-known Bulgarian jazz pianist Milcho Leviev in his first concert in Sofia after twenty years' exile. Spasov's subsequent albums *The Sand Girl*, *Welkya* and *Beyond the Frontiers* represent a successful folk-jazz fusion from one of Bulgaria's most exciting young players.

It's impossible to predict the **future** of Bulgarian music. During the 1990s, economic stagnation all but wiped out the network of folklore festivals that had kept traditional music alive in the past, and the folklore scene – now dependent on private sponsorship rather than state funding – is only just beginning to re-establish itself. It's certainly easier to catch live,

DISCOGRAPHY

The recommendations below largely concentrate on recordings available outside Bulgaria. You'll find a wide range of folk music cassettes and CDs on sale in shops and market stalls within the country itself, although the availability of specific titles is unpredictable. Generally speaking, it's well worth snapping up any recordings featuring the Koprivshtitsa festival, the Stambolovo festival, or big names like the Philip Kutev Ensemble, the Pirin Ensemble, Nadka Karadzhova, Teodosii Spasov or Ivo Papazov.

The Philip Koutev National Folk Ensemble, *Bulgarian Polyphony I* (JVC, VICG5001, UK). A startling collection of open-throat-style singing from one of Bulgaria's best-known folk ensembles. *Bulgarian Polyphony II* (JVC, VICG5002) and *Bulgarian a Capella* (JVC 5389 2) feature more of the same.

Ibro Lolov and his Gypsy Orchestra, *Gypsy Music From Bulgaria* (ARC, EUCD 1476, UK). Virtuoso playing from a Bulgarian-based family ensemble, concentrating on frenetic, wedding-band numbers.

Loznitsa, *Moods* (Black Crown Workalb1, UK). A tight band of excellent musicians playing material from all over the country, with vocals by Kalinka Vulcheva.

Ivo Papazov and his Orchestra, *Orpheus Ascending* and *Bàlkanology* (Hannibal HNBC 1363, UK). Both albums are splendid examples of Papazov's irrepressible style. The virtuoso clarinetist and his band play all sorts of goodies from their wedding bag. Fast and furious: Gypsies love it, musicologists despair. The *Balkanology* album includes more ethnically diverse material and, with the allusion to Charlie Parker, perhaps a touch more jazz.

Quartette Slavei, *Bulgarian Polyphony IV* (JVC, VICG5344, UK). Four female singers (including Nadka Karadzhova) from the Philip Kutev ensemble, performing traditional village songs.

Teodosii Spasov, *Beyond the Frontiers* and *Welkya* (both Gega New, Bulgaria). Stunning fusion of folk, jazz and contemporary classical music from Bulgaria's most popular *kaval* player. Spasov's earlier *Sand Girl* and *Dàlàg Pàt* (both Balkanton) occasionally turn up in Sofia record shops.

Trio Bulgarka, *The Forest Is Crying* (Hannibal HNBC1342, UK). The three singers perform a cappella of Bulgarian favourites re-recorded for a Western audience, and accompanied by one of Bulgaria's best instrumental groups, the Trakiiskata Troika (Thracian Trio). There's more of the same on **Various**, *Balkana: the Music of Bulgaria* (Hannibal HNBC 1335, UK), when the two groups are joined by various guests.

Various, *Bulgarian Music Anthology vols 1 to 5* (Harmonia Mundi, UK). A series of recordings documenting rural music traditions, with each CD

concentrating on a particular geographical region. Harmonia Mundi are also responsible for *The Great Voices of Bulgaria vols 1 to 3*, which feature traditional choral music in modern, arranged form.

Various, *Le Mystère des Voix Bulgares Vol.1* (4AD, UK). Classic melodies and arrangements performed beautifully by the Women's Choir of the Radio and Television. Indispensable. There are two further volumes on 4AD, and a fourth album *Ritual* (Elektra Nonesuch), which combines traditional Bulgarian Christmas songs with a selection of Sephardic Jewish melodies.

Various, *Folk Music of Bulgaria* (Topic, TSCD905, UK). Probably the best general introduction to Bulgarian music currently available, drawing varied pieces from a wide geographical area. Excellent sleeve notes, too.

Various, *The Rough Guide to the Music of Eastern Europe* (World Music Network, RGNET 1024, UK). Wide-ranging collection with a strong Bulgarian bias. The comparisons with the other Balkan countries featured on this disc (notably Macedonia) are instructive.

Various, *Stambolovo '88* (Balkanton VNA (or BHA) 12367/8, Bulgaria). Selection of wild and wonderful experiments by some of the wedding bands who took part in the 1988 Stambolovo festival. They come from all over the country and give some idea of the diversity of Bulgarian styles and their modern development.

Various, *Koprivshtitsa '76* and *Koprivshtitsa '86* (Balkanton BHA 2067 and 11902/903, Bulgaria). Recordings of some of the best amateur musicians and groups that have taken part in the great festival at Koprovshtitsa. Highly recommended if you can find them.

Various, *Village Music of Bulgaria* (Elektra Nonesuch, USA). Excellent selection, including a stunning performance of the song "Izlel e Delyo haidutin" by Valya Balkanska, which was the first Bulgarian song in space, when it travelled on the spacecraft "Voyager" as an example of earth culture.

Various, *Two Girls Started to Sing ...* (Rounder, US). Field recordings made in 1978–88 in village locations around Bulgaria. This is music as it is really lived and performed. Good notes, too.

folk music in Bulgaria now than at any time since the changes of 1989; see p.43 for a list of annual events and festivals. On a more negative note, many younger folk musicians have abandoned roots music to work in the more lucrative sphere of commercial folk-pop, leaving traditional folk music in the hands of an older generation who aren't always open to ideas of innovation and development. The best hope for the survival of folk as a living musical form lies with ground-breaking figures such as Teodosii Spasov, who enjoys something akin to mass popularity in Bulgaria, and other jazz-folk crossover merchants such as Ivo Papazov.

This article – an edited extract from The Rough Guide to World Music (*Rough Guides, 1999*) – *was researched and written by Kim Burton.*

LANGUAGE

Bulgarian is a South Slavonic tongue closely related to Slovene and Serbo-Croat, and more distantly to Russian, which most Bulgarians learned at school beore 1989. Since then, English language studies have become increasingly popular, but you'll still find that English is widely understood only in Sofia, Plovdiv, and the ski and beach resorts favoured by British holidaymakers. Those who acquire some Bulgarian will find that even the smallest effort reaps great rewards.

THE CYRILLIC ALPHABET

Most signs, menus and so on are in the **Cyrillic alphabet**, but along highways you'll also see signs in the Roman alphabet. For easy reference in the course of this guidebook, you'll find **town names** boxed in both alphabets at the beginning of each chapter. And note that at train stations, the Roman version won't be visible before the train pulls out unless you sit up front.

There are different ways of **transcribing** Cyrillic into Latin script (for example, "Cherven Bryag" or "Aerven Brjag" for ЧЕРВЕН БРЯГ; "Târnovo" or "Turnovo" for ТЪРНОВО) but – with a few notable exceptions like "Bulgaria" and "Sofia" instead of "Bâlgariya" and "Sofiya" – we've tried to adhere to the following system. This shows Cyrillic characters in capital and lower-case form, with their Roman transcription and a roughly equivalent sound in English.

It's useful to know that putting the word *da* before **verbs** makes an infinitive (*iskam da kupya*, "I want to buy"); while *ne* is used to form the negative (*ne iskam*, "I don't want"). Use of the particle *li* turns the sentence into a question – *imate li . . .?* is "do you have . . .?"

А а	a as in father	П п	p as in pot
Б б	b as in bath	Р р	r as in rasp
В в	v as in vat	С с	s as in sat
Г г	g as in gag	Т т	t as in tap
Д д	d as in dog	У у	u as in rule
Е е	e as in den	Ф ф	f as in fruit
Ж ж	zh like the 's' in measure	Х х	h as in loch (aspirated)
З з	z as in zap	Ц ц	ts as in shuts
И и	as in bit (or '*bee*', at the end of a word)	Ч ч	ch as in church
		Ш ш	sh as in dish
Й й	i 'y' as in youth	Щ щ	sht like the last syllable of sloshed
К к	k as in kit	Ъ ъ	â like the u in but
Л л	l as in like	Ь ь	(this character softens the preceding consonant)
М м	m as in met		
Н н	n as in not	Ю ю	yu as in you
О о	o as in got (never as in go)	Я я	ya as in yarn

In practice there are the odd **exceptions** to this pronunciation: Bulgarians pronounce ГРАД (town) as "grat" instead of "grad", for example. But the system generally holds good and if you follow it you'll certainly be understood.

The most important thing is to work on the **pronunciation** of certain sounds (Ж, Х, Ц, Ч, Ш, Щ, Ь, Ю and Я in the alphabet) and attuning your ear to Bulgarians' throatily mellow timbre. Most Bulgars sway their heads sideways for "**yes**" and nod to signify "**no**", but a few do things "our way", increasing the possibility of misunderstandings which can leave both parties floundering through *da*s and *ne*s.

Two widely available **self-study courses** offering an accessible introduction to the everyday language are *Colloquial Bulgarian* (Routledge) and *Teach Yourself Bulgarian* (Hodder & Stoughton), both of which are accompanied by optional cassettes. Once in Bulgaria itself, you'll find an increasing number of Bulgarian-English **dictionaries** and phrase books at bookshops and street stalls.

BULGARIAN WORDS AND PHRASES

BASICS

Do you speak English/ German/French	*Govorite li angliiski/ nemski/frenski?*	good day/evening	*dobâr den/vecher*
yes – okay	*da – dobre*	good night	*leka nosht*
no/not	*ne*	goodbye	*dovizhdane*
I don't understand	*ne vi razbiram*	please speak more slowly	*govorete po-bavno, ako obichate*
please – excuse me	*molya – izvinete*	please write it down	*bihte li ya napisali?*
thank you	*blagodarya* (or *merci*)	what's this called?	*kak se kazva tova?*
you're welcome	*nyama zashto*	come here!	*ela!*
how are you?	*kak ste?*	go on!	*haide!*
what's up?	*kakvo ima?*	that's enough!	*stiga!*
hi!	*zdravei*	on holiday	*na pochivka*
good morning	*dobro utro*	on a business trip	*na komandirovka*

REQUESTS

Have you got . . .?	*Imate li. . . ?*	Where can I buy . . .?	*Kâde moga da si kupya . . . ?*
a single/double room	*Staya s edno leglo/dve legla*	The bill, please	*Smetkata, molya*
How much for the night?	*Kolko se plashta na vecher za leglo?*	How many/how much?	*Kolko?*
It's too expensive	*Mnogo e skâpo*	Please give me . . .	*Daite mi. . . molya*
Haven't you a cheaper room?	*Nyamate li po-evtina staya?*		

For more on *accommodation* and *eating* see p.30 and p.33.

REACTIONS

good, bad	*dobro, loshe*	my/mine, ours, yours	*moe, nashe, vashe*
expensive, cheap	*skâpo, evtino*	what, which?	*kakvo?*
difficult, interesting	*trudno, interesno*	how?	*kak?*
beautiful, calm	*hubavo, spokoino*	this, that	*tova, onova*
big, little/few	*golyamo, malko*		
new, old	*novo, staro*		
early, late	*rano, kâsno*		
hot, cold	*toplo, studeno*		

NB. If you're uncertain about a noun's gender it's easiest to give the qualifying adjective or pronoun a neuter ending (as above).

SIGNS

entrance, exit	ВХОД, ИЗХОД	pause/lunch break	ПОЧИВКА
open, closed	ОТВОРЕНО, ЗАТВОРЕНО	closed for repairs	НА РЕМОНТ
vacant, occupied	СВОБОДНО, ЗАЕТО	attention/danger	ВНИМАНИЕ
admission free	ВХОД СВОБОДЕН	no smoking	ПУШЕНЕТО ЗАБРАНЕНО
day off	ПОЧИВЕН ДЕН		

continued overleaf

GETTING ABOUT

here	tuka	Stop!	Spri!
there	tam	Are there connections	Ima li vrâzka za...?
How can I get there?	Kak moga da otida do tam?	for...?	
Which bus to the	S koi avtobus moga	Where do I change?	Kâde tryabva da
centre?	da otida v tsentra?		smenya?
Is this the bus for...?	Tozi li e avtobusât za...?	Please reserve me...	Molya, zapazete mi...
Is this the train to...?	Tozi li e vlakât za...?	two sleepers/seats	dve legla/mesta
Where are you going?	Za kâde pâtuvate?	Which platform for	Na koi kolovoz se namira
Is it near?	Blizo li?	the .... train?	vlakât za...
Where do I get	Na koya spirka da slyaza		
off for...?	za...?	See p.23 for more help with transport.

TIME AND DATES

What's the time?	Kolko e chasât?	March	Mart
When?	Koga?	April	April
today, tomorrow	dnes, utre	May	Mai
(the day before)	(za)vchera	June	Yuni
yesterday		July	Yuli
in the mornings	sutrinta	August	Avgust
in the afternoons	sled obed	September	Septemvri
this week	tazi sedmitsa	October	Oktomvri
from . . . until . . .	ot . . . do . . .	November	Noemvri
January	Yanuari	December	Dekemvri
February	Fevruari		

Monday	ponedelnik	ПОНЕДЕЛНИК
Tuesday	vtornik	ВТОРНИК
Wednesday	sryada	СРЯДА
Thursday	chetvârtâk	ЧЕТВЪРТЪК
Friday	petâk	ПЕТЪК
Saturday	sâbota	СЪБОТА
Sunday	nedelya	НЕДЕЛЯ

NUMBERS

1	edin, edna, edno	12	dvanaiset	40	chetiriiset
2	dve, dva	13	trinaiset	50	petdeset
3	tri	14	chetirinaiset	60	shestdeset
4	chetiri	15	petnaiset	70	sedemdeset
5	pet	16	shestnaiset	80	osemdeset
6	shest	17	sedemnaiset	90	devetdeset
7	sedem	18	osemnaiset	100	sto
8	osem	19	devetnaise	500	petstotin
9	devet	20	dvaiset	1000	hilyada
10	deset	21	dvaiset i edno		
11	edinaiset	30	triiset		

USEFUL SLANG TERMS

Borets (pl. bortsi)	Literally "wrestler"; strong man employed by gangsters	Krâchma	Literally "tavern"; a real dive
Chenge	Policeman, "cop"	Mente	Fake (as applied to cigarettes, designer clothes, watches etc)
Gadzhe	Girlfriend or boyfriend	Mutra (pl. mutri)	Gangster

GLOSSARY

ALAFRANGA Term for the combination of native woodwork and textiles with Western fashions in nineteenth-century interior design (from *à la française*); or painted niches and walls in National Revival-style houses.

BANYA Public bath or spa.

BASHIBAZOUKS Murderous bands of *pomaks* (see overleaf) and Turks, employed to punish rebellions against Ottoman rule.

BEY Turkish provincial governor.

BLATO Marsh or reed-encircled lake.

BOLYARIN Medieval Bulgarian nobleman (a *bolyarka* is a noblewoman).

CARAVANSERAI Hostelry for merchants in Ottoman times.

CHARDAK Balcony or porch.

CHARSHIYA A bazaar or street of workshops, once a typical feature of Bulgarian towns.

CHERGA Handwoven rug. With a simpler design than a kilim, and often taking the form of a long thin runner.

CHERKVA Church (see also *Tsârkva*).

CHERNO MORE Black Sea.

CHESHMA Public drinking fountain.

CHETA Unit of resistance fighters (originally applied to the Bulgarian Legion of the 1860s).

CHIFLIK Farm, or small administrative unit in Ottoman times.

CHORBADZHII Village headmen (literally, "Soup makers") or rich landowners; also pejorative term for those who collaborated during the Ottoman occupation.

DERE Stream.

DUPKA Hole, den or cave.

DVORETS Palace.

DZHAMIYA A mosque (also spelt DJAMI or DZHAMIJA).

ESONARTHEX Short porch before the narthex of a church.

EZERO Lake.

FIRMAN Sultan's seal of authorization.

GORA Forest, hill or mountain (Sredna Gora – Central Range).

GRAD City or town. The oldest quarter is often known as the *Stariyat grad* or the *varosh* (see overleaf).

GRADINA Garden.

GUBER Fleecy rug.

HADZHI Man who has made the pilgrimage to Mecca (if a Muslim), or to Jerusalem (if a Christian).

HAIDUK Outlaw, bandit.

HAIDUTIN Outlaw, freedom fighter. Plural: *haiduti*

HALI Market hall.

HALISHTE Soft blanket or fleecy rug.

HAN Inn or caravanserai.

HISAR Fortress.

HIZHA Hikers' chalet or mountain hut.

IGUMEN Father-superior of a monastery.

IZVOR A spring.

JANISSARIES Elite military fighting corps raised from foreigners whom the Turks abducted during childhood (under the hated *devşirme* system), and indoctrinated with fanatical loyalty to the sultan.

KÂRDZHALI Turkish outlaws, particularly active in the late eighteenth and early nineteenth centuries.

KÂSHTA House.

KAZA Small Ottoman administrative unit.

KHAN (or HAN) Supreme ruler of the Bulgar tribes and, later, the first Bulgarian state; the title is of Central Asian origin.

KILIM Woollen carpet, featuring a complex central design within a border.

KITENIK See *Guber*.

KOBILITSA Yoke used for carrying buckets.

KOLEDA Christmas.

KOLEDAR Christmas carol singer.

KOMITADZHI Another word for *Cheta* (see above).

KONAK Headquarters of an Ottoman *chiflik* or region; including the governor's residence, a garrison and a prison.

KORSO Evening promenade.

KOZEK See *Guber*.

KOZYAK Goat-hair rug.

KREPOST Fortress.

KUKER Mummer; a man dressed in carnival

costume to celebrate winter nearing its end, a ceremony that usually takes place on the first Sunday before Lent.

KVARTAL Suburb.

KVARTIRA Room (*chastni kvartiri* – private rooms).

LIBERATION, THE The attainment of Bulgaria's independence from Ottoman rule, following the Russo-Turkish war of 1877–78.

MAGISTRALA Main highway.

MAHALA Quarter or area of town occupied by a particular ethnic or religious group (*tsiganska-ta mahala* – the gypsy quarter).

MALKO Small or little (Malko Târnovo – Little Târnovo).

MANASTIR Monastery.

MINDER Couch or seat built into a room (plural, *minderi*).

MOGILA Burial mound.

MOST Bridge.

NAOS Innermost part of an Orthodox church.

NARTHEX Entrance hall of Orthodox church.

NATIONAL REVIVAL Nineteenth-century upsurge in Bulgarian culture and national consciousness. Sometimes called the Bulgarian renaissance.

NATIONAL REVIVAL STYLE Architecture developed during the eighteenth and nineteenth centuries, characterized by the use of oriels and decorative features such as carved wooden ceilings, stylized murals and niches. Best seen in Târnovo, Tryavna and Plovdiv.

NOS Cape.

ODYALO Blanket.

ORIEL Angular or curved bay window projecting from the upper floor of a house.

OSVOBOZHDENIETO The Liberation (see above).

PAMETNIK Monument or memorial.

PÂT Road.

PAZAR Market.

PESHTERA Cave (see also *dupka*).

PLANINA Mountain.

PLOSHTAD (Pl.) Town square.

POMAKS Bulgarians who converted to Islam during the Turkish occupation, or their descendants; mainly resident in the Rhodopes.

POP Orthodox priest.

PROHOD Mountain pass.

PROLOM Gorge or defile.

RAYAH (or RAYA) "The Herd", as the Ottomans called and treated the non-Muslim subjects of their empire.

REKA River.

SÂBRANIE Parliament, assembly

SELO Village.

SHOSE Avenue or highway.

SOFRA Low table with a circular top of copper or brass.

SURVAKAR Boy who goes from house to house wishing people a happy new year by hitting them on the back with a *survaknitsa*.

SURVAKI New Year.

SURVAKNITSA Decorated twig borne by a *survakar*.

SVETI (Sv.) Saint; blessed or holy. Sveta is the feminine form: Sveta Bogoroditsa is the Holy Virgin; Sveta Troitsa is the Holy Trinity.

TEKKE Dervish lodge.

TELL Mound of earth left by successive generations of human settlement. Tells in the Plain of Thrace provide evidence of Bulgaria's Neolithic and Bronze Age inhabitants.

THRACIANS Inhabitants of Bulgaria during the pre-Christian era.

TSÂRKVA Church.

TURBE Small Islamic mausoleum.

TURISTICHESKA SPALNYA Tourist hostel, providing cheap dorm-type accommodation.

ULITSA (Ul.) Street.

VELIKDEN Easter.

VELIKO Great (Veliko Târnovo – Great Târnovo).

VAROSH Central quarter of old Balkan town.

VÂZRAZHDANE National Revival (see above).

VILAYET Large Ottoman administrative unit; province.

VOYVODA Leader of a *Cheta*.

VRÂH Summit or peak.

YAZOVIR Reservoir, artificial lake.

ACRONYMS

BKP Bulgarian Communist Party.

BSP Bulgarian Socialist Party (successor to the BKP).

BZNS Bulgarian Agrarian National Union.

DPS (*Dvizhenieto za prava i svobodi*). The Movement for Rights and Freedoms – a party supported by Bulgarian Muslims and ethnic Turks.

DS (*Dâzhavna Signurnost*). State security police.

IMRO (Internal Macedonian Revolutionary Organization). Macedonian separatist organization, predominantly terroristic from 1893 to 1934.

SDS (*Sâyuz na demokratichnite sili*). Union of Democratic Forces – a coalition of right-of-centre forces.

INDEX

A

accommodation 30
airlines
  in Australasia 13
  in Bulgaria 95
  in North America 11
  in the UK 5
Aladzha Monastery 343
Albena 344
Aleko 89
Apriltsi 199
Arbanasi 211–214
Asenovgrad 301

B

Bachkovo Monastery 302–305
Balchik 346
Balkan Range 145–160
banks 19
Bansko 124–127
Batak 314
Belogradchik 159
Berkovitsa 153
bibliography 411
Blagoevgrad 118–122
Blue Rocks 270
books 411
border crossings
  into Greece 299
  into Romania 166
  into Turkey 299
Borovets 115–117
Boyana 89
Bozhentsi 222
Burgas 359–363
buses
  to Bulgaria 26
  within Bulgaria 9

C

Cape Kaliakra 348
Chepelare 306
Cherni Osâm 199
Chiprovtsi 156–158
churches 52
costs 18
crime 53
Cyrillic alphabet 422

D

Danube River 161
Devin 311
Dobrich 181–184
domestic flights 29
Dragalevtsi 87
drink 36
driving 26
Dryanovski Monastery 218
Dupnitsa 105
Durankulak 350

E

Elena 217
Elenite 352
embassies
  in Bulgaria 96
  Bulgarian, abroad 15
  Romanian 8
  Yugoslav 8
entertainment 47
Etâra 225
Etropole 187

F

festivals 41
flights to Bulgaria
  from Australasia 12
  from North America 10
  from the UK 3
flights, domestic 29
food 32
football 47

G

Gabrovo 223
gay life 55
glossary 425
Golden Sands 343
Gotse Delchev 130
Greece, crossing into 299
gypsies 409

H

Harmanli 298
Haskovo 297
health 15
Hisar 251
history 379–396
hitching 28

I

information 20
insurance 16
Iskâr Gorge 147–149
Isperih 235

K

Kalofer 257
Kârdzhali 318
Karlovo 255
Kavarna 347
Kazanlâk 257–263
Kilifarevo Monastery 215
Kiten 370
Koprivshtitsa 243–250
Kotel 272
Kranevo 344
Krâstova gora 304
Kremikovtski 90
Kyustendil 103

L

Lake Srebârna 181
language 422
Lopushanski Monastery 158
Lovech 194–196

M

Macedonia 122, 397
Madara Horseman 231
Madzharovo nature reserve 320
Magura Cave 160
Malyovitsa 118
Manastir 305
maps 21
media, the 40
Melnik 135–138
monasteries 52
money 18
Montana 155
mosques 53
Mount Vihren 129
Mount Vitosha 86
museums 51
music 415
Muslims 405

N

national holidays 43
Nesebâr 352–357

O

outdoor activities 48

P

package holidays 3
Pamporovo 307
Panagyurishte 250
Pazardzhik 281
Pernik 101
Petrich 141
phones 40
Pirin Mountains 118–135

Pleven 189–194
Pliska 233
PLOVDIV 282–296
  accommodation 286
  Archeological Museum 289
  bars 294
  bus stations 283, 296
  campsites 287
  Chomanov House 291
  Danov House 289
  Dzhumaya Mosque 288
  entertainment 295
  Ethnographic Museum 291
  Hindlian House 291
  Imaret Mosque 288
  Kuyumdzhiioglu House, see Ethnographic Museum
  Museum of National Liberation 292
  Old Plovdiv 289–293
  ploshtad Dzhumaya 288
  restaurants 293
  Roman theatre 293
  tourist information 286
  train station 283, 296
police 53
Pomorie 358
post offices 39
Preobrazhenski Monastery 214
Predel Pass 123
Preslav 230
Primorsko 369
public holidays 43

R

Radomir 102
Razgrad 234
Rhodope Mountains 300–321
Ribaritsa 188
Rila Monastery 108–111
Rila Mountains 105–118
River Ropotamo nature reserve 369
Romanian embassies 8
Rozhen Monastery 139
Rupite 140
Rusalka 349
Ruse 170–177
Rusenski Lom 178

S

Samokov 113–115
Sandanski 132
Shipka Pass 264
Shiroka Lâka 310
Shumen 226–230
Silistra 180
Slânchev Bryag 351
Sliven 269
Smolyan 308

SOFIA 59–98
accommodation 65
airport 62, 97
Aleko 89
Aleksandâr Nevski memorial church 81
Banya Bashi Mosque 71
bars 93
Borisova Gradina 85
Boyana 89
bus stations 63, 97
cafés 93
Chapel of Sveta Paraskeva 71
Church Historical Museum 71
Church of Sveta Nedelya 71
discos 95
Dragalevtsi 87
football 95
Freedom Park 85
Ivan Vazov House-Museum 82
Largo, the 76
Mausoleum of Knyaz Aleksandâr Batenberg 84
Mount Vitosha 86
music 94
National History Museum 75
ploshtad Aleksandâr Batenberg 77
ploshtad Aleksandâr Nevski 80
ploshtad Sveta Nedelya 70
public transport 64
restaurants 91
Synagogue 74
SS Cyril and Methodius Foundation 81
theatre 94
tourist information 64
train station 63, 97
travel agents 64
Zoopark 86
Sozopol 363–368
Stara Planina 145–160, 184–238
Stara Zagora 266
Strandzha, the 372
Sunny Beach 351
Sveshtari 235–238
Sveta Troitsa Convent 214

T
taxis 26
Teteven 188
Thracian Horseman 333
Tolbuhin 181–184
tour operators
in Australasia 13
in North America 11
in the UK 5
tourist information 20
trains 23
to Bulgaria 7
within Bulgaria 23
Trigrad 312

Troyan 196
Troyan Monastery 198
Troyan Pass 197
Turkey, crossing into 299
Tryavna 219–222
"Turkish region", the 321

V
VARNA 326–342
accommodation 330
Aquarium 336
Archeological Museum 332
bars 339
bus station 327, 341
cafés 339
City Art Gallery 332
City Historical Museum 335
entertainment 340
Ethnographic Museum 334
Evksinograd Palace 337
Museum of Medical History 335
National Revival Museum 333
Natural History Museum 336
Navy Museum 336
nightlife 340
Park of Fighting Friendship 337
restaurants 339
Sea Gardens 336
Stone Forest 338
Sveti Konstantin 338
train station 327, 341
VELIKO TÂRNOVO 201–211
accommodation 204
Asenova quarter 208
Bazaar 205
bus station 204
Museum of the National Revival and the Constituent
    Assembly 206
restaurants 210
Sarafina House 205
Sveta Gora 210
train station 204
Tsaravets 206
Velingrad 315
Vidin 162–166
visas 14
Vratsa 149–152

Y
Yagodina 312
Yugoslav embassies 8

Z
Zabârdo 306
Zemen Monastery 102
Zheravna 274
Zlatni pyasâtsi 343

Can you help Nina?

Nobody to call Mum and Dad
No place to call home

Nina has lived in a Bulgarian orphanage for most of her life. She has distant memories of a mother and father who brought her here, simply because they were too poor to look after her properly. She and nearly 37,000 other institutionalised children are suffering. They are frightened, lonely and confused.

The damage of orphanage life is deep. Many ex-orphanage children end up on the streets, in mental institutions or even prison. **Without our help, they face a bleak and lonely future.**

Nina needs to experience life in a family as soon as possible. With your help The European Children's Trust (formerly The Romanian Orphanage Trust) can put her and others like her, on a path to a stable future.

> ● **Just £28 could help our team of Childcare Officers give a lonely child warmth, security and a family of their own.**

64 Queen Street, London, EC4R 1HA

A moment of your time now to call 01273 299399 or cut the form could transform a lonely young life.

I enclose £_____ to help Bulgarian orphanage children. Cheques to The European Children's Trust. Or debit my Access/Visa/CAF card

Card no ._____Expiry Date _____

Signature _____Date _____

Mr/Mrs/Miss/Ms _____

Address _____

_____Postcode _____

Telephone no. _____

Return to: Tanya Barron, (BRG/1), Bulgaria Appeal, The European Children's Trust, FREEPOST KE8359, 64d Queen Street, LONDON, EC4B 4AR or call 01273 299399 NOW. Registered Charity No. 803070

☐ Please send me information on sponsoring a child in eastern Europe

The European Children's Trust
Giving every child a real home

Please act NOW – and be a voice for these children